Stress and Fatigue
in Human Performance

Wiley Series on
Studies in Human Performance

Series Editor

Dennis H. Holding

University of Louisville
Kentucky, USA

Human Skills
edited by Dennis H. Holding

Biological Rhythms, Sleep,
and Performance
edited by Wilse B. Webb

Stress and Fatigue in Human Performance
edited by Robert Hockey

Further titles in preparation

Stress and Fatigue in Human Performance

Edited by

Robert Hockey

Department of Psychology
University of Durham
England

JOHN WILEY & SONS
Chichester · New York · Brisbane · Toronto · Singapore

Library of Congress Cataloging in Publication Data:

Main entry under title:
Stress and fatigue in human performance.
    (Wiley series on studies in human performance)
    Includes bibliographical references and indexes.
    1. Performance. 2. Stress (Physiology). 3. Stress
(Psychology). 4. Fatigue.   I. Hockey, Robert. II. Series.

BF481.S87   1983   155.9   82-13490
ISBN 0 471 10265 2

British Library Cataloguing in Publication Data:

Stress and fatigue in human performance. — (Wiley
    series on studies in human performance)
    1. Stress (Physiology)   2. Neurophysiology
    I. Hockey, Robert
    616.89   QP82.2.S8
    ISBN 0 471 10265 2

Phototypeset by Dobbie Typesetting Service, Plymouth, Devon, England
Printed by Page Bros. (Norwich) Limited

List of Contributors

ALAN D. BADDELEY	Director, MRC Applied Psychology Unit, Cambridge, *England*.
D. ROY DAVIES	Reader, Department of Applied Psychology, University of Aston in Birmingham, *England*.
MICHAEL W. EYSENCK	Reader, Department of Psychology, Birkbeck College, University of London, *England*.
SIMON FOLKARD	Research Psychologist, MRC Perceptual and Cognitive Performance Unit, University of Sussex, Brighton, England.
PETER HAMILTON	Senior Lecturer, Department of Psychology, University of Stirling, *Scotland*.
G. ROBERT J. HOCKEY	Lecturer, Department of Psychology, University of Durham, *England*.
DENNIS H. HOLDING	Professor, Department of Psychology, University of Louisville, *USA*.
CHRIS IDZIKOWSKI	Research Psychologist, MRC Applied Psychology Unit, Cambridge, *England*.
DYLAN M. JONES	Senior Lecturer, Department of Applied Psychology, University of Wales Institute of Science and Technology, Cardiff, Wales.
TIM H. MONK	Research Scientist, Institute of Chronobiology, Cornell Medical Centre, White Plain, N.Y., *USA*.
RAJA PARASURAMAN	Associate Professor, Department of Psychology, Catholic University of America, Washington, D.C., *USA*.
JERRY D. RAMSEY	Professor, Department of Industrial Engineering and Biomedical Engineering, Texas Tech University, Lubbock, Texas, *USA*.
WOLFGANG SCHÖNPFLUG	Professor, Institute für Psychologie der Freien Universität Berlin, *West Germany*.
VIVIAN J. SHACKLETON	Lecturer, Department of Applied Psychology, University of Aston in Birmingham, *England*.

DAVID M. WARBURTON   Reader, Department of Psychology, University of Reading, *England.*

KEITH WESNES   Resarch Fellow, Department of Psychology, University of Reading, *England.*

Contents

Series Preface xi
Preface xiii

1. **Monotony and Boredom** 1
   D. Roy Davies, Vivian J. Shackleton, and Raja Parasuraman
   The Problem of Definition 1
   Monotony and Boredom in Working Environments 4
   Laboratory Studies of Monotony and Boredom 14
   The Alleviation of Boredom 24
   Summary 25
   References 25

2. **Heat and Cold** . . . . *Jerry Ramsey* 33
   Thermoregulation 33
   Acclimatization and Adaptation 36
   Indices for Defining Thermal Levels 37
   Physical Performance in the Heat 39
   Perceptual–Motor Performance in the Heat 41
   Summary Analyses of Performance in the Heat 47
   Effects of Cold Environment on Manual Dexterity 53
   Perceptual–Motor Performance in the Cold 54
   Performance at Levels of Comfort 55
   Summary 56
   References 57

3. **Noise** . . . . *Dylan Jones* 61
   Sound: Measurement and Analysis 61
   Hearing 64
   Intermittent and Variable Noise 68
   Continuous Noise 71
   Field Studies 80
   Other Non-auditory Effects 82

Conclusions and Practical Implications...................... 86
Summary.. 88
References.. 88

4. **Circadian Rhythms and Shiftwork** 97
Tim Monk and Simon Folkard
Shiftwork as a Potential Stressor 97
The Role of Circadian Rhythms 98
Shiftwork and Performance 107
Other Factors in Shiftwork 113
Conclusions and Practical Implications..................... 116
Summary.. 118
References.. 119

5. **Fear and Dangerous Environments**......................... 123
Chris Idzikowski and Alan Baddeley
Anxiety and Fear 123
Methodological Problems 125
Uncontrolled Dangerous Environments 126
Subjective and Physiological Changes 130
Performance in Dangerous Environments.................... 132
Fear and Arousal 138
General Conclusions 140
Summary.. 141
Acknowledgement 141
References.. 141

6. **Fatigue**.. *Dennis Holding* 145
Definitions of Fatigue 145
Physical Fatigue 147
Perceptual Fatigue 149
Fatigue During Skilled Performance 152
Consequences of Fatigue 155
Attitudes Towards Risk and Effort 159
Final Remarks... 161
Summary.. 163
References.. 164

7. **Incentives** .... *Michael Eysenck* 169
Learning and Memory................................... 170
Major Determinants of Incentive Effects 173
Incentive and Motivation................................ 174
Task Characteristics.................................... 179

Performance Efficiency....................................... 184
Individual Characteristics 188
Intrinsic and Extrinsic Motivation 191
Conclusions and Practical Implications...................... 193
Summary.. 196
Acknowledgement 197
References 197

8. **Stress and Drugs** 203
   Keith Wesnes and David Warburton
   Stressors.. 203
   The Stress Response 205
   The Benzodiazepines 211
   Alcohol 218
   Nicotine 224
   The Pattern of Performance Changes Produced by the Drugs 232
   Summary.. 233
   Acknowledgements 235
   References 235

9. **Diurnal Variation** .... *Simon Folkard* 245
   The Physiological Basis of Performance Rhythms 246
   Time-of-day Effects in Performance 249
   The Complication of Memory................................. 254
   Individual Differences 259
   The Influence of Arousal.................................... 262
   Practical and Theoretical Conclusions....................... 266
   Summary.. 268
   References 269

10. **Anxiety and Individual Differences** .... *Michael Eysenck* 273
    The State–Trait Approach................................... 273
    Anxiety as an Organismic State............................. 276
    Effects of Anxiety on Performance 278
    Effort and Worry 285
    Summary of Performance Effects 291
    The Treatment of Anxiety 292
    Summary.. 294
    Acknowledgements 295
    References 295

11. **Coping Efficiency and Situational Demands** .. *Wolfgang Schönpflug* 299
    Orientation and Control 300

Demands and Efficiency 301
Capacity, Demand and the Role of Fatigue 305
Competence and Effort 309
Regulation of Demands and Competence 315
Broader Issues... 322
Final Remarks... 325
Summary 325
References 326

12. **The Cognitive Patterning of Stress States**....................... 331
    Robert Hockey and Peter Hamilton
    The State Analysis of Stress Effects 332
    Arousal and Performance Change 335
    Strategies for Stress Research 340
    A Map of the Noise State................................... 342
    Comparison of Stress States 346
    Mental States... 356
    Summary 359
    Acknowledgement 359
    References 360

13. **Current Issues and New Directions**................*Robert Hockey* 363
    Major Themes in Stress Research 363
    Emergent Directors 368
    Summary 372
    References 372

Author Index 375
Subject Index 391

Series Preface

Research on human performance has made considerable progress during the past forty years, reaching a respectable depth of analysis in several areas while, at the same time, becoming broader in scope. As a result, there have emerged a number of theoretical ideas which impinge on the general development of experimental psychology and, moreover, a great deal of knowledge has been obtained in ways which encourage direct, practical application. The series of *Studies in Human Performance*, well represented in this volume, is intended to explain these ideas and their applications in adequate detail.

Several of the books in the series are monographs while others, like the present text, are edited volumes. Although writing a monograph is often regarded as the more difficult assignment, producing an edited volume presents a considerable challenge. On one hand, it provides an opportunity to bring to bear a concentration of expertise which is otherwise unattainable; on the other hand, the multiplicity of contributors carries with it a risk that the overall result may be disorganized, or, literally, incoherent. In the *Human Performance* series, every effort has been made to counter the disadvantages attendant on using the edited format, while preserving the advantages of drawing upon special knowledge. The chapters have been commissioned in accordance with an integrated plan for each volume, information about each chapter has been circulated among the contributors in order to ensure cohesion, and editorial control has extended to the level of difficulty as well as to the format of each text.

The result of these preparations should be a series of books which combine readability with high standards of scholarship. The aim has been to supply a good deal of content, but within an expository framework which emphasizes explanation rather than mere reporting. Thus, although each volume contains sufficient material for the needs of graduate students or advanced undergraduates in experimental psychology, the books should provide readily accessible information for applied psychologists in many areas. In addition, it is hoped that the books will be useful to practitioners in ergonomics, to persons with interdisciplinary interests in production and industrial engineering, in physical education and in exercise physiology, and to psychologists in other fields.

The present volume presents a selection and integration of the stress research findings most relevant to the understanding of human performance. In order to accomplish this result it has been necessary to make a number of decisions concerning both the scope and the goals of the book. Stress research comprises a broad and rather ill-defined area, deriving its theoretical emphases and its methodology from at least two main traditions. At one extreme, stress has been regarded as little more than a convenient label for the group of environmental factors typified by noise, heat, and cold, together with those more individual variables which, like sleep loss, seem to share enough common features to warrant extending the classification. At the other extreme, the investigation of stress has been typified by the use of motivational and attitudinal concepts, like anxiety and perceived control, coupled with a greater reliance on medical, physiological, or social measures rather than on human performance scores.

The book deals capably with the environmental stressors, although by providing insights into their mechanisms rather than by simply cataloguing their effects. At the same time, however, the editor has attempted to incorporate into the volume the most valuable material from the medical and social traditions. A further challenge has been to integrate the results from two somewhat divergent experimental fields, combining the work on fatigue with that on stress. The concepts to be integrated are theoretically compatible but, in practice, derive from largely independent literatures and research personnel. A similar problem faced the preceding volume in this series, on *Biological Rhythms, Sleep and Performance*, in which sleep research was presented as interrelated with the work on circadian and other biological rhythms. In the present case, the concept of arousal again offers some degree of unification, although it is evident that the concept requires considerable qualification in order to retain any real utility.

Like the previous volume, the present book may therefore lay claim to making an appreciable theoretical contribution, despite its primary function as an explanatory text. Nevertheless, the level of explanation satisfies the overall objective of the series, that each book should be within the grasp of any educated person who has the motivation to study its subject matter.

DENNIS H. HOLDING
Series Editor

Preface

The last twenty years or so have seen the emergence of stress as a central concept in psychological thinking. From being a topic which was originally conceived in relation to disease and illness, through a period of being considered only of relevance to the problems of industrial and military operations, stress has now become the most generally accepted term for those aspects of behaviour which relate to bodily states, environmental changes, and the like. There is even a marked tendency to use the term stress to cover *all* types of motivational state, at least within the context of human behaviour; this usage of stress often coincides with the use of the concepts arousal and activation. There have been many attempts to clarify terminology in this area. Should stress be reserved for *marked* departures from some typical state or set of body parameters, on the one hand, or environmental conditions on the other? Alternatively, can we consider *all* environmental and bodily changes to result in a graded form of the stress response? Are there clear-cut criteria for the physiological and biochemical concomitants of stress, or are these only typical for certain kinds of state, particularly extreme ones?

In the present book I have made no attempt to address such issues directly. It is, of course, essential to be able to define our terms and be clear about the way in which we use of theoretical concepts: psychology certainly has an over-abundance of only half thought-out 'explanations' of behaviour, and very few even half-right solutions. What I have tried to do is to present a clear picture of what is known about the effects of stress and fatigue, without being too concerned to avoid areas of overlap between chapters, or gaps resulting from the absence of certain specialist topics. The book is the result of many hands, an arrangement which, like many others, has its advantages and its drawbacks. The principal gain is that experienced researchers in different fields are able to combine their knowledge within a single volume, yet still provide differing viewpoints on central issues common to us all. Amongst other considerations, this prevents us from presenting what would be a premature picture of the state of this knowledge. The major disadvantage is that the coverage can never be quite as systematic as if a single author were responsible for the whole book, nor the treatment of individual topics quite as even. Considerable effort has been made to ensure appropriate links between chapters, and a suitable balance of the content within each. Any deficiencies remaining in any aspect of the book's structure must, however, rest with the editor.

Authors were asked to consider the problem primarily from the point of view of a particular stressor, rather than using, say, type of task as the principal organizing factor. The reason for this lies mainly in my belief that we have neglected the job of describing what each environmental or bodily change does to our behaviour. By focusing on a particular task, say vigilance or short-term memory, there is a strong tendency to find that different stressors have rather similar effects. Unless we take the (still unusual) step of analysing our data in reasonable detail, there are not many ways in which they *could*, in fact, vary. Instead, our authors have tried to show what it is like to work in loud noise or under incentives, when one feels anxious or bored; they have also tried to include a broad range of performance situations in their analysis. Of course, both task-oriented *and* stressor-oriented approaches are necessary. They tell us rather different things, but they should, in principal, allow us to converge on the truth from two orthogonal patterns of findings. The various chapters in this book illustrate the influence of the two approaches to various degrees.

In addition to this largely conceptual reason, the kind of organization which I have used may also be justified on pragmatic grounds. It is, I think, a more natural one, and provides a clearer basis for applying our knowledge to the community at large. This aim is rarely central to research in experimental psychology, and there is no overwhelming reason why it should be. For this *particular* area of knowledge, however, it would seem rather sad if our efforts could not be turned to practical good, even if this may only, at the present time, be possible at some fairly elementary level. Even more obvious than the emergence of stress as a psychological concept is its increasing acceptance as a major factor in the shaping of our everyday lives. Stress is now a part of popular language and popular thinking, and the community has a right to expect that the research we do will have some practical effect on the myriad problems associated with it in the personal lives of its members. This is not to say that practical aims should be uppermost in our presentation of material: indeed, it would be quite impracticable to attempt such a goal in the present state of our knowledge. Many of the chapters, particularly the earlier ones, do offer considered implications of research for real-life problems, however, and we have tried throughout to relate theoretical and practical themes wherever possible.

Finally, a word about the scope of the book. I have restricted the focus of our concern to the area of *human performance*, although other aspects of human behaviour are considered in many places, these include the person's physiological and subjective states, his attitudes, health, and social behaviour. Our approach is not concerned, however, solely with the study of performance as a measure of efficiency. Although we examine task-related behaviour in the execution of instructions to comply with a set of task goals, we also consider qualitative changes in performance — strategies, individual differences in the patterning of behaviour, and so on. The earlier chapters in this book, broadly speaking, are more concerned with the traditional problems of applied stress research, with the behaviour of people under environmental conditions normally found in the working environment: monotony, heat and cold, noise, shift work, danger, and incentives. The later chapters are, on the whole, less directly concerned with the working environment, and concentrate more on conceptual and theoretical issues: the nature of arousal, anxiety, and bodily stress response, patterns of performance change across various stressors, strategies for coping with stress, and so on. The division is arbitrary, however: there is much theory and discussion of broad issues in the early chapters, much of practical relevance in the later ones. The arrangement was determined primarily by what seemed an intuitively satisfying transition from one topic to the next.

In the execution of my editorial duties I have been impressed by and grateful for the understanding, patience, and flexibility of purpose shown by my fellow authors. Perhaps they really do appreciate the peculiar traumas involved in editing a book rather than writing it oneself. I am also deeply indebted to the editorial staff of John Wiley & Sons, whose cheerful advice and assistance was a constant source of encouragement. On the production side much of the typing was carried out by Lindy Luke, often at very short notice, while the most accommodating of colleagues, Malcolm Rolling, redrew and photographed all the figures, to achieve at least an *appearance* of consistency from us all. As general editor of the series Dennis Holding deserves special mention in dispatches for his unbelievable patience and belief that the book would indeed get finished, as well as for his useful tips on the subtle craft of editorship. Finally, I want to extend my warmest thanks to my wife and children, Jenny, Joanna, and Gareth, for putting up with all the chaos and bad moods, and just for being around.

Robert Hockey
Durham, 1982

Stress and Fatigue in Human Performance
Edited by G. R. J. Hockey
© 1983 John Wiley & Sons Ltd.

Chapter 1

Monotony and Boredom

D. Roy Davies, Vivian J. Shackleton, and Raja Parasuraman

'I soon learned that variety is not the spice, but the very stuff of life', wrote Christopher Burney after experiencing 18 months in solitary confinement (Burney, 1952, p.16). Monotony is the opposite of variety and is a characteristic of the environment as perceived by an individual. It is usually associated with an environment which is unchanging, or which only changes in a repetitive and highly predictable fashion, and over which the individual's degree of control is perceived to be minimal. Just as a varied environment, which generally contains novel and unpredictable elements, tends to provoke interest, sometimes regarded as a basic human emotion (see Izard, 1978), so an unvaried environment often provokes boredom, which can also be considered to be an emotion (Arnold, in Appley and Trumbull, 1967, p.398). Boredom, therefore, can be regarded as an individual's emotional response to an environment that is perceived to be monotonous.

THE PROBLEM OF DEFINITION

In this chapter we examine the effects of monotony and boredom on the performance of industrial and laboratory tasks. Although monotony has been generally thought to be an important aspect of many industrial jobs and to be associated with undesirable effects on work performance and satisfaction, comparatively little research directly concerned with monotony and boredom exists and much of it is beset by methodological problems. Furthermore, although there is some agreement as to what constitutes a monotonous environment or a monotonous task, there is little consensus among researchers as to the definition of boredom. Barmack (1937), in a review of early conceptions of boredom, noted that 'Boredom is generally described as an attitude, which involves at least one distinguishing feature, namely dissatisfaction with work or situation' (p.9), and observed that this dissatisfaction had been attributed to 'a subjective dislike for uniformity' (Munsterberg, 1913), to 'the increased effort necessary to suppress distracting stimuli' (Myers, 1920), and to 'a feeling of fatigue resulting from a developed inadequacy of blood circulation to the work' (McDowell and Wells, 1927). Barmack's own researches on the physiology of mental effort, which are briefly discussed below, led him to distinguish between a feeling of boredom and an attitude of boredom. He considered the former to be associated with 'depressed or inadequate vital activity . . . caused in part by an attitude of boredom, or possibly by the decreased dynamic effectiveness of a particular motive' (Barmack, 1937, p.68), and thought of the latter as 'a phenomenon of conflict between the tendency to continue and the tendency to get away from a situation which has become unpleasant, principally because one is responding or may respond to it with inadequate physiological adjustments caused in turn by inadequate motivation' (Barmack, 1937, p.68; original italics removed). There are thus two components of Barmack's view of boredom, a feeling of boredom, attributable to a low level of physiological arousal, and an attitude of boredom which results from a motivational conflict, well described by Fenichel (1934), who suggested that boredom arises 'when we must do what we do not want to do and must not do what we want to do' (p.271). Writing from a psychoanalytic perspective, Fenichel defined boredom as 'a state of instinctual tension in which the instinctual aims are repressed but in which the tension as such is felt' (p.271).

The association between boredom and a state of low arousal, implicit in Barmack's analysis of boredom, has not passed unchallenged. Berlyne (1960), for instance, in common with many investigators of exploratory behaviour in animals (Fowler, 1967; Isaac, 1962; Myers and Miller, 1954; Zimbardo and Miller, 1958) and in children (Kubose, 1972) regarded boredom as a drive 'that is reduced through divertive exploration and aroused when external stimuli are excessively scarce or excessively monotonous' (p.187). Berlyne conceded that 'It is tempting to suppose that the conditions that make for boredom will produce exceptionally low arousal, and that low arousal, as well as high arousal, must therefore be aversive' (pp.188–189), citing Hebb (1955) as a proponent of this hypothesis. Berlyne argued, however, in favour of the view that boredom is the result of an increase in arousal level, although little direct evidence was put forward in support of this view. A few psychophysiological studies that bear on Berlyne's suggestion have since been conducted and these are discussed in a later section.

Boredom has also been associated with feelings of repetitiveness, of unpleasantness, or disagreeableness (Wyatt, 1929) and of constraint (Geiwitz, 1966). In a survey of white-collar workers, supervisors, and managers and a small sample of production workers, Guest, Williams, and Dewe (1978) found that the reasons given for feelings of boredom at work included constraint, meaninglessness, lack of interest and challenge, repetitiveness, and the never-ending nature of the job. However, Guest *et al.* emphasized that people differ widely among themselves in their perceptions of the nature and causes of boredom; for example, whether or not a job was regarded as repetitive seemed to depend on whether it was viewed in terms of process or content. As Guest *et al.* observed: 'If the job was seen as a process, which was basically repeated for each case with a number of minor variations, then it was judged as repetitive. If it was viewed in terms of the content, then it was seen as varied' (p.7).

Baldamus (1951) has suggested that the effects of monotony and repetitiveness should be distinguished from what may be described as 'content boredom'. For example, a book may not be repetitious yet may produce a state of extreme boredom; content boredom is thus probably due to a mismatch between the reader's interests and the book's content, and has little to do with the variety of stimulation provided. Another distinction between types of boredom has been made by Bernstein (1975), who differentiated between 'chronic bordeom', described as 'chronic feeling state that constitutes a malady', and 'responsive boredom', which is 'an affective response to an appropriate external situation'. This distinction is reminiscent of that made between 'trait' and 'state' anxiety (e.g., Spielberger, 1966; Zuckerman, 1976; see Eysenck, Chapter 10 this volume). Csikszentmihalyi (1975) suggested that both anxiety and boredom result from discrepancies between the demands imposed by a task and the performer's competence to deal with them. Anxiety occurs when task demands greatly exceed competence, while boredom is produced when the demands of the task lie well within the performer's capabilities. A related view, that boredom is associated with 'underload', was expressed by Welford (1965) who suggested that 'typically boring situations seem to be those in which attention is required but little information is conveyed' (p.438). The association of boredom with underload serves to distinguish boredom from fatigue, which Welford regarded as resulting from the chronic overloading of the sensory, central, or response mechanisms involved in task performance.

In a discussion of individual differences among industrial workers in the response to job enlargement, Hulin and Blood (1968) pointed out that the traditional view of industrial monotony has been that the increasing fragmentation and specialization of the work process, resulting in highly simplified tasks with short cycle times, leads to increased monotony, which Hulin and Blood defined as the 'perception of the *sameness* of the job from minute-to-minute, perception of the unchanging characteristic of the job' (p.42, their italics). The automobile assembly line is often taken as the quintessential example of the effects on work content of job fractionalization and specialization, and Terkel (1977) provides an account of an assembly line job given by a 27-year-old spot-welder on the 3.30 p.m. to midnight shift at the Ford Assembly Plant in South Chicago:

> I stand in one spot, about two- or three-feet area, all night. The only time a person stops is when the line stops. We do about thirty-two jobs per car, per unit. Forty-eight units an hour, eight hours

a day. Thirty-two times forty-eight times eight. Figure it out.
That's how many times I push that button.

The noise, oh it's tremendous. You open your mouth and you're
liable to get a mouthful of sparks. (Shows his arms) That's a burn,
these are burns. You don't compete against the noise. You go to
yell and at the same time you're standing to maneuver the gun to
where you have to weld (Terkel, 1977, pp.151–152).

The perception of monotony has been regarded as giving rise to feelings of
boredom and dissatisfaction with the job, the outcome being increased
absenteeism, turnover, and restriction of output. But, as Hulin and Blood
argued, this traditional view takes no account of possible individual differences
both in the perception of and in the response to industrial monotony and they
cited several examples of studies in which jobs with extremely short cycle times
were not invariably perceived as monotonous, or in which jobs that were so
perceived were also regarded as satisfying. Indeed, it appears that even car
workers rarely cite monotony as a reason for job dissatisfaction (Form, 1973),
and in an analysis of data collected by Caplan, Cobb, French, van Harrison, and
Pinneau (1975) from 23 different occupational groups, Kasl (1978) found that
although machine paced assembly workers described their jobs as being simple and
boring and as requiring little attention or concentration, their level of general
job satisfaction was not greatly different from that reported by other blue-collar
workers whose jobs were more attention demanding, more complex, and more
interesting. Furthermore, while there is some evidence suggesting a causal
relationship between dissatisfaction with work and both absenteeism and turnover
(see Davies and Shackleton, 1975; Porter and Steers, 1973; Taylor, 1968), the
belief that dissatisfaction with work causes absenteeism has also been considered
to be empirically unsupported (Nicholson, Brown, and Chadwick-Jones, 1976).

We turn now to a survey first of industrial studies and second of laboratory
studies of monotony and boredom in an attempt to determine (1) whether
boredom is reliably, and uniquely, associated with work decrement or other
performance changes; (2) whether boredom is reliably associated with changes
in psychophysiological activity; (3) whether individual differences in boredom
susceptibility are related to individual differences in performance, and also to
other variables such as age, intelligence and personality; and (4) whether
manipulations either of the task being performed, or of the work environment,
produce related changes in boredom and efficiency.

MONOTONY AND BOREDOM IN WORKING ENVIRONMENTS

Early industrial studies

The adverse effects of monotony on industrial efficiency were discussed in one
of the earliest textbooks of industrial psychology (Münsterberg, 1913).

Münsterberg was an experimental psychologist from the University of Freiburg who was recruited by William James to direct the psychological laboratory at Harvard (see Allen, 1967). However, the first research programme to investigate fatigue and monotony in industrial settings was initiated by the British Industrial Fatigue Research Board (IFRB), established in 1918 as a successor to the Health of Munitions Workers Committee of 1915–1917. In 1929 the IFRB became the Industrial Health Research Board (IHRB) which was disbanded in 1947. The IFRB had close links with the National Institute of Industrial Psychology (NIIP) which was established in 1921, since the NIIP's founder and first director, C. S. Myers, formerly an experimental psychologist at Cambridge University, was a member of the IFRB's Committee on Industrial Psychology. Much of the IFRB's research on monotony and work was conducted by Wyatt and his collaborators and Wyatt's autobiographical sketch (Wyatt, 1950) provides a useful and interesting account of the background of these studies.

Rose (1975) has described British industrial psychology during the 1920s as being 'largely isolated from American developments. . . . It was highly organised and the bulk of its effort was concentrated on the full exploration of a limited range of problems' (p.66), most of which related to the physical aspects of work. One of the most important of such problems was fatigue, which 'appeared to be a relatively easily conceived and measured condition' (p.69) although this over-simplified view did not endure for long. Many of the early reports of the IFRB were thus concerned with discovering the optimal length of the work spell so as to ensure maximum output, as well as with the optimal number of rest pauses and their distribution through the work period, and showed, in general, that in many jobs shorter hours resulted in higher output (Osborne, 1919; Vernon, 1919, 1920a,b). In subsequent studies changes through the working day in the rate of work at many different repetitive jobs were investigated over many weeks, in an attempt to establish 'output curves' characteristic of different tasks under varying conditions; these included the payment system adopted, the degree of pacing of the work, the batch size requirement, and the worker's length of service. Analysis of these output curves suggested that considerable hour-to-hour variations in output took place. In general the rate of work increased from the start of the work shift in the morning, decreased towards the end of the morning, increased again at the beginning of the afternoon, and then declined once more. Superimposed upon these general trends were occasional spurts of increased output either during or at the end of a shift.

As Wyatt recounts in his autobiography, a great deal of time and effort was devoted, unsuccessfully, as it turned out, to the search for a measure of fatigue. However, Wyatt came to believe that 'in most repetitive processes, the main obstacle to efficiency was not fatigue but boredom' since 'By this time the hours of work had been reduced, the spells of work were shorter and the replacement of manual by mechanical methods of production tended to focus attention on the mental rather than the bodily effects of work' (Wyatt, 1950, p.70).

Among the tasks studied by Wyatt and Langdon (1932) in their investigation of inspection processes in industry were the inspection of cartridge cases for 'high caps', the inspection of tiles for size and quality, the examination of metal cases, and the inspection of photographic paper for surface defects. In general they found that the efficiency of inspection tended to vary with time at work and concluded that 'There is reason to believe that boredom is responsible for a greater loss in output than fatigue' (p.50).

Wyatt and his associates also thought that 'Boredom . . . is a psychical state which may exist quite apart from fatigue, and must be separately considered in any industrial inquiry' (Wyatt and Fraser, 1928, p.2). Wyatt's researches on monotony and boredom can be divided into three areas of investigation: first, attempts to distinguish between output curves attributable to boredom and to fatigue; secondly, attempts to reduce the monotony of the work environment or of the work itself; and thirdly, attempts to provide correlates of boredom susceptibility (Wyatt, Fraser, and Stock, 1929; Wyatt, Langdon, and Stock, 1937).

These investigations involved observation of, and interviews with, experienced women workers in different factories engaged on such repetitive industrial tasks as tobacco weighing, chocolate packing, and soap wrapping. Each group of workers was observed for several weeks and mean levels and variabilities of output, subjective reports of boredom and fatigue, and conversation and other behaviour, such as yawning, were all recorded. The majority of workers on these jobs reported themselves as experiencing moderate or severe boredom at some time during the working day, most commonly in the middle of the morning and shortly after the beginning of the afternoon spell of work. These reports of boredom tended to be associated with marked increases in the variability of the time taken to complete each cycle of the work operation, which also occurred, to a lesser extent, with fatigue. Increases in restlessness were also apparent.

Boredom and output

Wyatt *et al.* (1937) also reported that distinct patterns of output were characteristic of fatigue and boredom. They suggested that whereas the mean output curve tended to fall in a step-wise fashion during the work spell when the operator was interested in the work but was suffering from progressive fatigue, it tended to rise in much the same manner when the work was 'distasteful' and the operator 'severely bored' (Wyatt *et al.*, 1937, p.29). The increase in output during the work spell under conditions of severe boredom was attributed in part to 'the pleasurable anticipation induced by the approaching end of work' and in part to the requirement for the worker 'to produce a minimum output in each spell' (Wyatt *et al.*, 1937, p.29). Wyatt *et al.* thus argued that 'the shape of the output curve may be used as a fairly reliable indication of the amount of boredom experienced by the worker' (p.30).

Table 1. The relation between assessments of boredom and changes in output during the work spell, as shown by idealized output curves: (a) continuous fall, (b) continuous fall with rise at the end of the work period, (c) immediate fall followed by a continuous rise, (d) continuous rise. Data for a group of 68 women workers, from Wyatt, Langdon, and Stock (1937).

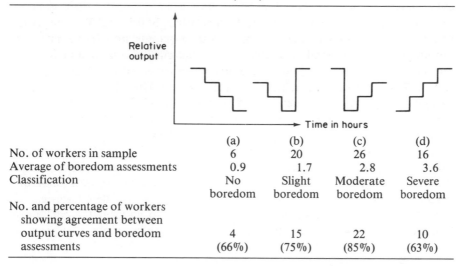

	(a)	(b)	(c)	(d)
No. of workers in sample	6	20	26	16
Average of boredom assessments	0.9	1.7	2.8	3.6
Classification	No boredom	Slight boredom	Moderate boredom	Severe boredom
No. and percentage of workers showing agreement between output curves and boredom assessments	4 (66%)	15 (75%)	22 (85%)	10 (63%)

Idealized examples of four output curves, thought to be associated with varying amounts of boredom, are shown in Table 1, although no examples of actual output curves were presented by Wyatt *et al.* The assessments of boredom also shown in Table 1 were obtained from a sample of 68 women workers, each of whom was given a lengthy interview structured around 13 questions, some of which presupposed that the operators were bored by their work (for example 'Which is the more boring, the morning or the afternoon? Why?' and 'When you find you are bored and time seems to drag, what do you do?'). The responses to these questions were then weighted on a six-point scale 'according to the presence or absence of boredom symptoms' (p.4), the final assessment of boredom being the average weighted response. The workers were then continuously observed throughout the working day and their output recorded at 15-minute intervals for a period, in some cases, of two or three months, although details of the tasks on which they were engaged are imprecise and it is unclear whether or not they were all working at the same job. The output curves thus obtained were then compared with the idealized output curves (a, b, c, and d in Table 1) and with the boredom assessments obtained from the structured interviews. As Table 1 indicates, only 22 out of the 68 workers exhibited either a 'no boredom (fatigue)' or a 'severe boredom' output curve, the remaining 46 producing mixed 'fatigue and boredom' curves. Table 1 also shows the degree of agreement between the output curve and the boredom assessment in each case.

It is perhaps not surprising that several criticisms of the procedures used by Wyatt and his collaborators have been made (Hulin and Blood, 1968; Murrell, 1962, 1971; Smith, 1953) and that subsequent attempts to establish an output curve characteristic of boredom have failed to replicate their findings (Roethlisberger and Dickson, 1941; Rothe, 1946; Smith, 1953). One of the principal difficulties has been that, more often than not, no reliable pattern in output records is discernible, so that the 'output curves' obtained prove to be unclassifiable. Even on the rare occasions where some pattern does emerge, it can usually be explained in terms of talking (see Murrell, 1965, p.412) or 'personal and operational delays and auxiliary work' (Dudley, 1958), which tend to be grouped either at the start or at the end of the work period. Since these factors are likely to be associated with lowered output, the shape of the output curve may be attributed to either 'warm up' or 'fatigue' effects despite the fact that the rate of work may show no change or even improve at these times. Although, therefore, it is possible that feelings of boredom and tiredness show consistent changes through the working day (Nelson and Bartley, 1968), clearly insufficient evidence exists to warrant the conclusion that there is a curve of output uniquely associated with boredom.

Varied and unvaried work

Wyatt and his collaborators also attempted to find ways of alleviating boredom and of improving output through increasing the variety of the work being performed by requiring operators to alternate between two or more tasks for varying lengths of time. Since laboratory studies had suggested that this procedure was effective in increasing output (Vernon, Wyatt, and Ogden, 1924; Wyatt, 1924), similar studies were conducted in industrial settings. Wyatt and Fraser (1928), for example, examined the output of women workers engaged in tobacco weighing and packing under three conditions. In the first, the workers remained on one task, either weighing or packing, throughout the work spell; in the second, weighing was exchanged for packing, and vice versa, once in each work spell, while in the third condition the exchange occurred twice. Increases in output of 11.2 and 13.8 per cent were obtained in the second and third conditions (compared to the first), and feelings of boredom were also reduced. Similar, although smaller, increases were obtained with the operations of rolling and cutting cigarettes, and with the alternation of two tasks involved in the manufacture of bicycle chains. However, no difference in output was found between uniform and varied work conditions in handkerchief folding when two different styles of folding were alternated.

But the effects of increasing the variety of work appeared to depend upon the number of times that different tasks were alternated. A large number of changes in work operation during the day reduced output by interfering with the 'swing of the work', a concept similar to 'traction' (Baldamus, 1961). Baldamus regarded traction as to some extent counteracting feelings of boredom or tedium and defined it as follows:

> Traction . . . in a sense . . . is the opposite of 'dis-traction'. It is a feeling of being pulled along by the inertia inherent in a particular activity. The experience is pleasant and may therefore function as a relief from tedium. It usually appears to be associated, though not always, with a feeling of reduced effort, relatively to actual or imagined situations where it is difficult to maintain continuity of performance (Baldamus, 1961, p.59).

A number of different types of traction are described in detail by Baldamus including *object traction* (the experience derived from visualizing an object which one feels urged to complete), *batch traction* (the desire to complete a batch of articles), *process traction* (the pleasant feeling of being guided or pulled along by the chemical or physical nature of such production processes as melting or casting), *machine traction* (feelings of being drawn by the machine), and *line traction* (pleasant feelings derived from the movement of objects passing along as one works on them).

Baldamus's ideas were drawn from introspections of his own experiences of repetitive work and may be criticized as being somewhat unrepresentative. However, some support for the experience of four types of traction (object, batch, line, and general production traction) was supplied by interview data and observation of women assembly workers in an electronics firm (Turner and Mitclette, 1962). The experience of batch traction was further confirmed by observation and interviews in a meat factory (Dickson, 1973) and by experiments in a metal-working firm (Smith and Lem, 1955).

Anecdotally, car production lines give rise to some of the most repetitive and boring of industrial jobs and two studies of car assembly plants throw light on the relationship between repetition and boredom. In a frequently cited study Walker and Guest (1952) interviewed 180 car assembly workers in their homes about their attitudes and feelings towards work on the assembly line. Walker and Guest pointed out that not all assembly line jobs were the same, and observed that, in general, jobs associated with high levels of machine pacing and repetitiveness were particularly disliked, although a minority of workers regarded such jobs as an exciting challenge. They also reported a tendency for the amount of rated interest in a job to vary directly with the number of operations performed; the greater the number of operations, the higher the rated interest in the job. Grubb (1975) found that workers engaged on sub-assembly tasks involving the complete fabrication of a unit (and therefore more operations) reported lower levels of boredom than workers engaged on the installation of a single part, or on the installation of a variety of parts at a single stage of the assembly operation. However, the differences between the three groups were small. Larger differences between the groups were recorded when the perception of time was measured. Tasks involving the complete manufacture of a production unit were perceived as significantly shorter in duration than those involving only partial fabrication, and there was a significant positive relation between estimates of task duration and levels of rated job boredom within each of the three work groups. Grubb noted that this finding supported Ornstein's (1970) view of the relation between the experience of boredom and the perception of time, a view also put forward by Wyatt (1929) who maintained that the bored individual is likely to over-estimate the duration of time. However, results obtained by Kerr and Keil (1963) in a correlational study conducted in a small manufacturing plant fail to support this hypothesis. In this study time was estimated to pass reliably more slowly by employees engaged on long-cycle 'variety-type' jobs than by those working at short-cycle 'monotony-type' jobs. The relation between 'time drag' and boredom clearly merits further investigation.

Industrial tasks have been described by Cooper (1973) as extending along two relatively independent variety dimensions: physical variety and skill variety. These two kinds of variety were distinguished in the following way:

> Physical Variety refers to the amount of physical differentiation in the individual's surroundings: differentiation of operation, physical setting, and other people . . . . Skill variety describes the application of knowledge and skill to task problems and is similar to those theoretical positions which identify the exercise of skill and knowledge with self-actualisation . . . and self expression . . . in work . . . . Skill Variety is here defined in terms of Task Uncertainty and Response Uncertainty (Cooper, 1973, pp.392–394).

The physical variety dimension, as noted above, appears to influence both the level of output and the incidence of boredom, and aspects of work which can be conceptualized in terms of physical variety also seem to affect rates of absenteeism and turnover (Baldamus, 1951; Turner and Lawrence, 1965).

Cooper also cited a number of studies which have attempted to relate skill variety to measures of work performance and satisfaction. Vroom (1962) showed that self-expression (which Cooper maintains is defined in terms similar to skill variety) for oil refinery workers was positively correlated with job satisfaction. Lodahl (1964) found that intrinsic job satisfaction among car assembly line workers loaded quite substantially on a skill variety factor. In a study of telephone company employees, Hackman and Lawler (1971) found the degree of autonomy, a further aspect of skill variety, to be significantly and positively correlated with measures of rated job performance (the quantity and quality of output and the overall effectiveness of the worker) and also with job satisfaction. A negative correlation with absenteeism was obtained.

In general, then, varied work is associated with increases in output and reductions in boredom, and several attempts have been made to redesign or restructure both blue-collar and white-collar jobs so that they become less monotonous, in the expectation that beneficial consequences, both for the firm and the individual worker, will follow. Numerous examples of successful attempts to enlarge or enrich jobs, together with the results observed in follow-up studies are provided by Birchall (1975) and O'Toole (1973) among others. Yet as the study by Guest *et al.* (1978), referred to above, indicated, many workers still find elements of their jobs boring even after the jobs have been redesigned or restructured. Not everyone agrees, therefore, that job enrichment can solve the problems of monotony and boredom resulting from the division and fragmentation of the work process, and some of the criticisms that have been advanced are outlined in the final section of this chapter.

Effects of music on output and job attitudes

A different method of introducing variety into the work situation is to provide music during all or part of the work period. Studies of the effects of music upon industrial output were first carried out in the United States shortly before the First World War. At this time, managements in different industries, influenced by the 'scientific management' approach of F. W. Taylor, were seeking new ways of motivating workers to produce more per unit time, without increasing costs or lowering quality. It was expected that studies of music in the work situation would reveal that music increased output, particularly in monotonous and repetitive jobs, that the onset of boredom and fatigue would be delayed, and that attitudes in the job would be influenced in a favourable direction. However, according to reviews of the effects of music in industrial situations (for example, Uhrbrock, 1961) there is not a great deal of evidence that music improves output very much, and some studies suggest that the quality of output tends to be impaired. Where music improves output, it seems to do so on simple and repetitive tasks as opposed to more complex ones. However, the experience of the operator is also a factor. The output of experienced operators tends to be unaffected by music, while that of inexperienced operators tends to show some improvement. Improvements in output with music have also been linked to time of day, with greater improvement occurring in the morning than the afternoon.

Although studies of the effects of music upon output have been somewhat inconclusive, studies concerned with job attitudes have produced rather clearer findings. A number of studies (Kerr, 1943, 1945; Kirkpatrick, 1943; McGehee and Gardner, 1949; Newman, Hunt, and Rhodes, 1966; Smith, 1947) suggest that factory employees prefer working where music is played rather than where it is not, although it also appears that from 1 to 10 per cent of individuals (depending on the study) are annoyed by it. These tend to be older workers. Instrumental music, as opposed to vocal, tends to be preferred.

The effects of music on performance in industrial situations have thus been difficult to detect, although positive results have occasionally been obtained (for example, Fox, 1975; Wyatt *et al.*, 1937). The general failure to observe improvements in output may be attributed in part to the use of many different kinds of music, the use of many different kinds of task, and the employment of insensitive measures of performance. On the other hand, attitudes to music at the workplace tend to be favourable.

According to Knight (1929), 'Music seems to act as a "tonic", freshening the worker who has become bored by the monotony of a repetitive task. It is not, therefore, an adequate substitute for a rest pause where the work involves muscular fatigue calling for periodic, physical recuperation' (p.85). Knight reviewed several studies concerned with work and rest conducted under the auspices of the Health of Munitions Workers Committee, the IFRB, and the National Institute of Industrial Psychology and concluded that reducing the length of the working day to 8 hours led to decreases in accidents, spoiled work, and sickness and absence rates, together with increases in both hourly and daily output, except where the speed of work was largely determined by the rate of operation of a machine. Rest pauses provided during the working day, thus reducing the length of the work spell, were also found to be effective in improving the quality and quantity of output, particularly in repetitive monotonous work, and in reducing sickness rates. Knight suggested that 'The rest pause should be introduced at about the time when the output has just reached its maximum' since 'Working activity is then about to decrease' (p.77). The determination of the optimal location of rest pauses during the work spell thus required an analysis of the output curve, which would take different forms for different jobs. Similarly, the optimal length of rest pauses was held to depend upon the demands made by a particular task.

Correlates of boredom and susceptibility

As Smith (1955) points out, 'Industrial investigation established very early . . . that jobs with all the appearance of being repetitive were not always considered monotonous by the workers . . . . Investigations of clerical workers, school teachers and professional workers, on the other hand, have repeatedly indicated that many persons find each of these more varied kinds of work boring' (p.322). Some attempts have therefore been made to find reliable correlates of the susceptibility to boredom with the aim, presumably, of providing a profile of the easily bored worker. Ideally, such workers could then be identified through selection procedures and assigned to less monotonous jobs. Yet despite the claim of Viteles (1932) that 'it is to the susceptibility of the individual and not to the task, that the responsibility for the feeling of boredom must in large part be ascribed' (p.547), such an approach is essentially static rather than dynamic, since it minimizes the importance of the interaction between task and personal characteristics which gives rise to the experience of boredom. Certainly there appears to be little evidence from industrial studies that boredom is a general characteristic. Wyatt *et al.* (1937), for example, recorded the incidence of boredom symptoms in the same group of women workers employed for monthly periods on each of five different jobs. These were, in order of expressed preference: 1. Packing boxes (14lb) with chocolates; 2. Packing boxes (4lb) with chocolates; 3. Cornering cardboard boxes, a process known as 'staying'; 4. Making paper crackers, and 5. Bundling chocolates. From the data provided by Wyatt *et al.* it is possible to compute Spearman rank collection coefficients between the levels of boredom reported for each of these five tasks: these are shown in Table 2. As Table 2 indicates, half of the ten correlation coefficients are positive, half are negative, and none reaches an acceptable level of significance.

Table 2. Correlation coefficients (Spearman r_s) between boredom assessments obtained from women workers with respect to five different industrial tasks (see text for details). Correlations computed from the data of Wyatt, Langdon, and Stock (1937).

Task	2	3	4	5
1. Packing chocolates (14lb)	+ 0.373	−0.297	−0.467	+ 0.091
2. Packing chocolates (4lb)	—	−0.009	−0.403	+ 0.197
3. 'Staying'		—	−0.382	+ 0.140
4. Making paper crackers			—	+ 0.152
5. Bundling chocolates				—

In presenting the data, Wyatt *et al.* observed that 'it will be noticed that each worker was bored by some processes but was comparatively free from boredom when employed on other types of work', although they were careful to point out that this observation 'does not preclude the possibility that some individuals would be bored by all kinds of repetition work. Neither does it prove that boredom in repetition work is specific rather than general' (p.15).

The evidence for a general trait of susceptibility to boredom in industrial situations is thus far from compelling. Nevertheless, examples of characteristics which have been reported to be related to boredom susceptibility include age, intelligence, extroversion, restlessness in daily habits and leisure activities, life satisfaction, and authoritarianism (Burnett, 1925; Hill, 1975a; Smith, 1955; Stagner, 1975; Thompson, 1929; Wyatt *et al.*, 1929, 1937). The easily bored worker is thus portrayed as being younger, more intelligent, less extroverted, more creative, more restless, less satisfied, and less authoritarian. However, some of the studies on which these conclusions are based employed very small samples, and there is a lack of agreement between them with regard to both intelligence and extroversion as correlates of the susceptibility to boredom. Furthermore, since the great majority of industrial workers engaged on monotonous jobs, particularly the automobile assembly line (see Stagner, 1975) tend to be below the age of 35, it may be difficult to obtain adequate samples of older workers in order to make age comparisons with respect to boredom. It appears, therefore, that there is insufficient reliable evidence to warrant any firm conclusions being drawn concerning correlates of boredom susceptibility.

LABORATORY STUDIES OF MONOTONY AND BOREDOM

Laboratory studies of monotonous work have tended to focus upon performance changes occurring in tasks which are simulations of repetitive industrial or military tasks and have attempted to relate such changes to task and environmental variables, to individual and group differences, and, more rarely, to subjective reactions, such as reports of boredom. Although a number of different tasks, such as sorting and assembly tasks, pursuit rotor tasks, mental arithmetic and problem-solving tasks have been employed in laboratory studies of monotony and boredom, the vigilance task has probably been more widely used than any other. This task demands continuous attention while conveying relatively little information requiring action, and thus matches Welford's (1965) definition of a 'typically boring situation' referred to above.

Mackworth's studies of vigilance in radar operators

Vigilance tasks are tasks in which attention is directed to one information display (although occasionally more than one) over long, unbroken, periods of time, for the purpose of detecting infrequent changes in the state of the display which are extremely difficult to discriminate. Such tasks are also known as 'monitoring' or 'watchkeeping' tasks, and resemble in many respects the tasks performed by some industrial inspectors and by some radar and sonar operators. Indeed, vigilance research began as an attempt to solve a serious practical problem. Mackworth (1950) noted that 'towards the end of 1943, the Royal Air Force asked if laboratory experiments could be done to determine the optimum length of watch for radar operators on anti-submarine patrol, as reports had been received of overstrain among these men' (p.12). Furthermore, 'there was evidence that a number of potential U-boat contacts were being missed', and after some preliminary experiments had been carried out by Mackworth, Coastal Command began an operational study of the detection of submarines by radar operators, the results of which suggested that after about 30 minutes on watch a marked deterioration in efficiency rapidly occurred. Thus, as Mackworth later put it in a communication to Jerison, 'the essential feature of the vigilance story was that its origins were without any theoretical background' (Jerison, 1970, p.130).

Mackworth's research programme began with an examination of the working conditions of Coastal Command airborne radar operators. These operators were mainly engaged in flying sorties over the Bay of Biscay and westward, from Cornwall, to the mid-Atlantic. As the result of a report from Middle East Command, Coastal Command had recommended that radar watches should last for no longer than one hour, although in practice the length of watch varied from 30 minutes to 2 hours (Craik and Mackworth, 1943). The radar operator's task was often a matter of waiting for nothing to happen since the anti-submarine search patrols were frequently unproductive. 'False alarms' were not unusual; for example, Spanish fishing vessels in the Bay of Biscay were registered on the radar screen and were indistinguishable from military vessels until visual contact was established. Mackworth observed that 'the chance of an aircraft pilot agreeing to investigate a contact reported by his radar observer was only 1 in 8; there was no more than 1 chance in 30 that any such contact investigated would prove to be an enemy submarine' (1950, p.12). The radar operator worked in isolation, except for occasional telephone calls, and no check on his efficiency was made. The target he was searching for was difficult to discriminate, being a small spot of light about 1 millimetre in diameter appearing on a radar screen covered in 'noise'. The target was present for a few seconds and if action was to be taken, it had to be taken quickly.

Mackworth designed a laboratory task which simulated the essentials of the radar operator's job. The task, known as the 'clock test', consisted of a blank clock face with a white background, around which traversed a black pointer, moving in discrete steps. Occasionally, in fact 12 times during each 30 minutes, the pointer moved through twice its normal distance and these 'double jumps' were the signals the observer had to detect by pressing a response key. The observers in Mackworth's experiments were experienced and inexperienced radar operators and it was found that almost all of them showed a decrement in performance over the 2-hour watch period. After the first half-hour of observation the detection rate was around 85 per cent, after 1 hour around 77 per cent, and after 2 hours around 72 per cent. Similar performance decrements were obtained by Mackworth in two other monitoring tasks, the 'synthetic radar test' and the 'main listening test'. Decrements with time at work in the performance of other tasks such as compensatory tracking (Siddall

and Anderson, 1955) and vernier gauge setting (Saldanha, 1955) have also
been obtained.

Individual and group differences

Many of the factors employed in monotonous industrial tasks in attempts to
reduce boredom and increase output have also proved effective in improving
performance in vigilance tasks. These include varying the length of the work
spell (Mackworth, 1950), the provision of music during task performance
(Davenport, 1972; Davies, Lang, and Shackleton, 1973; Ware, Kowal, and
Baker, 1964), and the introduction of rest pauses (Bergum and Lehr, 1962;
Colquhoun, 1959; Mackworth, 1950). However, none of these studies
examined the incidence of boredom. But groups of individuals differing in
boredom have been shown to perform at different levels in monotonous work
situations. Thackray, Bailey, and Touchstone (1977), for example, examined
the relation between ratings of boredom and monotony and a variety of
physiological measures taken during the performance of a 60-minute air-
traffic-control task. At the beginning and end of the experimental session 45
subjects were given nine-point scales on which they rated their levels of
boredom, monotony, irritation, attentiveness, fatigue, and strain. The
boredom and monotony scale scores obtained at the end of the experiment
were summed for each subject and two sub-groups, each of eight subjects,
were selected, one a High Boredom and the other a Low Boredom group.
There were no differences between the groups in the boredom/monotony
scores obtained at the beginning of the task. The two groups were then
compared with respect to performance, assessed by response latencies, and to
physiological changes occurring during the task. The High Boredom group
produced significant longer response times, compared to the Low group, and
the proportion of long response times increased from the first half of the task
to the second for the High group but decreased for the Low group. The High
Boredom group also showed a greater increase in strain over the task and a
greater decrease in attentiveness. The only physiological measure which
discriminated between the two groups was heart rate variability, which
decreased with time at work for the Low Boredom group, while increasing for
the High group. This study provides some evidence suggesting that there may
be a constellation of factors distinguishing those subjects who become bored
during the performance of a monotonous task from those who do not. Davies,
Shackleton, and Lang (1972) reported significant positive correlations between
self-reports of boredom and of day-dreaming, and between boredom and
perceived task difficulty, during the performance of a self-paced problem-
solving task lasting for about half an hour. Significant negative correlations
were obtained between boredom and concentration, and between boredom
and the perceived expenditure of effort in the same situation.

Comparatively few laboratory studies of individual and group differences in the performance of monotonous tasks have been conducted, although such differences have been more thoroughly examined in the vigilance situation. Individual differences in vigilance performance tend to be considerable, and there are indications that this is also true of performance at industrial inspection tasks. For instance, Wyatt and Langdon (1932) noted that despite the fact that industrial inspectors and examiners were a highly selected group, individual differences in efficiency were large, and indeed somewhat greater than those observed in other forms of repetitive work. In the examining of metal cases, for example, there was a difference of 47 per cent between the best and the worst workers, and in some groups the quickest workers were found to work from two to three times as fast as the slowest. Variations in accuracy were generally less than those in speed, and speed and accuracy tended to be inversely related. Wyatt and Langdon suggested that 'some individuals are inherently incapable of maintaining a uniform attitude for any length of time. They are restless and easily disturbed and are obviously unsuitable for examining work' (p.46). However, although individual differences in inspection and examining work are clearly important, no reliable selection procedure exists for industrial inspectors, and there is a paucity of recent research concerned with the topic (see Wiener, 1975, for a review).

Individual differences in vigilance performance do not appear to be related to intelligence and differences in the levels of performance of men and women are slight (see Davies and Parasuraman, 1982; Davies and Tune, 1970). Age differences in vigilance also tend to be small, and only the dimension of introversion–extroversion seems to bear some relationship either to the overall level of efficiency or to the rate at which performance deteriorates with time at work. The overall level of performance of introverts is generally superior, although extroverts probably only exhibit a more rapid deterioration in efficiency with time in tasks possessing certain characteristics (see Davies and Parasuraman, 1982, for a review). But extroverts do appear to behave differently from introverts in monotonous task situations, even when the level of performance of the two groups is much the same. Davies, Hockey, and Taylor (1969), for example, found that extroverts selected brief periods of varied auditory stimulation significantly more frequently than did introverts during the performance of a visual vigilance task. In another condition of the same experiment, introverts chose to turn off continuous auditory stimulation significantly more often than did extroverts. In neither of these conditions were there any reliable differences in the performance of introverts and extroverts. In an ingenious experiment, Hill (1975b) demonstrated that, compared to introverts, extroverts manifested significantly greater response variety, assessed both in terms of the number of alternations among possible responses and in terms of the average entropy of the set of responses made, in a monotonous task requiring the picking up and placing of push pins into a piece of chipboard. Extroverts also showed increasing response variety over successive trial blocks while introverts did not.

Extroverts thus seem to prefer a greater variety of stimulation, whether externally produced or spontaneously generated, during the performance of a monotonous task. A significant positive correlation between extroversion and sensation seeking, as measured by the Sensation-Seeking Scale (SSS), developed by Zuckerman, Kolin, Price, and Zoob (1964), has also been reported (Farley and Farley, 1967, 1970). Later versions of the SSS (Zuckerman, 1974) have incorporated a general sensation-seeking scale and four factor scales: thrill and adventure seeking, experience seeking, disinhibition, and boredom susceptibility. However, sensation seeking does not appear to be related to performance in a monotonous task (Cahoon, 1970), and although it might well be expected that a significant positive relationship between extroversion and boredom susceptibility would be observed, the results from correlational studies are inconsistent and a reliable correlation in the expected direction has been obtained in just one study (Eysenck and Eysenck, 1968), and then only for male subjects. Furthermore, extroverts show marginally greater tolerance for conditions of sensory and perceptual deprivation, in which the amount and variety of stimulation is severely restricted (see Myers, 1969, for a review). There must be some doubt, then, as to whether extroverts are more easily bored than introverts since it is possible that their strategies for coping with monotony are more efficient. 'Distractibility' has been related to extroversion, or at least to the 'impulsivity' component of extroversion (Thackray, Jones, and Touchstone, 1973, 1974), and Gale, Morris, Lucas, and Richardson (1972) obtained a significant positive correlation between extroversion and scores on the Betts Vividness of Imagery Scale (Betts, 1909), with extroverts reporting more vivid imagery than introverts. Morris and Gale (1974) also found vivid imagery to be more prevalent among extroverts. It is possible, therefore, that extroverts are more likely to generate mental imagery in monotonous situations, which would produce less efficient task performance but also a reduction in the susceptibility to boredom.

Certainly the extent to which individuals engage in task-irrelevant subsidiary behaviours is likely to be inversely related to task performance. Antrobus, Coleman, and Singer (1967), for example, divided their subjects into High and Low day-dreaming groups, on the basis of their responses to a day-dreaming questionnaire, and found that although there was no significant difference in the overall level of vigilance performance, the efficiency of the High day-dreaming group deteriorated at a faster rate. This group also reported significantly more 'task-irrelevant thoughts' during the vigil, the incidence of which tended to increase with time on task. In an industrial study, Kishida (1977) showed that the efficiency with which bottle inspectors detected faults was a function of the time spent in subsidiary behaviours such as turning round, chatting, yawning, and so on. Here again, the incidence of these subsidiary behaviours increased with time at work.

Performance at a repetitive laboratory task has also been shown to predict efficiency in monotonous situations outside the laboratory. McBain (1970), for instance, collected a great deal of information on twenty 'line drivers' (long-distance lorry drivers). They performed a highly repetitive 42-minute paced task in the laboratory and they completed self-report questionnaires on boredom susceptibility. Supervisory ratings, traffic convictions, and objective driving measures were obtained, and observations were also made of the behaviour of the drivers on the road. McBain found that the number of errors on the repetitive laboratory task was a good predictor of accident rates of drivers, particularly errors made at the end of the task when boredom was presumably greatest. Interestingly, the task predicted 'non-preventable' accidents (defined by the employers only after thorough investigation of each accident) better than preventable accidents. This suggested that:

> The driver who is steady, conscientious and alert, who is able to orient himself to the total environment in which he operates, rather than just the immediate task, may be the one to whom virtually all accidents are preventable (McBain, 1970, p.517).

How drivers keep themselves alert is suggested by other measures taken by McBain. He found that the subjects who reported themselves as least susceptible to boredom tended to be the most experienced drivers. Contrary to expectation, they were the least consistent in response times on the experimental tasks and had more inconsistent engine speeds when driving. These inconsistencies as well as observations of the drivers on the road led McBain to suggest that the most experienced drivers were not as susceptible to boredom exactly because they engaged in behaviours which made the laboratory task and their job more varied. He notes that the results suggest that:

> . . . exposure to monotonous work conditions need not inevitably lead to lapses of attention followed by accidents, even though the individual so exposed may be susceptible to such work conditions . . . (a driver) . . . may learn behaviors that reduce the loss of efficiency associated with exposure to monotonous work conditions . . . Drivers spotlighted deer by the side of the road with practiced accuracy, signalled to other drivers, observed and commented on the idiosyncracies of other drivers, pointed out changes in road and other construction projects visible since they had last been seen, and in these and many other ways kept themselves almost constantly occupied (McBain, 1970, pp.517–518).

Exposure to a monotonous environment can exert adverse effects on subsequent task performance, as indeed can exposure to noise (see Cohen, 1980; Glass and Singer, 1972) and to some other stressors. Suedfeld (1969, 1975), for example, reviewed over 80 sensory deprivation experiments and demonstrated that exposure to sensory deprivation often facilitated the performance of simple tasks, but was much more likely to impair the performance of complex cognitive tasks. Tasks of moderate complexity, for the most part, showed no effects of exposure to sensory deprivation. Furthermore, Taylor (1961), in a small-scale study which appears not to have been replicated, found some evidence of the impairment of intellectual and cognitive abilities in long-term prisoners. Adverse effects of monotonous and repetitive jobs upon the health, both mental and physical, of workers have also been reported (see Cox, 1978, 1980; Fraser, 1947; Johannsson, 1978; Kornhauser, 1965), although the results of such studies are sometimes difficult to interpret.

Psychophysiological studies of boredom

Boredom, like other emotional states, has been thought to be accompanied by a shift in the level of activation or arousal. The concept of arousal developed from numerous attempts to relate variations in behavioural intensity, and in the quality of task performance, to physiological changes. Augmentations of behavioural intensity (along a continuum ranging from deep sleep to extreme excitement) were considered to be associated with increases in the level of physiological functioning, as reflected in measures of muscular, autonomic, and cortical activity (see Duffy, 1962). The development of the concept of an arousal continuum was also influenced by research on the neural systems involved in the maintenance of wakefulness, which indicated the importance of the ascending reticular activating system and the diffuse thalamic projection system (see Lindsley, 1960; Magoun, 1958). Research on the consequences of exposure to sensory deprivation demonstrated that perceptual and cognitive processes were severely impaired, and led Hebb (1955) to emphasize the contribution made by sensory variation to the preservation of the efficient functioning of the brain. Finally, research concerned with the effects on task performance of various stressors, such as loud noise, sleep deprivation, and heat, and with those of motivational factors such as the provision of incentives and knowledge of results, also lent credibility to the concept of arousal.

Out of this work came the arousal theory of stress (Broadbent, 1963, 1971), which assumes that there is a general state of arousal or reactivity which is increased by loud noise or by incentives and reduced by boredom or loss of sleep. The arousal theory of stress makes a further assumption, reminiscent of the Yerkes–Dodson law, that the relationship between the level of arousal and the level of performance takes the form of an inverted U. This assumption has sometimes also been made by classical activation theory (Malmo, 1959) but is apparently not essential to it (Duffy, 1972). The inverted-U hypothesis holds that task performance is efficient when the level of arousal is either much above or much below an optimal point, although the nature of the performance deficit at high and low levels of arousal may well be different.

Despite some well-founded criticisms from several different perspectives, which have been directed at the idea of a unidimensional arousal continuum (for example, Broadbent, 1971; Dement, 1973; Gale, 1977; Hamilton, Hockey and Rejman, 1977; Lacey, 1967; see Hockey and Hamilton, Chapter 12 this volume), arousal theory has provided the impetus for the relatively small number of psychophysiological studies of boredom that have been conducted. One of the principal questions addressed by such studies concerns whether boredom is a state of high or of low arousal, and the contrasting views of Berlyne and Hebb on this point were mentioned earlier in the chapter. The results of two experiments reported by London, Schubert, and Washburn (1972) provide support for Berlyne's hypothesis that boredom is a high arousal state. In their first experiment, in which an independent groups design was employed, it was found that women undergraduates exhibited significantly higher galvanic skin potential levels during the performance of a 40-minute visual monitoring task than during a 40-minute period spent in composing stories in response to a series of Thematic Apperception Test cards. Subjects who performed the monotonous task also reported themselves to have felt significantly more bored and to have been significantly less interested in what they were doing than did subjects who wrote stories. In a second experiment, in which soldiers performed both a repetitive letter-writing task and a task requiring the composition of stories in response to magazine pictures, London *et al.* found that mean heart rate levels, although not skin conductance levels, were significantly higher during the letter-writing task than during story composition. As in the first experiment, subjects also reported themselves to be significantly more bored, apathetic, sleepy, tired, and restless, and significantly less interested and energetic, following the more monotonous task (letter writing) than following the story composition task. The results of these experiments seem to indicate that when men and women are engaged on tasks which provoke boredom the level of autonomic arousal increases, as Berlyne suggested.

However, studies of the relation between arousal level, boredom, and efficiency during task performance provide some support for Hebb's view that boredom is associated with a state of low arousal. A recent review paper on boredom (Thackray, 1981) concludes that the findings from both laboratory and field studies suggest that feelings of boredom are accompanied by low or declining rather than high or increasing levels of arousal.

In several apparently monotonous and repetitive tasks performance decrements with time at work are accompanied by decreases in autonomic arousal or in the level of cortical activation. Concomitant declines in the level of activation (or arousal) and in the level of efficiency are frequently observed in vigilance situations (for example, Davies and Krkovic, 1965; Davies and Parasuraman, 1977; Griew, Davies, and Treacher, 1963; O'Hanlon and Beatty, 1976, 1977; Wilkinson, Morlock, and Williams, 1966), but they have also been reported for task situations involving pursuit motor performance (Barmack, 1937), simple addition (Barmack, 1937), tracking (Kornfeld and Beatty, 1977), a version of the Stroop test (Frankenhaeuser, Mellis, Rissler, Bjorkvall and Patkai, 1968), and serial reaction time (Thackray, Jones, and Touchstone, 1973, 1974). In many such tasks the incidence of boredom also becomes more frequent with time at work, so that boredom increases as the level of arousal declines. However, changes in performance can take place in the absence of changes in boredom ratings, and vice versa and, as Barmack (1937) noted, 'reports of boredom may occur without depressed vital activity' (p.67). Changes in psychophysiological activity with time on task may also be much the same for monotonous tasks and for more interesting or demanding tasks (Bailey, Thackray, Pearl, and Parish, 1976; Frankenhaeuser, Norheden, Myrsten, and Post, 1971), although the performance of otherwise repetitive tasks differing in the degree of load they impose, so that the subject is either 'over-' or 'under-loaded', may be associated with different patterns of or rates of change in physiological measures over the course of the task (Sales, 1970). But while there may be some differences in the average level of arousal between tasks experienced as interesting or boring, as the studies of London *et al.* (1972) indicate, similar declines in arousal appear to occur during the performance of a wide range of tasks, whether or not they are perceived as monotonous. A pattern of psychophysiological changes specific to the performance of monotonous tasks has not yet been isolated. A review paper by Smith (1981) states that studies have shown that boredom is associated with some indices of high arousal and some of low arousal simultaneously, and concludes that 'boredom is a complex response pattern consisting of a variety of changes'. Furthermore, in vigilance situations at least, performance decrements with time at work are not satisfactorily explained in terms of declines in arousal, and other kinds of explanation seem more appropriate (Davies and Parasuraman, 1977, 1982; Parasuraman, 1979, in press; Parasuraman and Davies, 1977).

In several studies Grandjean and his associates have employed critical flicker-fusion frequency (CFF), often thought to be an index of mental fatigue (see Grandjean and Perret, 1961, and Simonson and Brozek, 1952, for reviews), in the investigation of performance in monotonous tasks. Grandjean (1969) considered boredom and fatigue to be closely linked and suggested that 'the effects of monotony arise because initial stimulation of reticular activating system is lacking' (p.64), since the level of stimulation provided by the task situation and the work environment is insufficiently varied.

Typically, increases in mental fatigue, inferred from performance scores or subjective ratings, are associated with reductions in CFF. Small to moderate doses of hypnotic (Weber, Jermini, and Grandjean, 1975) and stimulating (Fussler, O'Hanlon, Weber, and Grandjean, 1979) drugs produce opposing effects on CFF and subjective ratings of state (fatigue, boredom, sleepiness, distractibility, and the ability to concentrate). Grandjean Baschera, Martin, and Weber (1977) argued that CFF would decline with time at work during the performance of a 3-hour monotonous task (counting nails at a fixed pace) but not during the performance of an 'activating' task of similar duration (in which subjects carried out psychomotor tests and listened to music). Their results supported this hypothesis, as Figure 1 shows. In addition, subjective ratings of motivation and the 'ability for action' decreased for the monotonous task but not for the activating task.

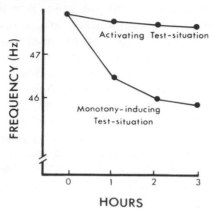

Figure 1. Critical flicker fusion (CFF) as a function of time spent at work on a monotonous counting task and in an activating test situation. From Grandjean *et al.* (1977).

In a further experiment Baschera and Grandjean (1979) examined temporal changes in CFF during the performance of three versions of the nail-sorting task. The three versions of the task differed in complexity: the first (low complexity) required subjects simply to sort nails into batches of 50, the second (moderate complexity) to sort them by colour and the number of markings, and the third (high complexity) to sort them also by colour and markings but in accordance with an elaborate set of rules. Different patterns of decline in CFF were observed for the three versions of the task with the low complexity version, regarded as the most monotonous, producing the earliest and greatest decline. CFF decrements with time at work have been reported for other monotonous tasks, such as packaging ball bearings (O'Hanlon, Weber, Fussler, and Grandjean, 1979) and in industrial work situations the amount of decline in CFF has been shown to be related to the frequency of task-irrelevant activities (Kishida, 1973) and to vary with the kind of shift (day or night) being worked (Grandjean, 1970).

THE ALLEVIATION OF BOREDOM

We have already considered, explicitly or implicitly, characteristics, and modifications, of task situations which may alleviate boredom. Some, such as the provision of music and of rest pauses, are relatively superficial; others, falling into the general category of job enrichment, involve more fundamental restructuring of the task or the working environment, and, as noted above, job enrichment techniques have been extensively applied to a variety of work situations (see, for example, Davis and Cherns, 1975). Briefly, job enrichment may involve operatives carrying out their own inspection of completed work; they may have more freedom to plan the job and to determine how it is done; they may receive increased recognition for job accomplishment, greater feedback, less supervision, and so on. These are all ways of changing the structure of the working environment in order to enhance its intrinsically-motivating properties, and have been shown to increase job satisfaction and the quality and quantity of output, decrease boredom, and reduce absenteeism and labour turnover. However, critics have argued that an enriched job is not desired by most blue-collar workers (see Reif and Luthans, 1972, for example), or that it is not a source of satisfaction to all workers, particularly those with urban, industrial backgrounds and those who choose to work in large firms (Hulin and Blood, 1968; Wall, 1973). Many workers almost certainly take it for granted that their work will be boring, just as they may take it for granted that it will be dirty or noisy; their interest is not in increasing satisfaction at work, but in earning money to increase satisfaction outside it. In any case job enrichment may not be possible for some extremely boring jobs, and the best solution in such cases might be to automate where it is possible to do so (for instance by employing 'robot' assemblers), and to make more extensive use of incentive schemes and job rotation where it is not.

On the other hand, favourable results of job enrichment programmes continue to appear in the literature, and many of the criticisms of such programmes have been countered. As Locke (1975) points out, people's work experiences largely determine the kind of satisfaction they report themselves as obtaining from their work; the fact that people do not claim to gain satisfaction from job factors such as autonomy and responsibility does not mean that they will not respond to them when they are provided. Some people have insufficiently varied work experience to enable them to predict accurately how they will respond to an entirely new job situation. Job enrichment practitioners report that it is very difficult to predict who will respond most favourably to an enriched job. Sometimes, indeed, the most 'troublesome' employees respond quite favourably (Maher, 1971).

In conclusion, tackling the problem of boredom and other negative aspects of the division of labour is difficult and job enrichment is not a panacea. Yet it is encouraging to note that much of the published work describing attempts at job enrichment has reported success of one kind or another. At both a practical and a theoretical level, there is a need to identify in greater detail the elements comprising job enrichment and to determine the relatively effectiveness of each element in producing improved morale and productivity.

SUMMARY

Boredom is here regarded as an individual's emotional response to an environment that is perceived to be monotonous, and this chapter examines the effects of monotony and boredom on the performance of industrial and laboratory tasks. The chapter begins by surveying definitions of monotony and boredom and proceeds to a review of industrial studies of boredom and output, varied and unvaried work, music, output, and job attitudes and correlates of the susceptibility to boredom. Laboratory investigations of monotony and boredom are then considered, including studies of vigilance, individual and group differences in boredom, and performance and psychophysiological correlates of the experience of boredom. The chapter concludes with a brief assessment of ways in which boredom might be alleviated.

REFERENCES

Allen, G. W. (1967) *William James*. New York: Viking Press.
Antrobus, J. S., Coleman, R., and Singer, J. L. (1967) Signal-detection performance by subjects differing in predisposition to daydreaming. *Journal of Consulting Psychology*, 31, 487–491.
Appley, M. H. and Trumbull, R. (eds.) (1967) *Psychological Stress*. New York: Appleton Century Crofts.
Bailey, J. P., Thackray, R. I., Pearl, J., and Parish, T. S. (1976) Boredom and arousal. Comparison of tasks differing in visual complexity. *Perceptual and Motor Skills*, 43, 141–142.
Baldamus, W. (1951) Type of work and motivation. *British Journal of Sociology*, 2, 44–58.
Baldamus, W. (1961) *Efficiency and Effort*. London: Tavistock.
Barmack, J. E. (1937) Boredom and other factors in the physiology of mental effort: An exploratory study. *Archives of Psychology*, 218, 1–83.
Baschera, P. and Grandjean, E. (1979) Effects of repetitive tasks with different degrees of difficulty on critical fusion frequency (CFF) and subjective state. *Ergonomics*, 22, 377–385.
Bergum, B. O. and Lehr, D. J. (1962) Vigilance performance as a function of interpolated rest. *Journal of Applied Psychology*, 46, 425–427.
Berlyne, D. E. (1960) *Conflict, Arousal and Curiosity*. New York: McGraw-Hill.
Bernstein, H. E. (1975) Boredom and the ready-made life. *Social Research*, 42, 512–537.

Betts, G. H. (1909) *The Distribution and Functions of Mental Imagery.* Teachers College, Columbia University, New York.
Birchall, D. (1975) *Job Design.* Epping: Gower Press.
Broadbent, D. E. (1963) Differences and interactions between stresses. *Quarterly Journal of Experimental Psychology*, **15**, 205–211.
Broadbent, D. E. (1971) *Decision and Stress.* London: Academic Press.
Burnett, I. (1925) An experimental investigation into repetitive work. *IFRB Report No. 30.* London: HMSO.
Burney, C. (1952) *Solitary Confinement.* New York: Clerke and Cockeran.
Cahoon, R. L. (1970) Vigilance performance under hypoxia. *Journal of Applied Psychology*, **54**, 479–483.
Caplan, R. D., Cobb, S., French, J. R. P., van Harrison, R., and Pinneau, S. R. (1975) *Job Demands and Worker Health.* US Department of Health, Education and Welfare Publication, No. (NIOSH) 75–160.
Cohen, S. (1980) After effects of stress on human performance and social behavior: A review of research and theory. *Psychological Bulletin*, **88**, 82–108.
Colquhoun, W. P. (1959) The effect of a short rest pause on inspection efficiency. *Ergonomics*, **2**, 367–372.
Cooper, R. (1973) Task characteristics and intrinsic motivation. *Human Relations*, **26**, 387–413.
Cox, T. (1978) *Stress.* London: Macmillan.
Cox, T. (1980) Repetitive work. In C. L. Cooper and R. Payne (eds.), *Current Concerns in Occupational Stress.* Chichester: John Wiley & Sons.
Craik, K. J. W. and Mackworth, N. H. (1943) Unpublished report to RAF Coastal Command quoted in N. H. Mackworth (1950), *Medical Research Council Special Report*, No. 268. London: HMSO.
Csikszentmihalyi, M. (1975) *Beyond Boredom and Anxiety.* San Francisco: Jossey-Bass.
Davenport, W. G. (1972) Vigilance and arousal: Effects of different types of background stimulation. *Journal of Psychology*, **82**, 339–346.
Davies, D. R. and Krkovic, A. (1965) Skin conductance, alpha-activity and vigilance. *American Journal of Psychology*, **78**, 304–306.
Davies, D. R. and Parasuraman, R. (1977) Cortical evoked potentials and vigilance: A decision theory analysis. In R. R. Mackie (ed.), *Vigilance: Theory, Operational Performance and Physiological Correlates.* New York: Plenum.
Davies, D. R. and Parasuraman, R. (1982) *The Psychology of Vigilance.* London: Academic Press.
Davies, D. R. and Shackleton, V. J. (1975) *Psychology and Work.* London: Methuen.
Davies, D. R. and Tune, G. S. (1970) *Human Vigilance Performance.* London: Staples.
Davies, D. R., Hockey, G. R. J., and Taylor, A. (1969) Varied auditory stimulation, temperament differences and vigilance performance. *British Journal of Psychology*, **60**, 453–457.
Davies, D. R., Lang, L., and Shackleton, V. J. (1973) The effects of music and task difficulty on performance at a visual vigilance task. *British Journal of Psychology*, **64**, 383–389.
Davies, D. R., Shackleton, V. J., and Lang, L. (1972) The effects of complexity and uncertainty upon performance at a problem-solving task. *Psychonomic Science*, **27**, 193–194.
Davis, L. E. and Cherns, A. B. (1975) *The Quality of Working Life.* London: Collier Macmillan.
Dement, W. C. (1973) Commentary. In W. B. Webb (ed.), *Sleep: An Active Process.* Glenview, Illinois: Scott Foresman.

Dickson, J. W. (1973) The physical correlates of variety in work. *Human Relations*, **26**, 715–733.

Dudley, N. A. (1958) Output patterns in repetitive tasks. *Institute of Production Engineering Journal*, **37**, 187–198.

Duffy, E. (1962) *Activation and Behavior*. New York: John Wiley & Sons.

Duffy, E. (1972) Activation. In N. S. Greenfield and R. A. Sternbach (eds.), *Handbook of Psychophysiology*. New York: Holt, Rinehart & Winston.

Eysenck, H. J. and Eysenck, S. B. G. (1968) A factorial study of psychoticism as a dimension of personality. *Multivariate Behavioral Research*, Special Issue, 15–32.

Farley, F. H. and Farley, S. V. (1967) Extroversion and stimulus seeking motivation. *Journal of Consulting Psychology*, **31**, 215–216.

Farley, F. H. and Farley, S. V. (1970) Impulsiveness, sociability and the preference for varied experience. *Perceptual and Motor Skills*, **31**, 47–50.

Fenichel, O. (1934) Zur Psychologie der Langeweite (On the psychology of boredom). *Imago* (Leipzig), **20**, 270–281.

Form, W. H. (1973) Auto workers and their machines: A study of work, factory and job satisfaction in four countries. *Social Forces*, **52**, 1–15.

Fowler, H. (1967) Satiation and curiosity: Constructs for a drive and incentive-motivational theory of exploration. In K. W. Spence and J. T. Spence (eds.), *The Psychology of Learning and Motivation: Advances in Research and Theory, Vol. 1*. New York: Academic Press.

Fox, J. G. (1975) Vigilance and arousal. In C. G. Drury and J. G. Fox (eds.), *Human Reliability in Quality Control*. London: Taylor & Francis.

Frankenhaeuser, M., Mellis, I., Rissler, A., Bjorkvall, C., and Patkai, P. (1968) Catecholamine excretion as related to cognitive and emotional reaction patterns. *Psychosomatic Medicine*, **30**, 109–120.

Frankenhaeuser, M., Norheden, B., Myrsten, A. L., and Post, B. (1971) Psycho-physiological reactions to understimulation and overstimulation. *Acta Psychologica*, **35**, 298–308.

Fraser, R. (1947) The incidence of neurosis among factory workers. *IFRB Report No. 90*. London: HMSO.

Fussler, C., O'Hanlon, J. F., Weber, A., and Grandjean, E. (1979). Electroencephal-ography and other psychophysiological measurements related to vigilance performance under two conditions of arousal. *Paper presented at the 7th Congress of the International Ergonomics Association, Warsaw, Poland.*

Gale, A. (1977) Some EEG correlates of sustained attention. In R. R. Mackie (ed.), *Vigilance, Theory, Operational Performance and Physiological Correlates*. New York: Plenum.

Gale, A., Morris, P. E., Lucas, B., and Richardson, A. (1972) Types of imagery and imagery types: An EEG study. *British Journal of Psychology*, **63**, 523–531.

Geiwitz, P. J. (1966) Structure of boredom. *Journal of Personality and Social Psychology*, **3**, 592–600.

Glass, D. and Singer, J. E. (1972) *Urban Stress*. New York: Academic Press.

Grandjean, E. (1969) *Fitting the Task to the Man: An Ergonomic Approach*. London: Taylor & Francis.

Grandjean, E. (1970) Fatigue. *American Industrial Hygiene Association Journal*, **31**, 410–411.

Grandjean, E. and Perret, E. (1961) Effects of pupil aperture and of the time of exposure on the fatigue induced variations of the flicker fusion frequency. *Ergonomics*, **4**, 17–23.

Grandjean, E., Baschera, P., Martin, E., and Weber, A. (1977) The effects of various conditions on subjective states and critical flicker frequency. In R. R. Mackie (ed.), *Vigilance: Theory, Operational Performance and Physiological Correlates.* New York: Plenum.

Griew, S., Davies, D. R., and Treacher, A. C. C. (1963) Heart rate during auditory vigilance performance. *Nature*, **200**, 1026.

Grubb, E. A. (1975) Assembly line boredom and individual differences in recreation participation. *Journal of Leisure Research*, **7**, 256–269.

Guest, D., Williams, R., and Dewe, P. (1978) Job design and the psychology of boredom. *Paper presented at the 19th International Congress of Applied Psychology, Munich, West Germany.*

Hackman, J. R. and Lawler, E. E. (1971) Employee reactions to job characteristics. *Journal of Applied Psychology Monographs*, **55**, 259–286.

Hamilton, P., Hockey, G. R. J., and Rejman, M. (1977) The place of the concept of activation in human information processing theory: An integrative approach. In S. Dornic (ed.), *Attention and Performance, VI.* Hillsdale, New Jersey: Erlbaum.

Hebb, D. O. (1955) Drives and the CNS (conceptual nervous system). *Psychological Review*, **62**, 243–254.

Hill, A. B. (1975a) Work variety and individual differences in occupational boredom. *Journal of Applied Psychology*, **60**, 128–131.

Hill, A. B. (1975b) Extraversion and variety-seeking in a monotonous task. *British Journal of Psychology*, **66**, 9–13.

Hulin, C. L. and Blood, M. R. (1968) Job enlargement, individual differences and worker responses. *Psychological Bulletin*, **69**, 41–55.

Isaac, W. (1962) Evidence for a sensory drive in monkeys. *Psychological Reports*, **11**, 170–181.

Izard, C. E. (1978) *Human emotions.* New York: Plenum.

Jerison, H. J. (1970) Vigilance, discrimination and attention. In D. I. Mostofsky (ed.), *Attention: Contemporary Theory and Analysis.* New York: Appleton Century Crofts.

Johansson, G. (1978) Social, psychological and neuroendocrine stress reactions in highly mechanical work. *Ergonomics*, **21**, 583–599.

Kasl, S. V. (1978) Epidemiological contributions to the study of work stress. In C. L. Cooper and R. Payne (eds.), *Stress at Work.* Chichester: John Wiley & Sons.

Kerr, W. A. (1943) Where they work: Workplace performance of 228 electrical workers in terms of music. *Journal of Applied Psychology*, **27**, 438–442.

Kerr, W. A. (1945) Experiments on the effects of music on factory production. *Applied Psychology Monographs*, No. 5.

Kerr, W. A. and Keil, R. C. (1963) A theory and factory experiment on the time-drag concept of boredom. *Journal of Applied Psychology*, **47**, 7–9.

Kirkpatrick, F. H. (1943) Music in industry. *Journal of Applied Psychology*, **27**, 268–274.

Kishida, K. (1973) Temporal change of subsidiary behavior in monotonous work. *Journal of Human Ergology*, **2**, 75–89.

Kishida, K. (1977) A study on subsidiary behavior in monotonous work. *International Journal of Production Research*, **15**, 609–621.

Knight, R. (1929) Work and Rest. In C. S. Myers (ed.), *Industrial Psychology.* London: Oxford University Press.

Kornfeld, C. M. and Beatty, J. (1977) EEG spectra during a long-term compensatory tracking task. *Bulletin of the Psychonomic Society*, **10**, 46–48.

Kornhauser, A. (1965) *Mental Health of the Industrial Worker.* New York: Wiley & Sons.

Kubose, S. K. (1972) Motivational effects of boredom on children's response speeds. *Developmental Psychology*, **6**, 302–305.

Lacey, J. I. (1967) Somatic patterning and stress: Some revisions of activation theory. In M. H. Appley and R. Trumbell (eds.), *Psychological Stress: Issues in Research.* New York: Appleton Century Crofts.

Lindsley, D. B. (1960) Attention, consciousness, sleep and wakefulness. In J. Field, H. W. Magoun, and V. E. Halls (eds.), *Handbook of Physiology. Section 1, Volume 3.* Baltimore: Williams & Wilkins.

Locke, E. A. (1975) Personnel attitudes and motivation. *Annual Review of Psychology,* **26**, 457–480.

Lodahl, T. M. (1964) Patterns of job attitudes in two assembly technologies. *Administrative Science Quarterly*, **8**, 483–519.

London, H., Schubert, D. S. P., and Washburn, D. (1972) Increase of autonomic arousal by boredom. *Journal of Abnormal Psychology*, **80**, 29–36.

McBain, W. N. (1970) Arousal, monotony and accidents in line driving. *Journal of Applied Psychology*, **54**, 509–519.

McDowell, R. J. S. and Wells, H. M. (1927) The Physiology of monotony. *British Medical Journal*, **1**, 414–415.

McGehee, W. and Gardner, J. E. (1949) Music in a complex industrial job. *Personnel Psychology*, **2**, 405–417.

Mackworth, N. H. (1950) Researches on the measurement of human performance. *Medical Research Council Special Report*, No. 268. London: HMSO.

Magoun, H. W. (1958) *The Waking Brain.* Springfield, Illinois: Charles C. Thomas.

Maher, J. R. (ed.) (1971) *New Perspectives in Job Enrichment.* New York: Van Nostrand Reinhold.

Malmo, R. B. (1959) Activation: A neuropsychological dimension. *Psychological Review*, **66**, 367–386.

Morris, P. E. and Gale, A. (1974) A correlational study of variables related to imagery. *Perceptual and Motor Skills*, **38**, 659–665.

Münsterberg, H. (1913) *Psychology and Industrial Efficiency.* New York: Houghton.

Murrell, K. F. H. (1962) Operator variability and its industrial consequences. *International Journal of Production Research*, **1**, 39–50.

Murrell, K. F. H. (1965) *Ergonomics.* London: Chapman & Hall.

Murrell, K. F. H. (1971) Industrial work rhythms. In W. P. Colquhoun (ed.), *Biological Rhythms and Human Efficiency.* London: Academic Press.

Myers, A. K. and Miller, N. E. (1954) Failure to find a learned drive based on hunger: Evidence for learning motivated by 'exploration'. *Journal of Comparative and Physiological Psychology*, **47**, 428–436.

Myers, C. S. (ed.) (1920) *Mind and Work.* London: University of London Press.

Myers, T. I. (1969) Tolerance for sensory and perceptual deprivation. In J. P. Zubek (ed.), *Sensory Deprivation: Fifteen Years of Research.* New York: Appleton Century Crofts.

Nelson, T. M. and Bartley, S. H. (1968) The pattern of personal response arising during the office work day. *Occupational Psychology*, **42**, 77–83.

Newman, R. I., Hunt, D. L., and Rhodes, F. (1966) Effects of music on employee attitude and productivity in a skateboard factory. *Journal of Applied Psychology*, **50**, 493–496.

Nicholson, N., Brown, C. A., and Chadwick-Jones, J. K. (1976) Absence from work and job satisfaction. *Journal of Applied Psychology*, **61**, 728–737.

O'Hanlon, J. F. and Beatty, J. (1976) Catecholamine correlates of radar monitoring performance. *Biological Psychology*, **4**, 293–304.

O'Hanlon, J. F. and Beatty, J. (1977) Concurrence of electroencephalographic and performance changes during a simulated radar watch and some implications for the arousal theory of vigilance. In R. R. Mackie (ed.), *Vigilance: Theory, Operational Performance and Physiological Correlates.* New York: Plenum.

O'Hanlon, J. F., Weber, A., Fussler, C., and Grandjean, E. (1979). Monotony effects in repetitive tasks. I. Interrelations between performance, physiological functions and subjective state. *Paper presented at the 7th Congress of the International Ergonomics Association, Warsaw, Poland.*

Ornstein, R. E. (1970) *On the Experience of Time.* Harmondsworth: Penguin.

Osborne, E. E. (1919) The output of women workers in relation to hours of work in shell-making. *IFRB Report No. 2.* London: HMSO.

O'Toole, J. (ed.) (1973) *Work in America.* Report of a Special Task Force to the Secretary of Health, Education and Welfare. Cambridge, Massachusetts: MIT Press.

Parasuraman, R. (1979) Memory load and event rate control sensitivity decrements in sustained attention. *Science,* **205,** 924–927.

Parasuraman, R. (in press) The psychobiology of sustained attention. In J. S. Warm (ed.), *Sustained attention in Human Performance.* Chichester: John Wiley & Sons.

Parasuraman, R. and Davies, D. R. (1977) A taxonomic analysis of vigilance performance. In R. R. Mackie (ed.), *Vigilance: Theory, Operational Performance and Physiological Correlates.* New York: Plenum.

Porter, L. W. and Steers, R. M. (1973) Organisational, work and personal factors in employee turnover and absenteeism. *Psychological Bulletin,* **80,** 151–176.

Reif, W. E. and Luthans, F. (1972) Does job enrichment really pay off? *California Management Review,* **15,** 30–37.

Roethlisberger, F. J. and Dickson, W. J. (1941) *Management and the Worker.* Cambridge: Harvard University Press.

Rose, M. (1975) *Industrial Behaviour.* London: Allen Lane.

Rothe, H. F. (1946) Output curves among butter wrappers: I. Work curves and their stability. *Journal of Applied Psychology,* **30,** 199–211.

Saldanha, E. (1955) An investigation into the effects of prolonged and exacting visual work. *Medical Research Council Applied Psychology Unit Report,* No. 243/55.

Sales, S. M. (1970) Some effects of role overload and role underload. *Organisational Behavior and Human Performance,* **5,** 592–608.

Siddall, G. J. and Anderson, D. M. (1955) Fatigue during prolonged performance on a simple compensatory tracking task. *Quarterly Journal of Experimental Psychology,* **7,** 159–165.

Simonson, E. and Brozek, J. (1952) Flicker fusion frequency. Background and applications. *Physiological Reviews,* **32,** 349–378.

Smith, H. C. (1947) Music in relation to employee attitudes, piece-work production, and industrial accidents. *Applied Psychology Monographs,* No. 14.

Smith, P. C. (1953) The curve of output as a criterion of boredom. *Journal of Applied Psychology,* **37,** 69–74.

Smith, P. C. (1955) The prediction of individual differences in susceptibility to industrial monotony. *Journal of Applied Psychology,* **39,** 322–329.

Smith, P. C. and Lem, C. (1955) Positive aspects of motivation in repetition work: effects of lot size upon spacing of voluntary work stoppages. *Journal of Applied Psychology,* **39,** 330–333.

Smith, R. P. (1981) Boredom: a review. *Human Factors,* **23,** 329–340.

Spielberger, C. D. (ed.) (1966) *Anxiety and Behavior.* New York: Academic Press.

Stagner, R. (1975) Boredom on the assembly line: Age and personality variables. *Industrial Gerontology,* **2,** 23–44.

Suedfeld, P. (1969) Changes in intellectual performance and in susceptibility to influence. In J. P. Zubek (ed.), *Sensory Deprivation: Fifteen Years of Research.* New York: Appleton Century Crofts.

Suedfeld, P. (1975) The benefits of boredom: Sensory deprivation reconsidered. *American Scientist*, **63**, 60–69.

Taylor, A. J. W. (1961) Social isolation and imprisonment. *Psychiatry*, **24**, 373–376.

Taylor, P. J. (1968) Personal factors associated with sickness absence. *British Journal of Industrial Medicine*, **25**, 106–118.

Terkel, S. (1977) *Working*. Harmondsworth: Penguin.

Thackray, R. I. (1981) The stress of boredom and monotony: A consideration of the evidence. *Psychosomatic Medicine*, **43**, 165–176.

Thackray, R. I., Bailey, J. P., and Touchstone, R. M. (1977) Physiological, subjective and performance correlates of reported boredom and monotony while performing a simulated radar control task. In R. R. Mackie (ed.), *Vigilance: Theory, Operational Performance and Physiological Correlates*. New York: Plenum.

Thackray, R. I., Jones, K. N., and Touchstone, R. M. (1973) Self-estimates of distractibility as related to performance decrement on a task requiring sustained attention. *Ergonomics*, **16**, 141–152.

Thackray, R. I., Jones, K. N., and Touchstone, R. M. (1974) Personality and physiological correlates of performance decrement on a monotonous task requiring sustained attention. *British Journal of Psychology*, **65**, 351–358.

Thompson, L. A. (1929) Measuring susceptibility to monotony. *Personnel Journal*, **8**, 172–197.

Turner, A. N. and Lawrence, P. R. (1965) *Industrial Jobs and the Worker. An Investigation of Response to Task Attributes*. Graduate School of Business Administration, Harvard University.

Turner, A. N. and Miclette, A. L. (1962) Sources of satisfaction in repetitive work. *Occupational Psychology*, **36**, 215–231.

Uhrbrock, R. S. (1961) Music on the job: Its influence on worker morale and production. *Personnel Psychology*, **14**, 9–38.

Vernon, H. M. (1919) The influence of hours of work and of ventilation on output in tinplate manufacture. *IFRB Report No. 1*. London: HMSO.

Vernon, H. M. (1920a) Fatigue and efficiency in the iron and steel industry. *IFRB Report No. 5*. London: HMSO.

Vernon, H. M. (1920b) The speed of adaptation of output to altered hours of work. *IFRB Report, No. 6*. London: HMSO.

Vernon, H.M., Wyatt, S., and Ogden, A. D. (1924) On the extent and effects of variety in repetitive work. *IFRB Report, No. 26*. London: HMSO.

Viteles, M. S. (1932) *Industrial Psychology*. New York: Norton.

Vroom, V. H. (1962) Ego-involvement, job satisfaction and job performance. *Personnel Psychology*, **15**, 159–177.

Walker, C. R. and Guest, R. H. (1952) The man on the assembly line. *Harvard Business Review*, **30**, 71–83.

Wall, T. D. (1973) Ego-defensiveness as a determinant of reported differences in sources of job satisfaction. *Journal of Applied Psychology*, **58**, 125–128.

Ware, J. R., Kowal, B., and Baker, R. A. (1964) The role of experimenter attitude and contingent reinforcement in a vigilance task. *Human Factors*, **6**, 111–115.

Weber, A., Jermini, C., and Grandjean, E. P. (1975) Relationship between objective and subjective assessment of experimentally induced fatigue. *Ergonomics*, **18**, 151–156.

Welford, A. T. (1965) Fatigue and monotony. In O. G. Edholm and A. L. Bacharach (eds.), *The Physiology of Human Survival*. London: Academic Press.

Wiener, E. L. (1975) Individual and group differences in inspection. In C. G. Drury and J. G. Fox (eds.), *Human Reliability in Quality Control*. London: Taylor & Francis.

Wilkinson, R. T., Morlock, H. C., and Williams, H. L. (1966) Evoked cortical response during vigilance. *Psychonomic Science*, **4**, 221–222.

Wyatt, S. (1924) On the extent and effect of variety in repetitive work. Pt.B: The effect of changes in activity. *IFRB Report, No. 26*. London: HMSO.

Wyatt, S. (1929) Boredom in industry. *Personnel Journal*, **8**, 161–171.

Wyatt, S. (1950) An autobiography. *Occupational Psychology*, **24**, 65–74.

Wyatt, S. and Fraser, J. A. (1928) The comparative effect of variety and uniformity in work. *IFRB Report No. 52*. London: HMSO.

Wyatt, S. and Langdon, J. N. (1932) Inspection processes in industry. *IFRB Report, No. 63*. London: HMSO.

Wyatt, S., Fraser, J. A., and Stock, F. G. L. (1929) The effects of monotony in work. *IFRB Report, No. 56*. London: HMSO.

Wyatt, S., Langdon, J. N., and Stock, F. G. L. (1937) Fatigue and boredom in repetitive work. *IFRB Report, No. 77*. London: HMSO.

Zimbardo, P. G. and Miller, N. E. (1958) Facilitation of exploration by hunger in rats. *Journal of Comparative and Physiological Psychology*, **51**, 43–46.

Zuckerman, M. (1974) The sensation seeking motive. *Progress in experimental personality research*, **7**, 79–148.

Zuckerman, M. (1976) General and situation-specific traits and states: New approaches to assessment of anxiety and other constructs. In M. Zuckerman and C. D. Spielberger (eds.), *Emotions and Anxiety*. Hillsdale, New Jersey: Erlbaum.

Zuckerman, M., Kolin, E. A., Price, L., and Zoob, I. (1964) Development of a sensation-seeking scale. *Journal of Consulting Psychology*, **28**, 477–482.

Chapter 2

Heat and Cold

Jerry D. Ramsey

The thermal environment is one of the natural conditions within which all persons are required to perform various activities. A person commonly operates within a microclimate generated by clothing or shelter within this ambient climatic state. Physiological responses to these thermal conditions vary widely between individuals, and within the same individual from one period to the next. Even so, the human's basic physiological relationships with thermal environments are well established.

The relationships between thermal environment and psychological activity or perceptual–motor performance is less well established. This chapter concentrates on this area and attempts to summarize and evaluate observations from the literature concerning a variety of topics, including thermoregulation, acclimatization, thermal indices, performance of physical work, performance on physical work, performance on combined physical and mental work tasks, and perceptual–motor task performance. Additionally discussed are factors affecting performance, such as brief exposures to high temperatures, skill and motivation, combined stressors, and work within the comfort range.

THERMOREGULATION

The human as a homeothermic animal has highly developed abilities to maintain heat balance within very narrow limits around 37°C (98.6°F). Although the human can function with environmental temperatures that range from -30°C (22°F) to $+80$°C (176°F) and beyond, a variation of plus or minus 4°C (7°F) in the core temperature will impair both physical and mental work capacity (Astrand and Rodahl, 1970). Core temperature, which cycles in a circadian rhythm in a response to the metabolic activities and demands of the individual, reaches a level during the midnight–early morning period which is 1°C (2°F) or more below the peak reached in the mid-afternoon–evening period (see Chapters 4 and 9).

33

Heat balance

There are several factors which have direct and major contributory influence on the degree of heat storage within the human. The basic thermodynamic process of heat exchange between the individual and his environment can be represented as follows:

$$\pm S = M \pm C \pm R \pm D - E,$$

where

S = body heat storage,
M = energy metabolism or body heat production,
C = convective heat exchange,
R = radiative heat exchange,
D = conductive heat exchange, and
E = evaporative heat exchange.

A state of thermal equilibrium is indicated when S approaches zero in this heat balance equation. The metabolic heat production, M, is always a positive factor; even under basal or resting conditions the body oxidizes fuel (food) and is generating heat in the metabolic process. The convective heat exchange, C, represents thermal exchange between the body and the fluid/air which surrounds it and may be either positive or negative depending upon whether air temperature is above or below the temperature of the skin, 35°C (95°F). Radiative heat exchange, R, may also be either positive or negative depending upon whether the human body represents the hot or cold radiative body in the environment. The body heat gain from radiation can be very high because the sun, furnaces, and other large sources can generate considerable electromagnetic radiation. Conversely, body heat loss due to radiation is a much smaller quantity since the temperature differential is normally much lower. Conductive heat exchange, D, is normally considered to be negligible in thermal balance considerations, since human sensory receptors do not normally allow voluntary contact between extremely hot or extremely cold bodies for a duration long enough to transfer much heat conductively. Evaporative heat exchange, E, which is always a negative factor in this equation, represents the major mechanism for dissipation of stored body heat.

Physiological response

The hypothalamus serves as the neural controller for the human thermal regulation process. It utilizes sensory information from core, muscle, skin, and chemoreceptors to control sweating mechanisms, vasomotor changes in the blood vessels, and motor neurons of the muscles, which in turn affect the level of temperature in the body itself. (For an information-flow model of this process, see Milsum, 1966.) Metabolic work or exercise, excretion, and also the thermal environment in which the human exists, serve as the external drivers to this regulating system. For example, upon entry into a high temperature environment: skin receptors would sense the temperature differential between body and environment, storage of heat within the core temperature would be sensed as thermal exchange takes place, the hypothalamus would initiate appropriate vasodilation so that more blood could flow through the vessels nearer the surface as an aid in the transfer of heat from the core to the surface for further heat exchange with the environment, heart rate would increase in order to increase the flow of blood to the skin, and sweating would be initiated in order to enhance evaporative heat loss. Conversely, upon entrance into a colder environment vasoconstriction would be initiated so that the blood flow would be restricted near the surface and in the appendages, and would circulate primarily through the core, vital organs, and brain areas in order to maintain the critical body functions at their required temperatures. The fingers and toes, because of their relatively small radii and relatively large blood flow, are both effective heat loss structures and also the areas affected first by the vasoconstriction process during cold exposure.

The vasomotor activity represents the body's initial response to changing environmental conditions, and is also a primary regulating mechanism when thermal variation is minimal. Sweating, however, provides the major ability of the human for losing heat to the surroundings. There is no single stimulus to initiate sweating, but rather it responds to complex interaction of blood, skin, glandular, and heat sensors. Sweat rates of 1 litre per hour are considered the maximum levels which can be substained over a work day without avoiding fatigue of the sweating mechanism. Thirst does not normally provide an adequate stimulus to guarantee replacement of body water loss during sweating. High levels of relative humidity result in little or no differential in vapor pressure between the environment and the wetted skin, and thus adversely affect the ability to lose heat evaporatively.

Another important physiological response relates to the ability of the thermoregulatory process to maintain, over a broad range of temperatures and at a given work load, a relatively constant storage level of heat. With increasing environmental temperatures, however, the point is reached where the prescriptive zone is exceeded and an environmentally driven zone is entered (Lind, 1963), and a significant increase in core temperature is initiated. This relationship has served as the basis for describing threshold values for exposure to hot occupational environments (Ramsey, 1975).

Clothing effects

An external factor important to thermal equilibrium is the effect of clothing. Clothing can serve as a protection against radiant heat exposure, but it normally serves as a deterrent to evaporative heat exchange. Both the thickness and the impermeability of clothing affect the ability to transfer heat between the human and his environment. For environments colder than the human body the increase in clothing insulation value, normally measured in 'clo' units, will help retard loss of heat from the body to the environment. The use of impermeable garments is not recommended even in cold weather, however, since sweating will occur within the microclimate created between the garment and the skin. One clo is approximately equivalent to the thermal insulation required by a resting nude person to maintain comfort in a normally ventilated room at 21°C (70°F) and 50 per cent relative humidity. Clothing consisting of a long sleeve shirt, trousers, and jacket represent about 1 clo, and clothing insulation greater than 4 clo is bulky to the point of interference with walking or performing normal tasks. An arctic sleeping bag can provide 10–15 clos of protection.

ACCLIMATIZATION AND ADAPTATION

Repeated exposure to a given level of work and thermal environment will result in a series of significant physiological adjustments as response to the given set of conditions. Typical acclimatization to heat shows a significant lowering of the body temperature and heart rate, and an increase in efficiency of the sweating mechanism during thermal exposure over a period of time. It is generally agreed that an exposure period of at least 2 to 4 hours per day and a duration of 5 to 10 days will result in physiological adaptation such that the total strain on an individual is considerably reduced during that specific level of heat and work. Acclimatization to the cold environment is much less dramatic or efficient and is best indicated as increases in metabolism, reduction of shivering reaction, and reduction of cold discomfort or pain due to more precise vasoconstriction. Repeated localized exposure such as to the hand will tend to cause increase blood flow through the area as part of the adaptation process.

There is considerable evidence from people living in the arctic or in the tropic regions of the world that not only have clothing habits been developed to be consistent with their environment, but these people typically have a higher level of tolerance to their environment. Part of this can be attributed to the physiological changes that have occurred as part of the acclimatization over a short-term period, and also to the life experience influences which have occurred over seasons, or indeed generations, in that particular environment. The psychological factors of expectancy and human will are also very important; a person might function quite well in both the sauna and on the ski slopes, but if required to perform normal work activity in either of these environments would feel they represent very undesirable work environments.

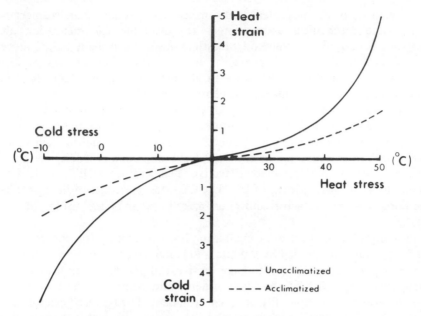

Figure 2. Schematic representation of the effect of acclimatization. From Macpherson (1974). (Reproduced by permission of Taylor and Francis Ltd.)

A summary schematic representative of the effect of acclimatization in the heat and cold is shown in Figure 2. Although the point of thermal neutrality remains basically unchanged, the imposition of heat or cold stress produces less physiological strain in the acclimatized individual (Macpherson, 1974).

INDICES FOR DEFINING THERMAL LEVELS

Heat indices

Air temperature or dry bulb temperature is generally measured using a mercury and glass thermometer, or other thermally sensitive elements exposed to the air. Wet bulb temperature is normally obtained by placing a wetted wick over a thermally sensitive instrument and artificially producing a flow of air across the wick. The ability to remove heat from the wick-covered thermal sensor is directly related to the vapour pressure or relative humidity of the air. Relative humidity is the measure of the amount of moisture contained in the air, as a percentage of the total amount of moisture which the air could hold at a given temperature. Relative humidity can be determined from a psychometric chart if the dry bulb and wet bulb temperatures have been measured. The thermal environment can be completely defined by these two measures plus the velocity of air movement and a measure of radiant heat. Numerous electrical and mechanical anemometers are available for measuring air velocity. A commonly use method of estimating mean radiant temperature is as a function of globe temperature. A globe thermometer is a hollow copper sphere typically 15cm (6in.) in diameter which is black on the outside and has a thermal sensor at the centre of the sphere.

Several indices have been developed as means of combining important thermal variables into a single index number. The Effective Temperature (ET) scale represents an empirically developed, subjective index relating equivalent levels of warmth as a function of dry bulb, wet bulb, and air velocity variables (ASHRAE, 1972). A Corrected Effective Temperature (CET) scale has been developed as a refinement of ET. The CET acknowledges radiant heat as an important thermal factor and thus greatly expands the utility of the ET index.

A meaningful index to use for evaluating hot working environments is the Heat Stress Index, originated by Belding and Hatch (1955). This index utilized heat transfer equations representing convective, radiant, and evaporative heat exchange characteristics of the environment, and compares these with the maximum evaporative capability of an environment. The required evaporative heat loss, E_{req}, is a function of the metabolic heat generation plus the radiative and convective characteristics of the environment, whereas the maximum evaporative capability of an environment, E_{max}, depends on the movement and vapor pressure of the air. The Heat Stress Index (HSI) is a function of the ratio of E_{req} to E_{max} and gives a single number which incorporates all the physiological and environmental factors into a single index of heat strain. The HSI serves as a useful tool in identifying individual thermal and work components and determining their influence on the total heat strain that can be expected. Engineering controls or administrative exposure changes can be tested for their influence within the HSI models as an aid in determining the best design for an environment.

Another index which has recently found much use for describing thermal environments associated with both physiological and psychological heat stress is the Wet Bulb Globe Temperature (WBGT) (NIOSH, 1972; Ramsey and Morrissey, 1978). Unlike Effective Temperature which must be obtained from a chart or nomograph, the WBGT can be measured directly with three instruments: dry bulb (db), natural wet bulb (nwb), and the globe (g) thermometers. The natural wet bulb utilizes the natural movement of the air in the environment as an indicator of the cooling power of the vapour pressure/air movement combination. The WBGT can be calculated as follows:

$$\text{WBGT indoors} = 0.7\,\text{nwb} + 0.3\,\text{g},$$
$$\text{WBGT outdoors} = 0.7\,\text{nwb} + 0.1\,\text{db} + 0.2\,\text{g}.$$

Cold indices

The Windchill Index represents the most universally accepted scale for describing the combined effects of air temperature and wind velocity. This index provides a more accurate description of cold thermal conditions than does air temperature alone since freezing capability increases with higher air movements. Although this index was developed using the freezing rate of a container of water, it does provide a useful means for estimating those combinations likely to freeze human flesh.

A useful format for windchill information, modified to assume calm conditions of 6 km/h (4 mile/h) wind speed, is shown in Table 3. This chart depicts the cooling power of wind on exposed flesh, expressed as an equivalent chill temperature. Temperature and wind speed combinations in the 'little danger' area pose potential cold injury problems unless skin is completely dry and exposure time is below 5 hours.

PHYSICAL PERFORMANCE IN THE HEAT

The effects of hot environments upon physical work output and performance are well understood and documented. Physical work in a hot environment generates physiological changes which are readily measurable (e.g. body temperature, heart rate, oxygen consumption, and blood chemistry), and the metabolic cost of various activities have been well calibrated, defined, and tabulated. Factors affecting physical capability to do work in the heat include physical fitness, general health, age, sex, nutritional status, and also the mental willingness to perform under a physical workload and heat. Even under the positive conditions of high physical fitness, high strength, and high levels of health and motivation, continuous muscular activity results in a build-up of fatigue and in a reduction of performance capability. Fatigue onset is also greatly enhanced by other working conditions and stressors that are often associated with work in the heat, e.g. noise, dust, fumes, hypoxia, vibration, and confinement. Heat not only impacts negatively on measurable physiological responses; loss of performance during physical activity in the heat can also be measured directly in the terms of reduced production, output, quality, or repetitions per unit time.

There are many reported studies involving exercise or physical work effects on the performance of perceptual–motor tasks. Benor and Shvartz (1971) measured the performance of visual and auditory vigilance while exercising on a treadmill in temperatures from 30 to 50°C (86 to 122°F). Reaction time was not affected by the body temperature increase but the detection rate deteriorated significantly, suggesting a 'short-term mobilization mechanism' for reaction time performance. Conversely, Shvartz *et al.*, (1976) found that exercise had adverse effects on simple reaction time.

Table 3. Cooling power of wind on exposed flesh, expressed as an equivalent temperature (under calm conditions). From U.S. Army Research Institute of Environmental Medicine.

Estimated wind speed (km/h, mile/h)	Actual thermometer reading (°C/°F)											
	10/50	4.4/40	−1.1/30	−6.7/20	−12.2/10	−17.8/0	−23.3/−10	−28.9/−20	−34.4/−30	−40/−40	−45.6/−50	−51.1/−60
	Equivalent chill temperature (°C/°F)											
Calm	10/50	4.4/40	−1.1/30	−6.7/20	−12.2/10	−17.8/0	−23.3/−10	−28.9/−20	−34.4/−30	−40/−40	−45.6/−50	−51.1/−60
8/5	8.9/48	2.8/37	−2.8/27	−8.9/16	−14.4/6	−20.6/−5	−26.1/−15	−32.2/−26	−37.8/−36	−43.9/−47	−55.6/−68	−55.6/−68
16/10	4.4/40	−2.2/28	−8.9/16	−15.6/4	−22.8/−9	−31.1/−24	−36.1/−33	−43.3/−46	−50/−58	−56.7/−70	−63.9/−83	−70.6/−85
24/15	2.2/36	−5.6/22	−12.8/9	−20.6/−5	−27.8/−18	−35.6/−32	−42.8/−45	−50/−58	−57.8/−72	−102.8/−85	−72.8/−99	−80/−112
32/20	0.0/32	−7.8/18	−15.6/4	−23.3/−10	−31.7/−25	−39.5/−39	−47.2/−53	−55/−67	−63.3/−82	−71.1/−96	−73.3/−110	−86.7/−124
40/25	−1.1/30	−8.9/16	−17.8/0	−26.1/−15	−33.9/−29	−42.2/−44	−50.6/−59	−58.9/−74	−67.7/−88	−75.6/−104	−83.3/−118	−91.7/−113
48/30	−2.2/28	−10.6/13	−18.9/12	−27.8/−18	−35.2/−33	−44.4/−48	−52.8/−63	−61.7/−79	−70/−84	−78.3/−108	−87.2/−125	−95.6/−140
56/35	−2.8/27	−11.7/11	−20.0/4	−29.4/−21	−37.3/−35	−46.1/−51	−55.0/−67	−63.3/−82	−72.2/−88	−80.6/−113	−88.4/−129	−98.3/−145
64/40	−3.3/26	−12.2/10	−21.1/−6	−29.4/−21	−38.4/−37	−47.2/−53	−56.1/−69	−102.8/−85	−73.3/−100	−82.2/−116	−91.1/−132	−100/−148

(wind speed greater than 64 km/h (40 mile/h) have little additive effect)

Little danger
In 5 hours with dry skin Maximum danger of false sense of security

Increasing danger
Danger from freezing of exposed flesh within 1 minute

Great danger
Flesh may freeze within 30 seconds

Trenchfoot and immersion foot may occur at any point on this chart

Mackworth (1961) utilized a heavy pursuit-meter which required a combination of perceptual–motor tracking and muscular load from handling the heavy pointer. In this study significant decrements in performance were observed as the thermal load was increased.

Russell (1957) conducted a study over a range of temperatures between −10 and 40°C (14 and 104°F). Tactual sensitivity was shown to decrease at both the high and low temperature extreme, whereas kinaesthetic sensitivity was effected only by temperatures below the comfort range and after extended duration of exposure. Grip strength was also tested and similarly showed deterioration at both high and low temperature extremes.

Physical strength appears to be minimally affected by increasing levels of temperature. Exposure of high enough intensity and duration to generate localized or general fatigue will affect performance, but prior to exposure extremes there does not seem to be general heat effects. Perceptual–motor performance with exercise appears to follow the same pattern, i.e. work which creates muscular fatigue will negatively affect muscular-based perceptual–motor performance, but has less direct effect on primary cognitive tasks such as those involving reaction time.

PERCEPTUAL–MOTOR PERFORMANCE IN THE HEAT

Whereas decreases in the capabilities to do physical work are relatively predictable, human performance is much more variable and unpredictable when it involves sedentary work, low metabolic costs, perceptual–motor, or mental activities. Although exposure to environmental temperature extremes commonly yield physiological, psychological, or mental responses which indicate some change in performance, the precise effects of environmental stress are difficult to predict as a result of the complex interaction of the individual with the task and environment.

There are many work tasks which involve a limited degree of muscular effort but a high level of mental or perceptual–motor effort. Many tasks found in the industrial, military, and general work environment have this characteristic. Attempts to isolate the effects of heat on these types of tasks are numerous in the literature, but in general represent data obtained under laboratory conditions where many variables are controlled and thermal effects can be measured as an independent variable affecting performance. Most of the reported data is from male populations, although there are a few reports of female sedentary performance (Ramsey and Pai, 1975). Military and college student subjects are well represented in reported data, and differences in these population characteristics must be considered when evaluating or extrapolating results from individual studies. The military subject normally represents a more controlled experimental environment, whereas the college student subject is much more likely to be affected by variations in sleep, nutrition, alcohol, and fatigue to a degree that is beyond the experimenter's control. There is also evidence that college students can perform better at tasks requiring concentration, high levels of attention, and effective ways of approaching a complex task.

Sedentary tasks

A very comprehensive set of studies on performance in the heat were conducted partially as paired studies by Pepler (1958) in Singapore and Mackworth (1961) in England. Based on this series of studies, Mackworth indicated a critical region around 27–30°C (81–86°F) ET above which performance is adversely affected for acclimatized man. Pepler's observation that performance decrement occurs at ±3°C (5°F) from a basic ET of 27°C (81°F) were not substantiated in a follow-up study by Chiles (1958). Chiles did suggest that 43°C (109°F) ET was at the upper limit for unimpaired mental performance for unprotected subjects. Differences between military and student subject populations used in the two respective studies have been suggested as contributory to the apparent contradictory findings between Peper and Chiles.

Azer *et al.* (1972) demonstrated a significant loss of tracking performance and poor reaction time for subjects in 35°C (95°F) high humidity, although performance at 35°C (95°F) moderate humidity or 37.8°C (100°F) moderate humidity did not show significant decrements. Furthermore, the 'peripheral field of awareness was not significantly affected by any of the environments'. A review of perceptual–motor tasks, i.e. time estimation, reaction time, vigilance, tracking, and skilled-cognitive tasks, performed under elevated temperatures was reported by Grether (1973). He found that tapping and reaction time actually got faster with elevated temperatures and that vigilance also improved, with an optimum at 26.7°C (80°F) ET. Other tasks, however, showed only minor effects up to around 29.4°C (85°F) ET, i.e. levels within physiological adjustment capability, and then performance decrements above that level.

The majority of investigations concerning vigilance tasks depict a normal performance decrement which begins within about 20 minutes duration of work on the task. The effect of heat on the performance of this type of task is an amplification of the drop in performance which is normally expected (Mortagy and Ramsey, 1973).

Research on mental performance frequently demonstrates no significant relationship as a function of heat. Givoni and Rim (1962) report no difference in performance scores on a dominoes task at conditions of 25°C (77°F) or 43°C (109°F). In a study by Bartlett and Gronow (1953) no decremental effects were noted on various mental performance tasks when exposed to air temperatures between 22.5 and 32.8°C (72.5 and 91°F) ET. Edholm (1963) reported no significant differences when performing intelligence or memory tasks between comfort levels and higher ambient conditions. Mental tasks involving anagram solution under various levels of high temperature and high humidity were investigated by Fine *et al.* (1960). They were unable to establish any negative effects on performance due to either the high temperature or high humidity levels. Subjects sustained equivalent complex mental performance at exposure levels of 21 and 35°C (70° and 95°F) under high and low humidity conditions.

Brief high-temperature exposures

Brief exposures at high temperature levels have also been studied by several investigators. A study by Blockley and Lyman (1951) investigated extremely high temperatures and brief duration exposures while performing simulated pilot tasks. The levels chosen were 71°C (160°F)/61 minutes, 83.3°C (200°F)/29 minutes, and 113°C (235°F)/21 minutes. Performance decrements became more serious only toward latter stages of exposure, i.e. from 4 to 13 minutes before the exposures were terminated due to physiological responses reaching hazardous levels. Iampietro *et al.* (1969) investigated pilots performing complex performance tasks under conditions of low humidity and very high temperature. Decrement was observed at 71°C (160°F), but not at 60°C (140°F), for a 30-minute period.

Poulton and Kerslake (1965) exposed 12 experienced subjects to temperatures of 25°C (77°F) and 45°C (113°F) with low humidity. Subjects were required to perform simultaneously a memorization and a monitoring task, and upon initial exposure to the heat, subjects were found to perform better in the hotter environment. After the initial stimulating effects of the heat, however, a general decrement in performance was observed. They suggested that 'man may be able to work efficiently for a short period when first entering an enclosed space such as a cockpit with a temperature of 45°C, provided that he starts reasonably cool and that humidity is kept low and the air movement adequate'.

Pepler (1958) reports initial enhancement of perceptual–motor performance to occur during the first few minutes of high temperature exposure. Similar effects were noted by Ramsey *et al.* (1975) and Ramsey and Pai (1975) where actual improvements or enhancements in performance were noted during initial exposure to what would be considered high and debilitating levels of thermal exposure. After continued exposure at high temperatures, performance did drop markedly, but the initial improvement effects were very clear.

The degree of task difficulty as a factor affecting performance has not been adequately defined, and this lends to the inconsistency observed in assessing performance effects due to climate. In those cases where heat effects on perceptual–motor performance have been reported, there seems to be a strong influence on the muscular aspects of performance, i.e. reduction of the manipulative or motor ability of the subject. Bell and Provins (1962) in their topical review of temperature and human performance state that available derived data are insufficient for a completely satisfactory classification of heat effects, and until all factors are adequately defined the relationship between heat stress and performance decrement cannot be wholly established.

Skill and motivation

The use of incentives as a means of retarding performance losses in the heat has proved only partially successful. Mackworth (1961) investigated performance of a physical pull-task which involved muscular activity of a single arm. The 'good skill' subjects performed at a higher level, but showed greater loss of performance under conditions of increasing heat. The use of additional incentives to either good or average subjects did not counteract the performance losses due to increasing heat load.

Bell and Provins (1962) also noted that subjects in tasks which are associated with high skill are most sensitive to the effects of adverse thermal conditions. Mackworth (1961) studied telegraphy operators who were categorized as having poor to good skill levels. The poor operators who found the task 'hard going' showed the most decrement in heat conditions. This is in contradiction to the above cited pull-task study, where the best performers showed the most adverse effects due to high temperature. These apparent conflicting findings can be partially explained by noting differences in arousal conditions between these tasks. The poor telegraphy performers were already mentally loaded, and the arousing nature of heat created overload which negatively effected the performance. The poor physical (pull-task) performers were under-loaded compared to the best group, and additional heat created an arousal effect that enhanced their output (Provins, 1966). In general tasks and subjects associated with high psychological costs are more sensitive to the effects of adverse thermal conditions (Bell and Provins, 1962).

Secondary tasks are sometimes utilized as a more sensitive indicator of performance effects due to a hot environment. Bursill (1958) studied subjects on a primary pursuit rotor/secondary peripheral light response task at temperatures between 18 and 35°C (65 and 95°F) ET. He showed a decrease in perceptual signal detection performance at the high temperature if the primary task was difficult, but no thermal effects if the primary task was easier.

A person in the heat generally does a poor job of relating their own thermal discomfort, drowsiness, boredom, and estimates of the job performance to their actual performance score and/or time on duty (Ramsey *et al.*, 1974). Mackworth (1961) also noted that most subjects, when asked for subjective responses, preferred to work at a medium speed and most indicated discomfort at a higher temperature level, although actual data showed that performance was best at the slow speed and the more moderate temperature. Reddy and Ramsey (1976), in investigating simple tasks in moderate thermal conditions, noted that in the judgement of the subjects, boredom represented a bigger problem than did drowsiness or fatigue. The total disagreeable responses were more numerous at a 25.6°C (78°F) level than at either higher or lower temperatures, and this also correlated with the poorer performance results obtained at the middle temperature. Gafafer (1964) indicated that subjective effects of anxiety, irritability, general lassitude, decrease in morale, and inability to concentrate are all functions of exposure to hot environments.

Combined stressors

Since heat is often encountered in combination with some other adverse environment, combined environmental stressors have been commonly investigated. Poulton and Edwards (1974a) investigated tracking, visual vigilance, and a five-choice task under combined stressors of mild heat and low frequency noise. The combined effects of the two stressors were smaller than the sum of the two separate effects. This is as anticipated based on the inverted-U relationship of arousal theory (but see Chapter 12). The effect of combined stressors of heat and noise on tracking tasks were also studied by Dean *et al.* (1964). Subjects who were highly skilled pilots were shown to maintain their performance for brief periods (20 minutes) in temperatures as high as 43°C (109°F) and noise levels as high as 110 dB. The combined effects of heat and noise were reported in a study of 144 male and female subjects by Bell (1978). He found performance decrements associated with high noise levels of 95 dBA and high temperatures of 35°C (95°F) were additive for a secondary task of number processing, but neither heat nor noise affected performance on the primary pursuit-rotor task.

High altitude and heat are also commonly encountered in combination. In investigating the physical performance of Nepalese subjects, Lahiri *et al.* (1976) showed that a 'hot, humid environment at sea levels is as much incapacitating as is hypoxia at high altitude'. The combined effects of altitude at 4300 meters (14,100ft) and heat at 88 per cent relative humidity/35°C (95°F) air temperature on the performance of complex perceptual–motor tasks were reported by Fine and Kobrick (1978). Although individuals responded differently to a variety of 'artillery fire direction' tasks, all showed significant and similar effects due to heat and to altitude. Poulton and Edwards (1974b) reported the combined effects of heat and motion sickness drugs on a battery of perceptual–motor tasks. Decrements in performance occurred in some instances, but for the less sensitive measures the decrement was found only with the two stressors in combination.

The composite of research concerning combined stressors supports the notion that the performance results obtained are highly variable and are a direct function of the stressor levels and the specificity of the tasks utilized in the study.

Acclimatization and perceptual–motor performance

Results are far from conclusive concerning perceptual–motor performance as affected by degree of acclimatization. The acclimatized individual will in general be more tolerant and physiologically more able to work in a hot environment without adverse effects upon performance. Edholm (1963) studied a business task using acclimatized and unacclimatized subjects and was able to detect differences in their performance on this type task. Ramsey *et al.* (1975) summarized a variety of perceptual–motor and heat studies which reported acclimatized and unacclimatized subjects. Considerable variability in the results were noted, but a general tendency was observed that unacclimatized subjects demonstrated more performance variability than did the acclimatized individuals.

Elevated body temperature and arousal

Wilkinson *et al.* (1964) studied perceptual–motor tasks of addition and vigilance while core temperature was maintained between 37.3 and 38.5°C (98 and 101.3°F). Compared with normal temperature performances, addition was impaired and vigilance was improved at the high body temperature. At the lower temperature an improvement in addition and an impairment in vigilance was indicated. After the subject became acclimatized no corresponding improvement in performance was observed at the elevated body temperature. Body temperature at 38.5°C (98°F) was shown by Fox *et al.* (1963) to adversely affect arithmetic tasks. Studies of body temperature versus performance on perceptual–motor tasks in general show no consistent correlation between performance and core temperature, except that both the decrement and body temperature rise with increases in thermal exposure level (Carpenter, 1946; Pepler, 1958; Mackworth, 1961). See Chapters 4 and 9, however, for effects of natural diurnal variation in body temperature, or of changes produced by shift work. Raising the body temperature has two kinds of effects on performance according to Poulton (1970). He reports that increasing body temperature will increase the level of arousal and improve performance on simple vigilance, but impair performance on complex calculation tasks.

Holmberg and Wyon (1969) in their observation of classroom behaviour in moderate heat supports the effects of arousal in that 27°C (81°F) indicated poorer performance than was observed at either 20 or 30°C (68 or 86°F). The arousal effect is clearly indicated in the study by Ramsey *et al.* (1975), which showed that none of four perceptual–motor tasks investigated yielded performance decrements during the first 30 minutes at 40.5°C (105°F) WBGT temperature. Although subjects were physically exhausted and noticeably stressed by this exposure, it appeared that, with effort by the individual and the arousal or simulating effect generated by the heat, a person keeps his mental and simple motor skill abilities at a high level of performance during short work bouts.

Some of the apparent inconsistencies between performance and body temperature relate to the fact that a body temperature expressed in terms of core or deep body temperature has an attendant lag time that is not normally associated with a reported oral temperature. Provins (1966) reports that human skilled performance tends to be affected more by a rise in body temperature than to the climatic factors themselves. Accordingly, 'an hypothesis is proposed which explains the increase in body temperature in terms of an increase in general levels of arousal . . .', and heat stress effects on performance tend to occur 'when the degree of activation exceeds the optimum value for performance on the task concerned'.

SUMMARY ANALYSES OF PERFORMANCE IN THE HEAT

Unimpaired mental performance

Wing (1965) attempted to bring some degree of order to the wide variety of experimental results reported in the literature concerning thermal stress, exposure time, and human performance. He summarized the results of 15 different studies which involved sedentary tasks or mental performance and which had reported well-defined levels of temperature and duration. This data, as summarized by Wing, became the basis for a suggested upper limit exposure for unimpaired mental performance reported by the National Institute for Occupational Safety and Health (NIOSH, 1972). This recommendation from NIOSH, as depicted in Figure 3, made this statement: 'For sedentary jobs where continuous unimpaired mental performance is required, no employee shall be exposed to conditions which exceed the limits set forth in this figure.' The NIOSH document refers to the Wing report in these terms: 'It is quite apparent from these studies that thermal stress is an important factor where the worker has to make critical decisions, make fine discriminations, or have to perform fast or skillful actions because safety will depend on constant alertness.'

Ramsey *et al.* (1975) attempted to validate the NIOSH proposed upper limit by measuring performance on four different sedentary tasks at temperatures ranging between 29 and 40.5°C (85 and 105°F) WBGT and for work periods up to 2 hours. Results of this study suggested that the upper limit for unimpaired mental performance is not well represented as a single line, due to the large number of variables affecting human performance. It is logical

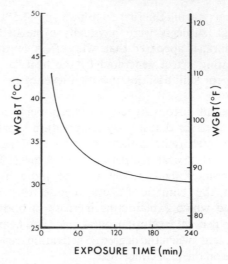

Figure 3.   Upper limits of exposure for unimpaired mental performance. NIOSH
(1972). (Reproduced with permission.)

to anticipate that a relationship similar to that of Figure 3 exists between
duration of exposure and ambient temperature level. It is likely, however, that
this would be better represented as a range of temperatures associated with
each exposure time and within which the likelihood of performance
impairment is increased. Additionally, the compensating and adaptive nature
of the human operator plus the arousing nature of heat would support a higher
temperature limit for work exposures of brief duration.

Isodecrement curves

A comprehensive summary of perceptual–motor performance in hot environments is presented by Ramsey and Morrissey (1978). This study includes data
from those studies in the literature which provided temperature and exposure
time data as they affect performance on a variety of perceptual–motor tasks
categories, including: tracking, vigilance, eye–hand coordination, reaction
time, and mental tasks. The diversity of research findings reported in the
literature are a function not only of thermal effects, but also of differences in
tasks, experimental conditions, and subjects' experience, skill, age, motivation,
physical condition, sex, degree of acclimatization, general health, and
nutritional state. These differences lend to the difficulty in generalizing results
from a specific study to a broader population and set of conditions. Another
factor complicating the intercomparisons of experimental results is the use of a
variety of thermal indicators, e.g. dry bulb, wet bulb, relative humidity, Wet
Bulb Globe Temperature, Effective Temperature, with and without a reported

air movement or radiant heat load. An investigator will typically report performance in terms of either one or some combination of these thermal indicators. Ramsey and Morrissey provided a common basis for evaluating and comparing this research data by converting the thermal environment of each study analysed into an estimated Wet Bulb Globe Temperature (WBGT) value. The WBGT was selected as an index which indirectly incorporates the psychometric factors of air temperature, humidity, mean radiant heat, and air movement into a single indicator. The WBGT has much current acceptance as a meaningful index for assessing occupational exposure to hot occupational environments (WHO, 1969; Astrand *et al.*, 1975; NIOSH, 1972; ISO, 1982).

Each individual study included in this analysis was initially categorized by a specific temperature level in WBGT and the duration of exposure. Correspondingly, the reported effects on performance at each temperature–time combination were categorized as: no change in performance, a slight performance decrement, a significant performance decrement, or a performance improvement. Figure 4 includes the summary of those studies of tracking tasks in the heat which had reported temperature, time, and performance data in a retrievable format. Figure 4 shows for the task category of tracking: the exposure time scale running from 8 to 125 minutes, the author and year of the reported study, the number of subjects in the study, and a bar with coded symbols indicating the effects on performance at each reported temperature–time combination. Also included is a sub-task identification (e.g. pursuit or compensatory) that falls within the general category of tracking.

Summary data from the literature concerning performance on reaction time tasks in the heat is presented in Figure 5 using the same format described above, but with sub-tasks identified as simple or complex. Similar analysis was also conducted using summary data for these tasks: mental tasks, with sub-tasks of coding, multiplication, mental arithmetic, and short-term memory; vigilance tasks, with auditory and visual sub-tasks; complex tasks, with a variety of perceptual–motor subtasks; and eye–hand coordination tasks, with maze tracing and manual manipulation sub-tasks (Ramsey and Morrissey, 1978).

The presentation of research findings in this summary form provides a useful means of comparing the experimental features and results of the various studies of a given task category. It also presents general patterns and trends which are sometimes obscured by the specific details and contradictory findings reported in individual studies.

The individual discrete data points, defining performance effects at a particular temperature–time combination by a specific researcher, became a data input point for a multiple regression model. The model was used for developing predictive equations and a series of isodecrement, or equal-decrement, curves describing relationships between the exposure time, exposure temperature, and significance of performance changes. Performance

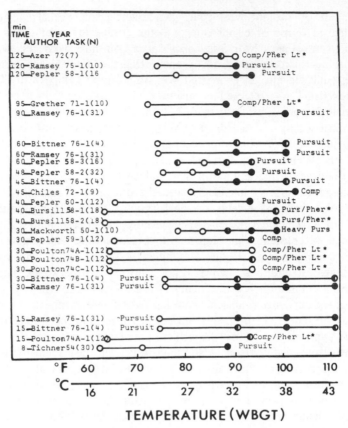

Figure 4. Performance of tracking tasks in the heat. (Figure reproduced from Ramsey and Morrissey, vol. 9, pp.66–71 of *Applied Ergonomics*, published by IPC Science and Technology Press Ltd, Guildford, Surrey, U.K.)

effects in the predictive models were coded as a −1 if performance decrement was indicated, as a 0 if no change of performance was indicated, and as a +1 if performance enhancement was indicated. Using this data, sets of models were developed to describe the relationships for each task category. Isodecrement curves were representing conditions of increasing likelihood of impaired motor performance were generated by setting predictive equations equal to decrement levels of 0.0, −0.3, −0.5, −0.8, and −1.0, and then solving in turn for temperatures and exposure times that represent each of these levels. Temperature–time combinations below the −0.3 curve have little likelihood of yielding performance decrements, whereas those above the −0.8 curve have high likelihood. Increasing likelihood of significant performance decrement occurs along the intermediary curves in between.

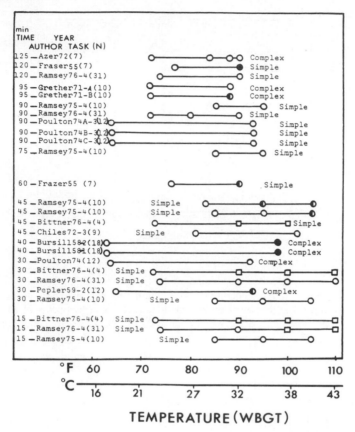

Figure 5. Performance of reaction time tasks in the heat. (Figure reproduced from Ramsey and Morrissey, vol. 9, pp.66–71 of *Applied Ergonomics*, published by IPC Science and Technology Press Ltd, Guildford, Surrey, U.K.)

Analysis of the isodecrement curves for each task category indicate that the temperature–time effects fall into two basic patterns. The data and corresponding isodecrement curves for reaction time and mental tasks are shown in Figure 6. The isodecrement curves superimposed over the numerous data points from the literature indicated little performance decrement along lower isodecrement curves, with increases in both time and temperature increasing the likelihood of impaired performance. Conversely, isodecrement curves for tracking, complex tasks, and vigilance tasks (Figure 7) indicate that increasing temperature level is much more degrading to performance than is increasing exposure time.

According to Ramsey and Morrissey (1978) these data summaries and models do not represent a 'final work in defining performance in the heat, but

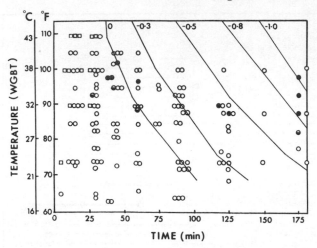

Figure 6. Temperature–time effects on mental-reaction time performance — isodecrement curves. (Figure reproduced from Ramsey and Morrissey, vol. 9, pp.66–71 of *Applied Ergonomics*, published by IPC Science and Technology Press Ltd, Guildford, Surrey, U.K.)

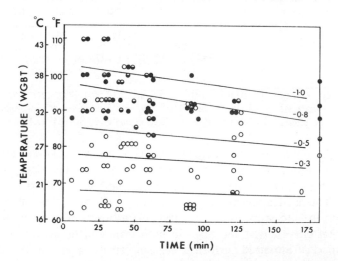

Figure 7. Temperature–time effects on combined tracking, vigilance, and complex tasks — isodecrement curves. (Figure reproduced from Ramsey and Morrissey, vol. 9, pp.66–71 of *Applied Ergonomics*, published by IPC Science and Technology Press Ltd, Guildford, Surrey, U.K.)

they do summarize a large amount of diverse data into a form which can aid in the prediction and decision-making processes' concerning heat and task performance.

EFFECTS OF COLD ENVIRONMENT ON MANUAL DEXTERITY

Many studies of performance in the cold have emphasized the effects of cold on the hands. Since the individual when required to work in the cold normally has a protective insulative layer of clothing consistent with the degree of cold environment, the internal microclimate of the body is less variable under normal cold exposure conditions. The hands, however, rapidly reach a limit in terms of ability to add insulating covering since normal dexterity and general hand work is adversely affected by increased thermal insulation and protection.

Loss of manipulative ability is amplified by loss of flexibility in the muscles of the forearm and finger, and also in the joints, probably due to an increase in synovial fluid viscosity. Local cooling of the hand or fingers produces stiffness of the joint and restriction of the joint movement. Cooling of the forearm alone causes loss in dexterity due to an increase in muscle viscosity of the long flexors and extensors of the fingers (Provins and Clark, 1960). Studies generally seem to suggest that local cooling of the hand or arm causes a significant decrement in manual dexterity, regardless, within limits, of the general body temperature.

The whole body frequently encounters a different and warmer temperature exposure in normal cold work situations than do the hands, and this factor is much reflected in the literature. Lockhart (1966) conducted a study in which the body temperature and the hand temperature were maintained at different levels. In one condition both the body and hand were warm, and the other conditions consisted of body and hand both cold, body warm and hand cold, or body cold and hand warm. On a series of manipulative tasks cold hand and body yielded the poorest performance. Warming the hands, even with the body remaining cold, improved the performance consistently, but there still remained a performance decrement which resulted from the sensations of cold on the man's brain and not exclusively to losses to the hand motor skills. Gaydos and Dusek (1958) report significant decrement in manual dexterity occurring when hand-skin temperature was lowered to about 11.5°C (52.7°F), but no impairment when hand-skin temperature was maintained at 27°C (80.6°F) or higher, even though the body surface was cooled in both conditions. Subjects' performance was equally poor when either the hands alone or the entire body was exposed to the cold.

An interesting study by Clark and Cohen (1960) required men in a comfortable temperature to put their hands in a cold box and tie knots in a rope. Greater loss in performance occurred with slow cooling rates, and it was noted that decrements continued even after hands were rewarmed to original temperatures. Conversely, Bensel and Lockhart (1974) investigated performance on a battery of six manual dexterity tasks during whole body cold exposure and observed that faster rates of hand cooling yielded the most decrease in manipulative performance. Kiess and Lockhart (1970) also studied performance decrements which occurred with lowered temperatures of the hand and suggested that hand warming may preserve psychomotor dexterity despite moderate lowering of the skin temperature. Provins and Clarke (1960) identified 6°C (42.8°F) as the minimum finger temperature for no impairment of tactual discrimination sensitivity. Dusek (1957) stated that finger temperatures below 15.6°C (60°F) created significant decrement in manual performance. Below 10°C (50°F) the onset of pain produces extensive loss of manual abilities, and below 4.4°C (40°F) tactual discrimination is lost, as is the ability to perform fine manipulative movements.

PERCEPTUAL–MOTOR PERFORMANCE IN THE COLD

Sedentary tasks

There is general consensus that loss of perceptual–motor performance in the cold is primarily a deterioration of motor capabilities rather than mental deterioration resulting from the cold. The opportunity to periodically rewarm or remove the hands from cold exposure provides great benefits in the retardation of losses of manipulative motor skills.

The influence of cold upon the efficiency of man was studied by Horvath and Freedman (1957), who quartered 22 men in a room with −30°C (−20°F) temperature for up to 2 weeks. Subjects showed significant performance decrements on manipulative and writing tasks, but neither mental performance on a code test or visual performance appeared to be affected by the cold. Lockhart *et al.* (1975) tested 32 subjects on a series of manual tasks with under-surface temperatures ranging between 9 and 18°C (48 and 64°F). Performance on all tasks decreased with lowered surface temperatures. Poulton *et al.* (1965) reported performance losses as a function of lower body temperature in a study using watchkeeping tasks, and conducted on-board ship in the Arctic. As body temperature fell it was accompanied by significant delay and inaccuracy in reporting of the watch. Perceptual–motor tasks such as tracking appear to be more adversely affected by moderate cold than are reaction–time tasks. When temperature or wind chill are extreme, the reaction time also degrades, due more likely to discomfort than to interference with the visual process. Teichner and Kobrick (1955) tested military subjects who were living in chambers maintained at 13 or 24°C (55 or 75°F). Those in lower temperature were markedly impaired in performing the pursuit motor tasks and were also less sensitive to radiant heat pain. The performance of tracking tasks in environments of 13, 21, 30, and 38°C (55, 70, 85 and 100°F) by Teichner and Wehrkamp (1954) suggested performance decrement both above and below 21°C (70°F). On the other hand, Teichner (1958) demonstrated that reaction time was not significantly affected by temperatures down to −37°C (−34.6°F) in still air, but increasing wind speed with the cold greatly reduced the reaction-time performance.

Other factors

Dietary and nutritional factors have the potential of affecting subjects' performance in the cold. Controlled studies in the laboratory by Mitchell *et al.* (1946) indicate that subjects exposed to low temperature performed differently on a variety of visual and psychomotor tasks based upon their diet. The psychomotor performance decrements and skin-cooling showed the most negative effects due to a high protein diet, followed by high carbohydrate diet. The high fat content diet provided the highest relative temperature and also the best performance. Higher metabolic rates increase total body heat; the high basal metabolic rate of the Eskimo can be attributed, in part, to the high fat content of their diets.

Surry (1968) states that the relationships between cold and accident rate are more likely a result of reduced sensitivity in fingers and toes, slowing down of movement itself, and interference from bulky clothing, rather than a loss of cognitive abilities in the cold.

Confounding of mental and motor effects

Attempts to empirically evaluate mental performance effects due to cold often result in a confounding due to the necessity of reporting mental scores or performance in the form of some motor output activity, e.g. writing with pencil, movement of switch, lever, or indicator. Such experimental conditions and factors have the potential of biasing an individual's mental performance score in the cold, as it is often impossible to separate the influence of losses in motor ability.

PERFORMANCE AT LEVELS OF COMFORT

The subjective feeling of thermal comfort is very important to humans and the topic has been much studied (ASHRAE, 1972). The same comfort conditions seem to apply to a person during their entire adult life, regardless of location in the world, time of day, or season (Fanger, 1970). There appears to be a correlation between 'comfort' and an individual's performance on perceptual–motor tasks, although the relationship is not easily defined. For continuous, repetitive mental work, with most populations the optimum thermal level is generally located in comfortably cool conditions.

Langkilde *et al.* (1973) observed that mental work was performed at the same level by subjects working at their individually preferred temperatures, or at temperatures ±4°C (7.2°F) from their preferred temperature. At warmer temperatures, subjects tended to over-estimate their performance and also indicated a higher degree of sleepiness and fatigue. Typewriting performance of males and females was studied by Wyon (1973). Subjects who regularly worked for several hours at 20–24°C (68–75°F) air temperature performed significantly better on typewriting in the cooler temperature. Holmberg and Wyon (1969) studied classroom performance and determined that reading speed and comprehension deteriorated over 30 per cent when the room temperature was raised from 20 to 30°C (69 to 86°F). They observed that moderate heat stress appears to lower the level of arousal of children. The effect of moderate heat on poorly motivated subjects was to decrease performance on routine tasks demanding concentration, whereas for well-motivated subjects performance was maintained; but only by exerting increased efforts.

Since the conditions of thermal comfort represent only minor excursions of the temperature, the effects of energy conservation practices have important performance implications. An air temperature of 25.6°C (78°F) at moderate relative humidity of 45 per cent and wearing light clothing or shorts is considered mid-comfort range for sedentary work (ASHRAE, 1972). Reddy and Ramsey (1976) investigated the performance of perceptual–motor tasks at mid-comfort, 25.6°C (78°F), plus the upper, 29°C (84°F), and lower, 20°C (68°F), extremes of comfort. In this study two of the four tasks evaluated actually showed improved performance at the lower temperature level. Physiological responses during the three temperature exposures also failed to demonstrate any major undesirable effects at any level. Subjective responses indicated that 20°C (68°F) was predoinantly considered as cool while the other temperatures were more often considered as neutral. The reduction in subjective comfort, however, was not accompanied by corresponding decrements in performance on perceptual–motor tasks.

SUMMARY

Performance on a specific task and under a specific set of thermal conditions is difficult to predict owing to the wide range of individual operator characteristics that relate to their handling of thermal loads and to their skill in performing the specific task. Summarized below, though, are some general relationships which may be useful for making decisions concerning design of work tasks in thermal environments.

Performance in a thermal environment and for exposure periods which yield general fatigue will also yield general performance decrements. Acclimatization will aid the physiological adjustments and reduce the fatigue cost of a task. With perceptual–motor tasks the effect is less pronounced, although there is some evidence that acclimatization reduces performance variability and improves performance.

Performance at perceptual–motor tasks during brief exposure to high temperature levels has been shown to cause only minor decrement or even enhancement of performance due to the arousal aspects of the heat. Hot temperature seems to affect skilled or trained personnel differently depending on the level of mental or physical load existing at non-heat-stress levels. If the work task does not load the operator, the addition of heat creates an arousal effect that will enhance the performance, but if the work task has already created an overload situation, additional heat will tend to degrade the performance.

Different types of perceptual–motor tasks are affected differentially by heat. This factor compounds the difficulty of predicting performance on combination tasks or real-life tasks. There are, however guidelines (isodecrement curves) for categories of tasks which may be useful in predicting relationships between heat, duration of exposure, and performance decrement.

The most significant effect of cold exposure is the loss of manipulative ability of the hands. Any action taken to reduce the intensity or exposure time to cold by the hands has a potential for helping reduce these performance losses, although the positive effect may be minimal.

Cognitive or mental tasks are much less affected by the cold than are motor tasks; however, it is often difficult to separate these effects since results of mental activity are generally reported by some motor movement which is more likely to be affected by cold. Perceptual–motor performance within the comfort zone is generally best at the lower end of this range.

REFERENCES

ASHRAE (1972) Physiological principles, comfort, and health. In *ASHRAE Handbook of Fundamentals*, Chapter 7. New York: American Society Heating, Refrigerating, and Air Conditioning Engineers, p.7.

Astrand, I., Axelson, O., Eriksson, U., and Olander, L. (1975) Heat stress in occupational work. *AMBIO*, **4**, 37–42.

Astrand, P. O. and Rodahl, K. (1970) *Textbook of Work Physiology*. New York: McGraw-Hill Book Company.

Azer, N. Z., McNall, P. E., and Leung, H. C. (1972) Effects of heat stress on performance. *Ergonomics*, **15**, 681–691.

Bartlett, D. J. and Gronow, D. G. C. (1953) The effect of heat stress on mental performance. FRPC Report 846, Royal Air Force Institute of Aviation Medicine.

Belding, H. S. and Hatch, T. F. (1955) Index for evaluating heat stress in terms of resulting physiological strains. *Heating Piping Air Conditioning*, **27**, 129–135.

Bell, C. R. and Provins, K. A. (1962) Effects of high temperature environmental conditions on human performance. *Journal of Occupational Medicine*, 4, 202–211.

Bell, P. A. (1978) Effects of noise and heat stress on primary and subsidiary task performance. *Human Factors*, 20, 749.

Benor, D. and Shvartz, E. (1971) Effect of body cooling on vigilance in hot environments. *Aerospace Medicine*, 42, 727–730.

Bensel, C. K. and Lockhart, J. M. (1974) Cold-induced vasodilation onset and manual performance in the cold. *Ergonomics*, 17, 717–730.

Blockley, W. V. and Lyman, J. (1951) Studies of human tolerance for extreme heat: IV. Psychomotor performance of pilots as indicated by a task simulating aircraft instrument flight. Tech. Report No. 6521, U.S. Air Force.

Bursill, A. E. (1958) The restriction of peripheral vision during exposure to hot and humid conditions. *Quarterly Journal of Experimental Psychology*, 5, 113–129.

Carpenter, A. (1946) The effect of room temperature of the resistance box test: A performance test of intelligence. Royal Naval Personnel Report 46:318, England.

Chiles, W. E. (1958) Effects of elevated temperatures on performance of a complex mental task. *Ergonomics*, 2, 89–96.

Clark, R. E. and Cohen, A. I. (1960) Manual performance as a function of rate of change in hand-skin temperature. *Journal of Applied Physiology*, 15, 496.

Dean, R. D., McGlothlen, C. L., and Monroe, J. L. (1964) Effects of combined heat and noise on physiology and subjective estimates of comfort and performance. Aerospace Technology, The Boeing Company, DZ-90 540.

Dusek, E. R. (1957) Effect of temperature on mental performance. In *Protection and Functioning of the Head in Cold Climates*. Washington, D.C.: National Academic Science Natural Resource Council.

Edholm, O. G. (1963) Heat acclimatization studied in the laboratory and the field a multi-disciplinary approach. *Ergonomics*, 6, 304–305.

Fanger, P. O. (1970) *Thermal Comfort: Analysis and Applications in Environmental Engineering*. New York: McGraw-Hill Book Company.

Fine, B. J. and Kobrick, J. L. (1978) Effects of altitude and heat on complex cognitive tasks. *Human Factors*, 20, 115–122.

Fine, B. J., Cohen, A., and Crist, B. (1960) Effect of exposure to high humidity at high and moderate ambient temperatures on anagram solution and auditory discrimination. *Psychological Report*, 7, 171.

Fox, R. H., Goldsmith, R., Hampton, I. F. G., and Wilkinson, R. T. (1963) The effects of a raised body temperature on the performance of mental tasks. *Journal of Physiology*, 167, 22–23.

Gafafer, W. M. (1964) *Occupational Diseases: A Guide to their Recognition*. U.S. Department of Health, Education and Welfare, USGPO, Washington, D.C.

Gaydos, H. F. and Dusek, E. R. Effects of localized hand cooling versus total body cooling on manual performance. *Journal of Applied Physiology*, 12, 377–380.

Givoni, R. and Rim, Y. (1962) Effect of the thermal environment and psychological factors upon the subject's responses and performance of mental work. *Ergonomics*, 5, 99–114.

Grether, W. R. (1973) Human performance at elevated environmental temperature. *Aerospace Medicine*, 44, 747–755.

Holmberg, I. and Wyon, D. P. (1969) The dependence of performance in school on classroom temperature. *Educational and Psychological Interactions*. School of Education, Malmo, Sweden, No. 31, pp.1–20.

Horvath, S. M. and Freedman, A. (1947) The influence of cold upon the efficiency of man. *Journal of Aviation Medicine*, 18, 158–164.

Iampietro, P. F., Chiles, W. D., Higgins, E. A., and Gibbons, H. L. (1969) Complex performance during exposure to high temperatures. *Aerospace Medicine*, **40**, 1331–1335.

International Organisation for Standardisation (ISO) (1982) *Hot Environments— Estimation of the Heat Stress on Working Man based on WBGT Index.* 150/TC 159, Geneva, Switzerland.

Kiess, H. O. and Lockhart, J. M. (1970) Effects of level and rate of body surface cooling on psychomotor performance. *Journal of Applied Psychology*, **54**, 386–392.

Lahiri, S., Weitz, C. A., Milledge, J. S., and Fishman, M. C. (1976) Effects of hypoxia, heat, and humidity on physical performance. *Journal of Applied Physiology*, **40**, 206–210.

Langkilde, G., Alexandersen, K., Wyon, D. P., and Fanger, P. O. (1973) Mental performance during slight cool or warm discomfort. *Archives Des Sciences Physiologiques*, **27**, 511–518.

Lind, A. R. (1963) A physiological criterion for setting thermal environmental limits for everyday work. *Journal of Applied Physiology*, **18**, 51–56.

Lockhart, J. M. (1966) Effects of body and hand cooling on complex manual performance. *Journal of Applied Psychology*, **50**, 57–59.

Lockhart, J. M., Kiess, H. O., and Clegg, T. J. (1975) Effect of rate and level of lowered finger surface temperature on manual performance. *Journal of Applied Psychology*, **60**, 106–113.

Mackworth, N. H. (1961) Researches on the measurement of human performance. In *Selected Papers on Human Factors in the Design and Use of Control Systems.* New York: Dover, pp.174–331.

MacPherson, R. K. (1974) Thermal stress and thermal comfort. In *Man Under Stress.* Taylor and Francis Ltd, pp.46–50.

Milsum, J. H. (1966) *Biological Control Systems Analysis.* New York: McGraw-Hill Book Company.

Mitchell, H. H., Glickman, N., Lambert, E. H., Keeton, R. W., and Fahnstock, M. K. (1946) The tolerance of man to cold as affected by dietary modifications: Carbohydrate versus fat and the effect of frequency of meals. *American Journal of Physiology*, **146**, 84.

Mortagy, A. K. and Ramsey, J. D. (1973) Monitoring performance as a function of work/rest schedule and thermal stress. *American Industrial Hygiene Association Journal*, **34**, 474–480.

NIOSH (1972) *Criteria for a Recommended Standard-Occupational Exposure to Hot Environments.* Washington, D.C.: National Institute for Occupational Safety and Health, USGPO-HSM 72-10269.

Pepler, R. D. (1958) Warmth and performance: An investigation in the tropics. *Ergonomics*, **2**, 63–68.

Poulton, E. C. (1970) *Environment and Human Efficiency.* Springfield, Illinois: Charles C. Thomas.

Poulton, E. C. (1974a) Interactions and range effects in experiments on pairs of stresses. *Journal of Experimental Psychology*, **102**, 621–628.

Poulton, E. C. (1974b) Interaction of the loss of a night's sleep with mild heat task variables. *Ergonomics*, **17**, p.59.

Poulton, E. C. and Edwards, R. S. (1974a) Interactions and range effects in experiments on pairs of stresses: Mild heat and low-frequency noise. *Journal of Experimental Psychology*, **102**, 621–628.

Poulton, E. C. and Edwards, R. S. (1974b) Interactions, range effects and comparisons between tasks in experiments measuring performance with pairs of stresses: Mild heat and 1 mg. of 1-hyoscine hydrobromide. *Aerospace Medicine*, **45**, 735-741.

Poulton, E. C., Hitchings, N. B., and Brooke, R. B. (1965) Effect of cold and rain upon the vigilance of lookouts. *Ergonomics*, **8**, 163-168.

Poulton, E. C. and Kerslake, D. McK. (1965) Initial stimulating effect of warmth upon perceptual efficiency. *Aerospace Medicine*, **36**, 29-32.

Provins, K. A. (1966) Environmental heat, body temperature, and behaviour: An hypothesis. *Australian Journal of Psychology*, **18**, 118-129.

Provins, K. A. and Clarke, R. S. J. (1960) The effect of cold on manual performance. *Journal of Occupational Medicine*, **2**, 169-176.

Ramsey, J. D. (1975) Heat stress standard: OSHA's Advisory Committee Recommendations. *National Safety News*, **1975**, 89-95.

Ramsey, J. D., Dayal, D., and Ghahramani, B. (1975) Heat stress limits for the sedentary worker. *American Industrial Hygiene Association Journal*, **36**, 259-265.

Ramsey, J. D., Halcomb, C. G., and Mortagy, A. K. (1974) Self determined work/rest cycles in hot environments. *International Journal of Production Research*, **12**, 623-631.

Ramsey, J. D. and Morrissey, S. J. (1978) Isodecrement curves for task performance in hot environments. *Applied Ergonomics*, **9**, 66-72.

Ramsey, J. D. and Pai, S. B. (1975) Sedentary work by females in hot environments. In *Proceedings 19th Annual Meeting of the Human Factors Society*, pp.498-500.

Reddy, S. P. and Ramsey, J. D. (1976) Thermostat variations and sedentary job performance. *ASHRAE Journal*, **18**, 32-36.

Russell, R. W. (1957) Effects of variations in ambient temperature on certain measures tracking skill and sensory sensitivity. Report 300, U.S. Army Medical Research Laboratory, Fort Knox, Wyoming.

Shvartz, E., Meroz, A., Mechtinger, A., and Birnfeld, H. (1976) Simple reaction time during exercise, heat exposure, and heat acclimation. *Aviation, Space, and Environmental Medicine*, **47**, 1168-1170.

Surry, J. (1968) *Industrial Accident Research: A Human Engineering Appraisal.* Toronto, Canada: Ontario Department of Labour.

Teichner, W. H. (1958) Reaction time in the cold. *Journal of Applied Psychology*, **42**, 54-59.

Teichner, W. H. and Kobrick, J. L. (1955) Effects of Prolonged exposure to low temperature on visual-motor performance. *Journal of Experimental Psychology*, **49**, 122-126.

Teichner, W. H. and Wehrkamp, R. F. (1954) Visual-motor performance as a function of short duration ambient temperature. *Journal of Experimental Psychology*, **47**, 447-450.

Wilkinson, R. T., Fox, R. H., Goldsmith, R., Hampton, I. F. G., and Lewis, H. E. (1964) Psychological and physiological responses to raised body temperature. *Journal of Applied Physiology*, **19**, 287-291.

Wing, J. I. (1965) A review of the effect of high ambient temperature on mental performance. Aerospace Medical Research Laboratories, AMRL-TR-65-102.

World Health Organization (1969) Health factors involved in working under conditions of heat stress. Technical Report Series # 412, Geneva, Switzerland.

Wyon, D. P. (1973) The effects of moderate heat stress on typewriting performance. International Symposium on Quantitative Prediction of Effects of Thermal Environment on Man, Strasbourg, France.

Stress and Fatigue in Human Performance
Edited by G. R. J. Hockey
© 1983 John Wiley & Sons Ltd.

Chapter 3

Noise

Dylan M. Jones

It is difficult to over-state the importance of sound for our well-being. Sounds made by our vocal tract have been shaped by language and through them we convey and receive much of our knowledge of the world. The spoken word shaped and extended human culture, and in the burgeoning intellect of the infant it is central to sensory experience. Through music, sounds provide the basis for intense aesthetic experience. These developments are, in evolutionary terms, relatively recent. In the more remote past the auditory organ served as sentinel to our senses, and this function is still clearly discernible by its broad catchment area and its multifarious connections to areas of the brain concerned with alertness. But the ear was not fashioned with the prospect of industrial revolution in mind. Its superlative sensitivity and scope of action have made it victim to the culmination of the last few hundred years of industrial and social development. Much of what we now hear is, in one sense or another, unwanted, and it is this element of unwantedness which defines a sound as noise.

The purpose of this chapter is to outline these unwanted effects, the more insidious but nevertheless damaging effects occasioning fatigue and stress being the primary focus. The discussion is divided into three major portions: the first reviews the effect of noise on hearing both in its effects of auditory fatigue and on the detection of other wanted sounds; the second describes the stressful properties of noise on performance in the laboratory setting; and scope of the final section encompasses those stressful effects found in the field including effects of performance and productivity as well as social behaviour and health. As a necessary prelude to these topics there follows a brief account of the nature and measurement of sound.

SOUND: MEASUREMENT AND ANALYSIS

Sound is propagated through media which possess mass and elasticity by the successive collision of molecules. Consider, for example, the pattern of changes arising from the motion of a piston shown in Figure 8. As it moves to

61

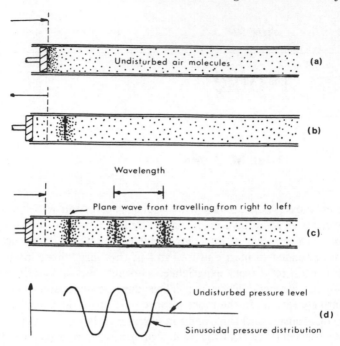

Figure 8. Pressure changes brought about by oscillation of a piston in a tube.

the right, molecules immediately adjacent to the surface of the piston become compressed. The pressure in this layer is now higher than at points farther away from the source (Figure 8a). As time passes, this pressure change is imparted to the next layer by successive molecular collision (Figure 8b). The molecules 'pass on' this change in pressure by moving about their stable positions rather than by travelling along the tube. Movement of the piston to the left produces just the opposite effect: causing the distribution of molecules to be rarefied, the layer adjacent to the piston becomes less dense, the pressure decreasing.

If the piston exhibits successive left and right movements alternate layers of compression and rarefaction will be generated (Figure 8c). One way of describing the sound thus produced is to plot the distribution of pressure along the tube at a particular instant, in this case taking the form of alternate excursions above and below the normal pressure in the tube. The resulting wave may vary in two main ways. First, the size of the excursions of the piston will be reflected in the height, or amplitude, of the wave. Secondly, the frequency of oscillation of the piston will be reflected in the frequency of the peaks in the wave, measured as the number of such cycles per second (expressed in Hertz, Hz). Changes in amplitude are heard as changes in loudness, while changes in frequency are heard as changes in pitch.

The range of frequencies to which the ear is sensitive may encompass a range as large as 20–20,000 Hz, known as the audio frequency spectrum. Most of the sounds that we commonly encounter are composed of pressure variations at a number of different frequencies. The case described above considered the generation of simple tones, so-called pure tones, but the more complex tones also share with them the property of evoking the sensation of pitch. The pitch of a sound containing several frequency components is taken to be the frequency of a pure tone which matches it in pitch. The relative contribution of each of the frequency components to the overall sound may be assessed by examining the distribution of energy at each frequency, resulting in an *amplitude spectrum*.

The expression of the amplitude of the wave is more problematical simply because of the enormous range of intensities to which the ear can respond, the ratio of the loudest to the faintest being in the order of $10^{11}:1$. This range is encompassed by the use of the logarithmic decibel scale. The decibel (dB) gives an index of the ratio between two quantities; the one of interest relative to a fixed standard. In the case of sound level measurement involving pressure, the decibel is defined as: $dB = 20 \log (P_1/P_2)$ (where P_1 is the pressure produced by the measured sound and P_2 is a standard pressure). A value of 20 micropascals has been adopted for the standard pressure since it corresponds to the minimum audible sound pressure detectable by the human ear. Levels of sound specified in this way are referred to as Sound Pressure Levels (SPLs). Because of its logarithmic nature caution has to be exercised over the use of the decibel scale. For example, a doubling of sound pressure corresponds to an increase in SPL of 6 dB; similarly, a multiplication of sound pressure by a factor of ten increases the SPL by 20 dB.

Commercially available meters are used to measure the overall sound level, and sophisticated versions also provide facilities for analysis of the frequency composition of the sound (cf. Bruel, 1976; Kohler, 1982; Wells, 1979). While the range of function may vary from model to model, two features are common to all. First, a microphone transforms fluctuations in pressure into electrical signals which are then amplified and presented on a digital or analogue display. Secondly, one or more weighting networks selectively attenuate certain portions of the audio frequency spectrum. Three such networks are usually provided—A, B, and C—and their response characteristics are shown in Figure 9. Each involves different degrees of de-emphasis of low and high frequencies relative to those in the middle (1,000–4,000 Hz) of the range. The A-weighting effectively simulates the response of the ear at low levels but is widely used in the measurement of sounds at all levels because of its strength in predicting subjective reaction to noise (Pearsons, 1974).

More sophisticated meters incorporate filters which allow measurement of

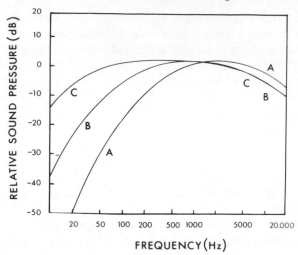

Figure 9. Weighting networks typically employed in sound level meters.

sound levels within specified frequency bands. Simple filters pass on for recording sounds from a range of frequencies covering one octave (that is, between two frequencies whose ratio is 2:1) although this range may be as small as a third or a quarter of an octave when more detailed analysis is required. By examining the levels from filters of this sort, set, in turn, to cover the whole of the audio spectrum, a picture of the amplitude spectrum emerges. Other special facilities include provision for the recording of fast and slow changes in level and for measurement of the peak value of an impulse.

Certain precautions should be observed when making measurements with a sound level meter and the reader is advised to consult the technical literature (Cunniff, 1977; Peterson, 1979).

HEARING

Noise interferes with our perception of sound in two main ways: by inducing hearing loss and by masking the detection of a wanted sound. That effect of noise occasioning deafness is of primary concern, principally because the handicap extends beyond the period of exposure and may be irreversible. Yet, although the phenomena associated with noise-induced hearing loss are well known, their effects on handicap and details of the responsible mechanism are shrouded in controversy. Such details are not simply of academic value, but are central to the formulation of policy regarding noise exposure and compensation for noise-induced hearing loss.

Hearing loss

Three types of hearing loss resulting from exposure to noise are usually distinguished (Burns, 1973). First, a *Temporary Threshold Shift* (TTS) referring to a short-lived impairment of sensitivity to sound in the period following exposure (usually measured 2 minutes after exposure). Secondly, a *Noise-Induced Permanent Threshold Shift* (NIPTS) resulting from prolonged exposure to loud noise where impairment of hearing is not reversible. Finally, another type of permanent change is distinguished, that of *acoustic trauma* from a single intense exposure. Our focus is on the first two types of loss simply because of their ubiquity in the occupational setting.

With TTS the maximal decrease in sensitivity does not appear for frequencies immediately adjacent to the stimulating spectrum but at points relatively remote from it. For exposure to a band of noise one or two octaves wide, TTS will be maximal one-half to one octave above its upper boundary. Exposure to pure tones may produce effects as remote as two octaves above their frequency (van Dishoeck, 1948; Ward, 1962). If TTS for continuous noise is less than 25 dB, its growth and recovery are exponential, the asymptote reached in 8–12 hours. Losses greater than 25 dB for TTS are regarded as especially severe since they require more than the usual 16 hours between successive 8-hour shifts of work for complete recovery. The elevation of threshold may be less when the energy is spread over a band of frequencies than when concentrated in a narrow range (at least for frequencies below 1,000 Hz) or when the spectral composition of the noise is changed during exposure or when the noise is intermittent (Ward, 1962).

The pattern of development of NIPTS is also well established. With broadband industrial noise, NIPTS appears initially in the 4–5 kHz range, greater loss appearing with increasing exposure, with a peak loss sometimes appearing at about 4,000 Hz (Burns, 1973). Loss in this region tends to increase rapidly at first, reaching an asymptote within a decade (Taylor *et al.*, 1965); however, any loss at lower frequencies may not be subject to this asymptotic fall-off (cf. Nixon and Glorig, 1961). While the description of the phenomena described thus far command consensus, issues connected with developing an acceptable level of exposure offering protection from handicap are far more troubled. Part of the problem lies in the weakness of association between TTS and NIPTS. A firm association between the two would, of course, be of enormous prognostic value, but the weight of evidence must compel even the most sanguine of readers to conclude that NIPTS is not *simply* the result of accumulated TTS.

Part of this difficulty may arise because measured NIPTS may arise from sources other than those found in occupational noise exposure. Hearing loss increases with age (*presbyacusis*); with the action of noxious non-acoustic factors such as industrial chemicals, ototoxic drugs, or illness (*nosoacusis*;

Ward, 1980); and results from noise to which a person is exposed, willingly, outside the work setting (*socioacusis*; cf. Cohen *et al.*, 1970). Without an accurate estimate of the contribution of each of these sources to hearing loss, the attribution of NIPTS to occupational exposure is correspondingly ambiguous. Estimates of this sort are usually based on retrospective accounts from exposed individuals often contaminated by lapses of memory or inadequate objective records of exposure. The picture is further complicated by the fact that indices derived from each type of source may not be additive (Corso, 1976; Spoor, 1967).

Despite these uncertainties about the genesis of NIPTS, evidence from large-scale analyses of hearing loss in industrial workers identifies the threshold for hearing loss as being long-term exposure to 80 dBA, with an additional 2 dB loss for every unit of dBA above this level (Passchier-Vermeer, 1974; Robinson *et al.*, 1973). While most people would agree that a low recommended maximum is ethically desirable, its realization is constrained by technical and economic considerations (Bruce, 1976; Ollerhead, 1973). Furthermore, there is by no means general agreement that even moderately pronounced impairments in the 3–6 kHz region produce handicap in either the reception of speech or the appreciation of music (Kryter, 1973). Standards for noise exposure are largely based on changes in the ability to detect pure tones and, to date, no measure of social handicap has been standardized.

Masking

Noise may directly interfere with the detection of signals; this effect is known as *masking*. Vital signals such as alarms or auditory cues to the operation of machinery may be lost, but the most pervasive and well-documented effect of masking is that upon speech.

The means by which pure tones are masked by narrow bands of noise is relatively well understood and forms the basis of our knowledge of the way masking occurs with non-speech stimuli. One of the most notable features of this process is the asymmetrical way in which a narrow band of noise interferes with the detection of sound above and below its boundaries, those higher in frequency showing more masking than those which are a corresponding distance below the masker. This effect arises because the pattern of excitation produced on the basilar membrane (that part of the ear responsible for converting sound waves to neural impulsed) is asymmetric. Masking of this sort occurs when two sounds are contemporaneous; however, perception of a tone may also be impaired by a preceding masker and vice versa (Elliott, 1971). Masking may also be *central* when the threshold of a signal presented in one ear is elevated by the presence of a masker in the other ear.

Speech, by virtue of its wide spectral distribution and high information content, presents a less straightforward case. What is heard is often as much to do with the effect of noise on the speaker as it is upon the listener. Part of the speaker's natural response to background noise is to raise the level of his voice, but elevations of vocal effort do not have a one-to-one correspondence with the change in the level of the noise: typically they are of the order 3–5 dB for every 10 dB increase in background level (Pearsons, 1980). As vocal output increases from a whisper (at about 40 dBA) to a shout (at about 80 dBA) the average spectral composition of speech also changes, frequencies in the region of 1,000 Hz predominate, with frequencies below this becoming less evident (Webster, 1979). The level of speech which is naturally adopted in the absence of competing sounds lies in the range 50–65 dBA (measured 1 m from the speaker) although the acoustic qualities of the particular setting may change this value. Recommended maxima of noise depend, among other things, on how long the talker is expected to sustain his vocal output. Over a distance of 1 m communication with a normal unraised voice may be adjudged satisfactory in noise to a level of 78 dBA but a limit of 70 dBA is recommended for sustained discourse (see Figure 10).

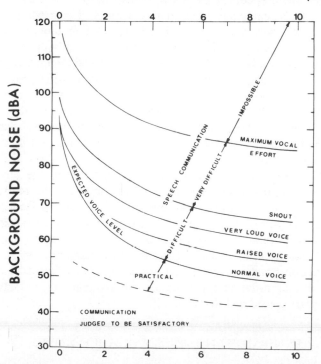

Figure 10. Quality of speech communication as a function of the A-weighted background noise level and talker-to-listener distances for different levels of vocal effort. From Miller (1974). (Reproduced by permission of J. D. Miller and the American Institute of Physics.)

Although the intelligibility of speech in broad-band noise is largely dependent upon the ratio between signal (speech) and noise levels, the effect of the type of material to be transmitted is often as great. The masking effect of noise becomes markedly less when the message is one of few possibilities than when it is one of many (Miller *et al.*, 1951). Moreover, the effects of masking will be less if the voice is familiar (Schubert and Parker, 1955) or if the individual is practiced at listening-out for sounds in a particular noisy setting (Tobias and Irons, 1974). The spectrum of speech ranges from 100 Hz to 8 kHz with most of the energy concentrated up to 6 kHz. Noise within this range will produce masking, but no part of the speech spectrum is particularly vulnerable. Because of the multi-dimensional nature of coding in speech the listener can resort to a variety of cues to maintain intelligibility. It is possible to simulate the effects of masking by selectively excluding certain portions of the speech spectrum. Excluding those speech frequencies above 1,900 Hz has a roughly similar effect to excluding those below this value, in each case performance is about 70 per cent of the level of performance when the spectrum is intact (French and Steinberg, 1947).

Even when the difficulties of communication in noise are apparently circumvented the listener may have to pay a residual cost for the effort of listening. For example, material previously learned in quiet may be more rapidly forgotten when, in the intervening period, the individual undertakes a period of listening in noise (Rabbitt, 1966, 1968). The difficulty of listening to speech may only become apparent when demands from other sources become more pressing: deterioration may only be evident on a secondary task performed during listening, even if the secondary task contains no component of speech (Broadbent, 1958). In each of these examples subjects overcame the difficulty of masking by focusing their resources on that aspect of the setting, with a consequent diminution of spare capacity.

Thus far those effects of noise which are manifested in the physiological fatigue of the sense organ or by direct interference with the registration of signals have been outlined. Both will have psychological consequences: on the well-being of those deafened by it, in the loss of vital information, in the restriction of the subtlety of conversation, and in the effort expended in listening and making oneself heard (Jones and Broadbent, 1979). The next section focuses on psychological effects of a slightly different kind, namely those effects of loud noise on performance and productivity. Effects found in the laboratory are considered first.

INTERMITTENT AND VARIABLE NOISE

Noise whose intensity changes during exposure can be broadly classed into two types: *variable noise*, whose level changes within a specified range but is seldom completely quiet, the changes being relatively slow, possibly accompanied by changes in spectral composition, and *intermittent noise*, which exhibits sharp elevations in level from quiet. In addition to the level and range, the important parameters are the frequency and regularity of the noise.

Changes in level

Several early studies demonstrated that changes in performance were confined to a short period following both the onset and offset of the noise burst (Ford, 1929; Morgan, 1916). The magnitude of the change in intensity in part determines the extent of the depression in performance. For example, Teichner *et al.* (1963) required subjects to identify one of five possible codes in sequences of ten letters. All subjects inspected the first 150 sequences in 81 dB white noise, but for the remaining 50 sequences the level of noise was either increased (to 93 or 105 dB), decreased (to 57 or 69 dB) or remained the same (control group). A change of level, in either direction, decreased the rate of improvement relative to that found for the control group. Moreover, this slowing in the rate of improvement was more pronounced with the larger changes in intensity. Similar effects were found by Shoenberger and Harris (1965) with the qualification that effect of change will be attenuated when the task is well practised. In both studies the effect on performance was proportional to the change in noise level and symmetrical: an increase or decrease in level giving a roughly equivalent change. Exceptions to this case may include longer tasks, asymmetry being observed in a study by Corcoran *et al.* (1977) in a test of sustained attention. A switch in level from 90 to 70 dB half-way through the vigil produced an overall decline in detection of signals over the vigil but a switch from 70 to 90 dB improved detection.

Noise bursts

If loud bursts of noise are presented occasionally, the effects on performance tend to be localized to at most the 30 seconds following its onset, although periods of disruption as short as 2 or 3 seconds are more commonly reported. Motor skills are sensitive to noise bursts in this way, both when the response required is continuous (May and Rice, 1971), or discrete (Fisher, 1972). Some components of a task may be more susceptible to disruption than others. Fisher (1972, 1973) found a slowing of response in a serial reaction task only when the noise bursts (at 80 dB) arrived during the execution of the response. Effects on specific elements of the task were also found by Woodhead (1964) in a mental arithmetic task, bursts of noise at 100 dB arriving during the intake of information being more damaging than those arriving in the subsequent period of mental calculation. This suggests that the effects of a short burst are due to an effect of distraction on the intake of information either during the inspection of a complex stimulus (Salamé and Wittersheim, 1978) or in the monitoring of a motor response. Based on findings from the laboratory, the upper limit to the range of this localized effect is in the order of half a minute, found by Woodhead (1958, 1959). Using bursts of rocket noise at 95 dB presented during a decision-making task she was also able to demonstrate that the effects were not due to the change in level of stimulation but to the intensity of the noise by showing that this localized effect of noise was markedly attenuated by wearing ear defenders.

When changes in level became more frequent the nature of effects on performance become more complex. This is due in part to the loss of novelty with repeated presentation of noise and also due to increased skill in the performance of a task. The experimental subject may assemble a picture of the likelihood of noise bursts, gaining tactical advantage either by applying compensatory effort or by skilful anticipation of the required response. This means that unless a fine-grained analysis of performance is undertaken, emphasizing temporal and strategic aspects of the response, the effects of intermittent noise may not appear. Unless the study of noise bursts takes into account their action on particular task elements again the effect will be rather small: the bursts coinciding with those sensitive elements only on some occasions. Similarly, if the demands made by the task vary over a wide range, bursts may only occasionally appear when demands are high.

Intermittent noise

Both the proportion of time for which the noise is on and the duration of the task play a part in determining the effects of frequent bursts of noise on performance. This is particularly true where the bursts appear regularly. By examining the effect of different lengths of time for which the noise (at 100 dB) was on in a 5-second cycle, Teichner *et al.* (1963) found search speed in a visual task to be an increasing function of the on–off ratio early in the exposure (up to 3 minutes) but in the later stages (to a limit of 12 minutes) to be a progressively steepening decreasing function of exposure (see Figure 11). Early in the exposure intermittent noise serves as a distractor, the shorter bursts being more distracting, but that late in the task the same noise serves an alerting function. Evidence from this study of the effects of prior exposure to these noises reinforces this picture: the early effect of distraction being attenuated but the later arousing effect undiminished.

Studies using a lower maximum level and smaller range of intensity show trends supporting the notion of two effects of noise. An on-time of roughly 60 per cent over a range of 95–70 dB was found by Hartley (1974) to reduce the deleterious effect of continuous noise (at 95 dB) on long responses (or gaps) in a serial reaction task but only in the later stages of a 40-minute exposure. Variable noise also has the property of improving performance after exposure has proceeded for some time; this is particularly true for tasks requiring sustained attention (e.g. McGrath, 1960).

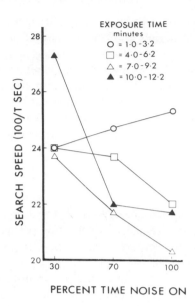

Figure 11. Effects of percent 'on' time of noise at four stages of exposure on the speed of visual search. From Teichner *et al.* (1963). (Reproduced by permission of W. H. Teichner and Taylor and Francis Ltd.)

The effect of the regularity of bursts of noise during performance is relatively little studied. Eschenbrenner (1971) compared the effects of 50, 70, and 90 dB presented continuously and noise with an average 50 per cent on-time being periodic or aperiodic. As expected, performance was poorest in periodic noise and loud noise, but the effect of periodicity did not depend on the level of the noise, a result at variance with expectations from other settings. Most of what is known of the effects of unpredictability comes from studies of the after-effects of exposure which are described below.

Unfortunately, most studies of intermittent noise have failed to equate noise dose at different levels of intermittency. Clearly, continuous noise and intermittent noise with an on-time of 30 per cent are far from equivalent in the total energy to which the individual is exposed. This is particularly serious since it is likely to underestimate the magnitude of the effect to be found in the work setting.

CONTINUOUS NOISE

A wide range of tasks has been studied in conditions where noise is loud and continuous. The studies to be described fall into three broad classes: monitoring, motor skills, and cognition. The differences within each class of task are often as great as those between classes and any simple generalization about the sensitivity of a certain class of task must be qualified by a consideration of specific details of the task demands and the measure of performance which is of interest.

Reviewers of noise research have long since complained that loud noise can have generally positive or negative effects or indeed no effects on performance. If we forsake the expectation that task performance can be couched in terms of elevations or depressions on a single index and instead expect a subtle interplay of different levels of adjustment to noise exposure a good many of the findings will become intelligible.

Monitoring

Under this heading are considered tasks requiring the detection of faint signals appearing infrequently and irregularly over long periods of time, called *vigilance tasks*, their closest counterpart in the work setting being the inspection of items for faults.

When signals arise from a single source, noise does not impair performance (e.g. Blackwell and Belt, 1971; Jerison, 1957; Tarrière and Wisner, 1962). Adverse effects of noise are more likely to appear when attention to several sources of signals is required. For example, Broadbent (1954) used 20 sources of signals each monitored for an excursion of a dial which remained in a 'danger zone'. Noise at 100 dB increased the proportion of particularly slow responses. In another version of the task involving the detection of dimly glowing lights (thus making the task easier) no overall effect of noise was found. However, detailed analysis of the speed of response over different parts of the display revealed that responses were slowed for those lights in front of the subject with those to each side showing a slight speeding of response.

Direct evidence of the effect of the number of sources is presented in a series of studies by Jerison and his co-workers. Detection of occasional double jumps in a clock dial was found to be unimpaired by noise at 113 dB over a vigil lasting 105 minutes (Jerison, 1957). When the number of clocks was increased from one to three and the vigil extended to 120 minutes, loud noise produced markedly fewer detections at the end of the vigil (Jerison, 1959), but as the number of clocks increased so did the overall number of signals per hour (by a factor of 6) and the number of single ticks (by a factor of 3). One particular feature of the nature of response suggests that when three clocks were present subjects adopted a more risky approach to the reportage of signals: the number of false alarms (reporting a signal when none was present) was increased relative to that found in the case when only one clock was monitored.

These various effects become comprehensible when the confidence with which judgements about the presence of a signal are taken into consideration. Broadbent and Gregory (1965) compared the effects of noise on confidence in detecting signals appearing on one or three sources, when the probability of a signal was relatively high and on one channel, when the probability of a signal was low (these last two conditions corresponding to Jerison's tasks). Subjects were asked to judge whether each event was a signal using three categories of response: 'sure yes', 'unsure', and 'sure no'. Noise (at 100 dB) tended to increase the use of the two extreme categories of response, but only in those cases where the probability of a signal was high, be the signals from one or three sources. Responses in noise become more extreme, subjects being more prepared to assert that they were sure that a signal was there or not there.

Most experiments using noise only have as their index of vigilance performance reports about the presence of a signal, without any judgement of confidence. However, from what is known about vigilance performance in quiet, Broadbent's analysis suggests that the effects of noise largely depends on the prevailing task demands. By making the signals very unlikely to occur or by making signals very noticeable, responses of the doubtful kind become rare, the increase in certainty brought about by noise being manifested in an increased number of reports of signals. When signals are probable or not very noticeable the proportion of doubtful judgements become more frequent, an increase of confidence in this case decreasing the number of responses to signals (Broadbent, 1979; Broadbent and Gregory, 1963).

The prevailing level of confidence will also have effects on the number of times an individual will check the current state of a display. In order to chart the way in which such observations are made in noise, Hockey (1970b) examined the pattern of inquiry into the state of a system in which faults would occasionally appear on one of three displays, subjects pressing a button to observe briefly the current state of a display. Noise (at 100 dB) was found to increase the incidence of two successive observations before a fault was reported, as if subjects required further confirmation before committing themselves to a response. Another feature of Hockey's study was that faults appeared on one source more often than on others. Here, noise increased the tendency for subjects to sample the source which contained the highest proportion of faults. This observation tends to confirm the suspicion first noted in Broadbent's '20 lights' task that in noise not all parts of the display are regarded with equal weight. The further study of this tendency has employed tasks containing two elements of different sorts, with priority being assigned to one of the elements.

One task of this type attempts to mimic the demands made by driving, using a tracking task designated as high priority (akin to the steering component in driving) coupled with the detection of lights arranged in a wide semi-circle in front of, and equidistant from, the subject. Hockey (1970a) used a task of this kind, examining performance in sessions each lasting 40 minutes in either 70 or 100 dB white noise. The results (see Figure 12) show that noise produces changes in efficiency in a complex way. Overall, the detection of lights at the

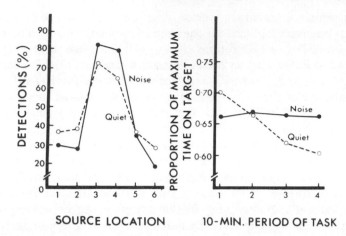

SOURCE LOCATION   10-MIN. PERIOD OF TASK

Figure 12. Effects of noise on performance in a multi-component task on (a) the detection of lights and on (b) pursuit tracking. (a) from Hockey (1970a); reproduced by permission of Academic Press. (b) From Hockey (1978); reproduced by permission of Van Nostrand Reinhold.

periphery of the display (locations 1, 2, 5, and 6 in Figure 12a) is poor relative to that for the central pair. Loud noise exaggerates the differences in efficiency between the two sectors, the detection of central lights becoming more efficient, peripheral lights less so. Tracking (Figure 12b) shows a marked deterioration over the period in quiet, while in noise performance remains steady. In noise attention is focused on the dominant part of the task (encompassing the tracking task and the central lights) at the expense of the less dominant part of the display.

Several details of this attentional change have been elucidated since these findings were published. One problematic issue was whether noise narrowed the *visual* field or the *attentional* field. It now appears that noise leads to a focusing on more subjectively or objectively probable sources of information regardless of their spatial location (Hockey, 1970a, 1970b). It is known too that noise does not distort the perception of the probabilities of events (Hamilton *et al.*, 1977) so that the effect is unlikely to be due to a further separation by noise of the subjective probabilities of central and peripheral lights. Thus, the effect is strategic, resources being invested in some activities at the expense of others. The extent of such a trade-off in noise will of course depend on both the qualitative and quantitative demands made by each component and the interpretation by the individual of the instructions concerning priority. It is therefore hardly surprising that detailed changes in this type of task will bring about different patterns of response to noise, leading, in some cases, to an impairment in tracking, but with no effect on watchkeeping (Loeb and Jones, 1978), in others to an impairment in both primary and secondary tasks (Finkleman *et al.*, 1977), in others to an overall deterioration in the primary task in noise together with an advantage for central over peripheral detection (Hartley, 1981), and to cases showing no effects on either task (Forster and Grierson, 1978).

The notion that attention is somehow concentrated or made more selective by noise is difficult to substantiate. Part of the difficulty stems from the absence of a satisfactory metric for changes in attentional capacity and our ignorance of the laws which govern the way performance on one task is traded-off for performance on another. The evidence, however, does compel us to regard changes induced by noise as being strategic rather than mechanical or involuntary and in turn helps to explain why performance may apparently improve or decline in different task settings.

Before leaving our discussion of monitoring, findings from another class of vigilance tasks should be mentioned for which the theoretical picture is not clear, but which nevertheless show effects for noise as low as 80 dB. The task in this case contains a substantial verbal component, each signal being a particular combination of digits in a stream of digits. In one study Beningus *et al.* (1975) found low-frequency noise in the range of 11–350 Hz at 80 dBC increased the number of missed signals during a vigil. In another study Jones *et al.* (1979) found effects of 80 or 85 dBC in four versions of the task, but found that small variations in the number of either non-signals or signals changed the nature of the effect.

Selectivity in perception

The trend for noise to focus attention on dominant aspects of the setting has already been noted in connection with multi-component tasks. Rather than study the effects of dominance by arbitrarily assigning priorities to parts of a complex display, a number of experiments have attempted to capitalize upon the natural response tendencies of the individual. For example, Millar (1980) found that noise improved the perception of faint words when preceded by a word frequently associated with it in everyday use, but not when preceded by an infrequent associate.

Evidence of changes in perceptual selectivity from a range of studies using the Stroop test is more equivocal. This test is used to study the competition between two response tendencies. In the part of the test of primary interest, words which are the names of colours are printed in an ink of a different hue. The requirement is for the name of the ink to be reported, suppressing the natural tendency for the word to be given. The results of this conflict, where the dominant response is said to interfere with the non-dominant response, can be assessed by comparing it with the speed of response to either monochrome words or to patches of colour. Both Houston and Jones (1967) and Houston (1969) found that a relatively short exposure to variable noise at 75 dB decreased interference; evidence that noise made perception more rather than less selective. Increased interference has been found, but only at the end of a 30-minute exposure, performance early in exposure showing decreased inter-ference (Hartley and Adams, 1974).

Speeded responses

Responses in discrete trials involving visual stimuli show no effect of noise either when there is only one stimulus and response or when there are many (e.g. Stevens, 1972). However, when serial reaction is required, response to one stimulus serving to bring on the next in an unpredictable sequence, loud noise may increase the incidence of errors or produce unduly long pauses in response. Studies using a version of this task with five lights as stimuli and five discs for response (the 5-choice task) have shed light on a number of features of the response to noise.

In one of the few studies examining effects of the spectral composition of sound on performance, Broadbent (1957) compared noises containing equal energy in the 100–2,000 Hz range with one covering the 2,000–5,000 Hz range at levels of 80, 90, and 100 dB. There were no effects of noise on the number of correct responses, but the number of errors increased at 100 dB only for the higher frequency noise. Wilkinson (1963) confirmed that a similar effect occurs with 100 dB broad-band noise, the increase in the number of errors becoming more noticeable toward the end of the test.

Like those studies of multi-source monitoring in noise, the effects of length of exposure on serial reaction have received scrutiny. Hartley (1973) attempted to discriminate between two classes of account for the tendency for noise to have its effect at the end of the period of work. One possibility is that execution of the task results in some kind of fatigue or stress which builds up as the period of work proceeds, noise, through its action as a stressor, acting to exacerbate this tendency. The other possibility is that the effects of task and noise are independent: the cumulative effect of prior work being unnecessary for the effect of noise to be manifested. These alternatives were examined by studying 20 minutes of serial reaction performance preceded by either task performance or rest and by either noise or quiet. The main conclusion of the study was that the effects of noise and test duration are independent: both increase gaps (unduly long response times) and errors, but the combined effect of prior noise and prior performance do not act synergistically. Many details of the theoretical underpinnings to the effects of stress on serial reaction performance remain to be discovered. One approach, in line with the strategic framework we have been suggesting, is that of Rabbitt (1979) who advocates a further detailed analysis of the processes governing the high-level control of the speed of the response.

Cognition

Much recent research has been concerned with assessing the effects of modest levels of noise, often no higher than 85 dB, on a range of tasks which make heavy demands upon memory. The pattern of changes which have been observed suggest a subtle adjustment of processing strategies in noise, sometimes showing effects on one aspect of performance, but not on others. However, in most cases the length of exposure has been extremely short and very little is known about the endurance of such effects.

Recall of a list of words drawn from a few classes of meaning tends to show clustering: words of similar meaning are recalled together even if they were not presented close together in the original list. Loud noise influences this tendency to cluster. Originally, the effect was found by Hörmann and Osterkamp (1966) to depend on the personality of the subject: in noise, those better able to suppress Stroop interference produced larger more cohesive clusters, whilst those susceptible to interference produced a more fragmented cluster pattern. However, more recent work has demonstrated that noise may reduce clustering for groups not distinguished in this way and at levels as low as 75 dBC (Daee and Wilding, 1977). A detailed analysis indicates that noise produces quite complex changes in the way in which category members are reported. Noise (at about 80 dBC) increases the tendency to make an initial perfunctory report of a few members of each category followed by several reports of words each from a different category. Thus, the overall number of words reported is not reduced in noise, but they are produced in a fashion which is both less coherent and organized. The extent of the effect of noise depends in large part on the opportunity for such fragmentation to take place and is thus crucially dependent upon the nature of the list to be remembered. When the total membership of a category is small (and thus the list is likely to include all the exemplars of a category) or when the words employed are poor examples of a category (showing little clustering even in quiet) the effects of loud noise are markedly reduced (Smith *et al.*, 1981).

Dornic (1975), on the basis of evidence of the effects of a variety of agents, including information overload and alcohol, concluded that stress increases the tendency to 'parrot-back' a list of items. In noise this tendency, manifested in improved memory for the order in which words were presented, has been demonstrated in several ways. For example, Hamilton *et al.* (1972) found that if retrieval of the list is required in the original order of presentation then noise improves performance. Orders of retrieval different to those at presentation may result in slightly poorer performance in noise. The adoption in noise of such a rudimentary strategy for remembering may in part reflect a state of caution; the lower incidence of incorrect guesses in noise tends to support the idea that noise induces caution. This effect is not simply one arising indirectly from the forgetting of words since it may be observed when members of the list are a set known to the subject in advance (Wilding and Mohindra, 1980) or when the words from the list are given unexpectedly to the subject who is required to place them in their original order (Daee and Wilding, 1977).

Like the skilled tasks already mentioned, noise also shifts the bias of attention in multi-component memory tasks. Studies by Hockey and Hamilton (1970) and Davies and Jones (1975) used the technique of presenting a short word-list with each word in one of four locations. Initially, the instructions made mention only of the recall of the words, but after the words were recalled memory for the locations of the words was also tested. Noise improved the recall of words (and in one study improved recall in correct order) but depressed the recall of locations. A similar trend was found by Cohen and Lezak (1977) using a combination of nonsense syllables with photographs portraying a range of social settings. Again, a test of memory for incidental material contained in the photographs was unexpectedly applied after recalling the syllables showed loud intermittent noise to depress performance and recall of the syllables was unaffected by noise.

In many of the tasks described above noise was present only during the period when the materials were initially displayed, but it is possible that the effects arise at retrieval, an effect of having just been in noise. Earlier in the discussion effects of the offset of noise were briefly reported and we now turn to consider these in greater detail.

After-effects

As an incidental feature of their results several researchers have noted that the effects of loud noise on performance may extend beyond the period of exposure. The experience of noise as the first treatment in a study sometimes has an influence carrying over to subsequent noise-free sessions. Following an initial exposure to noise performance may be depressed (Broadbent, 1954; Jerison, 1959) or elevated (Frankenhaeuser and Lundberg, 1974) even when the times of testing are weeks apart. Thus, noise may have its effects quite remote from the time of exposure, suggesting the action of enduring strategies in task performance (Jones *et al.*, 1981).

Just as noise may have a temporary effect due to its onset, the offset of the sound will also temporarily impair efficiency (e.g. Hartley, 1973). A series of studies by Glass and Singer (1972) focused on the development of these short-term after-effects and concluded that cognitive factors served to mediate their development—that they were not simply a hangover from noxious stimulation, but could be augmented or diminished depending on the attitude of the individual. Exposure to 25 or 30 minutes of intermittent noise peaking at 108 dB produced after-effects which took the form of reduced persistence at problem-solving, increased interference in the Stroop test, and, less consistently, in a reduction in the number of errors detected in a proof-reading task.

However, when subjects were told that they could switch off the noise (but did not exercise this option) or when the noise bursts were made more predictable (either by their regularity or by signalling their onset) the after-effects of exposure were attenuated. Subsequent reports have not only confirmed that after-effects occur with random intermittent noise (Gardner, 1978; Moran and Loeb, 1977; Percival and Loeb, 1980; Rotton *et al.*, 1978) but also extended it to include continuous noise, whether steady state (Broadbent, 1980; Hartley, 1973) or variable (Rotton *et al.*, 1978; Sherrod *et al.*, 1977).

The work of Glass and Singer (and the kindred work on 'learned helplessness'; Miller and Norman, 1979) point to the importance of the individual's perception of the noisy setting. The extent to which persons feel to be in control of the noise and the ability to predict or govern its onset, appears to be crucial in mediating disruption of both mood and performance. Particularly since such factors have also been identified as determinants of annoyance by noise (Graeven, 1975) perceived control may be a potent variable in shaping the disruption of performance in settings outside the laboratory.

Interactions with other stresses

The primary aim of examining the joint action of noise and other stressors is to identify those combinations which suggest that the effect arises via a common mechanism, by acting either synergistically (having a more than additive effect in combination) or antagonistically (one stressor cancelling the effect of another).

Heat has a characteristically different effect to noise on serial reaction (Pepler, 1959) but shows similarities in its effect upon multi-component tasks (Bursill, 1958). Nevertheless, in combination their effects do not interact (Bell, 1978; Viteles and Smith, 1946). Again, the effect of alcohol on the distribution of attention seems similar to that of noise, but nevertheless each wields an independent effect (Hamilton and Copeman, 1970).

Sleep loss and noise have consistently been shown to have antagonistic effects. Each stressor in isolation produces its deleterious effects on serial reaction at the end of a period of work. Performance of sleep-deprived individuals actually improves when loud noise is also present, manifested in a reduction of the number of errors (Wilkinson, 1963). Hartley and Shirley (1977) also found antagonistic effects of noise and sleep loss in a test of visual vigilance. The expected effect of noise in reducing judgements of intermediate confidence was cancelled out by sleep loss. Thus, the effects of sleep loss and noise seem to be qualitatively similar but opposite, the alerting quality of noise counteracting the soporific effect of sleep loss.

The joint effects of noise and incentive appear to depend in large part on the way in which incentive is given. If it takes the form of accumulated knowledge of results of individual and group serial reaction performance, incentive interacts with loud noise by increasing the frequency of gaps (Corcoran, 1962; Wilkinson, 1963). When in the same task accumulated knowledge of results is augmented by immediate feedback of the incidence of gaps (responses in excess of 1.5 seconds) and errors there is neither an overall effect of feedback nor an interaction between feedback and noise (Hartley, 1974). Moreover, the effect of incentive in the form of monetary reward for correctly remembering items from a list does not interact with noise. Using the task combining memory for words and locations (with incentive to remember the words) a number of studies have found that incentive improved the recall of words in their correct order without any change in the incidental element of recalling locations (e.g. Fowler and Wilding, 1979). This pattern is quite different to that found in noise; typically noise gives rise to a decline in recall of locations and a slight improvement in the recall of words. Moreover, when present together with effects of noise and monetary incentive do not interact (Davies and Jones, 1975).

Finally, a few studies have been able to show that the time of testing is an important variable. Blake (1971) found noise at 100 dB increased the numbers of letters cancelled in a text in an early morning test (at 0800 hours) but not at a slightly later time in the morning (at 1030 hours). A study by Mullin and Corcoran (1977) testing at the early morning time and at a very much later one (at 2030 hours) again found noise to improve performance in a vigilance task at the early, but not the later time of day.

Save that effect with sleep deprivation, evidence of interactions with loud noise does not present a coherent picture. From what is known, the patterning of response to single stresses may not be sufficient to predict their joint action.

In the next section we turn to consider evidence of effects on efficiency in a broader perspective, from settings outside the laboratory.

FIELD STUDIES

Relatively few field studies have been conducted, and while acknowledging that this is a less than ideal state of affairs, it must be recognized that the methodological difficulties are many and the opportunities for study few. Work and classroom settings have been the major foci of study.

Effects in the classroom

External noises, from traffic and aircraft, interfere directly with classroom behaviour. Experimental work suggests that this takes the form of less student participation, less attentiveness, and a shift from discussion to the use of lectures (Ward and Suedfeld, 1973). That academic achievement is also impaired is demonstrated in some studies (e.g. Bronzaft and McCarthy, 1975), but not in others (Weinstein and Weinstein, 1979). Effects of noise on academic achievement may arise from the disruption of teaching activities (cf. Crook and Langdon, 1974) rather than from some enduring change in pupil motivation or competence. However, recent work by S. Cohen and his colleagues indicates that noise may have effects manifested outside the noisy setting.

Poor auditory discrimination and reading ability were found by Cohen, Glass, and Singer (1973) to characterize children who lived in the noisier apartments near a busy freeway. Moreover, this deficit was greater for those children who had lived in the noisy apartments longer. More broad-ranging effects were found by Cohen *et al.* (1981) in a study examining the effects of aircraft noise on children attending school near a busy airport. At school, these children were exposed to peak levels as high as 95 dBA from flights passing over at an average rate of one per 2½ minutes. In addition to achievement scores from standard tests of academic ability, measures on a number of tasks assessing attentional strategies, persistence at problem solving, and cognitive performance were taken in the quiet of a mobile laboratory. Scores from two sessions a year apart enabled the investigators to examine the effects of both adaptation to noise and the effects of acoustic treatment of some of the classrooms. No evidence of adaptation was found either in the children's rating of the distracting effect of the noise or on two aspects of performance: the ability of children from noisy schools to resist auditory distraction and to display a lack of persistence (or helplessness) in solving geometric puzzles. Acoustic treatment of the classrooms produced a modest reduction in problem-solving ability (but not persistence) together with an improvement on some measures of academic achievement. Surprisingly, children's perception of noise interference and auditory distractability failed to show any effect of acoustic treatment. This finding is open to several interpretations. One is that since the effects of noise are long-lasting, noise reduction may take some time before the effects are noticeable. Coupled with the fact that only some of the classrooms had been treated, the slow process of a pupil's adaptation may have been cut short by a move to an untreated classroom. Yet another possibility is that exposure to loud noise outside the classroom may also diminish the effects of abatement (cf. Cohen *et al.*, 1980).

Occupational settings

Indices of efficiency based either on company records of accidents for workers exposed to noise or changes in productivity as a result of a reduction in noise level have been employed in the study of noise at work. A study by Kerr (1950) is typical of the first approach, investigating the correlates of accidents in over 12,000 employees on one site. Of the 40 factors under scrutiny mean noise level proved to be one of the most potent, correlating positively with accident frequency but not with accident severity.

A more complete analysis of the incidence of accidents provided in a series of studies by A. Cohen and his co-workers. Records for a 5-year period of over a thousand workers showed accidents to be more frequent in noisy areas (95 dBA or above). The incidence was particularly high in younger and less experienced workers in noisy settings, perhaps reflecting the susceptibility of untrained individuals, for whom task demands are high. This evidence is particularly convincing since a later study of the same population was able to show a reduction in accidents following the introduction of ear defenders (Cohen, 1974, 1976).

Two early studies managed to show an effect of noise on productivity. In one, by Weston and Adams (1932), a group of ten weavers wore ear defenders on alternate weeks for 6 months. Efficiency of production increased for all subjects by an average of 12 per cent when ear defenders (reducing the noise level by some 15 dB) were worn, although there is the possibility that this coincided with a period when thermal conditions were favourable to weaving. In a later study (Weston and Adams, 1935) a slightly different approach was adopted, comparing two groups of workers matched for skill. The group working with ear defenders improved their output by over 10 per cent. This effect was more marked at the end of the work period (both morning and afternoon) suggesting that low levels of noise help to sustain efficiency over long periods. The tendency for a group of workers under study to show improvements in efficiency simply as a result of receiving the experimenter's attention—known as the Hawthorne effect (Roethlisberger and Dickson, 1939)—may have played a role in bringing about improvements in productivity. However, in both studies increased output was found in workers who did not favour the wearing of ear defenders.

A more recent industrial study is one by Broadbent and Little (1960). The rate of work and the incidence of operator errors were compared for the task of perforating cine film at work stations with and without acoustical treatment (with levels of 89 and 99 dB, respectively). No differences were found for the rate of work, but the number of errors (especially of the type involving breakages of film) was markedly reduced at the treated stations. Since, for reasons associated with the scheme of payment, the operators moved periodically from machine to machine, the difference in errors cannot be ascribed to a sampling error or to a Hawthorne effect.

In the next section the emphasis on efficiency is less marked, attention is given to the general well-being of noise exposed groups.

OTHER NON-AUDITORY EFFECTS

Social behaviour

Effects of noise on the community have been found in naturalistic settings for such factors as truancy, care of dwellings, police arrests (Damon, 1977) and on social interaction (Appleyard and Lintell, 1971), but in each case they can be accounted for by, for example, differences in socio-economic class and traffic flow between the areas under scrutiny. Field experiments attempt to overcome the methodological shortcomings of naturalistic studies by introducing noise and studying specific social acts. In some, social responsiveness has been measured by the nature and degree of help offered to those in distress. For example, Mathews and Canon (1975) examined the effects of noise on helping an experimenter's confederate recover dropped books. In both the laboratory and field setting the presence of noise at 85 dB reduced the incidence of helping. However, Page (1977), using a similar setting with noise at 91 dB, found only a diminution in the help offered by females.

Further details of the effect of noise on helping are contained in a series of studies examining the granting of street interviews. Both Boles and Hayward (1978) and Korte *et al.* (1975) showed that the level of environmental input (including the intensity of noise as a component) reduced the proportion of subjects willing to grant an interview. Their findings are in line with Milgram's (1970) viewpoint that environmental overload leads to the blocking of some inputs, among them social ones, leading to a lack of cooperation. This view is difficult to reconcile with the detailed results. In particular, Korte *et al.* found that the number of people who refused an interview increased in noise rather than the number ignoring the request. This suggests that when verbal interaction may be involved the presence of others is not simply attenuated but actively evaluated (Jones *et al.* 1981). Such evaluations may also govern the helping of another, while the masking of auditory cues to the presence of another may play a synergistic role in shaping social behaviour. The aversive properties of noise may also serve to speed an individual's passage through a noisy setting (Korte and Grant, 1980) adding to the possibility that aspects of that setting may be ignored. Noise may also bring about inattentiveness to social cues in a manner analogous to that found for multi-component tasks in the laboratory by focusing attention on the dominant aspects of the social setting at the expense of non-dominant features (Cohen, 1978; Cohen and Lezak, 1977).

Loud noise also brings about changes of attitude to others. This is manifested both in the way that individuals or social settings are judged and by the degree of engagement with others. The behaviour of a group engaged in a competitive game is judged as more disorganized, disagreeable, and threatening by its members when the game is played in loud noise (Edsell, 1976). Even when others are judged from questionnaire responses, noise changes the degree of attraction. Attractiveness of others depends in large part on the discrepancy between the parties' attitudes. This is particularly marked when the factor 'intolerance for ambiguity' is taken into account. Those individuals tolerant of ambiguity do not show a marked discrepancy in their liking for similar and dissimilar others. When judgements of attractiveness are made in loud noise (at 84 dB) those subjects normally showing tolerance of ambiguity become more like their intolerant counterparts: their judgements become more directly associated with the degree of similarity (Bull *et al.*, 1972). Further details of the effects of noise on interpersonal judgements have been provided by Siegel and Steele (1980). They found that distracting noise at 70 dB increased the likelihood of extreme judgements of fictitious individuals. Noise in this case did not impair the intake or encoding of information about the individuals to be judged but in some way disrupted the weighting and integration of evidence. Notably this change was not restricted to negative judgements of individuals, positive attributes were also more emphatically rated. This change is reminiscent of that effect of noise found in confidence judgements of the detection of signals, although it is probably too early to conclude that adoption of extremes of judgement is a general and pervasive effect of noise.

Evidence from other sources indicates that noise may also increase the risk of hostile behaviour. In one study by Konečni (1975) subjects were asked to assess the 'creativity' of responses produced by the experimenters' confederate, giving electric shocks when they felt the response to be inadequate. The presence of complex or loud (97 dB) sound increased the number of shocks given but only if the subject had previously been insulted by the confederate Green and O'Neal, 1969).

It is clear that no single mechanism is responsible for the effects of noise on social behaviour. At least three factors must be considered: (i) changes in the weighting of judgements; (ii) the masking of cues to the presence and action of others; and (iii) the aversiveness of the noise coupled with the opportunities for escape.

Health

Everyday experience of distress and discomfort occasioned by noise leads us to regard as intuitively reasonable the notion that noise may have effects on mental and physical health. However, the evidence for a clear causal relation is equivocal.

Long-term effects of noise on physical health are thought to arise from the cumulative effect of repeated elicitation of the short-term physiological changes, but no evidence is available of the likelihood of reinstituting such responses from daily exposure to the same sound.

Intensity, rather than the annoyance value of noise, has been the major independent variable in those studies examining the effects of noise on health. The major focus of interest has been those ailments associated with the heart and circulation. A higher incidence of changes in peripheral circulation coupled with evidence of irregularity in the beating of the heart and disturbances of equilibrium was found in noise-exposed individuals among over one thousand steel workers (Jansen, 1961). Whether these changes arose solely from exposure to noise is doubtful, on the grounds that noisy jobs tend also to expose workers to a variety of environmental agents (among them heat, vibration, and noxious chemicals) and, above all, to danger. The confounding effect of exposure to danger may in part account for the incidence of hypertension in children from noisy urban areas (Karsdorf and Klappach, 1968). Children in a noisy urban area with a high traffic flow (1,000 cars/hour) had a higher mean blood pressure than children from quieter areas with low traffic flow (59 cars/hour). Here the element of danger from traffic in the noisy area may have accounted for, or contributed to, the elevation of blood pressure. Some studies in the occupational setting have found an association between the incidence of noise-induced deafness and that of hypertension (Jonsson and Hansson, 1977). One interpretation of these findings is that chronic exposure sufficient to bring about deafness also gives rise to elevated blood pressure (Jonsson, 1978). However, evidence from a class of studies examining cross-cultural differences suggests that hypertension may predispose an individual to hearing loss (e.g. Rosen, 1970).

Several studies have found a broad range of effects, often highlighting isolated symptoms. Two in particular attempt to overcome the difficulties of sampling by using a control group. In one, Ohrström and Björkman (1978) compared the symptomatology of workers exposed to periodic noise in a machine shop with workers in three textile plants each producing different levels of continuous noise. A little under half of the workers in the loudest textile plant reported subjective fatigue while only a quarter of those in the machine shop did so. Annoyance was however greater in the machine shop. Complaints of headaches were rare in the machine shop but much more frequent in the mills. Several factors may, however, have contributed to these findings: male workers in the machine shop were engaged in self-paced skilled work, in contrast to the machine-paced repetitive work undertaken by young females in the mills.

Similar interpretative difficulties rest with a large-scale study by A. Cohen (1974). The effect of noise on absence from work due to illness, accidents, and diagnosed medical problems, were investigated over a 5-year period by examining records at two major plants. One plant manufactured large boilers, the other electronic missile and weapon components. Workers drawn from high noise areas (in levels of 95 dBA or more) exhibited a higher incidence of problems on all three of the measures under investigation than workers from quiet areas (with levels of 80 dBA or less). Especially prevalent in those exposed to loud noise were allergies, respiratory and gastrointestinal disorders, and complaints associated with musculoskeletal, heart, and circulatory conditions. However, larger differences in the incidence of these ailments appeared when compared by job type and although attempts were made to examine the effects of noise levels in comparable jobs the job titles allowed considerable variation in the nature of each job. A follow-up study (Cohen,

1976) found evidence of a reduction in job accidents and medical problems as a result of introducing ear protection.

Few studies have examined the effects of noise in the occupational setting on mental health. Evidence of increased emotional tension was found by Jansen (1967) but the method of assessing symptoms was highly subjective and the effect was found in only a few symptoms from a very large number assessed. Most of the evidence on mental illness is contained in retrospective studies of admission rates to psychiatric hospitals from communities exposed to aircraft noise.

Higher rates of admission from noisy areas were found by Abbey-Wickrama, a'Brook, Gattoni, and Herridge (1969) in a study covering a 2-year period of 'high' and 'low' noise areas in the London Borough of Hounslow. These results were subsequently challenged on the grounds that the two samples were demographically different (Chowns, 1970) and several attempts have been made to replicate the findings with smaller samples, but without notable success. For example, Herridge (1972) found similar but less marked trends restricted to first admissions. Similar but non-significant trends were found by Gattoni and Tarnopolsky (1973) when, in a re-analysis of the original data, one source of bias (an old people's home in a high noise area) was removed. More recent work on mental health in noise settings points to the fact that the exposure is not the primary factor producing organic or psychiatric morbidity. Sensitivity to noise, in the view of Tarnopolsky *et al.* (1978) is '. . . a personality characteristic, a predisposing or high risk factor for psychiatric morbidity . . .', which '. . . helps to identify a predisposition and may even indicate morbidity; the noise itself, however, has not determined these factors . . .' (pp. 231–232).

Unfortunately, studies of the effects of airport noise on mental health are faced to a greater or lesser degree with a number of methodological difficulties: (i) the matching of different groups on socio-demographic variables; (ii) the possibility that patients from within the area of interest attend hospitals outside the area; and (iii) the restriction of the level of exposure to two usually extreme levels of noise, so that those effects of intermediate levels are absent (Hand *et al.*, 1980; Jansen, 1980).

CONCLUSIONS AND PRACTICAL IMPLICATIONS

So pervasive are the effects of noise that the impact of the body of evidence reviewed here seems modest in comparison with the magnitude of the problem. For some, like those effects on auditory fatigue and the direct effects of masking, a number of firm recommendations may be made.

(1) For an 8-hour working day the overall level of noise should be less than 85 dBA. The most economical means of reducing the level is to use ear defenders. Unfortunately, ear defenders tend to become uncomfortable after

prolonged use and do not improve either the intelligibility of speech or the detection of alarms.

(2) Improvements in the ratio of signal to noise will obviously reduce the effects of masking. If noise is concentrated in a narrow band, signals should be at frequencies remote from it, preferably in the region below its lower boundary.

(3) Speech will be satisfactorily received at levels of noise below 80 dBA, although if discourse has to be sustained a maximum noise level of 70 dBA will avoid fatigue in the speaker. In each case, however, listening or speaking in noise may have undesirable psychological side-effects.

(4) Practical means for reducing the effects of masking on inner speech include: (i) amplifying speech (although there will be an upper limit to the ear's tolerance for such sounds); (ii) excluding noise by the use of networks of headphones and noise-cancelling microphones; and (iii) restricting the range of vocabulary to an agreed or well-known set of words.

Reaching conclusions about those effects arising from the stressful action of noise is more problematical. This is primarily because much of the research has been carried out in the laboratory and evidence of its association with field results is, at best, tenuous. Whether the subtle effects we have been describing, resulting from short-term exposures to noise, will have any material consequence on productivity seems possible, but unlikely. Loud noise is usually only one element in a generally inhospitable working environment and factors such as the reliability of machinery and the method of payment may overwhelm the relatively minor effects of noise. However, the very limited evidence from the interaction of stresses bodes us to be cautious: noise may interact with other factors to produce a critical state of the organism and viewed in this way its effects can be profound.

With these reservations in mind, the following summary gives those findings about which there is general agreement.

(5) Intermittent noise produces both local and general effects, especially when the noise is unpredictable. The primary determinant in this case is the change in intensity of the noise. General effects extend beyond the period of exposure, their magnitude being in part determined by the attitude of the individual.

(6) Infrequent bursts of noise may have localized effects (particularly on the intake of information), the impairment in performance being a function of the noise level.

(7) Adverse effects of continuous noise are particularly noticeable in complex multi-component tasks, attention being diverted away from elements of low priority. The extent of the attentional change depends in large part on the demands made by each task element.

(8) When compared to continuous noise, variable noise may aid alertness at the end of a long vigil.

(9) Judgements become more extreme in noise: more confidence is expressed about the adequacy of a decision even though, on the basis of sensory evidence, it might be unwarranted. This effect may be found in cases as diverse as the detection of simple visual signals and the judgements of other persons.

(10) Tasks containing a heavy memory component are susceptible to disruption at relatively low levels of noise. This sensitivity may be more apparent than real and may in part be due to the ease with which the subtle strategic changes, commonly found in tasks of this type, may be discerned in cognitive tasks. Changes may take place in the organization of the response, particularly in the order in which items are reported, at levels of noise as low as 80 dBC. It is noteworthy that in tasks of this sort noise may improve performance.

(11) Evidence of the effect of noise on mental and physical health is equivocal.

(12) Social aspects of the response to noise include a reduction in helping behaviour, a more extreme or negative attitude to others, and in some cases noise may potentiate overt aggressive behaviour.

The consequences of noise, in any particular setting, will embrace deafness, masking, and performance, forming a conglomeration of effects, the contribution of each factor being difficult to predict. These manifold effects do not lend themselves to a simple generalization and, given the place of sound in our sensory world, it would be foolish to search for one.

SUMMARY

Three facets of human response to noise are distinguished. The first concerns the way in which loud noise brings about hearing loss. Both short- and long-term effects are distinguished. Difficulties associated with the establishment of limits to occupational exposure to noise are discussed. Second is the effect of noise on the perception of sounds: masking. While primary effects relating to the perception of speech and simple sounds are relatively well understood, little is known on the secondary effects of masking, in the effort involved in listening and making oneself heard. The third area encompasses the effects of noise on efficiency and well-being. Evidence of the relation between noise and mental or physical health is equivocal. Efficiency as assessed by laboratory tasks is influenced by noise in a complex way, with the effect largely depending on the prevailing task demands and the attitude of the individual. On both an individual and social level the human response in noise is more extreme and less elaborated than that in quiet. A number of practical recommendations are given.

REFERENCES

Abbey-Wickrama, I., a'Brook, M. F., Gattoni, W. G., and Herridge, C. F. (1969) Mental hospital admissions and aircraft noise. *Lancet*, **2**, 1275–1277.

Appleyard, D. and Lintell, M. (1971) Environmental quality of city streets: The residents' viewpoint. *Journal of the American Institute of Planners*, **38**, 84–101.

Bell, P. A. (1978) Effects of noise and heat stress on primary and subsidiary task performance. *Human Factors*, **20**, 749–752.

Beningus, V. A., Otto, D. A., and Krelson, J. H. (1975) Effects of low frequency random noises on performance of a numerical monitoring task. *Perceptual and Motor Skills*, **40**, 231–239.

Blackwell, P. J. and Belt, J. A. (1971) Effect of differential levels of ambient noise on vigilance performance. *Perceptual and Motor Skills*, **32**, 734.

Blake, M. J. F. (1971) Temperament and time of day. In W. P. Colquhoun (ed.), *Biological Rhythms and Human Performance*. London: Academic Press.

Boles, W. E. and Hayward, S. C. (1978) Effects of urban noise and sidewalk density upon pedestrian co-operation and tempo. *Journal of Social Psychology*, **104**, 29–35.

Broadbent, D. E. (1954) Some effects of noise on visual performance. *Quarterly Journal of Experimental Psychology*, **6**, 1–15.

Broadbent, D. E. (1957) Effects of noises of high and low frequency on behaviour. *Ergonomics*, **1**, 21–29.

Broadbent, D. E. (1958) *Perception and Communication*. London: Pergamon.

Broadbent, D. E. (1979) Human performance in noise. In C. M. Harris (ed.), *Handbook of Noise Control, 2nd Edition*. New York: McGraw-Hill.

Broadbent, D. E. (1980) Low levels of noise and the naming of colours. In J. V. Tobias *et al.* (eds.), *Proceedings of the Third International Congress on Noise as a Public Health Problem*. Rockville, Maryland: American Speech-Language-Hearing Association.

Broadbent, D. E. and Gregory, M. (1963) Vigilance considered as a statistical decision. *British Journal of Psychology*, **54**, 309–323.

Broadbent, D. E. and Gregory, M. (1965) Effects of noise and of signal rate upon vigilance analysed by means of decision theory. *Human Factors*, **7**, 155–162.

Broadbent, D. E. and Little, F. A. J. (1960) Effects of noise reduction in a work situation. *Occupational Psychology*, **34**, 133–140.

Bronzaft, A. L. and McCarthy, D. P. (1975) The effects of elevated train noise on reading ability. *Environment and Behaviour*, **7**, 517–527.

Bruce, R. D. (1976) The costs and benefits of implementing 90 and 85 dB(A) noise exposure standards. In G. Rossi and M. Vigone (eds.), *Man and Noise*. Turin: Edizioni Minerva Medica.

Bruel, P. V. (1976) Determination of noise levels. In G. Rossi and M. Vigone (eds.), *Man and Noise*. Turin: Edizioni Minerva Medica.

Bull, A. J., Burbage, S. E., Crandall, J. E., Fletcher, C. I., Lloyd, J. T., Ravenberg, R. L., and Rockett, S. L. (1972) Effects of noise and intolerance of ambiguity upon attraction for similar and dissimilar others. *Journal of Social Psychology*, **88**, 151–152.

Burns, W. (1973) *Noise and Man*. London: John Murray.

Bursill, A. E. (1958) The restriction of peripheral vision during exposure to hot and humid conditions. *Quarterly Journal of Experimental Psychology*, **10**, 113–129.

Chowns, R. H. (1970) Mental hospital admissions and aircraft noise. *Lancet*, **2**, 467.

Cohen, A. (1974) Industrial noise and medical, absence and accident record data on exposed workers. In W. D. Ward (ed.), *Proceedings of the International Congress on Noise as a Public Health Problem*. Washington: U.S. Environmental Protection Agency.

Cohen, A. (1976) The influence of a company hearing conservation program on extra-auditory problems in workers. *Journal of Safety Research*, **8**, 146–162.

Cohen, A. J., Anticaglia, R., and Jones, H. H. (1970) Noise-induced hearing loss. *Archives of Environmental Health*, **20**, 614–623.

Cohen, S. (1978) Environmental load and the allocation of attention. In A. Baum *et al.* (eds.), *Advances in Environmental Psychology, Vol. 1.* Hillsdale, N.J.: Lawrence Erlbaum.

Cohen, S. and Lezak, A. (1977) Noise and inattentiveness to social cues. *Environment and Behavior*, **9**, 559–572.

Cohen, S., Glass, D. C., and Singer, J. E. (1973) Apartment noise, auditory discrimination and reading ability in children. *Journal of Experimental Social Psychology*, **9**, 407–422.

Cohen, S., Evans, G. W., Krantz, D. S., and Stokols, D. (1980) Physiological, motivational, and cognitive effects of aircraft noise on children: Moving from the laboratory to the field. *American Psychologist*, **35**, 231–243.

Cohen, S., Evans, G. W., Krantz, D. S., Stokols, D., and Kelly, S. (1981) Aircraft noise and children: Longitudinal and cross-sectional evidence on evidence on adaptation to noise, and the effectiveness of noise abatement. *Journal of Personality and Social Psychology*, **40**, 331–345.

Corcoran, D. W. J. (1962) Noise and loss of sleep. *Quarterly Journal of Experimental Psychology*, **14**, 178–182.

Corcoran, D. W. J., Mullin, J., Rainey, M. T., and Firth, G. (1977) The effects of raised signal and noise amplitude during the course of vigilance tasks. In R. Mackie (ed.), *Vigilance: Theory, Operational Performance and Physiological Correlates.* New York: Plenum.

Corso, J. F. (1976) Presbycusis as a complicating factor in evaluating noise-induced hearing loss. In D. Henderson *et al.* (eds.), *Effects of Noise on Hearing.* New York: Raven Press.

Crook, M. A. and Langdon, F. J. (1974) The effects of aircraft noise in schools around London Airport. *Journal of Sound and Vibration*, **34**, 221–232.

Cunniff, P. F. (1977) *Environmental Noise Pollution.* London: John Wiley & Sons.

Daee, S. and Wilding, J. M. (1977) Effects of high intensity white noise on short-term memory for position and sequence. *British Journal of Psychology*, **68**, 335–349.

Damon, A. (1977) The residential environment, health and behavior: simple research opportunities, strategies, and some findings in the Solomon Islands, and Boston, Massachusetts. In L. E. Hinkle and W. C. Loring (eds.), *The Effect of the Man-Made Environment on Health and Behavior.* Atlanta: Center for Disease Control.

Davies, D. R. and Jones, D. M. (1975) The effects of noise, and incentives upon retention in short-term memory. *British Journal of Psychology*, **66**, 61–68.

van Dishoeck, H. A. E. (1948) The continuous threshold or detailed audiogram for recording simulation deafness. *Acta Otolaryngologica*, **78**, 183–192.

Dornic, S. (1975) Some studies on the retention of order information. In P. M. A. Rabbitt and S. Dornic (eds.), *Attention and Performance, V.* New York: Academic Press.

Edsell, R. D. (1976) Social stress and community psychology. *American Journal of Community Psychology*, **6**, 1–14.

Elliot, L. L. (1971) Backward and forward masking. *Audiology*, **10**, 65–76.

Eschenbrenner, J. A. (1971) Effects of intermittent noise on the performance of a complex psychomotor task. *Human Factors*, **13**, 59–63.

Finkleman, J. M., Zeitlin, L. R., Romoff, R. A., Friend, M. A., and Brown, L. S. (1979) Conjoint effect of physical stress and noise stress on information processing performance and cardiac response. *Human Factors*, **21**, 1–6.

Fisher, S. (1972) A 'distraction effect' of noise bursts. *Perception*, **1**, 223–236.

Fisher, S. (1973) The 'distraction effect' and information processing complexity. *Perception*, **2**, 78–89.

Ford, A. (1929) Attention-automisation: An investigation of the traditional nature of mind. *American Journal of Psychology*, **41**, 1–32.

Forster, P. M. and Grierson, A. T. (1978) Noise and attentional selectivity: A reproducible phenomenon? *British Journal of Psychology*, **69**, 489–498.

Fowler, C. J. H. and Wilding, J. (1979) Differential effects of noise and incentives on learning. *British Journal of Psychology*, **70**, 149–154.

Frankenhaeuser, M. and Lundberg, U. (1974) Immediate and delayed effects of noise on performance and arousal. *Biological Psychology*, **2**, 127–133.

French, N. R. and Steinberg, J. C. 61947) Factors governing the intelligibility of speech sounds. *Journal of the Acoustical Society of America*, **19**, 90–119.

Gardner, G. T. (1978) Effects of federal human subjects' regulations on data obtained in environmental stressor research. *Journal of Personality and Social Psychology*, **36**, 628–634.

Gattoni, F. and Tarnopolsky, A. (1973) Aircraft noise and psychiatric morbidity. *Psychological Medicine*, **3**, 516–520.

Green, R. G. and O'Neal, E. C. (1969) Activation of cue-elicited aggression by general arousal. *Journal of Personality and Social Psychology*, **11**, 289–292.

Glass, D. C. and Singer, J. E. (1972) *Urban Stress: Experiments on Noise and Social Stressors*. New York: Academic Press.

Graeven, D. B. (1975) Necessity control and predictability of noise annoyance. *Journal of Social Psychology*, **95**, 85–90.

Hamilton, P. and Copeman, A. (1970) The effect of alcohol and noise on components of a tracking and monitoring task. *British Journal of Psychology*, **61**, 149–156.

Hamilton, P., Hockey, G. R. J., and Quinn, J. G. (1972) Information selection, arousal and memory. *British Journal of Psychology*, **63**, 181–189.

Hamilton, P., Hockey, G. R. J., and Rejman, R. (1977) The place of the concept of activation in human information processing theory: An integrative approach. In S. Dornic (ed.), *Attention and Performance, VI*. New York: Lawrence Erlbaum.

Hand, D. J., Tarnopolsky, A., Barker, S. M., and Jenkins, L. M. (1980) Relationships between psychiatric hospital admissions, and aircraft noise: a new study. In J. V. Tobias, G. Jansen, and W. D. Ward (eds.), *Proceedings of the Third International Congress on Noise as a Public Health Problem*. Rockville, Maryland: American Speech-Language-Hearing Association.

Hartley, L. R. (1973) Effect of prior noise or prior performance on serial reaction. *Journal of Experimental Psychology*, **101**, 255–261.

Hartley, L. R. (1974) Performance during continuous and intermittent noise, and wearing ear protection. *Journal of Experimental Psychology*, **102**, 512–516.

Hartley, L. R. (1981) Noise does not impair by masking: A reply to Poulton's 'Composite Model for Human Performance in Continuous Noise'. *Psychological Review*, **88**, 86–89.

Hartley, L. R. and Adams, R. G. (1974) Effects of noise on the Stroop test. *Journal of Experimental Psychology*, **102**, 62–66.

Hartley, L. R. and Shirley, E. (1977) Sleep loss, noise, and decisions. *Ergonomics*, **20**, 481–482.

Herridge, C. F. (1972) Aircraft noise, and mental hospital admissions. *Sound*, **6**, 32–36.

Hockey, G. R. J. (1970a) Effect of loud noise on attentional selectivity. *Quarterly Journal of Experimental Psychology*, **22**, 28–36.

Hockey, G. R. J. (1970b) Signal probability and signal location as possible bases for increased selectivity in noise. *Quarterly Journal of Experimental Psychology*, **22**, 37–42.

Hockey, G. R. J. and Hamilton, P. (1970) Arousal, and information selection in short-term memory. *Nature*, **226**, 866–867.

Hörmann, H. and Osterkamp, J. (1966) Über den einfluss von Kontinvierlichem Lärm auf die Organisation von Gedächtrisinhalten. *Zeitschrift für Experimentelle und Angewandte Psychologie*, **13**, 31–38.

Houston, B. K. (1969) Noise, task difficulty, and Stroop color-word performance. *Journal of Experimental Psychology*, **28**, 403–404.

Houston, B. K. and Jones, T. M. (1967) Distraction and Stroop color-word performance. *Journal of Experimental Psychology*, **74**, 54–56.

Jansen, G. (1961) Adverse effects of noise on iron and steel workers. *Stahl und Eisen*, **81**, 217–220.

Jansen, G. (1980) Research on extraaural noise since 1973. In J. V. Tobias *et al.* (eds.), *Proceedings of the Third International Congress on Noise as a Public Health Problem*. Rockville, Maryland: American Speech-Language-Hearing Association.

Jerison, H. J. (1957) Performance on a simple vigilance task in noise and quiet. *Journal of the Acoustical Society of America*, **29**, 1163–1165.

Jerison, H. J. (1959) Effects of noise on human performance. *Journal of Applied Psychology*, **43**, 96–101.

Jones, D. M. and Broadbent, D. E. (1979) Side-effects of interference with speech by noise. *Ergonomics*, **22**, 1073–1081.

Jones, D. M., Chapman, A. J., and Auburn, J. C. (1981) Noise in the environment: A social perspective. *Journal of Environmental Psychology*, **1**, 43–59.

Jones, D. M., Smith, A. P., and Broadbent, D. E. (1979) Effects of moderate intensity noise on the Bakan vigilance task. *Journal of Applied Psychology*, **64**, 627–634.

Jonsson, A. (1978) Noise as a possible risk factor for raised blood pressure in man. *Journal of Sound and Vibration*, **59**, 119–121.

Jonsson, A. and Hansson, L. (1977) Prolonged exposure to a stressful stimulus (noise) as a cause of raised blood pressure in man. *Lancet*, **3**, 86–87.

Karsdorf, G. and Klappach, H. (1968) Einfluss des verkehrslarms auf Gesundheit und Leistung bei obserchulen einer grosstadt. *Zeitschrift fur die Gesamte Hygiene*, **14**, 52–54.

Kerr, W. A. (1950) Accident proneness and factory departments. *Journal of Applied Psychology*, **34**, 167–170.

Kohler, H. K. (1982) The measurement of noise. In D. M. Jones and A. J. Chapman (eds.), *Noise and Society*. Chichester: John Wiley & Sons.

Konečni, V. J. (1975) The mediation of aggressive behavior: Arousal level versus anger and cognitive labeling. *Journal of Personality and Social Psychology*, **32**, 706–712.

Korte, C. and Grant, R. (1980) Traffic noise, environmental awareness, and pedestrian behavior. *Environment and Behavior*, **12**, 408–420.

Korte, C., Ypma, A., and Toppen, A. (1975) Helpfulness in Dutch society as a function of urbanization and environmental input. *Journal of Personality and Social Psychology*, **32**, 996–1003.

Kryter, K. D. (1973) Impairment to hearing from exposure to noise. *Journal of the Acoustical Society of America*, **53**, 1211–1234.

Loeb, M. and Jones, P. D. (1978) Noise exposure, monitoring, and tracking performance as a function of signal bias and task priority. *Ergonomics*, **21**, 265–277.

Mathews, K. and Canon, L. (1975) Environmental noise level as a determinant of helping behavior. *Journal of Personality and Social Psychology*, **32**, 571–577.

May, D. N. and Rice, C. G. (1971) Effects of startle due to pistol shot on control precision performance. *Journal of Sound and Vibration*, **15**, 197–202.

McGrath, J. J. (1963) Irrelevant stimulation, and vigilance performance. In D. N. Buckner and J. J. McGrath (eds.), *Vigilance: A Symposium*. London: McGraw-Hill.

Milgram, S. (1970) The experience of living in cities. *Science*, **167**, 1461–1468.

Millar, K. (1980) Word recognition in loud noise. *Acta Psychologica*, **43**, 225–237.

Miller, G. A., Heise, G. A., and Lichten, W. (1951) The intelligibility of speech as a function of the content of the test materials. *Journal of Experimental Psychology*, **41**, 329–335.

Miller, I. W. and Norman, W. H. (1979) Learned helplessness in humans: A review and attribution-theory model. *Psychological Bulletin*, **86**, 93–118.

Miller, J. D. (1974) Effects of noise on people. *Journal of the Accoustical Society of America*, **56**, 729–764.

Moran, S. L. V. and Loeb, M. (1977) Annoyance, and behavioral aftereffects following interfering, and non-interfering aircraft noise. *Journal of Applied Psychology*, **62**, 719–726.

Morgan, J. J. B. (1916) The overcoming of distraction, and other resistances. *Archives of Psychology*, **5**, 1–84.

Mullin, J. and Corcoran, D. W. J. (1977) Interaction of task amplitude with circadian variation in auditory vigilance performance. *Ergonomics*, **20**, 193–200.

Nixon, J. C. and Glorig, A. (1961) Noise induced permanent threshold shift at 2000 cps and 4000 cps. *Journal of the Acoustical Society of America*, **33**, 904–908.

Öhrström, E. and Björkman, M. (1978) Medical symptoms in noisy industries *Journal of Sound and Vibration*, **59**, 115–118.

Ollerhead, J. B. (1973) Noise: How can the nuisance be controlled? *Applied Ergonomics*, **September**, 130–138.

Page, R. A. (1977) Noise and helping behavior. *Environment and Behavior*, **9**, 311–334.

Passchier-Vermeer, W. (1974) Hearing loss due to continuous exposure to steady state broad-band noise. *Journal of the Acoustical Society of America*, **56**, 1585–1593.

Pearsons, K. S. (1974) Systems of noise measurement. In W. Dixon Ward (ed.), *Proceedings of the International Congress on Noise as a Public Health Problem*. Washington: U.S. Environmental Protection Agency.

Pearsons, K. S. (1980) Communication in noise. In J. V. Tobias *et al.* (eds.), *Proceedings of the Third International Congress on Noise as a Public Health Problem*. Rockville, Maryland: American Speech-Language-Hearing Association.

Pepler, R. D. (1959) Warmth, and lack of sleep: Accuracy or activity reduced? *Journal of Comparative Physiology and Psychology*, **52**, 446–450.

Percival, L. and Loeb, M. (1980) Influence of noise characteristics on behavioral aftereffects. *Human Factors*, **22**, 341–352.

Peterson, A. P. G. (1979) Noise measurements: Methods. In C. M. Harris (ed.), *Handbook of Noise Control, 2nd Edition*. London: McGraw-Hill.

Rabbitt, P. M. A. (1966) Recognition memory for words correctly heard in noise. *Psychonomic Science*, **8**, 383–384.

Rabbitt, P. M. A. (1968) Channel capacity, intelligibility, and immediate memory. *Quarterly Journal of Experimental Psychology*, **20**, 241–248.

Rabbitt, P. M. A. (1979) Current paradigms, and models in human information processing. In V. S. Hamilton and D. W. Warburton (eds.), *Human Stress and Cognition*. Chichester: John Wiley & Sons.

Robinson, D. W., Shipton, M. S., and Whittle, L. S. (1973) *Audiometry in Industrial Hearing Conservation*. Teddington: National Physical Laboratory.

Roethlisberger, F. J. and Dickson, W. J. (1939) *Management, and the Worker*. Cambridge, Massachusetts: Harvard University Press.

Rosen, S. (1970) Noise, hearing, and cardiovascular function. In B. L. Welch and A. S. Welch (eds.), *Physiological Effects on Noise*. London: Plenum.

Rotton, J., Olszewski, D., Charleton, M., and Soler, E. (1978) Loud speech, conglomerate noise, and behavioural aftereffects. *Journal of Applied Psychology*, **63**, 360–365.

Salamé, P. and Wittersheim, G. (1978) Selective noise disturbance of the information input in short-term memory. *Quarterly Journal of Experimental Psychology*, **30**, 693–704.

Schubert, E. D. and Parker, C. D. (1955) Addition to Cherry's findings on switching speech between the two ears. *Journal of the Acoustical Society of America*, **27**, 792–794.

Sherrod, D. R., Hage, J. N., Halpern, P. L., and Moore, B. S. (1977) Effects of personal causation, and perceived control on responses to an aversive environment: The more control, the better. *Journal of Experimental Psychology*, **13**, 14–27.

Schoenberger, R. W. and Harris, C. S. (1965) Human performance as a function of changes in acoustic noise levels. *Journal of Engineering Psychology*, **4**, 108–119.

Siegel, J. M. and Steele, C. M. (1980) Environmental distraction, and interpersonal judgements. *British Journal of Social and Clinical Psychology*, **19**, 23–32.

Smith, A. P., Jones, D. M., and Broadbent, D. E. (1981) The effects of noise on recall of categorized lists. *British Journal of Psychology*, **72**, 299–316.

Spoor, A. (1967) Presbycusis values in relation to noise induced hearing loss. *Laryngoscope*, **82**, 1399–1409.

Stevens, S. S. (1972) Stability of human performance under intense noise. *Journal of Sound and Vibration*, **21**, 35–56.

Tarnopolsky, A., Barker, S. M., Wiggins, R. D., and McLean, E. K. (1978) The effect of aircraft noise on the mental health of a community sample: A pilot study. *Psychological Medicine*, **8**, 219–233.

Tarrière, C. and Wisner, A. (1962) Effets des bruits significatifs et non significatifs au cours d'une épreuve de vigilance. *Travail Humain*, **28**, 1–28.

Taylor, W., Pearson, J., Mair, A., and Burns, W. (1965) Study of noise, and hearing in jute weaving. *Journal of the Acoustical Society of America*, **38**, 113–120.

Teichner, W. H., Arees, E., and Reilly, R. (1963) Noise, and human performance: A psychophysiological approach. *Ergonomics*, **6**, 83–97.

Tobias, J. V. and Irons, F. M. (1974) Perception of distorted speech. In W. D. Ward (ed.), *Proceedings of the Second International Congress on Noise as a Public Health Problem*. Washington: U.S. Environmental Protection Agency.

Viteles, M. S. and Smith, K. R. (1946) An experimental investigation of the effect of change in atmospheric conditions, and noise upon performance. *Transactions of the American Society of Heating and Ventilation Engineers*, **52**, 167–182.

Ward, L. M. and Suedfeld, R. (1973) Human responses to highway noise. *Environmental Research*, **6**, 306–326.

Ward, W. D. (1962) Damage risk criteria for line spectra. *Journal of the Acoustical Society of America*, **34**, 1610–1619.

Ward, W. D. (1980) Noise-induced hearing loss: Research since 1973. In J. V. Tobias *et al.* (eds.), *Proceedings of the Third International Congress on Noise as a Public Health Problem*. Rockville, Maryland: American Speech-Language-Hearing Association.

Webster, J. C. (1979) Effects of noise on speech. In C. M. Harris (ed.), *Handbook of Noise Control*. London: McGraw-Hill.

Weinstein, C. S. and Weinstein, N. D. (1979) Noise and reading performance in open space school. *Journal of Educational Research*, **72**, 210–213.

Wells, R. J. (1979) Noise measurements: Methods. In C. M. Harris (ed.), *Handbook of Noise Control, 2nd Edition*. London: McGraw-Hill.

Weston, H. C. and Adams, S. (1932) The effect of noise on the performance of weavers. *Industrial Health Research Board Report No. 65, Part II*. London: H.M.S.O.

Weston, H. C. and Adams, S. (1935) The performance of weavers under varying conditions of noise. *Industrial Health Research Board Report No. 65.* London: H.M.S.O.

Wilding, J. and Mohindra, N. (1980) Effects of subvocal suppression, articulating aloud, and noise on sequence recall. *British Journal of Psychology,* **71,** 247–262.

Wilkinson, R. T. (1963) Interaction of noise with knowledge of results, and sleep deprivation. *Journal of Experimental Psychology,* **66,** 332–337.

Woodhead, M. M. (1958) Effects of bursts of loud noise on a continuous visual task. *British Journal of Industrial Medicine,* **15,** 120–125.

Woodhead, M. M. (1959) Effect of brief loud noise on decision making. *Journal of the Acoustical Society of America,* **31,** 1329–1331.

Woodhead, M. M. (1964) The effects of bursts of noise on an arithmetic task. *American Journal of Psychology,* **77,** 627–633.

Stress and Fatigue in Human Performance
Edited by G. R. J. Hockey
© 1983 John Wiley & Sons Ltd.

Chapter 4

Circadian Rhythms and Shiftwork

Timothy H. Monk and Simon Folkard

It has been said that there are only two things wrong with shiftwork: having to work when you ought to be asleep, and having to sleep when you ought to be awake. This highlights the fact that shiftwork problems result primarily from man's nature as a diurnal rather than a nocturnal creature. Thus, although shiftwork has been with us since Roman times (normal city traffic in those days being restricted to the night hours), there is little doubt that shiftwork involves a pattern of behaviour that is basically unnatural to the human animal. That a pattern of behaviour is unnatural does not, of course, imply that it is necessarily harmful, and a recent review of health consequences of shiftwork came to largely negative conclusions (Harrington, 1978). However, shiftwork is something that has to be consciously coped with, and should thus be considered as at least a potential stressor, which for some people can have disastrous effects on their well-being, safety, and efficiency.

SHIFTWORK AS A POTENTIAL STRESSOR

The rapid growth in shiftwork over the last few decades has meant that society can no longer rely upon a small pool of people who happen to be able to cope happily with shiftwork. In both Europe and the United States it has been estimated that about 20 per cent of the work-force is currently engaged in some sort of shift system. Thus, it has become necessary to find out more about shiftwork and shiftworkers, so that any detrimental effects on people who are unable to cope with shiftwork can be ameliorated. In Europe, in particular, this has resulted in quite a substantial body of research. The present chapter is concerned with presenting an overview of this research, setting it in the context of human circadian (24-hour) rhythms.

For the worker to successfully cope with shiftwork there are essentially three factors which have to be 'got right', namely sleep, social and family life, and circadian rhythms. All three are interrelated, such that a failure in any one of

97

them can negate any positive effects accrued from success with the other two. Sleep forms the major preoccupation in the life of many shiftworkers. On average, rotating shiftworkers get about 7 hours less sleep per week than their dayworking counterparts (Bjerner and Swensson, 1953). Very often the patterning of work, leisure, and sleep is changed by the shiftworker on night-shift so that sleep is taken straight after work rather than after a period of recreation. This has the advantage of allowing the early evening to remain free for recreation, and allows the attitude that one might simply have been rather late in getting to bed; i.e. the experience of a delay in the sleep/wake cycle, rather than a complete inversion of it. It does mean, however, that for any further lateness in going to bed the likelihood of a good day's sleep can be quite dramatically reduced.

This introduces the second factor which is that of the social problems inherent in night-work. In most households, mornings are basically rather noisy times, with the chatter of radios, roar of vacuum cleaners, and the general chaos of a family going off to work or to school. Social tensions and strains for the shiftworker can often thus occur simply as a product of the night-worker's need for peace and quiet conflicting with his wife's need to run a family household. Parenthetically, the female shiftworker is very often expected to perform household management duties as well as her work, and for her the 'sleep debt' can become quite enormous. Other social problems accrue from evening working which very often precludes enjoyment of television, pubs, and cinemas. The negative effects of these social problems have been catalogued by a variety of authors (reviewed by Walker, 1978).

The third factor, that of circadian rhythms and their adjustment (or, rather, the lack of it) has dominated much of the recent research in the shiftwork area. Thus, much of this chapter will be concerned with the daily 24-hour rhythms which provide a temporal structure to life, and with what happens to these rhythms when the structure is disrupted by the need to work at night. That a structure exists is obvious, with dramatic differences in behaviour and physiology between the states of sleep and wakefulness, and an overwhelming preponderance of sleep during the hours of darkness. What is less obvious is the complex pattern of gradual physiological and psychological changes that underlie this cycling of sleep and wakefulness, and the degree to which this pattern is self-sustaining and internal to the organism. Only when these more subtle factors are understood can the problems of the shiftworker be properly tackled.

THE ROLE OF CIRCADIAN RHYTHMS

The nature of circadian rhythms

The first misapprehension to be dispelled is that the homeostatic mechanisms of man are perfect, and provide an internal physiological environment that is utterly constant. Although this misapprehension appears to have been particularly resilient, there is now a wealth of evidence contrary to it (e.g. Conroy and Mills, 1970), and it is now generally accepted that there are regular, non-trivial fluctuations in almost every physiological measure over the 24-hour period. Because these fluctuations take the form of a rhythm having a period of about a day, the term 'circadian rhythms' has been coined to describe them (Halberg, 1969).

One of the more easily measured physiological circadian rhythms is that in body temperature. Contrary to popular belief, body temperature in the healthy human does not remain constant at exactly 37°C (or 98.6°F) over the day but varies rhythmically, with a difference of about 0.5°C (1°F) between peak and trough values. The minimum value occurs in the early hours of the morning, with a pronounced rise over the early waking hours and a gentler rise over the rest of the day, reaching a peak in the early evening (see the broken curve in Figure 16, p.105).

The timing of trough (during sleep) and peak (during wakefulness) temperatures suggests a second misapprehension, namely that circadian rhythms are merely simple reactions to changes in the person's gross behaviour or immediate environment. Such factors are labelled exogenous factors, and one might hypothesize that circadian rhythms are totally exogenous, being simply the product of measures having a low value during times of sleep and inactivity and high values during wakefulness and exertion. Clearly, the way to test this hypothesis is to place the subject in a constant time-free environment, keep him awake, and regulate his activities and diet. If the circadian rhythms still persist then one must attribute them to some internal *endogenous* time-keeper rather than to the exogenous factors, which in this case have been rigidly controlled. An excellent example of such a study is provided by Froberg *et al.* (1975) who investigated a variety of physiological and psychological circadian rhythms in 29 subjects who experienced 72 hours of sleep deprivation.

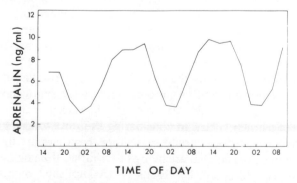

Figure 13. The average adrenaline excretion rate of 29 subjects experiencing 72 hours of sleep deprivation. After Froberg *et al.* (1975).

A typical result is shown in Figure 13 which plots the mean level of adrenaline excretion as a function of time. The clear evidence of a circadian rhythm refutes the idea that rhythms are simply exogenous reactions to changes in environment or gross behaviour.

Having shown that endogenous rhythms do exist, the question clearly arises as to the form that the internal clock (or clocks) might take. Those that have sought to answer this question for the human have invariably used a bunker, or isolation suite, in which a person can be incarcerated for several weeks or months, remaining totally isolated from all time cues. This technique has been used extensively by Jurgen Aschoff and his colleagues at Erling-Andechs, who have now run over 200 subjects in their bunkers (Wever, 1979). Aschoff and Wever found that although there were some interindividual differences, most subjects settled down to a 'day' that was about one hour longer than normal (i.e. a 25-hour circadian rhythm). Thus, after about 3½ weeks the subject effectively 'loses' a day. The rhythm is referred to as *free-running* under these conditions.

The investigation of free-running circadian rhythms provides insights into the internal clock or clocks that might comprise the circadian system. Although a wide range of physiological and psychological measures have been studied, most attention has focused upon two rhythms, the sleep/wake cycle, and the temperature rhythm. Usually these two rhythms 'free run' to the same period, although the normal phase relationship between them does sometimes break down. Thus, for example, the peak of the temperature rhythm might move from the end of the waking day to the beginning. This is referred to as *internal dissociation*.

More interesting from a theoretical point of view are the cases in which the two rhythms 'free run' to different periods. Thus, for example, the sleep/wake cycle might have a period of 33 hours, whilst the temperature rhythm has a period of 25 hours. This is known as *internal desynchronization* (Wever, 1975) and occurs in about 30 per cent of subjects during the first month of a free-running experiment, and in almost all subjects in longer experiments. Its occurrence is crucial in indicating that there must be more than one clock (or, more accurately, oscillator) controlling the circadian system. Both Wever (1979) in Germany and Moore-Ede *et al.* (1981) in the United States believe that there are two groups of oscillators: the Group 1 oscillators, primarily controlling the temperature rhythm (and comparatively endogenous) and the Group 2 oscillators, primarily controlling the sleep/wake cycle (and comparatively exogenous). Thus, in considering the shiftworker's problem of adjusting to a new routine one should remember that there are likely to be at least two internal body clocks that are being re-set rather than one.

The setting or re-setting of the clocks is accomplished by time cues or *zeitgeber* (from the German for 'time giver'). The inaccuracy of the internal clocks (as indicated by free-running periods unequal to 24 hours) suggests that even in a normal diurnal routine, *zeitgeber* are at work keeping the circadian system at an appropriate phase to the (exactly) 24-hour cycle of clock time. In man, *zeitgeber* may either by physical (e.g. sunrise, sunset) or social (e.g. clock time, traffic noise). When disruptions of the routine occur, these *zeitgeber* will act upon the circadian system, either attempting to bring it into phase with the new routine or, conversely, actually discouraging adjustment. As Table 4 shows, there are differences in the way that physical and social *zeitgeber* will operate, dependent upon the type of change that is occurring. Shiftwork appears to be the situation with the least encouragement towards adjustment.

Table 4. The ways in which social *zeitgeber* (such as clock time and traffic noise) and physical *zeitgeber* (such as sunrise and sunset) influence the phase adjustment of circadian rhythms to different disruptions of routine.

Change	Influence of social *zeitgeber*	Influence of physical *zeitgeber*
Transmeridianal flight	Encouraging adjustment	Encouraging adjustment
Daylight saving time	Encouraging adjustment	Discouraging adjustment
Shiftwork	Predominantly discouraging adjustment	Discouraging adjustment

Shift systems

From the above discussion of circadian rhythms it becomes clear that the pattern with which morning, evening, and night-shifts are worked is important in two respects. First, the *rate* with which shifts change will determine the degree of circadian rhythm phase adjustment that can occur, with little or no phase adjustment occurring when only one or two shifts of a particular type are worked before changing to a different type. Secondly, the *direction* of rotation would also seem to be important. Although there is little direct evidence in this respect, the fact that endogenous rhythms tend to be longer than 24 hours, together with data from the jet-lag area (see below), suggests that rotation in the order *morning, evening, night* might facilitate adjustment rather better than the direction *night, evening, morning*, since the latter requires a phase advance, or shortening, of the circadian rhythm. (See Wever, 1979, though for a critical discussion of this issue.)

Although there are many different types of shift system it is possible to create three broad categories. The first category comprises 'permanent' shift systems, where any one individual only ever works one sort of shift. The classic example of this is the night-watchman whose job is only there during the hours of darkness. Other examples are office cleaners, who work either evenings or very early in the morning, and night nurses. Recently there has also been a growth in the 'twilight' shift, where housewives are encouraged to come into a factory between about 5.0 p.m. and 9.0 p.m. while their husbands look after the children.

At the other end of the scale is the category known as 'rapidly rotating' shifts. Under this type of system the worker never has more than one or two shifts in a row, before changing to a different time. Thus, he might work two morning-shifts, followed by two evening-shifts, followed by two night-shifts, followed by two or three days off, the cycle then repeating itself. This type of system is particularly popular in Europe, and is referred to as the 'Continental' or 'Metropolitan' system.

In between the permanent and rapidly rotating shift systems are the slowly (i.e. weekly, fortnightly, or monthly) rotating methods. This type of shift system is probably the one used most frequently, particularly when the system is not continuous (i.e. when there are times or days when there is no one working); it is particularly prevalent in Britain and North America.

Circadian rhythms and work efficiency

Just as there are circadian rhythms in physiological measures, so also are there circadian rhythms in performance efficiency. These are discussed more fully in Chapter 9. The present section will merely present a summary of the major results in order to provide a basis for discussing performance changes during adjustment to shiftwork.

Following the work of Kleitman (1939, revised 1963) and Colquhoun (1971) and his associates, it has become accepted that for many tasks there is a strong parallelism between the circadian rhythms of temperature and performance. Thus, performance at these tasks is held to show a steep rise from early to mid-morning, a more gradual rise to an evening peak (perhaps interrupted by a post-lunch dip), followed by a sharp decline into the hours of sleep. Tasks in which such a pattern is particularly clear are visual scanning tasks in which the subject is required to work his way through visual material, finding and indicating targets (Monk, 1979). However, in contrast to such tasks, those that are more complex, and involve a high working memory load show a very different time-of-day trend. Thus, for example, performance at a task measuring immediate memory for material presented in prose shows a *decline* over the waking day, with a *trough* in the early evening (Folkard and Monk, 1980). Thus, any explanation of circadian performance rhythms has to account not only for the rhythms themselves, but also for the differences in time-of-day function that are observed for different tasks.

Circadian performance rhythms have commonly been explained in terms of an arousal model. This model postulates that there is an underlying rhythm in basal arousal which is broadly parallel to the circadian temperature rhythm. Performance is then held to be related to arousal level via the Yerkes–Dodson 'inverted-U'. Thus, the form that the time-of-day function takes is held to depend upon the arousal level that is optimal for performance at that particular task. Simple repetitive tasks and/or vigilance tasks are held to have a high optimal arousal level, and thus exhibit time-of-day functions broadly parallel to the presumed arousal rhythm, and hence to the temperature rhythm. In contrast, complex and/or high memory load tasks are held to have a low optimal arousal level, and thus to show a decline over the waking day, in roughly inverse phase to the temperature rhythm. A formal quantification of this arousal model has recently been presented (Monk, 1982). An elegant demonstration of the breakdown of the parallelism between performance and temperature rhythms with increased memory load has been provided by Folkard, Knauth, Monk, and Rutenfranz (1976); see Figure 14.

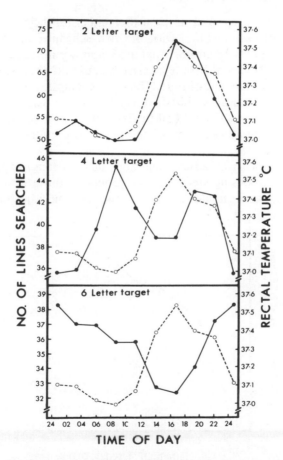

Figure 14. The circadian rhythm of two subjects' performance on low (two letter), medium (four letter) and high (six letter) memory load versions of a visual search task (●————●), together with that in rectal temperature (○————○). From Folkard and Monk (1979). (Reproduced by permission of the Human Factors Society Inc.)

The arousal model would also predict that material would be best remembered in the long term following presentation later in the waking day, and again there is some evidence to support this (see Chapter 9). Thus, from an applied point of view it is clear that to ascertain the times of best and worst performance one must take into account the components of the task that the worker is being asked to perform. It would, moreover, appear that the memory load of the task might be an important index in that respect, although even within the broad field of memory the difference between short- and long-term memory is important.

Physiological aspects of adjustment

If one requires people to work at night then either (a) their circadian systems will adjust to become 'in tune' with the new schedule, or (b) they will be required to work and sleep at times that are inappropriate relative to the phase of their circadian rhythms. Problems arise because the process of adjustment takes a considerable amount of time. Thus, for example, it was found that for two subjects in a laboratory shiftwork study (Monk, Knauth, Folkard, and Rutenfranz, 1978) up to 12 days had to elapse before the phase (time of peak) of their rectal temperature rhythms had shifted to be fully in phase with the new routine (Figure 15).

Because this process of adjustment does take so long, expert opinion is divided into two opposing views. In one group are those who hold the view that the primary goal should be one of encouraging adjustment, and that

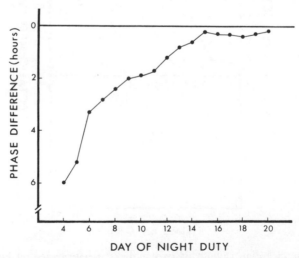

Figure 15. The phase adjustment curve (number of hours that rhythm is 'out of phase' with new routine) for the circadian rectal temperature rhythm of two subjects working 21 consecutive night shifts. After Monk *et al.* (1978).

permanent shift systems should thus be favoured, with the shiftworker being encouraged (by the provision of special housing and recreational facilities, for example) to maintain that schedule even on his days off. The latter point is important, since although there is evidence that adjustment to night-work may be facilitated in experienced night-workers (Folkard, Monk, and Lobban, 1978), the strength of the *zeitgeber* favouring a day-oriented schedule (Table 4) can result in very rapid loss of nocturnal orientation in circadian rhythms (Van Loon, 1963). The advantages of a permanent form of shift system are that the night-shift efficiency would then be comparable to that of the day-shift, and that the night-worker's sleep would be no worse than that of the dayworker.

In the other group are those who maintain that although desirable from a strictly circadian point of view, perfect adjustment is in most cases impossible to attain. They argue that only in very extreme cases such as the Arctic Circle or politically totalitarian regimes, can the commitment to a nocturnal way of life be absolute. These experts would thus favour the use of rapidly rotating shift systems, where long runs of duty on a particular shift are specifically avoided. In such situations the circadian rhythms remain effectively diurnal (day-oriented) with some flattening, but little or no shifting of phase (see, for example, Figure 16). They consider such a lack of adjustment to be a positive advantage since they believe that the process of repeatedly re-entraining (or re-setting) the circadian system is potentially more harmful than that of living, for a few days at a time, with a circadian system that is at an entirely inappropriate phase. The disadvantages of a rapidly rotating system are (a) that night-shift performance may be impaired (but see later section), and (b)

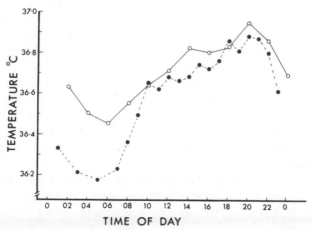

Figure 16. Circadian oral temperature rhythm (O———O) of six subjects working in a rapidly rotating 12-hour shift system, with either three or four 24-hour cycles from each subject. After Monk and Embrey (1981). A 'standard' oral temperature rhythm from 73 diurnal subjects is also included for comparison (●————●). After Colquhoun (1971). (Reproduced by permission of Pergamon Press Ltd.)

that a sleep debt may quickly build up, requiring that two or three days off are given after each (short) run of night duty (Rutenfranz *et al.*, 1977).

Inevitably, with such a difference between these two positions, there are strong arguments in favour and against both viewpoints. However, both 'camps' would undoubtedly agree that although there is no good solution to the shiftwork problem (apart from abolishing it!), slowly rotating shift systems, where people work a week or more on a particular shift before changing to the next shift, are undesirable from almost all points of view. Such systems suffer from the disadvantage of both rapidly rotating and permanent shift systems, without attracting the benefits of either of them. Thus, they involve a sufficient number of night-shifts for the worker's circadian rhythms to become disrupted, but an insufficient number for them to become adjusted to the change in the sleep/wake cycle.

Fatigue and sleep loss

Whatever the specific cause, the main side-effects of shiftwork that are apparent to the worker himself are those of fatigue and sleep loss. As mentioned earlier, sleep becomes a major preoccupation of the shiftworker, and it is possible to make generalizations about the amount of sleep taken by day and at night, with about 2 hours less sleep in the former than in the latter (Rutenfranz *et al.*, 1977).

It is not only the night-shift, however, that creates problems of sleep duration. Knauth *et al.* (1980) studied the duration of sleep associated with various shifts and combinations of shifts. Even when sleep was taken at night, these authors found that because of the time needed to travel to work, etc. significantly less sleep was taken before a morning shift. Thus, problems can arise even for the shiftworker who is on a 'double day' shift system, alternating between 'morning', (e.g. 0600 to 1400) and 'evening' (e.g. 1400 to 2200) shifts. This emphasizes the need for care in the choice of 'changeover' times, for even a 0600 start will probably require the worker to set his alarm clock for 0500. The problem is one of balancing the desire for an early finish to both shifts (so that more of the afternoon is 'free' for the morning shift, and that the evening shift can get to bed on time) with that for a more reasonable starting time in the early morning.

Although sleep (or rather the lack of it) is undoubtedly an important contributory factor to the problem of shiftwork, one must be careful to recognize that it is very often more of a symptom than a cause. It can be tempting to believe that if only the night-worker's bedroom could be soundproofed sufficiently, then all his problems would disappear. This, however, is not the case, as was indicated by a study of night nurses carried out by Folkard, Monk and Lobban (1979). In developing a questionnaire to predict suitability for shiftwork (see p.114) they found a factor R_s (rigidity of sleeping habits) to be an important (negative) predictor of circadian adjustment. Interestingly, high R_s types also reported their day-sleeps to be more disturbed by noise of various types than did low R_s types (i.e. flexible sleepers). Since the housing conditions of the two groups were essentially the same, one might conclude that having one's day-sleeps disturbed by noise is as likely to be a *result* of shiftwork adjustment problems as a *cause* of them.

SHIFTWORK AND PERFORMANCE

Laboratory studies

Because of the difficulties involved in obtaining permission to carry out studies, the irregularity of many shift systems, and possible contamination by a variety of factors, much research on shiftwork performance has taken place in the laboratory. Most of these studies have used simple 'immediate processing' and monitoring tasks to assess performance efficiency and have used subjects who lack shiftwork experience. The basic finding in these 'experimental' shift-work investigations has been that the circadian rhythm in performance efficiency adjusts rather slowly and, like the temperature rhythm (Figure 16), takes at least twelve successive nights before becoming completely adjusted to the new schedule (Colquhoun, Blake, and Edwards, 1968a, 1968b, 1969; Knauth and Rutenfranz, 1976). Thus, the parallelism between temperature and performance on this type of task has been found to persist even under these unusual conditions.

From these results, it has been argued the adjustment of circadian rhythms should be beneficial to night-shift performance since it would result in higher temperatures and hence better performance (see Colquhoun, 1971). In view of this, the best shift system for maintaining high levels of productivity and safety for this type of task has been argued to be a permanent one in which the night-workers are persuaded to remain on a nocturnal routine on their rest days. Although such a measure is rather extreme, there are situations, such as the control room of a chemical plant or nuclear reactor, where the potential cost to society of an accident is high enough to warrant it.

However, this recommendation does not apply when the night-worker's task involves a working memory load. As we have already seen (in Figure 14, for example), the parallelism between temperature and performance does not hold for such tasks. Indeed, there is a *negative* relationship between temperature and the performance of tasks with a high working memory load. This means that performance on this type of task should actually be rather good on the night-shift, provided there was *no* disruption, or adjustment, of the shiftworker's circadian rhythms (Folkard *et al.*, 1976; Folkard and Monk, 1979).

Laboratory studies have also been used to investigate the rate with which different circadian performance rhythms adjust their phase to the new

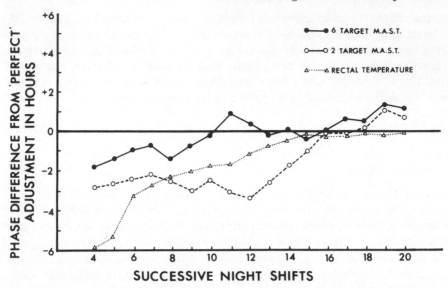

Figure 17. The process of phase adjustment in the circadian rhythms of performance on high (six target) and low (two target) memory load versions of a visual search task, and in rectal temperature. After Folkard and Monk (1979). (Reproduced by permission of the Human Factors Society Inc.)

schedule. Monk, Knauth, Folkard, and Rutenfranz (1978) studied the phase adjustment of low (2-MAST) and high (6-MAST) memory load visual search performance to 21 consecutive night-shifts. From Figure 17 it is clear that there were marked differences in rate of adjustment between different versions of the test, with the phase of the low memory load version adjusting at the same rate as that of rectal temperature, whilst that of the high memory load version adjusts considerably faster. This confirmed an earlier finding from a field study by Hughes and Folkard (1976), discussed in a later section.

From laboratory studies one is thus left with the conclusion that simple (low memory load) performance will tend to parallel the temperature rhythm, adjusting rather slowly, and generally indicating poor night-shift performance. However, for complex (high memory load) tasks, laboratory studies suggest the counterintuitive prediction, that night-shift performance will initially be better than day-shift performance, with phase adjustment actually being harmful to the former. They also suggest that such a phase adjustment would be rather more rapid than that of the temperature rhythm.

Field studies

There are remarkably few field studies of actual shiftwork performance. In fact, until very recently there appeared to have been only six published studies

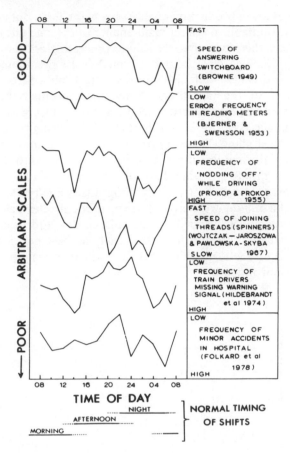

Figure 18. Variations in job performance over the 24-hour period. After Folkard and Monk (1979). (Reproduced by permission of the Human Factors Society Inc.)

that report relatively continuous, 24-hour 'real-life' performance measures. Nevertheless, from Figure 18 it is clear that there is a fair agreement among these studies that an impairment of performance occurs during the night shift. Thus, performance on the night-shift was found to be slower both in answering a switchboard (Browne, 1949) and in tying threads (Wojtczak-Jaroszowa and Pawlowska-Skyba, 1967), and less accurate in reading meters (Bjerner and Swensson, 1953). There was also some evidence that a decrease in alertness at night might cause accidents to be more frequent then (Prokop and Prokop, 1955; Hildebrandt, Rohmert, and Rutenfranz, 1974; Folkard, Monk, and Lobban, 1978). However, the 'real-life' nature of these studies has meant that it has been extremely difficult to control for possible 'contamination' by other factors. This point is illustrated by the study of Meers (1975) who found clear evidence of lower production quality on a night-shift, but also found that this might be attributable to poorer maintenance of the machine involved.

It would seem, therefore, that for simple processing and monitoring tasks the laboratory findings have been confirmed, with predominantly inferior performance on the night-shift. More interesting from a theoretical point of view is the test of the laboratory prediction that high memory loaded performance would be better performed at night than during the day. This has recently been undertaken (Monk and Embrey, 1981) using process controllers in a large chemical plant. These controllers had a high memory loaded job, entering coded information into the computer which controlled the plant. They worked a rapidly rotating 12-hour shift system and their circadian rhythms appeared to remain effectively diurnal (see Figure 16, above). For a period of about a month, every error made by the controller was automatically logged by the computer. The resultant time-of-day function is plotted in Figure 19. From this function it is clear that the best performance (fewest errors) occurred on the night-shift, an effect which appears not to be due to any difference in workload.

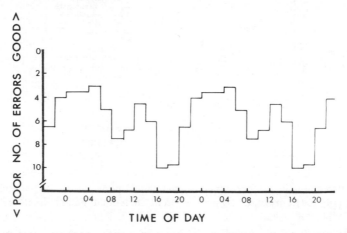

Figure 19. The circadian rhythm of 'on-job' performance taken from ten process controllers over a month's period. Improvements in performance (fewer errors) are represented by a rise. Two cycles of the 12 values defining the rhythm have been plotted. After Monk and Embrey (1981). Reproduced by permission of Pergammon Press, Ltd.

This finding is in line with the results of an earlier study which indicated that night nurses' immediate recall for training material is better following 0400 presentation than following 2030 presentation (Monk and Folkard, 1978; Folkard and Monk, 1980). The latter study also indicated (a) the importance of task differences (in this case elapsed time before recall), even within the broad field of memory, and (b) the importance of phase adjustment effects. With respect to the former, the study showed that (in line with theoretical predictions, see Chapter 9), *delayed* recall (i.e. that measured 28 days after presentation) showed the opposite effect to immediate recall, with 2030 presentation being associated with better performance than that associated with 0400 presentation. With respect to the latter, the study showed that the initial result only held for nurses whose circadian temperature rhythms remained diurnal (i.e. unadjusted). Moreover, the study found that different aspects of memory showed different rates of phase adjustment, both to each other and to the temperature rhythm. This confirmed the earlier field study of Hughes and Folkard (1976) which revealed quite dramatic differences between tasks in the degree of adjustment after 8 days of night work, expressed in terms of the percentage of variance accounted for by the pre-shift shape. These values were; body temperature 69 per cent, manual dexterity 45 per cent, visual search 59 per cent, but, for the two memory-based tasks, addition and verbal reasoning, 88 per cent.

In conclusion, these findings about high memory load tasks have two important implications. First, from a practical point of view they suggest that the more rapid the rotation of the shift system, the better will be performance on this type of task. Secondly, from a theoretical viewpoint, they provide strong evidence that the simple arousal theory of time-of-day effects may be inadequate. Thus, although the arousal theory can account for different trends over the day for different types of performance (since high arousal may benefit some types but impair others), it cannot account for different rates of adjustment of these rhythms to night-work, unless one postulates additional changes in overall levels of arousal. Indeed, no theory that assumes a single underlying factor to mediate time-of-day effects in performance can do so. This evidence on the rate of adjustment is verified in the jet-lag situation (see below) and is thus perhaps the strongest there is in the circadian rhythms area to support the necessity of a multi-factor arousal theory such as that outlined in Chapter 12.

In sum, although real-life shiftwork performance will often be lowest on the night-shift, the reason for this would appear to be dependent upon the type of task the shiftworker has to perform. For simple immediate processing tasks it may be low because of the lack of adjustment of the shiftworker's circadian rhythms. Thus, for these tasks permanent shift systems may prove to be optimal. However, for more complex working memory tasks, performance may be poor because of the more rapid adjustment that in this case lowers efficiency. For this latter type of task very rapidly rotating shift systems that minimize the disruption of the shiftworker's circadian rhythms may well be preferable.

Related phase shifts

In Table 4 we indicated that as well as shiftwork, there were two other situations, namely transmeridianal flight (jet-lag) and Daylight Saving Time

(DST) changes, in which a re-setting of the circadian system is required. There has been comparatively little study of the twice-yearly changes associated with DST systems. It would appear, however, that such changes can result in a disruption of sleep/wake cycles lasting up to a week (Monk and Folkard, 1976). Furthermore, autumn changes might be associated with improvements, and spring changes with impairments in mood upon awakening and performance efficiency during the week after the change (Monk and Aplin, 1980; Monk, 1980). This comparatively slow rate of adjustment of the circadian system to DST changes, relative to those connected with transmeridianal flight, suggests that the physical *zeitgeber* (which form the only difference between the two situations) may be more important to the circadian system than was originally thought. This is important in the shiftwork context, for our inability to control the physical *zeitgeber* may mean that even in (for the shiftworker) a perfect society, complete circadian rhythm adjustment may be unattainable because of the competing physical *zeitgeber* (see also Hughes and Folkard, 1976).

Much of the work concerned with jet-lag has been undertaken by Klein and his associates (e.g. Klein, Wegmann, and Hunt, 1972). The main findings are that phase adjustment to westbound flights is considerably faster than that to eastbound ones (whichever direction is 'homeward'), that a rough 'rule of thumb' for the latter is about one day per time zone crossed, that adjustment can be retarded by post-flight isolation in a hotel room, and that as well as phase adjustment effects, overall decrements in ('whole day') performance (and indeed decreases in rectal temperature) can also occur.

Klein *et al.*'s (1972) data also provide evidence for differences in the rate of phase adjustment between different tasks and between performance and temperature rhythms. Figure 20 (taken from Folkard and Monk, 1981b) shows not only that the high memory task (addition) appears to show a phase adjustment rather faster than symbol cancellation or temperature, but also that there are differences between the tasks in the directional asymmetry of phase adjustment. Thus, the westward direction is associated with the faster phase adjustment rate for symbol cancellation but (if anything) the slower phase adjustment rate for addition. These findings confirm the shiftwork results concerning the effect of memory load on phase adjustment of performance rhythms (e.g. Figure 17). Moreover, the directional asymmetry results suggest that the 'memory loaded' performance rhythm might (since it adjusts more quickly to a phase advance than to a delay) have a 'natural' period that is shorter than that associated with serial search performance. Folkard and Monk (1981b) also performed a re-analysis of the Monk *et al.* (1978) data which reinforced such a view, and pointed out that these results were contradictory to any unidimensional arousal model of performance rhythms. It would thus seem that explanations of circadian performance rhythms may well have to follow those of circadian physiological rhythms in postulating more than one underlying oscillator.

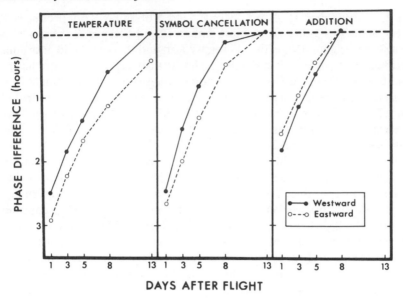

Figure 20. The phase adjustment of the circadian rhythms in body temperature and performance on different tasks to westward and eastward 6-hour time zone transitions. After Klein *et al.* (1972).

OTHER FACTORS IN SHIFTWORK

Individual differences

Even the most cursory investigation of shiftworkers 'in the field' reveals wide ranging individual differences, with some shiftworkers experiencing no problems at all, and others leading miserable lives, barely able to cope. There is thus an obvious benefit to be gained if some instrument can be developed to differentiate between the two types before they actually get themselves involved in and committed to shiftwork.

One technique has been to study the individual characteristics that are known to affect normal circadian rhythms. These variables, notably 'morningness' (whether one is a 'lark' or an 'owl') and extroversion are discussed in Chapter 9. In general, the circadian rhythms of evening types and of extroverts (especially those scoring high on neuroticism) have been found to adjust more rapidly than those of morning types or introverts (see Akerstedt and Froberg, 1976; Colquhoun and Folkard, 1978). (Also, since shiftworkers often 'sleep-in late' during the morning, one might expect evening types to cope better with shiftwork simply through being more able to do this than morning types.)

Another technique of enquiry has been to develop a purpose-built questionnaire specifically designed to predict shiftwork suitability. The 'Circadian

Type Questionnaire' (Folkard, Monk, and Lobban, 1979) produces three factors, namely rigidity of sleeping habits (Rigid Sleeper R_s versus Flexible Sleepers F_s); vigour (Vigorous V versus Languid L types; and morningness (Morning M versus Evening E types). The first two of these factors have been found to predict both differences in rate of physiological adjustment in night nurses, and differences in rate of sleep/wake cycle adjustment to a spring DST change (Folkard, Monk, and Lobban, 1979; Monk and Aplin, 1980). This line of research thus appears to be a promising one, although considerable development is clearly needed.

One fundamental problem with this whole general approach is that, as we have already seen, it is unclear whether the adjustment of circadian rhythms is desirable or undesirable. To some extent, the answer to this may depend on the type of task the shiftworker has to perform, but we also need to consider the shiftworker's health and social problems. Here again, opinion is divided between those who feel that the adjustment of circadian rhythms will minimize these problems, and those who argue that the maintenance of normal, day-oriented, circadian rhythms is better in this respect. Thus, for example, Reinberg *et al.* (1980) have recently shown normal rhythm amplitude to be inversely related to phase shift in shiftworkers, with a faster rate of phase adjustment (of the temperature rhythm) occurring in people whose normal (diurnal) rhythms exhibited a smaller natural amplitude. However, the group with the largest phase shift was the one least happy with shiftwork. Thus, for many the trouble with shiftwork may be that their circadian rhythms *do* readily adjust. This is highlighted by a recent study by Folkard and Monk (1981a) of computer operators on a weekly rotating shift system. Only one operator complained that he had problems coping with shiftwork, commenting that: 'I find shiftwork to be very unnatural and will soon be giving it up as it is having an adverse effect on my health—mainly tension and nervousness.' Despite this, his circadian rhythm in body temperature showed virtually perfect adjustment to his shift system.

Such findings do suggest that there may be certain situations and/or individuals for which the adjustment of circadian rhythms is undesirable. They thus highlight the fact that although there is considerable evidence on individual differences in the adjustment of circadian rhythms, this evidence cannot be used to make practical recommendations until we have determined whether or not such adjustment is to be encouraged.

A second fundamental question is that of whether circadian factors are so far outweighed by other factors as to be largely irrelevant to the question of shiftwork performance. Certainly, when the first author was a shiftworker, evening shift performance suffered simply from the fact that two out of the three members of the team were spending a considerable amount of time drinking at a local pub. Similarly, it is pointless to pontificate about day-sleeps and circadian rhythm adjustment if the night-worker is also trying to hold down a second job during the day ('moonlighting'), or is expected to look after a house and family as soon as she gets home from work in the morning. Thus, the major individual difference in shiftwork adjustment must be that of level of commitment (Folkard, Monk, and Lobban, 1978). Without a high level of commitment to the required routine, it may be largely irrelevant whether one is an extrovert or introvert, lark or owl.

Medical and social considerations

A number of studies have looked at the effects of shiftwork on health, and these have recently been reviewed by Harrington (1978). There appears to be no good evidence of reduced life expectancy in shiftworkers (Taylor and Pocock, 1972), or, on balance, of increased absence due to sickness (Harrington, 1978). Indeed, the only reliable detrimental effect of shiftwork on health would appear to be an increase in gastro-intestinal symptoms and diseases. However, Harrington (1978) points out that this could be due to impoverished catering facilities for night-workers rather than to any more fundamental cause.

Unfortunately, the existing evidence on these objective measures of health does not allow adequate comparison of the effects of different types of shift system. However, Tasto and Colligan (1978) reported *subjective* health measures from a sample of some 1,200 shiftworkers on a variety of different shift systems. They found that those on slowly rotating shift systems reported a greater incidence of gastric problems than those on a 'permanent' night-shift. Their sample did not include people on rapidly rotating systems so it is unclear whether this increased incidence of gastric problems occurs on such systems.

Other medical considerations relate to certain diseases or conditions which might indicate that a person should try to avoid shiftwork. Thus, for example, a diabetic shiftworker might have problems in balancing his sugar and insulin levels, and an epileptic shiftworker might find that his seizures increase in frequency due to the resultant sleep loss (Rutenfranz *et al.*, 1977). Also, the link between shiftwork and gastro-intestinal complaints would suggest that people with a tendency towards problems in that area should also try to avoid shiftwork. Generally with respect to health, shiftwork is probably best conceived as a stressor which may have little or no impact on the young, healthy individual, but which can dramatically aggravate otherwise minor complaints due to ill-health or increased age. Thus, in a recent survey of oil refinery workers, Koller *et al.* (1978) found that only 18.5 per cent of the shiftworkers believed that they would be able to continue with that kind of work until retirement.

The disruption of a shiftworker's social and family life is one of the most frequent sources of complaint and has been mentioned earlier. However, studies of shiftworkers' attitudes to different systems have produced somewhat conflicting findings. These studies have been reviewed in detail by Walker (1978). In general, shiftwork is disliked by those undertaking it, although there are some individuals who positively like it. This latter finding may explain the tendency for the early studies in this area to have found 'permanent' systems more acceptable, while the more recent studies have tended to obtain results favouring rapidly rotating shift systems. The incidence of shiftwork has doubled over the last 25 years (Walker, 1978) and it thus seems possible that in the past there were sufficient people who liked night-work to man permanent night-shifts. However, with the increased incidence of night-work it would seem that we no longer have sufficient numbers of such people, and thus have to employ people to work at night who dislike doing so.

The question as to the optimal form of shift system from a social point of view is thus not a simple one. Nevertheless, as Walker (1978) points out, an increasing number of firms are adopting rapidly rotating shift systems, often as a direct result of pressure from the shiftworkers. The advantage of such systems is that about 75 per cent of sleeps can be taken at the 'normal' time, and that in general 75 per cent of the shiftworker's life can be oriented to a normal diurnal pattern of life. Indeed, Wedderburn (1967) suggests that 'swiftly rotating systems may have hit on an optimum solution for both the physiological and social needs of man'.

CONCLUSIONS AND PRACTICAL IMPLICATIONS

General overview

The aim of this chapter has been to consider the various factors that are involved in shiftwork, setting them in the framework of man as an essentially diurnal creature. To do this one has to consider the circadian rhythms which underlie our pattern of sleep and wakefulness, and which are disrupted by the need to work at night. The ever-growing body of basic research on physiological rhythms that is being carried out in this area provides us with important information (e.g. about the periodicity of free-running rhythms, and number of internal clocks) which must be taken into account when tackling the applied problem of shiftwork. Basic research in circadian *performance* rhythms has also been important, in pointing to the need to consider the actual task that the worker is being asked to perform rather than thinking of performance as a single global entity. From these two pools of research, one can at least begin to ask the right questions about the phenomenon of shiftwork.

From the strictly applied end there is also a growing body of findings that are pertinent to the study of shiftwork. Thus, the study of sleep, health, and social problems provides data which serve to modify the conclusions one might wish to draw from consideration of purely basic research. Thus, for example, although one might wish to favour permanent shift systems as being the most suitable from a circadian point of view, the actuality of inferior sleep during the day, and reversions to a diurnal routine (for social reasons) during days off, can make such a suggestion unreasonable in practice.

The area is still a young one, with much research remaining to be done. However, there are certain gaps in our knowledge which are particularly striking. The most important of these is the key issue of whether shiftwork satisfaction (and/or health) really is linked to circadian rhythm adjustment in the direct way we have all assumed. Next is the issue of whether there are basic individual differences that can predispose some people to be happier with shiftwork than others. Third is the need for a large-scale multi-factor comparison of permanent, slowly rotating and rapidly rotating shift systems so that any relative advantages and/or disadvantages can be objectively evaluated. Probably the best way that all three goals could be accomplished would be a large-scale longitudinal study, following a cohort of brand new shiftworkers through their careers. Such a study would enable one to measure the circadian (and individual difference) characteristics of the worker before he or she actually started shiftwork. Then both longitudinal (years into shiftwork) and transverse (different individuals and/or shift systems) comparisons could be made.

Detailed conclusions

From the study of circadian rhythms in general, it would appear that such rhythms: (a) are often primarily endogenous, i.e. internal to the organism and self-sustaining; (b) are controlled by a variety of physical and social time cues (*zeitgeber*); and (c) often have a natural periodicity that is slightly greater than 24 hours. Thus, in practical terms one should bear in mind: (a) that such rhythms can take a long time (e.g. up to two weeks) to adjust; (b) that such adjustment can be helped along by the right *zeitgeber* (e.g. by making the shiftworker's environment less obviously day-oriented); and (c) that in a rotating shift system a shiftworker will probably find it more easy to stretch his rhythms (on a mornings–afternoons–nights schedule) than to shrink them (on a nights–afternoons–mornings schedule). Also, the suggestion that there are two groups of oscillators (clocks), one controlling the sleep/wake cycle the other the temperature rhythm, means that to have succeeded in adjusting the sleep/wake cycle does not necessarily imply that all the shiftworker's body clocks have been so re-set.

From the study of circadian performance rhythms one can conclude that it is wrong to make generalizations about the 'best form of shift system' for work efficiency, without taking into account the nature of the task to be performed. As with physiological circadian rhythms, a multi-oscillator approach would seem to be needed. Task differences in both normal diurnal rhythm and rate of phase adjustment suggest that a distinction should be made between simple repetitive or monitoring tasks and complex memory-loaded cognitive tasks. For the former, a permanent system would seem to be preferable, with the maximum possible phase adjustment. For the latter, adjustment should be discouraged by using rapidly rotating shift systems wherever possible. However, from this and many other points of view, the weekly rotating shift system should be avoided.

From the study of individual differences one might conclude that extroverts and/or evening types might show the most rapid phase adjustment, although one should remember that that might not always be an advantage. Also, it should be remembered that level of commitment is probably the most important individual difference.

Studies of sleep, health, and social problems point to shiftwork as a stressor which can exacerbate any existing problems which had hitherto been minor. The problem of inferior day-sleeps should not be ignored, and wherever possible a number of recuperative rest days should follow each run of night-duty. Health problems appear to be mainly gastro-intestinal and might be, at least partially, alleviated by the provision of adequate canteen facilities for the shiftworker. Social problems are the hardest to quantify and pin-down, and it is often tempting to either dismiss them as peripheral, or trivialize them. They are, however, crucial to the shiftworker's health, well-being, and efficiency. In living with shiftwork he is already suffering (to a greater or lesser extent) from one stressor; to burden him with the additional one of social and family problems is to court emotional disaster.

SUMMARY

The incidence of shiftwork has increased substantially over the last few decades in most industrialized countries. Thus, although some individuals positively enjoy shiftwork, a large number of people now employed on shift-systems find shiftwork stressful. One of the major reasons for this appears to be the disruption of the normal sleep/wake cycle which in turn is reflected in a disruption of the shiftworker's 'circadian' (around 24 hours) rhythms.

The degree to which these rhythms are disrupted depends both on the direction and speed of rotation of the shift-system, and on the degree of flexibility of the rhythm(s) under consideration. This is thought to have important implications for the scheduling of shift-systems. Thus, the optimal form of shift-system for maintaining high levels of performance efficiency and safety may depend on both the nature of the task being performed and the nature of the individual performing it. Much of the recent research in this area has been aimed at elucidating these effects. While some tentative conclusions can be drawn from these studies, there are many important questions that remain unanswered.

Perhaps the most fundamental of these is whether the detrimental effect of shiftwork on subjective health and social life is directly related to the disruption of circadian rhythms. Although it is commonly assumed to be so, the evidence to support this assumption is not strong. Despite this problem, some progress has been made towards minimizing the ill-effects of shiftwork. It now appears that there is no single optimum shift-system, but rather that the shift-system needs to be tailored to suit the needs of both the individual, and the task he performs.

REFERENCES

Akerstedt, T. and Froberg, J. (1976) Shift work and health-interdisciplinary aspects. In P. G. Rentos and R. D. Shepard (eds.), *Shift Work and Health*. Washington: US Dept of Health, Education and Welfare, HEW Publication No. (NIOSH) 76–203, pp.179–197.

Bjerner, B. and Swensson, A. (1953) Shiftwork and rhythm. *Acta Medica Scandinavica*, **Supple. 278**, 102–107.

Browne, R. C. (1949) The day and night performance of teleprinter switchboard operators. *Occupational Psychology*, **23**, 121–126.

Colquhoun, W. P. (1971) Circadian variations in mental efficiency. In W. P. Colquhoun (ed.), *Biological Rhythms and Human Performance*. London: Academic Press, pp.39–107.

Colquhoun, W. P. and Folkard, S. (1978) Personality differences in body-temperature rhythm, and their relation to its adjustment to night work. *Ergonomics*, **21**, 811–817.

Colquhoun, W. P., Blake, M. J. F., and Edwards, R. S. (1968a) Experimental studies of shift work. I: A comparison of 'rotating' and 'stabilized' 4 hour shift systems. *Ergonomics*, **11**, 437–453.

Colquhoun, W. P., Blake, M. J. F., and Edwards, R. S. (1968b) Experimental studies of shift work. II: Stabilized 8 hour shift systems. *Ergonomics*, **11**, 527–546.

Colquhoun, W. P., Blake, M. J. F., and Edwards, R. S. (1969) Experimental studies of shift work. III: Stabilized 12 hour shift systems. *Ergonomics*, **12**, 865–882.

Conroy, R. T. W. L. and Mills, J. N. (1970) *Human Circadian Rhythms*. London: Churchill.

Folkard, S., Knauth, P., Monk, T. H., and Rutenfranz, J. (1976) The effect of memory load on the circadian variation in performance efficiency under a rapidly rotating shift system. *Ergonomics*, **19**, 479–488.

Folkard, S. and Monk, T. H. (1979) Shiftwork and performance. *Human Factors*, **21**, 483–492.

Folkard, S. and Monk, T. H. (1980) Circadian rhythms in human memory. *British Journal of Psychology*, **71**, 295–307.

Folkard, S. and Monk, T. H. (1981a) Individual differences in the circadian response to a weekly rotating shift system. In A. Reinberg, N. Vieux, and P. Andlauer (eds.), *Night and Shift Work: Biological and Social Aspects*. Oxford: Pergamon Press, pp.365–374.

Folkard, S. and Monk, T. H. (1981b) Circadian rhythms in performance—one or more oscillators? In R. Sinz and M. R. Rosenzweg (eds.), *Psychophysiology 1980—Memory, Motivation and Event-related Potentials in Mental Operations*. Elsevier-North Holland (in press).

Folkard, S., Monk, T. H., and Lobban, M. C. (1978) Short and long-term adjustment of circadian rhythms in 'permanent' night nurses. *Ergonomics*, **21**, 785–799.

Folkard, S., Monk, T. H., and Lobban, M. C. (1979) Towards a predictive test of adjustment to shiftwork. *Ergonomics*, **22**, 79–91.

Froberg, J. E., Karlsson, C-G., Levi, L., and Lidberg, L. (1975) Circadian rhythms of catecholamine excretion, shooting range performance and self-ratings of fatigue during sleep deprivation. *Biological Psychology*, **2**, 175–188.

Halberg, F. (1969) Chronobiology. *Annual Review of Physiology*, **31**, 675–725.

Harrington, J. M. (1978) *Shiftwork and Health. A Critical Review of the Literature.* London: HMSO.

Hildebrandt, G., Rohmert, W., and Rutenfranz, J. (1974) Twelve and 24 hour rhythms in error frequency of locomotive drivers and the influence of tiredness. *International Journal of Chronobiology*, **2**, 175–180.

Hughes, D. G. and Folkard, S. (1976) Adaptation to an 8 h shift in living routine by members of a socially isolated community. *Nature*, **264**, 432–434.

Klein, K. E., Wegman, H. M., and Hunt, B. I. (1972) Desynchronisation of body temperature and performance circadian rhythm as a result of outgoing and home-going transmeridian flights. *Aerospace Medicine*, **43**, 119–132.

Kleitman, N. (1963) *Sleep and Wakefulness.* Chicago: University of Chicago Press.

Knauth, P., Landau, K., Droge, C., Schwitteck, M., Widynski, M., and Rutenfranz, J. (1980) Duration of sleep depending on the type of shift work. *International Archives of Occupational and Environmental Health*, **46**, 167–177.

Knauth, P. and Rutenfranz, J. (1976) Circadian rhythm of body temperature and re-entrainment at shift change. *International Archives of Occupational and Environmental Health*, **37**, 125–137.

Koller, M., Kundi, M., and Cervinka, R. (1978) Field studies of shiftwork at an Austrian oil refinery. I: Health and psychosocial well-being of workers who drop out of shiftwork. *Ergonomics*, **21**, 835–847.

Meers, A. (1975) Performance on different turns of duty within a three-shift system and its relation to body temperature—two field studies. In W. P. Colquhoun, S. Folkard, P. Knauth, and J. Rutenfranze (eds.), *Experimental Studies of Shiftwork.* Opladen: Westdeutscher Verlag, 188–205.

Monk, T. H. (1979) Temporal effects in visual search. In M. A. Sinclair and J. N. Clare (eds.). *Search and the Human Observer.* London: Taylor and Francis, pp.30–39.

Monk, T. H. (1980) Traffic accident increases as a possible indicant of desynchronosis. *Chronobiologia*, **7**, 527–529.

Monk, T. H. and Aplin, L. C. (1980) Spring and autumn daylight saving time changes: Studies of adjustment in sleep timings, mood and efficiency. *Ergonomics*, **23**, 167–178.

Monk, T. H. and Embrey, D. E. (1981) A field study of circadian rhythms in actual and interpolated task performance. In A. Reinberg, N. Vieux, and P. Andlauer (eds.), *Night and Shift Work: Biological and Social Aspects.* Oxford: Pergamon Press, pp.473–480.

Monk, T. H. (1982) The arousal model of time of day effects in human performance efficiency. *Chronobiologia*, **9**, 49–54.

Monk, T. H. and Folkard, S. (1976) Adjusting to the changes to and from daylight saving time. *Nature*, **261**, 688–689.

Monk, T. H. and Folkard, S. (1978) Concealed inefficiency of late-night study. *Nature*, **273**, 296–297.

Monk, T. H., Knauth, P., Folkard, S., and Rutenfranz, J. (1978) Memory based performance measures in studies of shiftwork. *Ergonomics*, **21**, 819–826.

Moore-Ede, M. C., Sulzman, F. M., and Fuller, C. A. (1981) *The Clocks that Time Us.* Boston, Mass.: Harvard University Press.

Prokop, O. and Prokop, L. (1974) Ermudung und einschlafen am steuer. *Deutsche Zeitschrift fur die gesamte gerichtliche Medizin*, 1955, **44**, 343. Cited by G. Hildebrandt, W. Rohmert, and J. Rutenfranz (1974) Twelve and 24 hour rhythms in error frequency of locomotive drivers and the influence of tiredness. *International Journal of Chronobiology*, **2**, 175–180.

Reinberg, A., Andlauer, P., Guillet, P., Nicolai, A., Vieux, N., and Laporte, A. (1980) Oral temperature, circadian rhythm amplitude ageing and tolerance to shiftwork. *Ergonomics*, **23**, 55–64.

Rutenfranz, J., Colquhoun, W. P., Knauth, P., and Ghata, J. N. (1977) Biomedical and psychosocial aspects of shift work: A review. *Scandinavian Journal of Work, Environment and Health*, **3**, 165–182.

Tasto, D. L. and Colligan, M. J. (1978) *Health Consequences of Shiftwork*. Menlo Park, California: Stanford Research Institute, Project URU-4426, Technical Report.

Taylor, P. J. and Pocock, S. J. (1972) Mortality of shift and day workers 1956–1968. *British Journal of Industrial Medicine*, **29**, 201–207.

Van Loon, J. H. (1963) Diurnal body temperature curves in shift workers. *Ergonomics*, **6**, 267–272.

Walker, J. (1978) *The Human Aspects of Shiftwork*. Bath: The Pitman Press.

Wedderburn, A. A. I. (1967) Social factors in satisfaction with swiftly rotating shifts. *Occupational Psychology*, **41**, 85–107.

Wever, R. (1975) The circadian multi-oscillator system of man. *International Journal of Chronobiology*, **3**, 19–55.

Wever, R. (1979) *The Circadian System of Man: Results of Experiments Under Temporal Isolation*. New York: Springer-Verlag.

Wojtczak-Jaroszowa, J. and Pawlowska-Skyba, K. (1977) Night and shift work. I: Circadian variations in work. *Medycyna Pracy*, 1967, **18**, 1. Cited by J. Wojtczak-Jaroszowa. *Physiological and Psychological Aspects of Night and Shift Work*, Washington, D.C.: US Department of Health, Education and Welfare, Publication No. (NIOSH), 76–203, pp.78–113.

Stress and Fatigue in Human Performance
Edited by G. R. J. Hockey
© John Wiley & Sons Ltd.

Chapter 5

Fear and Dangerous Environments

Chris Idzikowski and Alan D. Baddeley

In this chapter we will describe the nature of fear and its effects on performance. Emphasis will be placed on the evidence dealing with situations which involve the individual in physical danger. After defining anxiety and then fear, the methodological difficulties in collecting data in this area will be discussed. The main areas to be investigated will be combat, parachuting, and diving. The primary area of concern will be the behavioural effect of fear, but in order to give an adequate account it will also be necessary to describe the subjective and physiological concomitants of fear. Simple models which may be useful to our understanding of fear will be discussed.

ANXIETY AND FEAR

Mosso (1896) provides a vivid subjective description of the effects of apprehension, anxiety and fear:

> Never shall I forget that evening. From behind the curtains of the glass door I peered into the large amphitheatre crowded with people. It was my first appearance as a lecturer, and most humbly did I repent having undertaken to try my powers in the same hall in which my most celebrated teachers had so often spoken. All I had to do was communicate the results of some of my investigations into the physiology of sleep and yet, as the hour grew nearer, stronger waxed within me the fear that I should become confused, lose myself, and finally stand gaping, speechless before my audience. My heart beat violently, its very strings seemed to tighten, and my breath came and went as when one looks down into a yawning abyss . . . . As I cast the last glance at my notes, I became aware, to my horror, that the chain of ideas was broken and the links lost beyond recall . . . . Long periods which I thought myself

123

able to repeat word for word—all seemed forgotten . . . . There was a singing in my ears . . . . After a few sentences jerked out almost mechanically, I perceived that I had already finished the introduction to my speech . . . . Trembling of the hands . . . my knees shook . . . . My trembling voice . . . I was perspiring, exhausted.

The above account is useful since it contains many of the features that usually accompany anxiety and that have been investigated by later workers. In addition, Mosso's description expands on one of the more widely accepted present-day definitions of anxiety. Spielberger (1966) has defined anxiety as: 'a transitory emotional state characterised by subjective consciously perceived feelings of tension and apprehension and heightened autonomic nervous activity'. Figure 21 shows that the effects of public speaking on heart-rate appear much the same today as they were in Mosso's day!

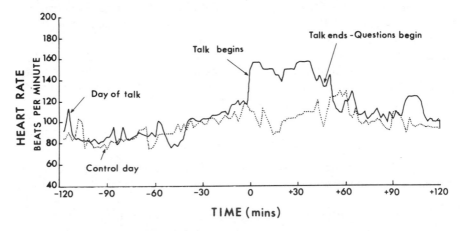

Figure 21. Heart-rate of subject A.S. when he presented a paper at a lunch-time seminar at the Applied Psychology Unit, Cambridge.

Both Mosso's description and Spielberger's definition refer to state-anxiety. Spielberger (1966) and Cattell (1972) both emphasized that it was necessary when measuring anxiety to differentiate between the individual's state of anxiety and the individual's predisposition towards anxiety (trait-anxiety). Of necessity, early theoretical accounts of anxiety did not formally contain this distinction but instead concentrated on varied mechanisms which were likely to produce anxiety (for example; Freud, 1936, 1959) or dealt with the effects of anxiety (for example; Taylor, 1951; Taylor and Spence, 1952; where anxiety was equated with drive), with little regard to the individual's proneness towards this state.

On the other hand, there has been less dispute as to the difference between anxiety and fear. Two main views have emerged: (1) fear may simply be regarded as a state of high anxiety, being placed on a continuum with a relaxed state on one pole and fear on the other (Martin, 1961), or (2) fear could be a state of anxiety with the eliciting conditions known.

A considerable number of studies and theoretical accounts of anxiety and fear exist but partly because of the early definitional ambiguities, and partly because of methodological inadequacies, only very few definitive studies in dangerous situations can be found.

METHODOLOGICAL PROBLEMS

Ethical problems arise if individuals are put into experimental situations which are designed to frighten them without the individual knowing that this is the purpose of the experiment. In attempting to avoid this problem, situations such as natural disasters, for example earthquakes, have been studied. These and other similar situations provide suitably dangerous environments for experiments but these situations are invariably inaccessible, unpredictable, affect the experimenter as much as the victims, and rarely allow any clear objective measure of performance. Consequently, these studies can only provide information of limited value.

Before analysing the behavioural effects of fear in more controllable situations (for example, parachuting) it is necessary first to establish that the individual is afraid. In order to do this it is desirable, because of the definitions given above, to have both a subjective assessment by the individual of his state of mind and a simultaneous assessment of his physiological state. If anxiety is indicated by the appropriate scores on a questionnaire, this does not necessarily mean that subjects are physiologically aroused; they may simply be filling out the questionnaire on the basis of what they *think* they should be feeling, as opposed to how they are *actually* feeling. Apart from the effect of the experimenter-demands and task-demands on subjective reports, there is the problem of how well a given individual can introspect. Many subjective anxiety measures rely partly on the individual's assessment of his own autonomic response and this ability varies widely between individuals (Mandler, Mandler, and Uviller, 1958). In fact, scores on one of the older anxiety questionnaires, the Taylor Manifest Anxiety Scale (TMAS), have not been found to correlate with autonomic state (measured objectively) during stress conditions (Mandler, Mandler, Kremen, and Sholitan, 1961).

Inferring that an individual is in an anxious state simply because of changes in physiological function is not sufficient as an index of anxiety, since other emotional states may lead to similar changes (Krause, 1961; Hodges, 1976). Taking just one autonomic measure is useful as long as it is not assumed that this measure will correlate with other autonomic measures. It has been known for some time that autonomic measures generally do not correlate with each other. The primary reason for this is the fact that individuals have specific response patterns in autonomic functions (Lacey, 1959; Lacey and Lacey, 1958). This 'response specificity' is constant over long periods and varies little with different stresses. Of all possible autonomic measures, heart-rate and galvanic skin response appear to be the most useful in monitoring anxiety (Elliott, 1974; Hodges, 1976).

A hostile or dangerous environment is one that generally requires an active and correct response for an individual to survive. Most people would consider situations such as combat, parachuting, and diving to be fear- or anxiety-provoking. However, it is important to remember that individuals put in these environments cannot simply be assumed to be anxious; as Lazarus (1966) points out, a situation may not induce anxiety in a person if that person does not perceive the situation as dangerous. The degree of anxiety may also vary depending on the individual's predisposition towards being anxious. As long as the above problems are borne in mind, it is worthwhile examining some of the data collected in dangerous environments.

UNCONTROLLED DANGEROUS ENVIRONMENTS

Effects of naturally-occurring stress

Andersson (1976) investigated the effects on small businesses following the flood damage caused by Hurricane Agnes (June 1972). By using questionnaires and structured interviews, he was able to assess the effects of the disaster on coping behaviour in owner-managers. He found a curvilinear relationship between perceived stress and how well the businesses were recovering. With low to moderate degrees of stress, there was an improvement in performance, whilst high levels of stress impaired performance. Obviously, this study cannot reveal very much about how individuals may react to varying stresses, but it does give a trend which can be found in research carried out on individuals.

Marshall (1947) and a team of psychiatrists interviewed large numbers of soldiers immediately after many Second World War battles. As this technique relied on the individual's memory, which could not be assumed to be accurate, Marshall attempted to determine what each individual had actually done and felt during an engagement by checking their accounts with their colleagues' accounts. He found that fear was widespread on the battlefield and that this was made worse by lack of communications and loneliness. Furthermore, he found that often only 15–25 per cent of the soldiers involved in an engagement actually fired their weapons.

When groups of people are in a fearful situation, social factors may be of paramount importance. These can be either positive, with the individuals in the group supporting each other, or negative, as suggested by expressions such as 'fear is infectious'. In extreme cases, such as that of a defeated army or a dance hall crowd trapped by a fire, panic may result, with more danger resulting from the stampeding crowd than from the original source of threat (Vetford and Lee, 1943). Such panic may disrupt large sections of society if there appears to be a major threat. A classic study of such behaviour is provided by Cantril's (1947) analysis of the disruption following a very realistic radio play about an invasion from Mars. A similar panic in a New Zealand community is described by McLeod (1975). This reaction followed the mistaken belief that a harmless substance released into the environment was toxic. It was feared in the early days of the Second World War that such panic would follow the bombing of civilians. In fact morale remained amazingly high; many ordinary people performed with extraordinary courage, and such indicators of social malaise as incidence of mental illness and suicide showed a reduction (Rachman, 1978). Radloff and Helmreich (1968) observed the behaviour of U.S. Navy divers taking part in the Sealab Project. This required them to live in an experimental underwater habitat at a depth which exceeded that of any previous habitat, and under conditions which were uncomfortable and potentially dangerous. Despite very cramped conditions, relationships between the divers were better than on the surface; the threat seemed to make the group more tolerant of personal quirks and petty irritations.

The tendency for controlled fear to raise morale and extreme fear to result in social breakdown and panic suggests something akin to the Yerkes–Dodson Law. However, since groups that have shown cohesiveness are rarely the same as those who subsequently panic, it would probably be unwise to assume a continuum rather than a dichotomy. It may well be that a level of fear that will inspire one group will destroy another.

We know very little about the social psychology of fear. It seems likely that the success of a group in responding positively to fear will depend in part on both its structure and leadership. What constitutes a good leader is however far from clear. One might imagine that the leader should be one who is immune to fear, and yet instances occur in which this is clearly not so. In one of these, a mine disaster, the person who emerged as group leader was one of the men who had originally shown the greatest fear and had apparently 'cracked' under the strain (Mende and Ploeger, 1966).

Combat stress

There have been some attempts at collecting physiological data in combat. It has been found that the heart-rate of pilots on bombing missions increases on take-off, increases again during the raid, and decreases after the pilots have returned to their base (Lewis, Jones, Austin, and Roman, 1967). There are also reports that phospholipid secretion increased in American airman involved in the Vietnam War (Austin, 1969) and conflicting evidence on corticosteroid levels (Bourne, Rose, and Mason, 1967). Secretion of testosterone and other androgens was found to decrease in American soldiers fighting in the same conflict (Rose, 1969).

It has been known for a considerable period that soldiers in the heat of battle are unlikely to fire their weapons. After the Battle of Gettysburg in the American Civil War, over 200 of the muzzle-loading rifles were found to have been loaded five or more times without being fired, and one had been loaded 21 times without being fired once (Walker and Burkhardt, 1965).

In the air, Grinker and Spiegel (1945) describe the varying degrees of anxiety they found in United States Air Force Personnel.

> . . . one may speak of mild anxiety states in which the subjective and motor signs of anxiety are present but function is not yet interfered with. The flier may have a tremor and feel constantly jittery and apprehensive or display severe tension and fear over the target area, and still be able to carry on his tasks in flying. In moderate anxiety states, the same symptoms may have progressed to the point where the flier makes mistakes in flying and now has his own incapacity to fear as well as the other conscious and unconscious sources of anxiety. This is the most common neurotic reaction among flying personnel. Severe anxiety states, with much regression of the ego, confusion in regard to the environment, mutism and stupor, are not seen in fliers but only in ground combat personnel who are submitted to more prolonged, continuous and severe punishment.

Clearly, severe cases of anxiety may not have survived long enough to be interviewed!

Reid (1945) analysed the calculation and plotting errors involved in measuring wind vectors by navigators on operational sorties. He found that compared to errors made over England, errors increased significantly once bombers made the enemy coast and increased even further as the bombers approached target. Errors declined when the bombers had crossed the coast on the return journey (suggesting that fatigue alone, or other accumulative stresses, were not the sole cause of the errors).

Walker and Burkhardt (1965) evaluated performance on complex weapon systems and tried to relate this to the degree of combat stress. Their results are shown in Figure 22.

Es is the ratio of error in combat to error during training and *A*, *B*, *C*, and *D* represent different degrees of combat severity: A = no losses, B = 2 per cent aircraft lost per raid, C = 5 per cent aircraft lost per raid (the limit of attrition warfare accepted by night bombing forces in the Second World War), and D = 10 per cent aircraft lost per raid (the average loss rate of the German

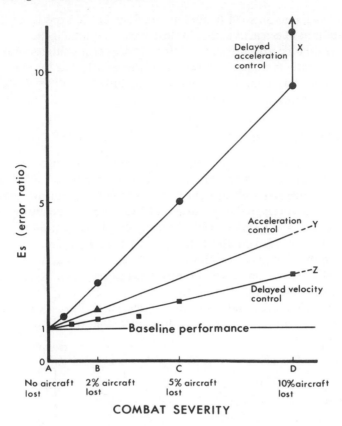

Figure 22. Performance decrement as a function of combat severity and weapon control. From Walker and Burkhardt (1965). (Reproduced by permission of Norman K. Walker Associates Inc.)

Air Force in the Battle of Britain).

The three lines represent different control systems, Line X represents acceleration with a 1.25-second lag. The points come from a number of guided bomb systems. The results show a decrement of up to 900 per cent as the combat situation becomes more and more dangerous, followed eventually by abandonment of control. Line Y represents an accelerational control with negligible lag. Line Z represents a velocity control with a short lag.

Although the above evidence does seem to indicate that adaptive performance deteriorates in dangerous situations, it is not possible to conclude with any degree of certainty that it is fear alone which is causing the breakdown. Various stresses such as fatigue, pain, and hunger, and varying degrees of motivation might just as well be influencing, if not causing the pattern of results. Also, individuals' perceptions of the dangerousness of the situations will vary, depending on such factors as previous battle experience, how long the combatant has been active since his last leave, and intelligence.

Clearly, the data derived from uncontrolled dangerous situations is useful in providing indications of how behaviour might be affected by fear, but since there are many confounding influences and little quantitative data, other dangerous situations need to be examined.

SUBJECTIVE AND PHYSIOLOGICAL CHANGES

Both sports and military parachuting have been investigated by various groups. Perhaps it is not too surprising to discover that most investigators find increases in subjectively-felt anxiety either preceding or during early jumps, either from high towers, balloons, or aircraft (military parachuting: Basowitz, Persky, Korchin, and Grinker, 1955; Halse, Blix, Ellertsen, and Ursin, 1978; sports parachuting: Epstein and Fenz, 1965; Grierson, 1975). Unfortunately, as in many of the dangerous situations that have been studied, most investigators have used differently-composed subjective measures, so it is not possible to give comparative estimates of subjective fear.

Various physiological and biochemical measures have been taken from parachutists (see Figure 23). During the time preceding the jump, and including

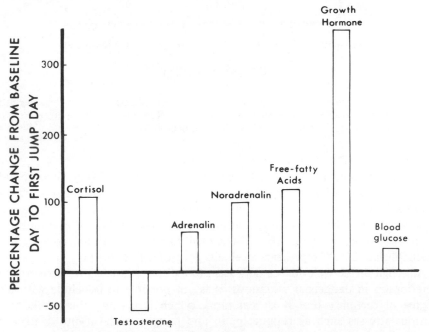

Figure 23. Biochemical changes in paratroopers on the day of their first aircraft descent. Adapted from Ursin *et al.* (1978).

the jump itself, the following measures show increased activation: heart-rate (Fenz and Epstein, 1967; Shane and Slinde, 1968, Grierson, 1975; Stromme, Wikeby, Blix, and Ursin, 1978); respiration (Fenz and Epstein, 1967); absolute skin conductance (Fenz and Epstein, 1967); adrenalin and noradrenalin secretion (Bloom, Euler, and Frankenhauser, 1962; Hansem, Stoa, Blix, and Ursin, 1978); growth hormone secretion (Weitzman and Ursin, 1978); blood glucose levels (Eide and Atteras, 1978); and hippuric acid excretion and blood glutathione (Basowitz *et al.*, 1955). Plasma prolactin, growth hormone, and thyrotropin secretion are also increased after the jump (Noel, Dimond, Earll, and Frantz, 1976). In contrast to other hormones testosterone secretion decreases (Davidson, Smith, and Levine, 1978).

Overall, there appears to be a monotonic and parallel increase in both subjective anxiety and objective physiological measures as the time before a known dangerous event decreases. In parachuting, greatest physiological arousal for novices occurs at the time of exit from the aircraft. Curiously, Epstein and Fenz (1965) found that maximal avoidance of the jump occurred a few seconds before the jump itself. This has occasionally, and probably mistakenly, been taken to mean that there is a dissociation between physiological and subjective measures, where the latter measures reached maximum before the former. The more likely explanation for their observed separation is the emphasis placed on 'avoidance' in their self-rating scales as opposed to fear. Grierson (1975), who used a more explicit 'fear' self-rating scale, found most fear at the time of exit.

In a similar vein, Epstein and Fenz compared novice jumpers with experienced jumpers on the avoidance ratings (Figure 24). With experienced jumpers, Epstein and Fenz found that maximal avoidance occurred the night before the jumper went to the airfield. This led them to speculate that with experience the point of greatest anxiety is displaced backwards in time. Again the problem with this speculation is the way avoidance was equated with anxiety. Grierson (1975) found that experienced jumpers reported relatively little fear and noted that the dominant response to jumping was one of pleasure.

Epstein and Fenz attained an interesting difference between the physiological measures observed from their experienced jumpers when compared with the pattern for novices. Experienced parachutists showed only a moderate increase in arousal and this elevation tended to occur before the parachutists were in the aircraft. This probably reflects the experienced jumper's excitement in anticipation of his forthcoming jump and aerial acrobatics.

Over the years, Fenz has extended his earlier findings (Fenz, 1975), and has noted that experienced but incompetent jumpers are those jumpers whose subjective and physiological response is still similar to that of novice jumpers. Also, in longitudinal studies, Fenz has been able to show in successful and experienced jumpers the diminution in physiological response and the reduction in fear. Furthermore, in a single-case study (Fenz and Jones, 1972)

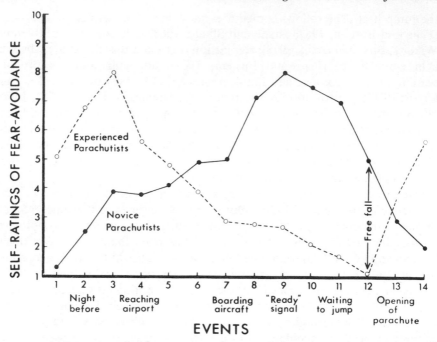

Figure 24. Mean self-ratings of avoidance of experienced and inexperienced sport-parachutists, before, during, and after their jumps. From Epstein and Fenz (1965). (Reproduced by permission of the American Psychosomatic Society Inc.)

he demonstrated that, by introducing an element of uncertainty into an experienced parachutist's jumps (by telling the sky-diver that his parachute would occasionally be packed incorrectly and therefore fail in a number of his following jumps), it was possible to cause a regression in physiological response towards a novice's response. Similarly, he found that the physiological response made by experienced parachutists on jumps immediately following accidents were the same as those who were inexperienced.

Clearly, both subjective and physiological measures change in situations that would be described, by most, as dangerous. Unfortunately, this does not provide any insight as to how anxiety will affect performance, or how much anxiety is needed before performance is affected.

PERFORMANCE IN DANGEROUS ENVIRONMENTS

Simulated danger

An early attempt at defining what processes might be affected by anxiety is provided by Berkun, Bialek, Kern, and Yagi (1962). These authors used soldiers in a contrived military exercise. As far as the soldiers were concerned, their function was to look out for aircraft. They were on their own and only had a radio-transmitter with which to communicate back to base. Three different situations were used to persuade the soldier that he was in immediate danger of losing his life or being seriously injured: (a) a series of explosions simulating a barrage of artillery shells coming in and bursting near the soldier; these explosions confirmed to the soldier reports he had heard on the radio suggesting that some shells were falling out of the designated target area; (b) a forest fire (in this situation the subject was enveloped by smoke); and (c) an accident with radio-active material producing dangerous fall-out in the soldier's area. In all of these situations the soldier's immediate key to rescue was the radio-transmitter, which inexplicably failed.

Berkun *et al.* measured how the subjects had felt during these situations by asking the subjects to fill in an affect check-list immediately after their 'rescue'. The check-list showed that the soldiers were frightened only in the artillery and radio-active fall-out situations. Blood and urine samples were also taken to provide biochemical measures (the level of 17-hydroxycortico-steroids). The biochemical measures showed all situations to be different from the control.

Berkun *et al.*'s performance measures were all derived from the way in which soldiers used the radio. They simply had to repair the radio as rapidly as possible: all the instructions necessary for this were present. Performance was tested by measuring how long it took the subject to start repair work, mechanical ability, manual dexterity, comprehension, and even vigilance (the subject had to watch out for a light which occasionally came on). Unfortunately, these measures were all combined in a single composite score, so it is not possible to know what aspects of performance might have been affected. What is of interest is that although the experimental groups were shown to be more stressed than the controls, only soldiers in the artillery situation showed significant decrements in the performance scores. However, this at least indicates that even if some levels of anxiety can be demonstrated to exist using subjective physiological measures, then performance need not necessarily be affected. Also, it is not possible to tell from a composite score whether some aspects of performance may have improved whilst others deteriorated.

Manual dexterity and motor skill

There are numerous well-known phrases in the English language which can provide clues concerning deficits that could be expected in frightening situations, and some of these have been investigated. For example 'shaking with fear' describes a gross failure of motor control, which seems to occur rarely, but does suggest an impairment that might be found. Research on divers has shown that manual dexterity is impaired under water, and,

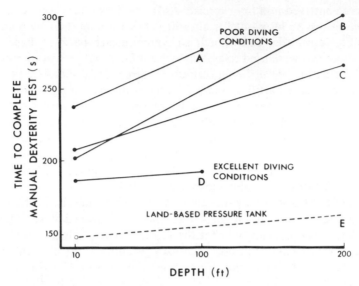

Figure 25. The combined effects of depth and anxiety on the screwplate of manual dexterity. Increasing depth coupled with poor diving conditions interacts to produce poorer performance. Sources: (A) Baddeley (1966); (B,C,E) Baddeley and Flemming (1967); (D) Baddeley *et al.* (1968)

furthermore, the more dangerous the dive the greater the impairment (see Figure 25). Commonly, manual dexterity performance is determined by measuring the time it takes to transfer nuts and bolts from one brass plate to another. Baddeley has noted this from a number of studies (Baddeley, 1966; Baddeley and Flemming, 1967; Baddeley, De Figuerdo, Hawkswell Curtis, and Williams, 1968; Davis, Osborne, Baddeley, and Graham, 1972). Initially it was found that impairment increased as the depth of the dive increased. This could not be explained away purely in terms of depth *per se*, since the early experiments included pressure chamber controls who were not as greatly impaired by increasing 'depth'. Baddeley *et al.* (1968) surprisingly found only a small effect of depth and, compared with the other studies, very fast completion times. The crucial difference between this and the other studies was that diving conditions were ideal. The experiment took place on the Southwest coast of Malta in very calm water, with a rocky bottom shelving rapidly down to a sandy plain at 100 feet. In the other experiments deep dives were conducted in the open sea where the diver had to go straight down into 'the blue' towards the sea-bed he could not see, a situation thought to be considerably more anxiety-provoking than the former.

Recently, Mears and Cleary (1980) have confirmed these findings in an underwater experiment in which divers performed a manual dexterity test; heart-rate was measured during the test and a self-report anxiety questionnaire was completed. They found a decrement of about 16 per cent between groups who were tested at a depth of 20 feet (low anxiety) and those tested at a depth of 100 feet (high anxiety).

Tracking tasks (those tasks in which a subject has to control some type of marker so that it follows a moving target) demand sensory and motor coordination. Hammerton and Tickner (1969) compared Regular Army (RA) men, RA trainees, and Territorial Army (TA) trainees in an acquisition tracking task performed shortly before a parachute jump from a balloon at 800 feet. When tested immediately before the jump, tracking performance was relatively impaired. The TA men, who were the least trained parachutists, and possibly the least used to coping with stress, were most severely impaired; the RA trainees were next in susceptibility, while the least affected were the trained RA parachutists.

There is little direct evidence from combat studies, although the data on bombing accuracy cited by Walker and Burkhardt, and mentioned above, could be indicative of deterioration in tracking ability. In a review of tracking performance, Bergstrom (1970) found many instances of impairment when subjects were, for example, stressed by electric shocks. It is unclear in the case of tracking tasks, however, whether impaired performance is due to deterioration in manual dexterity or to degraded sensory or perceptual processes.

Cognitive behaviour

There are some indications that anxiety may affect sensory and perceptual mechanisms. Fenz (1964) has used a word-association test in some of his experiments on sports parachutists. Some of the stimulus words varied along the dimensions of relevance to parachuting (for example *airport*, *jump*) and neutral words (for example *pencil*, *bicycle*) and finally anxiety words (for example *accident*, *fear*). Fenz measured the galvanic skin response (GSR) to the words, *auditory threshold*, *identification*, *memory*, and, of course, the associations produced. Subjects were tested two weeks before their jump, the day before their jump, and on the day of their jump. These results were compared with those of non-jump control subjects.

With GSR, Fenz found that the control subjects did not differ in their response to neutral words or to words which varied along the parachute-relevant dimension. These subjects, along with the novice parachutists, did, however, react strongly to anxiety-provoking words. In contrast, parachutists on all occasions reacted strongly to parachute-related words as relevance increased; moreover, this reactivity increased overall as the time between testing and the jump was reduced. The GSR findings have been extended by Fenz, who compared experienced parachutists (more than 100 jumps) with novices (Fenz and Epstein, 1968). He found that experienced jumpers reacted in much the same way as novices did to words of low relevance to parachuting;

unlike novices, experienced jumpers were not as reactive to high parachute-relevant words. Fenz and Epstein regarded this differential response as an indication of some fundamental coping mechanism associated with the mastery of stress.

Two weeks before their jump, subjects' absolute auditory threshold was measured using a tone of 800 Hz which followed the presentation of one of the stimulus words. The thresholds of parachutists was found not to differ from that of the controls. On the day of the jump, however, auditory threshold for the novices was significantly higher. Fenz's data also indicated that more anxiety words were misperceived by novices on the day of their jump than at any other time, in contrast with the control subjects. (Grierson, 1975, in a partial replication of Fenz's work, noted a similar effect, although the results were not statistically significant.) In the same vein, Simonov, Frolov, Evtushenko, and Sviridov (1977), who actually tested their parachutists on-board the aircraft as they were ascending towards the exit point, found that visual recognition of numbers (composed of dots and displayed against varying and distractive dotted backgrounds) deteriorated as 'emotional stress' increased. Emotional stress was measured by combining a number of electro-cardiographic (ECG) parameters. Basowitz *et al.* (1955) also found that men undergoing parachute training were poorer than controls in reproducing tachistoscopically-presented simple line figures.

Fenz (1964) required his subjects to produce associations to all of the three sets of words; he found no differences between the groups of subjects in associations produced. However, Fenz also tested his subjects using a modified version of the Thematic Apperception Test (TAT). In this test subjects were presented pictures of various scenes that were either completely, partly, or not at all related to parachuting. The subjects were required to tell a story which included the scene that was depicted by the picture. The results indicated that parachutists on the day of the jump explicitly denied their fear in the stories following the parachuting-related pictures, but produced an extreme number of fear responses to the pictures unrelated to parachuting. Grierson (1975) confirmed Fenz's TAT findings and also noted that novice parachutists' pleasure responses were higher than controls on the parachuting-related pictures. He also found that the fear content of neutral pictures declined in subjects who become more experienced jumpers (up to 20 jumps) and were noted to become competent. Incompetent or unsuccessful jumpers, on the other hand, continued to produce stories that contained many fear responses.

It is interesting to note that the Defence Mechanism Test developed by Kragh (1960) has been found useful in predicting the performance of Swedish airline pilots (Kragh, 1960) and Danish attack divers (Kragh, 1962). This test involves the tachistoscopic presentation of TAT-like pictures. Initially the exposure time is 20 milliseconds, and this is gradually increased to 500 milliseconds. After each exposure the subject has to write short comments about what he has just seen. Some of the pictures contain threatening elements. Subjects who were very slow to perceive this threat are claimed to be more likely to have flying accidents, a result which is interpreted by Kragh and his associates in psychoanalytic terms.

In experiments dealing with dangerous situations there has only been a moderate degree of success in detecting any cognitive effects. Fenz (1964) reported that novices seemed to suffer from a general memory deficit for neutral words. Basowitz *et al.* (1955) found that digit span appeared to be depressed in men who were under the stress of parachute training, although the effect was statistically unreliable. Berkun *et al.* (1962) used a task which might loosely be described as a complex cognitive task — form-filling. In their experiment, subjects were in a military plane when one of the engines stopped. The subjects were first told that the plane was about to ditch in the ocean and that it was necessary for them to fill out an 'emergency procedure' form for their insurance companies. These forms were deliberately composed so that they were misleading and difficult to fill in. After a period of time the plane landed back at the airport and the subjects had to fill in an affect check-list. Subjects also provided urine samples so that the level of 17-hydroxycortico-steroids could be measured. All the comparisons were made against the control group that had been taken up in the plane but had not experienced the simulated emergency. Both the subjective and biochemical measures indicated that the subjects had been frightened by the experience, and the performance measures indicated deterioration in form-filling.

Dual-task studies

So far, the experiments described have used only one performance task as the dependent variable. There is some evidence to indicate that if subjects have to perform simultaneously more than one task, then secondary task performance may deteriorate in frightening situations. Weltman, Smith, and Egstrom (1971), following an earlier observation in an open sea experiment (Weltman and Egstrom, 1966), found that novice subjects in a pressure chamber who thought that they were experiencing a 60-foot dive performed poorly on a peripheral light detection task, compared with a control group situated outside the chamber. Weltman *et al.* recorded heart-rate continuously throughout the experiment and used a subjective measure of anxiety, the Multiple Affect Adjective Check List (Zuckerman and Lubin, 1965). They found that the group exposed to the 'dive' had an average pulse-rate that was 10 beats per minute faster than the control group, although this did decrease slightly over time. In addition the Check List indicated that the 'divers' were more anxious than the controls. The central visual acuity task consisted of monitoring the direction of movement of a small gap in a moving Landolt circle. The peripheral task was to press a button on the occurrence of a 60-millisecond light flash, triggered randomly in time, and presented in the lower right-hand corner of an oval diving mask. Both groups performed equally well on the central task, but the anxious experimental group noticed only half as many peripheral light flashes as did the control group.

FEAR AND AROUSAL

This review has concentrated on the subjective, physiological, and behavioural responses to situations that contain either imminent or immediate threat to the life of the individual. As a result of this emphasis, many experiments have not been mentioned which manipulate anxiety or fear in other ways, for example physical threats of electric shock or other noxious stimuli; ego-threats such as examinations, public speaking, experimenter-induced failure or helplessness, demanding tasks. This narrow viewpoint has been taken simply in order to highlight the direct evidence available specifically on dangerous situations.

The literature presented has not been discussed with any particular theory of anxiety in mind, mainly because the sparse literature could probably be forced to fit into any of the theories available. We will, however, consider how behaviour in dangerous situations fits into arousal theory, since this is a framework that has been applied in a wide range of stress studies involving many different stressors.

Arousal and performance changes

Woodworth and Schlosberg (1954) define arousal as the level of excitation along a continuum that varies from deep sleep to emotional excitement. It is apparent that fear responses will lie towards the upper end of this continuum. As arousal and performance are supposed to be related in a curvilinear fashion, normally considered as an inverted-U (Yerkes and Dodson, 1908; Hebb, 1949), then performance decrements would be expected when an individual is frightened. The evidence derived from the fear literature does support this view. What is perhaps a little surprising, however, is the relative lack of decrement in some of the studies cited even when the subjective and physiological measures indicate that the individual is both frightened and highly aroused.

A number of possible reasons exist for the lack of large decrement when someone is afraid. It may simply reflect a measurement problem, so that even though large increments in subjective and physiological responses may be observed, these responses may only reflect relatively small increments in arousal. Another possibility is that the relationship between arousal and performance may not be a straightforward and continuous curvilinear function, but may be discontinuous. Performance may be maintained at the same level for relatively large increments in arousal until a break-point is reached, when a catastrophic deterioration occurs. Yet another, but perhaps more plausible reason, raised specifically by Baddeley (1972) for dangerous situations, and by Easterbrook (1959) for more general but emotionally arousing situations, would be to suggest that arousal acts by narrowing attention. In the general arousal literature there are numerous experiments which indicate that if an individual is aroused there is a tendency to miss peripheral or only occasionally relevant stimuli, or to perform poorly on peripheral tasks whilst maintaining or improving performance on central tasks (Zaffy and Bruning, 1966; Hockey, 1970a, 1970b): see Chapters 7, 10, and 12 this volume. Many of the observations made in dangerous situations have included only central tasks, as a result it is not known whether performance on peripheral tasks deteriorates.

Easterbrook postulated that narrowing of attention was caused by a reduction in the number of stimuli that are analysed by the individual. Wine (1971) in a review of the examination-anxiety literature has pointed out that impaired performance in high-anxiety individuals may occur because the individual divides his attention between self-relevant variables (e.g. worrying thoughts, self-blame) and task-relevant variables. Presumably, in frightening situations when there may be a great deal of autonomic activation, the individual's attention could be divided between the external demands of the situation, cognitive elaboration of those demands, and internal demands.

There is reasonable evidence to suggest that manual dexterity in central tasks is impaired by anxiety. This decrement might be caused in a number of ways. First, the individual's physiological state is likely to be very different in the frightened versus the non-frightened state and it is likely that the task was first learnt in non-anxious conditions. Consequently, state-dependent effects may occur. It has been shown that if subjects are given amphetamine (a drug which produces a physiological response similar to that produced by activation of the sympathetic nervous system) at the same time as they are learning, recall will be better if the subjects are again given amphetamine at the time of remembering (Bustamante, Jordan, Vila, Gonzalez, and Insua, 1970). Alternatively, the mechanisms which cause attentional deficits to external stimuli may also interfere with the execution of motor programmes. Yet another possibility comes from Spence-Hull learning theory (for example, Taylor and Spence, 1952). This theory is based on conditioning studies which equate anxiety with drive. The theory suggests that with increasing levels of anxiety, the probability of well-learned responses manifesting themselves increases: if these well-learnt responses happen to be the incorrect ones in a task, then task performance will deteriorate. Finally, the effect may simply be due to the disruption of normal muscle tone by anxiety; a tense subject will have tense muscles which impairs his normally smooth and skilled performance. Muscle tremor is easily seen in orchestral string players, and it is not surprising to find that excessive anxiety in these individuals will impair performance (James, Pearson, Griffith, and Newbury, 1977).

The effect of experience

It was pointed out in the section on parachuting that Fenz has found that as sky divers become more experienced, their autonomic reactivity to the sport diminishes. Fenz (1975) claims that this reflects a coping strategy (the sky diver learns to inhibit his anxiety). Although this may be the case, it is also possible that those people who become capable and experienced sky divers are those who have an innate ability to exert this control. One problem with looking at experienced sports parachutists is that this population has undergone great selective pressure. In sports parachuting in the United States, only 15 per cent of those who have jumped once come back for another jump, and a smaller percentage still return voluntarily for further jumps (Istel, 1961). Notwithstanding the problem of selectivity, it is interesting to note that the capable and experienced sky divers are those who quickly produce laboratory-induced conditioned cardiac responses (Fenz and Jones, 1974) and are those who do not deny their fear (Grierson, 1975). Another indication that experienced parachutists are a select population comes from an observation in combat studies. Generally, armed forces have learned that men can only withstand operating in battle conditions for limited periods of time before their fighting capability deteriorates. While parachutists may learn through experience that the activity is not as dangerous as it first seems, combatants who will probably experience the loss of fellow combatants are unlikely to do so.

GENERAL CONCLUSIONS

By combining the results of all the areas reviewed in this chapter, a general description of how an individual may respond in a dangerous situation can be built up. The magnitude of any response will depend on a number of factors: (a) the individual's predisposition towards feeling anxious (trait-anxiety) and being aroused (trait-arousal); (b) the individual's assessment of the dangerousness of the situation and his ability to cope with it; and (c) previous exposure. The precise pattern of physiological and biochemical responses will vary from individual to individual unless the situation is perceived as being extreme. In an extreme situation increases in heart-rate, respiration-rate, skin conductance, and muscle tension can be expected, as well as increases in the secretion of catecholamines and various other hormones. Behaviourally, deterioration can be expected in manual dexterity, in sensory-motor tasks such as tracking, and in performance of secondary tasks. It is probable that secondary task performance is reduced before central tasks are affected.

SUMMARY

In this chapter we have considered the effect of fear and danger on performance, subjective state, and bodily reactions. We have concentrated primarily on data provided by experiments conducted in controlled dangerous environments, primarily parachuting and diving, though available evidence from the results of natural disasters and war has also been examined.

The evidence suggests that when a situation has induced fear in an individual (as measured by subjective and physiological responses), then a deterioration in the efficiency of performance can be expected, especially in tasks involving sensory-motor skill or divided attention.

The findings are interpreted within the general arousal framework, which assumes an inverted-U relationship between arousal and performance.

ACKNOWLEDGEMENT

We gratefully acknowledge the support of the Army Personnel Research Committee of the Medical Research Council.

REFERENCES

Andersson, C. R. (1976) Coping behaviour as intervening mechanisms in the inverted U stress performance relationship. *Journal of Applied Psychology*, **61**, 30–34.

Austin, Jr., F. H. (1969) A review of stress and fatigue monitoring of naval aviators during aircraft carrier combat operations: Blood and Urine biochemical studies. In P. G. Bourne (ed.), *The Psychology and Physiology of Stress, with reference to special studies of the Viet Nam War*. London: Academic Press, pp.197–218.

Baddeley, A. D. (1966) The influence of depth on the manual dexterity of free divers: A comparison of open sea and pressure chamber testing. *Journal of Applied Psychology*, **50**, 81–85.

Baddeley, A. D. (1972) Selective attention and performance in dangerous environments. *British Journal of Psychology*, **63**, 537–546.

Baddeley, A. D. and Flemming, N. C. (1967) The efficiency of divers breathing oxy-helium. *Ergonomics*, **10**, 311–319.

Baddeley, A. D., De Figueredo, J. W., Hawkswell Curtis, J. W., and Williams, A. N. (1968) Nitrogen narcosis and performance under water. *Ergonomics*, **11**, 157–164.

Basowitz, H., Persky, H., Korchen, S., and Grinker, R. (1955) *Anxiety and Stress*. New York: McGraw-Hill Book Company.

Bergstrom, B. (1970) Manual missile guidance under short-term psychological stress. A literature review. *MPI Reports I*. Stockholm: Institute of Military Psychology.

Berkun, M. M., Bialek, H. M., Kern, R. P., and Yagi, K. (1962) Experimental studies of psychological stress in man. *Psychological Monographs*, **76**, No. 15.

Bloom, G., Euler, U. S., and Frankenhauser, M. (1963) Catecholamine excretion and personality traits in paratroop trainees. *Acta Physiol. Scand.* **58**, 77–89.

Bourne, P. G., Rose, R. M., and Mason, J. W. (1967) Urinary 17-OCHS levels, data on seven helicopter ambulance medics in combat. *Archives of General Psychiatry*, **17**, 104–109.

Bustamante, J. A., Jordan, A., Vila, M., Gonzalez, A., and Insua, A. (1970) State dependent learning in humans. *Physiology and Behaviour*, **5**, 793–796.

Cantril, H. (1947) The invasion from Mars. In T. M. Newcomb and E. L. Hartley, *Readings in Social Psychology*. New York: Henry Holt and Company.

Cattell, R. B. (1972) The nature and genesis of mood states: A theoretical model with experimental measurements concerning anxiety, depression, arousal and other mood states. In C. D. Spielberger (ed.), *Anxiety Current Trends in Theory and Research*. New York: Academic Press.

Davidson, J. M., Smith, E. R., and Levine, S. (1978) Testosterone. In H. Ursin, E. Baade, and S. Levine. *Psychobiology of Stress: A Study of Coping Men*. New York: Academic Press, pp.57–62.

Davis, F. M., Osborne, J. P., Baddeley, A. D., and Graham, I. M. F. (1972) Diver Performance: Nitrogen narcosis and anxiety. *Aerospace Medicine*, **43**, 1079–1082.

Easterbrook, J. A. (1959) The effect of emotion on the utilization and the organization of behaviour. *Psychological Review*, **66**, 183–207.

Eide, R. and Atteras, A. (1978) Blood glucose. In H. Ursin, E. Baade and S. Levine, *Psychobiology of Stress: A Study of Coping Men*. New York: Academic Press, pp.99–104.

Elliot, R. (1974) The motivational significance of heart rate. In P. A. Obrist, A. H. Black, J. Brener, and L. V. DiCara, *Cardiovascular Psychophysiology*. Chicago: Aldine Publishing Co., pp.505–537.

Epstein, S. and Fenz, W. D. (1965) Steepness of approach and avoidance gradients in humans as a function of experience: Theory and experiment. *Journal of Experimental Psychology*, **70**, 1–12.

Fenz, W. D. (1964) Conflict and stress as related to physiological activation, and sensory perceptual and cognitive functioning. *Psychological Monographs*, **78**, No. 8.

Fenz, W. D. (1975) Strategies for coping with stress. In I. Sarason and C. Spielberger (eds.), *Stress and Anxiety*. Washington: Hemisphere Publishing Company.

Fenz, W. D. and Epstein, S. (1967) Changes in gradients of skin conductance, heart rate and respiration rate as a function of experience. *Psychosomatic Medicine*, **29**, 33–51.

Fenz, W. D. and Epstein, S. (1968) Specific and general inhibitory reactions associated with mastery of stress. *Journal of Experimental Psychology*, **77**, 52–56.

Fenz, W. D. and Jones, B. (1972) The effect of uncertainty on mastery of stress: A case study. *Psychophysiology*, **9**, 615–619.

Freud, S. (1936) *The Problem of Anxiety*. New York: Norton.

Freud, S. (1959) *Beyond the Pleasure Principle*. New York: Bantam.

Grierson, A. T. (1975) Adaptation and motivation in sport parachuting. Unpublished M.A. dissertation, University of Edinburgh.

Grinker, R. R. and Spiegel, J. P. (1945) *Men Under Stress*. London: J. and A. Churchill Ltd.

Halse, K., Blix, A. S., Ellersten, B. and Ursin, H. (1978) Development of performance and fear experience. In H. Ursin, E. Baade, and S. Levine, *Psychobiology of Stress. A Study of Coping Men*. New York: Academic Press.

Hammerton, M. and Tickner, A. H. (1969) An investigation into the effects of stress upon skilled performance. *Ergonomics*, **12**, 851–855.

Hansen, J. R., Stoa, K. F., Blix, A. S., and Ursin, H. (1978) Urinary levels of epinephrine and norepinephrine in parachutist trainees. In H. Ursin, E. Baade, and S. Levine, *Psychobiology of Stress. A Study of Coping Men*. New York: Academic Press, pp.63–74.

Hebb, D. O. (1949) *The Organization of Behaviour: A Neuropsychological Theory*. New York: John Wiley & Sons.

Hockey, G. R. J. (1970a) Effect of loud noise on attentional selectivity. *Quarterly Journal of Experimental Psychology*, **22**, 28–36.

Hockey, G. R. J. (1970b) Signal probability and spatial location as possible bases for increased selectivity in noise. *Quarterly Journal of Experimental Psychology*, **22**, 37–42.

Hodges, W. F. (1976) The psychophysiology of anxiety. In M. Zuckerman and C. D. Spielberger (eds.), *Emotions and Anxiety*. Hillsdale, N.J.: Lawrence Erlbaum Associates.

Istel, J. (1961) Statistical report, *Parachutist*, **3**, 11–12.

James, I. M., Pearson, R. M., Griffith, D. N. W., and Newbury, P. (1977) Effect of oxprenolol on stage-fright in musicians. *Lancet*, **1977**, 952–954.

Kragh, U. (1960) The Defense Mechanism Test: A new method for diagnosis and personnel selection. *Journal of Applied Psychology*, **44**, 303–309.

Kragh, U. (1962) Predictions of success of Danish attack divers by the Defense Mechanism Test (DMT). *Psychological Research Bulletin*. Sweden: Lund University.

Krause, M. S. (1961) The measurement of transitory anxiety. *Psychological Review*, **68**, 178–189.

Lacey, J. I. (1959) Psychophysiological approaches to the evaluation of psycho-therapeutic process and outcome. In A. Rubenstein and M. B. Parloff, (eds.), *Research in Psychotherapy*. Washington, D.C.: American Psychological Association.

Lacey, J. I. and Lacey, B. C. (1958) Verification and extension of the principle of autonomic response-stereotypy. *American Journal of Psychology*, **71**, 50–73.

Lazarus, R. S. (1966) *Psychological Stress and the Coping Process*. New York: McGraw-Hill.

Lewis, C. E., Jones, W. L., Austin, F. H., and Roman, J. (1967) Flight research program: IX. Medical monitoring of carrier pilots in combat-II. *Aerospace Medicine*, **38**, 581–592.

Mandler, G., Mandler, J. M., Kremen, I., and Sholiton, R. D. (1961) The response to threat: Relations among verbal and physiological indices. *Psychological Monographs*, **75**, No. 9.

Mandler, G., Mandler, J. M., and Uviller, E. T. (1958) Autonomic feedback: The perception of autonomic activity. *Journal of Abnormal and Social Psychology*, **56**, 367–373.

Marshall, S. L. A. (1947) *Men against Fire*. New York: William Morrow.

Martin, B. (1961) The assessment of anxiety by physiological-behavioural measures. *Psychological Bulletin*, **58**, 234–255.

McLeod, W. R. (1975) Morphos poisoning or mass panic. *Australian and New Zealand Journal of Psychiatry*, **9**, 225–229.

Mears, J. D. and Cleary, P. J. (1980) Anxiety as a factor in underwater performance. *Ergonomics*, **23**, 549–557.

Mende, W. and Ploeger, A. (1966) The conduct and experience of miners under the acute stress of incarceration. *Der Nervnartz*, **1966**, May.

Mosso, A. (1896) *Fear*. London: Longman, Green and Co.

Noel, G. R., Dimond, R. C., Earll, J. M., and Frantz, A. G. (1976) Prolactin, thyrotropin and growth hormone release during stress associated with parachute jumping. *Aviation, Space and Environmental Medicine*, **1976**, 543–547.

Rachman, S. J. (1978) *Fear and Courage*. San Francisco: W. H. Freeman and Company.

Radloff, R. and Helmreich, R. (1968) *Groups under stress: Psychological Research in SEALAB II*. New York: Appleton-Century-Crofts.

Reid (1979) Fluctuations in navigator performance during operational sorties. In E. J. Dearnaley, and P. B. Warr, *Aircrew Stress in Wartime Operations*. London: Academic Press, pp.63–73.

Rose, R. M. (1969) Androgen excretion in stress. In P. G. Bourne (ed.), *The Psychology and Physiology of Stress*, with reference to special studies of the Viet Nam war. London: Academic Press, pp.117–147.

Shane, W. P., and Slinde, K. (1968) Continuous ECG recordings during free-fall parachuting. *Aerospace Medicine*, **39**, 597–602.

Simonov, P. V., Frolov, M. V., Evtushenko, V. F., and Sviridov, E. P. (1977) Effect of emotional stress on recognition of visual patterns. *Aviation, Space and Environmental Medicine*, **1977**, September, 856–858.

Spielberger, C. D. (1966) *Anxiety and Behaviour*. New York: Academic Press.

Stromme, S. B., Wikeby, P. C., Blix, A. S., and Ursin, H. (1978) Additional heart-rate. In H. Ursin, E. Baade, and S. Levine, *Psychobiology of Stress. A Study of Coping Men*. New York: Academic Press, pp.83–90.

Taylor, J. A. (1951) The relationship of anxiety to the conditioned eyelid response. *Journal of Experimental Psychology*, **41**, 81–92.

Taylor, J. A., and Spence, K. W. (1952) The relationship of anxiety level to performance in serial learning. *Journal of Experimental Psychology*, **44**, 61–64.

Ursin, H., Baade, E., and Levine, S. (1978) *Psychobiology of Stress. A Study of Coping Men*. New York: Academic Press.

Vetford, H. R. and Lee, S. E. (1943) The Coconut Grove fire: A study in scapegoating. *Journal of Abnormal and Social Psychology*, **38**, Clinical Supplement, 138–154.

Walker, N. K. and Burkhardt, J. F. (1965) The combat effectiveness of various human operator controlled systems. In *Proceedings of the 17th U.S. Military Operations Research Symposium*.

Weitzman, E. D. and Ursin, H. (1978) Growth hormone. In H. Ursin, E. Baade, and S. Levine. *Psychobiology of Stress. A Study of Coping Men*. New York: Academic Press, pp.91–98.

Weltman, G. and Egstrom, G. H. (1966) Perceptual narrowing in novice divers. *Human Factors*, **8**, 499–506.

Weltman, G., Smith, J. E., and Egstrom, G. H. (1971) Perceptual narrowing during simulated pressure-chamber exposure. *Human Factors*, **13**, 99–107.

Wine, J. (1971) Test anxiety and direction of attention. *Psychological Bulletin*, **76**, 92–104.

Woodworth, R. S. and Schlosberg, H. (1954) *Experimental Psychology*. New York: Holt, Rinehart and Winston.

Yerkes, R. M. and Dodson, J. D. (1908) The relation of strength of stimulus to rapidity of habit formation. *Journal of Comparative Neurology and Psychology*, **18**, 459–482.

Zaffy, D. J. and Bruning, J. L. (1966) Drive and the range of cue utilization, *Journal of Experimental Psychology*, **71**, 382–384.

Zuckerman, M. and Lubin, B. (1965) *Manual for the Multiple Affect Adjective Check List*. San Diego, California: Educational and Industrial Services.

Stress and Fatigue in Human Performance
Edited by G. R. J. Hockey
© 1983 John Wiley & Sons Ltd.

Chapter 6

Fatigue

Dennis H. Holding

Feeling tired is a common enough experience, but one which is surprisingly difficult to pin down in terms of experiments on fatigue. A broad definition of fatigue would encompass all the consequences resulting from deprivation of rest, thus including the effects of loss of sleep. However, although sleep loss has much in common with work fatigue, its effects are relevant elsewhere in the book (see Chapters 4 and 9) and are sufficiently separable to be neglected in what follows. There are problems enough in interpreting the consequences of physical work, but the difficulties are compounded when one tries to explain how it is that reading microfilms, checking dials or adding columns of figures are all tiring activities. Furthermore, fatigue can be quickly forgotten in a state of emergency or an excess of enthusiasm. Feeling tired does not necessarily correlate with physiological impairment, nor with reduced efficiency in work output or other kinds of human performance. As a result, the research literature dealing with attempts to find objective tests for fatigue contains many disappointing outcomes.

DEFINITIONS OF FATIGUE

These problems were well known to early workers in the field, so much so that Muscio (1921) argued that the concept of 'fatigue' should be entirely abandoned. It is not possible to devise an acceptable test of fatigue, he concluded, because there exist no observable criteria for fatigue, other than those provided by the test itself, against which the test might be validated. However, it is possible for research purposes to regard fatigue as an intervening variable, or perhaps as a hypothetical construct, with a status similar to that of psychological variables like hunger or associative strength. Hours of food deprivation operationally define hunger, and hours of work performance may be used to specify fatigue; more accurately, hours of work should be interpreted as 'hours on duty', since fatigue effects may occur irrespective of the amount of work done. This approach neglects some of the usual connotations of the term, excluding cases like chronic fatigue as well as sleep loss, but offers the only practical starting point for research. Even so, it must be admitted that the hours-of-work variable does not by itself reliably predict decrements on a fatiguing task, while it has even less predictive value for subsequent activities; this is not unusual in psychology, where predictions from a single variable may be less important than interactions, and where several dependent variables must be considered.

Some of the complications were clearly recognized by Bills (1934), who distinguishes sharply between subjective, objective, and physiological fatigue. Bartley and Chute (1947) concur, assigning the effects of fatigue into three broad categories. Measures of *work output* are performance data which include declines in all types of overt activity. They reserve the term *impairment* for physiological changes at the tissue level, including changes in neural and motor functions. All that remains to be designated as *fatigue* proper is the subjective residue of feelings of bodily discomfort and aversion to effort. This kind of formulation may have unpleasant theoretical overtones for modern readers, but it does serve to draw attention to some of the more elusive cognitive and motivational variables which seem to interfere with what one might otherwise wish to characterize as 'rest-seeking' behaviour. It is interesting, for instance, that Barmack (1939) saw fatigue as a motivated change of attention away from work, while Bartley and Chute (p.54) regard fatigue as 'a part of the individual's stance with reference to activity'; although a stance or attitude need not remain subjective. Holding (1974) has suggested how similar attitudinal factors can be operationalized and measured, as discussed in a later section.

Descriptions of fatigue have advanced very little since the early work. There have been repeated attempts at 'reductionism', typified by the assertion that fatigue is merely the accumulation of lactic acid in the muscles or, more recently (Tsaneva and Markov, 1971), that fatigue is determined by the production of a metabolite which raises the synaptic threshold between a nerve and the organ it controls. Probably the best regarded of the more general formulations, despite its failure to produce crucial research, has been the idea expressed by Bartley and Chute (1947) that fatigue represents a form of conflict. Presumably, although this is never made explicit, the conflict occurs between the demands of the task situation and the subject's aversion to effort.

A different development which had considerable impact on the human performance area was the wartime 'Cambridge Cockpit' work, summarized by Bartlett (1943) and reviewed in a later section, which emphasized the way in which the central organization of skill breaks down under fatigue. The methods established in this kind of research have been productive in evaluating the effects of time on task in situations where little physical work is demanded. On the other hand, Cameron (1973) has reasserted the importance of variables like anxiety, renewing the close links between fatigue and sleep disturbances, and suggesting that fatigue is a generalized response to stress over a period of time. Broadbent (1979) considers that the prospect of testing fatigue may now be more promising, provided that we accept the evidence of indirect 'indicator' tests. Tests of persistence, of colour–word confusion, and of apparent 'helplessness' seem to show some after-effects of work, which he attributes (a) to general depression of effort, and (b) to neglect of the minor, peripheral details of some tasks.

In reviewing the scattered evidence on the effects of fatigue, no attempt will be made to observe Bartley and Chute's (1947) rigid tripartite classification into impairment, work output, and subjective fatigue. Separating them would make exposition unnecessarily difficult while, in any case, it seems premature to assume that they are not interrelated. When people declare that they are tired, it seems implausible that they are only indicating a feeling of aversion or conflict. The statement seems to imply a prediction, suggesting that continued performance will suffer, that carelessness or skimping on the job will follow unless an extra effort is made, and so on. The statement may also contain a covert reference to physiological impairment, which is briefly reviewed as a preliminary step.

PHYSICAL FATIGUE

In some ways, the most direct approach to fatigue is to have people exert themselves until they drop, or at least until they can no longer put forth the required effort. This kind of procedure may be made to yield quite regular data, for subjects at any given level of motivation. Thus, Caldwell and Lyddan (1971) had army trainees pull repeatedly on a dynamometer handle, during trials separated by brief rest periods. Not surprisingly, the longer the rest period the greater was the recovery, but if we neglect this factor the data appear as in Figure 26. Clearly, the amount of strength which subjects exert decreases during a prolonged contraction, and over a series of trials. However, subjects who knew that they were to get 100-second rest pauses performed better, even on the first trial, than the subjects who were scheduled for 25-second rest pauses, which indicates that central factors like expectancy will influence the performance which is exhibited. In fact, the investigators reject a strictly mechanistic interpretation of their fatigue data, stressing instead the importance of motivation, instructional set, and pain tolerance. In general, the first limit encountered during physical exertion seems most often to be a psychological rather than a physiological boundary.

This kind of problem emerged quite early in the history of fatigue, with Ash's (1914) demonstration that the point at which subjects find it impossible to continue movements on a finger ergograph occurs well before muscular contractions become physiologically impossible. Thus, when his subjects were made to believe that the weight on the finger had been reduced, they found themselves able to begin the contractions again. The idea which this experiment

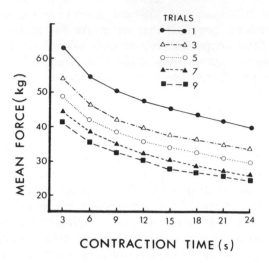

Figure 26. Strength decreases with length of contractions and with the number of successive contractions. From Caldwell and Lyddan (1971). (Reproduced by permission of Journal Publishing Affiliates.)

suggested, namely that the final limit to performance is set by central rather than peripheral factors, is also supported by more recent work. A good example is provided by Schwab (1953), who had people attempt to hang from a parallel bar for as long as possible, under different incentive conditions. Those who were promised a five-dollar reward managed to hang on for almost twice as long as controls, or subjects who were encouraged by the experimenter throughout the test. Jarrard's (1960) result is also interesting, since he showed that the number of times a weight is lifted is affected by the size–weight illusion; the smaller a given weight, the heavier it seems and the fewer the contractions.

The problem of physiological impairment has been attacked directly, although the findings do not altogether coincide. Reid (1929) continued contractions until they were no longer voluntarily possible, but found that he could still contract his muscles by electrical stimulation. However, Merton (1954) did manage to make voluntary contractions to the point where, with the local blood supply occluded, electrical stimulation was ineffective. Other similar evidence suggests that it is possible that peripheral limitations exist, although a recent survey of physiological findings (Simonson, 1971) concludes that the central versus peripheral issue in local muscular fatigue remains unsolved. The most recent experimental approach has been to 'fractionate' reaction times by separately measuring the pre-motor reaction time, which elapses between stimulus onset and the appearance of action potentials, and the motor time interval which occurs before electrical activity is converted into limb displacement. Hanson and Lofthus (1978) fatigued swimmers and tennis players with repeated handgrips on a dynamometer, finding that the pre-motor time became longer but the motor time did not. Although such data favour a central explanation of muscle decrement, Stull and Kearney (1978) found the reverse effect, with a change in the peripheral, motor time resulting from slightly more strenuous activity.

Although we cannot resolve the fundamental issue it seems clear that the possibility of peripheral fatigue is unlikely to be a factor in everyday performance, since no effect has been observed outside rather stringent conditions, like prolonged exertion at 70 per cent of maximum strength, or exertion sufficient to produce a 60 per cent strength loss. Of course, if exercise is sufficiently strenuous to incur an oxygen debt, the effects of accumulating lactic acid cannot be entirely neglected. Eventually, perhaps a distinction is needed between fatigue and exhaustion, although it is certainly clear that central factors play a very large part in determining physical performance.

PERCEPTUAL FATIGUE

Visual sensitivity

All of the senses show habituation or adaptation effects which are sometimes viewed as 'fatigue': in fact, the primary response in each modality is to change of stimulation. Loss of sensation occurs when skin pressure is evenly maintained, or when the same odour persists in the nostrils, or when a stabilized image is held in the same position on the retina, and so on. So-called auditory fatigue appears as a temporary threshold shift, such that sounds of constant pitch come to require greater loudness for detection; this is most often a local effect of impaired cochlear function, although Ward (1973) distinguishes five different forms of the effect. Our concern here is primarily wih the more generalized, long-term effects of perceptual fatigue.

Much of the relevant work has been on visual fatigue, since 'eyestrain' has been thought to constitute a practical problem—so much so that, in 1938, a committee of visual scientists was assembled by the U.S. National Research Council to deal with the potential problems arising from the growth of microfilm reading in libraries. Unfortunately, the chairman at the final meeting summed up as follows: 'At the symposium in Washington there was a group of individuals who together know as much, if not more, about fatigue than is known by anyone else. Yet, I think it is fair to say that probably the most outstanding thing about the meeting was the general uncertainty, not only as how to determine the presence of fatigue, but even as to just what visual fatigue was' (Bartley and Chute, 1947, p.44). However, a good many factual results have been obtained.

By the time of Bartley and Chute's review it appeared to have been established that visual thresholds remain essentially unchanged over time; although Berger and Mahneke (1954) have since shown apparent declines in visual acuity over a 1-hour session. A number of changes take place as a function of initial adaptation, the insertion of rest pauses, and changes of posture during rest, but the most systematic declines are in alertness rather than in sensitivity. Another short-term effect follows steady fixations which fatigue a part of the retina, such that enhanced sensitivity develops in adjacent areas. Coloured objects, particularly red, tend to become desaturated after prolonged fixations, although this again is a short-term phenomenon. Flicker fusion frequency, the rate at which a flashing light appears steady, tends to vary with hours of work and with lack of sleep, although there are many inconsistencies in the data. A recent paper (Volle, Brisson, Dion, and Tanaka, 1978) suggests that the difficulties arise because flicker fusion reflects both an arousal component provoked by the task and a depression component resulting from fatigue on the task.

There are also eye muscle effects, such as changes in accommodation, with some subjects showing reduced ability to focus on test objects over time. The range over which accommodation is possible may be reduced more after many, separate attempts than after sustained efforts; unfortunately, most often these changes do not coincide with reported feelings of tiredness. Measurements have also been made of convergence of the two eyes, which become more difficult over time in reduced illumination. Pupillary contractions seem to behave irregularly over time, but without systematic effects. Rate of blinking, on the other hand, seems to correlate reasonably well with reported visual fatigue; a good example from an industrial setting is shown in Figure 27. In general, as one progresses from more peripheral measurements towards more integrated behaviour, the signs of fatigue tend to increase. Thus, tests of

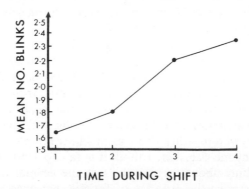

TIME DURING SHIFT

Figure 27. Mean number of blinks made by female machinists reading a test panel at various times during the afternoon shift. From Krivolahvy *et al.* (1969). (Reproduced by permission of Taylor and Francis Ltd.)

reading ability, especially using fine print, do often show decrements. The so-called conflict methods, in which the central control and co-ordination of pupillary reflexes and other oculomotor functions are tested, reveal increasing irregularities as reading and fixation tasks are extended over time.

Vigilance

Long-term visual tasks show most of the characteristics typical of vigilance tasks, in which declines in efficiency seem to result from lowered alertness. As originally conceived, vigilance tasks were those in which an operator had to detect the presence of infrequent, unpredictable, poorly discriminable signals. These characteristics are all manipulable in broader studies of sustained attention, most of which show decreases in the number of correct detections over prolonged periods of watch. Vigilance performance is improved by greater signal density, regularity, intensity, and duration, and by the increased probability of signals relative to other events; it is also improved by stimulants such as benzedrine, by rest pauses or interruptions, and by knowledge of results and rewards, but is impaired by loss of sleep and by some environmental stresses. The review by Loeb and Alluisi (1977) leads to the conclusion that several types of theory are required in order to account for all of the findings.

The general level of activation or arousal of the nervous system, more fully discussed in Chapter 12, is one factor which seems to determine vigilance effects. Thus, for example, loss of sleep is seen as depressing arousal and signal density as increasing arousal. However, there are discrepancies between various physiological and behavioural measures of arousal; techniques like skin resistance or muscle potential or cortical potential measurement may indicate increased arousal in conditions where fewer correct detections are made. In any case, arousal theories are currently too general to yield detailed predictions in many tasks. At an intermediate level of analysis, theoretical formulations of an expectancy type, or related conditioning or cognitive types, may be needed. The expected signal frequency, for example, partially determines performance, and it also appears that observing responses made by the subject are influenced by success or failure in detecting successive signals. At a similar level, filter theory describes instances of missed signals in terms of lapses by the attention mechanisms, thus relating vigilance phenomena to other experimental paradigms.

At yet another level of analysis, the statistical theory of signal detectability raises the question of whether correct detections are solely a question of sensory discrimination. Applications of the theory make it possible to disentangle changes in the discriminability of signals, against background or neural noise, from changes in the criteria which subjects use in reporting detections. Thus, a subject who obtains many correct detections may show by his commission of 'false alarms' that he is making rather risky judgements, or or even guessing, whereas a subject who gets many correct detections with few false positives is discriminating well. Until a few years ago the consensus of most researchers was that vigilance decrements were basically due to criterion changes, with subjects tending to become more cautious in reporting detections as time elapsed. However, Parasuraman and Davies (1977) have collected together a substantial number of studies which show decrements in sensitivity, instead of or in addition to changes in response criteria, and have made a classification of the tasks involved. It appears that the visual and auditory tasks showing declines in sensitivity are those which present a high event rate, with stimuli occurring every 2 or 3 seconds, and which demand an ability to make rapid perceptual comparisons involving memory.

FATIGUE DURING SKILLED PERFORMANCE

We have seen that physical effort tends to be reduced with repeated performance over time, as do various forms of perceptual efficiency, and that some measures of attentiveness or alertness fall with prolonged time on task. In each case, we are primarily concerned with the deterioration in an activity which is caused by performing that activity, rather than with the deterioration caused by a prior, fatiguing task. As Gagné (1953) pointed out, the tasks which show straightforward deterioration over time tend to be simple ones which present repetitive stimulation, as in the cases reviewed above. When more complex, and perhaps arousing, stimulus conditions obtain, the effects of prolonged work are often less direct. A good deal remains to be said about deterioration in skilled or complex tasks, before turning to the consequences of fatigue for other activities.

The Cambridge Cockpit studies

A major advance in analysing task fatigue was provided by the Cambridge Cockpit studies mentioned earlier, in which subjects sat for long periods, responding on aircraft controls to changes in a variety of instruments. The deterioration of skill over time, described by Bartlett (1943), was shown by a number of measures. As alertness declined, progressively larger deviations of the instrument readings came to be tolerated before any corrective action was taken; this apparently resulted from a shift in standards of performance, since the operators felt that they were remaining as efficient as they were at the outset. However, lapses in attention happened with increasing frequency, as operators became more easily distracted. Attention began to be reserved for items of central importance, like the course heading and speed indicators, while peripheral items like the fuel gauge were neglected. A similar constriction of attention towards central items has since been found in hot and humid conditions by Bursill (1958), and in noise by Hockey (1970), although the effect is by no means always obtained.

Further evidence of the deterioration of cockpit skill was that the skilled operators' responses became more variable, quite apart from any drop in their accuracy. This was partially evident in their timing, in that many correct actions were executed at the wrong time. In general, the skill seemed to lose cohesion, the overall pattern of action disintegrated into separate components, the instruments were apparently perceived one by one, and the appropriate control responses were no longer smoothly sequenced. There were also some interesting subjective observations: the operators' reports became less reliable; violent language gradually replaced mild sighs; errors were blamed on the apparatus, so that levers and switches were imagined to be recalcitrant; there was an increased awareness of physical discomfort, with external cues often ascribed to bodily origins. Davis (1948) has further suggested that any failure to meet implied or objective standards or performance causes anxiety, which in turn worsens the performance.

The nature of skill deterioration

Some of the other conclusions concerning the features of skill deterioration have also been carried further. For example, the broad picture of disorganization of performance has been verified by Bates, Osternig, and James (1977) who collected film records of the movements of highly skilled runners at the beginning and end of a relay race, analysing the running action into eight different phases of movement. Running became slower as fatigue mounted, primarily because of a reduction in stride length rather than a change in pace. However, the changes in movement patterns did not follow a uniform decrease. The times for components like foot descent and foot strike became longer, while the forward swing became faster and other measures remained constant. These kinds of change in the interrelationships of a sequence of movement components again suggest a breakdown in the organization of skill, at least with respect to the central control of timing.

The variability which often develops in responding can be measured directly, using statistical techniques. Fraser (1953) has recommended the use of z scores to give a standardized indication of the variability of responses; his data show that variability may increase during visual detection even when no other changes take place. Again, reaction times have long been known to become irregular during fatigue, a findings which Bills (1931) brought to prominence in his identification of 'blocks', or extra long response times, during prolonged colour naming; Broadbent (1958) has reviewed similar effects. However, choice reaction time is only one aspect of complex performance. It is most likely that fatigue and other stresses provoke separate changes in correct and error response times, at the same time as changes in speed–accuracy relationships, as subjects adapt their strategies to changed conditions. A promising model to account for these changes is described by Rabbitt (1981).

The practical implications of changes due to fatigue should be seen in long distance driving and flying, both areas which have been fairly extensively investigated. In fact, these skills hold up well under normal conditions, but increasing lapses of attention should occasionally result in accidents. Unfortunately, the accident rate is a coarse measure, and accidents eventuate from multiple causes, with the result that quite thorough studies reported by McFarland (1953) fail to show any clear effects of operational fatigue in long hours of flying, while driving accidents may actually decrease over hours at the wheel. Brown (1967), who has carried out a series of experiments on car driving, concludes that the most satisfactory way to assess driving fatigue is to make use of the subjective impressions of the tester. His own data failed to show any effects of prolonged driving on the performance of a subsidiary task, despite the fact that the extra loading imposed by the secondary task technique is often successful in revealing the effects of stress. Furthermore, scores on vigilance for the appearance of a light in the driving mirror actually improved during the driving session.

Some deterioration in skill was recorded by Herbert and Jaynes (1964), in a large-scale test of manoeuvring a three-quarter ton truck over a fatigue course. They used a composite score, based on items like backing into a maze, which did show a small decline over hours of rough driving. On the other hand, stronger effects can apparently be obtained in simulators, which provide controlled conditions and a variety of component scores, but perhaps less than real-life motivation. Dureman and Boden (1972) found that during 4 hours of simulated driving there were changes in the subjective ratings of fatigue, accompanied by changes in performance measures such as steering errors and braking reactions, and in several physiological measures including pulse-rate and skin resistance. The steering errors are shown in Figure 28, contrasting the curves for individual subjects. In addition, motivation was manipulated by offering the threat of electric shock, which increased arousal and reduced steering errors.

One of the many difficulties in investigating fatigue is that the different kinds of measure rarely coincide in the manner described above. It often happens that subjects feel tired but work efficiently, or suffer impairment without apparently recognizing their fatigue. Poffenberger (1928) found quite early that although 'feeling tone' decreased in all of his four cognitive tasks, performance was maintained in two, fell in one, and actually rose in the other. Similar discrepancies were observed quite recently by Pierson and Rich (1967) in a repetitive motor task. Work decrements in terms of movement and reaction time were minor and were uncorrelated with oxygen consumption measures of physiological cost, or subjective reports of fatigue. Clearly, one cannot rely on using self-reports to predict other kinds of decrement. Another kind of difficulty is that using interpolated tests, or separate final tests, instead of measurements taken from the task itself, often fail to reveal fatigue effects.

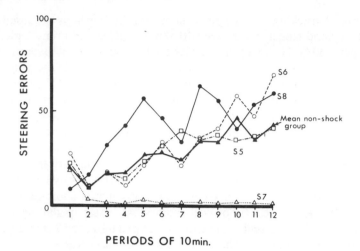

Figure 28. Steering errors tend to increase over time. The mean scores, and the scores for the four subjects (S5, S6, S7, and S8) who compose the non-shock group, are plotted separately. Note that S7 shows no evidence of fatigue. From Dureman and Boden (1972). (Reproduced by permission of Taylor and Francis Ltd.)

The question here is identical to the problem of the transfer of fatigue to subsequent tasks, an area where the effects are equally difficult to observe.

CONSEQUENCES OF FATIGUE

After-effects of work

If the concept of fatigue is to have any predictive value it should be possible to show the after-effects of fatigue on different tasks. Unfortunately, as indicated above, there are very few successful studies. One of the most dramatic failures to find fatigue effects was contributed by Chiles (1955). His subjects performed continuously in an aircraft simulator for as long as 56 hours without rest, with the exception that they were periodically required to go for testing on a tracking task. Towards the end of the experiment some of the subjects were so exhausted that they had to be carried to the test apparatus; nevertheless, their scores on the test were well within normal limits. This kind of difficulty, due to the apparent specificity of work deterioration, runs right through the literature of fatigue. An earlier example of the same kind was provided by Warren and Clark (1937), whose operators showed little or no decrements on a variety of mental and motor tests despite being kept on duty for as long as 65 hours.

Strenuous physical activity seems to fare no better in producing non-specific after-effects. Thus, Hammerton and Tickner (1968) obtained a very brief depression of tracking scores after violent exercise, perhaps explainable as an artefact of hand steadiness in line with known effects (Gutin, Fogle, Meyer, and Jaeger, 1974). However, the results of three subsequent experiments were completely negative when Hammerton (1971) explored the effects of a strenuous version (one foot up and down each second, for 200 seconds) of the Harvard step task, on a cognitive task of grammatical transformations. Whether the whole test followed the exercise, or only the initial part of the test was administered, in before-and-after designs, or whether the test was completely unfamiliar, being first met following the exercise, there were no differences between 'fatigued' and rested subjects. It is perhaps unsurprising that lighter exercise may even have a reverse effect, improving alertness and helping performance on a detection task involving short-term memory. Davey's (1973) subjects improved somewhat after pedalling a bicycle ergometer for 15–20 seconds, and more after pedalling for 2 minutes, but less again after 5 or 10 minutes. The data seemed to fit an inverted-U, arousal type of function, with optimum at the point where the subject had performed 20,000 foot-pounds of work.

If light exercise is directly compared with heavy exercise, both directions of effect may sometimes be observed. Dickinson, Medhurst, and Whittingham (1979) tried an accurate, reciprocal tapping task after different conditions of manual cranking on an ergometer. Light exercise always facilitated the tapping scores, but heavy exercise did depress the scores when the arm used in tapping was the fatigued arm, again showing the specificity of physical fatigue. This impression was reinforced in a second experiment where running on a treadmill, even to the point of voluntary exhaustion, continued to facilitate the tapping rather than impair it. Another complication is that when subjects in the first experiment were given a re-test, after a day's rest, even the group which had heavy exercise with the preferred arm showed no residual deficit. This suggests that the effects of fatigue are not only highly specific, but are limited to temporary performance rather than learning.

An experiment by Welford, Brown, and Gabb (1950) on fatigue in civilian air crews did suggest a learning effect, in that scores on their electrical problem-solving test remained poor on re-test for those who had first met the task while fatigued, but there have been no direct confirmations of the effect (which could arise as a consequence of anoxia in unpressurized aircraft). It is obviously possible, as Holding (1965) suggested with respect to massed versus distributed practice effects, that a temporary depression of performance will reduce the amount of effective practice undertaken, which in turn will have an indirect effect on learning scores. However, this possibility seems unimportant in the context of physical skills, where the question has been investigated most extensively, except in the special case where the fatiguing activity is maintained throughout the learning period (e.g. Pack, Cotten, and Biasiotto, 1974). The results vary somewhat according to the length of practice, the learning score employed, the interval before final test, and both the type and amount of fatiguing activity, but we may perhaps take the findings of Cotten, Thomas, Spieth, and Biasiotto (1972) as a representative example. In their study whole-body fatigue was induced by a stool-stepping procedure, while the test task consisted of bouncing a volleyball from a wall onto a target viewed in a mirror. The performance scores on successive trials, or 'learning curves', differed appreciably (see Figure 29) between rested subjects, subjects who were fatigued for 7 minutes before beginning the mirror-toss trials, and subjects who had fatigue bouts interpolated between the mirror-toss trials. However, the crucial test came on the following day when subjects were re-tested while fresh. There were no differences between the groups, implying that learning had been unaffected by the fatigue procedure.

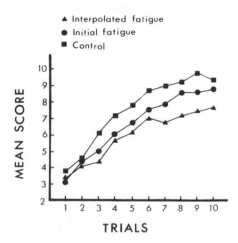

Figure 29. Motor skill performance during practice trials as affected by physical fatigue. These differences did not persist in later learning. From Cotten *et al.* (1972). (Reproduced by permission of Journal Publishing Associates.)

After-effects of fatigue have been found in a few isolated instances. The early work by Ryan and Warner (1936) did seem to indicate drops, and increased variability, in a variety of tests given after more than 8 hours driving on the road, the greatest effect appearing in the rather obscure skill of colour-naming. It is difficult to know how to explain these results, in view of the failures to identify flying fatigue reported by McFarland (1953), and especially since the essentially similar studies already mentioned yielded negative effects. It is possible, of course, that the effects were basically motivational, the subjects behaving as they knew they were expected to behave, although there is no evidence that this was the case. It may be that driving is a particularly stressful activity, especially since no automatic pilot is available, and that colour-naming is tapping into an aversion to mental effort; on the other hand, colour-naming improves in noise (Broadbent, 1978). In any case, fatigue after-effects are most often found when the test activity is very specifically related to the fatiguing activity. In the extreme case, this occurs when a second bout of the same exercise is affected by the first (Kearney and Stull, 1974). Less directly, Lance and Chaffin (1971) found that the fatigue induced by holding weights did transfer its effects to the movement times, particularly those for the secondary corrective movements, in a serial tracking task executed by the fatigued arm. One may reasonably conclude that the evidence for transfer of fatigue is extremely limited in scope.

Methodological difficulties with studies of after-effects

There seem to be three main reasons why attempts to find non-specific effects of fatigue should generally fail. The first is that interpolated or subsequent tests will usually incur the benefit indicated by the adage 'a change is as good as a rest'. This idea is consistent with the earlier conclusion that fatigue is dependent upon repetitive stimulation, and is indirectly confirmed by Adams' (1955) finding that watching others work, or losing the opportunity for a change of stimulation, is equivalent to losing a rest pause; it is also borne out by the early industrial studies, reviewed by Chambers (1961), which showed that switching from job to job gave higher output than remaining on a single task. Indeed, the anomalously positive result of Ryan and Warner (1936) might be explained by the fact that testing was itself repeated over 26 days, thus losing its novelty value and hence its capacity to bring about 'disinhibition' of the fatigue produced by driving.

Another possible reason for the failure of tests is the apparent ability of subjects to compensate, at least over short periods, for any deficit they have incurred. There is a distinction to be made here between open-ended tasks, in which the amount of work is elective and some decrements may be expected, and fixed-requirement tasks. If the task has a clearly defined goal, or standard of performance set by the experimenter, well-motivated subjects usually seem capable of meeting the requirements. This may involve extra effort, as several investigators have assumed, or sometimes a change in strategy; Welford (1958) has described ways in which older subjects may adjust their task strategies to compensate for the effects of ageing which, in some respects, resemble those of fatigue. There is little direct evidence for the idea of compensation after fatigue, despite its plausibility and intuitive appeal, although there is some support derived from Bills and Shapin's (1936) observation that a deterioration in cognitive performance, with subjects working at their own rate, could be postponed by introducing external pacing. Use of the secondary task technique should be effective in tapping the extra effort required for compensation, although it should be remembered that Brown's (1967) use of the method failed to measure driving fatigue.

The third reason for failure may quite simply be that interpolated tests have characteristically attempted to measure the wrong kind of effect. Even tests of cognitive function have not been directed towards the more central changes which are implied by aversion to effort, and by factors like increased irritability which seem to accompany carelessness.

ATTITUDES TOWARDS RISK AND EFFORT

We can be virtually certain that, other things being equal, fatigued subjects will choose to exert less effort. This is in accordance with Bartley and Chute's (1947) conclusions, and seems also to be true of the effects of noise, which Cohen and Spacapan (1978) view as inducing cognitive fatigue. Thus, for example, subjects persist less at insoluble problems (Glass and Singer, 1972) and attempt fewer arithmetic computations (Frankenhaeuser and Lundberg, 1977) when they are exposed to noise, in each case expending less effort. However, when fatigued persons say that they are 'too tired to bother', they seem to be indicating something more than a reluctance to undertake further effort; they may be implying a tendency towards carelessness or 'cutting corners'.

Carelessness and spoilage of materials have been reported (McFarland, 1953) for munitions workers putting in long hours. Again, the pilots in the Cambridge Cockpit experiments, with their disregard for peripheral instruments and lowered standards of accuracy, seem to have developed a degree of negligence which is tantamount to a willingness to take chances. Brown, Tickner, and Simmons (1970) found a quite explicit increase in risk-taking, as evidenced by testers' judgements of undue risk in overtaking by car drivers; although the speed of driving decreased somewhat between a first and fourth session of 3 hours driving, the proportion of risky overtaking manoeuvres increased by 50 per cent. These kinds of behaviour seem to imply the acceptance of greater probabilities of failure in the task, or even injuries, in return for savings in time or effort. It is clearly possible to make the trade-off explicit, thus quantifying an important result of fatigue.

Consequently, Holding (1974) has argued that a valuable test of non-specific fatigue should be provided by a paradigm in which the subject is presented with multiple routes to the goal of the task, each differently loaded for effort and for probability of success. Other things being equal, it is clear that subjects will choose the highest probability of success, or lowest risk of failure (Detambel, 1956). However, if probability of success is correlated with amount of effort, it can be predicted that the fatigued subject will shift his choices towards lowered effort, despite the lowered probability of success. Such a task will have the additional advantage of obviating any tendency towards compensation, since it offers no single correct standard for performance to which compensation might be directed. As for the problem of change constituting rest, its effect will depend upon the degree to which the effort required in the test resembles the effort demanded by the fatiguing task. However, it is possible that the factors measured are sufficiently central that the effect will be relatively immune to disruption by change.

After some initial experimentation, the COPE (choice of probability/effort) test has been developed as a three-choice task with 1, 2, or 3 units of effort associated with probabilities of 0.17, 0.33, or 0.50 of success. The basic paradigm can clearly be expressed in many forms. For a first full-scale test (Shingledecker and Holding, 1974), the apparatus was designed as an electrical fault-finding task, with effort represented by checking components containing 1, 2, or 3 resistors. A trial began with choosing a component for test; activating an ammeter, thus incidentally starting a timer; testing the appropriate resistors and logging the current flow; then pressing a button to obtain knowledge of results, thus stopping the timer. If the fault had been correctly identified, a red light and buzzer were activated, and the trial concluded; if not, another component was selected for test and the procedure was repeated until the fault was located. This test was used before and after normal activities by control subjects, and before and after a group of experimental subjects were fatigued by 24–32 hours of work on a battery of monitoring and cognitive tasks (Morgan and Alluisi, 1972).

During the pre-test trials, the scores gradually rose as subjects became aware of the probabilities, until they chose the highest probability about 50 per cent of the time. In the later test, the control subjects continued at the same level of choice, or slightly higher, but the fatigued subjects dropped their choice of high probability to about 25 per cent. Similar effects can be seen in Figure 30. It is clear, therefore, that fatigued subjects can be shown to make more risky

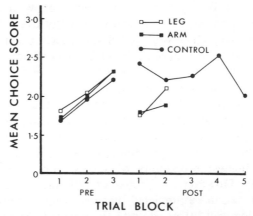

Figure 30. Mean choice scores before and after fatigue (or control) treatments. Low, middle, and high choices are given the respective values 1, 2, or 3, so that a drop in score indicates a shift towards lower probability and effort. From Barth *et al.* (1976). (Reproduced by permission of Journal Publishing Associates.)

choices despite the fact that the fatigue test is non-specific, both the stimuli and responses differing considerably between the fatiguing and test tasks. Furthermore, the decrement measured in the COPE test agrees substantially with subjective ratings of fatigue, which also separated the control and experimental subjects. A second experiment was designed to confirm whether the COPE test was measuring the same factors which determine subjective fatigue, using only control subjects whose level of fatigue varied naturally. There was in fact a correlation of 0.71 between risky choices and self-ratings of fatigue, suggesting that the test was appreciably sensitive to individual differences.

The next issue investigated was the degree to which fatigue is specific to motor or perceptual tasks. Barth, Holding, and Stamford (1976) began by exposing experimental subjects either to brief, intense physical exertion on an inclined treadmill or to long-term exertion on a bicycle ergometer, followed by testing on the largely perceptual resistor-checking device. As might be expected, there was virtually no effect beyond a difference in the error scores attributable to hand tremor, confirming the commonly made distinction between physical fatigue and perceptual or mental fatigue. Next, the effort component of the COPE design was embodied in a motor form. The choice was now between cranking an arm ergometer for 15, 30, or 45 seconds, again with probabilities of 0.17, 0.33, or 0.50 of eliciting a successful knowledge of results signal. Fatigue could be motor but non-specific, induced by pedalling a bicycle ergometer, or completely specific to arm-cranking.

The results, shown in Figure 30, are strikingly similar to the earlier data of Shingledecker and Holding (1974). The pre-test scores increase as the probabilities are learned, the post-test scores remain stable for the control subjects and drop for the experimental groups. The upper curve was continued for further trials in order to see whether performing the COPE test was itself fatiguing, which finally proved to be the case. There is some recovery during the post-test, understandably greater for the leg fatigue group than for the arm fatigue group. A similar recovery was present in the earlier data; in both cases it comes about because the subjects soon realize that choosing lower probabilities does not really save effort, owing to the design of the task. The initial drop after fatigue occurred as predicted, even when leg fatigue was measured by arm effort, confirming that non-specific fatigue engenders riskier choices when these promise to conserve effort. The COPE scores were again correlated with self-ratings of fatigue, which encourages the belief that a sharp distinction between subjective fatigue and measurable performance need not always be maintained.

FINAL REMARKS

The choice paradigm has further potential for measuring fatigue and can be expected to apply to a variety of tasks. In keeping with Kahneman's (1973) treatment of the cost of maintaining attention in terms of mental effort, cognitive versions of the COPE test may be based on the effort involved in tasks of visual search, mental rotation of figures, or arithmetic performance. Most recently, the COPE technique has been applied to a mathematical task (Holding, Baker, and Loeb, 1981). In this form the test is sensitive to the effects of prolonged work at arithmetic, and to the effects of superimposed noise. Furthermore, risky choices also occur as after-effects when testing is conducted after the noise is switched off. It also seems very possible that the technique will reveal deficits following other stresses, such as ambient heat, which in many ways resemble fatigue.

However, reluctance for exertion, whether mental or physical, cannot be the only measure of the central deterioration which is observed in skill fatigue and which might be expected to transfer to subsequent tasks. Furthermore, it is difficult to deny the anecdotal evidence that tasks with very high processing demands, like top-flight chess play, are affected by prior fatigue. More progress might be expected if after-effects could be predicted from a unified theory of the mechanisms of fatigue although, in view of the complexity of the concept of fatigue, such a theory may be impossible to formulate.

A promising generalization is due to Crawford (1961) who suggests that it is an increase in neural noise which underlies the after-effects of driving fatigue. The changed signal-to-noise ratio will account for sensory fatigue effects, the internal noise will impede decision processes, reaction times, and fine movement control, and will heighten irritability and discomfort. Such a view contrasts with the older assumption that nervous pathways, at least those subserving the fatigued performance, become more unresponsive as fatigue mounts. In the neural noise view the pathways are more rather than less responsive, but more of their output is random, so that efficiency goes down. The neural noise hypothesis has the disadvantage that it is not directly testable, at least by current methods. However, the contrast between increased neural noise and reduced neural function is rather directly analogous to the distinction between high and low states of arousal, which have attracted considerable research. Barring motivational complications, one might expect fatigued subjects to show signs of lowered arousal.

Arousal is more fully discussed elsewhere in this volume, but it is valuable to emphasize that such evidence as there is suggests that fatigue in general, like the vigilance data mentioned earlier, presents a mixed picture of arousal. For example, pilots in the simulated cockpit work showed a depression of attentiveness, but some over-activity in the form of wasted movements. For comparison we might note that, again depending on motivation, the effects of sleep loss may yield increased cortical activity but result in lowered detection rates (Wilkinson, 1964). Perhaps abandoning the use of arousal as a behavioural variable in favour of a more complex physiological classification may be necessary, if cumbersome; there is evidence (Pribram and McGuiness, 1975) to differentiate between a component of cortical arousal, a second component of response activation, and a third of co-ordinative effort. This division would separate, for instance, the over-activity from the decision effects, but does not solve all of the problems.

Speculation might be simpler if one could regard fatigue as the product of over-arousal in contrast with boredom resulting from under-arousal. Those fatigue effects which showed depression of activity would then be explained as after-effects, while the discrepant indices of increased arousal would be explained as products of stress during the process of fatigue. However, boredom and fatigue do not seem to be separable in this way, and even those studies directed at boredom have shown mixed effects. London, Schubert, and Washburn (1972) found that boring tasks, like repeatedly writing 'cd, cd, cd', led to increases in heart-rate and galvanic skin potential, rather than the reverse; and Bailey, Thackray, Pearl, and Parish (1976), in an air traffic control task, found increased body movement and heart-rate variability along with decreased blood pressure, mean heart-rate and skin conductance. A more sophisticated approach to arousal theory of the kind proposed by Hamilton, Hockey, and Rejman (1977), where stresses are seen as vectors describing the direction and amount of change in central control processes, may eventually provide an acceptable theoretical framework for detailed predictions concerning fatigue and boredom.

There remains a residue of relatively well-established empirical findings on fatigue. A good deal is known about both perceptual and motor deterioration during prolonged performance, and about the ways in which skill disintegrates during complex tasks. It seems relatively clear why later tests usually fail to show the effects of prior fatigue, although pitting risk against effort, in conditions where incentives towards compensation are avoided, does yield the predicted effects. Moreover, the fact that these measurements correlate well with subjectively rated fatigue offers hope that a fragmentary approach to the fatigue problem will be unnecessary; probably the rigid separation between work decrement and subjective fatigue, quite recently reiterated (Bartley, 1976), need not be maintained. Being tired may be a complicated state, in need of further explication, but there is no real need to abandon the concept of fatigue.

SUMMARY

Fatigue presents a complex problem for research, which can be made more manageable by considering only the effects of prolonged periods of work or duty. Physical fatigue is usually modifiable by incentives, since a psychological boundary precedes the physiological limit; it seems likely that even local muscular fatigue is centrally rather than peripherally determined. Perceptual fatigue is most evident in tasks with strong central components and may often be a function of decreased alertness or vigilance, which are thought to depend on arousal and expectancy. Fatigue effects are most readily measured during the actual performance of many tasks, appearing as direct decrements when stimulation is repetitive and showing a variety of the consequences of central deterioration in complex skills. On the other hand, interpolated or subsequent measurements on different tasks have not generally shown any after-effects of fatigue, for several reasons depending on change, compensation, and inappropriateness. However, methods which permit the subject a choice of responses have indicated changed attitudes towards acceptance of risk and avoidance of effort, for mental and motor fatigue, which are consistent with subjective expressions of tiredness; it is to be expected that other similar components of fatigue can be identified. Fatigue may perhaps be viewed as an increase in neural noise, although developments in arousal theory may eventually provide a better articulated description of the processes responsible for fatigue and other forms of stress.

REFERENCES

Adams, J. A. (1955) A source of decrement in psychomotor skills. *Journal of Experimental Psychology*, **49**, 390–394.

Ash, I. E. (1914) Fatigue and its effects upon control. *Archives of Psychology*, **4**, 1–61.

Bailey, J. P., Thackray, R. I., Pearl, J., and Parish, T. S. (1976) Boredom and arousal: Comparison of tasks differing in visual complexity. *Perceptual and Motor Skills*, **43**, 141–142.

Barmack, J. E. (1939) The length of the work period and the work curve. *Journal of Experimental Psychology*, **25**, 109–115.

Barth, J. L., Holding, D. H., and Stamford, B. A. (1976) Risk versus effort in the assessment of motor fatigue. *Journal of Motor Behavior*, **8**, 189–194.

Bartlett, F. C. (1943) Fatigue following highly skilled work. *Proceedings of the Royal Society*, Series B, **131**, 247–257.

Bartley, S. H. (1976). What do we call fatigue? In E. Simonson and P. C. Weiser (eds.), *Psychological Aspects and Physiological Correlates of Work and Fatigue*. Springfield, Ill.: C. C. Thomas.

Bartley, S. H. and Chute, E. (1947) *Fatigue and Impairment in Man*. New York: McGraw-Hill.

Bates, B. T., Osternig, L. R., and James, S. L. (1977). Fatigue effects in running. *Journal of Motor Behavior*, **9**, 203–207.

Berger, C. and Mahneke, A. (1954) Fatigue in two simple visual tasks. *American Journal of Psychology*, **67**, 509–512.

Bills, A. G. (1931) Blocking: A new principle in mental fatigue. *American Journal of Psychology*, **43**, 230–245.

Bills, A. G. (1934) *General Experimental Psychology*. New York: Longmans Green.

Bills, A. G. and Shapin, M. J. (1936). Mental fatigue under automatically controlled rates of work. *Journal of General Psychology*, **15**, 335–347.

Broadbent, D. E. (1958) *Perception and Communication*. London: Pergamon.

Broadbent, D. E. (1978) Low levels of noise and the naming of colors. *Third International Congress on Noise as a Public Health Problem*. Freiburg.

Broadbent, D. E. (1979) The Society's lecture: Is a fatigue test now possible? *Ergonomics*, **22**, 1227–1290.

Brown, I. D. (1967) Measurement of control skills, vigilance and performance of a subsidiary task during 12 hr of car driving. *Ergonomics*, **10**, 665–673.

Brown, I. D., Tickner, A. H., and Simmons, D. C. (1970) Effect of prolonged driving on overtaking criteria. *Ergonomics*, **13**, 239–242.

Bursill, A. E. (1958) The restriction of peripheral vision during exposure to hot and humid conditions. *Quarterly Journal of Experimental Psychology*, **10**, 113–129.

Caldwell, L. S. and Lyddan, J. M. (1971) Serial isometric fatigue functions with variable intertrial intervals. *Journal of Motor Behavior*, **3**, 17–30.

Cameron, C. (1973) A theory of fatigue. *Ergonomics*, **16**, 633–648.

Chambers, E. A. (1961) Industrial fatigue. *Occupational Psychology*, **35**, 44–57.

Chiles, W. D. (1955) *Experimental Studies of Prolonged Wakefulness.* Dayton, Ohio: W.A.D.C. Tech. Report No. 55–395.

Cohen, S. and Spacapan, S. (1978) The aftereffects of stress: An attentional interpretation. *Environmental Psychology and Nonverbal Behavior*, **3**, 43–56.

Cotten, D. J., Thomas, J. R., Spieth, W. R., and Biasiotto, J. (1972) Temporary fatigue effects in a gross motor skill. *Journal of Motor Behavior*, **4**, 217–222.

Crawford, A. (1961) Fatigue and driving. *Ergonomics*, **4**, 143–154.

Davey, C. P. (1973) Physical exertion and mental performance. *Ergonomics*, **16**, 595–599.

Davis, D. R. (1948) The disorder of skill responsible for accidents. *Quarterly Journal of Experimental Psychology*, **1**, 136–142.

Detambel, M. H. (1956) Probabilities of success and amounts of work in a multichoice situation. *Journal of Experimental Psychology*, **51**, 41–44.

Dickinson, J., Medhurst, C., and Whittingham, N. (1979) Warm-up and fatigue in skill acquisition and performance. *Journal of Motor Behavior*, **11**, 81–86.

Dureman, E. I. and Boden, C. (1972) Fatigue in simulated car driving. *Ergonomics*, **15**, 299–308.

Frankenhauser, M. and Lundberg, U. (1977) The influence of cognitive set on performance and arousal under different noise loads. *Motivation and Emotion*, **1**, 139–145.

Fraser, D. C. (1953) The relation of an environmental variable to performance in a prolonged visual task. *Quarterly Journal of Experimental Psychology*, **5**, 31–32.

Gagné, R. M. (1953) Task variables in fatigue. In W. F. Floyd and A. T. Welford (eds.), *Symposium on Fatigue.* London: H. K. Lewis.

Glass, D. C. and Singer, J. E. (1972) *Urban Stress.* New York: Academic Press.

Gutin, B., Fogle, R. K., Meyer, J., and Jaeger, M. (1974). Steadiness as a function of prior exercise. *Journal of Motor Behavior*, **6**, 69–76.

Hamilton, P., Hockey, G. R. J., and Rejman, R. (1977) The place of the concept of activation in human information processing theory: An integrative approach. In S. Dornic (ed.), *Attention and Performance, VI.* Hillsdale, N.J.: Erlbaum Associates.

Hammerton, M. (1971). Violent exercise and a cognitive task. *Ergonomics*, **14**, 265–267.

Hammerton, M. and Tickner, A. H. (1968) Physical fitness and skilled work after exercise. *Ergonomics*, **11**, 41–45.

Hanson, C. and Lofthus, G. K. (1978) Effects of fatigue and laterality on fractionated reaction time. *Journal of Motor Behavior*, **10**, 177–184.

Herbert, M. J. and Jaynes, W. E. (1964) Performance decrement in vehicle driving. *Journal of Engineering Psychology*, **3**, 1–18.

Hockey, G. R. J. (1970) Signal probability and spatial location as possible bases for increased selectivity in noise. *Quarterly Journal of Experimental Psychology*, **22**, 37–42.

Holding, D. H. (1965) *Principles of Training.* London: Pergamon.

Holding, D. H. (1974) Risk, effort and fatigue. In M. G. Wade and R. Martens (eds.), *Psychology of Motor Behavior and Sport.* Urbana, Ill.: Human Kinetics.

Holding, D. H., Baker, M. A., and Loeb, M. (1981) Work, noise, risk and effort. Paper to the annual meeting of the Human Factors Society, Rochester, October, 1981.

Jarrard, L. E. (1960) The role of visual cues in the performance of ergographic work. *Journal of Experimental Psychology*, **60**, 57–63.

Kahneman, D. (1973). *Attention and Effort.* Englewood Cliffs, N.J.: Prentice-Hall.

Kearney, J. T. and Stull, G. A. (1974) Fatigue patterns during second bouts of rhythmic and sustained exercise as a function of intertrial rest. *Journal of Motor Behavior*, **6**, 111–123.

Krivolahvy, J., Kodat, V., and Cizek, P. (1969) Visual efficiency and fatigue during the afternoon shift. *Ergonomics*, **12**, 735–740.

Lance, B. M. and Chaffin, D. B. (1971) The effect of prior muscle exertions on simple movements. *Human Factors*, **13**, 355–362.

Loeb, M. and Alluisi, E. A. (1977) An update of findings regarding vigilance and a reconsideration of underlying mechanisms. In R. R. Mackie (ed.), *Vigilance: Theory, Operational Performance and Physiological Correlates.* New York: Plenum Press.

London, H., Schubert, D. S. P., and Washburn, D. (1972) Increase of arousal by boredom. *Journal of Abnormal Psychology*, **80**, 29–36.

McFarland, R. A. (1953) *Human Factors in Air Transportation.* New York: McGraw-Hill.

Merton, P. A. (1954) Voluntary strength and fatigue. *Journal of Physiology*, **123**, 553–564.

Morgan, B. B. and Alluisi, E. A. (1972) Synthetic work: Methodology for assessment of human performance. *Perceptual and Motor Skills*, **35**, 835–845.

Muscio, B. (1921) Is a fatigue test possible? *British Journal of Psychology*, **12**, 31–46.

Pack, M., Cotten, D. J., and Biasiotto, J. (1974) Effect of four fatigue levels on performance and learning of a novel dynamic balance skill. *Journal of Motor Behavior*, **6**, 191–198.

Parasuraman, R. and Davies, D. R. (1977) A taxonomic analysis of vigilance performance. In R. R. Mackie (ed.), *Vigilance: Theory, Operational Performance Physiological Correlates.* New York: Plenum Press.

Pierson, W. R. and Rich, G. O. (1967) Energy expenditure and fatigue during simple repetitive tasks. *Human Factors*, **9**, 563–566.

Poffenberger, A. T. (1928) The effects of continuous work upon output and feelings. *Journal of Applied Psychology*, **12**, 459–467.

Pribram, K. H. and McGuiness, D. (1975) Arousal, activation and effort in the control of attention. *Psychological Review*, **82**, 116–149.

Rabbitt, P. M. A. (1981) Sequential reactions. In D. H. Holding (ed.), *Human Skills.* Chichester: John Wiley & Sons.

Reid, C. (1929) The mechanism of voluntary muscular fatigue. *Quarterly Journal of Experimental Physiology*, **19**, 17–42.

Ryan, A. H. and Warner, M. (1936). The effect of automobile driving on the reactions of the driver. *American Journal of Psychology*, **48**, 403–421.

Schwab, R. S. (1953) Motivation in measurements of fatigue. In W. F. Floyd and A. T. Welford (eds.), *Symposium on Fatigue.* London: H. K. Lewis.

Shingledecker, C. A. and Holding, D. H. (1974). Risk and effort measures of fatigue. *Journal of Motor Behavior*, **6**, 17–25.

Simonson, E. (1971) *Physiology of Work Capacity and Fatigue.* Springfield, Ill.: C. C. Thomas.

Stull, G. A. and Kearney, J. T. (1978) Effects of variable fatigue levels on reaction-time components. *Journal of Motor Behavior*, **10**, 223–232.

Tsaneva, N. and Markov, S. (1971) A model of fatigue. *Ergonomics*, **14**, 11–16.

Volle, M. A., Brisson, G. R., Dion, M., and Tanaka, M. (1978) Travail, fatigue et fréquence de fusion critique visuelle. *Ergonomics*, **21**, 551–558.

Ward, W. D. (1973) Adaptation and fatigue. In J. Jerger (ed.), *Modern Developments in Audiology*. New York: Academic Press.

Warren, N. and Clark, B. (1937) Blocking in mental and motor tasks during a 65-hour vigil. *Journal of Experimental Psychology*, **21**, 97–105.

Welford, A. T. (1958) *Ageing and Human Skill*. Oxford University Press.

Welford, A. T., Brown, R. A., and Gabb, J. E. (1950) Two experiments on fatigue as affecting skilled performance in civilian aircrew. *British Journal of Psychology*, **40**, 195–211.

Wilkinson, R. T. (1964) Effects of up to 60 hours' sleep deprivation on different types of work. *Ergonomics*, **7**, 175–186.

Stress and Fatigue in Human Performance
Edited by G. R. J. Hockey
© 1983 John Wiley & Sons Ltd.

Chapter 7

Incentives

Michael W. Eysenck

One of the most important (yet relatively neglected) areas of research in psychology concerns the effects of motivation on performance. At present, our knowledge is about as profound and accurate as that of thinkers who regard the terrestial globe as flat and who are frightened of falling over one of its edges. However, we do know that motivation involves an amalgam of internal and external factors. This can be seen very simply in the case of hunger, which is determined jointly by internal physiological conditions relating to the number of hours of food deprivation and by external stimuli providing information about the availability of food. While it is important to draw this conceptual distinction between internal and external factors, it is nevertheless true that the two factors interact with each other; for example, the incentive value of a bowl of rice is much greater for a half-starved peasant from the Third World than for a self-indulgent and bloated member of Western society.

A sweeping generalization that captures an important truth is that the history of research on motivation has shown a shift away from an emphasis on internal factors towards an increased awareness of the significance of external factors. Two key figures in this context are Charles Darwin and Fred Skinner. Darwin emphasized the major role played by biological and phylogenetic factors, and this led fairly directly to a theoretical position in which motivational forces were explained primarily in terms of a number of innate instincts. At the opposite extreme, Skinner has consistently focused on the importance of schedules of externally applied positive reinforcement (i.e. reward) in understanding the effects of motivation on behaviour. According to Skinner, behaviour only becomes predictable when we pay close attention to the precise patterning of external response-contingent rewards; in contrast, internal factors play the relatively modest role of determining the extent to which a stimulus is actually reinforcing at any given moment in time.

This chapter deals primarily with the effects of external motivational factors on performance. Many theorists have distinguished between two kinds of external factors: incentives and positive reinforcers or rewards. Incentive motivation has been defined as the energizing effect on behaviour of the anticipation of reinforcing events, which implies that incentives work 'forwards' on events which follow the motivating event. In contrast, it has been argued that the process of reinforcement works 'backwards' on responses preceding the reinforcing event. A further difference between reinforcers and incentives, it has often been asserted, is that reinforcing stimuli usually exert a relatively specific effect on behaviour (i.e. directly strengthening reinforced responses), whereas incentive stimuli have a non-specific energizing function.

Much of this conventional wisdom was convincingly refuted by Bindra (1974), who pointed out that the effects of reinforcing and incentive stimuli are both inferred on the basis of subsequent behaviour. This means that the empirical data do not provide strong evidence that reinforcers work 'backwards', whereas incentives work 'forwards'. The further contention that reinforcing stimuli always strengthen very specific patterns of responding is certainly erroneous. For example, Macfarlane (1930) found that rats were able to swim through a maze successfully when it was full of water, in spite of the fact that all of their previous experience with the maze had involved running through it for reward. Presumably the rats had acquired some kind of 'cognitive map' rather than a stereotyped sequence of specific responses during reinforced learning.

In sum, any complete theory of the effects of motivation on performance would include an analysis of both external and internal determinants of motivation. Incentive stimulation appears to be the most important external motivational factor, and constitutes the major focus of interest in this chapter. It is reasonable to assume that the behavioural effects of incentive stimuli resemble, or are identical to, the effects of reinforcing stimuli.

The second section of this chapter deals with work on the effects of incentive on learning and memory, an area of research which has attracted much interest. The third section deals with broader issues, and considers the major factors determining whether the effects of incentive on performance are beneficial or detrimental. The fourth section is concerned with the relationship between intrinsic and extrinsic motivation, and the final section provides a number of conclusions and speculations.

LEARNING AND MEMORY

The most thoroughly developed theory of the effects of incentive on learning and memory was proposed by Atkinson and Wickens (1971). Their theory relied heavily on the model of memory put forward by Atkinson and Shiffrin (1968), according to which information can only be retained over long periods of time provided that it has been processed in the short-term store, from which it is transferred or 'copied' into the long-term store. This transfer of information usually occurs as a result of rehearsal activity in the short-term store, and the strength of the representation in long-term memory is proportional to the length of time for which rehearsal continues. Within this theoretical framework, Atkinson and Wickens (1971) argued that incentive will improve retention to the extent that it augments the amount of rehearsal activity in the short-term store.

When people are asked to learn a list of items, half of which are associated with a small monetary incentive for correct recall and half with a large incentive, it is usually found that the high-incentive items are better recalled (Harley, 1965; Nelson, 1976; Eysenck and Eysenck, 1980). Cuvo (1974) attempted to assess the extent to which this effect was attributable to differential rehearsal. Subjects were presented with a mixture of high- and low-incentive items, and either rehearsed out loud during input or they counted backwards by threes between the presentation of each word so as to produce a comparably low level of rehearsal of high- and low-incentive words. In line with the theoretical position of Atkinson and Wickens (1971), there was a much reduced incentive effect when rehearsal activity was minimized.

More evidence concerning the importance of rehearsal was obtained by Eysenck and Eysenck (1980). They asked their subjects to rehearse out loud, and discovered that high-incentive words were rehearsed more often than low-incentive words, and also showed much better cued recall. However, they did not definitely establish a causal relationship between amount of rehearsal and probability of recall.

Eysenck and Eysenck (1980) also noted that Atkinson and Wickens (1971) emphasized the notion that incentive affects the amount or quantity of rehearsal. It is also possible that incentive affects the kind or type of processing. For example, if high-incentive stimuli were more likely than low-incentive stimuli to be processed semantically, this would probably produce the usual incentive effect (cf. Craik and Lockhart, 1972). In fact, Eysenck and Eysenck found that incentive increased the extensiveness or elaboration of processing, but it did not alter the type of processing.

All of the evidence discussed so far has been consistent with an extremely simple interpretation of the incentive effect: high-incentive stimuli receive more rehearsal and thus more thorough processing than low-incentive stimuli; this increased rehearsal mediates their greater memorability. Eysenck and Eysenck (unpublished) have cast some doubt on the adequacy of this theory. In the first place, it seems that the short-term storage system is more complicated than was assumed by Atkinson and Wickens (1971). Baddeley and Hitch (1974) argued for the replacement of the short-term store construct with that of working memory. The working memory system consists of two major components: (1) a modality-free central executive, and (2) a more peripheral articulatory loop. Eysenck and Eysenck found that the incentive effect involved working memory, and that both components were probably implicated.

In the second place, Atkinson and Wickens (1971) assumed that the greater amount of rehearsal given to high-incentive words would always lead to enhanced retention. However, they failed to consider the relationship between the conditions at storage and those at retrieval. When subjects are tested in a way which had not been expected (e.g. semantic retrieval cues following phonemic processing instructions), then there is no incentive effect at all (Eysenck and Eysenck, unpublished). The interaction between incentive and cue expectedness is shown in Figure 31. Thus, the greater rehearsal of high-incentive words does *not* lead to more thorough or extensive processing of all of the stimulus features or attributes of such words; rather, incentive produces greater elaboration of processing only for those attributes believed to be relevant to a subsequent retention test.

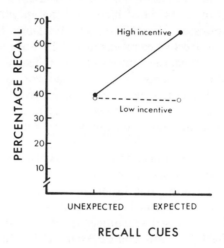

Figure 31. Cued recall as a function of financial incentive and cue expectedness. From Eysenck and Eysenck (unpublished).

Atkinson and Wickens (1971) argued that incentive could also affect retrieval. If information concerning the incentive values of to-be-remembered events is stored at input, then knowledge given at the time of testing regarding the appropriate incentive values associated with each item may increase the efficiency of the search process. In addition, it is likely that subjects will be prepared to spend more time attempting to retrieve high-incentive than low-incentive items, which should presumably increase the retrieval of high-incentive items.

While these suggestions are plausible, it has proved surprisingly difficult to demonstrate any effects of incentive on retrieval. Monetary incentive offered only at the time of recall has typically had no effect on retention (Wasserman, Weiner, and Houston, 1968; Weiner, 1966; Wickens and Simpson, 1968).

However, Loftus and Wickens (1970) found that high-incentive paired associates were better recalled than low-incentive paired associates when information about the incentive value of each pair was only available at the time of recall. In line with the reasoning of Atkinson and Wickens, subjects spent more time attempting recall with the high-incentive pairs, suggesting that the reason why incentive enhanced recall was because it led to increased memory search.

The conclusions which are warranted on the basis of the available research were expressed in the following way by Eysenck (1982):

> A major effect of incentive manipulations is to cause a re-allocation of attention in which certain stimuli (i.e., those associated with high incentives) receive a disproportionate amount of attention at the expense of other stimuli (i.e., those associated with low incentives). In the case of learning tasks, allocation of attention can be roughly indexed by rehearsal activity. The extra attention and rehearsal accorded to high-incentive stimuli simply lead to extra processing of the same kind as that given to low-incentive stimuli, rather than to processing of a different kind.

MAJOR DETERMINANTS OF INCENTIVE EFFECTS

The prevalent view during much of the history of psychology has been that incentives or rewards are beneficial for performance. The most renowned advocate of this point of view is undoubtedly Skinner, who has argued forcefully that a reward or reinforcer is any stimulus event that follows a response and thereby increases the strength (or probability of occurrence) of that response. While there are some uncertainties about the precise definition of a 'response', the clear implication is that rewards or reinforcers have a consistently facilitatory effect on performance. In view of the fact that so much of the research discussed in this chapter has used financial incentives, it is interesting to note that Skinner regards money as a 'universal, generalized reinforcer'.

Not everyone agrees that rewards or incentives are wholly beneficial in their effects. There are signs of a growing anti-reward campaign, as exemplified in the following quotation taken from Condry (1977, pp.471–472):

> Compared to non-rewarded subjects, subjects offered a task-extrinsic incentive choose easier tasks, are less efficient in using the information available to solve novel problems, and tend to be answer oriented and more illogical in their problem-solving strategies. They seem to work harder and produce more activity, but the activity is of a lower quality, contains more errors, and is

more stereotyped and less creative than the work of comparable nonrewarded subjects working on the same problems.

Condry's theoretical stance appears to be radically different to that of Skinner and more in line with the hypothesis originally proposed in the first Epistle of Paul to Timothy: 'Money is the root of all evil.'

How can we reconcile these different viewpoints? The answers to this and other questions depend on a detailed examination of four major factors, which are dealt with in the next four main sections:

(1) Incentive characteristics, such as the amount of incentive and the probability of attaining it.

(2) Task characteristics, including its complexity and duration.

(3) Performance characteristics, especially the comparability or otherwise of different measures of performance efficiency.

(4) Individual characteristics, including susceptibility to reward and susceptibility to frustration.

Accurate prediction of the behavioural consequences of incentive manipulations is only possible when due consideration is paid to all four factors. However, the writer is unaware of a single study in which these four factors were all systematically investigated! In fact, the typical study involves consideration of the effects of various incentive conditions on a single performance measure taken from a single task, with individual differences being ignored entirely.

Without giving away too much of the plot, it is relatively straightforward to identify the major reason for the contrasting views of Skinner and Condry. In most of his research, Skinner has used remarkably simple tasks which require the subject to produce routine and unchanging responses (e.g. lever pressing). The emphasis in such tasks is on performance rather than on the acquisition of new skills. In contrast, Condry's diatribe against reward centres largely on its apparently adverse effects when rather complex concept-attainment or problem-solving tasks are used. As a first approximation, then, incentives or rewards may tend to enhance performance on low-level, routine tasks but to impair performance on at least some kinds of cognitively demanding tasks.

INCENTIVE AND MOTIVATION

Size of incentive

The most obvious way in which incentive conditions can vary is in terms of the amount or size of incentive. While there has been relatively little systematic research, it appears that the relationship between amount of incentive and performance depends on the nature of the task. For example, Suedfeld and Landon (1970) looked at the effects of four levels of incentive (ranging from nothing to 7.50 dollars for being in the top 25 per cent of subjects and 30 dollars for having the best performance) on two different tasks. Incentive had no effect on the free-recall task, whereas performance on a more complex task (naming as many uses as possible for objects) was inversely related to incentive.

There is a dearth of research on the effects of really powerful incentives on performance. One of the few exceptions is a series of studies reported by Eysenck (1964), in which the high-incentive subjects were candidates for entrance to the apprentice training school of a large car manufacturer who were led to believe that their performance on a battery of tests would determine whether or not they were selected. Motivation among these subjects was presumably rather high for a second reason: only approximately 10 per cent of the applicants were selected for the apprenticeship. The low-incentive subjects had previously been accepted for the apprenticeship, and realized that the data being collected were irrelevant to their standing in the training school.

One of the most interesting of the rather bizarre gallimaufry of tasks used was the five-choice serial reaction task. In this task a light comes on at random and remains on until the appropriate response is made; responding to one light simultaneously switches off that light and illuminates another light at random. Willett (1964) found that the high-incentive subjects produced fewer correct responses and made approximately twice as many errors as the low-incentive subjects.

A related task was used by Eysenck and Warwick (1964); their task involved very complicated mutliple-choice reaction in which one finger, one foot, or the whole hand was required to produce each response. In contrast to the serial reaction task, this task was experimenter-paced rather than subject-paced. The high-incentive subjects performed considerably worse than the low-incentive subjects, producing approximately 30 per cent fewer correct responses.

It is instructive to compare these results with those obtained with milder incentives by Wilkinson, El-Beheri, and Gieseking (1972). They used both an easy and a difficult version of the serial reaction task (four- and ten-choice, respectively), and offered some of their subjects payment by results together with information about errors and unusually long response times. There was no effect of incentive on accuracy of performance, but the more motivated subjects performed both versions of the task more rapidly.

The pattern of results on the serial reaction task is consistent with the Yerkes–Dodson Law (Yerkes and Dodson, 1908), according to which there is a curvilinear relationship between arousal or motivation and performance, with intermediate levels of motivation being optimal for performance. However, it should be noted that the Yerkes–Dodson law is descriptive rather than explanatory, since it fails to indicate *why* there should be this curvilinear relationship. Furthermore, it cannot be said that the Yerkes–Dodson law has been found to apply across all tasks. Perhaps the most striking discovery of the research discussed by Eysenck (1964) is the great variation in the effects of very strong incentive on different tasks. While powerful incentive disrupted performance on the serial reaction task and the Tsai–Partington Number Tracing Test, it had no effect at all on forward and backward digit span or the initial stages of pursuit rotor learning, and actually enhanced performance on serial rote learning and on easy and difficult paired-associate learning. It is thus clear that no simple generalization can express the impact of powerful incentives on task performance.

Subjective probability of success

While it seems reasonable to assume that an individual's level of motivation will increase *pari passu* with the amount of incentive offered for successful performance, other factors also play a part in determining the effective level of motivation. For example, even an incentive as large as £1,000,000 for the accomplishment of a task which we believe to be impossible or nearly so (e.g. climbing the north face of the Eiger) would be unlikely to motivate most of us to buy climbing equipment and fly to Switzerland on the next plane. Clearly an individual's level of motivation is determined in part by the subjective probability of performing a task sufficiently well to obtain the incentive offered.

What is the probability of success at which motivation is maximal? Atkinson (1964) argued that the answer to that question depends on an individual's achievement motivation, which is usually assessed by combining scores for motive to achieve success based on the Thematic Apperception Test with scores for motive to avoid failure based on the Mandler–Sarason Test Anxiety Questionnaire. Those people with high achievement motivation (i.e. a stronger motive to achieve success than to avoid failure) are predicted to be maximally motivated when the probability of successful task completion is equal to 0.5. For those with low achievement motivation (i.e. a stronger motive to avoid failure than to achieve success) all achievement tasks are aversive in that they elicit fear; however, tasks where the probability of success is either very low or very high are allegedly more motivating than those where the probability of success is intermediate.

Atkinson and his associates have usually assessed motivation by observing the task difficulty selected by subjects when they are free to choose from a range of tasks. In a typical study, Atkinson and Litwin (1960) allowed subjects to select the distance from which they attempted to throw rings over a peg. All groups of subjects tended to prefer an intermediate distance, but this tendency was most pronounced in subjects with high achievement motivation. There is some evidence to suggest that people with high achievement motivation select tasks of intermediate difficulty because they regard such tasks as maximally informative concerning their ability (Trope, 1975).

In the above studies, no external incentives were offered for successful performance. When financial incentives are offered, subjects tend to select relatively easy tasks (Condry, 1977), presumably because this maximizes the probability of gaining the incentive payment. However, it is not clear that task selection provides an adequate measure of motivation. Revelle and Michaels (1976) discussed some of the key issues, and also proposed a modified version of Atkinson's theory. They claimed, with some empirical support, that moderately difficult tasks (with subjective probabilities of success between 0.1 and 0.5) should be extremely motivating, on the assumption that, 'When the going gets tough, the tough get going.' In contrast, there is very low motivation when the probability of success is less than 0.1, because, 'There is no point in banging your head against a brick wall.'

The role of goal-setting

It has usually been assumed, implicitly or explicitly, that the various factors discussed above combine to determine some internal motivational state. For Locke (1968), this internal state was represented by goal-setting, with the term 'goal' referring to what the individual is consciously trying to do. According to Locke, there is a linear relationship between goal difficulty and performance: 'The results are unequivocal: the harder the goal the higher the level of performance' (p.162). His main evidence was derived from 12 studies in which the relationship between performance and the difficulty of the subject's goal had been ascertained. The goals were either set by the experimenter, and their acceptance or otherwise determined by interview, or they were set by the subjects themselves. Several different tasks were used in these studies, including uses for objects, addition problems, toy construction, complex computation, reaction time, college achievement, and perceptual speed. Goal difficulty was measured on the basis of the percentage of trials on which subjects attained their goal; the overall rank-order correlation coefficient between goal difficulty and performance was a very respectable and significant +0.78.

Locke (1968) did not explain in any detail precisely why the setting of hard goals enhances performance, but he implied that there is greater effort and utilization of resources after relatively difficult goals have been set. However, it seems improbable that there is always a positive relationship between goal-setting and performance. The poor performance of very highly motivated would-be apprentices on several laboratory tasks (Eysenck, 1964), together with anecdotal evidence concerning the adverse effects of high motivation on some professional sportsmen and women, indicate that the setting of hard goals is not always beneficial to performance, perhaps because of the presence of anxiety and/or frustration.

In spite of these problems with Locke's theory, high goal-setting may still be a necessary, if not sufficient, prerequisite for improved performance. This kind of theoretical viewpoint was applied by Locke, Bryan, and Kendall (1968, p.104) to the effects of incentives: 'Incentives such as money should affect action only if and to the extent that they affect the individual's goals and intentions.' In one of their experiments they discovered that monetary incentive had no effect of a uses-for-objects task; this was explained by the further finding that incentive did not affect goal-setting. They also found that subjects who were assigned goals by the experimenter tended to set higher goals than subjects who set their own goals, and also produced more responses.

One of the reasons why incentive had no effect in the study by Locke *et al.* may have been that their monetary incentives were too low. Farr (1976) offered rather more money, and found that financial incentives led to the setting of much higher goals on an eight-category card-sorting task. As predicted, incentives also increased sorting speed; this cannot be attributed to a trade-off between speed and accuracy, because subjects were required to correct any errors that were made.

While most of the available data are consistent with the notion that incentives must affect goal-setting in order for them to affect performance, negative evidence was obtained by Pritchard and Curts (1973). Three groups of subjects all accepted the goal of performing a card-sorting task 30 per cent faster than their practise speed; different groups were offered nothing, 50 cents, or 3 dollars for goal attainment.

If goal-setting is the primary determinant of performance, then these three groups of subjects should have produced comparable performance. In fact, performance was better for subjects offered the 3-dollar incentive than for those in the other two conditions. An obvious possibility is that the high-incentive subjects actually set themselves a higher goal than the other subjects. However, post-experimental questioning provided no support for this conjecture; if anything, the high-incentive subjects were less committed to the goal than those in the no-incentive condition.

Terborg (1976) looked at the relationship between goal-setting and effort expenditure in a study in which subjects spent 5 hours a day for a week working through programmed texts concerned with some of the introductory principles of electricity. Effort was measured by the percentage of the available time that the participants spent working at the material. Goal-setting was positively related to effort, and to overall performance. In contrast, there was still a substantial influence of effort on performance when goal-setting was partialled out. One of the interesting implications of this study is that the effects of goal-setting on performance are mediated by effort.

According to Locke (1968), goal level corresponds to conscious intention and thereby motivates the subject. Thus, goal level is in a sense analogous to a dial that can be turned up or down, thereby regulating motivational intensity. There are some unanswered (and perhaps unanswerable) questions posed by this theoretical approach. In the first place, it seems unduly restrictive to claim that motivational forces are always accessible to consciousness. In the second place, questionnaire or post-experimental interviewing assessment of goal-setting is of unknown and possibly fairly low validity. To the extent that effort reflects goal-setting, it may be possible to use pupillary dilation as a measure, since Kahneman (1973) has argued that pupillary dilation provides a very sensitive measure of effort. If incentive leads to higher goal-setting, it might also be expected to produce greater pupillary dilation. Kahneman and Peavler (1969) found that pupillary dilation was greater during the learning of high-incentive than of low-incentive paired associates. The conclusion that incentive was affecting effort was strengthened by the further finding that those subjects having the greatest differences in pupillary dilation between high- and low-incentive items at the time of learning also had the largest recall differences between the two types of item.

In sum, an individual's level of motivation when performing a task is an amalgam of several factors, including the strength of incentive, the probability of obtaining the incentive, and the intrinsic characteristics of the task itself. The level of motivation can be indexed in an imprecise way by obtaining verbal reports of goal-setting or by taking various physiological measures (e.g. pupillary dilation). Widely differing account of the effects of motivational strength on performance have been offered. On the one hand, Locke (1968) argued that performance was always positively related to motivational strength, whereas Yerkes and Dodson (1908) claimed that an intermediate level of motivation was optimal for performance. In spite of the paucity of evidence, the latter position appears to be more tenable than the former.

TASK CHARACTERISTICS

Although it is almost a truism that the effects of incentive on performance depend on the nature of the task, there have been surprisingly few systematic attempts to identify those task characteristics which determine whether incentive improves or impairs performance. As a prelude to a more theoretical discussion, we will discuss some of the relevant evidence.

Effects of task variables

One of the more interesting studies was carried out by Glucksberg (1962). He used Duncker's functional fixedness problem in which a candle has to be mounted on a vertical screen, and a box of drawing pins and a book of matches are provided. Problem solution requires that the box is regarded as a platform rather than as a container. The task can be made relatively easy if the box is presented empty, or more difficult if it is initially full of drawing pins and matches. Low-incentive subjects were told that their solution time would be used to establish norms for this type of problem, whereas high-incentive subjects were informed that 5 dollars would be paid to each subject who was among the fastest 25 per cent in terms of speed of solution with 20 dollars going to the fastest subject.

When the task was presented in its easier version, there was no effect of incentive on speed of solution. However, high-incentive subjects took an average of some 3½ minutes longer than low-incentive subjects to solve the more difficult version of the candle problem.

A similar study was subsequently carried out by Glucksberg (1964). He used a different functional fixedness problem, in which a screwdriver had to be used to complete a circuit when the available wires turned out to be too short. There was no effect of financial incentive when it was made fairly clear that the screwdriver was relevant to task solution, but incentive increased the time to solution from 6 to 13 minutes on average when the relevance of the screwdriver was less obvious.

These two studies by Glucksberg indicate that a given level of incentive can have quite disparate effects on two versions of the same task. The implication of these findings appears to be that incentive reduces the flexibility of thought, and leads people to persevere in established modes of thinking even when these are counter-productive. The same message emerges from a later study by McGraw and McCullers (1979) in which subjects were presented with a series of 10 water-jar problems. Subjects had to imagine that they were pouring liquid from one jar to another in order to finish up with a specified amount of liquid in one of the jars. The first nine problems could only be solved by means of the same relatively complicated three-jar solution, thus establishing a mental set. The tenth problem, however, only had a simple two-jar solution.

Monetary incentive offered for correct solutions had no effect on speed of solution on the first nine problems. On the tenth problem, however, the mean solution time was 181 seconds for unmotivated subjects against 289 seconds for motivated subjects. Since it was important for the motivated subjects to get the answer right, it might be thought that they spent the extra time making sure that they had indeed solved the problem correctly. However, since they only had to check that '27 – 4' is equal to '23', it seems improbable that even today's college students would spend almost 2 minutes checking their answer.

The simplest explanation of the data is that incentive increases the tendency to cling to processing strategies that have proved successful in the past. In more technical terms, motivated subjects are more likely than unmotivated subjects to show a negative transfer effect, in which previously acquired skills are inappropriately applied to a new situation. At a more specific level, it is unfortunate that the data of McGraw and McCullers (1979) are insufficient to reveal exactly what the motivated subjects were doing during their attempts to solve the final problem. Finally, it should be noted that even the unmotivated subjects did not display any marked cognitive flexibility: their mean solution time of 181 seconds can be compared to the 25 seconds taken by both motivated and unmotivated subjects to solve the same problem in the absence of a prior mental set.

As a general rule of thumb, incentive is more likely to disrupt performance on cognitively complex tasks than on relatively routine tasks. More evidence of adverse effects of incentive on difficult tasks was obtained by Condry and Chambers (1978). A concept-attainment task was used, with one group of subjects being paid for each problem solved, and the other not. The paid subjects were more 'answer oriented', in that they began guessing at the answer earlier in the problem than unpaid subjects, and they also made more guesses *en route* to problem solution. The paid subjects also required as much, or more information before arriving at the correct solution, and they used available worksheets less extensively than unpaid subjects. Finally, when all of the subjects were asked to work out a problem and only suggest an answer when they were sure they had solved it, motivated subjects were more likely to guess before they had narrowed down the possible answers to one.

Condry and Chambers (1978) drew the following conclusions from their studies of incentivized and intrinsically motivated or non-incentivized subjects: 'Intrinsically motivated subjects attend to and utilize a wider array of information; they are focused on the *way* to solve the problem rather than the solution. They are, in general, more careful, logical, and coherent in their problem-solving strategies than comparable subjects offered a reward to solve the same problems' (p.69).

The tasks on which incentive consistently enhances performance tend to be those where the emphasis is one speed of responding. The best known of such tasks is the lever pressing for food often used in studies of operant conditioning. Another example is the reaction-time task, on which knowledge of results (which is often regarded as an incentive) has been found to produce faster reaction times (e.g. Blowers and Ongley, 1975).

An interesting pattern of results was obtained by Elliott (1970). Reaction times were interactively determined by incentives and by length of the foreperiod (i.e. the time between the warning stimulus and the signal requiring response) when blocks of trials with constant length of foreperiod were used. In this interaction, the beneficial effects of incentive were greater at the longer foreperiods. Similar results were reported by Elliott, Bankart, and Flaherty (1976), who used blocks of trials with preparatory intervals or foreperiods of 4 and 8 seconds. Their main finding was that incentive reduced reaction time more at the longer interval.

Why does incentive reduce reaction time to a greater extent at relatively long foreperiods? A speculative answer is suggested by a hypothesis proposed by Gottsdanker (1975, p.34): 'Preparation is an aversive state and as such is entered into only when profitable, but otherwise avoided.' Gottsdanker assumed that subjects would respond more rapidly when in a state of preparation or alertness. If motivated subjects are prepared to maintain the aversive state of preparation for longer periods of time than unmotivated subjects, this would account for the reported data.

Another activity in which the emphasis is on speed of performance is the cancellation task, which involves crossing out certain stimuli (e.g. all the 'e's) on a sheet of paper. Dey and Kaur (1965) discovered that people who were assigned hard output goals on a letter-cancellation task performed faster than those who were given easy goals. Feldman (1964) used an easy and a difficult version of a digit-cancellation task with high-incentive subjects (seeking a desired apprenticeship and low-incentive subjects (already accepted for the apprenticeship). Incentive augmented the number of correct responses on the easy task only, but this was achieved at the expense of a substantially increased error-rate.

Another experimental task on which the effects of incentive are predominantly beneficial is vigilance. In vigilance tasks the requirement is usually to spend an hour or more attempting to detect infrequent and inconspicuous signals (either visual or auditory). Most of the interest in this task has focused on the so-called vigilance decrement, i.e. the probability of detecting signals decreases over time.

Nachreiner (1977) used the relatively powerful incentive of informing some of his subjects that good performance on the vigilance task might lead to subsequent part-time work at the rate of approximately £4 per hour. This incentive produced an increase in the number of auditory signals detected, and also eliminated the vigilance decrement that was found with subjects not offered an incentive.

An unfortunate limitation of many studies in this area is that only detection data are reported. When information about false alarms (i.e. the reported detections of signals when none is present) is also provided, it is possible to calculate independent measures of observer sensitivity and of his or her decision criterion (i.e. the bias towards one or the other response alternative). As a result of such an approach, it turns out that the vigilance decrement is typically attributable to a progressive increase in the strictness of the response criterion (i.e. greater cautiousness of response) rather than to reduced sensitivity (see Broadbent, 1971, for a review).

A few researchers have addressed the issue of whether the effects of incentive on vigilance are due to changes in sensitivity or in the response criterion. Studies by Levine (1966) and Davenport (1968) on auditory vigilance, and by Davenport (1969) on vibro-tactile vigilance, all produced very similar patterns of results: financial incentives associated with signal detection had no effect on vigilance performance, whereas financial costs associated with missed signals or false alarms impaired detection. The latter finding was due to greater cautiousness of responding rather than to reduced sensitivity.

Sostek (1978) noted that most of these studies failed to include a control group receiving no incentive. He used a control group, and found that sensitivity in an auditory vigilance situation was increased by incentive. There were also effects on the response criterion: subjects threatened with the loss of 9 cents for each false alarm adopted a more stringent response criterion than the control group, and subjects who stood to lose 9 cents for every missed signal chose a relatively low response criterion.

Theoretical aspects of task variables

Is it possible to make any theoretical sense out of the confusing array of findings? As a starting point, let us consider the views of McGraw (1978). His quintessential argument was that there are two necessary pre-conditions which need to obtain in order for incentives to exert a detrimental effect on task performance: (1) the task must be sufficiently interesting on its own merits for extrinsic incentives to provide a superfluous source of motivation; and (2) the solution to the task must be relatively open-ended, so that the steps to that solution are non-obvious. In connection with the second point, McGraw suggested a distinction between algorithmic and heuristic tasks; in algorithmic tasks the route to the solution is well mapped and straightforward, whereas in heuristic tasks the first requirement is to develop an algorithm.

Within the framework of this theoretical orientation, tasks can be categorized as attractive or aversive, and as algorithmic or heuristic. Research on the effects of incentive on performance has not been based on a random selection of tasks from within this two-dimensional space; rather, the overwhelming emphasis has been on tasks that are both aversive and algorithmic. As a consequence it has too readily been assumed that incentive will nearly always enhance performance.

Perhaps the clearest example of the importance of the algorithmic–heuristic distinction occurs in the studies by Glucksberg (1962, 1964). In a sense, he discovered that incentive retarded problem-solving when a task was presented in a heuristic form, but no longer did so when the appropriate algorithm was made more obvious. Why does incentive disrupt the performance of heuristic tasks? According to McGraw (1978), the answer lies in the robust finding (which is documented below) that incentive reduces incidental learning. In McGraw's own words,

> Reward subjects might do less well on concept formation, problem solving, and those other tasks on which we have seen reward subjects to be inferior *precisely because* of their inferiority at incidental learning . . . The heuristic process needed for some intentional-task solutions can be said to feed on incidental thoughts and perceptions (p.55).

There is undoubtedly merit in McGraw's suggestions, but he ignored a number of important factors. In contradiction of his position, there are occasions on which incentive has been found to impair performance on tasks which are neither intrinsically interesting nor heuristic. For example, Willett (1964) noted that incentive impaired performance on the serial reaction task. This probably occurred because Willett was investigating the effects of a rather powerful incentive (i.e. a desired apprenticeship) on performance. As a general rule, the number of tasks adversely affected by incentive is likely to grow as the amount of incentive increases above some moderate level. Surprisingly, McGraw did not include amount of incentive as one of the determinants of whether or not incentive will impair performance.

There are also some studies in which incentive fails to impair performance of an interesting heuristic task. For example, McGraw and McCullers (1979) did not detect any effect of incentive on time to solve the initial water-jar problems in their study, in spite of the non-obvious nature of the appropriate algorithm. Incentive only worsened performance on that task when the algorithm changed on the last problem in the series. Thus, the critical factor may be the presence of an accessible but inappropriate algorithm, rather than (as McGraw argued) merely the absence of obvious steps to task solution.

McGraw's emphasis on the importance of task attractiveness is well-placed. Any attempt to predict whether incentive will enhance or worsen performance must take into account the extent to which non-incentivized subjects are intrinsically motivated to perform the task. The major problem is that it is difficult to measure task attractiveness. Whether or not a task is perceived as attractive depends on an interaction between the intrinsic qualities of the task and the subject's characteristics (e.g. intelligence, attitudes). Furthermore, it has not been sufficiently appreciated that there is a temporal dimension to task attractiveness: most tasks tend to become less attractive over time.

PERFORMANCE EFFICIENCY

One of the greatest limitations of most of the work in the area of incentive effects is the reliance on a single measure of performance efficiency. At the most general level, it is patently obvious that the use of two or more behavioural indices provides a more complete picture of the consequences of incentive manipulations than can be obtained through the use of only one dependent variable. More importantly, there are several cases in which the poverty of data collection has led to erroneous conclusions.

Some of the research discussed by Locke (1968) provides a useful cautionary tale. When people are asked to list a specified number of objects fulfilling various criteria (e.g. 'heavy, rough, and square'), it has been found that the number of objects listed is largely determined by the goal level (i.e. the

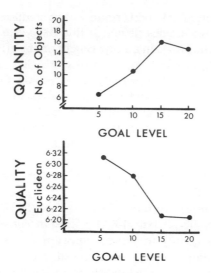

Figure 32. Quantity and quality of performance on an object-listing task as a function of incentive in the form of goal level. From Bavelas and Lee (1978).

specified number of objects). Such findings led Locke to conclude that performance efficiency is a direct function of goal level.

Bavelas and Lee (1978) challenged this conclusion. In one of their studies they asked different groups of subjects to attempt to list at least 5, 10, 15, or 20 objects that were 'hard, white, and edible' within seven minutes. They replicated the finding that the number of objects written down is greater as the goal level increases (see Figure 32). However, when they asked raters to evaluate the quality of the responses in terms of the extent to which they matched up with each of the three criteria, a very different picture emerged: the quality of performance was inversely related to goal level. In other words, high goal level led to a large quantity of responses, but only at the expense of reduced quality. It thus becomes difficult (if not impossible) to assess the overall effect of goal level on performance efficiency.

These results may reflect some kind of re-interpretation of the instructions by the subjects. If they are asked to produce numerous responses, they feel that the criteria for acceptable answers are to be (or at least can be) relaxed to some extent. When the subjects in the various groups were questioned, they usually referred to cognitive re-structuring, and practically never mentioned anything concerned with motivation level.

Speed and accuracy

One example of incentive having opposite effects on two different components of performance is the common finding of a speed–accuracy trade-off in which incentive increases speed of performance but reduces the accuracy of responding. One or two studies in which this happened have already been discussed (e.g. Feldman, 1964). In an experiment on the effects of the incentive of rivalry on intelligence-test performance, Maller and Zubin (1932) discovered that incentive had essentially no effect on the number of items correctly solved. However, a more detailed analysis revealed that incentive increased the number of items attempted (i.e. performance speed), and also produced a corresponding increase in the number of errors.

There are also some reports of incentive affecting speed–accuracy trade-off in the opposite direction, i.e. incentive reducing the speed of performance, but increasing accuracy. This pattern of results was obtained by Eysenck and Gillan (1964) in a mirror-drawing task.

It appears that incentive can more readily affect the speed of performance than its accuracy or quality. Adam (1972) offered incentives (money or praise) for either quantity or quality of performance on a task involving collating information from data-processing unit record cards. When there was an unannounced shift from rewarding quantity to rewarding quality, there was no discernible effect of incentive on performance; however, a shift in the opposite direction led to increased quantity and reduced quality.

Why are the quantitative aspects of performance more readily improved by incentive manipulations than are the qualitative aspects? Part of the answer may be that effort is more directly related to performance quantity (Terborg and Miller, 1978). It could alternatively be argued that incentive is an arouser, and it has been established that aroused people naturally respond rapidly but non-reflectively.

Dual-task studies

From a theoretical perspective, the most intriguing findings concern the effects of incentive on two concurrent tasks. A careful perusal of the literature uncovered 13 relevant studies, as follows: Bahrick, 1954; Bahrick, Fitts, and Rankin, 1952; Cohen, Telegdy, Laroche, and Getz, 1973; Davies and Jones, 1975; Dixon and Cameron, 1976; Dornbush, 1965; Harackiewicz, 1979; Johnson and Thomson, 1962; Kausler, Laughlin, and Trapp, 1963; Kausler and Trapp, 1962; McNamara and Fisch, 1964; Rubin, Shantz, and Smock, 1962; and Wolk and DuCette, 1974. In most of these studies the main task involved learning a list of items (geometrical forms, words, or nonsense syllables), whereas the subsidiary task was incidental learning of other stimuli (e.g. colours, additional words) presented concurrently with the main-task items.

Since more than one experiment was reported in some of these studies, there are 16 sets of relevant data. Incentives were found to produce significantly improved main-task performance in six of the 16 comparisons, and had no effect in the remaining ten. On the other hand, incentives only improved subsidiary-task performance in three cases, impaired performance in six comparisons, and had no effect in the other seven cases. This pattern of results suggests that incentive leads to a reallocation of attentional resources, with greater resources being invested in the main task (producing superior main-task performance) but with fewer resources being applied to the subsidiary task (leading to poor incidental-task performance).

It is certainly tempting to explain many of the effects of incentive in terms of increased attentional selectivity. Indeed, this is perhaps the single most plausible explanation of the fact that incentive frequently augments task performance. If incentive usually increases attentional selectivity, why is it that incentive has no beneficial effect or even impairs performance on complex and cognitively demanding tasks? The reason is that even subjects without incentive allocate nearly all of their attentional resources to such task; this is indicated by their extremely poor performance on a concurrent subsidiary task (Kahneman, 1973).

Before becoming too carried away by the theoretical notions espoused above, it is appropriate to consider the methodological deficiencies of the dual-task studies of incentive. In the first place, retention-test performance obviously provides an extremely indirect measure of attention. Secondly, it is much easier to assess attentional capacity when subjects are specifically asked to attempt to perform the subsidiary task; otherwise, subsidiary-task performance measures what individuals choose to do rather than what they are able to do. Thirdly, virtually all of the studies used rather different stimuli in the main and subsidiary tasks, so that the type of stimulus was confounded with task importance. As a consequence, differential effects of incentive on main and subsidiary tasks cannot be attributed unequivocally to task importance alone.

The theoretical idea that incentive increases attentional selectivity was put forward several years ago by Easterbrook (1959). He argued that high arousal, whether produced by incentive or other means, produced a narrowing of cue utilization. One of the differences between his position and the one favoured here is that Easterbrook regarded increased attentional selectivity as a relatively passive and automatic consequence of the arousal produced by incentive, whereas it is preferable to consider it as an active coping response to an altered payoff matrix.

According to Easterbrook's hypothesis, motivated subjects concentrate more intently than unmotivated subjects on the main task; as a result, they should be less distractible. In fact, we have found in recent unpublished work that the offer of large financial incentives for good performance on a letter-transformation task led to *increased* distractibility, at least when the distracting stimuli were very similar to the task stimuli. Presumably motivated subjects have less spare attentional capacity available for discriminating between task and non-task stimuli.

It is natural to enquire whether incentive improves or impairs performance on any aspect of performance emphasized explicitly or implicitly in the task instructions at the expense of impaired performance on non-emphasized performance. The characteristic pattern is for incentive to improve performance on any apsect of performance emphasized explicitly or implicitly in the task instructions at the expense of impaired performance on non-emphasized aspects. This pattern is especially likely to be found when the instructions emphasize speed of performance. Kruglanski, Stein, and Riter (1977) had something similar in mind when they suggested that motivated subjects operate in conformity with a 'minimax' principle: they restrict their performance to those aspects minimally required for the delivery of maximal rewards. In their own words, 'Extrinsically motivated subjects restrict their performance to activities indispensable to the delivery of contingent rewards' (p.146).

INDIVIDUAL CHARACTERISTICS

Even casual observation of professional sportsmen competing against each other for powerful incentives (e.g. the men's crown at Wimbledon) demonstrates that the effects of incentive on performance vary substantially from individual to individual. One major source of such individual differences concerns the extent to which a person is motivated by incentive or reward. However, there is another side to incentive manipulations: motivated subjects are more likely to experience negative affect if they feel (or are told) that their performance is poor. In other words, the prospect of failing to obtain a reward or incentive is likely to produce a state of frustration. This feeling of frustration induced by non-reward may resemble the feeling of anxiety produced by punishment (Gray, 1973), and is likely to impair performance on many tasks.

Extroversion and anxiety

The theoretical model proposed by Gray (1973) is very relevant at this point. He argued that individual differences in susceptibility to reward are related to the personality dimension of impulsivity: those low in impulsivity (i.e. stable introverts) are low in susceptibility to reward whereas those high in impulsivity (i.e. neurotic extroverts) have great susceptibility to reward. On the other hand, differences in susceptibility to punishment are related to the anxiety dimension: those low in anxiety (i.e. stable extroverts) are much less susceptible to punishment than those high in anxiety (i.e. neurotic introverts).

It follows from Gray's analysis that the beneficial effects of incentive should be greatest among extroverted subjects (especially neurotic extroverts), whereas the adverse effects of incentive should be most marked among high-anxiety subjects. Such evidence as is available tends to support those predictions.

Corcoran (1962) obtained very clear data in a study in which incentive in the form of fake feedback was introduced during the performance of a letter-cancellation task. Incentive had no detectable effect on the performance of introverts, but it improved the performance speed of extroverts by approximately 80 per cent.

In a further study, Corcoran (1962) examined the effects of a mild incentive on performance of the five-choice serial reaction task. Extroverts responded more than introverts to the incentive, especially under sleep-deprived conditions, where there was a correlation of $+0.59$ between extroversion and the size of the incentive effect. There is a more detailed discussion of the differential impact of incentive on introverts and extroverts in Eysenck (1981).

The prediction that incentive should be more likely to impair performance for high-anxiety than for low-anxiety subjects has been tested a number of times. The usual finding is that motivational factors worsen the performance of high-anxiety subjects, but improve or have no effect on low-anxiety subjects. Some of the relevant findings are discussed in Chapter 10. There is also evidence to indicate that anxious individuals are more susceptible to punishment than non-anxious individuals: for example, their performance is much more adversely affected by fake failure feedback.

Transient arousal changes

So far, we have only considered relatively permanent individual characteristics in the form of personality traits or dimensions. However, more transient states or moods also interact with incentive manipulations to determine behaviour. Broadbent (1971) has argued that the effects of incentive on performance are affected by an individual's level of arousal. More specifically, he claimed that incentive and other factors such as noise and sleeplessness affect the same arousal mechanism, and thus should interact with each other. It has usually been found that incentive enhances performance considerably more for sleep-deprived than non-deprived people, presumably because the sleep-deprived state is one of sub-optimal arousal. In contrast, the beneficial effects of incentive are reduced among subjects exposed to white noise, because noise has an alerting and arousing function (e.g. Wilkinson, 1963; see Figure 33).

Broadbent also suggested that different arousers have equivalent effects on performance; in the words of Broadbent (1978, p.1060): 'One of the interesting aspects of noise is the similarity of its effects to those of other conditions, such as financial incentives.' It is certainly true that both noise and incentive seem to increase attentional selectivity (Easterbrook, 1959), and they both often produce fast but rather inaccurate responding. However, there has been some dispute about just how much the behavioural effects of incentive resemble those of other arousers. For example, Fowler and Wilding (1979) found that white noise and monetary incentive had diametrically opposed

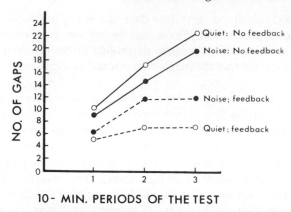

Figure 33. Mean number of slow reactions or gaps in the serial reaction task as a function of noise and feedback conditions. From Wilkinson (1963).

effects on the incidental learning of the spatial locations of to-be-learned words, with incentive improving incidental learning, but noise reducing it. This pattern of results led Fowler and Wilding to the following challenging conclusions: 'Noise appears to reduce attentional capacity whilst incentives appear to increase it . . . Distinctions between arousers exist and general explanations in terms of "arousal" are not adequate' (p.153).

Related findings were obtained by Eysenck in unpublished work. He used a letter-transformation task in which a given number of letters have to be added to between one and four letters. Thus, a sample one-letter problem is as follows: 'E + 4' for which the answer is 'I', and a sample four-letter problem is as follows: 'SNDG + 4' for which the answer is 'WRHK'. Modest financial incentive improved the speed of performance on all versions of the task by approximately 30 per cent, and the improvement was greater on three- and four-letter problems than on one- and two-letter problems.

In contrast, Hamilton, Hockey, and Rejman (1977) found that white noise speeded up performance on one-letter problems but led to a substantial slowing of performance on three- and four-letter problems. If we may assume that the demands on some short-term 'holding' mechanism are directly related to the number of letters requiring transformation, then the results indicate that noise impairs the efficiency of that short-term mechanism, whereas modest incentive tends to increase its efficiency. The beneficial effects of white noise on one-letter problems appears to be due in large measure to increased speed of transformation (Hockey, personal communication), and the same is true of incentive (Eysenck, unpublished data).

While the data of Fowler and Wilding and the findings from three- and four-letter problems suggest that incentive and noise do not have comparable effects on performance, there is a simple alternative explanation. If there is a curvilinear relationship between arousal and performance (Yerkes and Dodson, 1908), and if the modest financial incentives used in these studies were less arousing than the white noise, then it is possible that equivalence could be demonstrated if a greater variety of incentive and noise conditions were compared. However, we have found in recent unpublished work that larger financial incentive (up to £50 for successful performance) still enhances performance on the four-letter version of the letter-transformation task.

There are clearly good reasons for arguing that a motivated individual acts as if he or she were in a state of elevated arousal. In addition to the behavioural evidence, there are the physiological data reported by Wilkinson, El-Beheri, and Gieseking (1972); they found that incentive produced changes in pulse-rate, respiration-rate, and skin conductance level suggestive of an increase in arousal. However, the most direct effect of incentive is probably a cognitive re-allocation of processing resources, whereas with noise the main effect is on physiological arousal. Roughly speaking, the distinction is between an active and a passive effect.

In sum, the precise effects of incentive on performance depend in part upon semi-permanent personality characteristics, especially those relating to susceptibility to reward and punishment. In addition, transient internal states, especially those related to the level of arousal, have been found to augment or attenuate the behavioural effects of incentive manipulations.

INTRINSIC AND EXTRINSIC MOTIVATION

There is at least one important sense in which most of the research on incentive discussed in this chapter represents an extremely limited approach to motivation. This limitation can be seen most clearly in the context of Deci's (1975) interesting proposal that one should distinguish between intrinsic and extrinsic motivation. Intrinsically motivated activities are those for which there is no apparent reward other than the activity itself. Intrinsic motivation to perform a task will be present to the extent that engaging in that task increases an individual's feelings of competence and self-determination. In contrast, extrinsic motivation involves the use of extrinsic or external rewards (e.g. money, praise, food) which provide satisfaction that is independent of the activity itself.

Obviously we have been concerned primarily with extrinsic motivation. If there are any systematic differences in the ways in which intrinsic and extrinsic motivation affect behaviour, then the approach discussed in this chapter is rather limited. For example, it is likely that there is a difference in the time course of the two kinds of motivation: common sense indicates that extrinsic motivation is usually more transient than intrinsic motivation. Evidence that extrinsic rewards sometimes have very little long-term effect on behaviour comes from work on token economies, in which special groups of people (e.g. juvenile delinquents or mental patients) are given tokens for behaving in socially desirable ways; these tokens can later be exchanged for a variety of goods or privileges. In their review of the literature, Kazdin and Bootzin (1972) emphasized the ephemeral nature of any beneficial effects: 'There are numerous reports of token programmes showing behaviour change only while contingent token reinforcement is being delivered. Generally, removal of token reinforcement results in undesirable responses and a return to baseline or near baseline levels of performance' (p.359). In other words, token economies produce token learning.

A key issue in motivational theory is (or ought to be) the relationship between intrinsic and extrinsic motivation. It has conventionally been assumed that the effects of intrinsic and extrinsic motivation are independent and additive. Deci (1975) challenged this orthodoxy, arguing that intrinsic and extrinsic motivation are not independent, and do not simply summate. In particular, he claimed that increasing extrinsic motivation (e.g. by means of augmented incentive) can lead to reduced intrinsic motivation. The main way in which this occurs is by changing the perceived locus of causality. Intrinsically motivated behaviour is, by definition, regarded as self-determined. However, the provision of external rewards or incentives can alter the perceived locus of causality, making the individual feel that he or she is motivated by these externally controlled rewards rather than by internal factors. The feeling of being a 'pawn' controlled by external agencies has the consequence of reducing intrinsic motivation.

While incentive will often reduce intrinsic motivation, it can also enhance it. According to Deci (1975), intrinsic motivation not only involves feelings of self-determination; it also implicates feelings of competence. If incentive serves to provide information which strengthens the individual's feelings of competence, then it can actually lead to increased intrinsic motivation.

So much for theory—how much experimental support is there for these various hypotheses? Certainly the notion that extrinsic rewards can reduce intrinsic motivation has been confirmed several times, There are two main ways in which the strength of intrinsic motivation has been assessed: (1) the amount of time spent working on a specific task in a free-choice situation in which there are other things to do, and no extrinsic rewards are available; and (2) questionnaire measurement of task satisfaction or willingness to volunteer for a similar experiment.

In a classic study Deci (1971) used both measures of intrinsic motivation. Subjects participated in a problem-solving task called SOMA, which consists of a number of blocks that can be arranged to form a variety of patterns specified by the experimenter. There were three sessions, and the experimenter went out of the room for 8 minutes in the middle of each session. Subjects who were paid 1 dollar for each problem solved in the second session spent less time engaged in problem-solving activity during the experimenter's absence in the middle of the third session than did non-rewarded subjects. While this suggests that extrinsic rewards reduced intrinsic motivation, extrinsic rewards had no effect on rated task satisfaction.

Several other researchers have also found that intrinsic motivation is reduced by extrinsic rewards. However, despite its plausibility, there is little direct evidence that this effect is best attributed to the perception of extrinsic instrumentality as Deci supposed. An obvious alternative explanation is that rewarded subjects put more effort into the task and thus become more tired or frustrated, and as a consequence lose some of their intrinsic motivation for the task. However, an ingenious study by Kruglanski, Alon, and Lewis (1972) seems to eliminate this possibility. Several subjects participated in a series of games, after which they received a reward which they were erroneously told had been promised to them before they took part in the games. Thus, in this case extrinsic rewards could not possibly have affected their behaviour while participating in the games. Nevertheless, they reported less intrinsic interest in the games than non-rewarded subjects, presumably because they attributed their involvement in the games to extrinsic motivation.

At the practical level, an implication of this research is that the long-term consequences of incentive manipulations may be very different from their immediate effects. Incentives can manifestly be used to control and manipulate behaviour in various ways during the time incentive is offered; it does not necessarily follow that any immediate beneficial effects of incentive will continue to be present after incentive has been removed. Indeed, the work of Deci and others seems to suggest the exact opposite.

CONCLUSIONS AND PRACTICAL IMPLICATIONS

In drawing conclusions from the work in this area, one is tempted to echo the words of countless psychologists over the years who have decided that 'much more research clearly needs to be done'. However, it is possible to be somewhat more constructive, and to suggest a framework for such future research. We have argued that the effects of incentive on task performance can usefully be regarded as depending on four classes of variables: (1) the nature of the incentive; (2) the processes required by the task; (3) the aspects of performance selected for measurement; and (4) individual differences in mood or state and in semi-permanent personality characteristics.

It is probable that accurate prediction of task performance is possible only when all of these variables are considered jointly. While such a statement is hardly revolutionary or controversial, its implications have been almost universally ignored. There has never been an experimental study in which all four factors were manipulated simultaneously; indeed, it is customary to manipulate only one or two.

In spite of these limitations in the research, it is interesting to consider its potential relevance to 'real-life' situations like the work environment. It is unfortunate that we know more about extrinsic motivation than about intrinsic motivation, since it is very likely that the efficiency of work and the contentment of employees depend on intrinsic motivation more than on extrinsic motivation. Evidence supporting this point of view, and demonstrating the relative unimportance of financial incentives, was obtained in a classic study by Herzberg, Mausner, and Snyderman (1959). They asked engineers and accountants in management to indicate the most satisfying and the most dissatisfying aspects of their work. The six most frequently mentioned sources of satisfaction (in rank order) were as follows: (1) achievement; (2) recognition; (3) the work itself; (4) responsibility; (5) advancement; and (6) salary. Financial rewards were not especially prominent among the sources of dissatisfaction either, salary only coming in fourth position.

The work of Herzberg *et al.* (1959) has been criticized for being based on people in reasonably well-paid and interesting occupations. It is unlikely that a newspaper vendor would regard achievement and recognition as major sources of job satisfaction! Nevertheless, it is indisputable that there are several different potentially motivating factors in the work environment; as a consequence, it would often be naïve to assume that the introduction of a new piece-work system of payment will necessarily have a dramatic impact on productivity. Several of the motivating factors affecting employees emerge out of a social context, so that it is probably true to say that a social psychologist would be best equipped to predict the effects of incentive manipulations on work performance.

One of the major differences between laboratory studies and work situations is that laboratory experimentation typically involves unfamiliar tasks on which subjects are only given a modest amount of practice, whereas people at work are more likely to accumulate a vast amount of experience with a relatively familiar range of work activities. How are the incentive effects discussed in this chapter likely to be affected by practice? One of the most obvious effects of practise is to reduce effective task difficulty. For example, driving a car is initially an almost impossibly complex task, but with sufficient practise it becomes relatively straightforward. Since incentive typically enhances performance more on simple tasks than on difficult tasks, it seems likely that incentive would improve performance of a given work activity when it has been practised. On the other hand, practise can lead to the development of fixed modes of thinking which are maladaptive when circumstances change, and incentive may on occasion simply exacerbate any negative transfer effect.

When industrial psychologists consider the effects of financial incentives on work performance, they tend to emphasize factors such as the degree to which high output is seen as instrumental in leading to higher pay, the presence or absence of group norms opposing increased production, and the extent to which employees trust upper management. From the present perspective, it is surprising that so little attention has been paid to two other vitally important factors: (1) the nature of the work activity; and (2) the personality and other characteristics of the individual employee. One reason why industrial psychologists tend to de-emphasize the importance of the specific work activity is that they typically look at the effects of different piece-rate or other incentive systems *within a single work situation.* If they compared the effects of piece-rate systems across a variety of work activities, they would undoubtedly find interesting interactions between incentive conditions and work situations which would prove beyond peradventure the importance of the work activity in determining the effects of incentive.

Of course, industrial psychologists should not focus exclusively on the effects of incentive on work output. They should also be aware that incentive can act as a stressor causing an elevated state of physiological activity. We saw earlier in the chapter that incentive can produce changes in skin conductance, respiration-rate, and pulse-rate indicative of a general increase in physiological arousal, and incentive can also increase the circulation of the catecholamines adrenalin and noradrenalin.

The notion that incentive is a stressor resembling other stressors such as white noise is strengthened by the fact that the facilitatory effects of incentive are attenuated when subjects are exposed to intense white noise. While this kind of interaction between incentive and white noise has many possible interpretations, it is tempting to assume that white noise produces an internal state similar to that engendered by incentive, which thus minimizes the impact of incentive on performance.

In contrast, the circumstances in which incentive has its greatest beneficial effects tend to be those in which the individual is initially in a state of relatively low physiological arousal. Such a state occurs early in the morning (Blake, 1971) and in sleep deprivation (Wilkinson, 1961). An interaction between sleep conditions and incentive in the form of knowledge of results or feedback is shown in Figure 34. One of the implications of these various findings is that

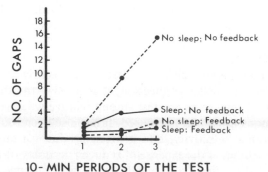

Figure 34. Mean number of slow reactions or gaps in the serial reaction task as a function of sleep and feedback conditions. Wilkinson (1961).

any enhancement effect of incentive on performance is achieved at some 'cost' in terms of stress and physiological arousal, and this should be borne in mind when incentive schemes are being devised for use in the work environment.

In spite of the evidence suggesting that incentive can be regarded as an arouser, it would be hazardous to ignore the conflicting findings. In particular, while white noise appears to decrease the capacity of some short-term storage mechanism (Hamilton *et al.*, 1977), incentive tends to have the opposite effect. It is a task for future research to delineate more precisely the similarities and dissimilarities between incentive and other arousers such as noise.

In addition to its effects on some internal arousal state, what else can be said about the effects of incentive? First, incentive alters the priorities accorded to environmental events, leading to increased attentional selectivity. Secondly, incentive tends to produce more rapid internal processing and external responding, often at the expense of accuracy. Thirdly, while the most obvious effects of incentive are motivational in nature, incentive can also lead to frustration and anxiety. This is especially likely when incentive is very high and/or the probability of attaining the incentive is low. As a consequence, there may be qualitative differences between the internal states produced by modest and very high incentives. Fourthly, it is much more difficult to demonstrate long-term improvements in peformance than immediate gains, in large measure because incentive tends to reduce or 'undermine' intrinsic motivation. Fifthly, incentive is most likely to enhance performance of monotonous, cognitively undemanding tasks, and least likely to benefit performance of interesting and complex tasks for which inappropriate processing strategies are readily accessible.

SUMMARY

Any systematic attempt to elucidate the effects of incentive on task performance must take account of a number of factors in addition to the nature of the incentive itself. Of particular significance are the processes required by the task and certain characteristics of the individual, such as his or her prevailing mood and personality.

It has been reasonably well established that incentive resembles various arousers or stressors; in this connection, it is noteworthy that the beneficial effects of incentive tend to be greatest among relatively de-aroused individuals and smallest among those highly aroused. It has also been found that incentive increases attentional selectivity, and it often produces a more rapid rate of responding, sometimes at the expense of reduced accuracy of performance. As a consequence, the effects of incentive on performance depend on the complexity of the task being performed: difficult tasks are less likely to benefit from incentive manipulations than are easy tasks.

In the real world, it is probably true that sources of motivation within the individual (intrinsic motivation) are more consequential than those imposed from outside (extrinsic motivation, which is exemplified by monetary incentive). Incentive may only affect performance temporarily, and may even have the unfortunate effect of reducing intrinsic motivation.

It is rather difficult to predict the effects of incentive on the efficiency with which people perform their jobs in the work situation. There are many reasons for this, such as the presence of many other potential sources of satisfaction to be derived from work and the fact that the effects of incentive on an individual within a group situation (such as in an office) may be very different to its effects on the same individual when on his or her own. In spite of these difficulties, there are some implications of laboratory research on incentive for industrial psychologists.

ACKNOWLEDGEMENT

Many thanks are extended to the Social Science Research Council for their generous financial assistance during the preparation of this manuscript.

REFERENCES

Adam, E. E. (1972) An analysis of changes in performance quality with operant conditioning procedures. *Journal of Applied Psychology*, **56**, 480–486.

Atkinson, J. W. (1964) *An Introduction to Motivation*. New York: Von Nostrand.

Atkinson, J. W. and Litwin, G. (1960) Achievement motive and test anxiety conceived as motive to approach success and motive to avoid failure. *Journal of Abnormal and Social Psychology*, **60**, 52–63.

Atkinson, R. C. and Shiffrin, R. M. (1968) Human memory: A proposed system and its control processes. In K. W. Spence and J. T. Spence (eds.), *The Psychology of Learning and Motivation: Advances in Research and Theory, Vol. 2*. London: Academic Press.

Atkinson, R. C. and Wickens, T. D. (1971) Human memory and the concept of reinforcement. In Glaser (ed.), *The Nature of Reinforcement*. London: Academic Press.

Baddeley, A. D. and Hitch, G. (1974) Working memory. In G. H. Bower (ed.), *The Psychology of Learning an Motivation: Advances in Research and Theory, Vol. 8*. London: Academic Press.

Bahrick, H. P. (1954) Incidental learning under two incentive conditions. *Journal of Experimental Psychology*, **47**, 170–172.

Bahrick, H. P., Fitts, P. M., and Rankin, R. E. (1952) Effects of incentives upon reactions to peripheral stimuli. *Journal of Experimental Psychology*, **4**, 400–406.

Bavelas, J. and Lee, E. S. (1978) Effects of goal level on performance: A trade-off of quantity and quality. *Canadian Journal of Psychology*, **32**, 219–240.

Bindra, D. (1974) A motivational view of learning, performance, and behaviour modification. *Psychological Review*, **81**, 199–213.

Blake, M. J. F. (1971) Temperament and time of day. In W. P. Colquhoun (ed.), *Biological Rhythms and Human Behaviour*. London: Academic Press.

Blowers, G. H. and Ongley, G. C. (1975) The effect of knowledge of results upon contingent negative variation in a reaction time situation with a variable foreperiod. *Physiological Psychology*, 3, 257-260.

Broadbent, D. E. (1971) *Decision and Stress*. London: Academic Press.

Broadbent, D. E. (1978) The current state of noise research: Reply to Poulton. *Psychological Bulletin*, 85, 1052-1067.

Cohen, J. S., Telegdy, G. A., Laroche, J. P., and Getz, Y. (1973) Cue utilization as a function of monetary incentive and learning efficiency. *Bulletin of the Psychonomic Society*, 1, 452-454.

Condry, J. (1977) Enemies of exploration: Self-initiated versus other-initiated learning. *Journal of Personality and Social Psychology*, 7, 459-477.

Condry, J. and Chambers, J. (1978) Intrinsic motivation and the process of learning. In M. R. Lepper and D. Greene (eds.), *The Hidden Costs of Reward: New Perspectives on the Psychology of human Motivation*. Hillsdale, N.J.: Erlbaum.

Corcoran, D. W. J. (1962) Individual differences in performance after loss of sleep. Unpublished Ph.D. thesis, University of Cambridge, England.

Craik, F. I. M. and Lockhart, R. S. (1972) Levels of processing: A framework for memory research. *Journal of Verbal Learning and Verbal Behavior*, 11, 671-684.

Cuvo, A. J. (1974) Incentive level influence on overt rehearsal and free recall as a function of age. *Journal of Experimental Child Psychology*, 18, 167-181.

Davenport, W. G. (1968) Auditory vigilance: The effects of costs and values on signals. *Australian Journal of Psychology*, 20, 213-218.

Davenport, W. G. (1969) Vibrotactile vigilance: The effects of costs and values on signals. *Perception and Psychophysics*, 5, 25-28.

Davies, D. R. and Jones, D. M. (1975) The effects of noise and incentive upon attention in short-term memory. *British Journal of Psychology*, 66, 61-68.

Deci, E. L. (1971). Effects of externally mediated rewards on intrinsic motivation. *Journal of Personality and Social Psychology*, 18, 105-115.

Deci, E. L. (1975) *Intrinsic Motivation*. London: Plenum.

Dey, M. K. and Kaur, G. (1965) Facilitation of performance by experimentally induced ego motivation. *Journal of General Psychology*, 73, 237-247.

Dixon, P. N. and Cameron, A. E. (1976) Personality and motivational factors on an intentional-incidental learning task. *Psychological Reports*, 39, 1315-1320.

Dornbush, R. L. (1965) Motivation and positional cues in incidental learning. *Perceptual and Motor Skills*, 20, 709-714.

Easterbrook, J. A. (1959) The effect of emotion on cue utilization and the organization of behaviour. *Psychological Review*, 66, 183-201.

Elliott, R. (1970) Simple reaction time: Effects associated with age, preparatory interval, incentive-shift, and mode of presentation. *Journal of Experimental Child Psychology*, 9, 86-107.

Elliott, R., Bankart, C. P., and Flaherty, B. (1976) Relation of heart-rate deceleration and simple reaction time. *Perceptual and Motor Skills*, 42, 1075-1084.

Eysenck, H. J. (1964) *Experiments in Motivation*. Oxford: Pergamon.

Eysenck, H. J. and Gillan, P. W. (1964) Speed and accuracy in mirror drawing as a function of drive. In H. J. Eysenck (ed.), *Experiments in Motivation*. Oxford: Pergamon.

Eysenck, H. J. and Warwick, K. M. (1964) The effects of drive level on a multiple-choice reaction task. In H. J. Eysenck (ed.), *Experiments in Motivation*. Oxford: Pergamon.

Eysenck, M. W. (1981) Learning, memory and personality. In H. J. Eysenck (ed.), *A Model for Personality*. Heidelberg: Springer.

Eysenck, M. W. (1982) *Attention and Arousal: Cognition and Performance.* Heidelberg: Springer.

Eysenck, M. W. and Eysenck, M. C. (1980) Effects of monetary incentives on rehearsal and on cued recall. *Bulletin of the Psychonomic Society*, 15, 245–247.

Farr, J. L. (1976) Task characteristics, reward contingency, and intrinsic motivation. *Organizational Behavior and Human Performance*, 16, 294–307.

Feldman, M. P. (1964) Response reversal performance as a function of drive level. In H. J. Eysenck (ed.), *Experiments in Motivation.* Oxford: Pergamon.

Fowler, C. J.H. and Wilding, J. (1979) Differential effects of noise and incentives on learning. *British Journal of Psychology*, 70, 149–153.

Glucksberg, S. (1962) The influence of strength of drive on functional fixedness and perceptual recognition. *Journal of Experimental Psychology*, 63, 36–41.

Glucksberg, S. (1964) Problem solving: Response competition and the influence of drive. *Psychological Reports*, 15, 939–942.

Gottsdanker, R. (1975) The attaining and maintaining of preparation. In P. M. A. Rabbitt and S. Dornic (eds.), *Attention and Performance, Vol. V.* London: Academic Press.

Gray, J. A. (1973) Causal theories and how to test them. In J. R. Royce (ed.), *Multivariate Analysis of Psychological Theory.* London: Academic Press.

Hamilton, P., Hockey, G. R. J., and Rejman, M. (1977) The place of the concept of activation in human information processing theory: An integrative approach. In S. Dornic (ed.), *Attention and Performance, Vol. VI.* Hillsdale, N.J.: Erlbaum.

Harackiewicz, J. M. (1979) The effects of reward contingency and performance feedback on intrinsic motivation. *Journal of Personality and Social Psychology*, 37, 1352–1363.

Harley, W. F. (1965) The effect of monetary incentive in paired associate learning using a differential method. *Psychonomic Science*, 2, 377–378.

Herzberg, F., Mausner, B., and Snyderman, B. (1959) *The Motivation to Work.* London: John Wiley & Sons.

Johnson, R. and Thomson, C. (1962) Incidental and intentional learning under three conditions of motivation. *American Journal of Psychology*, 75, 284–288.

Kahneman, D. (1973) *Attention and Effort.* Englewood Cliffs, N.J.: Prentice-Hall.

Kahneman, D. and Peavler, W. S. (1969) Incentive effects and pupillary changes in associative learning. *Journal of Experimental Psychology*, 79, 312–318.

Kausler, D. H., Laughlin, P. R., and Trapp, E. P. (1963) Effects of incentive-set on relevant and irrelevant (incidental) learning in children. *Child Development*, 34, 195–199.

Kausler, D. H. and Trapp, E. P. (1962) Effects of incentive-set and task variables on relevant and irrelevant learning in serial verbal learning. *Psychological Reports*, 10, 451–457.

Kazdin, A. E. and Bootzin, R. R. (1972) The token economy: An evaluative review. *Journal of Applied Behavioral Analysis Monographs*, no. 1:5(3).

Kruglanski, A. W., Alon, S., and Lewis, T. (1972) Retrospective misattribution and task enjoyment. *Journal of Experimental Social Psychology*, 8, 493–501.

Kruglanski, A. W., Stein, C., and Rider, A. (1977) Contingencies of exogenous reward and task performance: On the 'minimax' strategy in instrumental behaviour. *Journal of Applied Social Psychology*, 7, 141–148.

Levine, J. (1966) The effects of values and costs on the detection and identification of signals in auditory vigilance. *Human Factors*, 8, 525–537.

Locke, E. A. (1968) Toward a theory of task motivation and incentives. *Organizational Behavior and Human Performance*, 3, 157–189.

Locke, E. A., Bryan, J. F., and Kendall, L. M. (1968) Goals and intentions as mediators as mediators of the effects of monetary incentives on behaviour. *Journal of Applied Psychology*, **52**, 104–121.

Loftus, G. R. and Wickens, T. D. (1970) Effect of incentive on storage and retrieval processes. *Journal of Experimental Psychology*, **85**, 141–147.

Macfarlane, D. A. (1930) The role of kinaesthesis in maze learning. *University of California Publications in Psychology*, **4**, 277–305.

Maller, J. B. and Zubin, J. (1932) The effect of motivation upon intelligence test scores. *Journal of Genetic Psychology*, **41**, 136–151.

McGraw, K. O. (1978) The detrimental effects of reward on performance: A literature review and a prediction model. In M. R. Lepper and D. Greene (eds.), *The Hidden Costs of Reward: New Perspectives on the Psychology of Human Motivation*. Hillsdale, N.J.: Erlbaum.

McGraw, K. O. and McCullers, J. C. (1979) Evidence of a detrimental effect of extrinsic incentives on breaking a mental set. *Journal of Experimental Social Psychology*, **15**, 285–294.

McNamara, H. J. and Fisch, R. I. (1964) Effect of high and low motivation on two aspects of attention. *Perceptual and Motor Skills*, **19**, 571–578.

Nachreiner, F. (1977) Experiments on the validity of vigilance experiments. In R. R. Mackie (ed.), *Vigilance: Theory, Operational Performance, and Physiological Correlates*. London: Plenum.

Nelson, T. O. (1976) Reinforcement and human memory. In W. K. Estes (ed.), *Handbook of Learning and Cognitive Processes, Vol. 3*, London: John Wiley & Sons.

Pritchard, R. D. and Curts, M. I. (1973) The influence of goal setting and financial incentives on task performance. *Organizational Behavior and Human Performance*, **10**, 175–183.

Revelle, W. and Michaels, E. J. (1976) The theory of achievement motivation revisited: The implications of inertial tendencies. *Psychological Review*, **83**, 394–404.

Rubin, B. M., Shantz, D. W., and Smock, C. D. (1962) Perceptual constriction as a function of incentive motivation. *Perceptual and Motor Skills*, **15**, 90.

Sostek, A. J. (1978) Effects of electrodermal lability and payoff instructions on vigilance performance. *Psychophysiology*, **15**, 561–568.

Suedfeld, P. and Landon, P. B. (1970) Motivational arousal and task complexity. *Journal of Experimental Psychology*, **83**, 329–330.

Terborg, J. R. (1976) The motivational components of goal setting. *Journal of Applied Psychology*, **61**, 613–621.

Terborg, J. R. and Miller, H. E. (1978) Motivation, behaviour, and performance: A closer examination of goal setting and monetary incentives. *Journal of Applied Psychology*, **63**, 29–39.

Trope, Y. (1975) Seeking information about one's own ability as a determinant of choice among tasks. *Journal of Personality and Social Psychology*, **32**, 1004–1013.

Wasserman, E. A., Weiner, B., and Houston, J. P. (1968) Another failure for motivation to enhance trace retrieval. *Psychological Reports*, **22**, 1007–1008.

Weiner, B. (1966) Motivation and memory. *Psychological Monographs*, **80**, no. 18.

Wickens, D. D. and Simpson, C. K. (1968) Trace cue position, motivation and short-term memory. *Journal of Experimental Psychology*, **76**, 282–285.

Wilkinson, R. T. (1961) Interaction of lack of sleep with knowledge of results, repeated testing and individual differences. *Journal of Experimental Psychology*, **62**, 263–271.

Wilkinson, R. T. (1963) Interaction of noise with knowledge of results and sleep deprivation. *Journal of Experimental Psychology*, **66**, 332–337.

Wilkinson, R. T., El-Beheri, S., and Gieseking, C. C. (1972) Performance and arousal as a function of incentive, information load, and task novelty. *Psychophysiology*, **9**, 589–599.

Willett, R. A. (1964) Experimentally induced drive and performance on a five-choice reaction task. In H. J. Eysenck (ed.), *Experiments in Motivation*. Oxford: Pergamon.

Wolk, S. and DuCette, J. (1974) Intentional performance and incidental learning as a function of personality and task dimensions. *Journal of Personality and Social Psychology*, **29**, 90–101.

Yerkes, R. M. and Dodson, J. D. (1908) The relation of strength of stimulus to rapidity of habit-formation. *Journal of Comparative Neurology and Psychology*, **18**, 459–482.

Stress and Fatigue in Human Performance
Edited by G. R. J. Hockey

Chapter 8

Stress and Drugs

Keith Wesnes and David M. Warburton

The stress phenomenon is an integral part of normal everyday life. When we are in a state of relaxed wakefulness the stress response is very low, but as soon as we start to concentrate and do something, the brain prepares us for action both psychologically and physiologically, and the stress response may thus be viewed as a natural consequence of *any* human information processing activity. However, when the situation–person interaction is very uncertain, too intense and too prolonged, then distress occurs. Everyone's life is marked by particularly stressful life events, such as bereavement, and few of us are equipped to minimize the distress that results from these occurrences. However, such events are only isolated episodes in our lives and the commonest cause of the stress phenomenon are the demands of every-day life, which can produce distress when a person either feels or finds out that he cannot cope with them. Consequently, drugs which can control the stress phenomenon form an important part of our lives. In this chapter we will consider the stress phenomenon, the use of alcohol, nicotine, and the benzodiazepines to control it, and the consequences of their use for performance.

STRESSORS

The initiating factors in the stress phenomenon are termed *stressors*. A wide range of physical stimuli act as stressors, including exercise, restraint, heat, cold, noise, pain, shock, injury, and infection. All of these can elicit stress responses which are a simple monotonic function of the intensity of the physical stimulus. For mental work the stress response can be just as large as that produced by a physical stress, and can be directly proportional to the amount of information processed per unit time, with the largest responses being produced by information overload, when task demands exceed a person's capacities. Bainbridge (1974) has defined information-processing capacity as the processing operations and processing strategies which a person has available. An individual's level of performance will be a function of the processing capacity and the task demands, and a person's experience will be important in terms of the processing operations and processing strategies that have been developed. Most people work below maximum effort most of the time, and, although they can increase their effort to the maximum for short periods (Bainbridge, 1974), continuous work at maximum levels of effort results in more rapid onset of fatigue.

Thus, the stressful effects of work must be seen as an interaction between task demands, the person, and the environmental conditions. One way of viewing this interaction has been adopted from studies of elasticity in physics (Russell, 1953). A load is placed on a body to impose stress, the effects of this load can be measured as strain. In the present context stressor will refer to the imposed load on the information-processing system, and the consequences of the imposed load will be termed the *stress response*. This approach enables the physiological data to be related to that of the work psychologists. They proposed that stress is a consequence of the distribution of task demands over time, the mental load, and strain is a consequence of the individual processing capacity and the stress (Luczak, 1971). In this context stress and strain are being used in a quantitatively neutral sense, and do not imply that extreme demands are being made on the system, i.e. overload. The resulting performance will not necessarily reflect the amount of the processing performed (Bainbridge, 1974), because it will depend on the relation between mental capacity and the task demands, and this relation is almost certainly not linear. Luczak (1971) suggested that strain can be assessed by physiological measures so that the physiological stress response will reflect the mental effort which in turn is directly related to strain.

However, some psychological stimuli are stressors, not merely because of their mental load but because of their distribution in time. Information produces a much greater stress response if it is presented at unpredictable intervals than if it occurs regularly, even though the density of these stimuli over time is the same (Warburton, 1979). Thus, stressors must be quantified in terms of their uncertainty, and the stress response would be inversely proportional to their predictability. However, uncertainty of information cannot always be assessed without considering the individual perceiving it.

Situational uncertainty is the result of the many alternative meanings that the input has for the person, and with the available response choices for that person, so that certainty must be defined subjectively. For an individual there will be degrees of uncertainty about *whether* an event will happen, *what* event might occur, *when* it will happen, and *what* action can be taken. At work, stressors will depend both on how the person processes information and on how he perceives himself and his job with respect to the organization. Individuals will vary considerably in their appraisal of the same event, and even whether they perceive it as desirable or undesirable (Johnson and Sarason, 1979). Clearly, stressors cannot be defined independently of the person.

If psychological stressors must be considered with respect to the individual, and the stress response is a function of the person's evaluation of the input, the difference between 'psychological' stressors and 'physical' stressors disappears. All physical stressors (e.g. pain) have psychological effects and it is impossible to differentiate them in terms of the stress response.

THE STRESS RESPONSE

In this section it will be emphasized that the stress response must be viewed as a complex pattern of cognitive and physiological changes that prepare a person for mental and physical action, i.e. a mobilization of resources. Recent information-processing models are based on the idea that an individual is an active processor of information, not merely a passive channel. One of the assumptions of these models is that the individual has limited resources and so must allocate resources to one process or another on the basis of some sort of allocation strategy (Kahneman, 1973; Norman and Bobrow, 1975).

In most models effort is equated with arousal and it is postulated that an inverted U-shaped relation exists between performance and arousal. Since stressors may produce arousal, it is assumed that there is a stressor magnitude which is optimal for performance of a particular task, and stressor levels which are either less than, or greater than, this optimum level will produce inferior performance (Levi, 1972). However, Hockey (1979; Hockey and Hamilton, Chapter 12, this volume) argue that it is wrong to think of stressor effects as unitary changes, and show that stressors change the pattern of processing. Taking noise as an example, they show that there is a trade-off between information through-put and information storage. Thus, increasing the intensity of noise increases the selectivity of attention but lowers the capacity of primary memory; increases the selectivity of responses, but decreases the use of intermediate confidence categories; and increases the work-rate but lowers accuracy. Consequently, the changes in performance of a task will be partly a function of the different cognitive components involved. Altogether the cognitive stress response consists of a pattern of changes that has evolved for rapid mental and physical action.

Electrocortical arousal

A relationship between mental effort and neural processes has been suggested by Kahneman (1973) who proposed that the limited resources are related to physiological arousal, so that resources and arousal vary together in the low range of arousal levels by increasing and decreasing to match the task demands, and the allocation of resources is based on the level of arousal. We believe that the relevant subtype of arousal for mental effort is electrocortical arousal, and that an individual's electrocortical arousal can be related to his mental effort.

The electrocortical activity of the awake individual is usually divided into three types—alpha, beta, and theta. Beta activity consists of small amplitude (low voltage), fast waves (13–30 cycles per second), and is the most desynchronized activity, which is the usual activity of an alert person. Alpha activity has a larger amplitude, is much slower at 8–12 cycles per second, and is typical of relaxed wakefulness. The slowest activity in the awake subject is theta (4–7 cycles per second) which has a still larger amplitude and is typical of the drowsy person who is about to go to sleep.

When normal subjects have electrodes attached to their scalp for the first time they are uncertain about the test situation and the procedures. Records of electrocortical activity from the first session show a large amount of cortical desynchronization (beta activity) and very few of the more synchronized alpha waves (Lindsley, 1950), but as the person becomes more familiar with the situation and relaxes, the amplitude of the waves increases, frequency decreases, and alpha waves develop. However, if the subject is surprised or embarrassed there is again electrocortical arousal (see Lindsley, 1951). Thus, in a normal population of subjects an uncertain situation and apprehension increase beta activity, i.e. electrocortical arousal. Similar results have been obtained from patients who were suffering from chronic anxiety; beta activity was predominant and alpha activity was observed less frequently than with groups of normal subjects (Lader, 1975). When flashes of light are presented to a subject the electrocortical activity can be driven, and in anxious groups there is better driving at the higher frequencies than in normals, which shows that the endogenous rhythm is faster in the anxious groups (Lader, 1975).

Electrocortical arousal is controlled by the cholinergic pathways ascending from the mid-brain reticular formation (Warburton, 1981), and an important part for the stress response is the hippocampal pathway. The hippocampal formation is part of a feedback loop providing regulation of the activity in the ascending cholinergic electrocortical arousal pathways (Warburton, 1975; Gray, 1981), in order that redundant, i.e. 'expected', stimuli do not activate the cortex. This implies that there must be storage of information about simple predictable stimuli in the hippocampal formation, but analysis of more complex redundant stimuli occurs at the cortex which controls the mid-brain reticular formation via the hippocampal formation. Thus, feedback from the hippocampal formation to the mid-brain reticular formation maintains internal stability by diminishing the response to predictable events in the internal and external environments (Pribram, 1969). As a result, the amount of desynchronization depends on the amount of uncertainty in the environment, and a person reduces uncertainty by establishing expectancies about the world, but new information will increase uncertainty and so produce an increase in electrocortical arousal. Therefore the amount of this arousal will depend on the size of the match and mismatch between the person's expectancies and information input (see Pribram, 1967).

These changes in electrocortical activity with stressors provide an explanation for the cognitive shifts in information throughput and information storage that were mentioned both earlier, and elsewhere in this volume (see Chapter 12). A large number of studies have correlated drug-induced variations in electrocortical arousal with various aspects of information processing (see review of Warburton, 1979). They have shown that more synchronized cortical activity, such as theta and alpha activity, is correlated with both poorer selective attention and slower reactions, but with greater creative thinking and phantasizing. As the electrocortical activity becomes more desynchronized there is increased selective attention and faster responding, but thinking becomes more convergent and creative problem-solving is poorer. When there is abundant beta activity attention is very selective, primary memory is reduced, work-rate is high, but responses are stereotyped. This pattern of cognitive function is obviously ideal for mental and physical action in a highly stressful situation involving uncertainty and danger. The fuel for this action is mobilized by the stress hormones that are released in such a situation.

Hormone release by stressors

The hormonal stress response consists of the release from the adrenal glands of the catecholamines, adrenalin and noradrenalin, and the corticosteroids, including cortisone and corticosterone (see Figure 35). Catecholamines are released from the adrenal medulla by the brain via the pathways of the sympathetic nervous system. The control of corticosteroid secretion from the adrenal cortex is more complex; the median eminence of the hypothalamus secretes corticotrophin releasing factor (CRF) into a specialized blood vessel system to the adenohypophysis of the pituitary gland, where it triggers the release of adrenocorticotrophic hormone (ACTH). ACTH is carried via the general systemic circulation to the adrenal cortex, from where corticosteroids are released into the blood stream and act on many tissues throughout the body, including the brain. Catecholamines pass through the blood brain barrier very poorly and their major action is on tissues outside the brain.

Corticosteroid release in behavioural situations

The release of corticosteroids in a stress situation can be illustrated by considering the pattern of excretion in a unit of soldiers who were expecting an attack in Vietnam (Bourne, 1969). Common sense would suggest that all soldiers would show dramatic increases in corticosteroid production under the threat of combat, but in fact the ordinary soldiers showed a 40 per cent *decrease* in urinary corticosteroids on the day of an anticipated attack, and

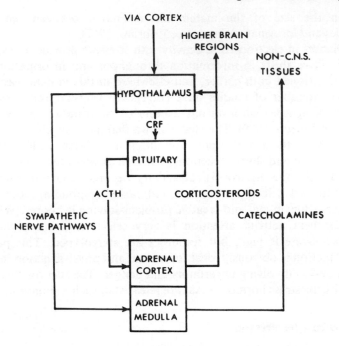

Figure 35. The hormonal stress response.

only the officer and radio operator showed 25 per cent increases. These unexpected changes can be related to the levels of uncertainty under which the two sets of soldiers were operating. On the day of the attack the ordinary soldiers performed routine tasks for which they had been highly trained, i.e. tasks involving little uncertainty. In contrast, the officer was required to stay alert for new instructions which might call for novel decisions and patterns of behaviour. The radio operator was in a similar position in the sense that he was transmitting and receiving new messages and so was dealing with high information inputs (uncertainty).

These results show that stress hormones are released by psychological stimuli which are just as potent as physical stimuli for triggering release (Mason, 1968). Uncertainty seems to be a common factor of many situations in which there is hormone release and this idea would relate to the idea of hormone release as an anticipation of action.

The stress steroid response was assessed in a milder stress situation involving public speaking (Bliss, Migeon, Branch, and Samuels, 1956). In one case subjects were told to talk about themselves in front of a one-way mirror for 15 minutes, and in the second case students were asked to evaluate a course, and told that their performance would determine their marks from the course. Higher levels of corticosteroids were found in the test situations than in the mirror situation. However, only small changes were found in subjects who were experienced public speakers, while subjects who felt that they did not know how to handle the situation had higher levels. Furthermore, these elevations of steroids in an experimental situation were smaller than Bliss *et al.* observed in a real-life emergency situation where the subjects were healthy individuals who had accompanied a person to a hospital emergency ward. Here the steroid levels increased by 90 per cent over levels for a similar control population. For the group, the greater the objective uncertainty the higher steroid output was elevated, but more importantly, the elevation was related to the amount of *subjective* uncertainty, i.e. there was an interaction between the individual and the situation, which determined the hormone response.

Corticosteroids pass easily through tissues, and so they pass through the blood–brain barrier from the cerebral blood vessels to act on the neurons of the brain. Studies of the effects of corticosteroids on brain chemistry have shown that brain levels of noradrenalin decrease after exposure to a variety of stressors (Levi and Maynert, 1964). This change can be interpreted as hormone feedback to the brain which activates adrenergic neurons. Serotonin neurons are also affected by the hormone feedback; injections of cortisol and corticosterone deplete serotonin, showing that steroid feedback releases the serotonin. Increased release would reduce the levels of serotonin if there was not a compensatory increase in synthesis. Evidence for corticosteroid control of synthesis has come from studies where synthesis inhibitors were not injected and the serotonin levels remained constant after stress. Further experiments have shown that increased synthesis is due to corticosteroids producing increased tryptophan hydroxylase activity, the synthesizing enzyme for serotonin. In summary, corticosteroids activate both noradrenergic and serotonin neurons.

If the feedback of corticosteroids acting on the neurochemical systems in the brain form part of the sensations experienced during stress, then we would expect increased symptoms of stress and even anxiety when corticosteroids are injected. After corticosteroid injections patients report a tense alert state marked by irritability and emotional lability. Anxiety was not always increased, which suggests that the corticosteroid only produced *proneness* to anxiety, and that anxiety was not experienced unless a cognitive compononent was present (see Warburton, 1979).

Catecholamine release in behavioural situations

Performance in any task which involves sustained attention is described as stressful by subjects. Frankenhaeuser and Patkai (1964) measured the catecholamine excretion of a group of students who were carrying out coding and proof-reading tasks under distracting conditions which would produce information overload. The excretion of catecholamines was increased but, although the secretion of adrenalin was greater and more consistent, small but highly significant correlations between noradrenalin excretion and performance in the later stages of the task were found. Accordingly, Frankenhaeuser hypothesized that catecholamine release served an adaptive purpose by increasing arousal which enabled the subject to sustain his concentration in boring and stressful tasks. If this interpretation is correct, the effects cannot be due to a direct effect on the brain arousal pathways, because the physiological concentrations of catecholamines in such situations do not pass from the blood to brain in measurable quantities.

Levi (1972) measured catecholamine levels in clerks working for a salary or paid for piece-work. During piece-work the number of processed invoices doubled without errors increasing, but their performance got worse during the late afternoon. There were higher levels of both adrenalin and noradrenalin levels under piece-work, but there were no differences between morning and afternoon in excretion rates. The subjects reported that they felt more fatigued during piece-work compared with salaried work. Contrary to Frankenhaeuser's hypothesis, there was dissociation between catecholamine excretion and performance as well as the subjective experience of fatigue.

Fatigue

Although the anatomical connections are not known, the release of cortico-steroids and catecholamines are usually highly correlated (Mason, 1968), both being increased in situations of uncertainty. Release in these circumstances makes sense in terms of the metabolic effects of the catecholamines and corticosteroids, which mobilize the energy resources to prepare body tissues for action. The advantage of having two groups of hormones with similar actions may be that the adrenal medullary system can provide a rapid short duration response because it is neurally activated, and the catecholamines are rapidly metabolized, while the corticosteroids provide a delayed but more sustained response.

Both corticosteroids and catecholamines raise the blood levels of carbohydrates and free fatty acids (Williamson, 1975), which makes available an increased supply of energy for physical and mental work. Thus, studies of carbohydrate and fat use in physical work of different intensities have found that during exhausting work there was a depletion of carbohydrates, but subjective symptoms of fatigue disappeared within 15 minutes of ingesting glucose, which increased the blood-sugar levels again (Christensen and Hensen, 1939). The central system has low reserves of sugar and depends on blood sugar for its supply of energy, and in man about 60 per cent of the liver sugar output supplies brain metabolism; exhaustion seems to be more a central nervous phenomenon than a lack of sugar for muscles (Åstrand and Rodahl, 1970). Thus, the hormone stress response mobilizes energy to partially prevent fatigue, and subjects with higher levels of catecholamines perform better not because catecholamines increase arousal, as Frankenhaeuser suggested, but rather because fatigue is reduced. Of course, sustained stress will result in a depletion of the fuel reserves and an onset of fatigue, even though the stress hormones are still being secreted at the same level, as in the studies of Levi (1972).

Summary

Modern cognitive theories emphasize the role of the person as an active processor of information, and as the task demands increase the amount of stress will increase. The amount of strain will depend on the processing capacity of the individual, and in order to perform effectively a person must allocate attentional resources to combat the imposed strain. The performance output will reflect the attentional effort. The cholinergic electrocortical arousal pathway controls the balance between throughput and storage. The hippocampal pathway of this system prevents redundant information producing electrocortical arousal, and thus stress hormone release. Corticosteroid and catecholamine release occurs in uncertain situations as electrocortical arousal increases. These hormones mobilize blood sugars and fats, the fuel for both mental and physical action, which, in the short term, promotes extra effort and higher performance. In the long term the sustained release of sugars and fats leads to depletion and fatigue, and mental work can be as exhausting as physical work because of the high levels of electrocortical arousal and the consequent stress response. Thus, the explicit theme of this section has been that the stress response is not limited to those classical situations in which the individual is subjected to pain, noise, rapid changes in temperature, and so on, but occurs whenever the individual is presented with stimuli which have a high informational content. While the stress response is a natural adaptive response to environmental information, there are limits to the degree and the duration of this response which individuals are either able or willing to endure, and in such instances individuals often take psychoactive substances in order to enable them to cope. These substances can either be prescribed by a doctor, or the individual can self-medicate with freely available drugs. In the next sections three of the most commonly used substances in such situations will be discussed, with regard not only to the mechanisms by which they enable the individual to cope, but also to the resulting effects such drugs have upon human psychomotor performance.

THE BENZODIAZEPINES

Between 10 and 20 per cent of adults in the Western world ingest drugs on a fairly regular basis to reduce anxiety and tension (Greenblatt, Shader, and

Koch-Weser, 1975). In the U.S. during 1977, the National Institute of Drug Abuse estimated that 5,000 million doses of benzodiazepines were prescribed, over 20 doses per head of the population. The first benzodiazepine was synthesized in the mid-1950s and the pharmacological properties of this drug were revealed in 1957 (Randall and Kappell, 1973). Following review and approval by the Federal Drug Administration in 1960, chlordiazepoxide hydrochloride (Librium) was introduced in the United States, followed three years later by diazepam (Valium), and two years later by oxazepam (Serax). There are now over 20 benzodiazepine derivatives marketed throughout the world (Sternbach, 1980), and the last 20 years has seen a consistent trend in the clinical preference for benzodiazepines over the previous drugs of choice — the barbiturates and the propranediol derivatives — such that the National Institute of Drug Abuse now estimates that benzodiazepines form 90 per cent of the tranquillizer market (Hughes and Brewin, 1979).

Stress and anxiety

The characteristic action of the benzodiazepines, which first brought the drugs under scrutiny as possible anti-anxiety agents, is to increase behavioural responses that are depressed by response-contingent punishment or conditioned fear. In such experiments animals are first trained to respond for food or fluid reward. When such behaviour has reached stable levels, an auditory or visual warning is presented which indicates that as long as it persists responses will still be rewarded but will also be punished by electric shock. This always leads to a suppression of responding, and the effect of benzodiazepines is to release this suppression, although the drugs have no consistent effects upon non-punished responding. These findings have been replicated in a large number of laboratories using a variety of different species (see review by Haefeley, 1978).

Besides these behavioural effects, benzodiazepines also decrease various indices of the stress response in both animals and man. For example, diazepam has been found to greatly reduce the Galvanic Skin Response (GSR) of monkeys exposed to brief electric shocks (Migler, 1975). Similarly, the increase of plasma corticosterone in irregularly foot-shocked rats has also been found to be reduced by the drug (Bassett and Cairncross, 1974). In man the benzodiazepines have been found to lower the GSR to the anticipation of electric shocks (Boucsein and Wendt-Suhl, 1976).

The clinical testing of the benzodiazepines has been comprehensively reviewed by Greenblatt and Shader (1974, 1978). In their second review of 24 studies carried out between 1974 and 1976, they reported that 18 had shown a strong reduction in neurotic anxiety compared to placebo, four a trend, and two no difference (Greenblatt and Shader, 1978). In these reviews, the authors also concluded that the literature indicated a reasonably consistent superiority of benzodiazepines over barbiturates in clinical efficiency.

The benzodiazepines have also been found to reduce anxiety in non-psychiatric patients. Steen and Hahl (1969) studied the effects of diazepam upon 800 patients who were undergoing a variety of surgical procedures. Compared to patients on placebo, those receiving diazepam showed reduced restlessness and apprehension both pre- and post-operatively. Other studies have found both chlordiazepoxide and diazepam particularly effective in reducing pre-operative anxiety (Tornetta, 1965; Crawford, 1973), and diazepam markedly reduces the severe post-operative anxiety and nervous tension which accompanies open-heart surgery (McClish, Andrew, and Tetrcault, 1968).

Cholinergic function

Evidence that the benzodiazepines decrease the turnover in hemispheric cholinergic neurones, by blocking the release of acetylcholine, comes from three main areas of study. First, the drugs block the convulsions, muscle spasms, and respiratory failure which are produced by anti-cholinesterases (Lipp, 1973; Johnson and Lowndes, 1974). Secondly, the benzodizepines block the convulsant activities of pentetraxol (Zbinden and Randall, 1967; Consolo, Garattini, and Ladinsky, 1975), a cholinergic stimulant which has been found to reduce brain acetylcholine levels (Longoni, Mulas, and Pepeu, 1974), and to produce a massive release of acetylcholine from the rat cerebral cortex (Mitchell, 1963). Thirdly, the benzodiazepines increase the hemispheric levels of acetylcholine in three separate species, while having no effect upon either acetylcholinesterase, choline, or choline acetyltransferase (Consolo, Garattini, and Ladinsky, 1975).

Human performance

Earlier we described the role played by the ascending reticular cholinergic pathways in human information processing. By blocking the release of acetylcholine, and thus lowering the activity in cholinergic pathways, we would predict that the benzodiazepines will lower the efficiency of human performance. This prediction is supported by a large number of studies which have investigated the effects of a variety of benzodiazepines upon a wide range of performance tasks. These studies, the majority of which have been recently reviewed (Hindmarch, 1980), indicate that the benzodiazepines increase both simple and complex reaction time, lower target detection, disrupt performance on the digit-symbol substitution test, impair the efficiency both of card-sorting and letter-cancellation, decrease the rate of tapping, lower mathematical efficiency, increase errors in motor-manipulation and complex-coordination tasks, lower the critical flicker fusion frequency, and disrupt both real and simulated driving. Because of the particularly long half-lives of some of the benzodiazepines, e.g. nitrazepam and flurazepam, the disruption of performance produced by these drugs can often be detected during the day following administration. We have studied the effects of nightly doses of flurazepam 30 mg, and temazepam 40 mg, upon the performance of a rapid information-processing task the next morning (Warburton, Wesnes, and Pitkethly, 1981). In this task subjects are required to monitor a continuous series of digits, presented visually at a rate of 100 per minute, and to detect and respond to runs of three odd or three even digits. As can be seen from Figure 36, the drugs lowered both the speed and the accuracy of detection, although this disruption was more marked with flurazepam.

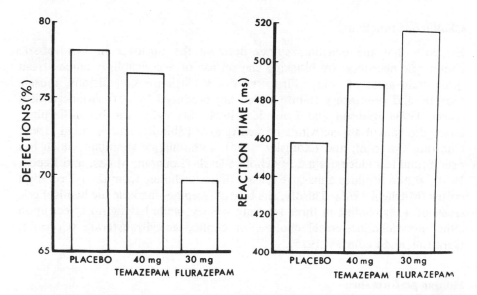

Figure 36. The effects of temazepam 40 mg and flurazepam 30 mg upon the percentage of correct detections and the reaction time in a rapid information-processing task.

Another characteristic action of the benzodiazepines is to disrupt memory, one of the advantages of using diazepam as a pre-anaesthetic being its ability to produce amnesia for pre-operative events (Bookman and Randall, 1975). Several studies have demonstrated that the disruption of memory occurs only for information presented after drug administration (e.g. Dundee and Pandit, 1972; Ghonheim and Mewaldt, 1975; File and Bond, 1979), suggesting that it is the registration phase of memory which is impaired.

A number of these studies have compared the effects of diazepam and scopolamine, a post-synaptic cholinergic antagonist (Dundee and Panditt, 1972; Ghonheim and Mewaldt, 1975, 1977). In these studies the drugs appear to have very similar effects, allowing for differences in dosage and half-life, which suggest that the effects of diazepam may well be mediated by the drug's effect upon cholinergic neurones. However, Ghonhaim and Mewaldt (1977) were able to almost completely counteract the effects of scopolamine upon memory by administering physostigmine, a drug which blocks acetylcholinesterase, whereas physostigmine had no effect upon the memory deficit produced by diazepam. The authors argued that the absence of effect of physostigmine upon the diazepam-induced memory deficit should be taken as evidence against the hypothesis that diazepam produces its effect upon memory performance as a result of its cholinergic effects. However, if the mechanisms by which scopolamine and diazepam disrupt cholinergic transmission are considered, an alternative explanation becomes evident. Scopolamine blocks cholinergic transmission by imitating acetylcholine and combining with the post-synaptic receptor, but then not altering the permeability of the post-synaptic membrane. Diazepam, however, appears to exert its action upon cholinergic neurones by blocking the release of acetylcholine (see previous section). In the case of a cholinergic synapse blocked by scopolamine, a decrease in the activity of acetylcholinesterase by physostigmine would increase the synaptic acetylcholine available to compete with scopolamine for post-synaptic receptor combination. Furthermore, not only would there be more acetylcholine available in the synapse, but it would also stay there for a longer period of time, which would also increase the likelihood of the neuro-transmitter combining with the post-synaptic receptor. On the other hand, there will be little benefit in blocking acetylcholinesterase activity in a neuron in which the release of acetylcholine is blocked by a benzodiazepine, because there would be little synaptic acetylcholine anyway.

Thus, these findings do not address the question of the neurochemical bases of the effects of the benzodiazepines upon memory. Furthermore, although the dependent variable in these studies is the recall of items of information, this need not indicate that a drug-induced deficit in recall results from an action of the drug upon memory processes. The benzodiazepines have been demonstrated to disrupt attentional efficiency in a wide variety of situations, and clearly such disruption could be the basis of the failures in recall observed in this research. At best it can be concluded that the mechanisms by which the drugs produce these effects are unclear, but to discuss these results in terms of actions of the drugs upon memory processes is quite unjustified.

Corticosteroids

Besides the ascending cholinergic reticular pathways, another cholinergic path-way has its origins in the ventral tegmental area but runs to the median eminence (Warburton, 1981). The function of this pathway is to trigger the release of CRF into the hypophyseal blood supply and thus emit ACTH from the anterior pituitary. By blocking cholinergic activity, the benzodiazepines would lower the ACTH-induced release of the corticosteroids into the bloodstream normally found in stressful situations, which would account for the previously discussed finding that diazepam lowered the levels of plasma corticosteroids in irregularly foot-shocked rats (Bassett and Cairncross, 1974).

Noradrenalin and dopamine function

The benzodiazepines have been found to decelerate the turnover of noradrenalin (Stein, Wise, and Berger, 1973). This effect is more markedly demonstrated in studies where the noradrenalin levels are increased by stress. For example, the benzodiazepines have been found to block the increase in noradrenalin turnover which typically accompanies electric shock (Taylor and Laverly, 1973). However, Stein, Wise, and Belluzzi (1975) argued that this change was not the basis of the anti-anxiety effect of the drug, and showed that repeated dosing with oxazepam resulted in a rapid tolerance to the decrease in noradrenalin turnover, although the drug maintained its anti-anxiety properties.

Dopamine turnover is also decreased by benzodiazepines. However, it is highly unlikely that this is related to the anti-anxiety actions of these compounds, because drugs such as neuroleptics reduce dopamine turnover to a greater degree, but do not exhibit an anti-anxiety effect (Haefely, 1978).

Serotonin function

Benzodiazepines reduce the rate of depletion of serotonin in the cortex and other parts of the brain (Lidbrink, Corrodi, Fuxe, and Olson, 1973) by blocking serotonin release (Chase, Katz, and Kopin, 1970). In contrast to the previously mentioned rapid tolerance to oxazepam-induced deceleration in turnover which occurs for noradrenalin, no such tolerance was observed for serotonin (Wise, Berger, and Stein, 1972). This finding suggests that serotonin is the neurotransmitter which is important in mediating the effects of the benzodiazepines upon anxiety, and this hypothesis has been thoroughly tested by Stein and his co-workers in an elegant series of studies. They argued that serotonin blockers and serotonin synthesis inhibitors would produce the same effects on behaviour as those produced by the benzodiazepines (Stein, Wise, and Berger, 1973). First, they injected methysergide, a serotonergic antagonist, and released the suppressed responding in a conflict situation. Similar results were obtained with para-chlorophenylalanine, the synthesis blocker, and the suppressed behaviour could be reinstated by the repletion of serotonin produced by its precursor, 5-hydroxytryptophan. Furthermore, both the serotonergic agonist, alpha-methyltryptamine, and serotonin enhanced the suppression of responding in the conflict situation, as would have been predicted from the other results. In a final test of the hypothesis, Stein *et al.*

injected oxazepam, releasing the suppressed responding, and then injected serotonin directly into the brain which restored the suppressed responding.

It has been proposed that the effects of the benzodiazepines upon serotonergic neurones are mediated by a primary action of the drugs upon GABAergic neurones (Haefely, 1978). GABAergic neurones are primarily inhibitory in nature and it is argued that by stimulating GABAergic activity, the benzodiazepines inhibit the release of serotonin. However, although the role of GABA in the anxiety effects of benzodiazepines still needs to be conclusively demonstrated, it is probable that such a role will eventually be shown. None the less, in terms of the experience of anxiety, the serotonergic action of these drugs would appear to be crucial, even though it may turn out to be a secondary effect to the actions of the benzodiazepines on GABA.

Summary

The benzodiazepines are particularly efficient drugs for reducing the stress response. Of the effects of the drugs upon the various neurotransmitters, only the cholinergic and serotonergic effects apepar to play a role in the reduction of the stress response.

By lowering cholinergic activity the drugs reduce the stress response in two ways. First, by reducing the activity of the cholinergic pathways controlling attention, the benzodiazepines will help to prevent information from raising cortical arousal, thus minimizing this aspect of the stress response. Consequently, the individual's awareness of stressful stimuli will be reduced, as will the likelihood that such stimuli will be recalled at a later date. Secondly, the activity in the cholinergic pathways controlling CRF release will be lowered, which will reduce the stress-induced release of the corticosteroids.

Despite these cholinergic effects, the main anti-anxiety action of the benzodiazepines would appear to result from the reduction in serotonergic activity which the drugs produce. The work of Stein *et al.* (1973) strongly implicates the serotonergic actions of the drugs in the characteristic reduction in punished responding, and as was discussed in an earlier section, serotonergic neurones play a large part in the actual experience of stress and anxiety. Further recent work upon a new benzodiazepine derivative suggests that a reduction in anxiety can be achieved without the disruption of psychomotor efficiency which is indicative of cholinergic blockade. The benzodiazepines discussed so far have all been 1,4 derivatives. However, clobazam, a 1,5 benzodiazepine derivative, while exhibiting anti-anxiety effects (Hunt, George, and Ridges, 1974) does not appear to impair psychomotor performance (e.g. Biehl, 1979; Hindmarch, 1979; Taeuber *et al.*, 1979), at least in the majority of subjects (Hindmarch, Hanks, and Hewett 1977), and there is some suggestion that the drug may actually improve performance (Biehl, 1979; Hindmarch, 1979; Hindmarch and Parrot, 1979). The interesting possibility here concerns the mechanism by which these possible improvements come about. The general absence of performance impairments with the drug would suggest to us that the drug does not produce a marked anti-cholinergic effect. However, it is unlikely that the drug will actually increase cholinergic activity, and it would thus appear that we are not looking at the effects of a drug which acts directly upon attentional mechanisms. Anxiety can disrupt performance, and it is possible that by reducing anxiety the drug is having a beneficial effect upon some subjects. The study of Biehl (1979) is of interest here because he selected subjects who had high neuroticism scores, and found that the drug produced an almost significant improvement in their readiness to brake in a real-life driving situation. Such subjects would be expected to show more anxiety in situations in which their performance was being monitored than subjects with lower neuroticism scores, and thus a reduction in anxiety without an impairment of efficiency may explain the trend towards better driving performance with the drug.

This is not to say that the cholinergic actions of the benzodiazepines are not important in reducing anxiety in some situations. For example, the amnesia for pre-operative events produced by the drugs is clearly of value, as are the hypnotic properties of flurazepam and temazepam. However, in some situations anxiety reduction without impaired information processing is clearly advantageous, and is certainly worthy of comprehensive future investigation.

ALCOHOL

Alcohol is one of the most widely self-administered drugs in the world. Firm knowledge of its use stems back to 6400 B.C. and it has been suggested that it was first used in the Palaeolithic Age, about 8,000 B.C. (Ray, 1972). Of the many alcohols only ethyl alcohol is sufficiently non-toxic to permit regular consumption. Despite the physical, social, and psychological damage which results from the misuse of the drug, it is banned in few countries in the world, and then for religious reasons. Very few adults in the Western world have not taken alcohol in one form or another, and moderate drinking is still generally considered to be a socially acceptable practice.

Alcohol is a small, fat soluble molecule which readily penetrates body membranes. It is particularly unusual in that it can be absorbed unchanged from the stomach, and far more rapidly from the small intestine. Because alcohol is rapidly and completely absorbed from the entire gastro-intestinal tract, only the rate of absorption can be varied. Three principle factors determine the rate of absorption. The first, and most important, is the amount of food in the stomach. Alcohol taken on a full stomach will take longer not only to reach the stomach walls, but also to pass through to the small intestine. The second is the presence of gas molecules in the beverage which will speed the passage of alcohol through the stomach to the small intestine. The third is the concentration of alcohol in the beverage: higher concentrations are absorbed more rapidly. Thus, for the maximum rate of absorption, a strong whisky and soda on an empty stomach is hard to beat!

Once alcohol is absorbed into the bloodstream it enters the hepatic circulation and passes almost immediately through the liver. From here it is carried throughout the body and enters all body fluids and tissues, including the central nervous system. While a small amount, less than 5 per cent, of the absorbed alcohol is excreted through the lungs, roughly 95 per cent of the alcohol is broken down by the enzyme alcohol dehydrogenase which is present primarily in the liver, and which is thus the factor which limits the rate of disappearance of alcohol from the body. In the liver, alcohol is first converted to acetaldehyde which is then itself broken down to acetic acid by aldehyde dehydrogenase. Unlike many other drugs the rate of metabolism is independent of the actual concentration of the drug in the bloodstream. Tolerance to the effects of alcohol has been demonstrated both in the short term and the long term (Cicero, 1978). Thus, after one drink, another has less effect than the first, and after several days' drinking subsequent doses have even less effect. The possible mechanisms for this tolerance are many, including alterations in drug metabolism or in the disposition and distribution of the drug, and cellular adaptations, and there would appear to be evidence to support each of these (Cicero, 1978).

Stress and anxiety

Alcohol is probably the most commonly used drug to alleviate stress and anxiety, and the well worn cliche 'you look like you need a drink', indicates the general acceptance that the drug has tranquillizing properties. These subjective effects of alcohol have been studied experimentally, and it has been found that moderate doses of alcohol produce initial feelings of reduced tension and euphoria (Williams, 1966; Lindman and Mellberg, 1976; Lindman and Taxell, 1976). This effect has been studied in detail by Persson, Sjoberg, and Svensson (1980) who found that alcohol increased feelings of pleasantness, activation, extroversion, calmness, social orientation, and control.

Acetaldehyde

Before considering the central nervous effects of alcohol, we must consider to what extent acetaldehyde, the first breakdown product of alcohol, is involved in these effects. It has been demonstrated that injection of acetaldehyde results in a rapid increase in brain acetaldehyde and produces physical dependence which has a degree of cross tolerance to alcohol (Oritz, Griffiths, and Littlejohn, 1974). However, following ethanol administration, very little acetaldehyde actually crosses the blood–brain barrier although the blood-levels are high. Furthermore, if pyrazole, a potent inhibitor of alcohol dehydrogenase, is injected following the administration of alcohol both the chronic and the acute effects of the drug are increased (Goldstein and Pal, 1971), which is exactly the opposite to what would be expected if these effects were due to acetaldehyde. Clearly, these findings indicate that acetaldehyde plays little or no part in the effects following alcohol administration, and in this account we shall attribute such effects to a direct action of alcohol on central nervous tissue.

Axonal conductance

Early studies of the effects of alcohol upon central nervous function indicated that the drug affected axonal membranes and lowered nerve conductance (Armstrong and Binstock, 1964). The mechanism for this effect could well be the lowering of central levels of calcium produced by alcohol (Ross, 1976), which would alter the permeability of the axonal membrane to both potassium and sodium. However, over the last 15 years it has become clear that despite this general effect upon neural transmission, the drug had differential effects upon the activity of the central neurotransmitters: acetylcholine, dopamine, noradrenalin, and serotonin.

Cholinergic function

Alcohol has been demonstrated to block the release of acetylcholine from cortical slices both *in vivo* (Carmichal and Israel, 1975; Phillis and Jhamandas, 1971) and *in vitro* (Kalant and Grose, 1967). Furthermore, the drug has also been found to disrupt the synthesis of acetylcholine (Smyth, Martin, Ross, and Beck, 1967). It is clear that, by blocking the synthesis and release of acetylcholine, alcohol will lower the transmission in the central cholinergic pathways originating in the ventral tegmental region.

Human performance

As discussed earlier, the ascending reticular cholinergic pathways control cortical arousal and thus determine the degree to which incoming information is evaluated. Inhibitory control is exerted over these pathways by the hippocampus, or by the cortex acting through the hippocampus, such that stimuli with low informational content are identified and prevented from increasing cortical arousal. As the stress response occurs in response to cholinergic activity in the ventral tegmental area, it is clear that a lowering of cholinergic activity will lower cortical arousal and prevent information from inducing the stress response. Furthermore, once electrocortical arousal is lowered it will be difficult for the individual to attend to particular stimuli and thus his awareness of stressful information will decrease.

From this account it is clear that alcohol should lower electrocortical arousal, and certainly the experimental evidence supports this. In both moderate and large doses alcohol slows the characteristic alpha frequency (Holmberg and Martens, 1955; Docter, Naitch, and Smith, 1966; Kalant, 1975; Knott and Venables, 1979). At blood alcohol concentrations (BACs) in the range 0.05–0.1 per cent this lowering of the dominant alpha frequency is in the range of 0.2–1 Hz. As the dose is increased so is the lowering of the alpha frequency to a maximum of 3 Hz at BACs of 0.2 per cent.

With this lowering of electrocortical arousal go the all-too-frequently observed changes in behavioural efficiency which result from alcohol administration. We all 'know someone' who has become drunk at some time or another, and the resulting impairments in articulation, concentration, skilled performance, balance, and memory are quite familiar to us. We are all equally aware that alcohol has been identified as a major contributor to motor accidents. For example, in Great Britain in the year preceding the introduction of legislation imposing a legal limit of alcohol in the blood of drivers of motor vehicles, 37 per cent of drivers killed on the roads had been drinking and 25 per cent had BACs exceeding 0.08 per cent. In the year following the introduction of legislation there was a 36 per cent decrease in the number of traffic fatalities during the main drink hours of 10 p.m. to 4 a.m., compared with a 7 per cent decrease over the rest of the day. This trend remained for the next five years although the maginitude of the decrease declined steadily (Sabey and Codling, 1975).

Several laboratory studies have investigated the pattern of changes in driving efficiency which follow alcohol administration by using driving simulators (Drew, Colquhoun, and Long, 1958; Landauer, Pococke, and Plott, 1974; Loomis and West, 1957). These experiments found that alcohol disrupts driving performance by impairing reaction time and steering efficiency, and also by lowering vigilance to speedometer readings.

In other studies of the effects of alcohol upon hyman psychomotor performance, the drug has been found to increase the reaction time of both single responses to single stimuli (Taeuber *et al.*, 1979; Taberner, 1980) and multiple responses to multiple stimuli (Indestrom and Cadenius, 1975), to lower the number of correct responses in a choice reaction test (Taeuber *et al.*, 1979), to impair persuit rotor performance (Siddell and Pless, 1971; Valeriote, Tong, and Durding, 1979) and complex coordination (Haffner *et al.*, 1973), to lower the critical flicker fusion frequency (Enzer, Simonson, and Ballard, 1944; Haffner *et al.*, 1973), to disrupt cancellation performance (Zirkle, McActee, King, and Van Dyke, 1960) and to lower efficiency in both undivided (Talland, 1966; Leigh, Tong, and Campbell, 1977) and divided attention tasks (Moskowitz and De Pry, 1968; Leigh *et al.*, 1977). We have

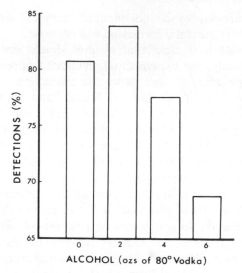

Figure 37. The effects of three doses of alcohol on the percentage of correct detections in a visual vigilance task.

studied the effects of alcohol upon the performance of a visual vigilance task in which the subjects had to detect pauses in the otherwise continuous movement of the second hand of a clock (Wesnes, Warburton, and Surman, unpublished data). As can be seen from Figure 37, the larger doses of the drug lowered the number of correct detections over the 60-minute testing period.

A number of studies have also found alcohol to disrupt memory for material persented following drug administration (Carpenter and Ross, 1965; Hartley, Birnbaum, and Parker, 1978; Miller and Dolan, 1974; Poulos, Wolff, Ziln, Kaplan, and Cappell, 1981), and others have demonstrated that this disruption only occurs for material presented at this time (Birnbaum, Parker, Hartley, and Noble, 1978; Parker, Birnbaum, and Noble, 1976). However, as with the benzodiazepines, these studies provide no evidence that alcohol acts directly upon memory processes, because the drug lowers attentional efficiency, which could account for the impaired memory performance.

Serotonergic function

It has been demonstrated that alcohol decreases serotonin turnover in the central nervous system most probably by inhibiting tryptophan hydroxylase, the enzyme necessary for the synthesis of serotonin (Ellingboe, 1978). As we discussed earlier, it appears that central serotonergic pathways are important for the experience of anxiety and that the corticosteroids increase the activity in these neurones. This decrease in the activity of these neurones produced by alcohol will to some extent reduce the experience of anxiety and tension, and it is quite possible that this is one of the mechanisms by which the drug was found to reduce tension and increase calmness in the studies discussed earlier.

Noradrenergic function

A number of studies have demonstrated that alcohol increases activity in central noradrenergic pathways (Ellingboe, 1978), although this increase is followed by a decrease several hours later (Hunt and Majchrowicz, 1974). The feedback mechanism by which corticosteroids attenuate their own release is believed to be via adrenergic neurones in the hypothalamus which have inhibitory control over CRF release (Warburton, 1981). This increased adrenergic activity would, together with the decrease of cholinergic activity, help to prevent the stress response-induced release of corticosteroids from the adrenal cortex.

One of the characteristic effects of alcohol is to induce euphoria. There is much evidence that the catecholaminergic pathways in the median forebrain bundle control mood and that activation of these pathways is rewarding. It is likely therefore that the euphoria resulting from alcohol administration is a result of the increased activity in catecholaminergic pathways controlling mood. Furthermore, the fall in noradrenalin turnover which is found to occur as the blood levels drop (Hunt and Majchrowicz, 1974) corresponds neatly to the decrease in euphoria observed in human subjects at this time (Myrsten, Hollstedt and Holmberg, 1975).

Summary

Alcohol is commonly believed to reduce tension and anxiety and experimental results support this. It is clear from this account that there are a number of ways in which the drug reduces the stress response. First, the drug lowers electrocortical arousal by lowering the activity in the ascending cholinergic reticular pathways and thus reduces the likelihood of the detection or the recall of stressful stimuli. Secondly, the drug blocks the release of corticosteroids by increasing adrenergic activity and decreasing cholinergic activity. Thirdly, by decreasing the turnover in central serotonergic neurones the drug reduces the experience of anxiety and tension. Fourthly, the drug activates the catecholaminergic pathways involved in reward and increases euphoria.

However, there are a number of contraindications for the use of alcohol to reduce stress. The cholinergic effects of the drug produce marked impairments in behavioural efficiency which have been found to make tasks such as driving particularly dangerous. Also, the drug markedly decreases glucose utilization in the brain (Nielsen, Hawkins, and Veech, 1975), and although the time-course of this effect indicates that it is not related to the immediate effects of the drug, this lowered glucose will increase mental fatigue after the direct effects of the drug have worn off. Furthermore, the increase in positive affect produced by the drug wears off as the blood levels decline, which may lead the individual to have another drink, but which further exacerbates the performance decrements which persist at this time (e.g. Jones, 1973). Finally, continued drinking results in depression (Mello, 1978).

Thus, alcohol is a useful and rapidly acting short-term anti-anxiety agent. A 'stiff drink' will help the individual to cope with a sudden shock, while a few drinks will help individuals to relax in social situations. However, the drug is not so useful in conditions of stress which persist over days due to the rapid tolerance which develops, the relatively short-lived euphoria it gives and the tendency for large doses to produce depression.

NICOTINE

Today very few, if any, smokers in the Western world are not aware of the health risks involved in the continuation of the habit, yet there has been only a small decline in smoking over the last 20 years. Clearly, there must be a powerful attraction to the habit which motivates smokers to continue smoking in spite of the health risks involved.

As one would expect, there have been a wide variety of explanations put forward to explain the attractiveness of smoking, ranging from those stressing the oral-manipulative pleasure of the habit to those which argue that it is based on a physiological addition to nicotine. Clearly, the great difficulty which theories of the former nature encounter is that nothing else besides tobacco will do for the vast majority of smokers. Smokers smoke only one particular leaf, *Nicotinia tabacum*, but if they smoked for the pleasure of orally manipulating a burning cylinder of leaves, surely other leaves would be as attractive. Certainly it would be a most remarkable coincidence that the hundreds of millions of smokers in the world today all restricted their smoking habit to one particular type of leaf, were it not for the fact that it was the *only* one which also contained nicotine. This is not to say that the rituals associated with smoking do not develop some autonomy over a lifetime of smoking. A '20-a-day' smoker will take in the order of 70,000 puffs each year. Together with the nicotine absorbed from each of these puffs, the smoker experiences a whole range of other sensations such as the feel of the cigarette, the flavour of the smoke, and the drawing of the smoke into the lungs. No doubt the close associations of these other sensations with nicotine will make them important to the smoker. However, the evidence indicates that although these sensations may become necessary for the smoker, they do not become sufficient for the maintenance of the habit, and are thus secondary to nicotine.

Stress and anxiety

When questioned about their motives for smoking, most smokers identify stress reduction and tranquillization as a major determinant of the habit. Phanishayi (cited by Matarazzo and Saslow, 1960) found that 60 per cent of smokers gave its relaxing effect as a major reason for smoking. Similarly, in a national sample of over 2,000 smokers, Ikard Green, and Horn (1969) found that 80 per cent scored high on the factor indicating that they either always or usually smoked for pleasurable relaxation. Furthermore, smokers report that they smoke when they are feeling stressed; Russell, Peto, and Patel (1974) found that 74 per cent of a general population and 88 per cent of a smoking clinic population reported that they smoked when feeling anxious or angry; using the same questionnaire it was also found that 80 per cent of a population of university undergraduates reported that they smoked when feeling this way (Warburton and Wesnes, 1978).

To complement these subjective reports a number of studies have looked at the relationships between smoking behaviour and situation. In one study it was found that people in stressful professions were more likely to smoke than those who were not (Russek, 1965). Similarly, a survey of executives revealed that heavy smoking (more than 20 per day) was more common in those under excessive stress, and one of the main reasons given by these individuals for this was the tranquillizing effects of the cigarettes (Pincherle and Williamson, 1971). We have studied the smoking behaviour of students in an examination period and compared this to their smoking during a quiet period of the university term (Warburton, Wesnes, and Revell, 1981). During the examination period the students smoked on average 33 per cent more cigarettes than during the quiet period. This increase was more marked during certain periods, such as the morning before an afternoon exam, when the students smoked on average 80 per cent more than they did on an equivalent morning during the non-examination period. Not only did the total number of cigarettes smoked during the examinations increase, but the students also rated their strength and depth of inhalation as being greater during this period. These findings were very consistent over the population studied, with only one student out of the 48 not reporting an increase in depth of inhalation during the examinations.

Thus, smokers feel that smoking helps them to relax and the intensity of smoking increases in times of stress. This suggests the possibility that individuals with a greater predisposition to stress and anxiety would be more likely to take up the habit. In the largest survey of male smokers (Eysenck, Tarrant, Woolf, and England, 1960; Eysenck, 1963) a very highly significant positive correlation was found between cigarette smoking and extroversion, but no relationship was found between smoking and neuroticism. Surveys carried out on both sexes, however, have found some relationship between cigarette consumption and neuroticism, at least for women (Meares, Grimwade, Bickley, and Wood, 1971; Walters, 1971; Dunnell and Cartwright, 1972). Our questionnaire survey of 259 student smokers (Warburton, Wesnes, and Revell, 1981) suggested that there may be two populations of smokers: those smoking less than 15 per day (light smokers), and those smoking 15 or more per day (heavy smokers). We found that for both sexes, heavy smokers were significantly more extroverted than light smokers, whereas no differences existed in the mean neuroticism scores of these two classes, supporting the findings of Eysenck. However, we then correlated the smoking and personality data for both sexes within the two classifications of smoker. For all four groups neuroticism was positively correlated with the number of cigarettes smoked each day, whereas no positive correlations were found for extroversion and this measure of smoking behaviour.

Taken together these findings suggest a relationship between neuroticism and smoking that has not previously been considered. First, the degree of extroversion is related to the type of smoker, i.e. light or heavy, which is in accordance with previous findings. However, our data also suggest that neuroticism is related to the number of cigarettes smoked once the smoker has become either a light or heavy smoker. Thus, we would suggest that the factors underlying extroversion act as a 'coarse tuner' which determines the general number of cigarettes smoked, while the factors underlying neuroticism act as a 'fine tuner' which determines the precise number of cigarettes smoked once the individual has become either a light or heavy smoker.

Strong support for the relationship between extroversion, neuroticism, and the development of the smoking habit has come from the work of Cherry and Kiernan (1976, 1978). A cohort of 2,735 young people have been followed for 25 years and at 16 years the subjects completed the Maudesley Personality Inventory *before* most of them had begun to smoke. At 20 years and 25 years they completed a smoking habits questionnaire, and it was found that the cigarette smokers as a group were more extroverted and neurotic than the non-smokers. Furthermore, the two personality characteristics were independent (i.e. additive) in their effect on the likelihood of becoming a regular smoker. Self-report of depth of inhalation indicated that deep inhalers had a higher mean neuroticism score than slight inhalers, who did not differ significantly from non-smokers.

If smoking were related to stress, then smoking withdrawal should increase stress. On the basis of considerable research in this area, Shiffman has concluded that: 'Subjective symptoms of irritability, anxiety, inability to concentrate and disturbances in arousal are characteristic of tobacco users in withdrawal . . .' (Shiffman, 1977, p.178). Furthermore, the increased anxiety following smoking withdrawal is more likely to occur among women, among whom there is the greatest proportion of neurotic smokers (Guildford, 1966; Shiffman, 1979).

Similarly, stress should be a factor in relapses of smokers attempting to quit the habit. An analysis of the situations which resulted in a return to smoking was made by Marlatt (1979) and Shiffman (1979). Retrospective reports indicated that 80 per cent of situations fell into three categories: coping with anxiety and other negative emotional states (43 per cent), social pressure (25 per cent), and coping with social stress (12 per cent). In the Shiffman (1979) study, two-thirds of the subjects were under stress at the time of relapse and anxiety was particularly common among ex-smokers who relapsed at work, which suggests that work-related anxiety was a contributory factor. Neurotics are more anxiety-prone and so it is not surprising that this group find it difficult to stop smoking, or relapse if they do (Cherry and Kiernan, 1978).

In summary there is strong evidence that smoking is related to stress. Smokers report that they smoke for the tranquillizing actions of cigarettes, and there is evidence that in times of stress they smoke more cigarettes and smoke these cigarettes more intensively. Besides this, neuroticism predisposes people to take up the habit, and when they have, the number of cigarettes they smoke is related to their degree of neuroticism. Finally, smoking withdrawal is characterized by increased anxiety, and stress is a major factor which leads to relapse.

Cholinergic function and electrocortical arousal

Nicotine is a classical cholinergic agonist. Armitage, Hall, and Sellars (1969) demonstrated that repeated injections of small doses of nicotine, similar to those received while smoking, produced an increase in the cortical release of acetylcholine together with electrocortical arousal. Essman (1973) studied the effects of the drug upon the storage pools of acetylcholine in the cerebral cortex and found that bound and vesicular levels of acetylcholine dropped dramatically following nicotine administration.

In man the characteristic action of cigarette smoking is to increase electrocortical arousal (Lambiase and Serra, 1957; Hauser Schwartz, Roth, and Bickford, 1958; Wechsler, 1958; Philips, 1971; Kenig and Murphree, 1973). Conversely, smoking withdrawal lowers the dominant alpha frequency (Murphree and Schultz, 1968; Ulett and Itil, 1969; Knott and Venables, 1979) and this trend is reversed by the smoking of a single cigarette (Ulett and Itil, 1969; Knott and Venables, 1979). Evidence that nicotine is responsible for this effect has come from studies which have demonstrated that injections of nicotine produce directly comparable increases in electrocortical arousal to those produced by smoking (Kenig and Murphree, 1975; Kumar, Cooke, Lader, and Russell, 1978).

Several studies have investigated both the location and the neurochemistry of the neurones which mediate the effects of nicotine upon electrocortical activity. Il'yuchenok and Ostrovskaya (1962) demonstrated that lesions above the mesencephalic reticular formation prevented the activation of electro-cortical arousal by nicotine, whereas lesions at the base of the brain stem which left the mid-brain reticular formation intact, permitted low doses of nicotine to produce the characteristic arousal response. In order to determine the neurochemistry of the neurones in the reticular formation which were activated by nicotine, these workers administered aminazine, and adrenergic blocker, and a number of nicotinic and muscarinic cholinergic blockers. Adrenergic blockade had *no* effects upon the actions of nicotine upon electro-cortical activity, whereas both muscarinic acid and nicotinic cholinergic blockade prevented nicotine from activating the cortex. Il'Yuchenok and Ostrovskaya concluded that their findings 'indicate that nicotine stimulates the cholinergic structures of the mesencephalic reticular formation . . . . The impossibility of preventing nicotine activation by preliminary aminazine administration shows that the excitation of adrenoreactive structures does not participate in the mechanism of this activation' (p.756). Subsequent studies have confirmed that the actions of nicotine upon electrocortical arousal can be blocked by lesions rostral to the mid-brain reticular formation (Domino, 1967; Kawamura and Domino, 1969), as well as by drugs which attenuate cholinergic transmission (Domino, 1967; Guha and Pradhan, 1976), but not by drugs blocking adrenergic activity (Guha and Pradhan, 1976).

These studies provide good evidence that cigarette smoking increases electrocortical arousal by acting upon the ascending cholinergic reticular pathways. This action would suggest that smoking will improve human efficiency.

Human performance

Two early studies demonstrated that smokers performed simulated driving tasks more efficiently when smoking than when not (Tarrière and Hartemann, 1964; Heimstra Bancroft and DeKock, 1967). Frankenhaeuser, Myrsten, Post, and Johansson, (1971) also found that smokers performed more efficiently in a continuous reaction time testing task when smoking than when not. Over the last 8 years we have been studying the effects of smoking and nicotine upon human performance. Our early findings have been summarized previously (Wesnes and Warburton, 1978; Warburton and Wesnes, 1979). We have found that smokers perform more efficiently in both visual and auditory vigilance tasks when smoking cigarettes than when either not smoking or smoking nicotine-free cigarettes. Furthermore, when performing the rapid information-processing task described earlier, smokers detected the targets more quickly and more accurately when smoking high nicotine cigarettes, than when smoking lower nicotine cigarettes, nicotine-free cigarettes, or when not smoking. To investigate the direct effects of nicotine we studied the effects of nicotine tablets upon visual vigilance. We found that the drug helped to reduce the decrement in correct detections which occurred over time in the placebo condition, while also reducing the number of false alarms. In a further study we investigated the effects of nicotine tablets upon the Stroop effect (see Chapter 3). The results are presented in Figure 38, from which it can be seen that nicotine markedly reduced the magnitude of the effect during the second stage of testing. This is evidence that nicotine markedly reduces the effect of distracting stimuli upon performance.

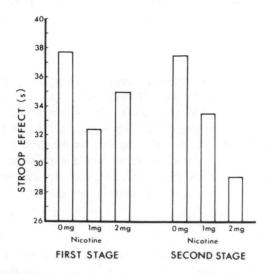

Figure 38. The effects of two doses of nicotine upon the magnitude of the Stroop effect in two successive stages of testing.

Since these early studies we have repeatedly replicated these effects of smoking, and further demonstrated the role of nicotine in them, the findings are now being prepared for publication.

Work from other laboratories has demonstrated that smoking has a detrimental effect upon both immediate memory (Andersson and Post, 1974; Andersson, 1975; Williams, 1980) and incidental memory (Andersson and Hockey, 1977).

Corticosteroids

By increasing cholinergic activity, nicotine should increase the release of corticosteroids. Kershbaum, Pappajohn, and Bellet (1968) studied the effects of nicotine on corticosteroids in man, rats, and dogs. In man there was a 22–77 per cent rise in plasma 11-hydroxycorticosteroid concentrations after heavy smoking, compared to a normal diurnal fall during non-smoking conditions.

The nicotine content of the cigarette smoke would appear to be primarily responsible for this increase since injections of nicotine caused rises in plasma corticosteroids of 64 and 58 per cent in dogs and rats, respectively. Hill and Wynder (1974) further confirmed this relationship. Non-nicotine cigarettes and very low nicotine cigarettes had no effect upon plasma corticosteroids, whereas a medium delivery cigarette produced a small increase and a high delivery cigarette a large increase in plasma corticosteroids. Repeated smoking of high nicotine cigarettes produced increases of 200 and 300 per cent after two and five cigarettes, respectively.

Noradrenergic function

Nicotine has been found to increase the central release of noradrenalin (Hall and Turner, 1972; Westfall, 1974), although this release can be blocked by cholinergic blocking drugs (Westfall, 1974). This release would thus appear to be a secondary effect of cholinergic stimulation and, as discussed earlier, is not involved in the electrocortical arousal produced by the drug. Furthermore, if this release were of marked significance, we would expect that the increased adrenergic activity would inhibit the release of corticosteroids, but as was clear from the previous section exactly the opposite is the case.

Adrenal catecholamines

Both cigarette smoking and cigar smoking have been found to increase the total urinary catecholamine output (Kershbaum *et al.*, 1968). However, studies of both plasma catecholamine (Hill and Wynder, 1974) and urinary catecholamine concentration (Ague, 1974; Frankenhaeuser, Myrsten, and Post, 1969), which have separately measured the levels of adrenalin and noradrenalin, have found only the former to rise after cigarette smoking.

Paradox of smoking and stress

The reader will no doubt be struck by an apparent paradox. With alcohol and the benzodiazepines, it was clear that their anti-anxiety effects could be explained by pointing out how well these drugs help to reduce the stress response. However, if one considers the physiological neurochemical, endocrinological, and electrophysiological actions of nicotine, it is only possible to conclude that the drug produces almost all the changes which one would associate with the stress response. Why then do smokers claim that the drug helps them to relax, smoke more in stressful situations, have personalities which suggest they are more susceptible to stress, and show signs of increased anxiety when they attempt to give up the habit? A number of theories which have been proposed to account for this paradox are reviewed by Gilbert

(1979), and three of the most plausible of these theories will now be discussed.

Eysenck (1973) proposed that smokers smoked for the change in arousal that nicotine produces. He argued that EEG was a suitable index of this arousal, and explained the paradox of smoking in highly arousing situations by proposing that there is an inverted-U-type of relationship between nicotine and arousal. Thus, small doses of nicotine will tend to increase arousal, whereas higher doses will lower arousal. He further proposed that different personality types would have different baseline levels of arousal, and therefore that a similar dose of nicotine would produce different effects in different people. For example, extroverts have low baseline levels of arousal and therefore smoke in order to increase their arousal, whereas neurotics have higher levels of arousal and smoke because the nicotine will lower their arousal. The major prediction from this theory must be that across a variety of situations involving different personality types smoking should sometimes increase electrocortical arousal and sometimes decrease it. However, in all of the studies of smoking and EEG described earlier, smoking was found to increase arousal, and this theory therefore is not consistent with the existing experimental evidence.

The second theory was put forward by Schachter (1973), who invoked the law of initial values to explain the paradox. The argument is that since nicotine increases arousal, the additional arousal induced by an emotional situation is less than it would be without the drug. As Gilbert (1979) points out, if the intensity of an emotion is a positive function of the deviation of autonomic activity from its baseline, such an explanation is plausible, but there is little or no data available with which to evaluate this theory.

The third theory, proposed by Jarvik (1970, 1973), assumes that nicotine's emotion-reducing properties are a produce of its action upon primary reward centres in the brain. However, as we have previously pointed out (Warburton and Wesnes, 1979, 1983), there are three weaknesses in this explanation. First, there is no evidence that nicotine acts directly upon the catecholaminergic pathways believed to be involved in reward. Secondly, the effects of nicotine upon the self-stimulation of these pathways are particularly weak in comparison with other drugs of abuse. Thirdly, smokers experience none of the intense pleasure reported by users of drugs such as amphetamine.

An alternative explanation centres on the smoking-induced improvements in attention which we have consistently been observed in our laboratory (Warburton and Wesnes, 1978, 1979; Knott, 1978, 1979). Any testing experience will result in some intrusion of thoughts and worries about competence during performance which may interfere with efficiency, but by improving attention nicotine will enable the individual to ignore these thoughts and will thus facilitate performance. This explanation clearly centres on the ability of nicotine to enable the individual to 'filter-out' distracting information, and is consistent with the previously described reduction in the Stroop effect produced by the drug. However, by increasing electrocortical arousal nicotine will also improve concentration and thus raise efficiency in tasks where there is little distraction. Furthermore, on the basis of such beneficial effects upon performance, the drug will help to reduce the anticipatory stress which precedes demanding tasks and experiences by increasing the self-perceived competence of the individual. Therefore we have extended our early explanation that nicotine reduces stress by enabling the individual to ignore distracting thoughts, to encompass those situations in which the individual has either justified or imagined doubts about his competence. Thus, nicotine may also reduce the perceived stress in a non-neurotic individual who simply wishes to perform a task well, irrespective of any distracting thoughts which may occur during task performance.

Summary

Smokers claim that cigarettes reduce tension; they smoke more intensively in times of stress, have personality characteristics indicative of a greater susceptibility to anxiety, experience stress when attempting to quit the habit, and cite stress as a major factor leading to a resumption of smoking. However, smoking produces all the electrophysiological, neurochemical, endocrinological, and behavioural changes which are typical of the stress response. In order to resolve this paradox we argue that it is the action of nicotine upon the cholinergic pathways controlling attention which reduces stress by enabling individuals to concentrate more efficiently. In neurotic subjects the drug will help them to filter-out distracting thoughts and thus enable them to perform more efficiently, increasing their perceived self-competence. In extroverted subjects the drug will maintain their electrocortical activation at levels sufficient to perform long and tedious tasks efficiently, also increasing their perceived self-competence. Furthermore, for both types of smoker, smoking will reduce anticipatory stress by increasing the confidence they have in their ability to perform and achieve. The advantage of this explanation over the others discussed in this section is that it is consistent with the known neuro-chemical, electrocortical, and behavioural effects of nicotine, and does not involve explanations which emphasize inter- and intra-individual bi-directional neurochemical and electrophysiological changes which have yet to be demonstrated.

THE PATTERN OF PERFORMANCE CHANGES PRODUCED BY THE DRUGS

Earlier we described the pattern of changes in psychomotor performance which Hockey has previously identified to result from noise-induced stress. We agree with Hockey that this pattern of changes is likely to be consistent for a wide variety of stressors, and would argue that nicotine, by increasing the physiological stress response, should produce a 'stressor' pattern of changes in performance. However, we would further predict that drugs such as alcohol and the benzodiazepines, by reducing the stress response, should produce an opposite pattern of changes. For nicotine, this prediction seems to hold: the work from our laboratory indicates that nicotine increases the selectivity of attention and raises the work-rate, while work from other laboratories indicates that the drug reduces primary memory capacity. However, while alcohol and the benzodiazepines lower work-rate, reduce the selectivity of responding, and disrupt selective attention, they also appear to reduce the capacity of primary memory. A difficulty in the interpretation of the latter studies is that these drugs disrupt attentional efficiency, and since these studies have only found memory losses for material presented after drug administration, it is not possible to decide whether the losses represent memory deficits or impaired attention. However, the findings of a recent study have shed much light on this problem. Parker, Birnbaum, Weingartner, Hartley, Stillman, and Wyatt, (1980) administered alcohol immediately after subjects had sorted 30 words into five categories. The subjects believed that this was simply a card-sorting task, but next day they were tested for both free and cued recall of these words. Those subjects who had received alcohol were able to recall significantly more words in both recall conditions than those subjects who had received a placebo. In a second experiment scenic slides were presented before alcohol or placebo administration and recognition was tested 3 hours later. Again, the subjects who had received alcohol performed significantly better than those on placebo. As the information was presented prior to drug administration, there could have been no attentional differences between the conditions. This study provides good support for the hypothesis that the drug improves memory processes, when attentional impairment is ruled out. Further material presented *after* alcohol administration was less well remembered than that presented after placebo, which strongly suggests that apparent memory deficits found in previous studies were in fact the result of the action of the drugs upon attention.

It would therefore appear that nicotine produces a stressor pattern of changes in performance, whereas alcohol and the benzodiazepines, by reducing the stress response, produce an opposite pattern. (See Hockey and Hamilton, Chapter 12).

SUMMARY

The stress response is a complex pattern of physiological and psychological changes which occur in individuals in response to a wide variety of physical and psychological stimuli. We have discussed the stress response in terms of everyday events, emphasizing its frequent occurrence in all our lives, in contrast to the view that it is an infrequently occurring set of dramatic bodily reactions to highly emotional and extremely dangerous situations. We have argued that the size of the stress response depends on the predictability of an environment as interpreted by the individual, and therefore that it is the interaction of the individual and the environment which is the crucial determinant.

People often take psychotropic drugs in order to enable them to cope with the experience of the stress response, and we discussed the three most commonly used substances for this purpose: the benzodiazepines, alcohol, and nicotine. We explained the actions of these drugs upon the stress response by describing the effects of these drugs upon the four major neurotransmitters: acetylcholine, dopamine, noradrenalin, and serotonin. Alcohol and the benzodiazepines both block cholinergic function, thus reducing the awareness of stressful stimuli and lowering the likelihood that such stimuli will be subsequently remembered. These drugs also block serotonergic function and therefore decrease the experience of anxiety. However, alcohol also increases noradrenergic function which induces euphoria. In contrast nicotine produces most of the physiological changes which form the stress response. The primary neurochemical action of the drug is to increase the activity in the ascending reticular cholinergic pathways, which heightens attentional efficiency and it is the improved psychological competence which results from this heightened attentional efficiency which we believe enables individuals to cope in stressful situations.

While the three drugs we have discussed all enable people to cope with the stress response, none of them can be considered to be ideal. All three have severe health risks associated with their long-term use and all three have unwanted side-effects in their short-term use. Often the disruptions of performance which result from alcohol and the benzodiazepines are unwanted side-effects, although in severe cases of anxiety a lowering of awareness is an important part of the therapeutic action of the drugs. However, it should be pointed out that the vast majority of studies of the psychomotor effects of alcohol and the benzodiazepines are carried out using healthy non-anxious volunteers. Thus, it might be argued that although the psychomotor efficiency of a non-anxious individual may be impaired by these drugs, the reduction in anxiety of a highly stressed individual may actually have beneficial consequences for performance. Although this argument is unlikely to hold for individuals who have received large doses of these drugs, it may hold in some instances for lower doses and is clearly worthy of more comprehensive experimental investigation.

Finally, although it has not been within the scope of this chapter to consider this subject more fully, it seems necessary to point out that whatever anti-anxiety effects the drugs discussed may have, and irrespective of the side-effects and health hazards which accompany their use, there is no justification in Western society for the widespread use of the drugs which exist today. Except in extreme cases the stress response is an adaptive response and an integral part of our everyday functioning, and we should not need drugs which help us to cope with it. For example, eyeglasses are of obvious benefit to people with impaired vision, but those with normal vision should not continuously use them in order to have greater visual acuity. Similarly, while drugs are occasionally useful in order to enable some individuals to cope with the demands of everyday life, and are sometimes useful in cases of extreme stress, they should not be used as props to enable us to cope with every uncertain situation which we encounter. Such use is misuse.

ACKNOWLEDGEMENTS

We thank Carreras-Rothmans Ltd, Farmitalia Carlo Erba Ltd, the Medical Research Council, and the Tobacco Research Council for financial support of the research described in this Chapter.

REFERENCES

Ague, C. (1974) Cardiovascular variables, skin conductance and time estimation; Changes after the administration of small doses of nicotine. *Psychopharmacologia*, **37**, 109–125.

Andersson, K. (1975) Effects of cigarette smoking on learning and retention. *Psychopharmacologia*, **41**, 1–5.

Andersson, K. and Hockey, G. R. J. (1977) Effects of cigarette smoking on incidental memory. *Psychopharmacology*, **52**, 223–226.

Andersson, K. and Post, B. (1974) Effects of cigarette smoking on verbal rote learning and physiological arousal. *Scandinavian Journal of Psychology*, **15**, 263–267.

Armitage, A. K., Hall, G. H., and Sellers, C. M. (1969) Effects of nicotine on electrocortical activity and acetylcholine release from the cat cerebral cortex. *British Journal of Pharmacology*, **35**, 152–160.

Armstrong, C. M. and Binstock, L. (1964) The effects of several alcohols on the properties of the squid giant axon. *Journal of General Physiology*, **48**, 265–277.

Åstrand, P. O. and Rodahl, K. (1970) *Textbook of Work Physiology*. New York: McGraw-Hill.

Bainbridge, L. (1974) Problems in the assessment of mental load. *Journale du Travail Humain*, **37**, 279–302.

Bassett, J. R. and Cairncross, K. D. (1974) Effects of psychoactive drugs on responses of the rat to aversive stimulation. *Archives of International Pharmacodynamics*, **212**, 221–229.

Biehl, B. (1979) Studies of clobazam on car-driving. *British Journal of Clinical Pharmacology*, **7**, 85s–90s.

Birnbaum, I. M., Parker, E. S., Hartley, J. T., and Noble, E. P. (1978) Alcohol and memory: Retrieval processes. *Journal of Verbal Learning and Verbal Behaviour*, **17**, 325–335.

Bliss, E. L., Migeon, C. J., Branch, C. H. H., and Samuels, L. Y. (1956) Reaction of the adrenal cortex to emotional stress. *Psychosomatic Medicine*, **18**, 56–76.

Bookman, P. H. and Randall, L. O. (1975) Therapeutic uses of the benzodiazepines. In L. Simpson (ed.), *Drug Treatment of Mental Disorders*. New York: Raven Press.

Boucsein, W. and Wendt-Suhl, G. (1976) The effect of chlordiazepoxide on the anticipation of electric shocks. *Psychopharmacology*, **48**, 303–306.

Bourne, P. G. (1969) Urinary 17-OHCS levels in two combat situations. In P. G. Bourne (ed.), *Psychology and Physiology of Stress*. New York: Academic Press, pp.95–116.

Carmichael, F. J. and Israel, Y. (1975) Effects of ethanol on neurotransmitter release by rat brain cortical slices. *Journal of Pharmacology and Experimental Therapy*, **193**, 824.

Carpenter, J. A. and Ross, B. M. (1965) Effects of alcohol on short-term memory. *Quarterly Journal of Studies on Alcohol*, **26**, 561–579.

Chase, T. N., Katz, R. I., and Kopin, J. J. (1970) Effect of diazepam on fate of intracisternally injected serotonin-C^{14}. *Neuropharmacology*, **9**, 103–108.

Cherry, N. and Kiernan, C. E. (1976) Personality scores and smoking behaviour. *British Journal of Preventative Social Medicine*, **30**, 123–131.

Cherry, N. and Kiernan, K. E. (1978) A longitudinal study of smoking and personality. In R. E. Thornton (ed.), *Smoking Behaviour: Physiological and Psychological Influences*. London: Churchill Livingstone.

Christensen, E. H. and Hansen, O. (1939) Arbeitsfähigheit und Ehrnähung. *Skandinavische Archiv für Physiologie*, **81**, 160–178.

Cicero, T. J. (1978) Tolerance to and physical dependence on alcohol: behavioural and neurobiological mechanisms. In M. A. Lipton, A. DiMascio, and K. F. Killam (eds.), *Psychopharmacology: A Generation of Progress*. New York: Raven Press.

Consolo, S., Garattini, S., and Ladinsky, H. (1975) Action of benzodiazepines on the cholinergic system. In E. Costa and P. Greengard (eds.), *Mechanisms of Action of the Benzodiazepines*. New York: Raven Press.

Crawford, T. I. (1973) Preanesthetic medication in elective surgery: Comparison of intravenous diazepam with meperidine. *Current Therapeutic Research*, **15**, 441–448.

Docter, R. F., Naitoh, P., and Smith, J. C. (1966) Electroencephalographic changes and vigilance behaviour during experimentally induced intoxication with alcoholic subjects. *Psychosomatic Medicine*, **28**, 605.

Domino, E. I. F. (1967) Electroencephalographic and behavioural arousal effects of small doses of nicotine: A neuropsychopharmacological study. *Annals of New York Academy of Sciences*, **142**, 216–244.

Drew, M. A., Colquhoun, W. P., and Long, M. A. (1958) Effect of small doses of alcohol on a task resembling driving. *British Medical Journal*, **1958**, 993–998.

Dundee, J. W. and Panditt, S. K. (1972) Anterograde amnesic effects of pethidine, hyoscine and diazepam in adults. *British Journal of Pharmacology*, **44**, 140–144.

Dunnell, K. and Cartwright, A. (1972) *Medicine Takers, Prescribers and Hoarders*. London: Routledge and Kegan-Paul.

Ellingboe, J. (1978) Effects of alcohol on neurochemical processes. In M. A. Lipton, A. DiMascio and K. F. Killam (eds.) *Psychopharmacology, A Generation of Progress*. New York: Raven Press.

Enzer, N. E., Simonson, E., and Ballard, G. (1944) The effects of small doses of alcohol in the central nervous system. *American Journal of Clinical Pathology*, **14**, 333–341.

Essman, W. B. (1973) Nicotine-related neurochemical changes: some implications for motivational mechanisms and differences. In W. L. Dunn (ed.), *Smoking Behavior: Motives and Incentives*. Washington D.C.: Winston, pp.51–65.

Eysenck, H. J. (1963) Personality and cigarette smoking. *Life Sciences*, **3**, 777–792.

Eysenck, H. J. (1973) Personality and the maintenance of the smoking habit. In W. L. Dunn (ed.), *Smoking Behavior: Motives and Incentives*. Washington D.C.: Winston.

Eysenck, H. J., Tarrant, M., Woolf, M., and England, L. (1960) Smoking and personality. *British Medical Journal*, **2**, 1456–1460.

File, S. E. and Bond, A. J. (1979) Impaired performance and sedation after a single dose of lorazepam. *Psychopharmacology*, **66**, 309–313.

Frankenhaeuser, M. and Patkai, P. (1964) Catecholamine excretion and performance under stress. *Perceptual and Motor Skills*, **19**, 13–14. 1964.

Frankenhaeuser, M., Myrsten, A-L., and Post, B. (1969) Psychophysiological reactions to cigarette smoking. Reports from the Psychological Laboratories, The University of Stockholm, No. 290.

Goldstein, D. B. and Pal, N. (1971) Alcohol dependence produced in mice by inhalation of ethanol: Grading the withdrawal reaction. *Science*, **172**, 288–290.

Ghonheim, M. M. and Mewaldt, S. P. (1975) Effects of diazepam and scopolamine on storage, retrieval and organizational processes in memory. *Psychopharmacologia*, **44**, 257–262.

Ghonheim, M. M. and Mewaldt, S. P. (1977) Studies of human memory: The interactions of diazepam, scopolamine and physostigmine. *Psychopharmacology*, **52**, 1–6.

Gilbert, D. G. (1979) Paradoxical tranquilizing and emotion-reducing effects of nicotine. *Psychological Bulletin*, **86**, 643–661.

Gray, J. A. (1981) Anxiety as a paradigm case of emotion. *British Medical Bulletin*, **37**, 193–198.

Greenblatt, D. J. and Shader, R. I. (1974) *Benzodiazepines in clinical practise*. New York: Raven Press.

Greenblatt, D. J. and Shader, R. I. (1978) Pharmacotherapy of anxiety with benzodiazepines and b- adrenergic blockers. In M. A. Lipton, A. DiMascio, and K. F. Killam (eds.), *Psychopharmacology: A Generation of Progress*. New York: Raven Press.

Greenblatt, D. J., Shader, R. I., and Koch-Weser, J. (1975) Pharmacokinetics in clinical medicine: Oxazepam versus other benzodiazepines. *Diseases of the Nervous System*, **36**, 6–13.

Guildford, J. S. (1966) Factors related to successful abstinence from smoking. American Institutes for Research, Pittsburgh.

Guha, D. and Pradhan, S. N. (1976) Effects of nicotine on E.E.G. and evoked potentials and their interactions with automatic drugs. *Neuropharmacology*, **15**, 225–232.

Haefely, W. E. (1978) Behavioural and neuropharmacological aspects of drugs used in anxiety and related states. In M. A. Lipton, A. DiMascio, and K. F. Killam (eds.), *Psychopharmacology: A Generation of Progress*. New York: Raven Press.

Haffner, J. F. W., Morland, J., Setekleiv, J., Stromsaether, C. E., Danielsen, A., Frivik, P. T., and Dybing, F. (1973) Mental and psychomotor effects of diazepam and ethanol. *Acta Pharmacologia et Toxicologia*, **32**, 161–178.

Hall, G. M. and Turner, D. M. (1972) Effects of nicotine on the release of 3-H Noradrenalin from the hypothalamus. *Biochemical Pharmacology*, **21**, 1829–1838.

Hartley, J. T., Birnbaum, I. M., and Parker, E. S. (1978) Alcohol and storage deficits: kind of processing. *Journal of Verbal Learning and Verbal Behaviour*, **17**, 635–647.

Hauser, H., Schwartz, B. E., Roth, G., and Bickford, R. G. (1958) Electroencephalographic changes related to smoking. *Electroencephalography and Clinical Neurophysiology*, **10**, 567.

Heimstra, N. W., Bancroft, N. R., and De Kock, A. R. (1967) The effects of smoking in sustained performance in a simulated driving test. *Annals of New York Academy of Sciences*, **142**, 295–306.

Hill, P. and Wynder, E. L. (1974) Smoking and cardiovascular disease—effect of nicotine on the serum epinephrine and corticoids. *American Heart Journal*, **87**, 491–496.

Hindmarch, I. (1979) Some aspects of the effects of clobazam on human psycho-motor performance. *British Journal of Clinical Pharmacology*, 7, 775–825.

Hindmarch, I. (1980) Psychomotor function and psychoactive drugs. *British Journal of Clinical Pharmacology*, 10, 189–209.

Hindmarch, I., Hanks, G. W., and Hewett, A. J. (1977) Clobazam, a 1,5 benzo-diazepine derivative and car driving ability. *British Journal of Clinical Pharmacology*, 4, 573–578.

Hindmarch, I. and Parrott, A. C. (1979) The effects of repeated nocturnal doses of clobazam, dipotassium clorazepate and placebo on subjective ratings of sleep and early morning behaviour and objective measures of arousal, psychomotor performance and anxiety. *British Journal of Clinical Pharmacology*, 8, 325–329.

Hockey, G. R. J. (1979) Stress and the components of skilled performance. In V. Hamilton and D. M. Warburton (eds.), *Human Stress and Cognition*. London: John Wiley & Sons, pp.141–178.

Holmberg, G. and Mårtens, S. (1955) Electroencephalographic changes in man correlated with blood alcohol concentrations and some other conditions following standardised ingestion of alcohol. *Quarterly Journal of Studies in Alcohol*, 16, 411–424.

Hughes, R. and Brewin, R. (1979) *The Tranquilizing of America*. New York: Warner Books Inc.

Hunt, B. J., George, A. J., and Ridges, A. F. (1974) Preliminary studies in humans on clobazam (HR376) a new anti-anxiety agent. *British Journal of Clinical Pharmacology*, 1, 174P–175P.

Hunt, W. A. and Majchrowicz, E. (1974) Alterations in the turnover of brain norepinephrine and dopamine in alcohol-dependent rats. *Journal of Neurochemistry*, 23, 549–552.

Ikard, F. F., Green, D. E., and Horn, D. (1969) A scale to differentiate between types of smoking as related to the management of affect. *International Journal of the Addictions*, 4, 649–659.

Il'yutchenok, R. Y. and Ostrovskaya, R. V. (1962) The role of mesencephalic cholinergic systems in the mechanism of nicotine activation of the electroencephalogram. *Bulletin of Experimental Biological Medicine*, 54, 753–757.

Indestrom, C. M. and Cadenius, B. (1968) Time relations and the effects of alcohol compared to placebo. *Psychopharmacologia*, 13, 189–200.

Jarvik, M. E. (1970) The role of nicotine in the smoking habit. In W. A. Hunt (ed.), *Learning Mechanisms in Smoking*. Chicago: Aldine.

Jarvik, M. E. (1973) Further observations on nicotine as the reinforcing agent in smoking. In W. L. Dunn (ed.), *Smoking Behavior: Motives and Incentives*. Washington D.C.: V. H. Winston.

Johnson, D. D. and Lowndes, H. E. (1974) Reduction by diazepam of repetitive electrical activity and toxicity resulting from soman. *European Journal of Pharmacology*, 28, 245–250.

Johnson, J. H. and Sarason, I. G. (1979) Recent developments in Research on Life Stress. In V. Hamilton and D. M. Warburton (eds.), *Human Stress and Cognition*. London: John Wiley & Sons, pp.205–236.

Jones, B. M. (1973) Memory impairment on the ascending and descending limbs of the blood alcohol curve. *Journal of Abnormal Psychology*, 82, 24–32.

Kahneman, D. (1973) *Attention and Effort*. Englewood Cliffs, N.J.: Prentice-Hall.

Kalant, M. (1975) Direct effects of ethanol on the nervous system. *Federal Proceedings*, 34, 1930–1941.

Kalant, M. and Grose, W. (1967) Effects of ethanol and pentobarbital on release of acetylcholine from cerebral cortex slices. *Journal of Pharmacology and Experimental Therapy*, **158**, 386.

Kawamura, M. L. and Domino, E. F. (1969) Differential actions of m and n cholinergic agonists on the brainstem activating system. *International Journal of Neuropharmacology*, **8**, 105–115.

Kenig and Murphee, M. B. (1975) Effects of intravenous nicotine in smokers and non-smokers. *Federal Proceedings*, **32**, 805.

Kershbaum, A., Pappajohn, D. J., and Bellet, S. (1968) Effect of smoking and nicotine on corticosteroid secretion. *Journal of the American Medical Association*, **203**, 275–278.

Knott, V. J. (1978) Smoking, E.E.G. and input regulation in smokers and non-smokers. In R. E. Thornton (ed.), *Smoking Behaviour: Physiological and Psychological Influences.* London: Churchill-Livingston.

Knott, V. J. (1979) Psychophysiological correlates of smokers and non-smokers: Studies on cortical, autonomic and behavioural responsibility. In A. Remond and C. Izard (eds.), *Electrophysiological Effects of Nicotine.* Amsterdam: Elsevier.

Knott, V. J. and Venables, P. H. (1979) E.E.G. alpha correlates of alcohol consumption in smokers and non-smokers. *Journal of Studies on Alcohol*, **40**, 247–257.

Kumar, R., Cooke, E. C., Lader, M. H., and Russell, M. A. H. (1978) Is tobacco smoking a form of nicotine dependence? In R. E. Thornton (ed.), *Smoking Behaviour: Physiological and Psychological Influences.* London: Churchill Livingston.

Lader, M. (1975) *The Psychophysiology of Mental Illness.* London: Routledge & Kegan Paul.

Lambiase, M. and Serra, C. (1957) Fumo e sistema nervoso. I. Modificazioni del l'attivita electrica corticale da fumo. *Acta Neurologica Napoli*, **12**, 475–493.

Landauer, A. A., Pococke, D. A., and Plott, F. W. (1974) The effects of medazepam and alcohol on cognitive and motor skills used in car driving. *Psychopharmacologia*, **37**, 159–168.

Leigh, G., Tong, J. E., and Campbell, J. A. (1977) Effects of ethanol and tobacco on divided attention. *Journal of Studies on Alcohol*, **38**, 1233–1239.

Levi, L. (1972) Stress and distress in response to psychosocial stimuli. *Acta Medica Scandinavica*, **1972**, Supplement 528.

Levi, R. and Maynert, E. W. (1964) The subcellular localization of brain stem norepinepherine and 5-hydroxytryptamine in stressed rats. *Biochemical Pharmacology*, **3**, 615–621.

Lidbrink, P., Corrodi, M., Fuxe, K., and Olson, L. (1973) The effects of benzo-diazepines, meprobamate and barbiturates on central monoamine neurones. In S. Garattini, E. Mussini, and L. O. Randell (eds.), *The Benzodiazepines.* New York: Raven Press.

Lindman, R. and Mellberg, B. (1976) The effects of alcohol and threat-induced stress on mood and psychophysiological functions. *Psykologiska Rapporter*, **6**, 1–20.

Lindman, R. and Taxell, H. (1976) Subjective mood as a function of cognitive stress, alcohol and time. *Psychologiska Rapporter*, **7**, 1–10.

Lindsley, D. B. (1950) Emotions and the electroencephalogram. In M. L. Raymert (ed.), *Feelings and Emotions.* New York: McGraw Hill, pp.238–246.

Lindsley, D. B. (1951) Emotion. In S. S. Stevens (ed.), *Handbook of Experimental Psychology.* New York: John Wiley & Sons, pp.473–516.

Lipp, J. A. (1973) Effect of benzodiazepine derivates on soman-induced seizure activity and convulsions in the monkey. *Archives Internationales de Pharmacodynamie et de Therapie*, **202**, 244–251.

240 *Stress and Fatigue in Human Performance*

Longoni, R., Mulas, A., and Pepeu, G. (1974) Drug effect on acetylcholine level in discrete brain regions of cats killed by microwave irradiation. *British Journal of Pharmacology*, **52**, 429–430.

Loomis, T. A. and West, T. C. (1957) The influence of alcohol on automobile driving efficiency. *Quarterly Journal of Studies of Alcohol*, **19**, 30–46.

Luczak, H. (1971) The use of simulators for testing individual working. *Ergonomics*, **14**, 651–660.

Marlatt, G. A. (1979) A cognitive-behavioural model of the relapse process. In N. A. Krasnegar (ed.), *Behavioural Analysis and Treatment of Substance Abuse.* Washington, D.C.: National Institute on Drug Abuse.

Mason, J. W. (1968) 'Over-all' hormonal balance as a key to endocrine organization. *Psychosomatic Medicine*, **30**, 791–808.

Matarazzo, J. D. and Saslow, G. (1960) Psychological and related characteristics of smokers and non-smokers. *Psychological Bulletin*, **57**, 493–513.

McClish, A., Andrew, D., and Tetreault, L. (1968) Intravenous diazepam for psychiatric reactions following open heart surgery. *Canadian Anaesthetic Society Journal*, **15**, 63–79.

Meares, R., Grimwade, J., Bickley, M., and Wood, C. (1971) Smoking and neuroticism. *Lancet*, **2**, 770.

Mello, N. K. (1978) Alcohol and the behavioural pharmacology of alcohol: 1967–1977. In M. A. Lipton, A. DiMascio, and K. F. Killam (eds.), *Psychopharmacology: A Generation of Progress.* New York: Raven Press.

Migler, B. (1975) Conditioned approach: An analogue of conditioned avoidance; effects of chlorpromazine and diazepam. *Pharmacology, Biochemistry and Behaviour*, **3**, 961–965.

Miller, L. L. and Dolan, M. P. (1974) Effects of alcohol on short-term memory as measured by a guessing technique. *Psychopharmacologia*, **35**, 353–364.

Mitchell, J. F. (1963) The spontaneous and evoked release of acetylcholine from the cerebral cortex. *Journal of Physiology*, **165**, 98–116.

Moskowitz, H. and De Pry, D. (1968) Effect of alcohol upon auditory vigilance and divided attention tasks. *Quarterly Journal of Studies in Alcohol*, **29**, 54–63.

Murphree, H. B. and Schultz, R. E. (1968) Abstinence effects in smokers. *Federal Proceedings*, **27**, 220.

Myrsten, A-L., Hollstedt, L., and Holmberg, L. (1975) Alcohol induced changes in mood and activation in males and females as related to catecholamine excretion and blood-alcohol level. *Scandinavian Journal of Psychology*, **16**, 303–310.

Nielsen, R. H., Hawkins, R. A., and Veech, R. C. (1975) The effects of acute ethanol intoxication in cerebral energy metabolism. *Advanced Experimental Medical Biology*, **59**, 93–109.

Norman, D. A. and Bobrow, D. G. (1975) On data-limited and resource-limited processes. *Cognitive Psychology*, **7**, 44–64.

Oritz, A., Griffiths, P. J., and Littleton, J. M. (1974) A comparison of the effects of chronic administration of ethanol and acetaldehyde to mice: Evidence for a role of acetaldehyde in ethanol dependence. *Journal of Pharmacy and Pharmacology*, **26**, 249–260.

Parker, E. S., Birnbaum, I. M., and Noble, E. P. (1976) Alcohol and memory: Storage and state dependency. *Journal of Verbal Learning and Verbal Behaviour*, **15**, 691–702.

Parker, E. S., Birnbaum, I. M., Weingartner, H., Hartley, J. T., Stillman, R. C., and Wyatt, R. J. (1980) Retrograde enhancement of human memory with alcohol. *Psychopharmacology*, **69**, 219–222.

Persson, L-O, Sjöberg, L., and Svensson, E. (1980) Mood effects of alcohol. *Psychopharmacology*, **68**, 295–299.

Phillips, C. (1971) The E.E.G. changes associated with smoking. *Psychophysiology*, **8**, 64–74.

Phillis, J. W. and Jhamandas, K. (1971) The effects of chlorpromazine and ethanol on in vivi release of acetylcholine from the cerebral cortex. *Comparative General Pharmacology*, **2**, 306–310.

Pincherle, G. and Williamson, J. (1971) Smoking and neuroticism. *Lancet*, **2**, 981.

Poulas, C. X., Wolff, L., Ziln, D. H., Kaplan, H., and Capell, H. (1981) Acquisition of tolerance to alcohol-induced memory deficits in humans. *Psychopharmacology*, **73**, 176–179.

Pribram, K. H. (1967) The new neurology and biology of emotion: A structural approach. *American Psychologist*, **22**, 830–838.

Pribram, K. H. (1969) The neurobehavioral analysis of the binbic forebrain mechanisms: Revision and progress report. In D. Lehrman (ed.), *Advances in the Study of Behavior, Vol. 2*. New York: Academic Press.

Randall, L. O. and Cappell, B. (1973) Pharmacological activity of some benzodiazepines and their metabolites. In S. Garrattini, E. Mussini and L. O. Randall (eds.), *The Benzodiazepines*. New York: Raven Press.

Ray, O. S. (1972) *Drugs, Society and Human Behavior*. St Louis: C. V. Mosby.

Ross, D. H. (1976) Selective actions of alcohols on cerebral calcium levels. *Annals of New York Academy of Sciences*, **273**, 280–294.

Russek, H. (1965) Stress, tobacco and coronary disease in North American professional groups. *Journal of American Medical Association*, **192**, 189–194.

Russell, M. A. H., Peto, J., and Patel, U. A. (1974) The classification of smoking by factorial structure of motives. *Journal of the Royal Statistical Society*, **137**, 313–333.

Russell, R. W. (1953) Behaviour under stress. *International Journal of Psychoanalysis*, **34**, 1–12.

Sabey, B. E. and Codling, P. J. (1975) Alcohol and road accidents in Great Britain. In S. Israelstam and S. Lambert (eds.), *Alcohol, Drugs and Traffic Safety*. Ontario: Liquor Control Board.

Schachter, S. (1973) Nesbitt's paradox. In W. L. Dunn (ed.), *Smoking Behaviour: Motives and Incentives*. Washington D.C.: V. H. Winston.

Shiffman, S. M. (1977) The tobacco-withdrawal syndrome. In N. A. Krasnegor (ed.), *Cigarette Smoking as a Dependence Process*. Washington, D.C.: National Institute in Drug Abuse Mnograph.

Shiffman, S. M. (1979) Analysis of relapse episodes following smoking cessation. Paper presented at Fourth World Conference on Smoking and Health.

Siddell, F. R. and Pless, J. E. (1971) Ethyl alcohol: Blood levels and performance decrements after oral administration in man. *Psychopharmacologia*, **19**, 246–261.

Smyth, R. D., Martin, G. J., Moss, J. N., and Beck, H. (1967) The modification of various enzyme parameters in brain acetylcholine metabolism by chronic ingestion of ethanol. *Experimental Medicine and Surgery*, **25**, 1–6.

Steen, J. and Hahl, D. (1969) Controlled evaluation of parenteral diazepam as pre-anaesthetic medication. A statistical study. *Anaesthesia and Analgesia*, **48**, 549–554.

Stein, L., Wise, C. D., and Belluzzi, J. D. (1975) Effects of benzodiazepines in central serotonergic mechanisms. In E. Costa and P. Greengard (eds.), *Mechanisms of Action of Benzodiazepines*. New York: Raven Press.

Stein, L., Wise, C. D., and Berger, B. D. (1973) Antianxiety action of benzodiazepines: Decrease in activity of serotonin neurones in the punishment system. In S. Garattini (ed.), *The Benzodiazepines*. New York: Raven Press.

Sternbach, L. M. (1980) *The Benzodiazepine Story.* Basle: Editiones (Roche).

Taberner, P. V. (1980) Sex differences in low doses of ethanol on simple reaction time. *Psychopharmacology,* **70,** 283–286.

Taeuber, K., Badian, M., Brettel, H. F., Royen, Th., Rupp, W., Sittig, W., and Uihletin, M. (1979) Kinetic and dynamic interaction of clobazam and alcohol. *British Journal of Clinical Pharmacology,* **7,** 915–975.

Talland, G. A. (1966) Effects of alcohol on performance in continuous attention tasks. *Psychosomatic Medicine,* **28,** 596–604.

Tarriere, C. and Hartmann, F. (1964) Investigation into the effect of tobacco smoke and visual vigilance task. In *Ergonomics,* Proceedings of the 2nd I.E.A. Congress, Dortmund, 1964, pp.525–530.

Taylor, K. M. and Laverty, R. (1973) The effect of chlordiazepoxide, diazepam and nitrazepam on catecholamine metabolism in regions of the rat brain. *European Journal of Pharmacology,* **8,** 296–301.

Tornetta, F. J. (1965) Diazepam as preanaesthetic medication. *Anaesthetic Analgesics* (Cleve), **44,** 449–452.

Ulett, G. A. and Itil, T. M. (1967) Quantitative electroencephalogram in smoking and deprivation. *Science,* **164,** 969–970.

Valeroite, C., Tong, J. E., and Durding, B. (1979) Ethanol, tobacco and laterality effects on simple and complex motor performance. *Journal of Studies on Alcohol,* **40,** 823–830.

Walters, W. G. (1971) Smoking and neuroticism. *British Journal of Preventative and Social Medicine,* **25,** 162–164.

Warburton, D. M. (1975) *Brain, Drugs and Behaviour.* London: John Wiley & Sons.

Warburton, D. M. (1979) Neurochemical bases of consciousness. In K. Brown and S. Cooper (eds.), *Chemical Influences on Behaviour.* London: Academic Press, pp.421–462.

Warburton, D. M. (1981) Neurochemical bases of behaviour. *British Medical Bulletin,* **37,** 121–125.

Warburton, D. M. and Wesnes, K. A. (1978) Individual differences in smoking and attentional performance. In R. E. Thornton (ed.), *Smoking Behaviour: Physiological and Psychological Influences.* London: Churchill Livingston, pp.19–43.

Warburton, D. M. and Wesnes, K. (1979) The role of electrocortical arousal in the smoking habit. In A. Remond and C. Izard (eds.), *Electrophysiological Effects of Nicotine.* Amsterdam: Elsevier.

Warburton, D. M. and Wesnes, K. (1983) Mechanisms of habitual substance use. In A. Gale and J. Edwards (eds.), *Physiological Correlates of Human Behaviour,* vol. 1. London: Academic Press.

Warburton, D. M., Wesnes, K., and Pitkethly, G. (1981) Residual effects of temazepam and flurazepam on attentional performance. *Proceedings of the British Pharmacological Society,* in press.

Warburton, D. M., Wesnes, K., and Revell, A. (1981) Personality factors in self-medication by smoking. In W. Janke (ed.), *Response Variability to Psychotropic Drugs.* London: Pergamon.

Wechsler, R. L. (1958) Effects of cigarette smoking and intravenous nicotine in the human brain. *Federal Proceedings,* **17,** 169.

Wesnes, K. and Warburton, D. M. (1978) The effects of cigarette smoking and nicotine tablets on human attention. In R. E. Thornton (ed.), *Smoking Behaviour: Physiological and Psychological Influences.* London: Churchill-Livingston.

Westfall, T. C. (1974) Effect on nicotine and other drugs on the release of 3H-noradrenalin and 3H-dopamine from rat brain slices. *Neuropharmacology,* **13,** 693–700.

Williams, A. F. (1966) Social drinking, anxiety and depression. *Journal of Personality and Social Psychology*, **6**, 689–693.

Williams, D. G. (1980) Effects on cigarette smoking on immediate memory and performance in different kinds of smoker. *British Journal of Psychology*, **71**, 81–90.

Williamson, J. R. (1975) The effects of epinephrine on glucogenolysis and myocardial contractility. In H. Blaschko, G. Sayers, and A. D. Smith (eds.), *Handbook of Physiology: Endocrinology, Vol. 6. Adrenal Gland*. Washington D.C.: American Physiological Society.

Wise, C. D., Berger, B. D., and Stein, L. (1972) Benzodiazepines: Anxiety-reducing activity by reduction of serotonin turnover in the brain. *Science*, **177**, 180–183.

Zbinden, G. and Randall, L. O. (1967) Pharmacology of the benzodiazepines. Laboratory and Clinical Correlations. *Advances in Pharmacology*, **5**, 213–291.

Zirkle, G. A., McActee, D. B., King, P. D., and Van Dyke, R. (1960) Meprobamate and small amounts of alcohol. *Journal of the American Medical Association*, **173**, 1823–1825.

Stress and Fatigue in Human Performance
Edited by G. R. J. Hockey
© 1983 John Wiley & Sons Ltd.

Chapter 9

Diurnal Variation

Simon Folkard

This chapter is concerned with the effects of time of day on people's ability to perform various tasks. These diurnal variations in performance are thought to reflect the 24-hour rhythms that are now known to exist in the vast majority of biological functions. Under normal circumstances they result in predictable trends in performance over the day, with the precise nature of these trends being influenced by various factors such as the demands of the task and individual differences. Such time-of-day effects in performance have obvious practical implications in a variety of situations including the scheduling of school timetables and shiftwork systems (see Chapter 4).

There is currently a revival of interest in the effects of time of day on performance, and this is largely due to the fact that these effects have been interpreted as reflecting similar underlying changes to those that occur under stress. Thus, although it is perhaps difficult to conceive of some times of day as being more stressful than others, there has been a considerable cross-fertilization of ideas between this area and the others covered in this book. Indeed, there is some evidence that the effects of stress on performance differ markedly depending on the time of day. Loud noise, for example, has been found to have a far greater effect on performance in the early morning than later on in the day. This finding has been interpreted within the arousal theory that has dominated recent research in both the time-of-day and stress areas. Clearly, the influence of time of day has both theoretical and practical implications for the stress and performance area.

Following a brief introduction to 24-hour rhythms, the arousal theory of time of day effects in performance is considered. The early research in this area is then discussed, followed by a review of the basic trends in performance over the day. These basic trends in performance are shown to be dependent upon the demands of the task, differences between individuals, and the level of various other factors, including stressors, that are thought to affect arousal level. Finally, it is pointed out that the arousal theory cannot account for all the findings in this area, and receives little support from either subjective or physiological measures of arousal.

THE PHYSIOLOGICAL BASIS OF PERFORMANCE RHYTHMS

Underlying physiological rhythms

It is now generally accepted that circadian rhythms exist in the vast majority of physiological functions. Thus, for example, although we frequently consider 37°C to be the 'normal' body temperature, there is in fact a pronounced circadian rhythm in man's body temperature (see Chapter 4). 'Normal' temperature varies considerably over the day from a minimum of about 36.2°C in the early hours of the morning to a maximum of 36.9°C in the evening at 20.00. Physiological circadian rhythms such as this are thought to be controlled by 'biological clocks' or oscillators that are regulated by our physical environment. It is thought that the pineal gland, which appears to be sensitive to the light/dark cycle, plays some role in their regulation via its secretion of a hormone called melatonin. However, it is also known that for man environmental cues (usually referred to as *zeitgeber*, the German for 'time givers') other than the light/dark cycle may assist in this regulation. The most important of these other *zeitgeber* would appear to be our knowledge of clock time, and our general social environment.

If someone is isolated from these *zeitgeber* most of their rhythms persist, although the periodicity of these rhythms may deviate from 24 hours. Indeed, the degree to which a rhythm deviates from 24 hours can be regarded as a measure of its dependence on external (exogenous) factors as opposed to internal (endogenous) factors for its timing. For example, it is not uncommon for the temperature rhythm of people isolated from the *zeitgeber* in underground chambers to drift to a periodicity of 25 hours, while their sleep/wake cycle may change to as much as 36 hours. This suggests that the temperature rhythm is relatively endogenous, but the activity rhythm (i.e. sleep/wake cycle) is relatively exogenous. When people's rhythms 'stretch' like this they are described as 'free running'. If different rhythms 'free run' at different periodicities, as in the example just given, *internal desynchronization* occurs. In other words, two rhythms that usually have the same periodicity acquire different periodicities, and this has been used as evidence that there is more than one underlying oscillator. (See Wever, 1979, for a review of these studies.)

Under normal circumstances, it is, of course, extremely rare for people to become isolated from these *zeitgeber*, except perhaps in the Arctic and Antarctic circles. However, it is not unusual for a conflict to arise between an individual's circadian rhythms and the external *zeitgeber*. Thus, *external desynchronization* may occur whenever people are forced to adopt an unusual sleep/wake cycle such as that occasioned by crossing time zones, or working at night (see Chapter 4 for a full discussion of this matter).

Before considering the effects of these circadian rhythms on performance, it should be pointed out that whereas it is relatively easy to monitor physio-logical parameters 'around the clock', it is logically impossible to do so for performance measures. The reason is simply that man spends about one-third of his time asleep, during which he ceases to perform (at least in any normal sense of the word), but obviously continues to live and hence has a measurable temperature and heart-rate, etc. While there are ways in which researchers have attempted to overcome this problem, they all have their drawbacks. In view of this, it is common to refer to trends in performance over the day as 'time-of-day effects' or 'diurnal variations' rather than circadian rhythms. Nevertheless, most recent researchers in this area have assumed that these time-of-day effects reflect an underlying circadian rhythm (or rhythms) in the ability to perform various tasks.

The arousal theory of time-of-day effects

In recent years diurnal variations in performance have usually been interpreted as reflecting an underlying circadian rhythm in arousal. This arousal theory has commonly been attributed to Colquhoun (1971), although, in fact, it has developed over a considerable period of time, and can be traced back at least as far as Michelson (1897), who proposed a hypothetical function relating 'sleepiness' to time of day. This function was taken up by Gates (1916b) who combined it with the ideas of Howell (1897) that people sleep because of the 'anaemic' condition of the brain at night. Gates (1916b) argued that 'it would seem that although the return to consciousness (on awakening in the morning) is sudden, the complete re-adjustment of the anaemic condition takes place more slowly, since it is dependent on the cumulative effects of sensory experience and the increasing activity of the brain' (p.11). Thus, Gates postulated the existence of a circadian sleep/wakefulness rhythm, and suggested that wakefulness was highest in the mid-afternoon.

Somewhat more recently Kleitman (1939, revised 1963) observed a marked parallelism between the circadian rhythm in body temperature and that in speed of reaction times. As a result of this, he argued for a causal relationship between temperature and performance, suggesting that the improved performance at higher temperatures reflected that 'either (a) mental processes represent chemical reactions in themselves or (b) the speed of thinking depends upon the level of metabolic activity of the cells of the cerebral cortex, and by raising the latter through an increase in body temperature, one indirectly speeds up the thought process' (p.160). In support of this claim Kleitman presented extensive correlational data from a single subject between the spontaneous changes in body temperature associated with time of day, and the corresponding changes in simple reaction time. Subsequently, Rutenfranz, Aschoff, and Mann (1972) controlled for circadian changes by summing over the different times of day, and failed to find any relationship between temperature and performance. They therefore suggested that the correlation observed by Kleitman was due to independent circadian rhythms in temperature and performance that are 'in phase' with one another.

Undoubtedly the best case for the arousal theory of time-of-day effects is that put forward by Colquhoun and his associates (e.g. Colquhoun, 1971; Blake, 1971; Hockey and Colquhoun, 1972). Colquhoun (1971) also rejected Kleitman's notion of a causal relationship between temperature and performance, but argued that apart from a 'post-lunch decrement' in performance, circadian changes in body temperature parallel those in performance efficiency. Like Gates (1916b), Colquhoun assumed these variations in performance to reflect a circadian rhythm in 'sleepiness' which he equated with 'arousal' (or more strictly, the lack of it). He postulated that 'the general level of sleepiness falls (i.e. arousal rises) during the waking day, to reach a minimum somewhere in the evening' (Colquhoun, 1971, p.51). He further argued that people tend to feel sleepy after lunch, and thus show a 'post-lunch decrement' in arousal and performance, despite the failure of the circadian rhythm in temperature to reflect this decrement.

However, the best evidence that Colquhoun (1971) presented for this arousal theory was not the parallelism between temperature and performance observed by Kleitman, but the fact that time of day interacted with other factors commonly assumed to affect arousal level. Thus, Colquhoun noted that a number of studies had found sleep-deprived subjects to show more pronounced time-of-day effects in performance than non-sleep-deprived ones. He argued that this finding was interpretable in terms of the postulated 'inverted-U' function relating performance efficiency to arousal level (see Chapter 12 for a full discussion of this theory). Basically, this 'inverted-U' theory predicts that as arousal increases, so performance on a given task will improve in a negatively accelerating manner up to some optimal level of arousal. Beyond this optimum, further increases in arousal will result in a deterioration of performance.

From the present standpoint, the important aspect of this theory is that it predicts that the effect of a fixed change in arousal, due to some other manipulation, will vary depending on the time of day (and hence 'baseline' level of arousal). Colquhoun argued that sleep deprivation, which is held to reduce arousal level, would thus have a bigger detrimental effect on performance in the morning, when arousal is low, than in the evening when it is high. This would result in the observed 'amplification' of the time-of-day effect in the performance of sleep-deprived subjects. Further evidence that generally supports this arousal interpretation of time-of-day effects in performance was obtained by Blake (1971). In a series of studies, Blake proved the time-of-day effect in performance to interact with other factors thought to affect arousal level (namely extroversion, knowledge of results, and loud noise) in a manner that can be accounted for by the 'inverted-U' theory.

The work of Colquhoun and his associates has thus provided an extremely valuable framework in which to interpret the effects of time of day on performance, and has stimulated considerable interest in this area. However, it would now appear that this inverted-U theory may be over-simplistic. In addition, there are some recent findings in the time of day literature that it cannot account for, and these are discussed later in this chapter, and in Chapter 4.

TIME-OF-DAY EFFECTS IN PERFORMANCE

It has commonly been assumed that time-of-day effects in performance reflect a single circadian rhythm that is itself controlled by a single 'biological clock'. This implies that if an individual's performance on one task is low at a particular time of day, then his performance on all other tasks should also be low. This assumption has obvious attractions, especially in view of the parallelism held to exist between the time-of-day effect in performance and the circadian changes in body temperature. Indeed, it has even been argued that performance efficiency could be assessed indirectly by measuring body temperature, and that such a technique has the advantage of avoiding the use of '. . . time consuming performance tests which, in themselves, interfere with, or disrupt, the scheduled activities of the persons studied' (Kleitman and Jackson, 1950, p.309).

Despite the fact that there has long been ample evidence that this assumption of a single circadian performance rhythm is false, it has had a considerable impact on research in this area. It appears that this assumption is primarily attributable to Kleitman (1939, revised 1963), who concluded that 'most of the curves of performance can be brought into line with the known 24-hour body temperature curves' (p.161). However, in describing his performance measures, Kleitman points out that '. . . except for multiplication, the individual tests required little or no mental activity on the part of the subject' (p.151). Thus, his conclusions were based mainly on simple perceptual–motor tasks rather than more cognitive ones.

Unfortunately, Kleitman appears to have set a trend in that subsequent reviews in this area (Colquhoun, 1971; Hockey and Colquhoun, 1972; Broughton, 1975) have also largely concentrated on perceptual–motor performance, thus perpetuating the myth of a single performance rhythm paralleling that in temperature. To their credit, Hockey and Colquhoun (1972) did at least suggest that the performance of memory tasks may show a rather different trend over the day to that found for other tasks, and point to the need for a more detailed examination of the literature in this area. Broughton (1975) also notes that the trend for memory may differ, but fails to examine this literature in any detail.

In this section we shall first consider the early studies in this area, and then go on to examine the trend in performance efficiency over the day for different types of task.

Early studies

Research on the effects of time of day on performance efficiency has two early roots. One of these is the work of Lombard at Clark University in the U.S. (Lombard, 1887). Lombard was interested in the time-of-day effect, or circadian rhythm, in the magnitude of the 'knee jerk' and published the results of his pioneering investigations in 1887. This led two students of his, Dressler and Bergstrum, to look for time-of-day effects in performance efficiency *per se*. Like many early psychologists, Dressler (1892) tested his own performance over a prolonged period of time. He used the speed with which he could tap a morse-key as his measure of performance, and found it to steadily improve with practice over the first 4 weeks. However, he found that in the last 2 weeks of his 6-week study, his tapping got faster from 08.00 to 12.00, was rather slower again after lunch at 14.00, but then improved again up to 18.00. This trend over the day is fairly typical for studies using this type of task that have managed to overcome the problems of the practice effect.

Lombard's other student, Bergstrum (1894), was more concerned with 'mental activity' and examined performance on tasks such as memory, mental arithmetic, and reading, as well as simpler tasks similar to those used by Dressler. Bergstrum found time-of-day effects in the performance scores, but these were '. . . not of a single type such as would be required if a natural inherited rhythm of activity exists'. In other words, Bergstrum found that the trend in performance over the day differed from one person to another, and from one type of task to another. Subsequently, this lack of consistency in Bergstrum's results has sometimes been attributed to his failure to practise his subjects adequately, although there is now ample evidence that the trend in performance over the day is affected by both the type of individual and the type of task. Rather surprisingly, Bergstrum's most important finding has been almost totally ignored by subsequent researchers in this area: namely, that performance on more complex mental tasks shows a bigger variation over the day than that on simple tasks. This point will be taken up later in this chapter.

This early research by Lombard and his students appears to have been motivated primarily by theoretical interest rather than by any specific practical problem. In contrast, the other main root of research in this area developed from consideration of the best way to organize or schedule school timetables. This problem was being discussed in Prague as early as 1889 (see Halberg, 1973) although it was some years later that the first experimental studies of this problem were published. Among the earliest of these pedagogical studies was that of a German called Baade (1907), who examined children's speed at solving arithmetical problems at different times of day. Similar studies were also conducted in Britain (e.g. Winch, 1912a, 1912b) and the United States (e.g. Gates, 1916a, 1961b; Laird, 1925).

These early educational psychologists were well aware that the trends they observed in performance over the day were, at least in part, attributable to mental fatigue. Indeed, Gates (1916b) pointed out that it is extremely difficult to separate the effects of fatigue from any underlying temporal trend. Such a separation is, of course, extremely important if practical recommendations are to be made. Thus, for example, many of these early studies found immediate memory to be good at 10.00. However, it is unclear from their results whether this was due to an underlying circadian rhythm, or to the fact that the children had not been at school for as long as they had at later times in the day. If the latter were the case, then starting school 4 hours later might be expected to result in such memory being good at 14.00 rather than at 10.00. The question as to whether the effects of time of day on performance are due to circadian rhythms or to mental fatigue is thus an extremely important one, and one that the vast majority of studies in this area have failed to tackle, despite the early awareness of it.

Before turning to the more recent renewal of interest in the effects of time of day on performance, it is worth briefly considering the work of Ebbinghaus (1885) who pioneered the experimental study of human memory processes. By simplifying the problems in various ways, Ebbinghaus was able to bring the 'new experimental approach' of Wundt and Fechner to bear on memory processes. He did this by considering the rote learning and re-learning of lists of nonsense CVC (consonant–vowel–consonant) syllables, such as 'CAZ', by a highly disciplined and motivated subject (himself) under rigorously controlled conditions.

Ebbinghaus's main findings concerned the rate at which lists of nonsense syllables were initially learned and then forgotten (see Baddeley, 1976). However, in the present context the most pertinent fact is that he examined the influence of time of day on both these functions. In one series of studies he learned lists of syllables in sessions starting at 10.00, 11.00, and 1800. Learning was found to be over 20 per cent faster at 11.00 than at 10.00, but to have slowed down by over 30 per cent by 18.00. As Ebbinghaus commented: 'In the later hours of the day, mental vigour and receptivity are less' (p.66). However, he failed to find any evidence that the time at which a list was originally learned influenced the rate at which it was forgotten.

Although Ebbinghaus's pioneering work has had a vast impact on subsequent research on memory, his findings concerning the effects of time of day have been almost totally ignored. Indeed, Ebbinghaus himself appears to have been relatively uninterested in this aspect of his research. Nevertheless, his failure to find any effect of the time of day at which material is learned on the rate at which it is forgotten, may account for the almost universal concentration on immediate memory that has subsequently occurred in this area. This concentration is particularly unfortunate in view of the educational background to much of this research. It would now appear that Ebbinghaus's failure to find differences in the rate of forgetting was due to his use of nonsense material, since recent research suggests that the time of day at which meaningful material is presented may have a marked effect on its subsequent retention.

This early research on the effects of time of day on performance was reviewed by Freeman and Hovland (1934) who concluded that 'the balance of evidence apparently favours an afternoon superiority for sensory and motor performance, but there is little agreement as to the time when complicated mental work can be done most efficiently' (p.786). Subsequently, and perhaps consequently, interest in this area appears to have waned until a revival in the 1960s. This revival stemmed from a completely different practical problem, namely that of maintaining high levels of productivity and safety on various shift systems (see Chapter 4).

The form of performance rhythms

The idea that time-of-day effects in the performance of certain tasks parallel changes in temperature is, of course, supported by an abundance of experimental evidence. Hockey and Colquhoun (1972) characterized these tasks as those requiring an 'immediate processing' (or 'throughput') of information. Perhaps the best example of this type of task is the 'cancellation' or 'list searching' test that has frequently been used in studies in this area. These studies have all involved subjects searching through alphanumeric characters to find particular 'targets'. The precise nature of the 'targets' appears to be relatively unimportant, and has varied from tilted zeros embedded in a background of upright ones (Hughes and Folkard, 1976) to the successive occurrence of a particular alphabetic character in random lines of such characters (Fort and Mills, 1976). The results of these studies, in terms of the speed with which subjects searched through the characters, are shown in Figure 39, together with the results of similar studies by Blake (1967a) and Klein, Wegmann, and Hunt (1972). Also shown is the normal trend over the day in oral temperature after Colquhoun, Blake, and Edwards (1968).

In order to compare across the performance studies, the scores at each time of day have been expressed as a percentage of the overall mean for the study. It can be seen that performance on this type of task is about 7 per cent below average at 08.00, and about 5 per cent above average when it reaches its peak at about 20.00. It is worth noting that in the Blake (1967a) study there was a suggestion of a 'post-lunch decrement' in performance, but that apart from this one exception, there is a fair parallelism between the circadian changes

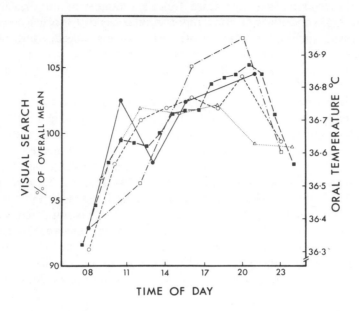

Figure 39. The time-of-day effect in serial visual search speed. After Blake (1967) ●————● ; Klein *et al.* (1972) Δ---------Δ; Fort and Mills (1976) ○— — —○; Hughes and Folkard (1976) □—·—·—□. Data are also shown for temperature (after Colquhoun *et al.*, 1968) ■————■. (Reproduced by permission of Lawrence Erlbaum Associates.)

in body temperature and those in performance efficiency on this type of task.

The failure of three of the studies shown in Figure 39 to show a 'post-lunch decrement' is somewhat surprising. Many of the early studies in this area (e.g. Kraepelin, 1893) found one, and it is generally accepted that one occurs. The only obvious difference between the studies shown in Figure 39 is that Blake used a rather more prolonged task (namely 30 minutes) than the other authors. Thus, it is possible that, like those associated with sleep-deprivation, post-lunch decrements only show up after people have been performing a given task for some time. Alternatively, this difference between the results of these studies could be attributable to the fact that Blake's subjects habitually had their main meal of the day at mid-day. Finally, there is some evidence that the post-lunch decrement is more marked in people who are relatively sleep-deprived (Hildebrandt, Rohmert, and Rutenfranz, 1974) and thus this difference could possibly reflect differences in the subjects' level of sleep deprivation.

Despite this problem of the inconsistency of the 'post-lunch decrement', the results shown in Figure 39 clearly agree as to the overall trend over the day fairly well: performance is low in the morning, high at about 20.00, and parallels the trend in oral temperature. Indeed, a number of authors, including Kleitman (1963) and Blake (1967a), report similar trends for other perceptual–motor tasks, such as reaction time, card-sorting speed, and vigilance performance. Thus, this improvement in performance over the day for perceptual–motor tasks requiring the immediate processing of information appears to have at least some generality.

The main exception to this 'through-the-day' improvement in performance is undoubtedly found with tasks of memory, or tasks involving a high working memory load (Baddeley and Hitch, 1974). However, before considering this evidence, it should be pointed out that some studies of perceptual–motor performance have also failed to find an improvement over most of the day. Thus, for example, Klein, Wegman, and Hunt (1972) report that reaction time was fastest at 09.00, while temperature reached its maximum at 21.00. Similarly, Buck (1976) found response speed to reach a maximum considerably earlier than the normal peak in body temperature. The reason for these discrepant results remains unclear, although it would appear that while visual search performance consistently reaches a maximum late in the day, that on tasks of motor speed may sometimes reach a maximum considerably earlier.

THE COMPLICATION OF MEMORY

In view of the educational background to much of the research in the time-of-day area, it is hardly surprising that memory tasks have been among the most extensively studied. Why these memory studies have been largely ignored in earlier reviews of this area is unclear, unless it is because they refute the idea of a single performance rhythm paralleling that in body temperature. Thus, for example, in one of the better of the early educational studies in this area, Gates (1916a) found markedly different trends over the day for performance on perceptual–motor and memory tasks. School children's performance on the perceptual–motor tasks improved over the whole of the school day, in line with the other results in this area. In contrast, their ability to repeat back a series of random digits, a classic test of short-term memory, reached an early maximum, at about 11.00, and then fell over the rest of the day. Subsequently, Gates (1916b) found a similar trend in the short-term memory of college students.

As a result of these findings, Gates (1916a, p.149) concluded that 'in general the forenoon is the best time for strictly mental work . . . while the afternoon may best be taken up with school subjects in which the motor factors are predominant'. While there is some reason to doubt the validity of this conclusion, there is clearly no doubt that Gates did not subscribe to the view of a single performance rhythm. Later studies, including that of Blake (1967a), have found very similar trends over the day on this type of memory task. However, the most convincing evidence that performance does not necessarily show a through-the-day improvement comes from studies that have used rather more realistic memory tasks.

Short-term memory

These studies have involved people reading short articles and then immediately afterwards being given a test on their memory for its contents. Both Laird (1925) and Folkard and Monk (1980) used this procedure and examined a wide range of times of day. Their findings are shown in Figure 40, in which the results for each time of day have again been expressed as a percentage of the overall mean to allow comparison between the studies. The trend in temperature from the Folkard and Monk study is also shown.

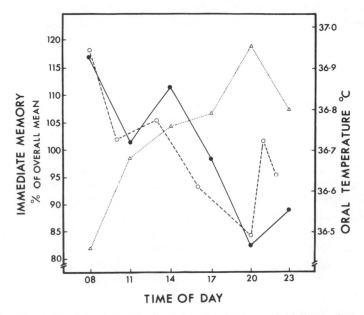

Figure 40. The time-of-day effect in the immediate memory for information presented in short passages of prose. After Laird (1925) ○———○; Folkard and Monk (1980) ●————● . Data are also shown for body temperature (after Folkard and Monk, 1980) Δ---------Δ. (Reproduced by permission of the British Psychological Society.)

Two important points should be noted from Figure 40. First, the trend in immediate memory over the day is virtually the opposite to that found for visual search performance, with such memory being highest at 08.00 and lowest at 20.00. Secondly, the magnitude of this effect, in terms of the percentage deviation from the overall mean, is considerably greater than that for visual search tasks, performance being over 15 per cent above average at

08.00 and 15 per cent below average at 20.00. This is, of course, in line with Bergstrum's (1894) finding that more complex mental tasks show a bigger variation over the day.

Long-term memory

Although these results from studies of immediate memory are incompatible with the idea of a single performance rhythm, they do not necessarily contradict the arousal theory of time-of-day effects. Thus, it is possible to argue that although the increase in arousal over the day improves visual search performance, it impairs short-term memory. Indeed, there is some evidence, albeit inconsistent, from studies using other arousal manipulations, that short-term memory may be impaired under high arousal (see Craik and Blankstein, 1975; and Chapter 12 of this volume). However, these studies have also consistently found that delayed memory (over about 15–20 minutes) is *superior* when the material has originally been presented under high arousal.

This latter finding obviously has important theoretical and practical implications for the time-of-day area. It suggests that although immediate memory is better in the morning, long-term memory should be superior following the presentation of material in the afternoon or evening. Clearly, if this were true, it would throw some doubt on the validity of the early recommendation that the morning is the best time to teach the more 'academic' school subjects.

The first authors to recognize that long-term memory should be better following afternoon or evening presentation were Baddeley, Hatter, Scott, and Snashall (1970). In fact, although their results tended to support this suggestion, they found no reliable effect of time of day on their measure of long-term memory. However, they used a rather unusual long-term memory task that involved the recall of lists of random digits. Subsequent studies using random lists of words (Hockey, Davies, and Gray, 1972; Folkard and Monk, 1979) have proved rather more successful in obtaining reliable effects on time of day on long-term memory that are consistent with this suggestion.

In view of the educational implications of this research, the other studies in this area have used rather more realistic memory tasks. Folkard, Monk, Bradbury, and Rosenthall (1977) examined school children's immediate and delayed (7-day) memory for a story that they were read at 09.00 or 15.00. In the immediate test the children that heard the story at 09.00 remembered about 10 per cent more than those who heard it at 15.00. However, a week later this pattern of results had reversed such that the children who had heard the story at 15.00 now remembered about 8 per cent more. Furthermore, this superior delayed retention following afternoon presentation was unaffected by the time of day at which the delayed memory test was itself given.

Subsequently, Folkard and Monk (1980) obtained similar results from a study of night nurses' memory for the information presented in an 'in-service training' film shown at 04.00 or 20.30. These times correspond fairly well to the normal minimum and maximum, respectively, of the circadian rhythm in body temperature, and hence in the postulated arousal rhythm. However, there is a complication since the nurses were night-workers and this might be expected to affect their circadian rhythms (see Chapter 4). Nevertheless, for those nurses whose circadian temperature rhythm was relatively unadjusted to night-work, the results supported the idea that presentation in the evening results in inferior immediate memory but superior delayed retention. Those seeing the film at 20.30 did about 18 per cent worse on the immediate test, but 20% per cent better on the delayed (28 days) memory test than those seeing it at 04.00. Again, this superior delayed retention following presentation at 20.30 was unaffected by the time of day at which the nurses were given the delayed memory test.

The nature of memory changes

The results of these studies suggest that the time of day at which information is presented has virtually opposite effects on immediate and delayed retention. Although this is in line with the predictions derived from the arousal theory, there are some uncertainties still to be resolved in this area. First, all but one of these studies of long-term memory have compared only two times of day, so it is impossible to infer the precise nature of the trend over the day. Secondly, there is some evidence that the arousal theory of time-of-day effects is over-simplistic in that it cannot easily account for some of the more recent findings in this area (as well as in other areas of stress research). Thirdly, the question must arise as to why these recent studies have found an effect of time of presentation on delayed retention when Ebbinghaus (1885) found absolutely no evidence for such an effect.

The first of these problems cannot be resolved without further experiments, while the second is taken up in the later sections of this chapter and in Chapter 12. However, it is possible to offer a reasonable explanation as to why Ebbinghaus found no effect of time of day on long-term memory. In order to do this we need to consider *how* time of day affects immediate and delayed retention, not in terms of the amount it affects it by, but in terms of the changes in the underlying processes responsible for our ability or inability to remember a particular bit of information. Studies of other arousal manipulations, such as loud noise, are important in this context in that they suggest that arousal affects the degree to which we attend to different aspects of the material to be remembered. These studies are considered in greater detail in Chapters 3 and 12, but, for example, Hockey and Hamilton (1970) found evidence suggesting that high arousal results in people paying less attention to the spatial location in which words are presented, but more attention to the words themselves.

Recent studies of time of day and immediate memory suggest a similar change in the degree to which different attributes are attended to. Basically it seems that as the day progresses, people pay less attention to the physical characteristics of words (e.g. their sounds), but more to their meaning; see Folkard (1982) for a review of this literature. Thus, it seems that the superior immediate memory in the morning may be due to more attention being paid to the physical characteristics of the information, while the superior delayed retention following afternoon or evening presentation is a result of greater attention being paid to the material's meaning. If this is the case, then Ebbinghaus's failure to find an effect of time of day on delayed retention is hardly surprising in view of his use of nonsense syllables that, by definition, are (effectively) devoid of meaning. It might also account for the fact that more realistic studies of memory have found bigger time-of-day effects since more realistic material is more meaningful.

Working memory

The evidence from these memory studies thus clearly refutes the idea of a single performance rhythm, and indeed indicates that different types of memory processes may show different trends over the day. Many of the tasks that people perform are, however, not pure memory ones, despite the fact that they are clearly more complex than the simple immediate processing tasks, such as visual search, considered in the previous section. These tasks, which include mental arithmetic, reading, and reasoning, have been characterized as involving working memory (Baddeley and Hitch, 1974), and are becoming more frequent in industrial situations due to the increased use of high technology. They have in common the fact that they involve both immediate processing and short-term memory.

Much of the experimental evidence suggests that performance on tasks of this type reaches a maximum at about mid-day. The results of two of these studies (Laird, 1925; Folkard, 1975) that examined mental arithmetic and performance on two verbal reasoning tasks, are shown in Figure 41. Clearly, performance showed a compromise function over the day between the decreasing trend for pure short-term memory, and the increasing one for immediate processing performance. There are, however, some atypical studies in this area that have found either a morning or an evening peak in performance. The reason for this would appear to be that the precise timing of the peak depends on the level of the memory load involved (Folkard, Knauth, Monk, and Rutenfranz, 1976).

It seems highly probable that the *effective* memory load involved in the performance of a given task will be affected by a number of factors including

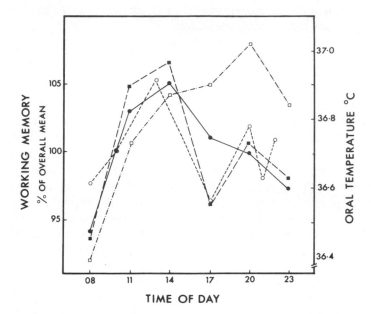

Figure 41. The time-of-day effect in performance speed on working memory tasks. After Laird (1925) ○————○; Folkard (1975) ■————■ and ●————●. Data are also shown for body temperature (after Folkard, 1975) □—·—·—□. (Reproduced by permission of Lawrence Erlbaum Associates.)

age, intelligence, and level of practice. With prolonged practice people may be able to adopt sophisticated strategies that have the effect of reducing the memory load and hence result in a later peak in performance. Similarly, what is only a moderate memory load for adults may be a high one for children, resulting in their showing an earlier peak in performance. Such an explanation could account for the late peak observed by Blake (1967a) for mental arithmetic, since his subjects were extremely highly practised; and for the early peak found for the same task by Rutenfranz and Hellbruegge (1957) since their subjects were children. Despite this complication, it is clear that the idea of a single rhythm in performance is untenable, and that task demands, and in particular the memory load, play an important role in determining the trend in performance over the day.

INDIVIDUAL DIFFERENCES

Another factor that affects the precise trend in performance over the day is the nature of the individual performing the task. As has already been pointed out, age and level of practice may affect the trend for working memory tasks by influencing the effective memory load. There are, however, more fundamental individual differences in temperament that affect the circadian rhythm in both physiological and performance measures.

Morning/evening types

The most extensively researched factor within this area is the difference between 'morning' and 'evening' types, or 'larks' and 'owls'. It has long been recognized that some people prefer to work in the morning, while others prefer to do so in the evening. Pillsbury (1903) was among the first to try to relate this difference to differences in the trend in various physiological and performance measures over the day. Subsequently, Kleitman (1939, 1963) divided people on the basis of whether their temperature rhythm showed an early or late peak, and found parallel differences in their performance rhythms. However, it appears that, in general, people do not differ all that much from one another in terms of the timing of their temperature peak. Thus, the recent data of Horne and Ostberg (1977) and Colquhoun (1979) suggests that over two-thirds of the population will have temperature peaks that are within a couple of hours of the average, namely 20.00. This implies that even extreme morning and evening types cannot differ very much in the timing of the peak of their temperature rhythms, and this is supported by the difference of only 65 minutes found by Horne and Ostberg (1977).

This failure to find large differences between morning and evening types in their temperature rhythms led some authors, including the present one, to assume that only small differences would be found in their performance rhythms. This assumption is based on the idea that the circadian rhythm in temperature parallels that in arousal, and that the latter mediates the changes in performance. Although we know that task demands can influence the nature of the relationship between temperature and performance, this evidence is still consistent with a circadian rhythm in arousal paralleling that in temperature. However, the results of a recent study by Horne, Brass, and Pettit (1980) throw considerable doubt on the idea that the arousal rhythm necessarily parallels that in temperature.

Horne *et al.* examined performance efficiency on a 'detection task' which would clearly be expected to parallel the time-of-day effect in temperature fairly closely. The subjects were selected as being very extreme 'morning' or 'evening' types on the basis of a paper and pencil questionnaire (Horne and Ostberg, 1976). The results from this study are shown in Figure 42. The left-hand panel shows the trends over the day in temperature for these extreme morning and evening types, and the right-hand panel the corresponding trends in performance.

The most important point to make about these results is that whereas the extreme morning and evening types had fairly similar temperature rhythms, they showed very different performance rhythms. Thus, while for the evening

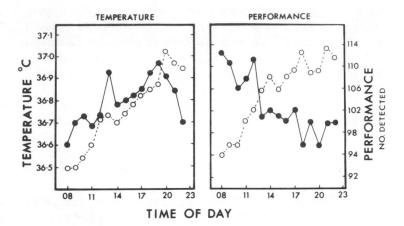

Figure 42. The time-of-day effect in body temperature and performance efficiency for extreme morning (●————●) and evening (○----------○) types. After Horne *et al.* (1980).

types there was a reliable positive relationship between temperature and performance, for the morning types there was a reliable *negative* one. Although these results are of limited practical relevance, since most people are neither extreme morning types nor extreme evening types, from a theoretical viewpoint they are extremely important. They are clearly inconsistent with the view that the circadian rhythm in arousal always parallels that in temperature. These findings of Horne *et al.* also indicate that individual differences in performance rhythms may be far greater than the small differences observed in the temperature rhythm would suggest.

Extroverts and introverts

The other main line of research in this area stems from the observation by Colquhoun (1960) that the performance of introverts was better than that of extroverts at 10.00, but that at 15.00 the reverse was true. This finding, which can be interpreted within the arousal theory since introverts are considered to be more aroused than extroverts (Eysenck, 1967), led Blake (1967b) to examine the circadian rhythm in temperature of these two types. He found differences rather similar to those found between morning and evening types. Thus introverts had slightly higher temperatures than extroverts in the morning, but slightly lower ones in the evening. Again, however, slightly larger differences were found for performance measures (Blake, 1971), although these were not as large as those shown in Figure 42.

More recently, Revelle, Humphreys, Simon, and Gilliland (1980) have pointed out that there are two 'sub-scales' to the dimension of extroversion.

Thus, 'extroverts' tend to be both highly sociable and highly impulsive, i.e. they do things 'on the spur of the moment'. These authors gave a highly cognitive working memory task to large numbers of undergraduates at 09.00 and 1900. The results were then examined in terms of the overall extroversion scores, the sociability scores, and the impulsivity scores. Their results clearly indicated that it was the impulsivity component of extroversion that was responsible for the different trends in performance over the day. Under normal conditions the performance of high impulsives improved from 09.00 to 19.00, while that of low impulsives either stayed the same, or declined. This finding is particularly impressive in view of the fact that the subjects were not extremes; the overall group being simply sub-divided into two sub-groups on the basis of their impulsivity scores.

Revelle *et al.* failed to obtain temperature measures from their subjects, but as a result of their findings M. W. Eysenck and Folkard (1980) re-examined some temperature data in terms of impulsivity. The circadian rhythm in temperature of both low and high impulsives was found to reach a maximum at 20.00, although the high impulsives showed a slightly bigger rise in temperature over the day. Thus, again, there is evidence suggesting that large differences may be found between individuals in terms of the trend in performance over the day, despite fairly small differences in the temperature rhythm.

The research in this area has thus indicated that individual differences are important in determining the trend in performance over the day, despite the small differences in the temperature rhythm. Whether people are morning or evening types, introverts or extroverts, or low or high impulsives, seems to be important in this respect. However, it must be pointed out that no studies have systematically attempted to determine whether these differences hold for all types of task. Whereas studies of the effects of task demands have examined a wide range of individuals, studies of individual differences have typically only used a single type of task. Thus, while differences between individuals may well have important applied implications, there is a clear need for a systematic research effort in this area before practical recommendations can be made.

THE INFLUENCE OF AROUSAL

Interactions of time of day with arousal manipulations

So far we have considered only the effects of task demands and individual differences in determining the trend in performance over the day. There are, however, a number of other factors that have been found to affect this trend, including sleep deprivation, noise, social isolation, knowledge of results, and drugs. The main thing these have in common is that they are all thought to either raise or lower an individual's arousal level. Indeed, research on the combined effect of these factors and time of day has been motivated almost entirely by theoretical considerations, rather than by any specific practical problems. Thus, it has been argued that if arousal increases over the day, and there is an 'inverted-U' shape function relating performance to arousal, other arousal manipulations should have a greater effect on performance in the morning than in the evening.

Studies that have examined the combined effects of time of day and *one* of these other factors have tended to obtain results that are consistent with this idea. Thus, loud noise has been found to improve performance on immediate processing tasks in the early morning, but to have little, if any, effect later in the day (Blake, 1971; Mullin and Corcoran, 1977). However, many of these studies have examined only two times of day, and two levels of the other arousal manipulation (e.g. noise). This procedure results in only three clearly distinguishable levels of arousal since; for example, it is not possible to determine *a priori* whether arousal is higher under loud noise at 08.00, or quieter noise later in the day. With only three levels of arousal the only pattern of results that the inverted-U function cannot account for is a drop in performance from low to medium levels of arousal, followed by an increase in performance from medium to high levels.

The critical studies for the arousal theory of time-of-day effects are thus those that have either examined several times of day under two or more levels of another arousal manipulation, or have examined the interaction between time of day and two or more other factors thought to affect arousal. There are very few studies that meet these requirements and most of these encounter one of two further problems. First, some of these studies have examined performance on vigilance tasks, and considered time on task to affect arousal level (e.g. Mullin and Corcoran, 1977). However, given the prolonged nature of such tasks, it is unclear whether, for example, a vigilance session run in the morning should result in a decrease in arousal over time on task due to 'boredom', or an increase in arousal due to time of day (see Colquhoun, Hamilton, and Edwards, 1975). Indeed, some studies have found the vigilance decrement to be greater in the morning (e.g. Blake, 1971), while others have found it to be greater in the afternoon (e.g. Jenkins, 1958).

Secondly, most of the other studies to satisfy these requirements have used extroversion as one of their factors thought to affect arousal level. Here, the interpretation of the results is complicated by the fact that extroversion may affect arousal level at a given time of day in two different ways. On the one hand, it has been argued that introverts are chronically aroused compared to extroverts, (e.g. Eysenck, 1967) and, in view of the inverted-U function, should therefore show less marked time-of-day effects. On the other hand, it has been suggested that there is a 'phase difference' in the circadian rhythms of introverts and extroverts (Blake, 1967b) such that the arousal level of introverts reaches a maximum earlier than that of extroverts. In view of these alternative interpretations as to the manner in which extroversion may interact with time of day, studies using this factor as one of those thought to affect arousal level cannot provide unequivocal evidence on the adequacy of the arousal theory.

The author is aware of only two studies that satisfy the requirements given above, *and* use neither time on task nor extroversion as one of their other factors thought to affect arousal level. In the first of these, Blake (1971) compared visual search performance, with and without knowledge of results (KR), at five different times of day. There was a significant interaction between time of day and KR, such that KR improved performance at 08.00, but had little effect at later times of day, and virtually no effect at 21.00, the latest time tested. While this interaction is interpretable within the arousal theory, there was no evidence that KR resulted in impaired performance in the evening. Thus, the interaction could equally easily be interpreted as reflecting a 'ceiling' effect.

In the second study, Davies and Davies (1975) examined the interaction between time of day (10.00 or 14.00), white noise level and age on a visual search task similar to that used by Blake (1971). Older subjects were argued to be relatively non-arousable and an interaction between these three factors was found, but only for the detection of difficult targets. The authors interpreted this interaction within the arousal framework. However, detailed examination of it reveals that it is *not* consistent with the arousal theory. Thus, at 10.00 loud noise impaired the performance of older (less arousable) subjects, but improved that of the younger subjects. The reverse was true at 14.00. This pattern is only consistent with the arousal theory if it is assumed that subjects were more aroused at 10.00 than at 14.00. In view of the post-lunch decrement such an assumption is possible, but is inconsistent with the improvement in the performance of older subjects found between these times.

Finally, Blake (1971) reports the correlations between extroversion and immediate memory performance for five different times of day. Since, in order to account for the decrease in immediate memory over the day, it has to be assumed that high arousal impairs immediate memory, extroverts should do better than introverts in the morning. In fact, Blake's results show the reverse trend to be the case, a finding that has been replicated by M. W. Eysenck and Folkard (1980). In sum, studies that have examined the interaction between time of day and other factors thought to affect arousal level have *not* provided unequivocal evidence favouring the arousal theory. While many of the findings can be accounted for within this arousal framework, this is in part due to the fact that the theory is very difficult to falsify. Indeed, the results of the few critical studies suggest that the arousal theory is inadequate, and that a multi-factor theory may be needed (see also Chapter 12).

Subjective and physiological measures of arousal

Further evidence on the inadequacy of the arousal theory comes from studies of subjective and physiological measures of arousal. Studies of the effects of time of day on subjective assessments of arousal or activation can be conveniently classified into two main types. First, a number of field studies (on for example, shiftwork) have used simple rating scales, such as a seven-point scale (Akerstedt, 1977), or a 10-cm visual analogue scale (Folkard, Glynn, and Lloyd, 1976; Folkard, Monk, and Lobban, 1978), on which subjects have assessed their level of 'alertness' at regular intervals. Data is available from control days that allow examination of the normal trend over the day in these ratings. Secondly, some authors have validated 'general activation' or arousal scales, derived from mood adjective check-lists, by showing them to be sensitive to time of day (Clements, Hafer, and Vermillion, 1976; Thayer, 1978).

A fair degree of agreement as to the trend over the day in self-rated activation has been found using these two rather different techniques. In view of the very different scores obtained, the results from these various studies are plotted as z scores in Figure 43. All these studies agree in showing a fairly sharp increase in activation between about 08.00 and 10.00, and then a more gradual increase to

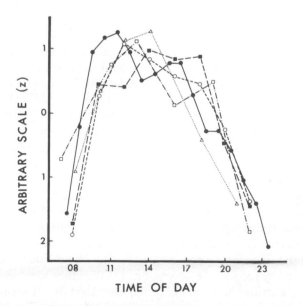

Figure 43. The time-of-day effect in self-rated alertness/activation level. After Akerstedt (1977) □—·—·—□; Clements *et al.* (1977) Δ----------Δ; Folkard *et al.* (1976) ○————○; Folkard *et al.* (1978) ■——————■; Thayer (1978) ●————————●.

reach a maximum between 11.30 and 14.00. They also agree in showing that self-rated arousal is considerably lower by 20.00 than at its peak. Thus, these studies do *not* show the 20.00 peak assumed by the arousal theory as outlined by Colquhoun (1971). Indeed, Thayer (1978) points out that the peak in self-rated arousal occurs considerably earlier than that in body temperature. Further studies of this sort have tested at only three (e.g. Taub and Berger, 1974) or five (e.g. Thayer, 1967) different times of day but have found trends consistent with that shown in Figure 43.

In contrast to these subjective measures, different psychophysiological measures of activation show little agreement as to when the peak occurs. This literature has been reviewed in detail elsewhere (e.g. Conroy and Mills, 1970; Akerstedt and Levi, 1978). Nevertheless, it is worth mentioning that, for example, the secretion of cortisol, which is thought to have an alerting function (Halberg, 1963), reaches a maximum between 05.00 and 08.00 (Akerstedt and Levi, 1978). In contrast, the secretion of both adrenalin and noradrenalin reaches a maximum rather later at about 14.00, despite the fact that the oscillators controlling these two rhythms would appear to differ (Akerstedt and Levi, 1978). Very few indices appear to support the view that arousal is at a maximum at 20.00, with the possible exception of metabolic rate which has been argued to mediate the circadian rhythm in body temperature (Kleitman, 1963).

PRACTICAL AND THEORETICAL CONCLUSIONS

Perhaps the main conclusion to be drawn from studies of the effects of time of day on performance is that the best time to perform a particular task depends on the nature of that task. As the early researchers in this area recognized, one of the obvious practical implications of this is in the educational field where timetables can be arranged to take account of these variations. However, as we have seen, the recommendation that the teaching of academic material should be confined to the morning is rather dubious in view of the superior delayed retention following afternoon presentation.

Unfortunately, there is no simple 'answer' as to the best time to teach these academic subjects. Although on the face of it the afternoon would seem preferable in view of the superior delayed retention, immediate or short-term memory is inferior at this time. This means that schoolchildren may have more difficulty in relating different bits of information to one another in the afternoon, and thus in grasping new concepts. They should also take longer to learn information 'by rote' in the afternoon. On the other hand, it seems that people pay more attention to meaning in the afternoon and it seems probable that this is responsible for the superior delayed retention. The best time to teach a particular subject will thus probably depend rather precisely on the nature of that subject, and the manner in which it is taught.

These sorts of considerations apply not only to the field of education, but to all work situations, where people have a variety of different tasks to perform. Thus, for example, Monk and Conrad (1979) point out that different clerical tasks may well be best performed at different times of day. In these situations it may also be possible to take account of individual differences in the trend in performance over the day, although as yet we know little about the combined effects of task demands and individual differences in determining the trend. Indeed, while in many situations it may prove possible to allocate particular tasks to different times of day, it may be impossible to do so differentially for each individual. Thus, practical considerations could result in either task demands, or individual differences, being taken into account, but not both. Which of these two factors should be considered as more important is as yet unclear, although to some extent it will obviously depend on the range of tasks being performed, and the individuals performing them.

From a more theoretical viewpoint, there are two main points to be made regarding the effects of time of day on performance. First, it is clear not only that performance efficiency varies over the day, but also that the effect of other arousal manipulations and stressors will be affected by the time of day. Unlike many sources of stress, time-of-day effects are unavoidable. This means that any study of the effects of stress needs to take account of the time of day at which it is conducted. Conclusions drawn from studies carried out in the morning may be limited to that time, while opposite conclusions could be true at other times of day. A similar argument could be put forward for other forms of stress; thus, the effects of anxiety may vary with the noise level of the environment. Ideally this means that any study of stress should be conducted at a range of different times of day, different levels of anxiety, and different levels of any other factor that may interact with those under consideration. Failing this, the levels of these factors should be clearly specified. As yet, very few experimental reports state the time of day at which the experiment was conducted.

The second, and perhaps more important, point to be made concerns the arousal theory of time-of-day effects. This theory has proved remarkably useful, and has successfully predicted interactions between time of day and various stressors. It also predicted that although immediate memory is superior in the morning, delayed retention should be superior following afternoon or evening presentation. Despite the counter-intuitive nature of this prediction, it has been borne out by the results of recent studies in this area. In general, arousal theory is consistent with the results of time-of-day studies, though a number of recent findings are inconsistent with it.

Perhaps the most damaging evidence is the fact that the performance of different tasks adjust to night-work at different rates (Chapter 4). This finding is quite impossible to account for within any theory that assumes only a single factor to mediate changes in performance, and points to the need for a multi-factor theory. The other problems include the failure of subjective and physiological measures of arousal to support this theory, the dissociation between temperature and performance for certain personality types, and the fact that the combined effects of time of day and other arousal manipulations are not always those that would be predicted.

In sum, the evidence suggests that while the unidimensional theory of arousal used in this area has proved useful, it is probably over-simplistic. It seems probable that there are at least two circadian factors responsible for time-of-day effects in performance. That responsible for the effects on immediate and working memory seems to be relatively exogenous, in that it adjusts to shifts in the sleep/wake cycle fairly rapidly. The other, that is probably responsible for the effects of time of day on simple tasks, such as visual search, and perhaps the effects on delayed retention, adjusts rather more slowly, and may thus be considered to be relatively endogenous (see Folkard and Monk, 1981). It remains to be determined whether these two circadian factors can account for all the effects of time of day on performance.

SUMMARY

Measures of human performance efficiency show more or less predictable variations over the day and night. These 'diurnal' variations are thought to reflect the underlying 24-hour, or 'circadian' rhythms now known to exist in most physiological parameters. In particular, it had been suggested in the past that there was a pronounced parallelism between variations in certain simple types of performance over the day, and those in body temperature. This parallelism gave rise to the arousal theory of time-of-day effects that assumed diurnal variations in performance to reflect an underlying circadian rhythm in basal arousal level.

This parallelism between changes in performance over the day and those in temperature is, however, now known to hold for only a limited range of tasks and individuals performing such tasks. The precise nature of the task demands, and, in particular, the memory load involved in performing the task, has been shown to exert a large influence on the trend in performance over the day. In addition, even for simple, non-memory loaded tasks, the parallelism beween temperature and performance has been shown to depend on the nature of the individual performing the task.

These findings, together with those on the interaction of time of day with other arousal manipulations, and the trends in other physiological measures of arousal over the day, suggest that a re-examination of the arousal theory of time-of-day effects is necessary. Nevertheless, it is undoubtedly the case that such effects exist, that they are relatively unavoidable, and that they have important practical, as well as theoretical, implications for the study of human performance efficiency.

REFERENCES

Akerstedt, T. (1977) Inversion of the sleep/wakefulness pattern; effects on circadian variations in psychophysiological activation. *Ergonomics*, **20**, 459–474.

Akerstedt, T. and Levi, L. (1978) Circadian rhythms in the secretion of cortisol, adrenalin and noradrenalin. *European Journal of Clinical Investigation*, **8**, 57–58.

Baade, W. (1907) Experimentelle und kritische Beitrage zur Frage such den sekundezen Wirkungen des Unterrichts insbesondere nuf die Empfunglichkeit des Schuters. *Pädagogische Monographien Band, III*, Nemnich Leipzig.

Baddeley, A. D. (1976) *The Psychology of Memory*. New York: Harper and Row.

Baddeley, A. D., Hatter, J. E., Scott, D., and Snashall, A. (1970) Memory and time of day. *Quarterly Journal of Experimental Psychology*, **22**, 605–609.

Baddeley, A. D. and Hitch, G. (1974) Working Memory. In G. Bower (ed.), *The Psychology of Learning and Motivation: Advances in Research and Theory, Vol. III*. New York: Academic Press.

Bergstrum, F. G. (1894) An experimental study of some of the conditions of mental activity. *American Journal of Psychology*, **6**, 247–274.

Blake, M. J. F. (1967a) Time of day effects on performance in a range of tasks. *Psychonomic Science*, **9**, 349–350.

Blake, M. J. F. (1976b) Relationship between circadian rhythm of body temperature and interoversion–extraversion. *Nature*, **215**, 896–897.

Blake, M. J. F. (1971) Temperament and time of day. In W. P. Colquhoun (ed.), *Biological Rhythms and Human Performance*. London: Academic Press, pp.109–148.

Broughton, R. (1975) Biorhythmic variations in consciousness and psychological functions. *Canadian Psychological Review*, **16**, 217–239.

Buck, L. (1976) Psychomotor test performance and sleep patterns of aircrew flying transmeridianal routes. *Aviation, Space and Environmental Medicine*, **1976**, 979–986.

Clements, P. R., Hafer, M. D., and Vermillion, M. E. (1976) Psychometric, diurnal and electrophysiological correlates of activation. *Journal of Personality and Social Psychology*, **33**, 387–394.

Colquhoun, W. P. (1960) Temperament, inspection efficiency, and time of day. *Ergonomics*, **3**, 377.

Colquhoun, W. P. (1971) Circadian variations in mental efficiency. In W. P. Colquhoun (ed.), *Biological Rhythms and Human Performance*. London: Academic Press, pp.39–107.

Colquhoun, W. P. (1979) Phase shift in temperature rhythm after transmeridian flight, as related to pre-flight phase angle. *International Archives of Occupational and Environmental Health*, **42**, 149–157.

Colquhoun, W. P., Blake, M. J. F., and Edwards, R. S. (1968) Experimental studies of shift work. 1: A comparison of rotating and stabilized 4 hour shift systems. *Ergonomics*, **11**, 437–453.

Colquhoun, W. P., Hamilton, P., and Edwards, R. S. (1975) Effects of circadian rhythm, sleep deprivation and fatigue on watchkeeping performance during the night hours. In P. Colquhoun, S. Folkard, P. Knauth, and J. Rutenfranz (eds.), *Experimental Studies of Shiftwork*. Opladen: Westdeutscher Verlag.

Conroy, R. T. W. L. and Mills, J. N. (1970) *Human Circadian Rhythms*. London: Churchill.

Craik, F. I. M. and Blankstein, K. R. (1975) Psychophysiology and human memory. In P. H. Venables and M. J. Christie (eds.), *Research in Psychophysiology*. London: John Wiley & Sons.

Davies, A. D. M. and Davies, D. R. (1975) The effects of noise and time of day upon age differences in performance at two checking tasks. *Ergonomics*, **18**, 321–336.

Dressler, F. B. (1892) Some influences which affect the rapidity of voluntary movements. *American Journal of Psychology*, **4**, 514–527.

Ebbinghaus, H. (1885) *Memory*. Republished in translation (1964). New York: Dover Publications.

Eysenck, H. J. (1967) *The Biological Basis of Personality*. Springfield, Illinois: Harper & Row.

Eysenck, M. W. and Folkard, S. (1980) Personality, time of day, and caffeine: some theoretical and conceptual problems in Revelle *et al. Journal of Experimental Psychology: General*, **109**, 32–41.

Folkard, S. (1975) Diurnal variation in logical reasoning. *British Journal of Psychology*, **66**, 1–8.

Folkard, S. (1982) Circadian rhythms and human memory. In: F. M. Brown and R. C. Graeber (eds.), *Rhythmic Aspects of Behaviour*. Hillsdale, N.J.: Lawrence Erlbaum Associates.

Folkard, S., Glynn, C. J., and Lloyd, J. W. (1976) Diurnal variation and individual differences in the perception of intractable pain. *Journal of Psychosomatic Research*, **20**, 289–301.

Folkard, S., Knauth, P., Monk, T. H., and Rutenfranz, J. (1976) The effect of memory load on the circadian variation in performance efficiency under a rapidly rotating shift system. *Ergonomics*, **19**, 479–488.

Folkard, S. and Monk, T. H. (1979) Time of day and processing strategy in free recall. *Quarterly Journal of Experimental Psychology*, **31**, 461–475.

Folkard, S. and Monk, T. H. (1980) Circadian rhythms in human memory. *British Journal of Psychology*, **71**, 295–307.

Folkard, S. and Monk, T. H. (1981) Circadian rhythms in performance — one or more oscillators? In R. Sinz and M. R. Rosenzwig (eds.), *Psychophysiology 1980 — Memory, Motivation and Event-related Potentials in Mental Operations*. Amsterdam: Elsevier North-Holland.

Folkard, S., Monk, T. H., Bradbury, R., and Rosenthall, J. (1977) Time of day effects in school children's immediate and delayed recall of meaningful material. *British Journal of Psychology*, **68**, 45–50.

Folkard, S., Monk, T. H., and Lobban, M. C. (1978) Short and long-term adjustment of circadian rhythms in 'permanent' night nurses. *Ergonomics*, **21**, 785–799.

Fort, A. and Mills, J. N. (1976) Der Einfluß der Tageszeit und des vorhergehenden Schaf-Wach-Musters auf die Leistungsfahigkeit unmittelbar nach dem Aufstehen. In G. Hildebrandt (ed.), *Biologische rhythmen und arbeit*. Springer-Verlag.

Freeman, G. L. and Hovland, C. I. (1934) Diurnal variations in performance and related physiological processes. *Psychological Bulletin*, **31**, 777–799.

Gates, A. I. (1916a) Diurnal variation in memory and association. *University of California Publications in Psychology*, **1**, 323–344.

Gates, A. I.(1916b) Variations in efficiency during the day, together with practise effects, sex differences, and correlations. *University of California Publications in Psychology*, **2**, 1–156.

Halberg, F. (1963) Circadian (about twenty-four-hour) rhythms in experimental medicine. *Proceedings of the Royal Society of Medicine*, **56**, 253–260.

Halberg, F. (1973) More on educative chronobiology, health and the computer. *International Journal of Chronology*, **2**, 87–105.

Hildebrandt, G., Rohmert, W., and Rutenfranz, J. (1974) Twelve and 24 hour rhythms in error frequency on locomotive drivers and the influence of tiredness. *International Journal of Chronobiology*, **2**, 97–110.

Hockey, G. R. G. and Colquhoun, W. P. (1972) Diurnal variation in human performance. In W. P. Colquhoun (ed.), *Aspects of Human Efficiency—Diurnal Rhythm and Loss of Sleep.* London: English Universities Press, pp.1–23.

Hockey, G. R. J., Davies, S. and Gray, M. M. (1972) Forgetting as a function of sleep at different times of day. *Quarterly Journal of Experimental Psychology,* 24, 386–393.

Hockey, G. R. J. and Hamilton, P. (1970) Arousal and information selection in short-term memory. *Nature,* 226, 866–867.

Horne, J. A., Brass, C. G., and Pettit, A. N. (1980) Circadian performance differences between morning and evening 'types'. *Ergonomics,* 23, 29–36.

Horne, J. A. and Ostberg, O. (1976) A self-assessment questionnaire to determine morningness-eveningness in human circadian rhythms. *International Journal of Chronobiology,* 4, 97–110.

Horne, J. A. and Ostberg, O. (1977) Individual differences in human circadian rhythms. *Biological Psychology,* 5, 179–190.

Howell, W. H. (1897) A contribution to the physiology of sleep upon plethysmographic experiments. *Journal of Experimental Medicine,* 2, 313.

Hughes, D. G. and Folkard, S. (1976) Adaptation to an 8-h shift in living routine by members of a socially isolated community. *Nature,* 264, 232–234.

Jenkins, H. M. (1958) The effect of signal-rate on performance in visual monitoring. *American Journal of Psychology,* 71, 647–661.

Klein, K. E., Wegmann, H. M., and Hunt, B. I. (1972) Desynchronization of body temperature and performance circadian rhythm as a result of outgoing and home-going transmeridian flights. *Aerospace Medicine,* 43, 119–132.

Kleitman, N. (1939, revised and enlarged 1963) *Sleep and Wakefulness.* Chicago: University of Chicago Press.

Kleitman, N. and Jackson, D. P. (1950) Body temperature and performance under different routines. *Journal of Applied Physiology,* 3, 309–328.

Kraepelin, E. (1893) Ueber psychische disposition. *Archives of the Journal of Psychiatry,* 23, 593–594.

Laird, D. A. (1925) Relative performance of college students as conditioned by time of day and day of week. *Journal of Experimental Psychology,* 8, 50–63.

Lombard, W. P. (1887) The variations of the normal knee jerk, and their relation to the activity of the central nervous system. *American Journal of Psychology,* 1, 5–71.

Michelson, M. (1897) Ueber die Tiefe des Schlafes. *Psychol Arbeiten,* 2, 84–117.

Monk, T. H. and Conrad, M. C. (1979) Time of day effects in a range of clerical tasks. *Human Factors,* 21, 191–194.

Mullin, J. and Corcoran, D. W. J. (1977) Interaction of task amplitude with circadian variation in auditory vigilance performance. *Ergonomics,* 20, 193–200.

Pillsbury, W. B. (1903) Attention waves as a means of measuring fatigue. *American Journal of Psychology,* 14, 277–288.

Revelle, W., Humphreys, M. S., Simon, L. and Gilliland, K. (1980) The interactive effect of personality, time of day and caffeine: A test of the arousal model. *Journal of Experimental Psychology: General,* 109, 1–31.

Rutenfranz, J., Aschoff, J., and Mann, H. (1972) The effects of a cumulative sleep deficit, duration of preceding sleep period and body temperature on multiple choice reaction time. In W. P. Colquhoun (ed.), *Aspects of Human Efficiency: Dirunal Rhythm and Loss of Sleep.* London: English Universities Press, pp.217–229.

Rutenfranz, J. and Helbruegge, T. (1957) Uber Tageschwankungen der Rechen-geschwindigkeit bei 11-jahrigen kinder. *Zeitschrift Kinderheilk,* 80, 65–82.

Taub, J. M. and Berger, R. J. (1974) Diurnal variations in mood as asserted by self-report and verbal content analysis. *Journal of Psychiatric Research,* 10, 83–88.

Thayer, R. E. (1967) Measurement of activation through self report. *Psychological Reports*, **20**, 663–678.

Thayer, R. E. (1978) Towards a psychological theory of multi-dimensional activation (arousal). *Motivation and Emotion*, **2**, 1–34.

Wever, R. (1979) *The Circadian System of Man: Results of Experiments Under Temporal Isolation*. New York: Springer-Verlag.

Winch, W. H. (1912a) Mental fatigue in day school children as measured by immediate memory, Part I. *Journal of Educational Psychology*, **3**, 18–28.

Winch, W. H. (1912b) Mental fatigue in day school children as measured by immediate memory, Part II. *Journal of Educational Psychology*, **3**, 75–82.

Chapter 10

Anxiety and Individual Differences

Michael W. Eysenck

The central focus of this chapter is anxiety, which is conceived of as an important aspect of individual differences. Within the prevalent conceptualization that regards psychology as being concerned with a stimulus–organism–response (S–O–R) sequence of events, anxiety clearly qualifies as an organismic state. This anxiety state has been defined by Spielberger (1972) as one that consists of 'unpleasant, consciously-perceived feelings of tension and apprehension, with associated activation or arousal of the autonomic nervous system' (p.29). Within this broad framework, one can meaningfully ask questions about the antecedent stimulus factors that produce the anxiety state, about the nature of the organismic state itself, and about the consequent effects of anxiety on cognitive processing and performance. The S–O–R conceptualization will be utilized in this chapter for heuristic and pedagogical reasons; it is, however, intended that adherence to this tripartite distinction in what follows will be less than Procrustean.

The basic theoretical orientation adopted in this chapter is the state–trait model. Accordingly, this approach will be outlined initially, followed by a consideration of criticisms to which it has been subjected. Some researchers, notably Mischel (1973), have argued that the state–trait theory cannot be reconciled with the empirical evidence; this view is not shared by the writer.

THE STATE–TRAIT APPROACH

It is probably merely stating the obvious to argue that there are pronounced individual differences in the ways in which people react to environmental stressors (e.g. intense noise, electric shock, ego threat, physical danger). However, there are substantial disagreements among psychologists concerning the most appropriate theoretical conceptualization of these individual differences. At one extreme, state–trait theorists (e.g. M. W. Eysenck, 1979; Spielberger, 1966) have argued that some individuals are, in general, more susceptible than others to anxiety when exposed to stressful situations; this susceptibility to anxiety is measurable by paper-and-pencil self-report questionnaires and is referred to as trait anxiety. State–trait theories assume, therefore, that those who are unusually anxious in one stressful situation will tend to manifest high anxiety in other stressful situations. At the other extreme, social learning theorists (e.g. Mischel, 1973) have claimed that people do not show cross-situational consistency in behaviour; rather, any individual's response to a given situation depends upon the particular conditioning history of that individual in the same or similar situations.

The state–trait approach draws a distinction (originally suggested by Cicero) between trait anxiety (defined by Spielberger, Gorsuch, and Lushene, 1970, p.3, as 'relatively stable individual differences in anxiety proneness') and state anxiety (defined by Spielberger *et al.*, 1970, p.3, as 'characterized by subjective, consciously perceived feelings of tension and apprehension, and heightened autonomic nervous system activity'). The best-known measuring instrument is the State–Trait Anxiety Inventory (Spielberger *et al.*, 1970), which provides self-report measures of both state and trait anxiety. The Inventory consists of two 20-item scales that ask people how they generally feel (trait anxiety), and how they feel 'right now' (state anxiety).

The basic interrelationships among the factors of trait anxiety, state anxiety, environmental stressors, and performance are shown in Figure 44. The major

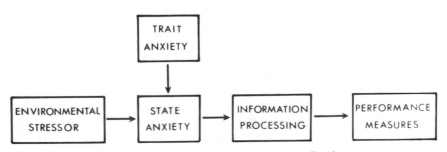

Figure 44. The basic state–trait conceptualization.

assumption is that transient states of anxiety are interactively determined by the individual's susceptibility to anxiety (trait anxiety) and by the degree of stress inherent in the situation. State anxiety affects information processing and behaviour more directly than trait anxiety, since the influence of trait anxiety is mediated by state anxiety.

A further assumption that has frequently been made is that individual differences in trait anxiety have a substantial hereditary component. The evidence for this has been discussed by Shields (1973), who reviewed work on neuroticism, a personality dimension that correlates approximately $+0.6$–$+0.8$ with trait anxiety. He concluded that a number of studies had obtained evidence of a significant hereditary component in anxiety or neuroticism.

The state–trait approach makes various predictions which have been investigated experimentally. Since state anxiety is allegedly affected by the degree of environmental stress, whereas trait anxiety is not, it follows that trait anxiety should be more stable or consistent than state anxiety across situations varying in stressfulness. This prediction has been confirmed a number of times (e.g. Allen, 1970; Martuza and Kallstrom, 1974), with state and trait anxiety usually being measured by means of the State–Trait Anxiety Inventory.

A related prediction is that there should be a relatively small difference in state anxiety between groups high and low in trait anxiety under non-stressful conditions, in which overall levels of state anxiety are relatively low, but that there should be a much larger difference under stressful conditions. A significant interaction between trait anxiety and degree of situational stress has been found several times (see Shedletsky and Endler, 1974, for a review). However, it is noticeable that the predicted interaction has mainly been obtained when stress involves threat to self-esteem (e.g. threat of failure), and not when stress involves physical danger (e.g. threat of electric shock).

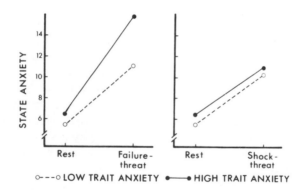

Figure 45. The effects of failure-threat and shock-threat on state anxiety for individuals differing in trait anxiety. Adapted from Hodges (1968).

The data of Hodges (1968) are relevant in this context; they are shown in Figure 45. The reason for this discrepancy in the data appears to be that most questionnaire measures of trait anxiety are primarily concerned with reactions to ego threat rather than to physical danger (Endler, Magnusson, Ekehammar, and Okada, 1976). These various findings imply that maximal state anxiety occurs in those circumstances in which there is congruence between the type of threat provided by the situation and the relevant facet of trait anxiety.

Mischel's (1969) main criticism of the state–trait approach is that it predicts that there will be behavioural consistency, whereas in actuality behavioural inconsistency is typically observed. However, since both trait and state anxiety are intervening variables, one must distinguish between consistency at the mediating level of states and traits, and consistency at the level of specific behavioural responses. In fact, while Mischel has concentrated his attack at the behavioural level, it is likely that a certain degree of behavioural inconsistency co-exists with a more obvious consistency at the mediating level. In other words, level of state anxiety (a mediating factor) can be quite well predicted on the basis of information about the stressfulness of the environment and the individual's level of trait anxiety, and thus there is some degree of consistency at the mediating level as the state–trait approach maintains. On the other hand, the exact pattern of responding is undoubtedly influenced by an individual's level of state anxiety, but it is also obviously affected by many other factors, thus leading to apparent inconsistency of responding. The task of predicting the effects of anxiety on behaviour within the context of the state–trait approach can often be achieved on the basis of 'moderator variables'. The essential notion is that the influence of any particular trait on behaviour is typically indirect, being affected or 'moderated' by a number of other traits, mediating variables, and situational factors.

In sum, the state–trait approach to anxiety is a valuable one; in particular, there is clear evidence that experienced or state anxiety is frequently determined conjointly by environmental stress and trait anxiety.

While the whole state–trait formulation has been criticized forcefully by Mischel on the grounds that individuals do not behave with the predicted cross-situational consistency, there are reasons for claiming that Mischel has misinterpreted the data. Furthermore, Mischel has attacked a simplistic form of state–trait model that predicts a direct, one-to-one correspondence between intervening variables such as states and traits and behavioural responses. In fact, state–trait theories usually argue that moderator variables produce an indirect, but theoretically predictable, relationship between central states and observable behaviour.

ANXIETY AS AN ORGANISMIC STATE

We have already seen that anxiety as a state is interactively produced by situational stress and trait anxiety, and that there is a discernible difference between stress involving physical danger and stress involving ego threat. An important question is the nature of the anxiety state or, more specifically, the various components of anxiety. One influential answer was suggested by Schachter and Singer (1962) in a classic article in which they put forward a general theoretical framework for the understanding of all emotional states. Their basic assertion was that experienced emotion is multiplicatively determined by the two factors of level of physiological arousal and cognitions about the arousing situation. People attempt to provide themselves with plausible cognitive interpretations of states of physiological arousal. If, as in the study reported by Schachter and Singer (1962), subjects are made aroused by a stimulant drug such as adrenalin, and they are told accurately what the effects of the drug will be, then arousal is interpreted cognitively as being attributable to the drug and little or no emotion is experienced. In other circumstances, an emotional interpretation of physiological arousal is preferred.

Some recent experimental evidence in broad agreement with the Schachter-Singer approach was obtained by Russell and Mehrabian (1977). They factor analysed scores from 42 verbal-report emotion scales, and discovered the existence of three orthogonal and bipolar dimensions (pleasure–displeasure, degree of arousal, and dominance–submissiveness). Russell and Mehrabian considered six scales measuring state anxiety, including the state-anxiety scale of the State–Trait Anxiety Inventory. Regression analysis of the data from these scales indicated that the most important component of anxiety is displeasure, followed by high arousal, and lastly submissiveness. If, as the theoretical approach of Schachter and Singer (1962) implies, the displeasure component of anxiety is based on cognitive appraisal, then anxiety resembles other emotional states in involving an amalgam of physiological and cognitive components. The fact that self-reported state anxiety is much more closely associated with displeasure than with high arousal may well be of relevance in explaining the relatively weak evidence of greater physiological arousal in anxious individuals (reviewed by M. W. Eysenck, 1977).

An important contemporary theory that also emphasizes the distinction between the physiological and cognitive components of anxiety was presented by Morris, Brown, and Halbert (1977). They pointed out that various factor analyses of Mandler and Sarason's (1952) Test Anxiety Questionnaire have indicated that test anxiety comprises the two conceptually distinct components of worry and emotionality. Emotionality involves changes in physiological functioning and accompanying unpleasant feeling states of uneasiness, tension, and nervousness; worry is the cognitive aspect of anxiety, involving conscious concern regarding one's performance and its consequences, negative task expectations, and negative self-evaluations.

While most of the empirical evidence relating to the proposed distinction between worry and emotionality is discussed below, one study illustrating the potential value of this distinction will be mentioned here. Spiegler, Morris, and Liebert (1968) found that worry scores were elevated, but emotionality scores were not, five days before an important examination for graduate students. Worry scores remained unchanged from immediately before to immediately after the examination, whereas emotionality scores decreased significantly.

Evidence has already been adduced that individuals high and low in trait anxiety respond differentially to ego threat but not to physical danger. A further difference between the effects of the two classes of stressor was discovered by Morris and Liebert (1973). They compared the effects of failure threat and of shock threat, and found that failure threat led to a substantial increase in worry but no increase in emotionality; on the other hand, shock threat produced an increase in emotionality, but had no effect on worry.

In sum, anxiety as a state can usefully be considered to comprise both physiological and cognitive components. These components are frequently referred to as emotionality and worry, respectively. There is suggestive evidence that stressors involving physical danger increase emotionality more than worry, whereas stressors involving ego threat have the opposite effect.

EFFECTS OF ANXIETY ON PERFORMANCE

There is a plethora of theories and experimental studies concerned with the effects of anxiety on performance. The first systematic theory of anxiety and performance was developed by Spence and his co-workers (Spence and Spence, 1966). According to this theory, anxiety affects retrieval and performance but does not affect learning. While this view was prevalent for many years, it is now obvious that it is inadequate (see M. W. Eysenck, 1981, for a discussion). Contemporary wisdom now holds that anxiety affects performance by producing changes in the selectivity and/or intensity of attention; within such an approach, anxiety can affect both the learning or acquisition of information and its subsequent retrieval. In what follows, we consider some of the relevant evidence that provides the basis for this support.

Task-irrelevant cognitive activities

Common sense as well as much of the available evidence support the contention that highly anxious people perform most tasks less successfully than non-anxious people. In view of the evidence implicating cognitive factors in anxiety, it is perhaps not surprising that several theorists (e.g. Morris *et al.*, 1977; Wine, 1971) have suggested that a major reason for the detrimental effects of anxiety on performance is the presence of task-irrelevant cognitive activities or worry associated with high anxiety. The argument was expressed in the following way by Sarason (1975): 'The highly test anxious person is one who is prone to emit self-centred interfering responses when confronted with evaluative conditions. Two response components have been emphasized by writers who espouse this view. One is emotional and autonomic — sweating, accelerated heart rate, etc. The other concerns cognitive events — e.g., saying to oneself while taking a test, "I am stupid", "Maybe I won't pass" ' (p.175).

In order to support the above hypothesis, there needs to be evidence both that high anxiety does, indeed, produce an increase in task-irrelevant cognitive activities, and that these irrelevant cognitions are causally responsible for the observed performance decrements. If one merely observes an increase in task-irrelevant cognition and a decrement in performance under high anxiety, and then explains the latter in terms of the former, there is the danger of committing the fallacy of *post hoc ergo propter hoc*. Ganzer (1968) studied the effects of audience presence and test anxiety on serial learning, and recorded the subjects' task-irrelevant comments while they were engaged in the learning task. High scorers on the Test Anxiety Scale, especially if they performed the task in the presence of an audience, emitted more task-irrelevant comments then the other groups of subjects; most of these comments were of an apologetic or self-evaluative nature.

It is perhaps reasonable to assume that anxiety-induced performance decrements will be due more to task-irrelevant thoughts or worry than to emotionality, and the relevant evidence has been reviewed by Morris *et al.* (1977). In one study, Doctor and Altman (1969) obtained answers to worry and emotionality questions from the Test Anxiety Questionnaire in terms of students' feelings immediately prior to taking an important examination. Worry and emotionality were both negatively related to examination performance, but worry was more strongly related to poor performance. In a related study by Morris and Liebert (1970), they found that correlations between worry and final examination scores, with emotionality partialled out, were negative and significant. In contrast, correlations between emotionality scores and grades, with worry partialled out, were statistically non-significant.

Deffenbacher (1978) required high and low scorers on the Test Anxiety Scale to solve difficult anagrams under conditions of high or low stress. The worst anagram-solving performance was shown by the high-anxiety subjects run under high stress, and it was in this condition that self-reported anxiety was greatest. According to post-experimental questionnaire responses, stressed high-anxiety subjects spent only 60 per cent of the available time actually engaged in the task, compared to approximately 80 per cent in the other conditions; these subjects also reported easily the highest level of worry (i.e. thinking about the consequences of doing poorly and about how much brighter others were). While the correlational nature of the data precludes any definite assignment of causality, the results are consistent with the hypothesis that anxiety impairs performance because subjects misdirect attention to task-irrelevant information processing.

Apart from the fact that the experimental evidence is less than compelling, there are further problems with the hypothesis under consideration. The most important of these is that theories that emphasize the role played by worry seem to predict that anxiety will always reduce the quality of performance; it is by no means obvious how they could account for the various facilitatory effects of anxiety on performance. An additional issue is that the mutual interference between task performance and task-irrelevant activities such as worry assumed by several theorists presumably depends upon the similarity of the two processing mechanisms. For example, if worry and related forms of verbal processing constitute the major form of task-irrelevant cognitive activity, then main tasks involving verbal processing should be more impaired than those dependent upon non-verbal processing. This prediction does not appear to have been examined experimentally.

Selective attention: Easterbrook's hypothesis

The theoretical approach discussed in the previous section attributes the effects of anxiety on performance to a malfunctioning of attentional processes. Another influential theory emphasizing the effects of anxiety and arousal on the selectivity of attention was proposed by Easterbrook (1959). He argued that states of high emotionality, arousal, and anxiety all produce restrictions in the range of cue utilization. The consequence of this progressive reduction in the range of cues used as anxiety or arousal increases, 'will reduce the proportion of irrelevant cues employed, and so improve performance. When all irrelevant cues have been excluded, however, . . . further reduction in the number of cues employed can only affect relevant cues, and proficiency will fall' (p.193).

Easterbrook's hypothesis has the important advantage of providing a potential mechanism to explain the Yerkes–Dodson Law (Yerkes and Dodson, 1908). This 'Law' postulated that there is an inverted-U relationship between arousal and performance, with the best level of performance being attained at intermediate levels of arousal. While the Yerkes–Dodson Law merely describes a predicted relationship between arousal and performance, Easterbrook's account based on attentional narrowing would explain this relationship.

In terms of experimental data, Easterbrook's notion that anxiety increases attentional selectivity has usually been investigated in paradigms incorporating both a main or primary task and a secondary or incidental task. If anxiety reduces the range of cue utilization, then non-anxious subjects should perform better than anxious subjects on the subsidiary task. In the various studies investigating this hypothesis, high- and low-anxiety groups were usually obtained either by using threat versus no threat of electric shock or by dividing subjects into anxiety groups on the basis of questionnaire data. In many of the studies the main task was intentional learning and the subsidiary task was incidental learning. Nineteen experimental comparisons of high- and low-anxiety groups on subsidiary-task performance were located; of the 19 comparisons, 7 revealed a non-significant effect of anxiety on performance, 12 produced the predicted significant adverse effect of anxiety on the performance of the subsidiary task, and none indicated an enhancement effect of anxiety. There is thus compelling evidence that anxiety is far more likely to have a detrimental rather than a facilitatory effect on performance of the subsidiary task. The relevant studies are discussed in more detail by M. W. Eysenck (1981).

Easterbrook's (1959) hypothesis is also relevant to the prediction that the optimal level of arousal for performance varies inversely with task difficulty or complexity (Yerkes and Dodson, 1908). There is quite good empirical support for an interaction of the expected type between anxiety and task difficulty, with high-anxiety subjects performing much worse than low-anxiety subjects on difficult tasks, but not on easy tasks (this evidence is discussed in more detail below). If one assumes that difficult tasks tend to incorporate more components or cues than easy tasks, then the narrowing of attention under high anxiety would have a greater detrimental effect on the performance of difficult tasks.

In spite of the strength of the experimental support for Easterbrook's hypothesis, I do not feel that it offers a generally satisfactory account of the effects of anxiety on performance. The hypothesis makes the strange assumption that performance decrements under high anxiety are mainly attributable to great concentration on only a few task elements. It seems to follow that high-anxiety subjects should spend a greater proportion of the time processing task-relevant information than low-anxiety subjects, whose broader range of cue utilization may well include non-task elements. In fact, in a study already discussed, Deffenbacher (1978) found that high-anxiety subjects actually reported spending far *less* time than low-anxiety subjects attending to task-relevant information.

There are other studies also indicating that high anxiety reduces rather than increases the ability to concentrate on the task in hand. For example, Nottelman and Hill (1977) investigated the anagram-task performance of children obtaining high and low scores on the Test Anxiety Scale for Children. High-anxiety children had significantly inferior anagram performance to low-anxiety children; of most immediate relevance, the high-anxiety children were observed to engage in substantially more off-task glancing.

A further difficulty with Easterbrook's hypothesis is the assumption that incentives, white noise, anxiety, and other variables associated with increased arousal all operate in a broadly similar manner by leading to increased attentional selectivity. There are several studies indicating quite clearly that this is an over-simplification. For example, Fowler and Wilding (1979) obtained diametrically opposed effects of incentives and white noise on the incidental learning of the spatial locations of to-be-remembered words; incentives enhanced incidental learning, whereas white noise reduced it. In spite of the inconclusive nature of the available evidence, it may be that the precise effects of arousing agents on performance depend importantly on the degree of worry associated with them.

The general expectation from Easterbrook's (1959) hypothesis is that arousing agents such as failure information and electric shock should have comparable effects on performance. In fact, as discussed by M. W. Eysenck (1979), the effects of failure and shock on the performance of high- and low-anxiety subjects are quite different. Failure feedback consistently impairs performance to a greater extent for high-anxiety than for low-anxiety subjects, but shock has the opposite effect. There are 14 experimental comparisons in the literature of the effects of shock on the learning performance of subjects varying in trait anxiety (Beach, 1959; Chiles, 1958; Deese, Lazarus, and Keenan, 1953; Glover and Cravens, 1974; Lazarus, Deese, and Hamilton, 1954; Lee, 1961). The performance of high-anxiety subjects was improved in nine cases by threat of shock and impaired five times, whereas that of low-anxiety subjects was improved once and reduced 13 times. In all but one of the 14 comparisons the performance of high-anxiety subjects was either less impaired or more improved than that of low-anxiety subjects by threat of shock.

While the differential effects of shock and failure on high- and low-anxiety subjects are hard to explain in terms of the notion that all arousers or stressors simply produce attentional narrowing, they can be accounted for by the present theoretical framework. Threat of failure increases worry rather than emotionality, whereas threat of shock heightens emotionality and not worry (Morris and Liebert, 1973). Since we have argued that performance decrements under high anxiety are largely attributable to worry and other task-irrelevant cognitive activities, it follows that failure should be more effective than shock in reducing performance for high-anxiety subjects.

It may well be the case that anxious individuals often display enhanced attentional selectivity as well as increased distractibility. However, it is less clear that the process of attentional narrowing under heightened arousal is as passive and invariant as Easterbrook implied. It is more plausible that, when a state of anxiety means that the total information-processing demands cannot be handled by the available processing capacity, the subjects adopts the strategy of restricting attention voluntarily to a small number of sources of information.

Attentional capacity: working memory

Baddeley and Hitch (1974) proposed an interesting theoretical framework for understanding some of the problems of attention and short-term memory. Their major innovation was the notion of 'working memory', which comprises the two conceptually separate components of a modality-free central processor and an articulatory loop. While the central processor is necessarily involved in the processing of information across a wide range of cognitive activities, use of the articulatory loop is largely optional; its function is to permit the temporary storage of a limited amount of information in a phonemic code at a relatively low 'cost' to the processing system.

Since working memory appears to be of central importance in information processing, it would clearly be of interest to investigate the relationship between anxiety and the capacity limitations of working memory. Since working memory is typically involved in the processing and temporary 'holding' of information, any anxiety-induced reduction in its capacity would inevitably have wide-ranging effects on the performance of many cognitive tasks. Since Baddeley and Hitch (1974) argued that working memory is involved in the digit-span task, there are grounds for regarding the effects of anxiety on digit-span performance as being of relevance. Unfortunately, the literature on the effects of anxiety on the capacity of working memory is extremely narrow, since almost all the work has concentrated on digit-span measures rather than any other index.

The relevant studies are discussed in more detail by M. W. Eysenck (1977, 1981). The most obvious division of the studies is into those concerned with trait anxiety and those concerned with situational stress or state anxiety. From the perspective of the state–trait approach, it would be predicted that digit-span would be more directly affected by state anxiety than by trait anxiety, and this expectation is borne out by the evidence. With respect to trait anxiety, the modal finding has been that there is no effect of anxiety on digit span. On the other hand, the typical finding is that stress is negatively related to performance; in addition, state anxiety is also associated with a reduction in span performance. Overall, nine out of eleven studies reporting a significant effect of state anxiety or of an environmental stressor on the capacity of working memory found that high anxiety reduced its capacity. An unanswered question is whether this effect is due to reduced efficiency of the modality-free central processor, or of the articulatory loop, or of both these components of working memory.

The finding that anxiety reduces working memory capacity may be relevant to the explanation of one of the most reliable effects of anxiety on performance. It has been found that anxiety interacts with task difficulty on a variety of learning tasks. The results from 12 studies were discussed by M. W. Eysenck (1981). In all 12 studies high anxiety improved learning performance on the easy task (significantly so in five cases). In ten of the studies high anxiety impaired performance on the difficult task (significantly so in two cases). This interaction has also been obtained with other kinds of task. Mayer (1977) investigated the effects of trait anxiety on the performance of various simple or rote problems (e.g. searching for the letter 'a'; simple mathematical operations) and more difficult cognitive problems (e.g. anagram solving; water jar problems). There was a highly significant interaction between anxiety and type of task in terms of the proportion of correct solutions. As can be seen in Figure 46, anxiety had little effect on rote problems, but the high-anxiety subjects were considerably inferior to low-anxiety subjects on cognitive problems.

The above findings are consistent with the Yerkes–Dodson Law (Yerkes and Dodson, 1908), which stated that moderate levels of arousal are optimal for performance, and that this optimal level of arousal varies inversely with

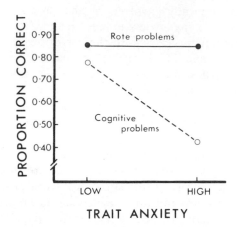

Figure 46. The effects of trait anxiety on the performance of role and cognitive problems. Adapted from Mayer (1977).

task difficulty. Unfortunately, Yerkes and Dodson did not provide any detailed explanation for the proposed interaction between arousal and task difficulty, nor did they delineate the crucial determinants of task difficulty. In terms of contemporary theoretical developments, it is reasonable to assume that 'difficult' tasks make greater demands on working memory capacity than do 'easy' tasks. Since the evidence indicates that working memory capacity is reduced under high anxiety, it follows that the detrimental effects of anxiety on task performance should be more pronounced on complex tasks than on simple ones. Of course, the usual interaction between anxiety and task difficulty is in line with this expectation.

One of the inadequacies of the studies in the literature is that task difficulty has typically been manipulated in ways which cannot readily be related to contemporary theoretical conceptions. An attempt to clarify matters has recently been carried out in our laboratory. Subjects performed a letter-transformation task (Hamilton, Hockey, and Rejman, 1977) in which between one and four letters were presented, each of which needed to be transformed by moving a given distance through the alphabet (up to a maximum of four letters forward) before the answer was given. A sample one-letter problem is 'D + 2', for which the answer is 'F', and a sample four-letter problem is 'RDGE + 4' (answer = 'VHKI'). The major finding was a highly significant interaction between trait anxiety and task difficulty as determined by the number of letters requiring transformation. In this interaction, anxiety had no effect on one- and two-letter problems, but greatly impaired performance on three- and four-letter problems. These findings strengthen the argument that anxiety reduces the ability to handle concurrent processing demands; alternatively, they suggest that anxiety reduces the available capacity of working memory. The results are very similar to those found for noise by Hamilton *et al.* (1977): see Chapter 12.

While easy and difficult tasks undoubtedly differ in terms of the demands which they make on working memory capacity, they clearly differ in other ways. For example, Tennyson and Wooley (1971) found that the mean level of state anxiety was significantly higher following a difficult task than following an easy task, perhaps because performance on a difficult task results in a feeling of failure due to the relatively slow rate of learning. The importance of this factor was demonstrated by Weiner (1966) and Weiner and Schneider (1971). They separated task difficulty and success–failure by giving their subjects false social norms indicating that they were succeeding at a difficult verbal learning task or failing at an easy learning task. Under these conditions, subjects high in anxiety performed better on the difficult task and worse on the easy task than subjects low in anxiety.

EFFORT AND WORRY

There is reasonable agreement among most researchers that many of the effects of anxiety on performance can best be explained in attentional terms. However, there is some dispute as to whether anxiety primarily leads to increased selectivity of attention (Easterbrook, 1959), or whether it leads to increased lability of attention and susceptibility to distraction (Morris *et al.*, 1977). A further possibility is that anxiety leads to both increased selectivity and lability of attention, a position endorsed by Wachtel (1967); such a theory obviously has no trouble in explaining the preponderantly negative effects of anxiety on performance.

Effectiveness and efficiency

A related approach has been developed recently by M. W. Eysenck (1979, 1981). He argued for the usefulness of a conceptual distinction between the terms 'effectiveness' and 'efficiency'. The difference is that efficiency is a measure of the quality of performance or behaviour, whereas effectiveness represents the relationship between the quality or efficiency of performance and the effort invested in it. The concept of 'effort' is discussed at length by Kahneman (1973). He argued that attention involves not only the selection of certain inputs rather than others, but also has an intensive component which, 'corresponds to effort rather than to mere wakefulness' (p.4). He further argued that the effective attentional capacity fluctuated continuously as a function of the immediate processing demands; the greater the level of effort expenditure, the greater the available attentional capacity.

The above considerations give us the following formula: processing effectiveness = (performance efficiency)/effort. Apart from any other reasons, the distinction between effectiveness and efficiency seems to be of value because there is indirect evidence that there are important differences between the effects of anxiety on each of the two factors. The position with respect to the overwhelming majority of studies on the effects of anxiety on various performance tasks is that the dependent variable or variables selected are merely measures of performance efficiency. It is worth noting that any effect of anxiety on the efficiency of performance is only informative with respect to effectiveness provided that the assumption is made that anxiety has no effect on effort expenditure.

Several pertinent observations were made by Kahneman (1973) in his book on attention and effort. He argued that the major determinant of the amount of effort expended by a subject performing a task was the evaluation of task demands. It is clear that the effective demands on anxious subjects are greater than those on non-anxious subjects. The reason for this is that the task-irrelevant cognitive activities associated with anxiety (e.g. decisions about the threat posed by certain external stimuli; the retrieval and contemplation of anxiety-related information; and the formation of appropriate cognitive coping strategies) all make substantial demands on the information-processing system. This means that the task-irrelevant information involved in worry must compete for space in the processing system with task-relevant information. In other words, the anxious subject is effectively in a dual-task situation, whereas the non-anxious subject is in a single-task situation. It is, perhaps, reasonable to assume that working memory is that part of the system most heavily involved in processing both task-relevant and task-irrelevant information. A consequence of the greater demands placed on anxious subjects is that they will typically respond with increased effort.

The apparent paradox that anxiety seems to lead to much task-irrelevant processing (e.g. worry), but nevertheless is sometimes associated with enhancement of task performance is explicable in terms of the framework developed here. It is assumed that the task-irrelevant cognitive processes associated with anxiety always reduce processing effectiveness. However, the extent to which anxiety impairs, or even enhances, performance efficiency depends largely on the extent to which anxious subjects attempt to *compensate* for this reduced effectiveness by means of an increase in mental effort. The argument may be clearer in terms of a homely metaphor. Consider two identical cars being driven up a hill. Performance efficiency is the speed at which each car is travelling, and effort corresponds to the extent to which the accelerator is depressed. If one car has a heavy trailer attached to it (analogous to task-irrelevant processing), then this car will proceed more slowly than the other one with identical usage of the accelerator, i.e. effectiveness suffers. The question as to whether the car pulling the trailer will travel faster or slower than the other car has no definitive answer: while its progress is slowed by the trailer, sufficient use of the accelerator will compensate for this. A crucial point is that even if the two cars travel at the same speed, this does not mean that they are functioning in the same way. Applied to people, anxious subjects may perform as efficiently as non-anxious subjects, but only at greater 'subjective cost' to the system.

There are three kinds of data that are relevant to the proposals outlined above, especially the important issue of measuring expended effort: (1) self-reports of perceived effort; (2) subsidiary-task performance; and (3) effects of motivational manipulations. Self-report data were collected by Dornic (1977). In one study, he found that neurotics and normals performed a series of tasks with comparable efficiency. However, neurotics increasingly rated the tasks as more difficult than did the normal subjects as task difficulty became greater, which may be regarded as indirect evidence that the neurotic subjects expended greater effort than the normal controls on the more demanding tasks. In another study, Dornic (1977) compared groups of stable extroverts (i.e. those low in anxiety) with neurotic introverts (i.e. those high in anxiety). The complexity or difficulty of the task was manipulated by altering both the number of information sources within a closed-system-thinking task (task load), and the distraction power of extra-task stimulation (environmental load). As can be seen in Figure 47, the two groups of subjects did not differ noticeably in terms of the efficiency of performance. However, it appears that comparability of performance efficiency is disguising substantial differences between the two groups of subjects with respect to perceived effort. As is shown in Figure 47, the results for perceived effort indicated a significant triple interaction involving task load, environmental load, and personality. The neurotic introverts expended more effort than the stable extroverts, particularly in the relatively more demanding conditions involving either a high task load or high extra-task load.

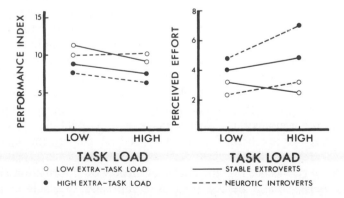

Figure 47. The effects of varying complexity of a closed-system-thinking task on performance and on perceived effort of stable extroverts (low anxiety subjects) and neurotic introverts (high anxiety subjects). Adapted from Dornic (1977).

It is also possible to measure effort expenditure in a somewhat more indirect manner. According to Kahneman (1973), spare processing capacity is inversely related to the amount of effort that the subject is devoting to the main task. One method of attempting to index this spare processing capacity is by measuring performance on a subsidiary or secondary task, the prediction being that performance on the subsidiary task should be inversely related to effort expenditure on the main task (plus any task-irrelevant processing associated with worry). The usual finding in studies investigating the effects of anxiety on primary and secondary or incidental tasks is that anxiety has no effect on the efficiency with which the main task is performed (M. W. Eysenck, 1979). However, it seems likely that this comparability of performance is concealing important effects of anxiety on processing effectiveness and on mental effort. In those experiments in which anxiety had no effect on the performance of the main task, there was a significantly detrimental effect of anxiety on the performance of the subsidiary task in ten cases, and no effect of anxiety in five cases. In none of the studies did anxiety enhance subsidiary-task performance. In terms of the theoretical analysis provided by Kahneman (1973), the implication is that anxious subjects were investing more effort and resources than non-anxious subjects in the primary task. As in the work by Dornic (1977), the message seems to be that anxiety has more clearly detrimental effects on processing effectiveness than on performance efficiency (at least so far as the main or primary task is concerned).

A further way of ascertaining the effects of anxiety on effort expenditure is by using instructions to manipulate the level of motivation. The basic prediction is that attempts to increase motivation will be more successful in improving the performance efficiency of low-anxiety subjects than high-anxiety subjects; the reason for this is that anxious subjects are putatively expending more effort than non-anxious subjects in the absence of motivational instructions. Some researchers have compared the effects of ego-involving (e.g. 'This is a test of intelligence') and task-involving (e.g. 'I want to see how well this apparatus works') instructions, the assumption being that ego-involving instructions are more likely to produce a high level of motivation. The consistent finding is that only low-anxiety subjects perform better under ego-involving than under task-involving instructions (see M. W. Eysenck, 1979, for further details). While this may mean that anxious subjects are nearer maximal effort expenditure than non-anxious subjects under task-involving instructions, it is also likely that ego-involving instructions produce anxiety through fear of failure.

In sum, there is evidence that the effects of anxiety on information processing and performance should be regarded as comprising two stages: (1) task-irrelevant cognitive activities (e.g. worry) reduce processing effectiveness and thus performance efficiency; and (2) there is an attempt to compensate for the reduction in processing effectiveness by means of increased effort; this compensatory process may succeed in preventing a reduction in performance efficiency, but at some extra 'cost' to the system. It is worth noting at this point that anxious subjects will not invariably expend more effort than non-anxious subjects. For example, if the subjective probability of success is minimal, then anxiety may very well be associated with a very low level of task involvement (cf. learned helplessness; Seligman, 1975). Furthermore, the data and theorizing described in this chapter are primarily relevant to task-intrinsic anxiety (i.e. anxiety caused by concern about task performance). It seems less likely that there would be an increase in effort under task-extrinsic anxiety (i.e. anxiety caused by external stimuli or events, such as physical danger).

Failure feedback

The hypothesis that high-anxiety subjects typically experience more worry and other task-irrelevant cognitive activities than low-anxiety subjects, and also exert more effort, may be of relevance in explaining the differential effects of failure feedback on those high and low in anxiety. Failure feedback usually leads to increased state anxiety, and this increase is greater for high-anxiety subjects than for low-anxiety subjects (Hodges, 1968). Since Morris and Liebert (1973) found that it was the worry component of anxiety rather than the emotionality component that was affected by failure, it is likely that a major consequence of failure feedback is to increase worry for high-anxiety subjects to a greater extent than for low-anxiety subjects. In addition, there are motivational consequences of failure feedback, with many subjects exerting enhanced effort after failure in an attempt to reduce the likelihood of subsequent failure. Since high-anxiety subjects are usually close to maximum effort expenditure under neutral conditions, the potential for increased effort is greater for non-anxious subjects.

It is thus reasonable to argue that the primary reaction of anxious subjects to failure is increased worry, whereas that of non-anxious subjects is increased effort. If worry reduces the available capacity of working memory, whereas increased effort enhances its capacity, the general expectation is that failure will improve the performance of low-anxiety subjects through enhanced effort, but that failure will lead to a performance decrement in high-anxiety subjects through increased worry. This analysis implies that there should be an interaction between type of feedback (failure versus neutral) and level of anxiety, a result that has been obtained several times (Gordon and Berlyne, 1954; Krugman, 1958; Lucas, 1952; Sarason, 1957; Walker, 1961). Moreover, high-anxiety subjects showed a consistent impairment of performance as a result of failure feedback in these studies, whereas low-anxiety subjects manifested either no effect or actually improved their level of performance.

An alternative approach to understanding the effects of failure experiences on people varying in anxiety was proposed by Weiner (1972), who claimed that there are four main perceived causes of failure on a performance task: lack of effort, bad luck, task difficulty, and lack of ability. He argued that these four factors could be conceptualized within a two-dimensional framework, with the two dimensions being locus of control (external versus internal) and stability over time (stable versus unstable). Within this framework, bad luck and task difficulty both refer to external factors, with bad luck being unstable and task difficulty being stable; lack of effort and lack of ability are internal factors, with lack of effort being unstable and lack of ability stable. In terms of the expenditure of effort following an experience of failure, Meyer (1970) reported that attribution of failure to the unstable and variable factors of bad luck and lack of effort was far more positively related to subsequent task effort than was attribution of failure to the stable factors of low ability and task difficulty. Not surprisingly, people are more inclined to increase effort if failure appears to be potentially reversible than if it does not.

The relevance of this cognitive approach to failure, based upon the perceived causes of failure, to work on anxiety was clarified by the work of Kukla (1972) and Weiner and Potepan (1970). They found that high-anxiety subjects are more inclined to ascribe failure to a lack of ability, whereas low-anxiety subjects are more likely to attribute failure to lack of effort. Since those high in anxiety invoke a stable factor to explain their failure, whereas those low in anxiety invoke an unstable factor, it follows that low-anxiety subjects should be more likely than high-anxiety subjects to respond to failure with increased effort. This conclusion is consistent with much of the evidence discussed previously.

Memory retrieval: experimental repression

There have been numerous attempts to investigate Freud's notion of repression or motivated forgetting. While there is little likelihood of psychologists being permitted to induce in a laboratory setting the life-crippling traumata alleged to produce clinically observed repression, it is quite straightforward to produce some anxiety by means of failure feedback, and then to investigate the effects of this anxiety on memory.

Zeller (1950) proposed three requirements for an adequate demonstration of experimental repression. The first is to ensure that the material in question has been learned by all of the subjects. The second is to show that an inhibitory factor (e.g. a failure experience) produces a significant decrease in the recall of the material, and the third is to demonstrate that removal of the inhibiting factor (e.g. indicating that the failure feedback was erroneous) results in a reinstatement of the ability to recall the material (return of the repressed). Holmes (1974) reviewed several studies using the approach advocated by Zeller that obtained evidence both for the occurrence of repression and for the return of the repressed.

Since there is evidence that failure increases worry and not emotionality (Morris and Liebert, 1973), it is reasonable to assume that the adverse effects of failure on retention are due to worry and other cognate task-irrelevant cognitive activities. There are some studies providing support for this interpretation rather than a more traditional Freudian account. For example, D'Zurilla (1965) did a study of the kind advocated by Zeller (1950), and obtained evidence of experimental repression. When he asked the subjects post-experimentally what they had thought about immediately after the feedback had been given, subjects receiving failure feedback were far more likely than other subjects to report thoughts that were quite irrelevant to the subsequent task of word recall. He concluded that the greater incidence of conflicting cognitive events for failure subjects probably reduced their recall performance.

SUMMARY OF PERFORMANCE EFFECTS

The experimental work on the effects of anxiety on task performance has produced a number of replicable findings which would need to be accounted for by any adequate theory of anxiety.

(1) Anxiety leads to increased task-irrelevant cognitive activities (e.g. worry).

(2) Anxiety leads to increased effort during task performance most of the time.

(3) Anxiety reduces digit-span performance (working memory capacity).

(4) Anxiety interacts with task difficulty, with adverse effects of anxiety growing as task difficulty increases.

(5) Adverse effects of anxiety are more apparent on subsidiary or incidental tasks than on main or primary tasks.

(6) Anxiety interacts with type of feedback (neutral versus failure), with high-anxiety subjects being more detrimentally affected than low-anxiety subjects by failure feedback.

(7) High-anxiety subjects are not more detrimentally affected than low-anxiety subjects by threat of electric shock; if anything, it is low-anxiety subjects who are more affected by shock.

(8) Anxiety induced by failure impairs the retrieval process.

(9) There is a closer relationship between state anxiety and performance than there is between trait anxiety and performance.

It has been argued somewhat speculatively that most, if not all, of these findings are predictable from a small set of initial assumptions. First, it is assumed that man has limited processing capacity, and that the worry component of anxiety pre-empts some of the available processing capacity. Secondly, it is assumed that anxious individuals characteristically attempt to compensate for the adverse effects of worry by increased effort expenditure.

Thirdly, it is assumed that the aspect of processing capacity most directly involved in mediating the effects of anxiety on information processing is the modality-free central processing component of working memory. This set of assumptions leads to the prediction that anxiety will much more consistently impair processing effectiveness than observed performance efficiency.

THE TREATMENT OF ANXIETY

On the assumption that anxiety comprises both physiological and cognitive components, it seems to follow that attempts to alleviate anxiety symptoms might prove successful whether they focused on reducing the level of arousal or on altering the ways in which people appraise states of arousal at the cognitive level. In practice, of course, it is highly likely that physiological and cognitive factors will have interactive effects on each other. There has been some dispute about the direction of causality. Schachter and Singer (1962) argued that there was initially a state of physiological arousal to which a cognitive label was attached, whereas Lazarus (1966) argued that the level of arousal *per se* is determined by cognitive appraisal, so that anxiety could be effectively reduced by appropriate cognitions. It is entirely possible that the causality can operate in either direction.

The typical approach adopted by Lazarus has been to manipulate cognitive processes, and then to assess the effects of these manipulations on physiological arousal. Subjects view a film that gives rise to emotional reactions related to anxiety; a subincision film shows a stone-age ritual in which adolescent boys have their penises deeply cut, while a safety film depicts a variety of workshop accidents. In the most dramatic of these, a board is caught in a circular saw and rammed with tremendous force through the midsection of a fellow worker, who dies writhing on the floor. Cognitive activity is manipulated during the viewing of the film by varying the accompanying sound track, and attempts are made to induce the defence mechanism of denial or of intellectualization. Denial is produced by indicating that the subincision film does not show a painful operation, or that the participants in the safety film are actors. Intellectualization is evoked during the subincision film by considering matters from the perspective of an objective anthropologist merely viewing strange customs, and is produced during the safety film by asking the viewer to look objectively at the situational dynamics. During the viewing of the film, various measures of autonomic arousal (e.g. heart-rate; galvanic skin response) are recorded continuously.

The major finding of the various studies is that the arousal or stress reactions to the films are substantially reduced by the defence mechanisms of denial and intellectualization, thus demonstrating that changes in cognitive appraisal can be effective in reducing physiological stress reactions. Lazarus and Alfert (1964) also found that this reduction in physiological stress relative to a control group receiving no sound track was especially large when the defence information was presented in its entirety before the film was viewed. They also reported that those individuals identified as being high in a personality disposition towards denial derived the most benefit from the denial message; the implication is that emotional reactions to stimulus events will be most reduced when an individual's personality structure is compatible with the manipulated defence.

It is clearly of clinical and theoretical interest to compare the effectiveness in reducing anxiety of cognitive coping strategies such as those investigated by Lazarus (1966) with other approaches based on reducing arousal, such as systematic desensitization. The essential ingredient of systematic desensitization is that people are trained to inhibit autonomic arousal by means of deep muscle relaxation while imagining or thinking about events that resemble more and more closely the original anxiety-evoking event.

The methods of systematic desensitization and of a cognitive modification technique combining systematic desensitization with an insight-oriented therapy designed to foster awareness of anxiety-engendered thoughts were compared with respect to the treatment of test anxiety by Meichenbaum (1972). He found that both forms of treatment were more effective than no treatment in improving academic performance (grade point average) and digit-symbol performance, and in reducing self-reported anxiety. While the cognitive modification procedure tended to be superior to systematic desensitization, the differences were mainly non-significant.

In a related study, Holroyd (1976) studied the relative effectiveness of four different treatment techniques in reducing test anxiety. The techniques were cognitive therapy (based exclusively on eliminating task-irrelevant ruminations and attentional focus), systematic desensitization (using muscle relaxation to inhibit autonomic arousal), combined cognitive therapy and desensitization, and pseudotherapy meditation (apparently impressive therapeutic procedures but no actual treatment). The students receiving cognitive therapy showed a significantly greater improvement in academic performance (measured by grade point average) than any of the other groups. They also showed the greatest improvement in digit-symbol test performance, and this was maintained at a one-month follow-up. The reduction in state anxiety experienced during the digit-symbol test was greatest for the cognitive therapy subjects. A final general finding was that the effectiveness of pseudotherapy and systematic desensitization was comparable, suggesting that non-specific treatment elements such as contact with an interested therapist and exposure to an impressive treatment ritual may account for the results obtained with systematic desensitization. The major conclusion, however, is that treatment focusing on the cognitive component of anxiety was more efficacious than treatment dealing primarily with the autonomic arousal component.

An experimental demonstration of the value of cognitive coping strategies even under very stressful conditions was provided by Girodo and Roehl (1976). They considered various groups of women reporting great fear of flying; one group was trained to emit positive self-coping statements, a second group was provided with detailed information about flying, and a third group was given no treatment. The groups of women then took a trip by plane; shortly before landing, when the plane was within one hundred feet of the runway, a loud emergency buzzer sounded, full throttle was applied to the engines, and the aircraft banked to one side and rose again rapidly. The group trained to emit self-coping statements was rather less terrified than the other group. However, the main message of this study seems to be that you would be well advised not to leave yourself to the tender mercies of unscrupulous psychologists!

In spite of the fact that the evidence clearly indicates that cognitive coping strategies can be effective in the treatment of anxiety, the precise processes involved are obscure. For example, consider the stress-inoculation procedure favoured by Meichenbaum (1976). This involves providing the anxious person with a conceptual rationale that induces him to believe in the applicability of the technique, it requires him to focus his attention on negative statements and evaluations, and then it requires him to emit positive self-coping statements. The success or failure of this procedure may depend on any or all of these various stages of treatment. In psychological terms, the production of self-coping statements may prevent one from focusing on external stimuli that could lead to anxiety responses; it may prevent negative and self-defeating evaluations being made; or it may be instrumental in leading to appropriate response patterns that minimize experienced anxiety. Until there is more progress in understanding why some forms of treatment are successful, there is little hope of reducing the high levels of *angst* and *weltschmerz* prevalent in industrialized societies!

SUMMARY

The psychometric approach to anxiety makes an important distinction between trait anxiety (the degree of susceptibility to anxiety in stressful conditions) and state anxiety (the transient experience of anxiety). State anxiety is interactively determined by trait anxiety and by the amount of stress in the immediate situation, and it is assumed that information processing and behaviour are more directly affected by state anxiety than by trait anxiety.

There is some evidence to suggest that anxiety consists of two major components: worry and emotionality. Performance on most tasks is more adversely affected by worry than by emotionality, perhaps because worry utilized some of the processing resources required for task performance.

While worry reduces the quality of performance, there is much evidence that anxious subjects attempt to compensate for this. As a consequence, it often happens that there is little obvious effect of anxiety on performance, but anxious subjects attain comparability of performance at greater 'cost' to themselves.

Attempts to alleviate anxiety symptoms have typically focused either on reducing the level of autonomic arousal or on providing the anxious individual with cognitive coping strategies. Both methods have been found to be effective, but there is some suggestion in the literature that treatment based on the cognitive component of anxiety is more efficacious than treatment involving the arousal component.

In sum, if we want to understand the effects of stressful environmental conditions on people's behaviour, it is essential to take notice of individual differences in susceptibility to stress. An appropriate way of incorporating such individual differences into theoretical conceptualizations is suggested by the state–trait model of anxiety.

ACKNOWLEDGEMENTS

Many thanks are due to the Social Science Research Council for their generous financial assistance during the preparation of this chapter. Thanks are also due to Christine Eysenck, who commented critically on an earlier version of the manuscript.

REFERENCES

Allen, G. J. (1970) Effect of three conditions of administration on 'trait' and 'state' measures of anxiety. *Journal of Consulting and Clinical Psychology*, **34**, 355–359.

Baddeley, A. D. and Hitch, G. (1974) Working memory. In G. H. Bower (ed.), *Recent Advances in Learning and Motivation, Vol. 8*. Academic Press, pp.47–89.

Beach, N. F. (1959) Paired-associates learning as a function of anxiety level and shock. *Journal of Personality*, **27**, 116–124.

Chiles, W. D. (1958) Effects of shock-induced stress on verbal performance. *Journal of Experimental Psychology*, **56**, 159–165.

Deese, J., Lazarus, R. S., and Keenan, J. (1953) Anxiety, anxiety reduction, and stress in learning. *Journal of Experimental Psychology*, **46**, 55–60.

Deffenbacher, J. L. (1978) Worry, emotionality, and task-generated interference in test anxiety: An empirical test of attentional theory. *Journal of Educational Psychology*, **70**, 248–254.

Doctor, R. M. and Altman, F. (1969) Worry and emotionality as components of test anxiety: Replication and further data. *Psychological Reports*, **24**, 563–568.

Dornic, S. (1977) Mental load, effort, and individual differences. *Reports from the Department of Psychology, The University of Stockholm*, No. 509.

D'Zurilla, T. (1965) Recall efficiency and mediating cognitive events in 'experimental repression'. *Journal of Personality and Social Psychology*, **1**, 253–256.

Easterbrook, J. A. (1959) The effects of emotion on cue utilization and the organization of behaviour. *Psychological Review*, **66**, 183–201.

Endler, N. S., Magnusson, D., Ekehammar, B., and Okada, M. (1976) The multi-dimensionality of state and trait anxiety. *Scandinavian Journal of Psychology*, **17**, 81–96.

Eysenck, M. W. (1977) *Human Memory: Theory, Research and Individual Differences.* Pergamon, pp.1–366.

Eysenck, M. W. (1979) Anxiety, learning, and memory: A reconceptualization. *Journal of Research in Personality*, **13**, 363–385.

Eysenck, M. W. (1981) Learning, memory, and personality. In H. J. Eysenck (ed.), *A Model for Personality.* Springer.

Fowler, C. J. H. and Wilding, J. (1979) Differential effects of noise and incentives on learning. *British Journal of Psychology*, **70**, 149–153.

Ganzer, V. J. (1968) Effects of audience presence and test anxiety on learning and retention in a serial learning situation. *Journal of Personality and Social Psychology*, **8**, 194–199.

Girodo, M. and Roehl, J. (1976) Preparatory information and self-talk in coping with the stress of flying. Unpublished manuscript, University of Ottawa.

Glover, C. B. and Cravens, R. W. (1974) Trait anxiety, stress, and learning: A test of Saltz's hypothesis. *Journal of Research in Personality*, **8**, 243–253.

Gordon, W. M. and Berlyne, D. E. (1954) Drive level and flexibility in paired associate nonsense syllable learning. *Quarterly Journal of Experimental Psychology*, **6**, 181–185.

Hamilton, P., Hockey, G. R. J., and Rejman, M. (1977) The place of the concept of activation in human information processing theory: An integrative approach. In S. Dornic (ed.), *Attention and Performance Vol VI*, Hillsdale, N.J.: Erlbaum.

Hodges, W. F. (1968) Effects of ego threat and threat of pain on state anxiety. *Journal of Personality and Social Psychology*, **8**, 364–372.

Holmes, D. S. (1974) Investigations of repression: Differential recall of material experimentally or naturally associated with ego threat. *Psychological Bulletin*, **81**, 632–654.

Holroyd, K. A. (1976) Cognition and desensitization in the group treatment of test anxiety. *Journal of Consulting and Clinical Psychology*, **44**, 991–1001.

Kahneman, D. (1973) *Attention and Effort.* Prentice-Hall, pp.1–216.

Krugman, A. D. (1958) A comparative study of the effect of induced failure, induced success and a neutral task upon the retentive processes of anxiety and normal subjects. *Dissertation Abstracts*, **18**, 662.

Kukla, A. (1972) Cognitive determinants of achieving behaviour. *Journal of Personality and Social Psychology*, **21**, 166–174.

Lazarus, R. S. (1966) *Psychological Stress and the Coping Process.* McGraw-Hill.

Lazarus, R. S. and Alfert, E. (1964) The short-circuiting of threat by experimentally altering cognitive appraisal. *Journal of Abnormal and Social Psychology*, **69**, 194–205.

Lazarus, R. S., Deese, J., and Hamilton, R. (1954) Anxiety and stress in learning: The role of intraserial duplication. *Journal of Experimental Psychology*, **47**, 111–114.

Lee, L. C. (1961) The effects of anxiety level and shock on a paired-associate verbal task. *Journal of Experimental Psychology*, **61**, 213–217.

Lucas, J. D. (1952) The interactive effect of anxiety failure and intra-serial duplication. *American Journal of Psychology*, **65**, 59–66.

Mandler, G. and Sarason, S. B. (1952) A study of anxiety and learning. *Journal of Abnormal and Social Psychology*, **47**, 166–173.

Martuza, V. R. and Kallstrom, D. W. (1974) Validity of the State–Trait Anxiety Inventory in an academic setting. *Psychological Reports*, **35**, 363–366.

Mayer, R. E. (1977) Problem-solving performance with task overload: Effects of self-pacing and trait anxiety. *Bulletin of the Psychonomic Society*, **9**, 283–286.

Meichenbaum, D. H. (1972) Cognitive modification of test anxious college students. *Journal of Consulting and Clinical Psychology*, **39**, 370–380.

Meichenbaum, D. H. (1975) Self-instructional methods. In F. H. Kanfer and A. P. Goldstein (eds.), *Helping People Change*. Pergamon.

Meyer, W. V. (1970) Selbstverantwortlichkeit und Leistungsmotivation. Unpublished Ph.D. thesis, Ruhr University, Bochum, West Germany.

Mischel, W. (1969) Continuity and change in personality. *American Psychologist*, **24**, 1012–1018.

Mischel, W. (1973) Toward a cognitive social learning reconceptualization of personality. *Psychological Review*, **80**, 252–283.

Morris, L. W., Brown, N. R., and Halbert, B. L. (1977) Effects of symbolic modeling on the arousal of cognitive and affective components of anxiety in preschool children. In C. D. Spielberger and I. G. Sarason (eds.), *Stress and Anxiety, Vol. 4*. Halsted, pp.153–170.

Morris, L. W. and Liebert, R. M. (1970) Relationships of cognitive and emotional components of test anxiety to physiological arousal and academic performance. *Journal of Consulting and Clinical Psychology*, **35**, 332–337.

Morris, L. W. and Liebert, R. M. (1973) Effects of negative feedback, threat of shock, and level of trait anxiety on the arousal of two components of anxiety. *Journal of Counseling Psychology*, **20**, 321–326.

Nottelman, E. D. and Hill, K. T. (1977) Test and anxiety and off-task behaviour in evaluative situations. *Child Development*, **48**, 225–231.

Russell, J. A. and Mehrabian, A. (1977) Evidence for a three-factor theory of emotion. *Journal of Research in Personality*, **11**, 273–294.

Sarason, I. G. (1957) Effects of anxiety and two kinds of failure on serial learning. *Journal of Personality*, **27**, 116–124.

Sarason, I. G. (1975) Anxiety and self-preoccupation. In I. G. Sarason and C. D. Spielberger (eds.), *Stress and Anxiety, Vol. 2*. Hemisphere/Wiley.

Schachter, S. and Singer, J. E. (1962) Cognitive, social and physiological determinants of emotional state. *Psychological Review*, **69**, 379–399.

Seligman, M. E. P. (1975) *Helplessness: On Depression, Development, and Death.* Freeman.

Shedletsky, R. and Endler, N. S. (1974) Anxiety: The state–trait model and the interaction model. *Journal of Personality*, **42**, 511–527.

Shields, J. (1973) Heredity and psychological abnormality. In H. J. Eysenck (ed.), *Handbook of Abnormal Psychology* (2nd edn). Pitman.

Spence, J. T. and Spence, K. W. (1966) The motivational components of manifest anxiety: Drive and drive stimuli. In C. D. Spielberger (ed.), *Anxiety and Behavior*. Academic Press, pp.291–326.

Spiegler, M. D., Morris, L. W., and Liebert, R. M. (1968) Cognitive and emotional components of test anxiety: Temporal factors. *Psychological Reports*, **22**, 451–456.

Spielberger, C. D. (1966) The effects of anxiety on complex learning and academic achievement. In C. D. Spielberger (ed.), *Anxiety and Behavior*. Academic Press, pp.361–398.

Spielberger, C. D. (1972) Anxiety as an emotional state. In C. D. Spielberger (ed.), *Anxiety: Current Trends in Theory and Research, Vol. 1*. Academic Press.

Spielberger, C. D., Gorsuch, R., and Lushene, R. (1970) *The State–Trait Anxiety Inventory (STAI) Test Manual Form X*. Consulting Psychologists Press.

Tennyson, R. D. and Woolley, F. R. (1971) Interaction of anxiety with performance on two levels of task difficulty. *Journal of Educational Psychology*, **62**, 463–467.

Wachtel, P. L. (1967) Conceptions of broad and narrow attention. *Psychological Bulletin*, **68**, 417–429.

Walker, R. E. (1961) The interaction between failure, manifest anxiety, and task-irrelevant responses in paired-associate learning. Unpublished Ph.D. thesis, Northwestern University.

Weiner, B. (1966) The role of success and failure in the learning of easy and complex tasks. *Journal of Personality and Social Psychology*, **3**, 339–344.
Weiner, B. (1972) *Theories of Motivation: From Mechanisms to Cognition*. London: Markham.
Weiner, B. and Potepan, P. A. (1970) Personality correlates and affective reactions towards exams of succeeding and failing college students. *Journal of Educational Psychology*, **61**, 144–151.
Weiner, B. and Schneider, K. (1971) Drive versus cognitive theory: A reply to Boor and Harmon. *Journal of Personality and Social Psychology*, **18**, 258–262.
Wine, J. (1971) Test anxiety and direction of attention. *Psychological Bulletin*, **76**, 92–104.
Yerkes, R. M. and Dodson, J. D. (1908) The relation of strength of stimulus to rapidity of habit-formation. *Journal of Comparative Neurology and Psychology*, **18**, 459–482.
Zeller, A. F. (1950) An experimental analogue of repression: II. The effect of individual failure and success on memory measured by recall. *Journal of Experimental Psychology*, **40**, 411–422.

Stress and Fatigue in Human Performance
Edited by G. R. J. Hockey
© 1983 John Wiley & Sons Ltd.

Chapter 11

Coping Efficiency and Situational Demands

Wolfgang Schönpflug

When Cannon (1914) introduced the term 'stress' into the psychophysiological literature he was dealing with highly dramatic internal shifts from anabolic to catabolic functions. Arguing from a biogenetic perspective, he assigned to phases of stress the release of 'power in the attack and in the defence or flight' (Cannon, 1914, p.275). His emphasis on highly dramatic states evoked by potent biological or cultural agents has not been preserved in more recent theoretical approaches. These tend to broaden the concept of stress by taking into account relatively minor changes of biological state. The most general definition is one proposed by Welford (1973). He assumed any departure from an 'optimum' to result in a stress state and conceived of stress 'as arising when motivating conditions are not reduced by the organism's actions' (Welford, 1973, p.568). In this formulation the concept of stress comes close to the concept of motivation, and coping with stress is hardly to be distinguished from goal-directed activity in general.

It will *not* be contended in this chapter that all motivating conditions are equivalent to stressors, and, therefore, that all human actions have to be regarded as attempts to cope with stress. However, it may prove valuable for further theorizing to treat stressing agents as motivating conditions, or rather as sources of demands. Then, behaviour under stress could be analysed as activity devised to meet these demands. By his actions a person will exert an influence on his environment, while being himself affected by it; thus, he may both reduce and augment the stressing features in his situation. If actions extend over time, a continuous transaction between the person involved and his environment will develop (Pervin and Lewis, 1978). From this perspective, states of stress mark a special relation between man and his environment (Lazarus and Launier, 1978), a relation which appears to be mediated by the concern for non-optimal conditions, i.e. for problems.

ORIENTATION AND CONTROL

Concern for non-optimal conditions or problems includes two basic components: *orientation* and *control*. Each of these can again be partitioned into at least two further components. Thus, orientation can be decomposed into

(a) a problem-identification process comprising the scanning of problem features, definition of problems, subjective appraisals, and goal setting, and

(b) a process of developing problem-solving strategies.

Control processes, on the other hand, can be decomposed into

(a) execution of problem-solving activity, and

(b) acquisition of new coping skills.

Orientation and control processes may be effective in problem finding and problem solving (cf. Getzels, 1979; Newell and Simon, 1972). It is possible to treat the stress situation as a problem situation, and to study the contribution of orientation and control to prevention, elimination, and modification of problem sources (Meichenbaum, 1977). This, however, is not the approach emphasized here. This chapter, while also being based on a problem-solving conception, concentrates rather on ineffective coping attempts and inappropriate assessment of the problem situation. It will be the induction of stress rather than its reduction by a person's activity which becomes the central issue.

If concern for a problem follows an orienting mode, failures in problem identification and shortcomings in the development of feasible problem-solving strategies will contribute to a state of stress. In this state feelings of worrying, helplessness, and uncertainty will dominate (Heckhausen, 1982; Sarason, 1975). If concern follows a control mode, over-exertion and feedback from unsuccessful attempts at controlling the situation may occur, which are likely to raise further difficulties. After ineffective control attempts, the individual either returns to the phase of problem identification or engages in compensatory activity (Schulz and Schönpflug, 1982). In either case the problem situation will be prolonged, if not aggravated.

From the actional (or transactional) perspective it is the concern for a problem which constitutes a state of stress. All kinds of concern may enhance the degree of stress. They may also mitigate it and play their part in the coping process. Therefore in the interests of coping the need for optimal selection of mediating processes arises. Competition may occur

(a) within the orienting mode (e.g. whether to reduce concern for a problem rather than to search for new coping strategies),

(b) within the control mode (e.g. which operation to apply), or

(c) between orienting and control (e.g. a choice between the immediate application of a well-practised skill or a search for a new coping strategy).

Each process will have its costs and benefits, and the selection should be based on balancing the account to provide an optimal relation between losses and gains. Such balancing procedures are observed most easily during the search for optimal operations in work situations (Sperandio, 1978), but should also occur as a more general phenomenon. Balancing of psychological costs and benefits may be regarded as a central issue for the regulation of internal states of stress and external stressors. It is referred to in this chapter as *behaviour economics.*

DEMANDS AND EFFICIENCY

Internal and external demands

Transactional models of stress have treated external stressors like work load, time pressure, or painful life changes as task demands (Holmes and Masuda, 1974; McGrath, 1976; Schönpflug, 1979). External demands, however, cannot operate within an individual unless they have been identified by him and internalized to become part of his set of internal demands. In stress theory this process has been dealt with as one of appraisal (Lazarus, 1966); in problem-solving theory as the transition from external to internal problem space (Newell and Simon, 1972). There are other demands which are internal from the outset. They relate to the individual's physical, cognitive, and emotional state and concern for his well-being. Obviously, external and internal demands are psychologically related, but in an asymmetric way. Whereas meeting external demands (e.g. safety control, environmental protection) is invariably instrumental for satisfying internal demands (e.g. relief from pain or annoyance), there are internal demands (like the need for cognitive consonance, or a reduction of muscular tension) which can eventually be responded to without reference to the environment (Schönpflug, 1979).

Apparently, the concern for stressors easily leads to a conflicting state. On the one hand, orientation and control are prerequisites for the elimination of threats and challenges, and therefore indispensable for the satisfaction of internal needs. On the other hand, orientation and attempts at controlling threatening and challenging conditions may put strain on a person and contribute to his disorganization, emotionality, and worries; these effects will not be in concordance with internal demands. From the economical point of view it is necessary to ask which coping attempts are likely to 'pay off' and which cannot be regarded as profitable.

Behaviour changes under stress

Psychological research has up to now succeeded in documenting changes in physiological arousal, emotionality, and subjective appraisal in stress situations and states of stress (e.g. Frankenhaeuser, 1975; Lazarus and Launier, 1978). There is also evidence for shifts in overt behaviour and cognitive functioning (Hockey, 1979; Schulz and Battmann, 1980) and of interference with ongoing primary activity (Näätänen, 1973). A case of reorganization of behaviour under stress is presented in a study by Werner (Schönpflug, 1974). Four groups of subjects had to write an essay on an incident during the 1972 Olympic Games at Munich. The four groups were exposed to noise differing in intensity from 45 to 105 dB. Two main tendencies were observed in this study as a function of noise intensity: the number of words and sentences written increased, but the number of subordinate clauses decreased. (While subjects under quiet conditions, for example, favoured sentences like: 'After addressing the council the secretary brought forward a motion', subjects under noise preferred as series of shorter sentences like: 'The secretary first addressed the council. Then he brought forward a motion'). With increasing stress subjects thus tended to produce more in terms of quantity, while the linguistic quality of their sentences (as expressed by subordination) decreased.

The evaluation of the pay-off of coping presupposes the identification of coping acts. The acts of coping to be observed most conveniently are control acts. Unfortunately, psychological experiments designed to check the effects of stress on behaviour and cognitive functioning have typically not permitted the subjects to control the stressing agents (like heat or noise), whereas experiments on the active control of stressing conditions like noise (e.g. Glass and Singer, 1972; Sherrod *et al.*, 1977) have usually not proceeded to study behaviour more carefully.

A study making provisions for both active control of a stressor and detailed behaviour analysis was done by Schulz (Schulz and Schönpflug, 1982, study I). Schulz confronted his subjects with mental tasks varying in difficulty. Different subjects were exposed to traffic noise varying in intensity between 0, 30–40, 50–60, and 70–80 dB. The subjects were permitted to press a button which terminated the noise for 40 seconds. From the data the following observation is relevant for the present discussion: in the 30–40 dB noise only the peaks were clearly audible (horn signals, fast cars), and these attracted the subjects' attention. Since diversion of attention was likely to interrupt the work on the mental task, subjects shut off the low noise as often as the loudest noise and more often than the clearly audible 50–60 dB noise. Probably as a consequence, the error rate with barely audible noise was twice as high as that found under quiet conditions and fell behind the error rate in the loud noise condition by only 25 per cent. These results give support to the possibility that the subject's attempts at external control of the noise might in this case have been more rather than less detrimental to work efficiency than the actual exposure to the noise. Under these conditions an attitude of terminating orientation on the low noise seems to be more economical than attempts at external control. The same does not hold true for loud noise, of course, since it seems very unlikely that attention can be averted from sound above 70 dB. Therefore, external control (if this is less detrimental than non-control) is to be favoured to loud noise. Although these observations need further corroboration, they do support the general view that orientation and coping have to be traded off on the basis of their demands and their efficiency.

Compensatory activity and efficiency

Efficiency is not to be equated with absolute achievement but rather with the relation between activity (regarded as psychological costs) and achievement (i.e. gains). Discussing data from anxiety research, Eysenck (1979) has proposed as an index of efficiency the ratio between performance and effort; interpretations from the Stockholm laboratory (Frankenhaeuser, 1976; Lundberg, 1982) follow the same line. In the Berlin laboratory, which allows long-term behaviour analysis, both time spent on control and the number of operations performed have been related to the number of correct solutions in order to obtain estimates of efficiency. The method was first applied in the above-mentioned studies carried out by Schulz. In his paradigm the subjects had to solve a series of mental tasks such as those occurring in public administration (e.g. checking of bills, responding to requests, deciding about complaints). A correct solution required (a) the search for relevant items of information, (b) memorizing of relevant information, and (c) drawing correct conclusions from the information memorized. In the recent versions of the experimental set-up, information is sequentially exposed on a screen; the item of information exposed and duration of exposure are controlled by the subjects by use of a keyboard. The main feature is that items which have

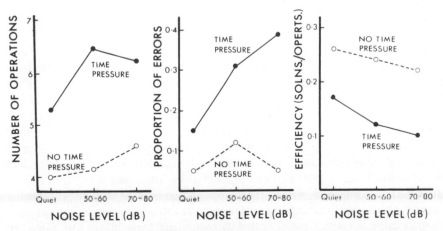

Figure 48. (a) Number of operations per task as a function of noise intensity and time pressure. (b) Proportion of errors as a function of noise intensity and time pressure. (c) Efficiency (number of correct solutions/number of operations) as a function of noise intensity and time pressure. From Schulz and Schönpflug (1982, study II).

already been exposed but then forgotten before the solution may be repeated; otherwise subjects risk making decisions in the absence of sufficient information. Typically, under stress, as induced by time pressure or noise, subjects show a decrement in memorizing, and either call for previously exposed information repeatedly or go ahead with risky decisions. The risk-taking behaviour will be treated later in this chapter. What is of interest here are repeated calls for information (Figure 48a), which can be classified, after failures in memorizing, as compensatory behaviour. As can be seen from Figure 48b, compensatory activity does not succeed in keeping the performance level constant. However, it would be expected that performance would suffer even more from time pressure and noise if no compensation occurs. As a result, the ration of correct solutions to the number of operations (the index of efficiency) drops considerably with increasing stress (Figure 48c).

There is further evidence that the extent of compensatory activity increases arousal, feelings of annoyance, and other symptoms of stress. However, there seems to be a considerable variation in the impact of compensatory activity depending on whether it succeeds in maintaining performance level or not. This compares well with observations in an industrial field study (Karasek, 1979). In this study it was shown that high demands lower work satisfaction only for less qualified individuals, whereas they may increase satisfaction for the more qualified ones. Obviously it is not load *per se* determining the degree of distress but rather lack of proficiency in handling the load. (This leads to the topic of the demand/capacity ratio which will be treated in the next section.) Whereas successful compensation may be classified as a case of effective coping, unsuccessful compensatory activity has to be interpreted as an example of an ineffective coping attempt.

Stress as a consequence of ineffective coping

Schulz's data demonstrate what already had been hypothesized by Neufeld (1976). Ineffective coping attempts form a major source of stress. They combine the costs of control with the costs of continued problem orientation. While they are continued, concern is directed towards the person involved, his arousal, his worries, his uncertainty of proceeding, his cognitive and behavioral disorganization. These are states which most probably will deviate from a person's internal demands. And, therefore, the concern for a primary task in phases of inefficiency may well be augmented by increased self-concern. This self-concern, combined with heightened arousal, may add a substantial component of emotional load to the existing amount of stress. If concern for internal states is finally not effective in regulating these states and does not restore the efficiency of coping with the primary problem source, a vicious circle may result. Inefficiency increases stress, and stress increases inefficiency.

Coping attempts, while being effective or ineffective in solving old problems, may generate new ones. Problem generation can be regarded as another way of increasing costs. The creation of self-related problems due to inefficient handling of a primary task is just one kind of problem generation. There are more explicit examples. A driver of an ambulance drives quickly in order to save a patient with a heart failure and hits a passenger in the street. In this case a new problem arises while an old problem remains unsolved. Or, a family moves away from an industrial area to escape from air pollution and unexpectedly faces annoyance by traffic noise in the new home. In this case an old problem is bartered for a new one. Unfortunately, there is just anecdotal evidence up to now for the phenomenon of problem generation. The phenomenon, however, deserves more intensive study because of its relevance for models of stress and for behavior economics.

With reference to the modes of problem concern and their efficiency, five activity patterns can be differentiated. They are listed in a more systematic way in Table 5 below. There are also tentative suppositions entered in the table relating to the intensity and duration of stress associated with these patterns. It is assumed that the accumulation of ineffective coping efforts and problem-generating acts increases the intensity of stress, while any failures in removing problems results in prolongation of this state, as long as problem orientation continues.

Table 5. Ineffective coping attempts and problem generation as sources of stress.

Concern for a problem?		Coping attempts effective?	Generation of new problem?	Stress	
Orientation	Control			Intensity	Duration
yes	no	no	no	low	long
yes	yes	yes	no	low	short
yes	yes	no	no	medium	long
yes	yes	yes	yes	medium	long
yes	yes	no	yes	high	long

CAPACITY, DEMAND, AND THE ROLE OF FATIGUE

In the field of mathematics the engagement in a problem ends if a solution is found or the problem is proved to be insoluble. This seems to be a good analogy for coping in general. Coping capacity can then be defined as a set of resources for limiting the concern with a problem; concern with a problem can either be terminated by solving the problem in question or by recognizing the futility of all problem-solving attempts. After termination of problem concern there will be no basis for the development of stress; in particular, inefficiency and self-concern will be avoided.

Stress as a function of demand and capacity

Termination of concern with a problem requires various kinds and varying amounts of individual resources. The resources may refer to problem orientation (effectiveness in stating and evaluating a problem, or in developing appropriate problem-solving strategies) or to control processes (manual or verbal skills, ability for self-regulation). The ratio between demands (or difficulties) of problems and capacities (or abilities) of individuals has been considered as a mediating factor of stress in both transactional and person-environment fit approaches. However, there is no agreement on the exact relation between the demand/capacity ratio and the degree of stress. McGrath (1976) and Lazarus and Cohen (1978) simply state that stress occurs if demands outbalance an individual's capacities. Harrison (1978), arguing from a person–environment fit point of view, assumes the lowest degree of stress if capacities and demands just match. Stress is assumed to increase if either demands outbalance capacities (the case of overload) or capacities exceed demands (the case of underload). Schulz and Schönpflug (1982) argue for just the opposite version. They hypothesize that stress will be most pronounced if capacities just match demands or if demands marginally exceed capacities. Under conditions of balance, they would expect the lowest degree of efficiency to be maintained for a longer period of time. In comparison, they predict higher efficiency if capacity exceeds demands, and earlier termination of ineffective performance if demands exceed capacity.

All views, except the person-environment fit version, regard a capacity reserve, the difference between resources available and the resources applied (Kahneman, 1973), as a protection from stress. The less an individual's capacity reserve, the more he should be vulnerable to additional demands. This issue can be nicely demonstrated with data from the above-mentioned study by schulz (Schönpflug and Schulz, 1979). As a reminder, these are based on decision times of subjects working on mental tasks while being exposed to traffic noise varying in intensity. As a form of subsidiary task, subjects can interrupt the noise by pressing a button. The tasks varied in difficulty, as classified in a pre-test on an independent sample of subjects. They were assumed to consume a portion of the subject's capacity, depending on difficulty. Exposure to noise or attempts to control noise were expected to consume another portion, depending on noise intensity. As can be seen from Figure 49a the relation between noise intensity and decision time is linear for tasks of medium difficulty. The function is negatively accelerated for difficult tasks, and positively accelerated for easy tasks. This means, from the economical points of view, that the cost of an increment of load in one task rises with the difficulty of a concomitant task — until an upper limit is reached.

The distinction between demands and capacities remains promising for conceptual reasons. From the methodological point of view, however, it suffers from a severe shortcoming: measures of difficulty and capacity cannot

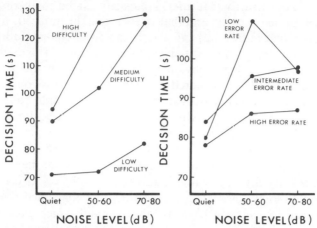

Figure 49. (a) Decision time for tasks varying in difficulty, as a function of noise intensity. (b) Decision time for subjects varying in error rate, as a function of noise intensity. (a) From Schönpflug and Shultz (1979); based on Schönpflug and Shultz (1979).

be assessed independently. They are typically calculated from the same pool of subjective responses. Typically, a sample of i subjects is confronted with a sample of t tasks, and thereby a matrix of $i \times t$ error scores or performance times is produced. Collapsing the data for each individual over the t tasks yields i capacity parameters, whereas collapsing the same data for each task over the i individuals yields t difficulty parameters. According to this procedure, difficulty measures clearly represent capacity characteristics of individuals rather than features of the task situation themselves. Following this logic, individuals classified as low in their capacity should suffer more from an increase in extra load than individuals classified as high. Under these assumptions, longer decision times could be predicted for low capacity individuals, and also a greater increase in decision time with increasing noise level.

To test the above predictions, subjects were assigned to three groups according to their total number of errors. When the three groups were compared on the basis of their total decision times, there were no significant differences between group means and no interaction of groups with noise intensity. A closer look at the data revealed that many of the wrong solutions were due to risky decisions. Therefore the times for correct decisions only were examined. The new data, as presented in Figure 49b, contradict the predictions derived above: subjects who make a high number of errors have the *shortest* not the longest decision times, even for correct solutions. They show the weakest response to noise and not the strongest. Is the failure of these predictions also a failure of the demand/capacity model from which the predictions were derived? Apparently this is not a necessary consequence. With another proposition added, the original model remains fully valid.

   The model states correctly that inferior capacity can be compensated for by extended and repeated activity, and that stress is thereby induced. It should be added, however, that individuals can also resign from compensating activity, and thereby avoid stress from excessive coping attempts. This is the attitude which low capacity subjects obviously favoured under the experimental conditions. They may have favoured a combination of low output and low activity as being more effective than alternatives, which might have turned out as a combination of slightly higher output and disproportionately higher commitment. Their attitude also prevented dramatic changes in activity in response to noise. A strong change in behaviour was, however, observed with the high capacity subjects in response to intermediate noise; they still engaged in compensatory activity. Typically, high capacity subjects also reduce their commitment with loud noise. It therefore has to be concluded that there are critical discrepancies between capacity and demand which may reduce the motivation for compensatory coping. The point will be followed up in the next section. It will be argued that the extent of coping activity is a joint function of competence and effort regulation.

Implications for fatigue

At this point the problem of fatigue may be considered. Cameron's conceptualization of fatigue 'as a generalized response to stress over a period of time' (Cameron, 1973, p.640) deserves support, but needs further elaboration. Fatigue obviously operates on the capacity component. It can be suggested that fatigue reduces capacity and therefore increases the vulnerability to stress. Indices of stress have been found to become more pronounced after prolonged work periods (e.g. Broadbent, 1954; Schönpflug and Schulz, 1979), and stress in general seems to interfere with the work–rest cycle (Wieland, 1981). There is also a relation between task difficulty and fatigue. Impairment in serial reaction tasks occurs more rapidly with high than with low difficulty (Bornemann, 1956/57; Schmidtke, 1965), while recovery with rest pauses is slower (Hacker *et al.*, 1978). In a straightforward analysis it could be argued that fatigue, by impairing capacity, also increases the demand/capacity ratio (in favour of demands) resulting in a state of stress. However, the issue may be more complex. As has been already shown in Figure 49b, a reduction in the capacity component may be associated with a drop in activity, a well-known symptom of fatigue, which has also been demonstrated as an effect of prolonged work periods and extended vigils (Davies and Tune, 1970; see Davies *et al.*, Chapter 1 this volume; Schmidtke, 1965). Although omissions may become a basis for inefficiency, a lower activity rate may also be associated with a lower incidence of ineffective and problem-generating behaviour. If this can be taken for granted, fatigue can be assumed to counteract stress. Indeed, in some studies, sleep loss has been found to counteract stress from noise during a choice-reaction task (e.g. Corcoran, 1962; Wilkinson, 1963).

COMPETENCE AND EFFORT

The components of capacity

The construct of capacity can be further decomposed. Common sense comprehends capacity as a joint function of ability and effort, and both achievement motivation theory (cf. Weiner, 1974; Heckhausen, 1977) and performance analysis (cf. Kahneman, 1973) have adopted these constructs. Ability or competence can be conceptualized as a repertory of mental and motor skills which remain stable over longer periods of time. This long-term component is to be contrasted with a dynamic process of effort or activation (or psychophysiological arousal) which, due to a trade-off between duration and intensity, is restricted to shorter periods of time. The dimensionality of both the long-term and the short-term components are far from being clarified. Undoubtedly there exists a large variety of technical, social, and epistemic abilities. Activation is, in contrast, treated as a process having a smaller number of dimensions. Physiological data do not give evidence for more than three types of arousal patterns, differentiating between executive behaviour, orienting behaviour, and acceleration of activity (Pribram and McGuinness, 1975). Subjective reports permit the differentiation of two factors designated as wakefulness and emotional involvement (Thayer, 1978). In addition, central (e.g. pulmonary, cardiac) and local factors (e.g. strain in muscles and joints) have to be distinguished (Ekblom and Goldberg, 1971). In total, there may be a few fairly generalized dynamic processes, activating a large number of specific possible behaviour patterns.

In a recent paper Schulz (1980) tries to separate different arousal patterns in a stressing situation, also contrasting conditions of mental and emotional involvement. The present chapter is confined to considering effort or activation as an energizing function allocating resources to ongoing activities and initiating behaviour change (Kahneman, 1973; Simon, 1967). The position is taken that the total amount of competence defines the maximal capacity of a subject, whereas the degree of effort or activation determines the proportion of total competence (or maximal capacity) which is utilized in a given situation. What remains to be clarified is the relation between capacity and effort. In an incremental model capacity is a monotonic function over the whole range of activation; maximal effort activates total capacity (model A). In addition truncated versions (B and C) of the incremental model may be considered: (B) the actual capacity always falls behind the total competence of an individual, because even maximal effort does not suffice in activating full capacity, and (C) the full amount of competence is already activated with

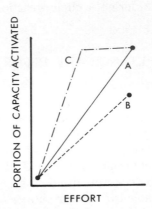

Figure 50. Models relating effort to capacity activated. A—incremental model, B and C —truncated versions of the incremental model. See text for explanation.

medium effort, so that full effort cannot be utilized. Again arguing from the economical point of view, the incremental model (A) is the most economical. The first alternative suffers from unusable spare capacity, the second from the possibility of inefficient use of effort. The three models are depicted in Figure 50.

The notion that capacity in general profits from rises in effort or activation has been controversial. Several authors have pointed out the disorganizing effects of high activation, or rather over-activation. This effect has already been referred to in an earlier section. What has to be added now is the notion of an optimal level of activation shifting to lower values with increasing task difficulty. This notion is commonly called the Yerkes–Dodson Law (Yerkes and Dodson, 1908).

The Yerkes–Dodson Law revisited

From empirical studies there are numerous examples of performance increments with increased effort in physical (e.g. Morgan, 1977) and mental work (Kahneman, 1973). Effort, as defined by subjective ratings or measures of physiological arousal, could also be shown to compensate for the effects of task difficulty (Hillgruber, 1912; Sjöberg *et al.*, 1979), depressing factors like alcohol (Düker, 1963), stressing agents like noise (Frankenhaeuser and Lundberg, 1974; Lundberg and Frankenhaeuser, 1978; Schönpflug and Schäfer, 1962), and fatigue (Warren and Clark, 1937). All these conditions have in common that they put high demands on capacity; thus, increases in effort may be interpreted as mobilizing resources and thereby contributing to coping.

The issue of over-activation appears to be more complex. The thesis of an optimal level of activation intuitively sounds very reasonable, and seems to be backed by anecdotal observations. However, it remains debatable whether the phenomenon could ever be demonstrated convincingly in laboratory situations (de Bonis, 1968; Hamilton, 1976; Näätänen, 1973). It can even be doubted whether researchers until now have really succeeded in inducing states of over-activation experimentally. Possibly, techniques designed to induce heightened activation (such as extra stimulation, air deprivation, or monetary reward) have just diverted the subject's attention (Näätänen, 1973), or have caused some other detrimental side-effects, like masking in noise (Poulton, 1977). Unfortunately, activation has in all relevant studies been inferred as an explanatory construct on the basis of stimulus conditions or performance. If direct physiological and subjective measures of activation were taken, two phenomena could be demonstrated which contradicted the principle of optimal activation as usually employed in the theory of stress:

(1) activation does not invariably rise as a function of stressful conditions, and

(2) performance deficits under stressful conditions are not invariably associated with excessive activation, but rather with signs of deactivation.

An early study demonstrating effects which are paradoxical in the light of the theory of optimal activation was published by Schönpflug and Schäfer (1962). The authors gave a serial learning task to six groups of subjects, varying the intensity of a 1,000 Hz tone between groups, and measured skin conductance as an index of activation. According to the theory of optimal activation they expected a monotonic relation between sound intensity and skin conductance. In addition, the theory predicted an inverted-U-shaped relation between intensity and skin conductance, on the one hand, and performance in the learning task on the other. What they actually found was a monotonic relation between skin conductance and performance, while the function relating the two dependent measures to sound intensity was cubic (Figure 51). Apparently, the variation of sound intensity had effects which cannot be described unidimensionally. When interview data were included, three dimensions could be distinguished.

(1) An arousing effect, dominating at a level of about 55 dbA; this was associated with a facilitation in performance rather than an impairment.

(2) An interfering effect of the sound, dominating at levels of 75–85 dbA; subjects reacted to interference by filtering techniques indicating in their self-reports that they were 'trying not to listen' to the sound.

(3) An effect of compensatory effort; with 95 dbA sound-filtering techniques were not successful, so subjects tried hard to tolerate the sound and to concentrate on the learning task.

In a follow up study (Schönpflug, 1964), physical workload on a bicycle ergometer was varied as an external stressor. Physical work was introduced instead of acoustical stimulation because it was assumed that muscular and

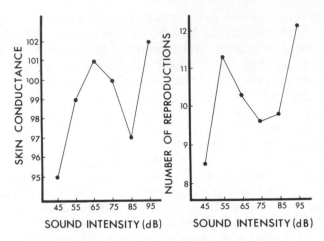

Figure 51. (a) Skin conductance in a learning situation, as a function of sound intensity. (b) Number of correct reproductions as a function of sound intensity. From Schönpflug and Schäfer (1962).

cardiovascular effects could not as easily be filtered out as the sensory effects in the Schönpflug and Schäfer study. There were five different groups, each carrying out a serial learning task, with skin conductance and heart-rate measured as indices of activation. Under conditions of minimal and maximal workload, two additional groups without a learning task were also observed. In this study the arousal effect enhancing both physiological activation and learning performance could be replicated for lower loads. There was no indication of a filtering effect. With learning under high load there was a drop in performance and in skin conductance, while heart-rate showed maximal values. If, however, maximal load was given without a learning task, both heart-rate and skin conductance reached maximal levels. Subjects were thus less variable in their response to physical load than to acoustical stimulation. High physical loads are more detrimental to performance than conditions of high intensity sensory stimulation. Therefore inverted-U-shaped curves relating performance to physical load are more likely, and have indeed been reported quite frequently in the literature (e.g. Lundberg, 1982). However, there are some doubts regarding over-activation as a cause for performance depression. Clearly, the two indices of activation diverge. Whereas heart-rate invariably rises with load, skin conductance is depressed under conditions of high load and learning, but not under high load without learning. The interpretation given in the study suggests that heart-rate is largely a function of physical expenditure and is not readily accessible to internal regulation. Skin conductance, on the other hand, is more a function of mental involvement, so can be controlled if it reaches excessive levels.

Effort regulation and fatigue

The idea of an internal regulation of activation or effort can be seen to be useful in considering the above-mentioned studies from the Berlin laboratory. In the first of these studies (Schulz and Schönpflug, 1982, study I), variation of traffic noises was shown to have considerable effects on behavior. With an increase in noise intensity the error-rate increased, and so did inefficiency. The number of operations rose until an intermediate noise level was reached, and then dropped (Figure 52a). The drop in the number of operations under high

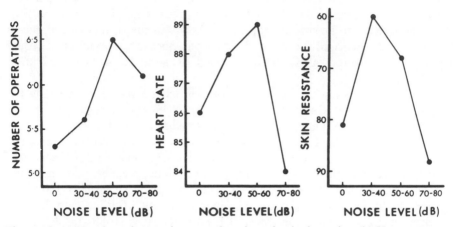

Figure 52. (a) Number of operations as a function of noise intensity. (b) Heart-rate as a function of noise intensity. (c) Skin resistance as a function of noise intensity. From Schulz and Schönpflug (1981, study I).

noise correlated well with a tendency for risky decisions. When heart-rate and skin conductance were measured as indices of activation they were related to an inverted-U-shaped fashion with noise intensity, as was the number of operations (Figures 52b,c). For these phenomena a consistent interpretation can be given referring to effort regulation as a mediating process. Compensatory activity in response to a mild increment in demand is mediated by an upward shift of effort, intentionally adjusting the actual capacity to the existing demands. Under the conditions of the study in question, however, high intensity noise provided a load which the subjects did not try to cope with by a further rise in effort. Under these conditions, they adopted a strategy of reducing their commitment to the task and conserving effort; thus, downward shifts of effort seem to mediate the reduction in coping activity.

As has been reported by Karasek (1979), highly efficient individuals can sustain high degrees of strain for extended periods of time and even seem to enjoy it. On the other hand, each model of stress should make provisions for the possibility that any individual may resign from a task if load becomes excessive. The theoretical problem is to define the conditions under which an individual will shift from a state of increased effort to one of effort reduction. One variable to be considered is obviously competence. In the other study of the Berlin series where data from individuals varying in the frequency of errors were presented (Figure 49), degree of activity can possibly be explained by effort regulation. High competence subjects may have been characterized by a higher effort increment with intermediate load, and they did not exhibit signs of effort reduction except at the most intense level of noise. Low competence individuals, on the other hand, may already have reduced their effort with the intermediate noise level. In general, maximal effort is to be expected with intermediate difficulty for the individual (Meyer and Hallermann, 1974). Another variable to be considered, especially within the framework of action theory, is the salience of the result of an action; more effort should be devoted to highly important tasks, or those used as a basis for self-evaluation (Heckhausen, 1977).

'Decline in the subject's desire to make himself do the task especially for long periods of time' (Carmichael *et al.*, 1949, p.696) and 'degradation of will' (Bornemann, 1956/57) have already been offered as descriptions of the nature of fatigue. These may be seen as clearly analogous to the recently favoured concepts of effort or activation. In addition, risky shifts have been observed in states of fatigue (Brown *et al.*, 1970). In fatigue, negligence concerning performance seems to be correlated with loss of effort. This has been demonstrated experimentally quite convincingly by Holding and his co-workers, using what they call the COPE paradigm (see Holding, Chapter 6, this volume). They gave subjects the choice between high effort activities yielding a high probability of success and low effort–low probability activities. With fatigue from previous mental work their subjects shifted to the low effort–low probability strategy (Shingledecker and Holding, 1974; Barth *et al.*, 1976). There is also, however, evidence for a compensation of fatigue by increments of effort (Bornemann, 1956/57; Cameron, 1973).

Thus, the same principle of effort regulation seems to operate in stress and in fatigue. If the demand–capacity ratio becomes unfavourable, due either to increasing demands in stressing situations or to reduced capacity in states of fatigue, effort may be raised in order to enhance capacity. This process of upward regulation is designed to restore a more favourable balance of capacity to demands, though downward shifts are also possible in effort regulation. There are two explanations for downward shifts: (1) lack of efficiency despite initially increased effort; in this case effort is reduced in order to adjust activity in relation to achievement, and (2) high psychological costs of effort; there is evidence that effort constitutes a major source of psychological costs, and that saving of effort becomes a potent principle in human life. This point will be resumed in the next section.

A demand/capacity interpretation of the Yerkes–Dodson Law

These results permit entirely new interpretations of the Yerkes–Dodson relationship:

(1) Performance is related to demands in an inverted-U-shaped fashion.

(2) The vertex of the function marks the point where demands and competence or total capacity are at balance.

(3) Up to this point increments of effort or activation can be effective in raising capacity and improving performance, as expressed in the left-hand side of the curve.

(4) Propositions (2) and (3) are valid only if costs of effort are not prohibitive to the individual; under the motive of effort-saving the vertex of the function will correspond to lower values than the subject's competence or maximal capacity.

(5) The more demands exceed the balance point the lower performance will be; this is the explanation for the drop in performance as illustrated in the right-hand side of the curve.

(6) Even under conditions of demands exceeding capacity, effort or activation may be continued or even increased.

(7) Since effort causes costs and does not grant benefits it is more likely that effort or activation will drop with increasing demands.

From propositions (6) and (7) follows the conclusion that a curvilinear relation between activation and performance may occur, but only in a few instances and for short periods of time. The regular case should be a linear correlation between performance and activation; such a correlation can be interpreted as the result of the economical adjustment of resources to output.

REGULATION OF DEMANDS AND COMPETENCE

Other strategies of matching demands and capacity are changes in aspiration level and in competence. Enhancement of demands due to stressing conditions, and impairment of capacity due to fatigue, can be compensated for by subjective reduction of aspirations and by augmentation of competence.

Changes in aspiration level

From a more intuitive perspective, the method of problem devaluation and of goal reduction has already been advocated by Ellis (1978). His rational-emotive therapy is designed to liberate us from the 'tyranny of shoulds' (Horney, 1965), and supposedly removes stress by negation of stressors. Indeed, explicit downward shifts in aspiration level have been observed in a recent study by Krenauer (Krenauer and Schönpflug, 1980). In this study high-school students were given three series of pattern recognition tasks. During the

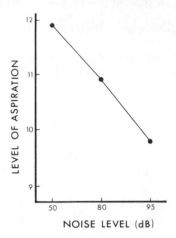

Figure 53. Level of aspiration as a function of noise intensity. From Krenauer and Schönpflug (1980).

series there were quiet conditions or traffic noise of 80 or 95 dB. The subjects heard demonstrations of the noise at the beginning of the experiment, and had each sound level once in the experiment for the duration of a whole series. Before each series, the sound level was announced, and the subject had to state the minimal score aspired to. Knowledge of noise level to be introduced could be shown to reduce aspiration level (Figure 53). When the causes of hits and failures were analysed after each recognition test, subjects attributed failures predominantly to noise and hits predominantly to effort. Downward shifts of aspiration may not only refer to quantitative aspects of performance as in Krenauer's study but also to qualitative aspects. Thus, a variety of investigations report qualitative changes in attention and performance under stress which can be interpreted as aspiration shifts. In monitoring tasks attention narrows to the location of the signals with the highest probabilities (Hockey, 1970); in running memory recent items are preferred to earlier ones (Hamilton *et al.*, 1977), and in more complex mental tasks executive operations (e.g. calculating sums) are reduced as compared to routine monitoring, such as checks of the validity of prices (Schulz and Battmann, 1980). Neglect of peripheral signals becomes more pronounced with prolonged stress, as well as with periods of sustained mental work (e.g. Bursill, 1958; Davies and Tune, 1970). It may be argued that broadly similar changes in the mapping of behaviour do occur under conditions attributed to fatigue and those of stress.

It should be noted that goal reduction facilitates performance but at the same time degrades achievement. This case has to be contrasted with the phenomenon of achievement degradation caused by actual interference. Adequate downward shifts of aspiration due to the anticipation of interference saves the psychological costs of dealing with actual interference effects. It thereby avoids stressful experiences which may become the result of unrealistic goal setting (Reykowski, 1972).

Changes in competence

The second strategy to be treated is that of upgrading competence and capacity by learning. Such a strategy has already been recommended by Meichenbaum and Novaco (1978). A special training of coping skills is included in their stress inoculation program. Even pure exposure to a stressor may be effective in adjustment to a stressor (Vossel and Laux, 1978). Training also seems to prevent effects of fatigue (Schmidtke, 1965; Hacker *et al.*, 1978).

Learning, however, cannot be treated as a mediator of adjustment to adverse conditions, only. Lack of learning or acquisition of inadequate habits and emotional reactions can also account for maladjustment and thereby produce conditions of stress and fatigue (Beech, 1978).

Psychological costs

Psychological costs include:
  (1) the loss of physical and mental health,
  (2) exhaustion of internal energy resources, and
  (3) exhaustion of external resources.

Loss of physical and mental health will commonly relate to decrements of competence (e.g. mental impairment, physical disadvantage). Exhaustion of internal energy resources will show up in difficulties of maintaining or raising effort. External resources mainly refer to technical and social aids which may contribute to coping and thus diminish individual task demands (e.g. Burke and Weir, 1978). All active modes of coping can result in any of these three types of costs. Inactive problem orientation can be assumed to consume internal energy as well, and may even endanger physical and mental health (cf. Lundberg, 1982; Shapiro, 1978).

From both the transactional and the behaviour economic points of view, these three types of costs should be made more explicit in future theories of stress and fatigue. From the transactional point of view, interactions with the environment contributing to costs should be further specified and incorporated in general psychological theories (e.g. inadequate coping resulting in accidents). Costs like loss of health, internal and external resources, constitute new problems for the individuals involved; their existence sets demands of rehabilitation and recovery (Wieland and Schönpflug, 1980). Although all types of costs mentioned deserve a more detailed treatment, the rest of this section will exclusively deal with energetic costs. They appear to represent the most general phenomenon, and are directly related to both stress and fatigue. A comparison of the competence and the effort component of capacity leads to the conclusion that neither the availability of a long-term repertory of skills nor its utilization *per se* constitute psychological costs, since skills are improved rather than impaired by frequent use. What should be regarded instead as the origin of coping costs is the expenditure of effort. Effort can be hypothesized to derive from an internal energy pool, and there is already some evidence of the biochemical basis of this energy pool (Schmidtke, 1965). Consumption from the pool can only be replaced after a time lag. The organism can be conceptualized as an economic system with limited energy resources and individuals seem to behave like many other such systems rationing energy by (a) saving effort in general, (b) calculating the pay-off between effort and outcomes, and (c) distributing effort over time. Clearly, problem orientation and coping attempts are associated with effort increments; therefore stress situations can be regarded as high cost situations. Where there are high costs and limited resources, there will also occur a state of exhaustion. Fatigue should be characterized as such a state, and therefore Cameron (1973) should receive support for his general contention that fatigue follows stress. Since a state of exhaustion in general does not match with internal needs for recreation, internal demands deriving from stress and fatigue will contribute to the states of self-concern described in an earlier section as a characteristic feature of stress.

Distributing effort expenditure over time becomes a major task in behaviour regulation. This point will be further clarified in two central issues, termination of problem orientation by effective coping and effort increment during fatigue. Problem orientation (e.g. worries, thoughts about help, etc.) may consume considerable amounts of energy, and it does so for unlimited time, as long as the problem continues. Control attempts may produce high costs, possibly higher than those involved in orientation. From a short time perspective, control activity does not pay off. If, however, control activity becomes effective within a short period of time, the costs of continued problem orientation may be outbalanced (see Table 5, p.305). Likewise, it may become economical to raise effort expenditure in a state of fatigue. Although fatigue has been described above as a state of exhaustion in which energy savings are required in general, a short-term increase of effort may be worthwhile if it is effective in dissipating the stressing and fatiguing conditions operating on a long-term basis. In this case, but only in this case, when fatigue sets demands for activity it can be treated as a stressor, as already has been done in the literature (Frankenhaeuser, 1975; McGrath, 1976).

A model of regulatory activity should also assign psychological costs to the four modes of regulation described in the preceeding sections:

(1) coping attempts by problem orientation and control activity,
(2) reduction of activity as a result of inefficiency,

(3) shifts in aspiration level, and

(4) increments of competence by learning.

Problem orientation and control will continuously go along with effort expenditure; type and amount of expenditure will depend on specific demands and capacities, and the search for the most economical coping strategy (see above) may form a major decision task. This task will, in all non-routine situations, augment the actual demands and, although being instrumental in terminating stress and fatigue, will be likely to both enhance these states and suffer from them itself (cf. Janis and Mann, 1977). Reduction of activity will avoid the effort associated with the selection and execution of coping behaviour. Shifts in aspiration level *per se* may be neutral in regard to costs, but since demands for coping follow subjective aspirations, upward shifts can be assumed to raise subsequent costs and downward shifts to decrease them.

Balancing of profits and costs in behaviour regulation will carefully need to include the costs of problems not coped with, i.e. the cost of continued problem orientation. Restraint from effective coping will only sufficiently succeed in saving effort if it is accompanied by adequate downward shifts in aspiration and in problem orientation in general. High concern for problems associated with a strategy of coping avoidance should form an experience of discrepancy which may turn out to be a source of stress in itself.

The role of learning

Another conflicting issue seems to be the increase of competence by learning. On the one hand, learning improves total capacity, and thereby helps to save effort. With increased total capacity both strategy selection and executive control are facilitated and abbreviated. Thus, in the long run, energy consumption is lowered. On the other hand, learning itself requires effort. This is documented by subjective reports and physiological data (Andreassi, 1966; Jennings and Hall, 1980; Schönpflug, 1963). For the individuals involved the question will arise as to whether immediate learning effort will pay off in the long run. The basic motivation for learning may be high in crisis and stress situations. But still there are two reasons for questioning its value in states of stress:

(a) learning may proceed too slowly to become effective in the current stress situation, and

(b) learning requirements may impose subsidiary tasks on an individual which are avoided because of their load.

The ambivalent impact of learning during states of stress has been demonstrated recently in a study by Schulz (1981). In a new version of his experimental design described above, subjects again had to make decisions on the basis of several pieces of information. The information had to be selected from a set of 15 items. In addition, a survey list was available presenting the content of each item and the position from which the item could be obtained. The subjects could expose both the survey list and the single item on a screen by pressing keys on the board (e.g. for the task 'checking of bills' the survey read: for 'list of orders'—press key 1; for 'price-list'—press key 2, etc.). Blocks of ten successive tasks were constant in type, and the same survey list could be used. Thus, subjects could save time and operations if they memorized the survey list instead of exposing it frequently, and this is what the subjects actually did. However, under 70 dbA noise this learning was significantly retarded in comparison with quiet conditions (Figure 54a). As a result of memorizing, more relevant information was called for without prior consultation of the survey list. Figure 54b presents the number of free calls, i.e. the calls for relevant information which were not immediately preceded by observation of the survey list. Subjects under noise made less free calls, so that they had to execute more operations in order to obtain the same amount of information as the subjects working under quiet conditions. Under the assumption that memorization of the survey at the beginning of each block is less demanding in the long run than frequent repetitions of the list, subjects under noise were engaging in a style of work which has to be classified as uneconomical. The failures of learning seem to affect performance at the end of each block in a special way. The number of calls exhibits a downward trend for both conditions. Since this downward trend affects mainly the search for specific information (and not calls for the survey list), subjects working under noise are more likely to be basing their decisions on minimal information (i.e. making risky decisions).

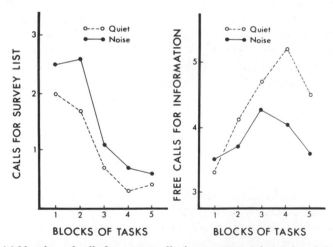

Figure 54. (a) Number of calls for a survey list in ten consecutive tasks of the same type, under noisy and quiet conditions. (b) Number of free calls for information (not immediately preceded by inspection of survey list) in ten consecutive tasks of the same type, under noisy and quiet conditions. From Schulz (1981).

Not only do Schulz's data demonstrate impairment of learning under stressful conditions (as do many other experiments) but they also illustrate the contribution of learning deficits to the state of stress. Still stronger effects may be expected if inadequate skills and strategies are acquired under stress (Beech, 1978), and costs of learning effort combine with costs of inefficient coping attempts and problem generation.

What seems to be true for stress may also hold for fatigue. If routine prevents stress it should also prevent fatigue as a consequence of stress. However, as was shown above, states of stress themselves seem to be adverse to efficient learning, and so are states of fatigue (cf. Monk *et al.*, 1978). Under these conditions, only preventative learning as advocated by Meichenbaum and Novaco (1978) offers the chance of being effective and economical. If routines and skills for handling situations of stress and fatigue cannot be acquired on actual demand, they can only be obtained in advance in situations of relaxation and alertness.

A model of regulatory behaviour

Different modes of regulation can be assumed to operate simultaneously and in combination. Benefits and costs for each mode will have to be calculated (a) separately, (b) in combination with other modes, (c) with reference to external and internal conditions, (d) for short periods of time, especially in their presence, and (e) for more extended periods of time. Calculations of this sort should yield parameters for a trade-off between different modes of regulation and different combinations of modes. On the basis of these parameters behaviour regulation may take place. Effective regulation will lead to minimizing costs; poor regulation towards maximizing them. Figure 55 presents the general model underlying the above propositions. Included in the

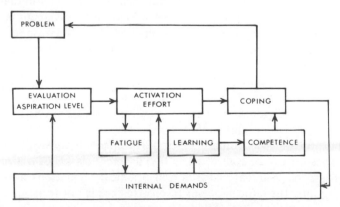

Figure 55. Model of a regulatory system operating towards maximizing or minimizing of costs. See text for details.

figure are the components of the described regulatory system and the interactions between the components emphasized in this Chapter. For the sake of simplicity the system is described in the text as adequately operating towards the minimization of costs. Demands for activity stimulation or release of excessive energy (e.g. Zuckerman, 1979) have not been considered as relevant for situations of stress and fatigue.

Within the proposed model, decreased problem orientation and problem evaluation, adequate coping, and lack of inadequate coping are assumed to be regulatory acts preventing and reducing stress and fatigue. By reversal of regulatory acts the possibilities of non-regulation leading to stress and fatigue are obtained: (a) prolonged problem orientation without attempting at coping (lack of control activity), (b) high appraisal of the problem in cases of high costs of coping (failure in problem devaluation), and (c) extension of coping (including learning) despite prolonged inefficiency (failure in deactivation).

BROADER ISSUES

Macrostressors and microstressors

In the light of the theoretical model outlined above, objective stressing agents have no direct impact on subjective experience and behaviour. Their effects are mediated and modified by internal processes of problem concern. Therefore, according to the model, stress effects are not predictable from the objective characteristics of the stressing agents only. Instead, a large variation in stress reactions between and within individuals has to be assumed. The variation may refer to the nature of stress responses (e.g. compensatory activity versus deactivation) as well as to intensity and duration. Correlations between objective features of stress situations and stress responses should, however, not completely be denied. Conditions of extreme stimulation and high personal challenge like heat, heavy work load, or involvement in combat, will rarely fail to evoke distinct reactions. Mild stimulation and minor impositions like the sound of dripping water, car break-downs, or personal quarrels will less regularly induce stress. Nevertheless, there are remarkable exceptions. Some individuals remain virtually unaffected in situations to which a large proportion of the population reacts as being stressful. On the other hand, some individuals may suffer tremendously from causes which the vast majority regard as insignificant.

For the purpose of easier communication, high probability stressors and low probability stressors can be contrasted as two different classes of *macrostressors* and *microstressors*. Whereas research and practical regulations have centred on macrostressors, the importance of microstressors is not to be under-rated. There is reason to believe that while macrostressors are gradually eliminated in civilized countries, stressful experiences from microstressors expand and gain practical importance. There may be a conspicuous analogy between the spread of stress and the spread of depression as described by McLean (1976). In analysing current trends of increasing depression in Western civilization, McLean points out that the proportion of 'classical' origins of depression (loss of spouse, unemployment, etc.) are receding, whereas the proportion of other causes, being evaluated from non-patients as minor mischiefs, rises. In this context, McLean has already introduced the term 'microstressor'.

The hypothesis should be considered that stress in modern life is induced by a variety of microstressors rather than a small number of single macrostressors. Documenting the frequency of microstressors in everyday life should form an important research task. An example is a recent survey about complaints on noise (Guski, 1976). In three environmental agencies where complaints were registered a considerable number of calls referred to low intensity emissions, which may appear to non-involved persons as normal occurrences in everyday life (e.g. noise from exhausts or from children playing).

A twentieth-century perspective on stress

Under the assumption that the reaction to microstressors is a typical phenomenon of maladjustment in modern civilization, the assessment of stressing incidences and stress responses in earlier periods becomes a challenging problem. Unfortunately, assessment of historical data which are psychologically valid is very difficult. Brunke, Sange, and Treziak (1978) have explored the feasibility of two methods: (a) content-analysis of newspaper reports, and (b) interviews with senior citizens ranging in age between 75 and 92 years. They inquired about sources of stress and reactions to stress since 1900, restricting themselves to a suburb of Berlin, and omitting the events related to the First and Second World Wars (e.g. air raids, reconstruction after the Second World War). Although their results are not far above the anecdotal level, three trends in their data deserve further attention.

(1) Reports on stressing agents increase in number since 1900. The increase in the quantity of stressing events goes along with changes in quality. Some stressors have only recently entered the stage (e.g. aircraft noise), whereas others have gradually disappeared (e.g. obligations of teenage girls to rear their infant brothers and sisters).

(2) Acquisition of new technologies permits more effective control of some types of stressor (e.g. birth-control devices, methods for increasing work productivity). But there is also evidence for a loss of social and technical skills which makes individuals more susceptible for some stressing conditions (e.g. allocation rules in private homes have become less rigid, which seems to encourage conflicts between persons sharing the same room).

(3) Evaluation of stressors follows the change of coping capacities. If coping capacity increases, potential sources of stress are rated as less severe (e.g. the prospect of unwanted parenthood is regarded as a minor factor due to the acquisition of effective birth-control techniques), whereas a loss of coping capacity goes along with higher ratings of stressfulness (e.g. lower class seniors describe the living conditions of their grandchildren as unpleasant if they have to share a room, whereas they regard the same, or even more uncomfortable, living conditions during their own childhood as neutral).

In group discussions with seniors it remained a controversial issue whether the total amount of stress has been growing from their childhood to higher age. 'Life is much easier now', was a statement with which almost all of the interviewees agreed. But there was also support for the statement: 'We were unhappy, sometimes, but we were more content than people are nowadays.'

Statements like 'Life used to be harder', in juxtaposition with the statement 'We were more content', may be related beyond the individual lives studied to the development of civilization in general. This may reflect the fact that (at least middle and lower class) people were living in a more stable environment, which offered a smaller number of stressors but a higher proportion of more severe occurrences of stress. The stability of the environment permitted a higher prediction rate, and also improved chances for developing coping skills. In contrast, modern life may be characterized by a higher number of potential stressors, giving less opportunity for adjustment and prediction. Due to improved health service, environmental protection programs, social service, etc. the proportion of severe stressors has, evidently, been cut down considerably, thus permitting mild stressors to attract attention.

Thus, microstressors *per se* may gain importance for four reasons:

(1) They all compete for high ranks of evaluation.

(2) As the absolute level of evaluation may remain low, there is less motivation for coping effort.

(3) Since stressors are not always predictable, there are no immediate coping strategies available.

(4) With a high rank (though not necessarily an absolutely high rating) in evaluation and a lack of both coping effort and strategy, persistence of the stressor and prolonged orientation on the stressor occurs.

Multiple stressors

These four reasons could already account for the experience of inefficiency and for a state of stressful self-concern as a result of this experience. There is, however, still another issue to be emphasized: with low demands and a high competition for priorities, microstressors serve as multiple problems. They pose a set of problems to be handled simultaneously.

The total stress induced by multiple problems should be determined by (a) the individual demands of single stressors, (b) the number of separate problems, and (c) the compatability of problems. These variables are already known from dual task studies (e.g. Bornemann, 1959; McLeod and Mierop, 1979). The analogy to the multiple task situation elucidates the difference between macrostressors and microstressors. It can be argued that macrostressors normally function as single agents, due to their difficulty. In contrast, microstressors operate by (a) accumulation of single problem demands, (b) basic co-ordinative demands, and (c) inflated co-ordinative demands due to incompatability of simultaneous coping procedures. In order to outbalance these demands, special skills of co-ordination and time sharing are required.

Concern for and coping with multiple demands constitutes rather complex activity patterns, and an elaborated theory of action should both aid in the analysis of these processes and profit from this analysis. The confrontation with different goals at the same time is also an issue to be looked at from the behaviour economic perspective. What are the benefits of dealing with several objectives simultaneously? What are the costs of simultaneous handling? How could costs and benefits change if the objectives were pursued in succession? What would be the advantages and disadvantages of different sequences? These may be difficult questions, and answers to these questions will include intricate decision-making.

FINAL REMARKS

A situation with a multiplicity of demands calls for a variety of detailed competences, for managerial skills, and eventually risky decision-making. Especially if real time needs are involved, it should be hard to avoid inadequate orientation and control. In such a situation, stress is almost inevitable. However, to find oneself in such a situation may not always be inevitable. Prospective planning, clear priority of decisions, and wise renunciation of goals of low priority may help to prevent multi-demand situations (Hacker *et al.*, 1978). Lack of prospective planning, inability in setting priorities, and blind fixation to various incentives may, in contrast, serve as the *via regia* to the creation of an entangling stress situation, finally also leading to fatigue. This, at least, is one of the lessons taught by the theory of action and its good companion, the theory of behaviour economics.

SUMMARY

Stress is analysed from transactional perspective as a state of inefficiency. It is characterized by (a) deficiencies in the control of a problem situation, (b) compensatory activity, (c) generation of new problems, (d) increased self-concern, and (e) continuous problem orientation. Two ways for the termination of stressful transactions are described: (a) effective coping with internal and external demands, and (b) limitation of coping attempts (eventually complete resignation).

Utility of coping attempts and of reductions in problem concern are evaluated as functions of the ratio between demands and capacity. The more the capacity component exceeds the demands the higher is the probability of efficient coping attempts; the more demands outbalance capacities the more likely is a reduction of coping attempts after a period of experienced inefficiency. Behaviour in stress situations is therefore directed towards regulation of the demand/capacity ratio. The ratio can be improved (a) by raising the capacity component (e.g. by the acquisition of a new skill or by increments in effort), or (b) by lowering demands (e.g. by reductions in aspiration level).

The choice of strategy can be explained within a model of behaviour economics. This model considers costs of effective and ineffective coping as well as the costs of non-coping with continued problem orientation. For stress situations, it is conceptualized as operating towards minimizing costs. By analogy to stress, fatigue is treated as state resulting from high energy consumption; in this state both inefficiency and effort-saving behaviour are assumed to dominate. Data from field and laboratory studies are presented which have guided the construction fo the above-mentioned model of behaviour economics.

REFERENCES

Andreassi, J. L. (1966) Some physiological correlates of verbal learning task difficulty. *Psychonomic Science*, **6**, 69–70.

Barth, J. L., Holding, D. H., and Stamford, B. A. (1976) Risk versus effort in the assessment of motor fatigue. *Journal of Motor Behavior*, **8**, 189–194.

Beech, H. R. (1978) Learning: Cause and cure. In C. L. Cooper and R. Payne (eds.), *Stress at Work*. New York: John Wiley & Sons, pp.149–172.

de Bonis, M. (1968) La loi de Yerkes–Dodson: Problèmes méthodologiques liés à sa vérification. *L'Année Psychologique*, **68**, 121–141.

Bornemann, E. (1956/57) Psychologie der Ermüdung. *Psychologie und Praxis*, **1**, 57–69.

Broadbent, D. E. (1954) Some effects of noise on visual performance. *Quarterly Journal of Experimental Psychology*, **6**, 1–5.

Brown, I. D., Tickner, A. H., and Simmons, D. C. (1970) Effect of prolonged driving on overtaking criteria. *Ergonomics*, **13**, 239–242.

Brunke, Ch., Sange, P., and Treziak, M. (1978) Belastungsfaktoren eines Großstadt-lebens. Unpublished thesis, Institut für Psychologie der Freien Universität Berlin.

Burke, R. J. and Weir, T. (1978) Sex differences in adolescent life stress, social support, and well-being. *Journal of Psychology*, **98**, 277–288.

Bursill, A. E. (1958) The restriction of peripheral vision during exposure to hot and humid conditions. *Quarterly Journal of Experimental Psychology*, **10**, 113–129.

Cameron, C. (1973) A theory of fatigue. *Ergonomics*, **16**, 633–648.

Cannon, W. B. (1914) The interrelations of emotions as suggested by recent physiological researches. *American Journal of Psychology*, **25**, 256–282.

Carmichael, L., Kennedy, J. C., and Mead, L. C. (1949) Some recent approaches to the experimental study of human fatigue. *Proceedings of the Academy of Sciences*, **35**, 691 (after Schmidtke, 1965).

Corcoran, D. W. J. (1962) Noise and loss of sleep. *Quarterly Journal of Experimental Psychology*, **14**, 178–182.

Davies, D. R. and Tune, G. S. (1970) *Human Vigilance Performance*. London: Staples.

Düker, H. (1963) Über reaktive Anspannungssteigerung. *Zeitschrift für experimentelle und angewandte Psychologie*, **10**, 46–72.

Ekblom, H. B. and Goldberg, A. N. (1971) The influence of physical training and other factors on the subjective rating of perceived exertion. *Acta Physiologica Scandinavica*, **83**, 399–406.

Ellis, A. (1978) What people can do for themselves to cope with stress. In C. L. Cooper and R. Payne (eds.), *Stress at Work*. New York: John Wiley & Sons, pp.209–222.

Eysenck, M. W. (1979) Anxiety, learning, and memory: A reconceptualization. *Journal of Research in Personality*, **13**, 363–385.

Frankenhaeuser, M. (1975) Experimental approaches to the study of catecholamines and emotion. In L. Levi (ed.), *Emotions—Their Parameters and Measurement*. New York: Raven, pp.209–234.

Frankenhaeuser, M. (1976) The role of peripheral catecholamines in adaptation to understimulation and overstimulation. In G. Serban (ed.), *The Psychopathology of Human Adaptation*. New York: Plenum, pp.173–182.

Frankenhaeuser, M. and Lundberg, U. (1974) Immediate and delayed effects of noise on performance and arousal. *Biological Psychology*, **2**, 127–133.

Getzels, J. W. (1979) Problem finding: A theoretical note. *Cognitive Science*, **3**, 167–172.

Glass, D. C. and Singer, J. E. (1972) *Urban Stress*. New York: Academic Press.

Guski, R. (1976) Eine Inhaltsanalyse von Lärmbeschwerden, die bei 'Umwelt-telephonen' eingehen. *Kampf dem Lärm*, **23**, 119–126.

Hacker, W., Plath, H. E., Richter, P., and Zimmer, K. (1978) Internal representation of task structure and mental load of work: Approaches and methods of assessment. *Ergonomics*, **21**, 187–194.

Hamilton, V. (1976) Cognitive development in the neuroses and schizophrenias. In V. Hamilton and M. D. Vernon (eds.), *The Development of Cognitive Processes*. London: Academic Press, pp.681–731.

Hamilton, P., Hockey, G. R. J., and Rejman, M. (1977) The place of the concept of activation in human processing theory: An integrative approach. In S. Dornič (ed.) *Attention and Performance VI*. Hillsdale: Lawrence Erlbaum, pp.463–486.

Harrison, R. V. (1978) Person–environment fit and job stress. In C. L. Cooper and R. Payne (eds.), *Stress at Work*. New York: John Wiley & Sons, pp.175–205.

Heckhausen, H. (1977) Achievement motivation and its constructs: A cognitive model. *Motivation and Emotion*, **1**, 283–329.

Heckhausen, H. (1982) Task-irrelevant cognitions during an exam: Incidence and effects. In H. W. Krohne and L. Laux (eds.), *Achievement, Stress and Anxiety*. Washington: Hemisphere, pp.247–274.

Hillgruber, A. (1912) Fortlaufende Arbeit und Willensbetätigung. *Untersuchungen zur psychologischen Philosophie*, **1**, Heft 6.

Hockey, G. R. J. (1970) Signal probability and spatial location as possible bases for increased selectivity in noise. *Quarterly Journal of Experimental Psychology*, **22**, 37–42.

Hockey, G. R. J. (1979) Stress and the cognitive components of skilled performance. In V. Hamilton and D. M. Warburton (eds.), *Human Stress and Cognition. An Information Processing Approach*. New York: John Wiley & Sons, pp.141–177.

Holmes, H. and Masuda, M. (1974) Life change and illness susceptibility. In B. S. Dohrenwend and B. P. Dohrenwend (eds.), *Stressful Life Events: Their Nature and Effects*. New York: John Wiley & Sons, pp.45–72.

Horney, K. (1965) *Collected Works*. New York: Norton (after Ellis, 1978).

Janis, I. L. and Mann, L. (1977) *Decision Making: A Psychological Analysis of Conflict, Choice, and Commitment*. New York: Free Press–Macmillan.

Jennings, J. R. and Hall, S. W. (1980) Recall, recognition, and rate: Memory and the heart. *Psychophysiology*, **17**, 37–46.

Kahneman, D. (1973) *Attention and Effort*. Englewood Cliffs: Prentice-Hall.

Karasek, R. A. (1979) A stress management model of job strain. *Administrative Science Quarterly*, **24**, 285–308.

Krenauer, M. and Schönpflug, W. (1980) Regulation und Fehlregulation im Verhalten III. Zielsetzung und Ursachenbeschreibung unter Belastung. *Psychologische Beiträge*, 1980, **22**, 414–431.

Lazarus, R. S. (1966) *Psychological Stress and the Coping Process*. New York: McGraw-Hill.

Lazarus, R. S. and Cohen, J. B. (1978) Environmental stress. In I. Altmann and J. F. Wohlwill (eds.), *Human Behavior and Environment, Vol. 1*. New York: Plenum, pp.89–127.

Lazarus, R. S. and Launier, R. (1978) Stress-related transactions between persons and environment. In L. A. Pervin and M. Lewis (eds.), *Perspectives in Interactional Psychology*. New York: Plenum, pp.287–327.

Lundberg, U. (1982) Psychophysiological aspects of performance and adjustment to stress. In W. Krohne and L. Laux (eds.), *Achievement, Stress and Anxiety*. Washington: Hemisphere, pp.75–91.

Lundberg, U. and Frankenhaeuser, M. (1978) Psychophysiological reactions to noise as modified by personal control over noise intensity. *Biological Psychology*, **6**, 51–59.

McGrath, J. E. (1976) Stress and behavior in organisations. In M. D. Dunette (ed.), *Social and Psychological Factors in Stress*. New York: Holt, Rinehart, and Winston, pp.1351–1395.

McLean, P. D. (1976) Depression as a specific response to stress. In I. G. Sarason and C. D. Spielberger (eds.), *Stress and Anxiety, Vol. III*. New York: John Wiley, pp.297–324.

McLeod, P. and Mierop, J. (1979) How to reduce manual response interference in the multiple task environment. *Ergonomics*, **22**, 469–475.

Meichenbaum, D. (1977) *Cognitive-Behavior Modification: An Integrative Approach*. New York: Plenum.

Meichenbaum, D. and Novaco, R. (1978) Stress inoculation: A preventive approach. In C. D. Spielberger and I. G. Sarason (eds.), *Stress and Anxiety, Vol. V*. Washington: Hemisphere, pp.317–330.

Meyer, W. U. and Hallermann, B. (1974) Anstrengungsintention bei leichten und schweren Aufgaben in Abhängigkeit von der wahrgenommenen eigenen Begabung. *Archiv für Psychologie*, **126**, 85–89.

Monk, T. H., Knauth, P., Folkard, S., and Rutenfranz, J. (1978) Memory based performance measures in studies of shiftwork. *Ergonomics*, **21**, 819–826.

Morgan, W. P. (1977) Perception of effort in selected samples of olympic athletes and soldiers. In G. Borg (ed.), *Physical Work and Effort.* Oxford: Pergamon, pp.267–277.

Näätänen, R. (1973) The inverted U-relationship between activation and performance — A critical review. In S. Kornblum (ed.), *Attention and Performance, Vol IV.* New York: Academic Press, pp.155–174.

Neufeld, R. W. (1976) Evidence of stress as a function of experimentally altered appraisal of stimulus aversiveness and coping adequacy. *Journal of Personality and Social Psychology*, **33**, 632–646.

Newell, A. and Simon, H. A. (1972) *Human Problem Solving.* Englewood Cliffs: Prentice-Hall.

Pervin, L. A. and Lewis, M. (1978) Overview of the internal–external issue. In L. A. Pervin and M. Lewis (eds.), *Perspectives in Interactional Psychology.* New York: Plenum, pp.1–22.

Poulton, E. C. (1977) Continuous intense noise masks auditory feedback and inner speech. *Psychological Bulletin*, **84**, 977–1001.

Pribram, K. H. and McGuinness, D. (1975) Arousal, activation and effort in the control of attention. *Psychological Review*, **82**, 116–149.

Reykowski, J. (1972) Efficiency of self-regulation and tolerance for stress. *Studia Psychologica*, **14**, 294–300.

Sarason, I. G. (1975) Anxiety and self-preoccupation. In I. G. Sarason and C. D. Spielberger, *Stress and anxiety, Vol. II.* Washington: Hemisphere/Wiley, pp.27–44.

Schmidtke, H. (1965) *Die Ermüdung.* Bern: Huber.

Schönpflug, W. (1963) *Über Aktivationsprozesse im Lernversuch.* Frankfurt a.M.: Kramer.

Schönpflug, W. (1964) Retention und Aktivation bei zusätzlicher Beanspruchung durch körperliche Tätigkeit. *Zeitschrift für experimentelle und angewandte Psychologie*, **11**, 130–154.

Schönpflug, W. (1974) Cognitive operations in stress. In J. Linhart (ed.), *Proceedings of the 2nd Prague Conference, Psychology of Human Learning and Problem Solving.* Praha: Univerzita Karlova, pp.213–217.

Schönpflug, W. (1979) Regulation und Fehlregulation im Verhalten I. Verhaltensstruktur, Effizienz und Belastung — theoretische Grundlagen eines Untersuchungsprogramms. *Psychologische Beiträge*, **21**, 174–202.

Schönpflug, W. and Schäfer, M. (1962) Retention und Aktivation bei akustischer Zusatzreizung. *Zeitschrift für experimentelle und angewandte Psychologie*, **9**, 452–464.

Schönpflug, W. and Schulz, P. (1979) *Lärmwirkungen bei Tätigkeiten mit komplexer Informationsverarbeitung.* Forschungsbericht 79-105 01 201. Berlin: Umweltbundesamt.

Schulz, P. (1980) Regulation und Fehlregulation im Verhalten. V. Die wechselseitige Beeinflussung von mentaler und emotionaler Beanspruchung. *Psychologische Beiträge*, **22**, 633–656.

Schulz, P. (1981) Die Beeinträchtigung von Lernprozessen durch Verkehrslärm bei unterschiedlich leistungsfähigen Personen. In A. Schick (ed.), *Akustik zwischen Physik und Psychologie.* Stuttgart: Klett-Cotta, pp.188–192.

Schulz, P. and Battmann, W. (1980) Die Auswirkungen von Verkehrslärm auf verschiedene Tätigkeiten. *Zeitschrift für experimentelle und angewandte Psychologie*, **27**, 592–606.

Schulz, P. and Schönpflug, W. (1982) Regulatory activity during states of stress. In W. Krohne and L. Laux (eds.), *Achievement, Stress and Anxiety.* Washington: Hemisphere, pp.51–73.

Shapiro, A. P. (1978) Behavioral and environmental aspects of hypertension. *Journal of Human Stress*, **4**, 9–17.

Sherrod, D. D., Hage, J. N., Halpern, Ph. L., and Moore, B. S. (1977) Effects of personal causation and perceived control on responses to an aversive environment: The more control, the better. *Journal of Experimental Social Psychology*, **13**, 14–27.

Shingledecker, C. A. and Holding, D. H. (1974) Risk and effort measures of fatigue. *Journal of Motor Behavior*, **6**, 17–25.

Simon, H. A. (1967) Motivational and emotional controls of cognition. *Psychological Review*, **74**, 29–39.

Sjöberg, H., Frankenhaeuser, M., and Bjurstedt, H. (1979) Interactions between heart rate, psychomotor performance and perceived effort during physical work as influenced by beta-adrenergic blockade. *Biological Psychology*, **8**, 31–43.

Sperandio, J.-C. (1978) The regulation of working methods as a function of work load among air-traffic controllers. *Ergonomics*, **21**, 195–202.

Thayer, R. E. (1978) Towards a psychological theory of multidimensional activation (arousal). *Motivation and Emotion*, **2**, 1–34.

Vossel, G. and Laux, L. (1978) The impact of stress experience on heart rate and task performance in the presence of a novel stressor. *Biological Psychology*, **6**, 193–201.

Warren, N. and Clark, B. (1937) Blocking in mental and motor tasks during a 65-hour vigil. *Journal of Experimental Psychology*, **21**, 97–105.

Weiner, B. (1974) *Achievement Motivation and Attribution Theory*. Morristown, N. J.: General Learning Press.

Welford, A. T. (1973) Stress and performance. *Ergonomics*, **16**, 567–580.

Wieland, R. (1981) Lärmwirkungen bei Entspannung und innerhalb des Arbeits-Erholungs-Zyklus. In Schick, A. (ed.), *Akustik zwischen Physik und Psychologie*. Stuttgart: Klett-Cotta, pp.180–187.

Wieland, R. and Schönpflug, W. (1980) Regulation und Fehlregulation im Verhalten. IV. Entspannung bei Angst und Lärmbelastung. *Psychologische Beiträge*, **22**, 521–536.

Wilkinson, R. T. (1963) Interaction of noise with knowledge of results and sleep deprivation. *Journal of Experimental Psychology*, **66**, 332–337.

Yerkes, R. M. and Dodson, J. D. (1908) The relation to the strength of stimulus to the rapidity of habit formation. *Journal of Comparative Neurology and Psychology*, **18**, 459–482.

Zuckerman, M. (1979) *Sensation: Beyond the Optimum Level of Arousal*. Hillsdale, N.J.: Lawrence-Erlbaum.

Chapter 12

The Cognitive Patterning of Stress States

Robert Hockey and Peter Hamilton

The view which we put forward in the present chapter is that the nature of stress effects can only be properly understood by considering the particular patterns of bodily and cognitive changes associated with different stressors as indicators of specific stress states. This view places our approach at the opposite pole from those which assume that the principal effects of stressors are exercised through their influence on a common mechanism, general arousal. Although we would not wish to deny the existence of such a common process we would argue that such a change must be appreciated as part of a whole constellation of changes, differing in detail from one state to the next. General arousal may be an important indicator in some situations, not in others. Thus, instead of focusing on the *similarities* between the performance patterns found under different conditions, our approach primarily examines the *differences* between such patterns. How many different patterns can be discerned? How well do these map onto the unidimensional arousal concept? What kind of theory is demanded by the data when they are expressed in this way? These are some of the more fundamental questions addressed in the present discussion.

At the outset it should be said that our emphasis is largely methodological. Our main concern is for the collection of data of sufficient complexity (breadth of cognitive function) for noise, for sleeplessness, for anxiety, and so on, to provide a useful basis for the development of theory. It is now apparent that stressors affect performance in ways which cannot be fitted comfortably into the simple arousal generalization. This was stated quite clearly even in Broadbent's (1971) analysis of the problem, though it has been convenient to play down these observations. It is now time to take these departures from the simple unidimensional theory seriously, and consider the arousal concept in relation to the detailed data on performance changes resulting from variations in the organismic state. Rather than treat these under a broad label, such as the 'general state' or even 'stress' or 'motivation', let us start by actually *describing the states associated with different environmental conditions*. They may not all turn out to be different but it is likely that they will vary on more than one dimension.

THE STATE ANALYSIS OF STRESS EFFECTS

The concept of state

Our conception of state is based on that adopted in the theory of dynamic systems and intelligent automata (e.g. Arbib, 1972), though our own use of the concept places it more firmly in the sub-set of *biological* systems (Bunge, 1980). Furthermore, our emphasis is on *mental* states (or *cognitive* states), rather than states of the whole organism, although this is a necessary simplification for the present. Any complex system may be envisaged as existing at a given point in time in any one of a (potentially infinite) number of states. The state space is defined as the set of all states the system can be in, and is represented by an *n*-dimensional array made up of the functional ranges for each property of the system. A particular state is defined as a point in this space, the resultant pattern associated with these system vectors. In practice the number of properties (indicator variables) is kept fairly low, so that only variables thought to be important in determining the system's behaviour are considered. Secondly, in any dynamic system the state space will be in constant flux. It is unlikely to be either valuable or possible to consider states which endure only briefly. In our analysis of the cognitive state, and the way in which it changes with environmental conditions, we shall consider only five main indicators, and concentrate on stressors which produce relatively sustained changes in state.

This kind of approach has been used successfully in the analysis of *behavioural states* in the young infant (e.g. Prechtl, 1974). The behaviour can be described in terms of constellations of observable indicators (eyes open or closed, respiration, presence of movements, etc.) which occur together as well-defined patterns. According to these criteria, Prechtl shows that five states can be determined, and may be represented by vectors on each of the indicator variables observed, as in Table 6. As he points out, the use of a greater number of indicators would not make the definition of each state easier, but rather would lead to the identification of other states, i.e. a more fine-grained classification. Furthermore, only patterns existing for a reasonable period of time are identified. The main point is that each state can only be described by a unique combination of vectors in the four-dimensional space (in this case) defined by the values for each of the system indicators considered. It is, of course, tempting to attach labels to states, and those in Table 6 may be seen as

Table 6. The patterns of behavioural states observed in the neonate. From Prechtl (1974).

State	Eyes open	Respiration regular	Gross movements	Vocalization
(1)	− 1	+ 1	− 1	− 1
(2)	− 1	− 1	− 1	− 1
(3)	+ 1	+ 1	− 1	− 1
(4)	+ 1	− 1	+ 1	− 1
(5)	0	− 1	+ 1	+ 1

corresponding roughly to increasing *levels of arousal*. They could be labelled sleep, drowsiness, alert inactivity, alert activity, crying, in ascending numerical order. On this basis, one could consider states to correspond to *bands* of relatively stable activity levels in the arousal continuum. This is misleading, however, since detailed analysis illustrates the qualitative distinctiveness of these states, and the state-specific dependency which characterizes responsiveness to stimulus events. We shall return to the problem of the explanatory status of the state concept towards the end of this chapter. Our adoption of the approach for analysing effects of stressors on performance is encouraged by the observation that changes in performance cannot easily be described in terms of general increments or decrements in level of competence, and furthermore, that many inconsistencies emerge from an attempt to map all these effects onto a single dimension of arousal. Rather, various stressors appear to affect behaviour in distinctive ways, as indexed by the direction and extent of changes in various common measures of task performance.

In translating the analysis of Table 6 into the current area we are faced with a number of problems, both of theory and of method.

The measurement of cognitive state

What do we mean by the term 'state' in the domain of human performance? What are the appropriate indicators for defining a state? Clearly, we cannot demonstrate the same kinds of spontaneous activity as those studied by Prechtl and his colleagues. The appropriate level for our purposes is that of the mental function. We would argue that the cognitive state is indicated by the pattern of cognitive behaviour demonstrated in the pursuit of criterion task demands. The adequacy of the system's response in producing behaviour appropriate to the short-term goals of laboratory tasks can be taken to reflect, reasonably well, the values of the mental functions represented in the present state of the system. Changes in the relative success in dealing with component goals of the task in the presence of a particular stressor may be assumed to reflect the cognitive pattern associated with the noise state, or with the incentive state, and so on. The balance of mental functions at any point in time is referred to as the *mental state* (or *cognitive state*), while the term *resource state* may be used when specific mental functions are implicated.

The indicators adopted in the infant behaviour studies are those which are readily observable through the use of non-invasive techniques (observation, EEG monitoring, etc.). How can we select appropriate measures for the analysis of mental states? To a certain extent our selection has to be arbitrary since no adequate taxonomy of mental behaviour exists, beyond the long-held distinction between emotion and reason. Within the more restricted area of cognitive activity there is almost nothing to build on, though it is now clear that the conception of capacity as an undifferentiated pool of general-purpose units may no longer adequately handle the data from divided attention and multiple component tasks (Allport, 1980). The question of what are the main functions of cognitive activity, or how many separate resources we have at our disposal, has been left traditionally to psychometrics. The emphasis in human performance has, instead, been on the integrated information-processing system (e.g. Broadbent, 1958; Welford, 1968). Even recent information processing analyses of resources such as that of Wickens (in press) appear to rely heavily in conception on psychometric models of the structure of intelligence, employing dimensions of encoding, response mode, and so on. The question is essentially a biological one, having its roots in the localization of brain function. Although anatomical considerations may well turn out to have greater importance for cognitive theory than is currently supposed (e.g. Kinsbourne, 1981), it is not necessary to think beyond the level of sub-systems capable of separate functional operation, or the degree of independence between functionally distinct components of information-processing models.

The question is one which deserves serious consideration. For the moment it is sufficient to assume that criteria do exist for selecting performance measures as the basis for inferring mental states. The set of indicators is purposively kept quite small in number (four or five) in order to prevent the inevitable increase in the number of states that may be discerned. Performance as a function of stress may then, by analogy with Table 6, be expressed as a set of vectors (or indicator profiles). We consider these issues in greater detail later in the chapter. The problem with such an approach is that mental criteria, unlike those used by Prechtl, are not all or none. Typically, response speed may be slightly greater, or STM recall marginally lower. Furthermore, both the effects of different stressors on the same indicator, and those of the same stressor on different indicators, are logically incommensurate. How can we make the statement that reaction time is increased by sleep deprivation, but not by prolonged work, when the comparison is between one night without sleep and a 1-hour work session? Do these operational forms of the stress manipulation achieve equivalent degrees of change of state? Similarly, can we say that heat affects serial responding more than it does STM? At the very least we assume equal task sensitivity, but at a more fundamental level we cannot compare changes in two different metrics, time and errors. Rabbitt (1979) has pointed out that misunderstandings such as these are quite common. Even more common is the mistake of comparing changes in two different mental functions when they expressed in units having the same name: e.g. a 5 per cent increase in errors in serial responding with a 15 per cent increase in errors in visual search. The only option for a state analysis at the present time is to express changes in indicator variables in purely qualitative terms. This means ignoring the size of effect across different tasks and measures on the one hand, and stress conditions on the other, and coding effects simply in terms of the overall direction of the effect; as a plus ($+$) or a minus ($-$), with the possibility of using zero (0) to indicate the absence of an effect (though not with any confidence, in view of the above problem). We would need to do this even though we may think that some stressors may always produce greater quantitative state changes than others, and even though some measures of cognitive state may always be more susceptible to change than others.

Before moving on to examine the development of theory in the stress literature it should be emphasized that the kinds of changes in cognitive state that we are discussing need not be the result of changes in the hardware of the system (such as reduced rates of information processing or changes in decay characteristics). Although such effects may occur under particular stress states, and thus limit performance of any task requiring that resource, changes may also take the form of a shift in strategy of resource deployment. In the latter case, while there is no reduction in the effectiveness of a particular process, it may nevertheless be employed less in a given state. This would depend on the task demands, as well as on factors influencing the pay-off associated with the component resources, in terms of effort or cost to the system. These points will become clearer below.

AROUSAL AND PERFORMANCE CHANGE

Stress effects as changes in arousal level

It has become usual to think of performance changes under stress as the result of a change in the level of arousal. This view is evident in many of the contributions to this volume, as it is in similar volumes. It probably has its origins in Cannon's (1915) discussion of the unified action of the sympathetic division of the ANS in response to environmental threat, and in Selye's original interpretation of stress (Selye, 1956) as a general state resulting from high levels of stimulation of many different kinds. The subsequent popularity of non-specific motivational processes such as drive, effort, and arousal (activation) in psychological theory has easily accommodated such a view of stress, though the identification of its effects on performance with changes in arousal level is comparatively recent. The first research to be discussed predominantly in such terms was that carried out at the Applied Psychology Unit, Cambridge, England, during the early 1960s (Corcoran, 1962; Broadbent, 1963). Only a few years earlier (e.g. Broadbent, 1958) stressors such as noise had been regarded as distracting the subject, causing failures of selective perception.

The main impetus for the arousal argument came from studies using a number of stressors on the same task of serial responding (the five choice serial reaction test). Not only were there differences in the effects of different stressors, but these appeared to fit into a consistent pattern. Incentives improved performance; noise, heat, and sleep loss made it worse. Incentives, noise, and sleep loss exercised their effects only towards the end of a half-hour work period, while heat did so throughout. What criteria could be used for classifying stressors according to their effects? The answer appeared to come from a number of studies which examined the combined effects of two stressors (Corcoran, 1962; Wilkinson, 1963; Broadbent, 1963). Sleep loss actually *reduced* the size of the impairment found with noise, though both individually impaired performance later in the work period. Incentives reduced the effect of sleep loss in the same way, though in this case the overall effects of the two stressors were opposite. In both cases the two conditions appeared to cancel each other to some degree. Of course, poor performance resulting from sleepiness may well benefit either from a noisy environment, which may serve to keep the subject awake, or from the presence of incentives, which may help to maintain his motivation. Both results are expected from the general arousal theory, though they would also fit several other interpretations. More convincing evidence for the arousal interpretation was provided by Wilkinson's (1963) finding that incentives actually *impaired* the performance of subjects already working in noise. The results of the two incentive studies are also discussed by Eysenck (Chapter 7), and represented graphically in Figures 33 and 34. Taking the findings as a whole, Broadbent (1963) made out a convincing case for the arousal explanation. His argument is illustrated in Figure 56. (1) Subjects normally operate at a level below the supposed optimum for the task. (2) Incentives increase arousal, so bring performance up to the optimum. (3) Sleep loss lowers arousal, and so reduces performance efficiency. (4) Noise increases the level of arousal, but by too much so that subjects are *over*-aroused. The movements along the arousal/performance function induced by interactions of the three stressors are self-explanatory.

This analysis has the advantage that it can account for outcomes of experiments where performance is improved by a stressor, as well as the more usual (or expected) result of reduced efficiency. Although heat impaired serial responding (as well as performance on other tasks) it does not normally interact with either noise (Bell, 1978) or sleep loss (Pepler, 1959). This, coupled with the observation (above) that its effects are present at the beginning of the testing session (unlke the other conditions discussed above), suggests that it

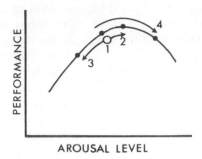

Figure 56. Hypothesized relation between arousal and performance in relation to effects of stressors in sequential choice reaction: (1) is the baseline condition just below the optimum level of arousal. Other numbers refer to the position on the inverted-U function produced by incentives (2), sleep loss (3), and noise (4). Arrows represent movement along the function.

affected a different mechanism and did not fit simply into the arousal picture. We will return to this point later.

For the moment let us acknowledge that the arousal level view of stress has been an enormously influential one. It has generated a number of important research programmes, many of which are discussed in previous chapters, and helped to dispel the clearly short-sighted assumption that, at least as far as human performance is concerned, stress is necessarily a 'bad thing'. On the other hand, we feel that it has been responsible for a considerable amount of uncritical theorizing and ill-founded experimental work. This is no fault of the theory, which was never designed to provide an explanation for *all* effects of stress, but rather an over-simplistic interpretation of its explanatory power and a failure to develop it in the light of ensuing results. Let us consider some of the problems of the simple theory.

Problems with the Yerkes–Dodson Law

The particular application of arousal theory referred to above is usually known as 'the inverted-U hypothesis'. It is a part of the more general relation between motivation and performance originally demonstrated in a study of discrimination learning in mice by Yerkes and Dodson (1908), and come to be called the Yerkes–Dodson Law. In this more general version the difficulty of the task is also a variable, so that it may be expressed in two parts:

(1) There is an optimum level of arousal for performance of any task, and
(2) The optimum is lower for more difficult tasks.

Despite the claims for empirical support for these generalizations (Broadhurst, 1959; Duffy, 1962) it is probably fair to say that neither statement has received unambiguous direct support from the manipulation of arousal within a single study. Freeman (1938) did find the expected curvilinear relationship by inducing physiological arousal through muscle tension, while Stennett (1957) demonstrated a similar relationship of performance with naturally-occurring changes in GSR. Generally speaking, however, the reason for the durability of the Yerkes–Dodson Law lies in its 'commonsense' appeal. While there is general support for the positive limb of the relationship, the detrimental effects of 'over-arousal' have been *assumed* rather than shown to occur by the results of experiment. It seems obvious to us all that while a little motivation will clearly improve our efficiency, one can be 'too keyed-up' or 'not relaxed enough' for some jobs. As with most beliefs of this kind there is probably some basis for such statements, but just what form would an explanation take. Näätänen (1973) has argued that the decrement in performance (sometimes) observed with high arousal may be attributable to the distracting effects of arousal-inducing tasks (e.g. Freeman's induced muscle tension), secondary anxiety effects, and the like. It is this inappropriate *patterning* of activation, rather than the high *level*, which is responsible for the downturn in performance. Even less directly studied is the second part of the hypothesis. Apart from the original demonstration, the evidence for a negative correlation between the point of optimum arousal and the difficulty of the task has been remarkably indirect: again it has a commonsense appeal. Surely a higher level of arousal is needed to run 100 metres in the Olympic final than to play chess against a grand master. One must agree that it seems unlikely that one could be *too* 'keyed up' for the former, while successful, chronically over-excited world chess champions are few and far between. While accepting this evidence from subjective experience we must nevertheless be careful to ask why this should be so (or, at least, why it appears to be so).

One analysis which attempts to provide a basis for these observations is that of Easterbrook (1959), based on a review of studies on the effects of emotional arousal on perceptual organization. The general form of the inverted-U function is said to result from an increasing reduction in the processing of environmental information as arousal level increases, starting with peripheral or secondary sources, then eventually restricting the use of even primary task information. Performance will clearly rise at first then fall as arousal level rises. More difficult tasks may be described as those in which successful performance depends on the use of information from a larger number of sources, or of a broader attentional strategy, so would clearly be expected to suffer from an increase in arousal at an earlier stage than simpler tasks. This analysis has proved generally successful in recent theoretical developments (Hockey, 1970a; Broadbent, 1971; Kahneman, 1973) and has come to be accepted as *the* 'explanation' of the everyday observations referred to above. What, then, are the problems with such a theory?

The main strength of Easterbrook's hypothesis is that it provides an account of the effects of arousal which are *independent of task performance*. In most studies where the Yerkes–Dodson Law is invoked as an explanatory concept this feature is missing; changes in arousal are inferred from changes in the dependent variable—a circular argument which makes the use of arousal theory entirely superfluous. Easterbrook does at least provide an answer to the question 'What does arousal do?'. It progressively reduces the range of environmental events considered by the cognitive system. In our terms, it produces a monotonic increase in the *selectivity* of attention. There is, in fact, considerable evidence for this conclusion from a number of recent sources (see, for example, Broadbent, 1971; Hockey, 1979; Mandler, 1979) though we shall have more to say on this point below. The problem is that an increase in selectivity does not appear to be the *only* change associated with high arousal, nor are the changes exactly the same for different conditions thought to give rise to high arousal. These issues are the main focus of the rest of this chapter. For the moment let us simply note that the success in demonstrating the relationship between selectivity and arousal, resulting from dramatic improvements in performance methodology in the last 20 years, may well have misled us into treating it as the *key* to the Yerkes–Dodson Law, rather than as a part of the puzzle. Our own work (e.g. Hockey, 1970a; Hockey and Hamilton, 1970) provides a good example of this error in theorizing. We badly need to find out what the other important dimensions of human performance are, and show how these *too* change as a function of environmental stress, emotional arousal, and the like. We would surely not wish to say that human cognitive activity varied only in terms of its degree of selectivity! Certainly, selectivity must be considered one of the most salient and general features of an organism's behaviour (Broadbent, 1958), though even attention theorists have preferred to regard selectivity and intensity as rather separate aspects of attention (e.g. Hebb, 1949). In particular, we may wonder what happens to memory function. Does that not play any role in the Yerkes–Dodson Law, or is the role restricted to the selective processing of events in memory (Broadbent, 1981)? There are other contenders for a place in the equation, but these will be discussed below.

And what of Easterbrook's explanation of the interaction with difficulty? Are we happy to accept an explanation in which difficult tasks are defined in terms of 'greater breadth of cue utilization'? Is not this circularity in a disguised form? While there may be some commonsense basis for accepting such a definition it does not help us much to classify tasks in advance. Subjective ratings of task difficulty are often surprisingly accurate, but not surely because subjects can estimate a task's breadth of cue utilization. We 'know' a task is more difficult, as cognitive theorists, because it appears to have a lower optimum level of arousal! Of course, the answer may well be that there are a number of reasons why a task may be difficult. It may indeed require a broad attentional strategy. (This could be defined operationally quite easily, for example as having more critical sources of information, or less redundancy in the sequential arrangement of signals across different sources.) On the other hand, it may be more difficult when it demands the use of working memory. For example, Folkard, Knauth, Monk and Rutenfrantz (1976) have demonstrated the potency of this variable in shifting the phase of the diurnal rhythm for visual search (see Chapter 4 of this volume), while Hamilton, Hockey and Rejman (1977) showed that an increase in memory load resulted in a change from a facilitatory to a detrimental effect of noise on rapid processing. More generally, difficulty may result from the necessity to make use of any internal cognitive process as opposed to tasks requiring attention to external events. Finally (for the moment, at least) difficulty may depend on the number of different processing resources required by the task, and the control problems involved in using them to meet the task requirements. As with the first part of the hypothesis it is surely important for us to be able to find ways of defining difficulty independently of the outcome of the experiment. Difficulty, in any case, is a quantitative variable which may have no simple mapping onto cognitive demands. Rather than resort to such a simple way out it would be more valuable to attempt to understand the qualitative nature of task requirements which provide the basis for such a classification.

STRATEGIES FOR STRESS RESEARCH

When we examine performance changes resulting from exposure to a stressor we have in mind some model of the human information-processing system, and this guides the kind of experiment or programme of experiments that we carry out. Earlier work, particularly in the applied field of environmental stress, tended to regard the human being as a fairly passive organism which was reduced in its efficiency by the presence of any unusual conditions. This view was formally analysed in its most useful form by Broadbent (1958), though he had introduced the important modification that information processing was essentially an active behaviour, requiring the subject to maintain and use various rules that determined which inputs were to be selected, stored, and so on. Broadbent argued that environmental stressors such as noise impaired efficiency by lowering the selectivity of intake (by diverting attention away from the task to the noise itself). An important demonstration of this is the finding that the kind of noise which is most effective at disrupting performance in serial responding (intense, high frequency noise) is also that which attracts the fastest reactions when it serves as the imperative signal in a reaction time experiment (Broadbent, 1957). Not only does the system process such signals more effectively, it cannot help doing so, even when they are irrelevant. The fact is that while noise may be distracting in this very direct sense, the two results may have no causal relationship. Broadbent's later (1971) interpretation of these two results is tempered with the evidence from the various other experiments on the same task showing interactions between stressors, discussed earlier in this chapter.

If noise is arousing (rather than distracting), then the impairment with intense high frequency noise is due to *over*-arousal, while the fast reaction times with the same noise may be the result of a quite different effect of stimulus intensity on the rate of accumulation of sensory evidence (Grice, 1968).

The results which we discussed earlier are the foundations of current conceptions of stressors as arousing (or dearousing). They can be seen, along with earlier work on distraction, as the result of a convergent research methodology in which, broadly speaking, similarities between the outcomes of studies employing different stressors are the main inputs to the theory. The strength of the Cambridge series of studies is that they used a single experimental task, serial responding (with the addition of a smaller number of studies on vigilance and tracking, which we shall leave aside for the moment), rather than attempting to compare results from different stressors with different tasks. The methodology is depicted diagrammatically in Figure 57, for a number of the stressors frequently used in those studies, and the one task.

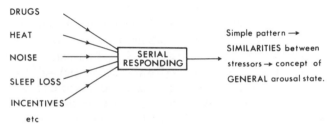

Figure 57. The narrow-band strategy for stress research (see text).

What emerges is predominantly a picture of a rather general state (arousal), derived from an observation of similarities between stressors on the basis of the measurement of a restricted (and simplified) set of performance measures. This, let us make quite clear, is an admirable research strategy, and this particular stress of studies represents the strategy at its best. Our reason for isolating it in this context is to compare it with an alternative strategy characterized by a divergent sampling of task environments for analysis of the effects of a single stressor. We have illustrated this methodology, roughly in the form it has taken in our own research over the past 10 years, for the stressor of noise (Figure 58). We have included serial reaction, as well as other situations we have not studied intensively ourselves, since these data form part of the total 'map' of this state. The point we would make is that such a strategy offers a different sort of evidence for a theory of stress effects. First, there is no justification for generalizing beyond the state induced in the subjects by noise; it is the specific *noise state* we are studying, rather than the general state of arousal. Secondly, when this strategy is carried out for a number of stressors,

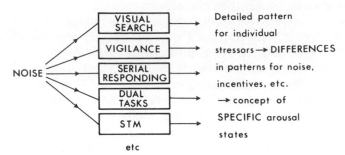

Figure 58. The broad-band strategy for stress research (see text).

the more detailed pattern of performance change associated with each will direct us towards *differences* rather than similarities between them. In addition to our experience with noise, the adoption of such a methodology in the field of circadian rhythms by Colquhoun's group (see Chapters 4 and 9 of this volume) has pointed towards a number of important ways in which the general theory is inadequate.

We have tried to avoid presenting these two strategies as alternatives in any absolute sense: of course, both approaches are necessary, and many research programmes actually dovetail the two. The Cambridge studies, as we mentioned above, also looked at performance on pursuit tracking and vigilance, though it is probably fair to say that the data from these other areas has had little impact on the theoretical orientation of the work. The use of different tasks and other measures (short-term memory, for example) may have resulted in greater interaction between the data from different tasks, but all the tasks used in this programme were designed to be sensitive to interruptions in task-oriented attention, and so overlapped considerably in their use of mental functions. Whereas the narrow band approach is partially dictated by the belief that the system operates as a single-channel general purpose processor, so the broad band approach can be seen to reflect a bias in theorizing towards multiple resources and specific processing components. In the former case it is important to avoid over-generalization, but equally, in the latter, we must be prepared to look for similarities of pattern. The difference is one of emphasis. Before examining patterns of mental function for different stress states, derived from the general literature, let us first illustrate the broad-band methodology in detail in the case of noise.

A MAP OF THE NOISE STATE

Noise has been studied more than perhaps any other environmental stressor, particularly in the context of human performance. In our own work we have been guided by the principles outlined in the broad-band methodology, primarily because we have been concerned to describe the total pattern of changes occurring under noise, as a specific state, rather than consider the data from such studies as applying directly to the concept of arousal level. The mapping exercise is quite complex, since it is necessary first to identify the relevant topographical features of cognitive states; what kinds of behaviour are we to look for in this area? Although our principal aim is to observe the landscape, our measurements must nevertheless be guided by theory. We shall consider these problems more fully in the next main section. For the moment let us summarize the current picture of cognition in the noise state. The detailed evidence is not considered in full here, though our arguments represent an extension of our previous descriptions of this pattern of changes (Hamilton, Hockey, and Rejman, 1977; Hockey, 1979). What is clear from research on noise is that it does *not* always impair performance. Instead, a qualitative pattern of effects is observed at a level more fundamental than that of efficiency. What seem to be the features of this pattern that stand out for the observer?

Selectivity of attention

There is now considerable evidence that noise is associated with a bias in the intake of information from dominant or high priority sources. The original demonstrations of this result as a shift in the relative efficiency of control and peripheral components of a complex tracking and monitoring task (Hockey, 1970a, 1970b, 1973) have been questioned on the grounds of replicability (Loeb and Jones, 1978; Forster and Grierson, 1978), though Hartley (1981) has recently confirmed the essential pattern of the effect. In addition, a similar change appears in simpler incidental memory tasks (Hockey and Hamilton, 1970; Davies and Jones, 1975; Wilding and Mohindra, 1980), though it is fair to say that these findings have also attracted some problems of replication (Niemi, von Wright and Koivunen, 1977). It seems clear that noise either produces an increase in selectivity, or that no effect is observed. There is no evidence to suggest that selectivity is reduced by noise. The problem of replicability of some of these results is an interesting one, and occurs elsewhere in the noise literature. We would argue that this is what might be expected in view of the strategic nature of the changes. They are critically dependent upon the appropriate induction of task set, often a delicate balance of priorities towards different activities encompassed by the overall task goal. The overwhelming conclusion is that noise increases the tendency to direct activities towards these dominant aspects of the overall goal.

Shifts in speed and accuracy

There is considerable evidence that noise produces a shift in the speed and accuracy with which fast 'throughput' tasks are conducted. The most general observation is that accuracy is reduced, a greater proportion of errors being found under noise in the continuous serial reaction task (see Broadbent, 1971) in a number of different studies. There is also a tendency for performance to be faster under noise, particularly towards the end of the work period, though such an effect may often be masked by the high rates of responding adopted by subjects in self-paced tasks. Currently there is not sufficient evidence for us to interpret these data confidently. It seems likely that there is a shift in the speed/accuracy trade-off function towards faster/less accurate responding, though it is less clear whether this is accompanied by a change in location of the function towards a slower RT band (or even a faster one). As yet there is no useful data on the distributions of correct and error RTs for noise. Rabbitt (1981) raises the possibility that the available evidence for noise (as well as for sleep loss and alcohol) may be consistent with a different interpretation. Stress may have the effect of reducing subjects' ability to monitor their response speeds in order to maintain an optimal balance between speed and accuracy. This would predict a pattern of increased RT variance and fast errors, with the same trade-off function. A shift towards a slower speed/accuracy function would show up as an increase in the proportion of errors in noise with no change in the RT distributions. Clearly, the present data do not allow us to be more precise than to suggest that noise does produce a shift in responding of the kind we have outlined. What is clear, again, is that noise does not *reduce* the proportion of errors in fast responding, nor decrease the mean rate of responding. The evidence strongly indicates the contrary in each case.

Memory function

A number of separate effects of noise on the storage and retrieval of information may be distinguished. Hamilton *et al.* (1977) showed that the last few items in a running memory presentation were recalled better in noise, though earlier items were not retained as well. This was interpreted as a reduction in the capacity of primary memory, resulting in the storage of a smaller number of recent items, on average, than under normal conditions. These were better retrieved, at the expense of reduced access to items five or more places back from the end of the sequence. A recent series of studies by Broadbent and Smith (personal communication) illustrates that noise may alter the strategies adopted in this kind of task. When instructions encourage the recall of items in their order of occurrence there is a tendency for noise to improve the recall of those early in the sequence, at the expense of more recent items. Such a result would locate the effect of noise in the output buffer, though the form of the effect is probably strongly affected by strategy decisions about the order of report, the number of items to be reported, and so on. A number of studies have found a reduction in immediate recall (for visually presented items) when noise is present, often coupled with an increase in recall in a delayed test (see

Hockey, 1979; Craik and Blankstein, 1975). We have found that short-term recall is not necessarily impaired by noise, at least in the paired-associate task. Here, when the order in which stimulus words are presented is changed from the familiarization trial to the test trial, noise does make it more difficult to recall the response that was paired with each stimulus. However, if the order of pairs is maintained, noise actually improves performance. It now seems clear that either positional or sequential information is preserved in this state, a view which has been recently confirmed in a series of experiments by Wilding (Wilding and Mohindra, 1980; Daee and Wilding, 1977).

In addition, there are good grounds for thinking that use of the working memory system is more limited in the noise state (unless immediate ordered retrieval is required). Hamilton *et al.* (1977) used an alphabet transformation task in which groups of letter sequences had to be transformed by counting forward say four places in the alphabet from each letter. Single letters and groups of two were processed quicker in noise, while groups of three or four were slower. The longer sequences required the holding of early transformations in working memory while carrying out the later transforms, until all four were completed. This proved a considerable load on the memory system, some subjects not being able to complete such a problem at all. Noise can be seen here as speeding up the processing rate in the absence of a requirement to hold information in memory, but preventing the efficient use of working storage. This is an example where difficulty can be defined operationally as the memory load involved in the task, and noise, obligingly, fits into the Yerkes–Dodson Law by facilitating 'simple' tasks and impairing 'difficult' versions. As we said before, it may well be that the involvement of the memory system is the main feature of task difficulty, but the simpler interpretation of this result is that noise has two separate effects: it increases processing speed, and it impairs working memory. The separate effects combine to provide spurious support for the simple arousal argument. In a more recent series of studies using this task (Hockey, McLean, and Hamilton, 1981) we have succeeded in partitioning the solution of each problem into its constituent components, letter by letter. Here, noise can be seen to have a direct effect of reducing the time taken by the transformation phase, while increasing that taken up by storing and updating operations. Summarizing these findings, noise may be considered to reduce the effectiveness of working memory, though it is not clear how much this is a structural limitation rather than a strategic one. Certainly, changes in strategy are evident in relation to order information, semantic coding, and recall order. This is one of the more active current areas of research in noise.

Other features

In addition to the characteristics already outlined, all of which can be considered in terms of a systematic classification of resources and their pattern of use, there are a number of other, perhaps less easily classified, features of performance change under noise. For example, decisions are made with greater confidence in this state, whether right or wrong. Broadbent (1971) and Broadbent and Gregory (1963, 1965) have shown that subjects make less use of a 'doubtful' category of confidence in vigilance tasks, while Hockey (1973) found that noise reduced the tendency to check sources of signals a second time when the information was unclear. We have also found in our memory studies that the rate of intrusions is usually low in noise, though omissions are more common. Subjects tend to either produce the correct response or omit the response entirely. Lastly, there is evidence that the selectivity seen in intake is found in tasks where no information is presented; in retrieval from memory (Eysenck, 1975) and in an event-prediction situation (Hamilton *et al.*, 1977). It is possible to show that all these features of the noise state can be made to fit a consistent overall view of the nature of the change (Hockey, 1979, pp.169–170): see Chapter 3 for a more detailed discussion of noise effects. Let us now consider other stress patterns.

COMPARISON OF STRESS STATES

In this section we attempt to illustrate the particular patterns of performance changes that occur with different stress conditions, and to compare stressors in terms of these overall patterns of change. The methodology of this follows closely that of Prechtl (1974), as described on pp.332–333, and depicted in Table 6. In order to summarize the evidence from stress studies in this way we need to decide on the appropriate entries for both rows and columns; (1) What stressors should we consider? (2) What indicators of performance should we adopt?

Stressors considered

We have used as our criteria of selection (a) stressors which have been used to study performance over a range of cognitive functions, and (b) a variety of stress conditions; ambient environmental changes (noise, heat), states arising from variations in normal and abnormal bodily conditions (time of day, sleepiness, fatigue, shiftwork), drug ingestion (amphetamine, tranquillizers, alcohol, and nicotine), and more general psychological stress (anxiety). We have also included incentive, a motivational variable. In addition, our selection has been tempered by the desire to consider as many of the stressors treated within the present volume as possible. Indeed, we are fortunate to be able to draw upon this body of evidence in sketching out our maps of these states. We have not been able to consider detailed differences between various manipulations of each of the stress variables, however. Our definitions are necessarily very general ones, though they encompass the typical quantitative ranges found in research. An indication of what is meant by each of the stressor terms used in our analysis is given in Table 7 below.

Indicator variables

The most difficult problem encountered in our attempt to map the effects of stressors onto cognitive function has been the selection of a set of suitable indicator variables. For noise we have not worried unduly about this problem for three reasons: (a) since we have been dealing with a single state change we have been content to combine data from different available sources and let these speak for themselves, (b) research on noise effects has, in any case, tended to cover a wide range of cognitive tasks, providing a broad data base for our mapping exercise, and (c) this research has been guided, more than has been the case with most stressors, by theories which assume a differentiated structure of human cognitive processes (particularly Broadbent's work, which we have found an invaluable basis for our own research). When we come to compare cognitive changes across a large number of stressors, however, there is a need for a standard taxonomy. Of course, whatever indicators we choose, there will inevitably be gaps in knowledge, or uncertainties about the reliability or interpretation of certain data. At the outset, we should say that we do not intend to justify the *details* of our state 'observations'. Rather, we hope to provide a reasonably accurate set of 'sketches' of cognitive life in each of the states resulting from exposure to the various stressors. More than anything else in this chapter, we would wish the urgent requirement for relevant state-oriented (broad-band) research to be recognized. Apologies aside, what indicators should we include?

Much research on stressors is rather unhelpful from this point of view. Performance is often indicated by 'a test of psychomotor performance', usually a combination of various components with no way of assessing their relative contribution to the adequacy of response. Some study of the factors to be considered may be rewarding. Let us first of all distinguish between those effects of stressors which are peculiar to the task situation and its demand characteristics (*strategic* variables) and those which reflect fundamental changes in the operating parameters of the system (*structural* variables). Among the former we might consider patterns of attention distribution, organization of internal thought sequences, tolerated speed/accuracy trade-off settings, and adopted criteria for decision. Examples of the latter are speed of information transmission, decay parameters for sensory storage, variations in working memory space, and level of muscular activity (response readiness). Thus, it is possible to distinguish between strategies of resource management and capacities of the available resources themselves.

In practice, unfortunately, this distinction is difficult to sustain. A good example is the relative failure of the statistical decision theory approach to the measurement of detection (and memory retrieval) processes. The original application of SDT methodology (e.g. Tanner and Swets, 1954) promised a solution to the problem of distinguishing perceptual sensitivity (a structural property) from response bias (a strategic one), in terms of two independent parameters of detection performance, d' and β. Although these are clearly of great value in describing the quality of performance, there are doubts that they relate clearly to psychological processes (Jerison, 1967), though Davies and Parasuraman (1982) have recently argued convincingly in favour of the general theory, rather than particular statistics. We would suggest that the theory *is* unrealistic. Decision criteria depend sometimes on signal quality; risky decisions are less necessary when clear information is available. The problem comes about by a failure to recognize that the human information processing system is an interactive, flexible one where information intake and motor output are *both* subject to strategic and structural factors. In any case, there is still insufficient data of the SDT type for us to include it in our analysis. Whatever its limitations it would certainly have been very useful to be able to include even approximate indices of information intake efficiency and output bias in our maps of the effects.

Two features of performance which do seem to reflect strategy are those of *attentional selectivity* and *speed/accuracy trade-off*. Two predominantly structural limitations are *speed of processing* and *capacity of short-term memory*. We provide brief arguments in favour of these below, with an additional indicator, that of *alertness*. This last feature is included as a baseline of behavioural intensity, roughly corresponding to subjective arousal, and inferred from a number of sources.

The five indicators adopted for the purposes of this analysis are outlined below.

(1) Alertness. Largely, this corresponds to the commonly accepted classification of stressors in terms of their effects on arousal level. In addition, we have taken into account subjective reactions and data from physiological activation as well as a general indication of vigilance performance. This is used here as a *criterion* variable for the state, from the point of view of a primary classification based only on directional changes in arousal. We can therefore group stressors according to alertness and then sort them by their patterns of effects across other performance variables.

(2) Selectivity. This reflects one of the most apparent features of cognitive activity, namely the relation between the subject and the task environment. In some states he may appear withdrawn, involvement with task priorities would be minimal, the frequency of task-irrelevant activities high, and so on. In others he may become almost totally dominated by the task, even obsessional, and seemingly unresponsive to other aspects of his environment. Within certain restrictions we can examine this behaviour in laboratory situations having an order of priority for the allocation of resources to two or more components (normally primary and secondary tasks). Here, selectivity (or *task*

set) refers to the extent that behaviour is oriented towards dominant sources of information or output modes at the expense of less dominant requirements. This variable has an important place in clinical theories of cognitive deficit (Korchin, 1964; Wachtel, 1967), and is, as we have already observed, the basis of Easterbrook's (1959) analysis of the Yerkes–Dodson Law.

(3) and (4) Speed and accuracy. We consider effects on both speed and accuracy in rapid decision-making. In the absence of speed/accuracy trade-off information it is not possible to separate strategy from structure directly. Instead, speed of processing is treated as a fundamental structural indicant unless accuracy effects appear to be negatively correlated with changes in speed. A change in the trade-off strategy is reflected by a shift of these two indices in opposite directions (faster, less accurate; slower, more accurate). This is necessarily crude in the absence of relevant data of the right kind about trade-off functions and RT distributions for correct and error responses (Rabbitt, 1981), but data on reaction time performance are the most widely available of all measures, and clearly reflects important changes of function for the system as a whole.

(5) STM capacity. Memory function seems separate from processing speed in a number of treatments of system function (e.g. Broadbent, 1971; Hamilton *et al.*, 1977). There is now evidence that these two processes might even be controlled in their diurnal variation through separate oscillators having different periods in free running rhythms (see Monk and Folkard, Chapter 4, this volume). Accordingly, performance in recalling brief sequences of items with short time delays is assumed to reflect the operation of a fundamental resource function. The variety of memory tasks and testing procedures employed makes this a surprisingly difficult task. There has been little systematic study of short-term memory as a function of stress. We have, nevertheless, been able to make satisfactory generalizations from the data available; sometimes this has involved making inferences from the effects of stressors on tasks which differ in memory load, though they themselves are not designed primarily for testing memory.

The indicators are presented in the table of stress effects which follows in the form of vectors. An increase in the property listed is given a plus (+) value if some indication for this exists in the literature (we have not tried to distinguish here between weak and strong effects), while corresponding reductions in the property are given a negative value (–). Only in fairly clear cases have we included such a vector value. A value of zero (0) is indicated in places where no effect is typically observed, or a small number of studies provided conflicting results, while (?) indicates the absence of relevant data.

Sketch maps of stress states

We have attempted to draw together the various strands of evidence concerning the pattern of changes found with different stressors and organismic states. A full review of this evidence is clearly not possible here, though it is dealt with elsewhere (Hockey and Hamilton, in preparation). Our interpretation of the data is based on fairly reliable and substantiated findings in some cases, on rather isolated results in others. In addition, we have been obliged to make qualitative assessments based on the prevailing balance of experimental outcomes in cases where the evidence is ambiguous. The end-product is a set of 'sketch maps' for these stressors. Their aim is to provide a rough guide to the terrain rather than a set of thoroughly surveyed maps. Our conclusions are summarized in Table 7. Stressors usually thought of as associated with an increase in arousal are grouped together, as are those usually regarded as dearousing. Heat stress is ambiguous in this respect (Poulton, 1970; Ramsey, Chapter 2 this volume), and is located in the middle of the table.

How many states?

It can be seen that there is a fair degree of communality in the cognitive patterning in these major clusters. This offers some support to the notion that some kind of general state concept (arousal or alertness) provides a reasonable rule of thumb for the prediction of detailed stress effects. Nevertheless, *within* these clusters, differences in the direction of effect between stressors seem sufficiently marked for us to conclude that a state formulation may be more representative of the 'true' situation than one based on levels of a general process. A common feature of this 'high arousal' cluster seems to be the relative 'speeding' of performance, though whether or not this is accompanied by an apparent trade-off against accuracy is dependent on the particular stressor. Noise and time of day are good examples of states which typically produce such a change in the balance of speed and errors, while this does not seem to occur either with nicotine or with tests carried out under moderate incentives. A difference also occurs in the effect on STM capacity. This is characteristically reduced for states of high arousal, but is clearly increased under incentive. Lastly, selectivity is typically increased for high arousal, though there is no clear evidence for such a change with time of day. This dissociation between changes in the indicator variables suggests four distinct patterns of high arousal, or five if heat is included here (Table 7 shows this to be different in a number of ways). These are sketched below, omitting the distinctive but inconsistent heat pattern.

(1) Anxiety (noise, amphetamine). These stressors change performance in similar ways. Against a background of increased alertness, selectivity (task set) is increased and rate of work tends to increase. There is a corresponding cost in terms of reduced accuracy of responding in speeded classification tasks, so that the overall nature of the state change may be related more to the 'high activity' of the system than to its efficiency as such. The (by now) well-

Table 7. The pattern of performance change associated with different stressors: see text for explanation.

Stressor or condition	Brief description of manipulation	Alertness	Selectivity	Fast responding		STM
				Speed	Accuracy	
Anxiety	High scorers on trait-state anxiety tests; induced by danger/threat	+	+	0	-	-
Noise	Continuous broad-band noise at about 80–100 dB	+	+	0	-	-
Amphetamine	Oral ingestion in normal clinical dosages	+	+	-	(?)	-
Nicotine	Smoking one or two cigarettes, or oral ingestion of nicotine tablets	+	+	+	0 (?)	-
Incentives	Augmented feedback, financial reward, or induced competitiveness	+	+	+	+	+
Time of day (p.m.)	Testing at later times of day (between about 1500 and 2100)	+	(?)	+	-	-
Heat	WGBT of about 30–40°C for up to 2–3 hours	+ (?)	+	0	-	0
Alcohol	Oral ingestion of about 0.2–0.5 g/kg (peak BA level about 0.04%)	-	+ (?)	-	-	-
Minor tranquilizers	Oral ingestion of benzodiazepines in normal clinical dosages	-	-	-	-	-
Sleep loss/night-work	One night without sleep/working at night before adaptation	-	-	-	-	0
Prolonged work/boredom	Continuous work for 30+ minutes on repetitive tasks	-	+ (?)	-	-	0
Time of day (a.m.)	Testing at earlier times of day (between	-	(?)	-	+	+

documented STM deficit is a feature of this group of effects. In the presence of the increase in task set this has to be interpreted as a genuine reduction in storage capacity.

(2) Nicotine. Nicotine produces changes very much like those of group 1, except that no speed/accuracy trade-off is implied. At the present time this may be taken to reflect a true shift in system parameters (increased speed, decreased storage), with strategic factors playing a secondary role.

(3) Incentives. This state is very similar to that produced by nicotine. The critical difference here is that STM performance is typically improved rather than impaired. The pattern suggests a general increase in task set (effort) with no apparent tendency for a trade-off in system parameters.

(4) Afternoon. Later points in the diurnal cycle produce speed/accuracy trade-off effects, like those of group 1. The changes are generally those of 'high arousal', except that no change in selectivity is apparent. As with groups 1 and 2, a true shift in system parameters is implied between speed and memory processes.

The same separation of states appears in the case of the 'low arousal' cluster. While there is certainly evidence for a broad pattern of results associated with conditions resulting in a reduction of alertness, inconsistencies again appear in the observed changes in all indicators except speed. No tendency for speed and accuracy to change in opposite directions is observed in any of these states, though particular studies sometimes find an increase in errors, say for sleeplessness, instead of a reduction in speed. In either case a true reduction of processing efficiency is implicated.

(5) Morning. This is only identified as a different state in terms of being the opposite of (comparison for) the pattern of changes found in the afternoon. STM is better at this time than later in the day while throughput is less efficient.

(6) Sleeplessness (night-work). Typically, within the reduced alertness pattern selectivity is reduced and speed (and/or accuracy) also reduced. In the presence of reduced task set the maintenance of STM cannot be interpreted as an effort effect (such as that found with incentives), and may be seen as a genuine lengthening of the decay constant for temporary storage. The effect is more marked, in fact, when active processing is minimized by task requirements, as in the running memory paradigm (Hamilton *et al.*, 1972).

(7) Boredom (prolonged work). Although a reduction in alertness is usually assumed to result from prolonged work, performance is rarely markedly affected. Typical effects show a reduction of speed but no change in memory capacity. Selectivity may, in fact, increase with time on task, so that the change may be largely a strategic compensation for loss of environmental input. In vigilance tasks there is clear evidence that the main change in detection behaviour is that of increased caution in responding, again a strategic change.

(8) Alcohol. In small doses (the state considered here) some attempt to compensate for the drug's depressant effects by increased selectivity may be

observed. Like the typical low arousal state (group 6), speed is reduced, but, unlike it, so is memory performance. The attempt to maintain task set is not sufficient to overcome this general reduction in state efficiency.

(9) Tranquillizers. The cognitive scene here is of unmitigated gloom. All features show evidence of reduced efficiency, with no attempt to compensate for the effects. It should be said that large dosages of alcohol may fall into this category, as compensatory activity is abandoned.

Even with such a simple analysis it is clear that stressors exercise their effects on cognitive behaviour by changes along a number of separate dimensions. While it is undoubtedly true that some of the 'high arousal' and some of the 'low arousal' patterns could be paired to make bipolar dimensions of state change (e.g. groups 1 and 6, 2 and 9, obviously 4 and 5), it is not quite true that these are entirely complementary. (Of course the last-mentioned *is*, since it is *defined* by comparison of the two states we have selected.) For example, sleep loss sometimes shows a compensatory tendency, in line with the pattern observed in noise and anxiety. Teichner (1968) argues that *all* stressors produce such a change, and both Hockey (1970c) and Youngling (see Teichner, 1968) provide evidence of *increased* selectivity under sleep loss. In the former case the effect was short-lived (though significant in the first 5 minutes of testing), then replaced by a marked reduction of selectivity. It is also clear that the patterns of changes we have documented cannot be made to fit easily into a *single* dimension. Even allowing for the reasonable assumption (in the context of arousal theory) that memory performance has a lower optimum level, the theory cannot accommodate a pattern in which both incentives and sleep loss can improve STM, and where the depressant alcohol impairs speed while increasing selectivity.

Of course, it may be the case that the conditions we have considered produce a number of separate effects, *in addition to* a change in arousal level which is primary. If this is true it can only be substantiated by a rather selective use of the data: accept results where they fit the theory, otherwise attribute them to 'special effects'. This kind of interpretation may save us from a plethora of stress states, but the onus is on advocates of such a view to demonstrate that these rogue results are indeed special. It is hard to see how this can be done without taking the physiological consequences of stressors seriously. For example, the 'alcohol state' is certainly a tenuous one. The effects depend markedly on dosage and factors concerning individual differences. It is known by workers in the field to be a rather complex drug, having a number of effects on CNS function (e.g. Wesnes and Warburton, Chapter 8 this volume). To 'explain away' its cognitive effects that do not quite fit the expected pattern it is necessary to recognize these complications and seriously consider the role of blood alcohol absorption functions, and the like. Certainly the practice of including this variable in an experiment simply because it is defined operationally as a depressant (or even a stimulant in small doses) can only lead to further confusion.

Some further observations

The rough sketches presented in the previous section are naturally of limited usefulness. We have been forced to compare effects across different forms of performance test and different manipulations of stressors. Nevertheless, we believe that the broad picture that results from this exercise gives a reasonable indication of the sorts of pattern that exist in the literature. We have been forced to make educated guesses to fill in cells where the data would not normally allow a confident interpretation. The validity of these details is not an issue here, since the exercise rests more on its methodological value. The analysis can, however, be sharpened in a few places where considerably *more* data are available than could be dealt with in Table 7.

First, there is now a considerable amount of data on the qualitative patterns of storage and retrieval in memory tasks for different 'arousers'. Noise is seen to increase the use of order information and to decrease semantic organization and clustering (Broadbent, 1981). Time of day, on the other hand, shows the opposite trend from morning to evening (see Folkard, Chapter 9 this volume). As arousal 'increases', the system makes more rather than less use of semantic information. Here, although both noise and later points in the diurnal rhythm are associated with relatively poor STM there may be quite different reasons for the two patterns of performance. The increased use of order in noise has also been found in the case of alcohol (thought to reduce arousal) by Dornič (1975), while prolonged work has no effect on immediate recall but increases the dependence of recall on the most recent information received (enhanced recency traded off for reduced primacy; Hamilton and Hockey, 1971).

Some of the patterns we have inferred from our superficial survey may be observed more or less direction in multiple-component tasks, such as the letter transformation task developed by Hamilton, Hockey, and Rejman (1977), and discussed earlier in this chapter. We have found that noise reduces the time taken for transformations involving minimal memory loads (0 or 1 item), while high memory load tasks take longer. Eysenck (Chapter 7 this volume) found that incentives improved performance on both kinds of task, confirming the difference between these two 'arousers'. In the same series of studies he confirmed the noise findings mentioned above (Eysenck, personal communication) and found that trait anxiety differences produced the same pattern of results as noise (Chapter 10 this volume). Hockey, McLean, and Hamilton (1981) were able to measure transformation speed and storage time separately, using a temporal decomposition technique. They showed that noise did indeed speed up the transformation phase and lengthen the duration of the storage phase whatever the memory load. The importance of this result is that the two opposite effects on speed and memory are obtained in the same task as modulations of the rhythmic control structure processing cycles of letter inputs. Hockey *et al.* (1981) also examined alcohol in the same way. The drug lengthened the time spent on *both* phases of the task, though storage time was only seriously impaired for high memory load tasks where order preservation was required. A parallel immediate recall experiment revealed that alcohol impaired memory for letter sequences, but again, the effect was confined to the loss of order information. These results illustrate that differences between stressors may be observed at the level of the detailed patterning of sequential control through complex activities, not only as generalized composites drawn from different sources. The bonus, in this case, is that the detailed results from the direct analyses mirror those obtained from our rather indirect mapping.

We have tried to avoid skipping too lightly over major theoretical issues, although these are not central to this chapter. Nevertheless, one or two observations should be made about the limitations of our methodology and interpretations. In the first place our attempt to distinguish between strategic and structural changes is less than satisfactory. Although we have seen that many of the effects of stressors must be interpreted against a background of changes in the way in which a subject approaches the task, it is not often possible to separate the two kinds of change in terms of observable performance measures. Given the current acceptance of resource allocation as an active feature of the human performance model (e.g. Rabbitt, 1979) we are urgently in need of the right kind of experiments to allow us to make this distinction. Current work in the field of noise (e.g. Broadbent, 1981) illustrates the enormous advantages of considering the relationship between possible strategic and structural aspects of state change, and Rabbitt (1979) has demonstrated how important this is for understanding the nature of stress effects in terms of their functional properties.

Secondly, we have made little mention of qualitative changes in state arising from quantitative changes in stressor level (e.g. a large increase in alcohol dosage or differences in the level of monetary incentive). Certainly, we would not assume that a higher level of stressor would merely produce the same pattern of indicator changes (albeit more clearly). Rather, and this will depend on the system response to each stressor, some changes may only become evident when some critical (threshold) level of tolerance in the system parameters is exceeded. This is possible for both strategic and structural processes, though may be expected more confidently, perhaps for the former. Whereas lower levels of noise, say, can be tolerated, or classified as harmless, above a certain level an individual may decide that he must introduce some form of coping. The appraisal of tolerance limits may, of course, be based on sensitivity to structural changes, but the shift in behaviour is the result of the active attempt to control the task environment. Schönpflug (Chapter 11 this volume) discusses some of the implications of this kind of effect. There are also problems of qualitative differences within stressors. Obvious examples of this are continuous and intermittent noise, deprivation of slow wave (stage 4) sleep versus deprivation of REM sleep, and monetary incentives versus social/

competitive incentives. All of these are potentially different states in our analysis, though there is not enough suitable data to enable us to deal with them effectively. Certainly, when we are able to include data from a wider range of stressors, all of which have been studied in sufficient behavioural detail, the number of discernible patterns will increase. The question of how many states *can* be distinguished is, as we have said, meaningless. The important question for the development of theory is to allow our research to display the variety of states it appears to, even when we confine our observations to major areas of interest. One state with a variable level of activation will no longer do, though, conversely, we do not need a state for *each* stressor. The nine patterns we have discerned may become 12 or 15 with the accumulation of evidence, or be reduced to three or four as our understanding of the functional properties of the system becomes more sophisticated. The important thing is to have the methodology to detect patterns (i.e. a broad-band research instrument), rather than allow adherence to a particular theory to determine which particular pattern we should search for. Before concluding, let us look more closely at what we have in mind when we discuss the state of the cognitive system, and what implications such a view has for the study of more stable (higher order) states than those found in the performance of laboratory tasks.

MENTAL STATES

Cognitive resources and task demands

A state conception of mental processes involves a number of assumptions about the relation between cognitive resources and the basis for organized mental activity. It may help to outline those that have guided our thinking.

Assumption 1. the system comprises a number of specific processing resources. These may or may not be structurally identifiable within the hardware of the CNS.

Assumption 2. Each resource is limited either in its rate of operation or in the space available for processing data, or both.

Assumption 3. The system also possesses a general resource (the executive or effort) which can direct control from one part of the system to another.

Assumption 4. The executive has access to a library of control procedures which may be used for operating on different resources. Control operations may be specific to a resource or generally applicable to a sub-set of resources.

Assumption 5. Resources may also be activated automatically when inputs to the system are highly compatible with outputs available to the resource.

Assumption 6. The system may be regarded as being in one of a large number of states, corresponding to the profile of the functional levels for different resources.

Assumption 7. A modal, or typical, state exists for any given individual, such that the pattern of resource levels remains comparatively stable when averaged over large time samples.

Assumption 8. States can be altered by environmental changes or stressors so that the modal state is modified in the direction of that which is typical for that condition.

Assumption 9. Stress-induced shifts of state do not impose strict limitations on system function, but represent qualitative changes in the ease of operation of different resources.

Assumption 10. The executive (effort) resource may be used to change the prevailing resource state in the direction of that which is optimal for performance of a particular task. The further state parameters are from their target values for the task the greater the effort required to attain that state. It may also be used to maintain the current state in the face of imposed changes in inputs to the system.

These assumptions are not meant to be considered as a theory in any formal sense, though they do make a number of quite specific predictions which are testable. In particular, Assumptions 1, 2, 3, 5, 7, 8, 9, and 10 can all be shown to have support from empirical studies of multiple-task performance and stress (e.g. Allport, 1980; Kahneman, 1973; Wickens, in press; Norman and Bobrow, 1973). We do not have space to defend them here, nor would we want to. They form the basis for a theoretical frame of reference in which we have developed our approach to the analysis of stress effects in particular, and to the control of complex mental activity in general. Many of the assumptions are highly consistent with the arguments of a number of current approaches, such as those above. We differ primarily in our emphasis on the adaptive and flexible nature of mental states. Two important mechanisms that we should single out for mention are those responsible for *state maintenance* and *state selection* (see Assumption 10) already included in our preliminary outline of the view (Hamilton *et al.*, 1977). State selection may be achieved passively (automatically) or through the operation of effort-directed control processes. State maintenance, on the other hand (loosely equivalent to concentration or focussing), is the direct result of effort. Whenever effort is involved, either in maintaining the present state or in moving to a new one, there may be some observable physiological cost to the system. In this sense the view is very much like that put forward by Kahneman (1973).

Characteristic states

Assumption 7 refers to the system being in an identifiable modal state for a given individual. This seems to us a valid application of the state terminology to the description of temperament or personality. An individual may be described in terms of the typical pattern of resource functions underlying his overt behaviour—his particular cognitive style, in other closely related terms.

He may be predominantly externally oriented, seeking contact with new environmental inputs, or he may be dominated by internal processing, such as that associated with thinking. He may be typically alert and attentive, or just as typically 'low key' or unresponsive. The content of his thinking activities may be characterized by passive memory search (reflecting or day-dreaming), or by active planning of new activities. In terms more closely associated with our own rough classification of indicator variables, he may appear rigidly oriented in the direction of his activity, or he may consider various possibilities more or less equally. Lastly, he may work quickly or slowly, whatever his skill level at the task, and typically make few or many errors.

All these are observable features of everyday human cognition, and they surely are the product of a comparatively stable mental state. States such as these we can call *enduring*, and they clearly have to be seen as the baseline for any changes produced by stressors, or by task demands. It is likely that individuals dominated by active use of memory processes, say, will be more successful in maintaining the state required for carrying out a 20-minute memory task, while those who are characterized by sensory intake should be more successful at detecting changes in external signals. This may be a promising line of research in the near future. There are no insurmountable problems to the analysis of real-life cognitive states, and a number of current approaches to the study of cognitive errors (e.g. Reason, in press; Broadbent, Cooper, Fitzgerald, and Parkes, 1981) provide encouragement for such a study. Can we provide a classification of temperament in terms of cognitive states? Surely this would represent a step forward in the study of individual differences, not only within human performance, but within the broader area of personality theory.

The states associated with stressors are usually *transient*. They may be transformed into a more typical state soon after contact with the stressor (by coping, or through state selection and maintenance in our terms), or they may persist for longer. Schönpflug (Chapter 11 this volume) has shown that this will depend on whether individuals attempt to cope, and whether coping is successful. In any case, other classes of transient states may be distinguished. Emotional states can be seen as a special case of stress states, arising from the presence of distinctive patterns of cognitive awareness. Izard (1972), for example, shows that anxiety may involve components of fear and at least two other fundamental elements from the set (distress, anger, shame, and interest–excitement). The awareness of affective quality is a feature of emotional states not normally involved in the response of the system to environmental change (e.g. to loud noise or to heat), while the input from autonomic and endocrine components of the response may add another distinctive dimension. Emotional states are rich in mental life, compared to the resource states we have been considering, though they can be seen as part of the same analysis of the system. We may also distinguish the transient state of mood, which may be seen either as a relatively controlled emotional state or as a less well-defined response to environmental events (in terms of hedonic tone or interest, for example). Mood changes may be spontaneous and relatively endogenous (e.g. Thayer, 1967) and they may vary cyclically over short or long periods. The search for switches for these subtle emotional states may again provide a useful source of evidence for the mechanism of state change and maintenance.

SUMMARY

The effects of stress on performance cannot easily be fitted into the framework of traditional arousal theory. Rather, they must be considered to be the result of a number of separate changes in underlying processes which give rise to an observed pattern of change. The concept of a multi-dimensional state is seen to be necessary to account for these changes, rather than variations along a single dimension. This chapter examines the central issues addressed by the arousal theory, illustrating the way in which arousal has been applied to results of experiments on the effects of stressors in performance. The Yerkes–Dodson Law has not been demonstrated directly and may be true in only a very general way. It fails to show what changes occur as a function of arousal, and how different processes may depend on each other.

Two complementary research methodologies are outlined for broadening our understanding of stress phenomena: (a) narrow-band, where a particular task is used to enable generalizations to be drawn from the effects of a number of stressors, and (b) broad-band, where the emphasis is on the description of performance changes across a wide range of tasks for a single stressor. The second method highlights differences between stressors that would otherwise be missed. Both approaches are seen to be necessary to provide an adequate basis for theories of the effects.

We illustrate the broad band methodology in the case of noise, then go on to describe patterns of stress effects for a wide range of conditions. The indicator variables selected are alertness, speed, accuracy, selectivity, and capacity of STM. From a simple analysis of data from the literature it is clear that the patterns of effects cannot be mapped onto a single underlying dimension, at least four 'high arousal' and five 'low arousal' patterns emerging. These are called *stress states*.

The assumptions about the processes underlying state change and resource functions in the system are outlined, and the applications to broader issues considered briefly.

ACKNOWLEDGEMENT

The support of the Social Science Research Council during the writing of this Chapter is gratefully acknowledged.

REFERENCES

Allport, A. (1980) Attention and performance. In G. Claxton (ed.), *Cognitive Psychology, New Directions*. London: Routledge and Kegan Paul.

Arbib, M. A. (1972) *The Metaphorical Brain*. New York: John Wiley & Sons.

Bell, P. A. (1978) Effects of noise and heat stress on primary and secondary task performance. *Human Factors*, **20**, 749–752.

Broadbent, D. E. (1957) Effects of noises of high and low frequency on behaviour. *Ergonomics*, **1**, 21–29.

Broadbent, D. E. (1958) *Perception and Communication*. London: Pergamon.

Broadbent, D. E. (1963) Differences and interactions between stresses. *Quarterly Journal of Experimental Psychology*, **15**, 205–211.

Broadbent, D. E. (1971) *Decision and Stress*. London: Academic Press.

Broadbent, D. E. (1981) The effects of moderate levels of noise on human performance. In J. V. Tobias and E. D. Schubert (eds.), *Hearing Research and Theory*. New York: Academic Press.

Broadbent, D. E. and Gregory, M. (1963) Vigilance considered as a statistical decision. *British Journal of Psychology*, **54**, 309–323.

Broadbent, D. E. and Gregory, M. (1965) Effects of noise and signal rate upon vigilance analysed by means of decision theory. *Human Factors*, **7**, 155–162.

Broadbent, D. E., Cooper, P. F., Fitzgerald, P., and Parkes, K. R. (1982) The cognitive failures question noise (CFQ) and its correlates. *British Journal of Clinical Psychology*, **21**, 1–16.

Broadhurst, P. L. (1959) The interaction of task difficulty and motivation. The Yerkes–Dodson law revisited. *Acta Psychologica*, **16**, 321–338.

Bunge, M. (1980) *The Mind–Body Problem*. Oxford: Pergamon.

Cannon, W. B. (1915) *Bodily Changes in Pain, Hunger, Fear and Rage*. New York: Appleton.

Corcoran, D. W. J. (1962) Noise and loss of sleep. *Quarterly Journal of Experimental Psychology*, **14**, 178–182.

Craik, F. I. M. and Blankstein, K. R. (1975) Psychophysiology and human memory. In P. M. Venables and M. J. Christie (eds.), *Researc in Psychophysiology*. Chichester: John Wiley & Sons.

Daee, S. and Wilding, J. M. (1977) Effects of high intensity noise on short-term memory for position in a list and sequence. *British Journal of Psychology*, **68**, 335–349.

Davies, D. R. and Jones, D. M. (1975) The effects of noise and incentives upon attention in short-term memory. *British Journal of Psychology*, **66**, 61–68.

Davies, D. R. and Parasuraman, R. (1982) *The Psychology of Vigilance*. London: Academic Press.

Dornič, S. (1975) Some studies on the resention of order information. In P. M. A. Rabbitt and S. Dornič (eds.), *Attention and Performance, Vol. 5*, London: Academic Press.

Duffy, E. (1962) *Activation and Behaviour*. New York: John Wiley & Sons.

Easterbrook, J. A. (1959) The effect of emotion on the utilisation and the organisation of behaviour. *Psychological Review*, **66**, 183–201.

Eysenck, M. W. (1975) Effects of noise, activation and response dominance on retrieval from semantic memory. *Journal of Experimental Psychology (Human Learning)*, **1**, 143–148.

Folkard, S., Knauth, P., Monk, T. H., and Rutenfrantz, J. (1976) The effect of memory load upon the circadian variation in performance efficiency under a rapidly-rotating shift system. *Ergonomics*, **19**, 479–488.

Forster, P. M. and Grierson, A. T. (1978) Noise and attentional selectivity: a reproducible phenomenon? *British Journal of Psychology*, **69**, 489–498.

Freeman, G. L. (1938) The optimal muscle tension for various performances. *American Journal of Psychology*, **51**, 146–150.

Grice, G. R. (1968) Stimulus intensity and response evocation. *Psychological Review*, **75**, 359–373.

Hamilton, P. and Hockey, G. R. J. (1971) Recency/primary ratio: A short test of task orientation. *Psychonomic Science*, **21**, 253–254.

Hamilton, P., Hockey, G. R. J., and Rejman, M. (1977) The place of the concept of activation in human information processing: An integrative approach. In S. Dornič (ed.), *Attention and Performance, Vol. 6*. Hillsdale, N.J.: Lawrence–Erlbaum.

Hartley, L. R. (1981) Noise, attentional selectivity, serial reactions and the need for experimental power. *British Journal of Psychology*, **72**, 101–107.

Hebb, D. O. (1949) *The Organisation of Behaviour*, New York: John Wiley & Sons.

Hockey, G. R. J. (1970a) Effect of loud noise on attentional selectivity. *Quarterly Journal of Experimental Psychology*, **22**, 28–36.

Hockey, G. R. J. (1970b) Signal probability and spatial location as possible bases for increased selectivity in noise. *Quarterly Journal of Experimental Psychology*, **22**, 37–42.

Hockey, G. R. J. (1970c) Changes in attention allocation in a multi-component task under loss of sleep. *British Journal of Psychology*, **61**, 473–480.

Hockey, G. R. J. (1973) Changes in information-selection patterns in multi-source monitoring as a function of induced arousal shifts. *Journal of Experimental Psychology*, **101**, 35–42.

Hockey, G. R. J. (1979) Stress and the cognitive components of skilled performance. In V. Hamilton and D. M. Warburton (eds.), *Human Stress and Cognition: An Information-Processing Approach*. Chichester: John Wiley & Sons.

Hockey, G. R. J. and Hamilton, P. (1970) Arousal and information selection in short-term memory. *Nature*, **226**, 866–867.

Hockey, G. R. J., McLean, A., and Hamilton, P. (1981) State changes and the temoral patterning of component resources. In J. Long and A. D. Baddeley (eds.), *Attention and Performance, Vol. 9*. Hillsdale, N.J.: Lawrence–Erlbaum.

Izard, C. E. (1972) *Patterns of Emotion*. New York: Academic Press.

Jerison, H. J. (1967) Signal detection theory in the analyses of human vigilance. *Human Factors*, **9**, 285–288.

Kahneman, D. (1973) *Attention and Effort*. Englewood Cliffs, N.J.: Prentice-Hall.

Kinsbourne, M. (1981) Single-channel theory. In D. H. Holding (ed.), *Human Skills*. Chichester: John Wiley & Sons.

Korchin, S. (1964) Anxiety and cognition. In C. Schearer (ed.), *Cognition: Theory, Research, Promise*. New York: Harper and Row.

Loeb, M. and Jones, P. D. (1978) Noise exposure, monitoring and tracking performance as a function of signal bias and task priority. *Ergonomics*, **21**, 265–272.

Mandler, G. (1979) Thought processes, consciousness and stress. In V. Hamilton and D. M. Warburton (eds.), *Human Stress and Cognition: An Information-Processing Approach*. Chichester: John Wiley & Sons.

Näätänen, R. (1973) The inverted-U relationship between activation and performance: A critical review. In S. Kornblum (ed.), *Attention and Performance, Vol. 4*. New York: Academic Press.

Niemi, P., von Wright, J. M., and Koivunen, E. (1977) Arousal and incidental learning: A reappraisal. *Reports from the Institute of Psychology, University of Turku, No.44*.

Norman, D. H. and Bobrow, D. G. (1973) On data-limited and resource-limited processes. *Cognitive Psychology*, **7**, 44–64.

Pepler, R. D. (1959) Warmth and lack of sleep: Accuracy or activity reduced. *Journal of Comparative and Physiological Psychology*, **52**, 446–450.

Poulton, E. C. (1970) *Environment and Human Efficiency.* Springfield, Ill.: Charles C. Thomas.

Prechtl, H. F. R. (1974) The behavioural states of the newborn infant (a review). *Brain Research*, **76**, 185–212.

Rabbitt, P. M. A. (1979) Current paradigms and models in human information processing. In V. Hamilton and D. M. Warburton (eds.), *Human Stress and Cognition: An Information -Processing Approach.* Chichester: John Wiley & Sons.

Rabbitt, P. M. A. (1981) Sequential reactions. In D. H. Holding (ed.), *Human Skills.* Chichester: John Wiley & Sons.

Reason, J. (In press) Lapses of attention. In R. Parasuraman and D. R. Davies (eds.). *Varieties of Attention.* New York: Academic Press.

Selye, H. (1956) *The Stress of Life.* New York: McGraw-Hill.

Stennett, R. G. (1957) The relationship of performance level to level of arousal. *Journal of Experimental Psychology*, **54**, 54–61.

Tanner, W. P. and Swets, J. A. (1954) A decision-making theory of visual detection. *Psychological Review*, **61**, 401–409.

Teichner, W. H. (1968) Interaction of behavioural and physiological stress reactions. *Psychological Review*, **75**, 271–291.

Thayer, R. G. (1967) Measurement of activation through self-report. *Psychological Reports*, **20**, 663–678.

Wachtel, P. (1967) Conceptions of broad and narrow attention. *Psychological Bulletin*, **68**, 417–429.

Welford, A. T. (1968) *Fundamentals of Skill.* London: Methuen.

Wickens, C. D. Processing resources in attention. In R. Parasuraman and D. R. Davies (eds.), *Varieties of Attention.* New York: Academic Press.

Wilding, J. M. and Mohindra, N. (1980) Effects of sub-vocal suppression articulating aloud and noise on sequence recall. *British Journal of Psychology*, **71**, 247–262.

Wilkinson, R. T. (1963) Interaction of noise with knowledge of results and sleep deprivation. *Journal of Experimental Psychology*, **66**, 332–337.

Yerkes, R. M. and Dodson, J. D. (1908) The relation of strength of stimulus to rapidity of habit-formation. *Journal of Comparative and Neurological Psychology*, **18**, 459–482.

Stress and Fatigue in Human Performance
Edited by G. R. J. Hockey
© 1983 John Wiley & Sons Ltd.

Chapter 13

Current Issues and New Directions

Robert Hockey

The previous twelve chapters have presented a broad coverage of stress and fatigue, principally from the point of view of performance changes. Because of the structure adopted in the volume, primarily based on the plan of considering each stressor separately, it seems necessary in this final chapter to provide an overview of the field as a whole. This will involve drawing together the various common strands that run through different contributions, and relating those to broad issues, central to current analyses of stress. In the final section of the book I hope to be able to outline some new directions for research, again building upon the foundations of the material presented in these chapters. While these are not new in any fundamental sense, they represent what I feel to be important shifts of emphasis in comparison with the work of the past 20 years.

MAJOR THEMES IN STRESS RESEARCH

Despite the fact that many authors have contributed to this book, all specialists in particular areas of the subject, there are a number of common threads that run right through the various contributions. It seems valuable to draw these together at this point in order to illustrate the major points of agreement in research on stress and performance. These are (a) the use of arousal theory, (b) the recognition of the importance of task demands, (c) the appreciation of individual differences, and (d) the emphasis on the interaction of field studies and laboratory experiments.

Arousal theory

Almost all the contributions make reference to arousal as the process underlying changes of performance with stress and fatigue. It is especially emphasized by Wesnes and Warburton (Chapter 8), who base the observed changes in performance resulting either from stress, or from attempts to cope with stress through the administration of drugs, on changes in electrocortical arousal. Other uses of the term are less specific than this, referring instead to broadly accepted notions such as the Yerkes–Dodson Law or the inverted-U relationship, or even more generally, to arousal as an alternative label for motivation. The strength of this conception is that it enables us to consider a large range of stress states within the same theoretical framework, and this has been very successfully done in some cases (see, for example Figure 56). On the other hand, as Hockey and Hamilton point out in Chapter 12, the uncritical acceptance of such a view may be extremely dangerous for the development of theory. It encourages over-generalization and premature grouping of separate findings.

Anxiety about such over-indulgent use of arousal theory is admitted by a number of the contributors. Eysenck (Chapter 10) is concerned that even the relatively sophisticated Easterbrook theory appears to be at odds with what information is available about cue utilization. Both he, and Hockey and Hamilton in Chapter 12, argue that it is a very serious mistake to group together all 'high arousal' stressors as if they were equivalent from the point of view of performance effects. Folkard, in Chapter 9, presents data that reinforce the idea that different dimensions of arousal, at least, must be entertained; with Monk (Chapter 4), he provides evidence of quite separate mechanisms for the rhythmic control of memory and speeded processing. This result is important, if it becomes firmly established, since a unitary arousal process cannot easily be used as the basis for two asynchronous bodily processes. Lastly, in Chapter 12, Hamilton and Hockey argue that a number of separate states can be discerned, at least in terms of performance changes observed under stress, and put the case for a qualitative rather than a quantitative arousal process.

The ubiquity of arousal theory in this book probably reflects the desire to be able to provide an account which is based on changes in bodily function. This is, understandably, more compelling in this area of psychology than in many others, since, as Selye originally pointed out so clearly (Selye, 1956), stressors are known to have widespread physiological effects. Wesnes and Warburton (Chapter 8) detail the bodily changes resulting from stress, as well as from attempts to alleviate it. Monk and Folkard (Chapter 4) illustrate the adaptation of bodily function required by shiftwork or trans-zonal jet flights. Ramsey (Chapter 2) reminds us of the very real physiological consequences of exposure to excessive heat or cold. Our use of arousal theory at least indicates that we are aware of the closeness of bodily processes to cognitive demands. Unfortunately, it is now clear that arousal is a far more complex process than originally conceived. If we are to continue to attempt to relate bodily and mental function (quite properly, in my opinion), it is clear that we need concepts more realistically suited to the task.

Task demands and the nature of performance effects

It has been clear for many years that stress effects in human performance may not be predictable from general knowledge or 'common sense'; they may be selective in terms of which human functions are affected, and often rather subtle. The traditional idea that any behaviour will be less efficient whenever unusual environmental conditions are present does not begin to even approximate the wealth of evidence presented in previous chapters. Part of the reason for the adoption of the arousal theory, of course, is that it may be used to account for unexpected results, such as improvement in performance under loud noise or high temperatures.

More specific than this observation, however, is the generalization that stressors may exhibit their effects primarily through particular kinds of performance function. A good example of this is provided by diurnal rhythm, where speeded processing is facilitated by testing later in the day, while working memory efficiency is impaired. Not only that, but a disruption of the normal rhythm by shiftwork or trans-zonal jet flights results in a far greater problem of adaptation for the former type of function than for the latter (see Chapters 4 and 9). Hockey (1970) showed that loud continuous noise tended to improve simple monitoring tasks (having a single source of signals or a low signal load), but to impair more complex ones. This argument is re-stated and extended by Jones in Chapter 3. Jones also argues that tasks having high memory loads may be particularly vulnerable to disruption by quite low levels of noise, though he suggests that this disruption may take the form of subtle changes in strategy rather than a fundamental reduction in the efficiency of the memory system. Such observations about strategy changes crop up in other chapters too, in addition to the extended treatment afforded it by Hockey and Hamilton in Chapter 12. Eysenck, in Chapter 10, clearly sees compensatory activity as very much a part of the state of being anxious and being required to carry out a task. Holding (Chapter 6) and Eysenck (Chapter 7) both treat strategic changes as the major effect of fatigue and incentives, respectively. Fatigue results in subjects making less effort and opting for low probability short-cuts to problems, while incentives tend to result in greater sustained effort and orientation to the task. Schönpflug, in Chapter 11, offers a sustained account of strategy changes as a central feature of behaviour under stress. Here choices of actions are seen to represent the adaptive or regulatory nature of coping.

In other chapters it is also apparent that an analysis of task characteristics in relation to patterns of performance change may reveal important insights into the nature of the stress effect. An unusual and interesting approach is demonstrated by Ramsey in Chapter 2 in relation to heat stress. Here, critical boundary curves are constructed for different combinations of exposure duration and temperature, representing various levels of decrement (iso-decrement functions). For tracking, monitoring, and combinations of the two, increases in temperature may be seen to be more serious than a lengthening of exposure time, while for cognitive tasks and choice reaction the two variables appear to contribute more or less equally to the increased likelihood of decrement. In addition, decrements are much more likely for the former group, whatever the conditions. Improvements in performance with increased temperature are rare, but may be found with simple RT tasks. Among the advantages that this analysis offers it is clear that such graphical summaries of results provide a valuable practical guide in designing environments for different jobs.

The classification of tasks is, however, rather arbitrary, determined largely by traditional notions of 'simple' and 'complex'. As was pointed out in Chapter 12, there *is* no readily available basis for classifying task demands. The division of function adopted by Jones in Chapter 3 is similar to our own, being based broadly on theoretical distinctions within experimental psychology. Clearly, there is a great need for the development of a widely-accepted taxonomy for performance functions if this relation between stress effects and task demands is to be made more generally useful and applicable to a wide range of work conditions.

Individual differences

We are all aware that some people always seem more stressed than others. Even when we allow for the obvious differences in circumstances between individuals there still remains something that we feel is attributable to the personality or temperament of the person. We say that they 'cannot cope with stress' as well as others. Is there any scientific basis for this observation?

In fact, although an interest in individual differences has long been central to experimental work on stress, we still know very little of real predictive value. There is, on the other hand, enough evidence now to suggest that some basis does exist for our everyday conclusions. Valuable discussions of individual differences are included by a number of contributors, notably Davies *et al.*, Monk and Folkard, Eysenck, Wesnes and Warburton, Folkard and Schönpflug. One of the more common measures of individual differences used in stress studies is that of temperament, as measured by the EPI or Heron inventory. Extroversion, in particular, is seen to be a temperament factor that correlates with the degree of performance change observed, though the direction of the effect is not always the same for different stressors or task conditions. It now appears (Revelle, Humphries, Simon, and Gilliland, 1980) that the impulsivity component of the extroversion factor may be more important than that of sociability, particularly in relation to circadian variation in efficiency. Folkard, in Chapter 9, has pointed out that these differences are not related to the phase of the body temperature cycle, normally seen to be closely related to performance. The task used by Revelle *et al.*, however, was heavily loaded on working memory, which, as Folkard and Monk have pointed out elsewhere (Folkard and Monk, 1981), may be quite dissociated from the temperature rhythm. Somewhat related to extroversion is the measurement of morning/evening types, also discussed by Folkard. Again, differences in performance rhythms are quite marked for groups differing in diurnal habits, even though temperature rhythms are very similar (Horne and Ostberg, 1976).

Extroversion is also implicated in effects of monotony, noise, incentives, drugs, sleep deprivation, and other stressors (Eysenck, 1982), though other factors have also been shown to be important. Michael Eysenck, in Chapter 7, argues that neuroticism may potentiate the beneficial or adverse effects of incentives, so that the performance of neurotic introverts (high-anxiety individuals) may be likely to suffer under high incentive, while that of neurotic extroverts is more likely to benefit. Stable individuals of either temperament type are less likely to show any effects. Of course, anxiety, as a trait characteristic, is likely to underly a great many of the differences that we know exist between individuals in the face of real-life stress. Eysenck's second chapter (Chapter 10) addresses itself directly to this area, locating the problem primarily in the 'worry' component of anxiety, rather than that of 'emotionality'. Eysenck also discusses the implications from work on attribution theory (Weiner, 1972). High anxiety appears to be associated with a tendency to attribute failure to a lack of self-ability, while individuals low in anxiety attribute failure more to a lack of effort: while the latter is reversible the former is not. High levels of trait anxiety may therefore be associated with a belief that nothing can be done to overcome stress or its resultant problems. Schönpflug, in Chapter 11, expands on this theme in great detail, focusing more on the efficiency of coping attempts and the assessment of psychological costs associated with coping. Although Schönpflug does not discuss the nature of the individual characteristics directly, his analysis clearly points towards the part played by the person in mediating effects of stress. In the present state of our knowledge it appears that we will need to examine these characteristics more closely than is possible using temperament or anxiety inventories, though much has been learned from using these instruments. A detailed study of individual behaviour under stress, of the kind attempted by Schönpflug and his colleagues, may be a more fruitful line of research in the long run.

Interaction between laboratory and field

In a book on stress and fatigue it would indeed be surprising if we were not able to offer some practical advice on how best to deal with these problems in the real world. What does seem quite striking, however, is how much contributors have felt able to draw upon field studies in presenting their arguments. This is particularly true, of course, for those chapters where the stressors dealt with are very much a feature of the working environment—those on monotony, heat and cold, noise and shiftwork. In all cases there is a clear gain from considering both kinds of evidence. In some cases the field data come from the few well-controlled examples of traditional industrial studies such as those of Wyatt on industrial fatigue, or Weston and Adams on noise effects. In other cases inferences can be made from published statistical data or naturalistic observations.

There are, of course, problems in using field data. The well-known Hawthorne effect warns us that any intervention in work places may result in wholesale changes in behaviour which may be quite unrelated to the specific effect of the treatment. On the other hand, it is clear that such problems can be overcome by particularly-well designed studies, such as that of Broadbent and Little (1960), mentioned by Jones. Furthermore, the need to consider practical data forces us into developing theories which have a realistic range of application. The traffic is not all one-way, however. In addition to making use of field information in developing our theoretical conceptions of stress, there has been considerable interest in applying what we know to the problems of the real world.

EMERGENT DIRECTIONS

It seems useful, in this final section, to sketch out what seem likely to be the major developments in the field in the near future. None of these is new, yet they have received only scant attention in the human performance literature of the last 20 years. For different reasons, I think they represent important new directions for our field of research. These are (a) the use of broad-band methodology, (b) the study of coping strategies, (c) the use of long-term study techniques, and (d) the study of everyday stress.

Broad-band methodology

Most of the chapters in this book have concentrated on a particular stressor or state. If we look closely enough we can see that the performance changes associated with these different conditions do not fall easily into the pattern expected from changes in a single underlying dimension of arousal. Chapter 12 examines these patterns directly and suggests the presence of a large number of state-specific profiles. In Chapter 12 we advocated the use of what we have called a broad-band research methodology in order to provide suitable data for adequately describing stress performance patterns. This amounts primarily to examining performance under particular stress states across a wide range of performance functions.

As we pointed out in the previous chapter, this approach represents primarily a change of emphasis away from research strategies which use particular tasks or paradigms with a wide range of stress conditions: most researchers manage to combine the two aims to some degree. Thus far, it is fair to say that only noise and circadian rhythms have been studied extensively with the broad-band method. Earlier work on sleep deprivation by Wilkinson (1964) was carried out very much in this spirit but became perhaps overly-concerned with the quest for *the* explanation of its effects on performance. Research on heat and cold has never been systematic enough to qualify as 'broad-band' in the sense meant here. Ramsey's impressive attempts to organize and integrate research findings in Chapter 2 are made more difficult than they might have been by the restricted range of performance functions covered by previous research efforts. In other cases (e.g. drugs or anxiety), while the range of tasks is quite extensive, there has been little attempt to provide any clear rationale for their selection or to relate performance measures to general theories of behaviour.

I am convinced that we need quite systematic application of this method in order to provide an adequate picture of the way in which different stressors affect behaviour. We can no longer assume that all stressors have the same effects on arousal (a view that is shared by several of the contributions, e.g. Eysenck and Folkard), so careful classification of similarities and differences becomes a central requirement for the development of suitable theories.

Coping strategies

A second area of development is likely to be an increase in the study of coping strategies. Although this has long been a central issue in clinical work on stress (Janis, 1958; Lazarus, 1966), it has only been considered seriously within the performance context since the publication of Glass and Singer's *Urban Stress* in 1972, and even then, only as a peripheral methodological problem. Whether a particular stressor affects a subject's performance or not can be shown to depend on (a) the degree of control he feels he is able to exercise over the environment, and (b) the extent to which he can adopt strategies for maintaining efficient performance.

Glass and Singer (1972) showed that noise only impaired performance when subjects considered that they had no control over it; the mere belief that the noise can be terminated if necessary is sufficient to prevent it affecting performance. This kind of result is now fairly common (see Cohen, 1980), either in the form of an amelioration of decrement during exposure to stress or a reduction in the size of after-effects. The most general kind of conclusion that emerges from such studies (e.g. Cohen and Weinstein, 1981) is that performance disruption is determined only partly by physical properties of the stressor. It also depends on the psychological characteristics of the situation; its predictability, controllability, social context, and so on.

There have been few attempts to study the actual strategies used by subjects in coping with stress, either in laboratory or in field studies. This is an area that has an obvious application, since it may reveal techniques that may be taught. It also again allows for a fruitful interaction of theory and application. The kind of approach adopted by Schönpflug and his colleagues (see Chapter 11), discussed above, suggests that these may be observed at both a gross level (e.g. turning off noises or leaving them on), or in a more subtle form (modifying the pattern of information processing in order to meet the demands of the task). The problem provides a promising stage for the interplay of traditional experimental psychology, personality, social psychology, and practical issues, and can be expected to grow in significance in the near future.

Long-term studies

The effect of exposure to stress under laboratory conditions probably owes something to the novelty of the situation. Subjects are rarely trained on the task for more than a minimum amount (sufficient to avoid gross errors or misunderstandings of requirements), and the combination of stressor and laboratory setting involves a degree of unfamiliarity rarely met in everyday life. We need to know how stressors affect people when they are familiar with them (as with working conditions or domestic problems), or when they have had an opportunity of learning to cope with them. We also need to study tasks which are well practiced, rather than continue to use only novel laboratory tasks. Do effects persist when subjects are tested for a large number of sessions, or do they vanish as coping strategies become available? Even more interesting do they change in character as both task and situation become more familiar?

I would like to see these important issues studied within the context of a longitudinal methodology, possibly trying to relate performance changes with subjective state and clinical measures over the course of adaptation to changing industrial or domestic demands, or even over the period of a course of treatment for depression or anxiety. On a more mundane, though more manageable level, it is important that we design experiments that will enable us to study changes in effects of stressors over reasonably long periods. For most psychological investigations an hour or two is the limit of our behavioural sample. For an analysis of response to stress that may offer some hope of application to broader areas of human life, a week or two should perhaps be considered a minimum. Rabbitt (1981) has demonstrated how valuable such an approach can be in illuminating the changes in performance associated with ageing; indeed, it is now widely agreed that longitudinal methods are the *only* ones that can provide suitable data on age changes.

In addition, again as Rabbitt (1981) has argued, it is essential that model of performance are capable of dealing with change, and not only with 'steady state' behaviour. In practical terms these considerations imply that research on stress (as well as on ageing) should probably be concentrated in a small number of long-term projects, each considering a wide range of behavioural indicators for a particular kind of stressor. Here, we need not worry too much about the 'purity' of our environment; of greater concern is its representativeness, whether centred on the family, the school, the office, or the factory. This has not been a tradition in stress research, except for a few military investigations. There are examples, however, that illustrate the value of the approach. Sheldon Cohen's work on adaptation of children living in the air corridor of Los Angeles airport (Cohen, Evans, Krantz, and Stokols, 1980) combines cross-sectional studies with a one-year follow up in order to assess possible effects of adaptation in schoolchildren. This work is particularly praiseworthy since it explicitly attempts to integrate laboratory findings into the study of realistic long-term problems. Other notable examples include some of the studies of urban and occupational stress carried out by Frankenhaeuser's group in Stockholm (e.g. Frankenhaeuser and Gardell, 1976), and Broadbent's analysis of the relations between job structure, cognitive processes, individual differences, and health in car workers (Broadbent and Gath, 1981). In all these studies the value of the research is enhanced by the great care taken in control and sampling of the populations, and the framing of questions to allow profitable interaction between practical problems and mainstream theory.

Stress in everyday life

Lastly, it seems necessary to extend our study of stress effects into the realm of everyday life. Much of what I have discussed in the previous section clearly overlaps with this point, since long-term studies are very much a part of the necessary methodology for research in naturalistic settings. The two are not synonymous, however, and it may be very useful to carry out cross-sectional studies in situations which have great ecological validity. There are, of course, a number of examples of this kind of approach. Idzikowski and Baddeley, in Chapter 5, discuss stress in parachutists and in divers. They also refer to moment-to-moment changes in heart-rate in people giving a research talk to an audience. Their current approach is to test people just before these kinds of anxiety-provoking activities on cognitive tasks as well as on physiological indicants of stress (Idzikowski and Baddeley, in preparation). Monk and Folkard (Chapter 4) have successfully applied laboratory-based notions of shiftwork adaptation and performance rhythms to a wide range of medical and industrual situations. Wesnes and Warburton (Chapter 8) relate their discussion of drug effects to real-life drug-oriented behaviour, such as smoking, as well as to their effects on the performance of laboratory tasks.

This application of laboratory techniques and task methodology to everyday life is, I think, long overdue. Despite much effort and good intentions we have benefited society at large rather less than we might have hoped. The success of the rather crude life change event index (Holmes and Rahe, 1967) in predicting susceptibility to general illness, myocardial infarction, and other health problems, does suggest that everyday stress can be usefully measured. It may not be too much to hope that performance measures may contribute to our understanding of chronic stress conditions, and help us to predict the onset of medical or social problems. Already, sophisticated measurement of heart-rate variability using power spectrum analysis (Mulder and Mulder, 1981) demonstrates dramatic changes in vascular control under variations in task load and practice, and indication of the mild cardiovascular stress resulting from attempts to cope with the demands of cognitive tasks. It is not a great step to ask whether these effects have anything in common with the executive stress syndrome. It may even help us to predict such dangers well before they arise.

SUMMARY

The chapter provides a brief overview of material presented in the book, and outlines some emerging developments in research methodology. First, it examines some current issues in stress research that are represented to various extents in previous chapters: these include arousal theory, task demands, individual differences, and the relation between laboratory and field studies. Secondly, four new directions in research are proposed, with greater emphasis being placed on broad-band methodology, coping strategies, long-term studies, and real-life behaviour. Reference to particular previous chapters is made throughout.

REFERENCES

Broadbent, D. E. and Gath, D. (1981) Symptom levels in assembly line workers. In G. Salvendy and M. J. Smith (eds.), *Machine Pacing and Occupational Stress.* London: Taylor and Francis.

Broadbent, D. E. and Little, E. A. J. (1960) Effects of noise reduction in a work situation. *Occupational Psychology*, **34**, 133–140.

Cohen, S. (1980) After-effects of stress on human performance and social behaviour. A review of research and theory. *Psychological Bulletin*, **88**, 82–108.

Cohen, S. and Weinstein, N. (1981) Non-auditory effects of noise on behaviour and health. *Journal of Social Issues*, **37**, 36–70.

Cohen, S., Evans, G. W., Krantz, D. S., and Stokols, D. (1980) Physiological, motivational and cognitive effects of aircraft noise on children. Moving from the laboratory to the field. *American Psychologist*, **35**, 231–243.

Eysenck, M. W. (1982) *Attention and Arousal: Cognition and Performance.* Springer-Verlag: Heidelberg.

Folkard, S. and Monk, T. H. (1981) Circadian rhythms in performance — one or more oscillators? In R. Sinz and M. R. Rosenzweig (eds.), *Psychophysiology 1980: Memory, Motivation and Event-related Potentials in Mental Operations.* Amsterdam: Elsevier, North-Holland.

Frankenhaeuser, M. and Gardell, B. (1976) Underload and overload in working life: Outline of a multidisciplinary approach. *Human Stress,* **2,** 35–46.

Glass, D. C. and Singer, J. E. (1972) *Urban Stress.* New York: Academic Press.

Hockey, G. R. J. (1970) Effect of loud noise on attentional selectivity. *Quarterly Journal of Experimental Psychology,* **22,** 28–36.

Holmes, T. H. and Rahe, R. H. (1967) The social readjustment rating scale. *Journal of Psychosomatic Research,* **11,** 213–218.

Horne, J. A. and Ostberg, O. (1976) A self-assessment questionnaire to determine morningness–eveningness in human circadian rhythms. *International Journal of Chronobiology,* **4,** 97–110.

Idzikowski, C. and Baddeley, A. D. (in preparation) Waiting in the wings: Apprehension, public speaking and performance.

Janis, I. L. (1958) *Psychological Stress.* New York: John Wiley & Sons.

Lazarus, R. S. (1966) *Psychological Stress and the Coping Process.* New York: McGraw-Hill.

Mulder, G. and Mulder, L. J. M. (1981) Task-related cardiovascular stress. In J. Long and A. D. Baddeley (eds.), *Attention and Performance, Vol. 9.* Hillsdale, N.J.: Lawrence–Erlbaum.

Rabbitt, P. M. A. (1981) Cognitive Psychology needs models for changes in performance with old age. In J. Long and A. D. Baddeley (eds.), *Attention and Performance, Vol. 9.* Hillsdale, N.J.: Lawrence–Erlbaum.

Revelle, W., Simon, M. S., Humphreys, L., and Gilliland, K. (1980) The interactive effect of personality, time of day and caffeine: A test of the arousal model. *Journal of Experimental Psychology (General),* **109,** 1–31.

Seyle, H. (1956) *The Stress of Life.* New York: McGraw-Hill.

Weiner, B. (1972) *Theories of Motivation: From Mechanisms to Cognition.* London: Markham.

Wilkinson, R. T. (1964) Effects of up to 60 hours sleep deprivation on different types of work. *Ergonomics,* **7,** 175–186.

Author Index

A'Brook, M. F., 86, *88*
Abbey-Wickrama, I., 86, *88*
Adam, E. E., 186, *197*
Adams, J. A., 158, *164*
Adams, R. G., 76, *91*
Adams, S., 82, *94*, *95*, 368
Ague, C., 230, *235*
Akerstedt, T., 113, *119*, 265, 266, *269*
Alfert, E., 292, *296*
Allen, G. W., 5, *25*
Allen, G. J., 275, *295*
Allport, D. A., 334, 357, *360*
Alluisi, E. A., 151, 160, *166*
Alon, S., 193, *199*
Altman, F., 279, *295*
Anderson, D. M., 16, *30*
Andersson, C. R., 126, *141*
Andersson, K., 229, *235*
Andreassi, J. L., 319, *326*
Andrew, D., 213, *240*
Antrobus, J. S., 18, *25*
Appley, M. H., 1, *25*
Appleyard, D., 83, *89*
Applin, L. C., 112, 114, *120*
Arbib, M. A., 332, *360*
Armitage, A. K., 227, *235*
Armstrong, C. M., 220, *235*
Arnold, M. B., 1
Aschoff, J., 100, 247, *271*
Ash, I. E., 147, *164*
ASHRAE, 37, 55, *57*
Astrand, I., 49, *57*
Astrand, P. O., 33, *57*, 210, *235*
Atkinson, J. W., 176, *197*
Atkinson, R. C., 170, 171, 172, *197*
Atteras, A., 131, *142*
Austin, F. H., 127, *141*, *143*
Azer, N. Z., 42, 50, 51, 57

Baade, W., 251, *269*
Baddeley, A. D., 123, 134, 139, *141*, *142*, 171, *197*, 251, 254, 256, 258, *269*, 282, 283, *295*, 371, *373*
Bahrick, H. P., 186, *197*
Bailey, J. P., 16, 20, *25*, *31*, 163, *164*
Bainbridge, L., 203, 204, *235*
Baker, M. A., 162, *166*
Baker, R. A., 16, *31*
Baldamus, W., 3, 9, 10, *25*
Ballard, G., 221, *336*
Bancroft, N. R., 228, *237*
Bankhart, C. P., 181, *198*
Barmack, J. E., 1, 2, 22, *25*, 146, *164*
Barth, J. L., 160, *164*, 314, *326*
Bartlett, D. J., 42, *57*
Bartlett, F. C., 146, 152, *164*
Bartley, S. H., 8, *29*, 146, 147, 149, 150, 159, 163, *164*
Baschera, P., 23, *25*, *27*
Basuwitz, H., 130, 131, 136, 137, *141*
Bassett, J. R., 212, 216, *235*
Bates, B. T., 153, *164*
Battmann, W., 302, 316, *329*
Bavelas, J., 185, *197*
Beach, N. F., 282, *295*
Beatty, J., 22, *28*, *29*, *30*
Beck, H., 220, *241*
Beech, H. R., 317, *326*
Belding, H. S., 37, *57*
Bell, C. R., 44, *58*
Bell, P. A., 45, *58*, 79, *89*, 336, *360*
Bellet, S., 229, *239*
Belt, J. A., 72, *89*
Beluzzi, J. D., 216, *241*
Beningus, V. A., 75, *89*
Benor, D., 39, *58*
Bensel, C. K., 54, *58*

Berger, B. D., 216, *241*, *243*
Berger, C., 150, *164*
Berger, R. J., 266, *271*
Bergstrum, B., 135, *141*
Bergstrum, F. G., 250, 256, *269*
Bergum, B. O., 16, *25*
Berkun, M. M., 132, 133, 137, *141*
Berlyne, D. E., 2, 21, *25*, 289, *296*
Bernstein, H. E., 3, *25*
Betts, G. H., 18, *26*
Bialek, H. M., 132, *141*
Biasiotto, J., 156, 157, *165*, *166*
Bickford, R. G., 227, *237*
Bickley, M., 226, *240*
Biehl, B., 217, 218, *235*
Bills, A. G., 146, 153, 158, *164*
Bindra, D., 170, *197*
Binstock, L., 220, *235*
Birchall, D., 11, *26*
Birnbaum, I. M., 222, 233, *235*, *237*, *240*
Bittner, K., 50, 51
Bjerner, B., 98, *119*
Björkman, M., 85, *93*
Bjurkvall, C., 22, *27*
Blackwell, P. J., 72, *89*
Blake, M. J. F., 80, *89*, 107, *119*, 195,
    197, 248, 252, 253, 254, 259, 261,
    263, 264, *269*
Blankstein, K. R., 256, *269*, 345, *300*
Bliss, E. L., 208, 209, *235*
Blix, A. S., 130, 131, *142*, *144*
Blockley, W. V., 43, *58*
Blood, M. R., 3, 4, 8, 24, *28*
Bloom, G., 131, *141*
Blowers, G. H., 181, *198*
Bobrow, D. G., 205, *240*, 357, *361*
Boden, C., 154, 155, *165*
Boles, W. E., 83, *89*
Bond, A. J., 214, *237*
Bookman, P. H., 214, *235*
Bootzin, R. R., 192, *199*
Bornemann, E., 308, 314, 325, *326*
Boucsein, W., 212, *235*
Bourne, P. G., 128, *141*, 207, *236*
Bradbury, R., 256, *270*
Branch, C. H. H., 208, *235*
Brass, C. G., 260, *271*
Brewin, R., 212, *238*
Brisson, G. R., 150, *166*
Broadbent, D. E., 20, 21, *26*, 68, 72, 73,
    76, 78, 79, 82, *89*, *92*, 147, 153, 158,

    164, *165*, 182, 189, *198*, 308, *326*,
    334, 336, 338, 339, 340, 344, 346,
    347, 349, 354, 355, 358, *360*, 368,
    371, *372*
Broadhurst, P. L., 337, *360*
Bronzaft, A. L., 80, *89*
Broughton, R., 249, *269*
Brown, C. A., 4, *29*
Brown, I. D., 154, 158, 159, *165*, 314,
    326
Brown, N. R., 277, *297*
Brown, R. A., 156, *167*
Browne, R. C., 109, *119*
Brozek, J., 22, *30*
Bruce, R. D., 66, *89*
Bruel, P. V., 63, *89*
Bruning, J. L., 139, *144*
Brunke, C., 323, *326*
Bryan, J. F., 178, *200*
Buck, L., 254, *269*
Bull, A. J., 84, *89*
Bunge, M., 331, 332, *360*
Burke, R. J., 317, *326*
Burkhardt, J. F., 128, 129, 135, *144*
Burnett, I., 14, *26*
Burney, C., 1, *26*
Burns, W., 65, *89*
Bursill, A. E., 44, 50, 51, *58*, 79, *89*, 152,
    165, 316, *326*
Bustamante, J. A., 139, *142*

Cadenius, B., 221, *238*
Cahoon, R. L., 18, *26*
Cairncross, K. D., 212, 216, *235*
Caldwell, L. S., 147, 148, *165*
Cameron, A. E., 186, *198*
Cameron, C., 146, *165*, 308, 314, 318, *327*
Campbell, J. A., 221, *239*
Cannon, W. B., 299, *327*, 335, *360*
Canon, L., 83, *92*
Cantril, H., 127, *142*
Caplan, R. D., 4, *26*
Cappell, H., 222, *241*
Carmichael, F. J., 220, *236*
Carmichael, L., 314, *327*
Carpenter, A., 46, *58*
Carpenter, J. A., 222, *236*
Cartwright, A., 226, *236*
Cattell, R. B., 124, *142*
Chadwick-Jones, J. K., 4, *29*
Chaffin, D. B., 158, *166*

Chambers, E. A., 158, *165*
Chambers, J., 181, *198*
Chase, T. N., 216, *236*
Cherns, A. B., 24, *26*
Cherry, N., 226, 227, *236*
Chiles, W. D., 42, 50, 51, *58*, 155, *165*, 282, *295*
Chowns, R. H., 86, *89*
Christensen, E. H., 210, *236*
Chute, E., 146, 147, 149, 150, 159, *164*
Cicero, T. J., 219, *236*
Clark, B., 155, *167*, 310, *330*
Clark, R. E., 53, *58*
Clarke, R. S. J., 53, 54, *60*
Cleary, P. J., 134, *143*
Clements, P. R., 265, *269*
Cobb, S., 4, *26*
Codling, P. J., 221, *241*
Cohen, A., 66, 82, 85, *89*
Cohen, A. I., 53, *58*
Cohen, A. J., 66, *90*
Cohen, J. B., 306, *328*
Cohen, J. S., 186, *198*
Cohen, S., 20, *26*, 78, 81, 83, *90*, 159, *165*, 369, 371, *372*
Coleman, R., 18, *25*
Colligan, M. J., 115, *121*
Colquhoun, W. P., 16, *26*, 102, 105, 107, 113, *119*, 221, *236*, 247, 248, 249, 252, 253, 260, 261, 263, 266, *269*, *271*, 342
Condry, J., 173, 174, 177, 181, *198*
Conrad, M. C., 267, *271*
Conroy, R. T. W. L., 99, *191*, 266, *269*
Consolo, S., 213, *236*
Cooke, E. C., 227, *239*
Cooper, P. F., 358, *360*
Cooper, R., 10, *26*
Copeman, A., 79, *91*
Corcoran, D. W. J., 69, 80, *90*, *93*, 189, *198*, 263, *271*, 308, *327*, 336, *360*
Corrodi, M., 216, *239*
Corso, J. F., 66, *90*
Cotten, D. J., 156, 157, *165*, *166*
Cox, T., 20, *26*
Craik, F. I. M., 171, *198*, 256, *269*, 345, *360*
Craik, K. J. W., 15, *26*
Cravens, R. W., 282, *296*
Crawford, A., 162, *165*
Crawford, T. I., 213, *236*

Crook, M. A., 81, *90*
Cunniff, P. F., 64, *90*
Curts, M. I., 178, *200*
Cuvo, A. J., 171, *198*
Czikszentmihalyi, M., 3, *26*

D'Zurilla, T., 291, *295*,
Daee, S., 77, 78, *90*, 345, *360*
Damon, A., 82, *90*
Darwin, C., 169
Davenport, W. G., 16, *26*, 182, *198*
Davey, C. P., 156, *165*
Davidson, J. M., 131, *142*
Davies, A. D. M., 264, *270*
Davies, D. R., 4, 16, 17, 22, *26*, *28*, *30*, 78, 80, *90*, 152, *166*, 186, *198*, 264, *270*, 308, 316, *327*, 343, 348, *360*, 366
Davies, S., 256, *271*
Davis, D. R., 153, *165*
Davis, F. M., 134, *142*
Davis, L. E., 24, *26*
De Bonis, M., 310, *326*
De Figueredo, J. W., 134, *141*
De Kock A. R., 228, *237*
De Pry, D., 221, *240*
Dean, R. D., 45, *58*
Deci, E. L., 191, 192, 193, *198*
Deese, J., 282, *295*, *296*
Deffenbacher, J. L., 279, 281, *295*
Dement, W. C., 21, *26*
Detambel, M. H., 159, *165*
Dewe, P., 2, *28*
Dey, M. K., 182, *198*
Dickinson, J., 156, *165*
Dickson, J. W., 9, *27*
Dickson, W. J., 8, *30*, 82, *93*
Dimond, R. C., 131, *143*
Dion, M., 150, *167*
Dixon, P. M., 186, *198*
Dixon, W. J., 82
Docter, R. F., 221, *236*
Doctor, R. M., 279, *295*
Dodson, J. D., 102, 127, 138, *144*, 175, 179, 191, *201*, 280, 281, 283, 284, *298*, 310, 314, *330*, 337, 338, 339, 345, 349, 359, *362*
Dolan, M. P., 222, *240*
Domino, E. I. F., 228, *236*, *239*
Dornbush, R. L., 186, *198*
Dornic, S., 77, *90*, 287, 288, *295*, 354, *360*
Dressler, F. B., 250, *270*

Drew, G. C., 221, *236*
Ducette, J., 186, *201*
Dudley, N. A., 8, *27*
Duffy, E., 20, 21, *27*, 337, *360*
Düker, H., 310, *327*
Dundee, J. W., 214, *236*
Dunnell, K., 226, *236*
Duraman, E. I., 154, 155, *165*
Durding, B., 221, *242*
Dusek, E. R., 53, 54, *58*

Earll, J. M., 131, *143*
Easterbrook, J. A., 139, *142*, 187, 189, *198*, 280, 281, 282, 285, *295*, 338, 339, 349, *360*
Ebbinghaus, H., 251, 257, 258, *270*
Edholm, O. G., 42, 46, *58*
Edsall, R. D., 83, *90*
Edwards, R. S., 45, *59*, 107, *119*, 252, 263, *269*
Egstrom, G. H., 137, *144*
Eide, R., 131, *142*
Ekblom, H. B., 309, *327*
Ekehammar, B., 275, *295*
El-Beheri, S., 175, 191, *200*
Ellertson, B., 130, *142*
Ellingboe, J., 222, 223, *236*
Elliot, R., 126, *142*, 181, *198*
Elliott, L. L., 66, *90*
Ellis, A., 315, *327*
Embrey, D. E., 105, 110, *120*
Endler, N. S., 275, *295*, *297*
England, L., 225, *237*
Enzer, N. E., 221, *236*
Epstein, S., 130, 131, 132, 135, 136, *142*
Eschenbrenner, J. A., 71, *90*
Essman, W. B., 227, *236*
Euler, U. S., 131, *141*
Evans, G. W., 371, *372*
Evtushenko, V. F., 136, *144*,
Eysenck, H. J., 18, *127*, 175, 177, 186, *198*, 225, 231, *236*, *237*, 261, 263, *270*
Eysenck, M. C., 171, 172, *199*
Eysenck, M. W., 3, 169, 171, 172, 173, 189, 190, *198*, *199*, 262, 264, *279*, 273, 277, 278, 280, 281, 283, 285, 288, *296*, 303, *327*, 336, 346, 354, 365, 366, 367, 369, *372*
Eysenck, S. B. G., 18, *27*

Fanger, P. O., 55, *58*
Farley, F. H., 18, *27*

Farley, S. V., 18, *27*
Farr, J. L., 178, *199*
Feldman, M. P., 182, 186, *199*
Fenichel, O., 2, *27*
Fentz, W. D., 130, 131, 132, 135, 136, 137, 140, *142*
File, S. E., 214, *237*
Fine, B. J., 43, 45, *58*
Finkleman, J. M., 75, *90*
Fisch, R. I., 186, *200*
Fisher, S. A., 69, *90*
Fitts, P. M., 186, *197*
Fitzgerald, P., 358, *360*
Flaherty, B., 181, *198*
Flemming, N. C., 134, *141*
Fogel, R. K., 156, *165*
Folkard, S., 97, 102, 103, 104, 105, 106, 107, 108, 109, 110, 111, 112, 113, 114, 115, *119*, *120*, 245, 252, 253, 255, 256, 258, 259, 262, 264, 265, 268, *270*, 340, 349, 354, *360*, 366, 367, 369, 371, *373*
Ford, A., 69, *91*
Forster, P. M., 75, *91*, 343, *361*
Fort, A., 252, 253, *270*
Fowler, C. J. H., 80, *91*, 189, 190, *199*, 281, *296*
Fowler, H., 2, *27*
Fox, J. G., 12, *27*
Fox, R. H., 46, *58*
Frankenhaeuser, M., 22, *27*, 78, *91*, 131, *141*, 159, *165*, 209, 210, 211, 228, 230, *237*, 301, 303, 310, 318, *372*, *328* 371, *373*
Frantz, A. G., 131, *143*
Fraser, J. A., 6, 8, *32*
Fraser, D. C., 153, *165*
Fraser, R., 20, *27*
Freedman, A., 54, *58*
Freeman, G. L., 252, *270*, 337, 338, *361*
French, J. R. P., 4, *26*
French, N. R., 68, *91*
Freud, S., 124, *142*, 290
Fruberg, J. E., 99, 113, *119*, *120*
Frolov, M. V., 136, *144*
Fussler, C., 23, *27*, *30*
Fuxe, K., 216, *239*

Gabb, J. E., 156, *167*
Gafafer, W. M., 45, *58*
Gagné, R. M., 152, *165*

Gale, A., 18, 21, *27*, *29*
Ganzer, V. J., 279, *296*
Garattini, S., 213, *236*
Gardell, B., 371, *373*
Gardner, J. E., 12, *29*
Gardner, G. T., 79, *91*
Gates, A. I., 247, 248, 251, 254, *270*
Gath, D., 371, *372*
Gattoni, F., 86, *91*
Gattoni, W. G., 86, *88*
Gaydos, I. H. F., 53, *58*
Geiwitz, P. J., 2, *27*
George, A. J., 217, *238*
Getz, Y., 186, *198*
Getzels, J. W., 300, *327*
Ghonheim, M. M., 214, *237*
Gieseking, C. C., 175, 191, *200*
Gilbert, D. G., 231, *237*
Gillan, P. W., 186, *198*
Gilliland, K., 261, *271*, 366, *373*
Girodo, M., 294, *296*
Givoni, R., 42, *58*
Glass, D. C., 20, *27*, 78, 79, 81, *90*, *91*,
    159, *165*, 302, *327*, 369, *373*
Glorig, A., 65, *93*
Glover, C. B., 282, *296*
Glucksberg, S., 179, 180, 183, *199*
Glynn, C. J., 265, *270*
Goldberg, A. N., 309, *327*
Goldstein, D. B., 220, *237*
Gonzales, A., 139, *142*
Gordon, W. M., 289, *296*
Gorsuch, R., 274, *297*
Gottsdanker, R., 181, *199*
Graeven, D. B., 79, *91*
Graham, I. M. F., 134, *142*
Grandjean, E., 22, 23, 24, *25*, *27*, *30*, *31*
Grant, R., 83, *92*
Gray, J. A., 188, *199*, 206, *237*
Gray, M. M., 256, *270*
Green, D. E., 225, *238*
Green, R. G., 84, *91*
Greenblatt, D. J., 211, 212, *237*
Gregory, M., 72, 73, *89*, 346, *360*
Grether, W. R., 42, 50, 51, *58*
Grice, G. R., 341, *361*
Grierson, A. T., 75, *91*, 130, 131, 136,
    140, *142*, 343, *361*
Griew, S., 22, *28*
Griffith, D. N. W., 140, *143*
Griffiths, P. J., 219, *240*

Grimwade, J., 226, *240*
Grinker, R. R., 128, 130, *141*, *142*
Gronow, D. G. C., 42, *57*
Grose, W., 220, *238*
Grubb, E. A., 10, *28*
Guest, D., 3, 11, *28*
Guest, R. H., 9, *31*
Guha, D., 228, *237*
Guildford, J. S., 226, *237*
Guski, R., 323, *327*
Gutin, B., 156, *165*

Hacker, W., 308, 317, 325, *327*
Hackman, J. R., 11, *28*
Haefeley, W. E., 212, 216, 217, *237*
Hafer, M. D., 265, *269*
Haffner, J. F. W., 221, *235*
Hahl, D., 213, *241*
Halberg, F., 99, *120*, 250, 266, *270*
Halbert, B. L., 277, *297*
Hall, G. H., 227, *235*
Hall, G. M., 230, *237*
Hall, S. W., 319, *328*
Hallermann, B., 314, *328*
Halse, K., 130, *142*
Hamilton, P., 21, *28*, 74, 77, 78, 79, *91*,
    163, *165*, 190, 196, *199*, 205, 233,
    257, 263, *269*, *270*, 284, 285, *296*,
    316, *327*, 339, 340, 343, 344, 345,
    346, 349, 350, 352, 354, 357, *361*, 365
Hamilton, R., 282, *296*
Hamilton, V., 310, *327*
Hammerton, M., 135, *142*, 155, 156, *165*
Hand, D. J., 86, *91*
Hanks, G. W., 217, *238*
Hansen, J. R., 131, *142*
Hansen, O., 210, *236*
Hanson, C., 149, *165*
Hansson, L., 85, *92*
Harackiewicz, J. M., 186, *199*
Harley, W. F., 171, *199*
Harrington, J. M., 97, 115, *120*
Harris, C. S., 69, *94*
Harrison, R. V., 306, *327*
Hartley, J. T., 222, 233, *235*, *237*, *240*
Hartley, L. R., 70, 75, 76, 78, 79, 80, *91*,
    343, *361*
Hartmann, F., 228, *242*
Hatch, T. F., 37, *57*
Hatter, J. E., 256, *269*
Hauser, H., 227, *237*

Hawkins, R. A., 223, *240*
Hawkswell Curtis, J. W., 134, *141*
Hayward, S. C., 83, *89*
Hebb, D, O., 2, 20, 21, *28*, 138, *142*, 339, *361*
Heckhausen, H., 300, 314, *327*
Heimstra, N. W., 228, *237*
Hellbruegge, T., 259, *271*
Helmreich, R., 127, *143*
Herbert, M. J., 154, *165*
Herridge, C. F., 86, *88*, *91*
Herzberg, F., 194, *199*
Hewett, A. J., 217, *238*
Hildebrandt, G., 109, *120*, 253, *270*
Hill, A. B., 14, 17, *28*
Hill, K. T., 281, *297*
Hill, P., 230, *237*
Hillgruber, A., 310, *327*
Hindmarch, I., 213, 217, *238*
Hitch, G. J., 171, *197*, 254, 258, *269*, 282, 283, *295*
Hockey, G. R. J., 17, 21, *26*, *28*, 70, 73, 74, 78, *91*, 139, *143*, 152, 163, *165*, 190, *199*, 205, 229, 232, 233, *235*, *238*, 248, 249, 252, 256, 257, *271*, 284, *296*, 302, 316, *327*, *328*, 331, 338, 339, 343, 345, 346, 350, 353, 354, *361*, 363, 365, *373*
Hodges, W. F., 125, 126, *143*, 275, 289, *296*
Holding, D. H., 145, 146, 156, 159, 160, 161, 162, *164*, *166*, 314, *326*, *330*, 365
Hollstedt, L., 223, *240*
Holmberg, I., 46, 55, *58*
Holmberg, G., 221, *238*
Holmberg, L., 223, *240*
Holmes, D. S., 290, *296*
Holmes, T. H., 301, *328*, 372, *373*
Holroyd, K. A., 293, *296*
Hormann, H., 77, *92*
Horn, D., 225, *238*
Horne, J. A., 260, 261, *271*, 367, *373*
Horney, K., 315, *328*
Horvath, S. M., 54, *58*
Houston, J. P., 172, *200*
Houston, B. K., 75, *92*
Hovland, C. I., 252
Howell, W. H., 247, *271*
Hughes, D. G., 108, 111, 112, *120*, 252, 253, *271*
Hughes, R., 212, *238*

Hulin, C. L., 3, 4, 8, 24, *28*
Hull, C. L., 139
Humphries, M. S., 261, *271*, 366, *373*
Hunt, B. I., 112, *120*, 252, 254, *271*
Hunt, B. J., 217, *238*
Hunt, D. L., 12, *29*
Hunt, W. A., 223, *238*

Iampietro, P. F., 43, *59*
Idzikowski, C. I., 123, 371, *373*
Ikard, F. F., 225, *238*
Il'Yutchenok, R. Y., 227, 228, *238*
Indestrom, C. M., 221, *238*
Insua, A., 139, *142*
Irons, F. M., 68, *94*
Isaac, W., 2, *28*
ISO, 49, *59*
Israel, Y., 220, *236*
Istel, J., 140, *143*
Itil, T. M., 227, *242*
Izard, C. E., 1, *28*, 358, *361*

Jackson, D. P., 249, *271*
Jaeger, M., 156, *165*
James, I. M., 140, *143*
James, S. L., 153, *164*
James, W., 5
Janis, I. L., 319, *328*, 369, *373*
Jansen, G., 84, 86, *92*
Jarrard, L. E., 148, *166*
Jarvik, M. E., 231, *238*
Jaynes, W. E., 154, *165*
Jenkins, H. M., 263, *271*
Jennings, J. R., 319, *328*
Jerison, H. J., 15, *28*, 72, 73, 78, *92*, 348, *361*
Jermini, C., 23, *31*
Jhamandas, K., 220, *241*
Johansson, G., 20, *28*, 228
Johnson, D. D., 213, *238*
Johnson, J. H., 204, *238*
Johnson, R., 186, *199*
Jones, B., 131, 140, *142*
Jones, B. M., 224, *238*
Jones, D. M., 61, 68, 75, 78, 80, 83, *90*, *92*, 186, *198*, 343, *360*, 365, 368
Jones, K. N., 18, 22, *31*
Jones, P. D., 74, *92*, 343, *361*
Jones, T. M., 75, *92*
Jones, W. L., 127, *143*

Jonsson, A., 85, *92*
Jordan, A., 139, *142*

Kahneman, D., 161, *166*, 179, 187, *199*, 205, *238*, 285, 286, 288, *296*, 306, 309, 310, *328*, 338, 357, *361*
Kalant, M., 220, 221, *238*
Kallstrom, D. W., 275, *296*
Kaplan, H., 222, *241*
Kappell, B., 212, *241*
Kappell, B., 212, *241*
Karasek, R. A., 304, 313, *328*
Karsdoff, G., 85, *92*
Kasl, S. V., 4, *28*
Katz, R. I., 216, *236*
Kaur, G., 182, *198*
Kausler, D. H., 186, *199*
Kawamura, M. L., 228, *239*
Kazdin, A. E., 192, *199*
Kearney, J. T., 149, 158, *166*
Keenan, J., 282, *295*
Keil, R. C., 10, *28*
Kendall, L. M., 178, *200*
Kenig, M. B., 227, *239*
Kern, R. P., 132, *141*
Kerr, W. A., 10, 12, *28*, 81, *92*
Kershbaum, A., 229, 230, *239*
Kerslake, D. McK., 43, *60*
Kiernan, K. E., 226, 227, *236*
Kiess, H. O., 54, *59*
King, P. D., 221, *243*
Kinsbourne, M., 334, *361*
Kirkpatrick, F. M., 12, *28*
Kishida, K., 18, 24, *28*
Klappach, H., 85, *92*
Klein, K. E., 112, 113, *120*, 252, 253, 254, *271*
Kleitman, N., 102, *120*, 247, 248, 249, 254, 260, 266, *271*
Knauth, P., 103, 104, 107, 108, *119*, *120*, 258, *270*
Knight, R., 12, *28*
Knott, V. J., 221, 227, 231, *239*
Kobrick, J. L., 45, 54, *58*, *60*
Koch-Weser, J., 212, *237*
Kohler, H. K., 63, *92*
Koivunen, E., 343, *361*
Kolin, E. A., 18, *32*
Koller, M., 115, *120*
Konecni, V. J., 84, *92*
Kopin, J. J., 216, *236*

Korchin, S., 130, *141*, 349, *361*
Kornfeld, C. M., 22, *28*
Kornhauser, A., 20, *28*
Korte, C., 83, *92*
Kowal, B., 16, *31*
Kraepelin, E., 253, *271*
Kragh, U., 136, 137, *143*
Krantz, D. S., 371, *372*
Krause, M. S., 125, *143*
Kremen, I., 125, *143*
Krenauer, M., 315, *328*
Krivolahvy, J., 150, *166*
Krkovic, A., 22, *26*
Kruglanski, A. W., 188, 193, *199*
Krugman, A. D., 289, *296*
Kryter, K. D., 66, *92*
Kubose, S. K., 2, *29*
Kukla, A., 290, *296*
Kumar, R., 227, *239*

Lacey, B. C., 126, *143*
Lacey, J. I., 21, *29*, 126, *143*
Lader, M., 206, *239*
Lader, M. H., 227, *239*
Ladinski, H., 213, *236*
Lahiri, S., 45, *59*
Laird, D. A., 251, 255, 258, 259, *271*
Lambiase, M., 227, *239*
Lance, B. M., 158, *166*
Landauer, A. A., 221, 239
Landon, P. B., 174, *200*
Lang, L., 16, *26*
Langdon, J. N., 6, 7, 13, 17, *32*
Langdon, F. J., 81, *90*
Langkilde, G., 55, *59*
Laroche, J. P., 186, *198*
Laughlin, P. R., 186, *199*
Launier, R., 299. 301, *328*
Laux, L., 317, *330*
Laverty, R., 216, *242*
Lawler, E. E., 11, *28*
Lawrence, P. R., 10, *31*
Lazarus, R. S., 126, *143*, 282, 292, 293, *295*, *296*, 299, 301, 306, *328*, 369, *373*
Lee, E. S., 185, *197*
Lee, L. C., 282, *296*
Lee, S. E., 127, *144*
Lehr, D. J., 16, *25*
Leigh, G., 221, *239*
Lem, C., 9, *30*

Levi, L., 205, 210, 211, *239*, 266, *269*
Levi, R., 209,
Levine, J., 182, *199*
Levine, S., 131, *142*
Lewis, C. E., 127, *143*
Lewis, M., 299, *329*
Lewis, T., 193, *199*
Lezak, A., 78, 83, *90*
Lidbrink, P., 216, *239*
Liebert, R. M., 277, 279, 282, 289, 291, 297
Lind, A. R., 35, *59*
Lindman, R., 219, *239*
Lindsley, D. B., 20, *29*, 206, *239*
Lintell, M., 83, *89*
Lipp, J. A., 213, *239*
Little, F. A. J., 82, *89*, 368, 372
Littleton, J. M., 219, *240*
Litwin, G., 176, *197*
Lloyd, J. W., 265, *270*
Lobban, M. C., 105, 106, 109, 114, 115, *119*, *120*, 265, *270*
Locke, E. A., 24, *29*, 177, 178, 179, 184, *199*, *200*
Lockhart, J. M., 53, 54, *58*, *59*
Lockhart, R. S., 171, *198*
Lodahl, T. M., 11, *29*
Loeb, M., 74, 79, *92*, *93*, 151, 162, *166* 343, *361*
Lofthus, G. K., 149, *165*
Loftus, G. R., 173, *200*
Lombard, W. P., 250, *271*
London, H., 21, 22, *29*, 163, *166*
Long, M. A., 221, *236*
Longoni, R., 213, *240*
Loomis, T. A., 221, *240*
Lowndes, H. E., 213, *238*
Lubin, B., 137, *144*
Lucas, B., 18, *27*
Lucas, J. D., 289, *296*
Luczak, H., 204, *240*
Lundberg, U., 78, *91*, 159, *165*, 303, 310, 312, 317, *327*, *328*
Lushene, R., 274, *297*
Luthans, F., 24, *30*
Lyddan, J. M., 147, 148, *165*
Lyman, J., 43, *58*

Macfarlane, D. A., 170, *200*
Mackworth, N. H., 14, 15, *26*, *29*, 41, 42, 44, 46, 50, *59*

MacPherson, R. K., 37, *59*
Magnusson, D., 275, *295*
Magoun, H. W., 20, *29*
Maher, J. R., 24, *29*
Mahneker, A., 150, *164*
Majchrowicz, E., 223, *238*
Maller, J. B., 186, *200*
Malmo, R. B., 21, *29*
Mandler, G., 125, *143*, 277, *296*, 339, *361*
Mandler, J. M., 125, *143*
Mann, H., 247, *271*
Mann, L., 319, *328*
Markov, S., 146, *167*
Marlatt, G. A., 227, *240*
Marshall, S. L. A., 126, *143*
Martens, S., 221, *238*
Martin, B., 125, *143*
Martin, E., 23, *27*
Martin, G. J., 220, *241*
Martuza, V. R., 275, *296*
Mason, J. W., 128, *149*, 208, 210, *240*
Masuda, M., 301, *328*
Matarazzo, J. D., 225, *240*
Mathews, K., 83, *92*
Mausner, B., 194, *199*
May, D. N., 69, *92*
Mayer, J., 156
Mayer, R. E., 283, 284, *296*
Maynert, E. W., 209, *239*
McActee, D. B., 221, *243*
McBain, W. N., 19, *29*
McCarthy, D. P., 80, *89*
McClish, A., 213, *240*
McCullers, J. C., 180, 184, *200*
McDowell, R. J., 2, *29*
McFarland, R. A., 154, 157, 159, *166*
McGehee, W., 12, *29*
McGrath, J. E., 301, 305, 318, *328*
McGrath, J. J., 70, *92*
McGraw, K. O., 180, 183, 184, *200*
McGuiness, D., 162, *166*, 309, *329*
McLean, A., 345, 354, *361*
McLean, P. D., 323, *328*
McLeod, P., 325, *328*
McLeod, W. R., 127, *143*
McNamara, H. J., 186, *200*
Meares, R., 226, *240*
Mears, J. D., 134, *143*
Medhurst, C., 156, *165*
Meers, A., 109, *120*
Mehrabian, A., 277, *297*

Meichenbaum, D. H., 293, 294, *296*, *297*, 300, 316, 321, *328*
Mellberg, B., 219, *239*
Mellis, I., 22, *27*
Mello, N. K., 224, *240*
Mende, W., 127, *143*
Merton, J., 148, *166*
Mewaldt, S. P., 214, *237*
Meyer, J., 156, *165*
Meyer, W. U., 314, *328*
Meyer, W. V., 290, *296*, *297*
Michaels, E. J., 177, *200*
Michelson, M., 247, *271*
Miclette, A. L., 9, *31*
Mierop, J., 325, *328*
Migeon, C. J., 208, *235*
Migler, B., 212, *240*
Milgram, S., 83, *92*
Miller, G. A., 68, *93*
Miller, H. E., 186, *200*
Miller, I. W., 79, *93*
Miller, J. D., 67, *93*
Miller, L. L., 222, *240*
Miller, N. E., 2, *32*
Mills, J. N., 99, *119*, 252, 253, 266, *269*, 270
Milsum, J. H., 35, *59*
Mischel, W., 273, 274, 275, 276, *297*
Mitchell, J. F., 213, *240*
Mitchell, H. H., 55, *59*
Mohindra, N., 78, *95*, 343, 345, *362*
Monk, T. H., 97, 102, 103, 104, 105, 106, 107, 108, 109, 110, 112, 114, 115, *119*, *120*, 255, 256, 258, 265, 267, 268, *270*, *271*, 321, *328*, 349, 366, 367, 371, *373*
Moore-Ede, M. C., 100, *120*
Moran, S. L. V., 79, *93*
Morgan, B. B., 160, *166*
Morgan, J. J. B., 69, *93*
Morgan, W. P., 310, *329*
Morlock, H. C., 22, *32*
Morris, L. W., 277, 278, 279, 282, 285, 289, 291, *297*
Morris, P. E., 18, *27*, *29*
Morrissey, S. J., 37, 48, 49, 50, 51, 52, 60
Mortagy, A. K., 42, *59*
Moskowitz, H., 221, *240*
Moss, J. N., 220, *241*
Mosso, A., 123, 124, *147*

Mulas, A., 213, *240*
Mulder, G., 371, *373*
Mulder, L. J. M., 371, *373*
Mullin, J., 80, *90*, *93*, 263, *271*
Munsterberg, H., 1, 4, 5, *29*
Murphree, M. B., 227, *239*, *240*
Murrell, K. F. H., 8, *29*
Muscio, B., 145, *166*
Myers, A. K., 2, *29*
Myers, C. S., 1, 5, *29*
Myers, T. I., 18, *29*
Myrsten, A. L., 22, *27*, 223, 228, 230, *240*

Näätänen, R., 302, 310, *329*, 338
Nachreiner, F., 182, *200*
Naitoh, P., 221, *236*
Nelson, T. M., 8, *29*
Nelson, T. O., 171, *200*
Neufeld, R. W., 304, *329*
Newbury, P., 140, *143*
Newell, A., 300, 301, *329*
Newman, R. I., 12, *29*
Nicholson, N., 4, *29*
Nielsen, R. H., 223, *240*
Niemi, P., 343
NIOSH, 37, 47, 48, 49, *59*
Nixon, J. C., 65, *93*
Noble, E. P., 222, *235*, *240*
Noel, G. R., 131, *143*
Norheden, B., 22, *27*
Norman, D. A., 205, *240*, 357, *361*
Norman, W. H., 79, *93*
Nottelman, E. D., 281, *297*
Novaco, R., 316, 321, *328*

O'Hanlon, J., 22, 23, *27*, *29*, *30*
O'Neal, E. C., 84, *91*
O'Toole, J., 11, *30*
Ogden, W., 8
Ohström, E., 85, *93*
Okada, M., 275, *295*
Ollerhead, J. B., 66, *93*
Olsen, L., 216, *239*
Ongley, G. C., 181, *198*
Oritz, A., 219, *240*
Ornstein, R. E., 10, *30*
Osborne, E. E., 5, *30*
Osborne, J. P., 134, *142*
Ostberg, O., 260, *271*, 367, *373*
Osterkamp, J., 77, *92*

Osternig, L. R., 153, *164*
Ostrovskaya, R. V., 227, 228, *238*

Pack, M., 156, *166*
Page, R. A., 83, *93*
Pai, S. B., 41, 43, *60*
Pal, N., 220
Panditt, S. K., 214, *236*
Pappajohn, D. J., 229, *239*
Parasuraman, R., 17, 22, *26*, *30*, 152, *166*, 348, *360*
Parish, T. S., 22, *25*
Parker, C. D., 68, *94*
Parker, E. S., 222, 233, *235*, *237*, *240*
Parkes, K. R., 358, *360*
Parrish, T. S., 163, *164*
Parrott, A. C., 217, *238*
Passchier-Vermeer, W., 66, *93*
Patel, U. A., 225, *241*
Patkai, P., 22, *27*, 209
Pawlowska-Skyba, D., 109, *121*
Pearl, J., 22, *25*, 163, *164*
Pearson, R. M., 140, *143*
Pearsons, K. S., 63, 67, *93*
Peavler, W. S., 179, *199*
Pepeu, G., 213, *240*
Pepler, R. D., 42, 43, 46, 50, *59*, 79, *93*, 336, *362*
Percival, L., 79, *93*
Perret, E., 22, *27*
Persky, H., 130, *141*
Persson, L. O., 219, *241*
Pervin, L. A., 299, *329*
Peterson, A. P. G., 64, *93*
Peto, J., 225, *241*
Pettit, A. N., 260, *271*
Philips, C., 227, *241*
Phillis, J. W., 220, *241*
Pierson, W. R., 154, *166*
Pillsbury, W. B., 260, *271*
Pincherle, G., 225, *241*
Pinneau, S. R., 4, *26*
Pitkethley, G., 214, *242*
Pless, J. E., 221, *241*
Ploeger, A., 127, *143*
Plott, F. W., 221, *239*
Pocock, S. J., 115, *121*
Pococke, D. A., 221, *239*
Pofenberger, A. T., 154, *166*
Porter, L. W., 4, *30*
Post, B., 22, *27*, 228, 229, 230, *235*

Potepan, P. A., 290, *298*
Poulas, C. X., 222, *241*
Poulton, E. C., 43, 45, 46, 50, 51, 54, *59*, *60*, 310, *329*, 350, *362*
Pradhan, S. N., 228, *237*
Prechtl, H. F. R., 331, 332, 333, 334, 346, *362*
Pribram, K. H., 162, *166*, 206, 207, *241*, 309, *329*
Price, L., 18, *32*
Pritchard, R. B., 178, *200*
Prokop, L., 109, *121*
Prokop, O., 109, *121*
Provins, K. A., 44, 47, 53, 54, *58*, *60*

Rabbitt, P. M. A., 68, 76, *93*, 153, *166*, 335, 344, 349, 355, *362*, 370, *373*
Rachman, S. J., 127, *143*
Radloff, R., 127, *143*
Rahe, R. H., 371, *373*
Ramsey, J. D., 35, 37, 41, 42, 43, 44, 45, 46, 47, 48, 49, 50, 51, 52, 55, *59*, *60*, 350, 365, 369
Randall, L. O., 212, 213, 214, *236*, *241*, *243*
Rankin, R. E., 186, *197*
Ray, O. S., 218, *241*
Reason, J. T., 358, *362*
Reddy, S. P., 45, 55, *60*
Reid, A., 128, *143*
Reid, C., 148, *166*
Reif, W. E., 24, *30*
Reinberg, A., 114, *121*
Rejman, M., 21, *28*, *91*, 163, *165*, 190, *199*, 284, *296*, *327*, 343, 354, *361*
Revell, A., 225, 226, *242*
Revelle, W., 177, *200*, 261, 262, *271*, 366, *373*
Reykowski, J., 316, *329*
Rhodes, F., 12, *29*
Rice, C. G., 69, *92*
Rich, G. O., 154, *166*
Richardson, A., 18, *27*
Ridges, A. F., 217, *238*
Rim, Y., 42, *58*
Rissler, A., 22, *27*
Riter, A., 188, *199*
Robinson, D. W., 66, *93*
Rodahl, K., 33, *57*, 210, *235*
Roehl, J., 294, *296*
Roethlisberger, F. J., 8, *30*, 82, *93*

Rohmert, W., 109, *120*, 253, *270*
Roman, J., 127, *143*
Rose, M., 5, *30*
Rose, R. M., 128, *141*, *144*
Rosen, S., 85, *93*
Rosenthall, J., 256, *270*
Ross, B. M., 222, *236*
Ross, D. H., 220, *241*
Roth, G., 227, *237*
Rothe, H. F., 8, *30*
Rotton, J., 79, *93*
Rubin, B. M., 186, *200*
Russek, H., 225, *241*
Russell, J. A., 277, *297*
Russell, M. A. H., 225, 227, *239*, *241*
Russell, R. W., 41, *60*, 204, *241*
Rutenfrantz, J., 103, 104, 106, 107, 108, 109, 115, *119*, *120*, *121*, 247, 253, 258, 259, *270*, *271*
Ryan, A. H., 157, 158, *166*

Sabey, B. E., 221, *241*
Salame, P., 69, *94*
Saldanha, E., 16, *30*
Sales, S. M., 22, *30*
Samuels, L. Y., 208, *235*
Sange, P., 323, *326*
Sarason, I. G., 204, *238*, 278, 289, *297*, 300, *329*
Sarason, S. B., 277, *296*
Saslow, G., 225, *240*
Schachter, S., 231, *241*, 276, 277, 292, *297*
Schäfer, W., 310, 311, 312, *329*
Schlosberg, H., 138, *144*
Schmidtke, H., 308, 317, *329*
Schneider, K., 285, *298*
Schönpflug, W., 299, 300, 301, 302, 303, 306, 308, 310, 311, 312, 313, 315, 317, 319, *328*, *329*, *330*, 355, 358, 365, 366, 367, 370
Schubert, D. S. P., 21, *29*, 163, *166*
Schubert, E. D., 68, *94*
Schultz, P., 300, 302, 303, 304, 306, 308, 309, 312, 313, 316, 319, 320, 321, *329*
Schultz, R. E., 227, *240*
Schvartz., E., 39, *58*, *60*
Schwab, R. S., 148, *166*
Schwartz, B. E., 227, *237*
Scott, D., 256, *269*
Seligman, M. E. P., 289, *297*

Sellers, C. M., 227, *235*
Selye, H., 264, 335, *362*, *373*
Serra, C., 227, *239*
Shackleton, V. J., 4, 16, *26*
Shader, R. I., 211, 212, *237*
Shane, W. P., 131, *144*
Shantz, D. W., 186, *200*
Shapin, M. J., 158, *164*
Shapiro, A. P., 317, *330*
Shedletsky, R., 275, *297*
Sherrod, D. D., 302, *330*
Sherrod, D. R., 79, *94*
Shields, J., 274, *297*
Shiffman, S. M., 226, 227, *241*
Shiffrin, R. M., 170, *197*
Shingledecker, C. A., 160, 161, *166*, 314, *330*
Shirley, E., 79, *91*
Shoenberger, R. W., 69, *94*
Sholitan, R. D., 125, *143*
Siddall, G. J., 15, *30*
Siddell, F. R., 221, *241*
Siegel, J. M., 84
Simmons, D. C., 159, *165*
Simon, H. A., 300, 301, 309, *329*, *330*
Simon, L., 261, *271*, 366, *373*
Simonov, P. V., 136, *144*
Simonson, E., 22, *30*, 148, *166*, 221, *236*
Simpson, C. K., 172, *200*
Singer, J. E., 18, 20, *25*, *27*, 78, 79, 81, *90*, *91*, 159, *165*, 276, 277, 292, *297*, 302, *327*, 369, *373*
Sjöberg, H., 310, *330*
Sjöberg, L., 219, *241*
Skinner, B. F., 169, 173, 174
Slinde, K., 131, *144*
Smith, A. P., 77, *94*
Smith, E. R., 131, *142*
Smith, H. C., 12, *30*
Smith, J. C., 221, *236*
Smith, J. E., 137, *144*
Smith, K. R., 79, *94*
Smith, P. C., 8, 9, 12, 14, *30*
Smith, R. P., 22, *30*
Smock, C. D., 186, *200*
Smyth, R. D., 220, *241*
Snashall, A., 256, *269*
Snyderman, B., 194, *199*
Sostek, A. J., 183, *200*
Spacapan, S., 159, *165*
Spence, J. T., 278, *297*

Spence, K. W., 124, 139, *144*, 278, *297*
Sperandio, J. C., 301, *330*
Spiegel, J. P., 128, *142*
Spiegler, M. D., 277, *297*
Spielberger, C. D., 3, *30*, 124, *144*, 273, 274, *297*
Spieth, W. R., 157, *165*
Spoor, A., 66, *94*
Stagner, P., 14, *30*
Stamford, B. A., 161, *164*, *326*
Steele, C. M., 84, *94*
Steen, J., 213, *241*
Steers, R. M., 4, *30*
Stein, C., 188, *199*
Stein, L., 216, 217, *241*, *243*
Steinberg, J. C., 68, *91*
Stennett, R. G., 338, *362*
Sternbach, L. M., 212, *242*
Stevens, S. S., 76, *94*
Stillman, R. C., 233, *240*
Stoa, K. F., 131, *142*
Stock, F. G. L., 6, 7, 13, *32*
Stokols, D., 371, *372*
Stromme, S. B., 131, *144*
Stull, G. A., 149, 158, *166*
Suedfeld, P., 20, *31*, 174, *200*
Suedfeld, R., 80, *94*
Surman, M., 222
Surry, J., 55, *60*
Svensson, E., 219, *241*
Sviridov, E. P., 136, *144*
Swensson, A., 98, 109, *119*
Swets, J. A., 348, *362*

Taberner, P. V., 221, *242*
Taeuber, K., 217, 221, *242*
Talland, G. A., 221, *242*
Tanaka, M., 150, *167*
Tanner, W. P., 348, *362*
Tarnopulsky, A., 86, *91*, *94*
Tarrant, M., 225, *237*
Tarrière, C., 72, *94*, 228, *242*
Tasto, D. L., 115, *121*
Taub, J. M., 266, *271*
Taxell, H., 219, *239*
Taylor, A., 17, *26*
Taylor, A. J. W., 20, *31*
Taylor, F. W., 11
Taylor, J. A., 124, 139, *144*
Taylor, K. M., 216, *242*
Taylor, P. J., 4, *31*, 115, *120*

Taylor, W., 65, *94*
Teichner, W. H., 50, 54, *60*, 69, 70, 71, *94*, 353, *362*
Telegdy, G. A., 186, *198*
Tennyson, R. D., 285, *297*
Terborg, J. R., 178, 186, *200*
Terkel, S., 3, 4, *31*
Tetreault, L., 213, *240*
Thackray, R. I., 16, 18, 21, 22, *25*, *31*, 163, *164*
Thayer, R. E., 265, 266, *272*, 309, *330*, 359, *362*
Thomas, J. R., 157, *165*
Thompson, L. A., 14, *31*
Thomson, C., 186, *199*
Tickner, A. H., 135, *142*, 155, 159, *165*
Tobias, J. B., 68, *94*
Tong, J. E., 221, *239*, *242*
Tornetta, F. J., 213, *242*
Touchstone, R. M., 16, 18, 22, *30*, *31*
Trapp, E. P., 186, *199*
Treacher, A. C. C., 22, *28*
Treziak, M., 323, *326*
Trope, Y., 176, *200*
Trumbell, R., 1, *25*
Tsaneva, N., 146, *167*
Tune, G. S., 17, *26*, 308, 316
Turner, A. N., 9, 10, *31*
Turner, D. M., 230, *237*

Uhrbrock, R. S., 11, *31*
Ulett, G. A., 227, *242*
Ursin, H., 130, 131, *142*
Uviller, E. T., 125

Valeriote, C., 221, *242*
Van Dishoeck, H. A. E., 65, *90*
Van Dyke, R., 221, *247*
Van Harrison, R., 4, *26*
Van Loon, J. H., 105, *121*
Veech, R., 223, *240*
Venables, P. H., 221, 227, *239*
Vermillion, M. E., 265, *269*
Vernon, H. M., 5, 8, *31*
Vetford, H. R., 127, *144*
Vila, M., 139, *142*
Viteles, M. S., 13, *34*, 79, *94*
Volle, M. A., 150, *167*
Von Wright, J. M., 343, *361*
Vossel, G., 317, *330*
Vroom, V. H., 10, *31*

Wachtel, P. L., 285, *297*, 349, *362*
Walker, C. R., 9, *31*
Walker, J., 98, 116, *121*
Walker, N. K., 128, 129, 135, *144*
Walker, R. E., 289, *297*
Wall, T. D., 24, *31*
Walters, W. G., 226, *242*
Warburton, D. M., 203, 204, 206, 207, 209, 214, 222, 223, 225, 226, 228, 231, *242*, 353, 363, 366, 371
Ward, L. M., 80, *94*
Ward, W. D., 65, 66, *94*, 149, *166*
Ware, J. R., 16, *31*
Warner, M., 157, 158, *166*
Warren, N., 155, *167*, 310, *330*
Warwick, K. M., 175, *198*
Washburn, D., 21, *29*, 163, *166*
Wasserman, E. A., 172, *200*
Weber, A., 23, *27*, *30*, *31*
Webster, J. C., 67, *94*
Wechsler, R. L., 227, *242*
Wedderburn, A. A. I., 116, *121*
Wegman, H. M., 112, *201*, 252, 254, *271*
Wehrkamp, R. F., *60*
Weiner, B., 172, *200*, 285, 289, 290, *298*, 308, *330*, 367, *373*
Weingartner, H., 233, *240*
Weinstein, C. S., 80, *94*
Weinstein, N. D., 80, *94*, 369
Weir, T., 317, *326*
Weitzman, E. D., 131, *144*
Welford, A. T., 3, 14, *31*, 156, 158, *167*, 299, *330*, 334, *362*
Wells, H. M., 2, *29*
Wells, R. J., 63, *94*
Weltman, G., 137, *144*
Wendt-Suhl, G., 212, *236*
Wesnes, K., 203, 214, 222, 225, 226, 228, 231, *242*, 353, 363, 366, 371
West, T. C., 221, *240*
Westfall, T. C., 230, *242*
Weston, H. C., 82, *94*, *95*, 368
Wever, R., 100, 101, *121*, 246, *272*
Whittingham, N., 156, *165*
WHO, 49, *60*
Wickens, C. D., 334, 357, *362*
Wickens, D. D., 172, *200*
Wickens, T. D., 170, 171, 172, 173, *197*, *200*
Wieland, R., 308, 317, *330*
Wiener, E. L., 17, *32*
Wiid, C., 226

Wikeby, P. C., 131, *144*
Wilding, J. M., 77, 78, 80, 90, 95, 189, 190, *199*, 281, *296*, 343, 345, *360*, *362*,
Wilkinson, R. T., 22, *32*, 46, *60*, 76, 79, 80, *95*, 162, *167*, 175, 189, 190, 191, 195, *200*, 308, *330*, 336, *362*, 369, *373*
Willett, R. A., 175, 184, *201*
Williams, A. F., 219, *243*
Williams, A. N., 134, *141*
Williams, D. G., 229, *243*
Williams, H. L., 22, *32*
Williams, R., 2, *28*
Williamson, J., 225, *241*
Williamson, J. R., 210, *243*
Winch, W. H., 251, *272*
Wine, J., 139, *144*, 278, *298*
Wing, J. I., 47, *60*
Wise, C. D., 216, *241*, *243*
Wisner, A., 72, *94*
Wittersheim, G., 69, *94*
Wojtczak-Jaraszowa, J., 109, *121*
Wolff, L., 222
Wolk, S., 186, *201*
Wood, C., 226, *240*
Woodhead, M. M., 69, 70, *95*
Woodworth, R. S., 138, *144*
Woolf, M., 225, *237*, *241*
Woolley, F. R., 285, *297*
Wyatt, S., 2, 5, 6, 7, 8, 10, 12, 13, 14, 17, *32*, 368
Wyatt, R. J., 233, *240*
Wynder, E. L., 230, *237*
Wyon, D. P., 46, 55, *58*, *60*

Yagi, K., 132, *141*
Yerkes, R. M., 102, 127, 138, *144*, 175, 179, 191, *201*, 280, 281, 283, 284, *298*, 310, 314, *330*, 337, 338, 339, 345, 349, 359, *362*
Youngling, M., 353

Zaffy, D. J., 139, *144*
Zbinden, G., 213, *243*
Zeller, A. F., 290, 291, *298*
Ziln, D. H., 222, *241*
Zimbardo, P. G., 2, *32*
Zirkle, G. A., 221, *243*
Zoob, I., 18, *32*
Zubin, J., 186, *200*
Zuckerman, M., 3, 18, *32*, 137, *144*, 322, *330*

Subject Index

Acclimatization to heat and cold, 36–37, 46
Acetaldehyde, 219–220
Adjustment to phase shifts, 98, 104–106, 111–113
  daylight saving time (DST), 111–112
  transmeridianal flight, 111–113
Adrenalin, 99–100, 207, 230, 266
  and smoking, 230
  circadian rhythm of, 99–100, 266
  role in stress response, 207
After-effects of stress, 20, 78–79, 155–159
  monotony, 20
  noise, 20, 78–79
  sensory deprivation, 20
  work, 155–159
Ageing, 155, 264
Aircraft noise, 81, 371
Alcohol, 218–224, 352–355
  alleviation of anxiety by, 219
  and performance, 220–222, 352–355
Alertness, 248, 265–266, 348, 351
  as indicator of system, state, 348, 351
  circadian rhythm of, 248, 265–266
Alphabet transformation task, 284–285, 345, 354
Amphetamine, 139, 350–352
Anxiety, 3, 123–141, 209, 212–213, 218–219, 225–227, 230–295, 350–352, 354, 358
  and experience, 240
  and extraversion, 188–189
  as a physiological state, 123–124
  as a subjective state, 130–132
  as an organismic state, 276–278
  effects on learning, 281–282
  effects on performance, 132–138, 278, 350–352, 354
  effects on working memory, 282–286
  emotional patterning of, 358
  emotionality component of, 277–279, 282
  physiological indices of a, 24–128, 130–131, 135–137
  role of corticosteroids in, 209
  role of effort and worry in, 285–291
  role of failure feedback in, 289–290
  state and trait, 3, 124, 273–276, 283
  Taylor Manifest Anxiety Scale (TMAS), 125
  test, 277–279
  treatment of, 292–294
  worry component of, 139, 285–291
  use of alcohol for, 219
  use of benzodiazapines for, 212–213
  use of smoking for, 225–227
Arousal, 2, 20–22, 74–75, 78, 80, 83, 111–112, 138–140, 151–152, 162–163, 178, 189–191, 195–196, 205–207, 221, 227–228, 233, 247–249, 262–238, 280–282, 309–312, 314–315, 331–359, 363–364
  and attentional selectivity, 74–75, 78, 80, 83, 152, 189–190, 196, 205, 233, 280–282, 338–339, 343, 350–352
  and boredom, 2, 20, 22
  and effort, 178
  and fear, 138–140
  and performance, 331–359
  and the inverted-U hypothesis, 20–21, 138, 263, 310–312, 314–315, 336–338
  and the Yerkes–Dodson law, 20, 175, 179, 191, 310–312, 314–315, 336–340, 345
  electrocortical, 22, 205–207, 221, 227–228

patterning of, 338
physiological indices of, 163, 179, 191, 265–266, 311–312
state theory, 163, 331–359
subjective, 265–266
theory, probems of interpretation of, 21, 331, 337–340
theory of time of day effects, 247–249
transient changes in, 189–191
Aspiration level, 315–316
Attention, 14–20, 72–75, 78, 80, 83, 151– 153, 182, 205, 214, 222, 228–229, 280–282, 338–339, 343, 346, 348, 351–352, 354
lapses of, 152–153
selectivity of, 74–75, 78, 80, 83, 205, 280–282, 338–339, 343, 350–352
sustained, 14–20, 72–75, 151–152, 182, 214, 222, 228–229, 346, 348, 351– 352, 354
see also Prolonged work, Vigilance
Attribution theory, 289–290

Behavioural states, 332–333
Benzodiazapines, 211–218, 351, 353
and anxiety, 212–213
and performance, 213–215, 251, 353
Blinking and fatigue, 150
Body temperature, 33–36, 46–47, 99–100, 102–105, 107, 246–248, 253–255
circadian rhythm of, 33, 99–100, 102– 105, 107, 108, 112–113
elevated core temperature, 46–47
Boredom, 1–25, 163, 351–352
alleviation of, 24–25
and fatigue, 22–23, 163
and performance, 14–24, 351–352
corelates of, 12–24
definitions of, 1–4
effects of music on, 11–12
effects of variety of work on, 8–11
in working environments, 3–14
individual differences in, 16–20
laboratory studies of, 14–24
psychophysiology of, 20–24

Cambridge Cockpit studies, 146, 152–153, 159
Cancellation task, 182, 231, 252
Capacity, 204, 282–288, 305–315, 349– 353, 356–357

and effort, 285–289, 308–315, 356–357
STM capacity as indicator of system state, 349, 350–353
Catecholamines, 99–100, 130–131, 207– 211, 230, 266
adrenalin, 99–100, 130, 266
in the stress response, 207–211
noradrenalin, 130, 207, 230, 266
see also Adrenalin
Characteristic states, 357–359
Cholinergic pathways, 206, 213, 215, 220, 227–228
Circadian rhythm, 33, 97–119, 245–268
and adjustment to phase shifts, 98, 104–108, 112
and performance, 102–104, 107–113, 249–259
and zeitgebers, 100–101, 112, 246
field studies of, 108–111
freerunning, 100, 246
in shiftwork, 97–119
individual differences in, 113–115, 259– 262
laboratory studies of, 107–108
of adrenalin, 99–100, 266
of alertness, 265–266
of body temperature, 33, 99–100, 103– 105, 107–108, 112–113, 246–248, 257, 260–262
of sleep/wake cycle, 100, 112, 246
physiological basis of, 246–249
Clothing insulation unit (Clo), 36
Clustering in free recall, 77
Cognitive appraisal of stress and fatigue, 147–148, 204, 276–277, 300, 365, 369–370
Cognitive resources, 356–357
Cognitive states, 332, 356–359
Cognitive tasks, 43, 52, 77–78, 135–137, 179–181
Cold environments, 53–55
Combat stress, 126–130
and fear, 126
and performance, 128–130
Combinations of stressors, 45–46, 79–80, 189–191, 262–264, 324–325, 336
Comfortable temperatures for performance, 55–56
Comparison of stress states, 346–356
Compensatory activity under stress, 286, 303–304, 350, 352–353, 365

Continuous noise, 71–80, 342–346, 350–352
  see also Noise
COPE task, 159–162, 314
Coping strategies, 292–294, 299–326, 369–370
  and compensatory activity, 303–304
  in treatment of anxiety, 292–294
  orientation and control as, 300–301
  stress and ineffective, 304–305
Corticosteroids, 130, 137, 207–211, 215–216, 229–230, 266
  role in the stress response, 207–211
Costs of adapting to stress, 130–132, 154, 159–161, 289, 317–319, 350, 372
Critical flicker fusion (CFF) frequency, 22–23, 213, 221

Dangerous Environments, 123–141
  and performance, 132–138
  combat, 126–128
  combat flying, 127
  diving, 127, 133–135, 137–138
  parachuting, 130–132, 135–137, 140
  simulated danger, 132–133, 137
Daylight Saving Time (DST), 111–112
Demands, 22, 179–184, 204, 301–308, 365–366
  of tasks, 22, 179–184, 204, 365–366
  stress and environmental, 301–308
Diurnal variation, 97–119, 245–268, 351, 352–354
  see also Circadian rhythm
Diving and performance, 127, 133–135, 137–138
Dopamine, 216
Driving and stress, 19, 154, 157, 162, 213, 221
Drugs and stress, 23, 139, 204–235, 351–355
  alcohol, 218–224, 352–355
  alertness effects, 23
  amphetamine, 139, 350–352
  benzodiazapines, 211–218, 351, 353
  nicotine, 224–232, 351–352
Dual tasks, 44–45, 51–52, 73–75, 78, 137–139, 186–188, 280–282, 342–343, 348

Effective temperature (ET), 38
Effectiveness and efficiency in anxiety, 285–289

Efficiency, 4–12, 14–24, 41–56, 68–82, 102–104, 107–111, 128–130, 132–134, 151–158, 184–188, 194–195, 249–259, 278–289, 301–305, 335–340
  and demands, 301–305
  and effectiveness, 285–289
  of applied work, 4–12, 81–82, 107–111, 128–130, 132–134, 194–195, 368
  of performance, 14–24, 41–56, 68–80, 103–104, 151–158, 184–188, 249–259, 278–285, 335–340
Effort, 68, 157, 159–161, 179, 285–291, 312–314, 356–357
  and anxiety, 285–291
  and fatigue, 157, 159–161, 312–314
  and incentives, 179
  and processing capacity, 285–289, 308–315, 356–357
  of listening, 68
Electrocortical arousal, 22, 205–207, 221, 227–228
Emotionality, 277–279, 282
  see also Anxiety
Emotional states, 358–359
Environmental noise, 80–86
  see also Noise
Experience and stress, 140, 370
Extraversion, 17–18, 188–189, 231, 261–263, 367
Eyestrain and fatigue, 149

Failure feedback and anxiety, 289–290
Fatigue, 5–6, 22–23, 39, 76, 85, 106, 128–130, 145–164, 210–211, 305–308, 312–314, 317–319, 321, 346
  after-effects of, 155–159
  and boredom, 22–23
  and capacity, 305–308
  and effort, 159–161, 312–314, 317–318
  and performance, 147–161
  and prolonged work, 76
  and stress, 210–211, 308, 317–319, 321, 346
  combat, 128–130
  definitions of, 145–147
  during skilled performance, 152–155
  in shiftwork, 106
  industrial, 5–6, 39, 85
  perceptual, 149–152
  physical, 147–149
  risk and effort aspects of, 159–161

Fear, 123–141
  see also Anxiety, Dangerous environments
Field studies of stress and fatigue, 4–14, 80–86, 108–116, 126–138, 150, 154, 156–158, 221, 225–227, 304, 323–324, 367–368, 370–372
  alcohol, 221
  dangerous environments, 126–138
  fatigue, 150, 154, 156–158
  monotony and boredom, 4–14
  noise, 80–86
  of stress reactions, 323–324
  shiftwork, 108–116
  smoking, 225–227
  versus laboratory studies, 367–368, 370–372
  work stress, 304
Flying and performance, 127

GABA and benzodiazapines, 217
Globe temperature, 38

Hawthorne effect, 82
Health and stress, 84–86, 115–117, 371–372
Hearing loss, 65–66
  masking of speech by noise, 66–68
  temporary threshold shift (TTS), 65
Heart rate, 21, 36, 123–124, 126, 131, 136–137, 163, 195, 292, 312–313
Heat, 33–57, 79, 332, 350–351
  acclimatization, 36–37
  and performance, 39–53, 55–56, 79, 332, 350–351
  indices for defining thermal levels, 37–39
  thermoregulation, 33–36
Heat indices, 37–38, 49
Heat stress index, 38
Hippocampal formation and the stress response, 206
Hypoxia, 45

Impulsivity, 18, 262, 366
Incentives, 169–197, 264, 336, 351–352, 354
  and attention, 173
  and learning, 170–173
  and memory, 170–173
  and motivation, 174–179

and performance, 184–188, 264, 336, 351–352, 354
individual differences in the effects of, 188–191
major determinants of, 173–174
role of task characteristics, 179–184
Indicators of system state, 333–335, 347–349
Individual differences in stress effects, 16–20, 83–84, 106–107, 113–115, 188–191, 260–264, 273–295, 357–359, 266–367
  ageing, 264
  anxiety, 188–189, 273–295, 367
  extraversion, 17–18, 113, 188–189, 231, 261–263, 366–367
  impulsivity, 18, 262, 366
  in boredom susceptibility, 16–17
  in cognitive state, 357–359
  in fatigue, 161
  in sleeping habits, 106–107, 113–114
  morning/evening types, 113, 260–261, 367
  sensation-seeking, 18
  sex differences, 83
Industrial Fatigue Research Board (IFRB), 5, 12
Intermittent noise, 61–64
  see also Noise
Inverted-U hypothesis, 20–21, 138, 263, 310–312, 314–315, 336, 338
  see also Arousal
Isodecrement curves for performance in the heat, 48–53, 365–366

Jet lag, 111–113

Laboratory versus field studies, 367–368
Learning and stress, 170–173, 251–252, 256–258, 266, 281–282, 320–322
  effects of anxiety on, 281–282
  effects of incentives on, 170–173
  role in coping, 320–322
  time of day effects in, 251–252, 256–258, 266
Letter transformation task, 284–285, 345–354
Levels of processing in memory, 171–172
Life stress, 301, 372
Long-term memory, 110–111, 137, 170–173, 290–291
  see also Memory

Macrostressors, 322–323
Mapping of stress states, 343, 349–353
Masking of speech, 66–68
Memory, 77–78, 103–104, 107, 110–112, 137, 171–173, 229, 251, 254–259, 267, 282–285, 290–291, 339–340, 343–345, 349–355, 366–367
  and arousal, 257–258, 267
  and comprehension, 257
  as indicator of system state, 349–355
  free recall, 77, 256
  immediate and delayed recall, 110–111, 255–256, 267, 344–345
  incidental recall, 78, 229, 343
  levels of processing, 171–173
  load in processing, 103–104, 107, 110–112, 339–340, 345
  order effects in recall, 344–345
  paired-associate learning, 77
  prose recall, 255–256
  rehearsal, 171–173
  repression, 290–291
  running memory, 344
  serial recall, 77, 137, 251, 254, 256
  working memory, 171–172, 258–259, 282–285, 339–340, 345, 366–367
Mental states, 332, 356, 359
  see also States
Mental health and stress, 86
Microstressors, 322–323
Monotony, 1–25
  see also Boredom
Mood states, 358–359
Moning/evening types, 113, 260–261
Motion sickness, 45
Motivation, 44–45, 191–193
  and performance in heat, 44–45
  intrinsic and extrinsic, 191–193
  see also Incentives
Motor skill, 42–45, 53–55, 109, 133–135, 152–155, 250
Multiple stressors, 324–325
  see also Combinations of stressors
Music and work output, 11–12

Neonates, behavioural states of, 332–333
Neural noise and fatigue, 162, 164
Nicotine, 224–232, 352
  and anxiety, 225–227
  and performance, 228–229, 352
Noise, 45, 61–88, 139, 158, 162, 189, 205,

Noise *continued*
  232, 263–264, 302–303, 306, 311–312, 315, 320, 336, 341–346, 350–352, 354–355
  and performance, 45, 68–82, 139, 158, 162, 189, 205, 232, 263–264, 302–303, 306, 311–312, 315, 320, 336, 341–346, 350–352, 354–355
  bursts, 69–70
  continuous, 71–80
  effects on hearing, 65–66
  intermittent and variable, 68–71
  measurement, 61–64
  state, 341–346
Noise state, 341–346
  see also Noise
Noradrenalin, 130, 207, 230, 266

Occupational noise, 81–82
  see also Noise

Paired-associate learning, 77
Parachuting, 130–132, 135–137
  and anxiety, 130–132
  and performance, 135–137
Perceived control of noise, 79, 302–303, 369
Perceptual fatigue, 149–152
  see also Fatigue
Performance under stress, 14–24, 39–56, 68–82, 102–104, 107–113, 132–139, 147–161, 170–196, 205, 213–215, 220–222, 228–229, 232, 249–259, 263–264, 278–285, 302–303, 306, 311–312, 315, 320, 332, 336, 341–346, 350–352, 354–355
  anxiety and fear, 132–138, 278–285, 350–352, 354
  circadian rhythms and shiftwork, 102–104, 107–113, 249–259, 351–352, 354
  cold, 53–56
  drugs, 139, 213–215, 220–222, 228–229, 350–355
  fatigue, 147–161
  heat, 39–53, 55–56, 332, 350–351
  incentives, 170–196, 264, 336, 351–352, 354
  monotony and boredom, 14–24, 351–352

noise, 45, 68–82, 139, 158, 162, 189, 205, 232, 263–264, 302–303, 306, 311–312, 315, 320, 336, 341–346, 350–352, 354–355
Performance patterns, 232–233, 331–359
Performance rhythms, 102–104, 107–113, 249–259
see also Circadian rhythm
Physical fatigue, 147–149
see also Fatigue
Physiological indices of activation, 20–24, 124–128, 130–131, 135–137, 163, 179, 265–266, 311–312
Post-lunch decrement in performance, 248, 253
Practical recommendations from stress research, 24–25, 47–48, 86–88, 116–118, 193–196, 266–267
Practice, effects on performance under stress, 194, 370–371
Problem solving, 180–181, 183
Processing capacity, 204, 282–288, 305–315, 349–353, 356–357
and effort, 285–289, 308–315, 356–357
STM capacity as indicator of system state, 349, 350–353
Prolonged work, 1–25, 42–53, 54, 72–76, 78–80, 86–87, 107–110, 147–164, 182, 189, 194–195, 214, 222, 228–229, 308, 316, 334, 336–337, 351–353
see also Boredom, Fatigue, Vigilance

Reaction time, 22, 45, 69–70, 76, 79–80, 175, 178, 185–186, 189–190, 195–196, 213–214, 221, 250–254, 336–337, 340–344, 348–353
serial reaction, 22, 45, 69–70, 76, 79–80, 189–190, 195–196, 336–337, 340–342, 344
speed/accuracy trade off, 175, 178, 185–186, 196, 343–344, 348–353
speed of response, 213–214, 221, 254
Regulatory behaviour and stress, 321–322
Rehearsal, 171–173
see also Memory
Repression, 290–291
Running memory, 344

School, effects of stress on, 80–81, 250–251, 254, 256, 266, 371
environmental noise, 80–81, 371

time of day, 250–251, 254, 256, 266
Selectivity of attention, 74–75, 78, 80, 83, 152, 189–190, 196, 205, 233, 280–282, 338–339, 343, 350–352
see also Attention
Serial responding, 22, 45, 69–70, 76, 79–80, 189–190, 195–196, 336–337, 340–342, 344
see also Reaction time
Serial recall, 77, 137, 251, 254, 256
see also Memory
Serotonin, 209, 216–217, 222–223
Sex differences, 83
Shift systems, 101, 104–107, 111, 115
see also Shiftwork
Shiftwork, 97–119
and health, 115–117
experimental studies of, 107–108
field studies of, 108–111
shift systems, 101, 104–107, 111, 115
sleep of shiftworkers, 98, 106, 116
sleep/wake cycle in 98–100, 106, 112
Short-term memory, 77–78, 103–104, 110–112, 171–173, 229, 251, 254–259, 267, 282–285, 339–340, 343–345, 366–367
see also Memory
Signal detection analysis in vigilance, 72–73, 151–152, 182–183, 346–348
Situational demands, 301–308
and capacity, 305–308
and efficiency, 301–305
role of fatigue, 308
Skilled performance, 42–45, 53–55, 109, 133–135, 152–155, 250
Skin conductance, 21, 131, 163, 292, 311–313
Sleep, 98–100, 106–107, 112–114, 116, 118, 246
effects of shiftwork on, 116, 118
habits, 106–107, 113–114
sleep/wake cycle, 98–100, 106, 112, 246
Sleep loss, 79, 99–100, 105–107, 115, 118, 195, 248, 336–337, 351–352
and adrenalin rhythm, 99–100
and performance, 79, 195, 248, 336–337, 351–352
associated with shiftwork, 105–107, 115, 118
Sleep/wake cycle, 98–100, 106, 112
Sleeping habits, 106–107, 113–114

Smoking, 224–232
  see also Nicotine
Social behaviour under stress, 82–84, 97–98, 101–102, 115–116, 126–127, 323–324
  danger, 126–127
  historical perspective, 323–324
  noise, 82–84
  shiftwork, 97–98, 101–102, 115–116
Sound, measurement of, 61–64
Speed/accuracy trade off, 175, 178, 185–186, 196, 343–344, 348–353
  see also Reaction time
State, 331–359
  behavioural, 332–333
  cognitive, 332
  indicators of system, 333–335, 347–349
  mental, 332, 356–259
  systems analysis of, 332
  see also Stress states
State dependent learning, 139
Strategy changes under stress, 73–74, 158–161, 191, 257–259, 285–289, 295, 302–304, 315–316, 326, 339, 344–345, 347–355, 369–371
  see also Coping strategies
Stress, 47–53, 84–86, 97–98, 101–102, 115–117, 123–138, 205–213, 219, 225–227, 230–233, 274–276, 292–294, 299–326, 331–359, 363–372
  and anxiety, 123–138, 212–213, 219, 225–227, 274–276, 292–294
  and drug effects, 212, 219, 225–226, 230–232
  and fatigue, 210–211, 308, 317–319, 321, 346
  and health, 84–86, 115–117, 371–372
  and information processing, 205, 211, 233, 301–302, 316
  as a consequence of ineffective coping, 304–305
  as a function of demands and capacity, 305–308
  combat, 127–130
  coping with, 292–294, 299–326, 369–370
  historical perspective on, 323–324
  in everyday life, 323–324, 371
  in social behaviour, 82–84, 97–98, 101–102, 115–116, 126–127, 323–324
  naturally occurring, 126–127

physiological concomitants of, 130–131, 205–211, 299
research, 158–159, 262, 363–372
states, 331–359
  see also Anxiety, Arousal, Performance under stress, Stressors
Stress research, 158–159, 262, 363–372
  see also Stress
Stress response, 203–211
Stress states, 331–359
  comparison of different, 346–356
  mapping of, 343, 349–353
  noise state, 341, 342–346
  see also Noise, State, Stress, Stressors
Stressors, 1–25, 33–57, 61–88, 97–119, 123–141, 145–164, 169–197, 204–235, 245–268, 273–295, 322–325, 336, 346–347, 349–356, 358
  anxiety and fear, 123–141, 273–295
  combinations of, 45–46, 79–80, 189–191, 262–264, 324–325, 336
  danger, 123–141
  differences between, 336, 346–347, 349–356
  drugs, 204–235
  fatigue, 145–164
  heat and cold, 33–57
  historical perspective on, 323–324
  incentives, 169–197
  macrostressors, microstressors and multiple stressors, 322–325
  monotony and boredom, 1–25
  nature of, 203–205, 358
  noise, 61–88, 349–356
  shiftwork and time of day, 97–119, 245–268
  see also Performance under stress
Stroop test, 22, 75, 77, 78, 158, 229

Task factors in stress effects, 22, 48–53, 71–78, 107–113, 179–184, 205, 249, 252–259, 266–268, 280–285, 287, 333–335, 339–356, 365–366
Thermal equilibrium, 34
Thermoregulation, 34–36
  role of hypothalamus, 34
  role of sweating, 35
Time of day effects in performance, 97–119, 245–268, 351–354
  see also Circadian rhythm

Tracking, 22, 42, 45, 50–52, 73–74, 135, 158, 221, 343
Tranquillizers, 211–218, 351, 353
  see also Benzodiazapines
Transmeridianal flight, 111–113

Variable noise, 68–71
  see also Noise
Variety of work and performance, 8–11
Vigilance, 14–20, 22–23, 41–42, 51–52, 72–75, 151–152, 182–183, 222, 228–229, 346, 348
  and drugs, 222, 228–229
  and heat, 41–42, 51–52
  and incentives, 182
  and noise, 72–75, 346
  arousal level in, 22–23, 151–152
  as indicator of system state, 348
  individual and group differences in, 16–20

Mackworth's studies, 14–16
signal detection analysis of, 72–73, 151–152, 182–183, 346–348
Visual search, 102–103, 108, 252–253

Wet bulb globe temperature (WBGT), 38, 49
Wet bulb temperature, 37
Wind chill index, 39
Working memory, 171–172, 258–259, 282–285, 339–340, 345, 366–367
  see also Memory
Worry, 139, 285–291
  see also Anxiety

Yerkes–Dodson law, 20, 175, 179, 191, 310–312, 314–315, 336–340, 345
  see also Arousal